VOICES

VOICES

READINGS FROM EL GRITO

A JOURNAL OF CONTEMPORARY MEXICAN AMERICAN THOUGHT

1967 — 1973

OCTAVIO IGNACIO ROMANO-V., Ph.D.

Editor

A QUINTO SOL BOOK
1973

65781

QUINTO SOL PUBLICATIONS, INC.
P.O. Box 9275
Berkeley, California 94709

First Printing: June 1971

Second Printing (Revised): July 1973

Library of Congress Catalogue Card Number: 73-85535
ISBN Number: 0-88412-059-7

Cuando el sol se baja y la gente ha cenado, el pueblo mexicano se aviva y se oyen las voces del barrio; la gente mayor, los jóvenes, los chicos, los perros . . . .

Rolando R. Hinojosa-S.
Kingsville, Texas
May, 1973

The voices from the barrios have got to be heard. These velvet voices, like the Mexican grito, are long and from the deepest pits of the soul: the voices from long-burdened mothers crying in despair, the voices of poverty stricken children for homes and food, the voices of hard-working men whose manhood is challenged by poverty and their pride by discrimination. There are the voices of junkies and wise old men and women, and there are the voices of tamale sellers on street corners or of pachucos on dead-end streets.

Luis Javier Rodríguez
San Gabriel, Califas
May, 1973

THE CONTRIBUTORS IN THIS VOLUME

Salvador Enrique Alvarez

"Mexican-American Community Organizations"
El Grito, Volume IV, Number 3 (Spring 1971).

"The Legal and Legislative Struggle of the Farmworkers, 1965-1972"
El Grito, Volume VI, Number 2 (Winter 1972-73).

SALVADOR ENRIQUE ALVAREZ. Associate Professor of Planning, San Jose State University. U.S. Catholic Conference, Division for the Spanish Speaking, West Coast Office Farm Labor Committee. He was instrumental in developing the School of Social Work, San Jose State University. Mr. Alvarez is also a contributing editor for *El Grito.*

Samuel R. Alvidrez

"Narcotics and Drug Use Trends in California"
El Grito, Volume IV, Number 1 (Fall 1970).

SAMUEL R. ALVIDREZ. Born in Las Cruces, New Mexico, raised in San Jose, California. Extensive studies in Social Criminology at Fresno State University, Fresno, California. Recently he has traveled extensively in Mexico in pursuit of his studies.

Ronald D. Arroyo

"La Raza Influence in Jazz"
El Grito, Volume V, Number 4 (Summer 1972).

RONALD D. ARROYO. Born in Honolulu, Hawaii. Raised in the Mission District of San Francisco, California. B.A., University of San Francisco, M.A., San Diego State University, in counselling. Mr. Arroyo has taught classes in counselling at the University of Santa Clara and at Fort Chapman College. He has received many favorable comments on his article on La Raza influence in jazz by people who were not aware of this aspect in history. Presently he has compiled lectures with music for presentation in schools and for civic groups.

César E. Chávez

"The Mexican-American and the Church"
El Grito, Volume I, Number 4 (Summer 1968).

CESAR E. CHAVEZ. Born in Yuma, Arizona, of a migrant farm working family. As a consequence, he attended 36 different grammar schools throughout the Southwest. Mr. Chávez was active in the Community Service Organization for eighteen years, before beginning the organization of farmworkers initially in Delano, California. The impact he has had in organizing farm labor, and his pioneering work in labor union services to the workers, will be felt for many decades to come.

Thomas M. Martínez

"Advertising and Racism: The Case of the Mexican-American"
El Grito, Volume II, Number 4 (Summer 1969).

THOMAS M. MARTINEZ. A.B., Sociology, University of Illinois. M.A., University of California at Davis. Ph.D., University of California at Berkeley. Mr. Martínez has been Director of Seminars on Mexican-Americans at Stanford University, and hosted a television program on Chicano issues in San Francisco. Recently he has been teaching in Chicano Studies, University of California at Riverside.

Miguel Montiel

"The Social Science Myth of the Mexican-American Family"
El Grito, Volume III, Number 4 (Summer 1970).

MIGUEL MONTIEL. Born in Nogales, Arizona where he attended public schools. Recently, Mr. Montiel has conducted extensive studies in Santa Clara County, California and he is presently teaching at the School of Social Welfare, University of California, Berkeley.

Steve Moreno

"Problems Related to Present Testing Instruments"
El Grito, Volume III, Number 3 (Spring 1970).

STEVE MORENO. Born in Denver, Colorado. Received his B.A. and M.A. in guidance and counseling from Colorado State College and also his Ph.D. in school psychology from the same institution. Presently Mr. Moreno is a professor of elementary education at San Diego State University, San Diego, California.

Frank Ortega

"Special Education and Mexican-Americans"
El Grito, Volume IV, Number 4 (Summer 1971).

FRANK ORTEGA. Born in Albuquerque, New Mexico. B.A. in History at the University of New Mexico. M.A. in special education at San Diego State University, California. Past president of Delano Chapter, Association of Mexican-American Educators. Member of the American G.I. Forum. He is Special Education instructor at San Dieguito High School.

Raymond V. Padilla

"Apuntes Para la Documentación de la Cultura Chicana"
El Grito, Volume V, Number 2 (Winter 1971-72).

"A Critique of Pittian History"
El Grito, Volume V, Number 4 (Summer 1972).

RAYMOND V. PADILLA. Born in Jalisco, México. He has attended universities in Michigan and California. A prolific and very articulate researcher, Mr. Padilla has become well known for his forthright approach to contemporary studies of Chicanos. Currently he is conducting research on education and the Chicanos.

Jorge H. Del Pinal

"The Penal Population of California"
(Written especially for VOICES, Revised Edition)

JORGE H. DEL PINAL. Born in Guatemala. Currently engaged in extensive research in demography at the University of California, Berkeley.

Manuel Ramirez III

"The Relationship of Acculturation to Educational Achievement"
El Grito, Volume IV, Number 4 (Summer 1971).

MANUEL RAMIREZ III. Born in Roma, Texas. B.A. and Ph.D. in psychology at the University of Texas at Austin. Presently he is Associate Professor of Chicano Studies and Psychology at the University of California at Riverside. He has done extensive work in bilingual education.

Richard Rodríguez
Gloria L. Rodríguez

"Teresa Urrea: Her Life, as it Affected the Mexican-U.S. Frontier"
El Grito, Volume V, Number 4 (Summer 1972).

RICHARD RODRIGUEZ and GLORIA L. RODRIGUEZ have devoted many hours in their research of their subject matter. Presently, they are retracing the history of Santa Teresa as it took place.

Octavio I. Romano-V.

"The Anthropology and Sociology of the Mexican-Americans"
El Grito, Volume II, Number 1 (Fall 1968).

"The Historical and Intellectual Presence of Mexican-Americans"
El Grito, Volume II, Number 2 (Winter 1968-69).

"Social Science, Objectivity, and the Chicanos"
El Grito, Volume IV, Number 1 (Fall 1970).

"Notes on the Modern State"
El Grito, Volume IV, Number 3 (Spring 1971).

OCTAVIO I. ROMANO-V. Born in Mexico City. Raised in "Old Town" in National City, California. B.A. and M.A. in anthropology at the University of New Mexico. Ph.D. in anthropology at the University of California at Berkeley. Presently he is Associate Professor, Behavioral Sciences, School of Public Health, University of California at Berkeley.

Guadalupe Salinas

"Mexican-Americans and the Desegregation of Schools in the Southwest"
El Grito, Volume IV, Number 4 (Summer 1971).

GUADALUPE SALINAS. Born in McAllen, Texas. He attended public schools in Galveston (Honor Graduate), graduated *cum laude* in Political Science at the University of Houston in 1970. He is a member of MAYO. Formerly Associate Editor of the Houston Law Review (University of Houston) and Chairman of the Chicano Law Students Association at Houston. Presently a practicing lawyer, Mr. Salinas is with M.A.L.D.E.F. (Mexican-American Legal Defense and Education Fund) in San Antonio, Texas.

Armand Sánchez

"Affluence Amid Poverty"
El Grito, Volume III, Number 4 (Summer 1970).

"The Definers and the Defined"
El Grito, Volume IV, Number 4 (Summer 1971).

ARMAND SANCHEZ. Born in Flagstaff, Arizona. B.A. in Liberal Arts, University of San Francisco. M.A. in Spanish at Stanford University. M.S.W. in Social Work at Fresno State University. Director of the Chicano Planning Project, Social and Rehabilitation Services (H.E.W.) in San Jose. Currently, Mr. Sánchez is Dean of the School of Social Work at San Jose State University, San Jose, California.

Rosaura Sánchez

"Nuestra Circunstancia Lingüística"
El Grito, Volume VI, Number 1 (Fall 1972).

ROSAURA SANCHEZ. A large part of her linguistic studies has been done in Texas. Recently, she moved to California where she continues her research. Presently she is teaching at the University of California at San Diego.

Fernando D. Vázquez

"El Acre: A Study of Space"
El Grito, Volume VI, Number 1 (Fall 1972).

FERNANDO D. VAZQUEZ. Through personal experience, Mr. Vázquez is extremely familiar with the San Joaquin Valley in California. Currently, he is a graduate student in Sociology at the University of California at Berkeley.

CONTENTS

PART II — CUESTIONES BIBLIOGRAFICAS

PART III — LA HISTORIA

PART IV – LA EDUCACION

PART V – CHICANOS EN EL ESTADO MODERNO

CONTENTS

INTRODUCTION

Second Edition

In mid-1971, while writing the introduction to the first edition of VOICES, perhaps the last thought in my mind was the possibility that so soon after I would be writing an introduction for the second edition. Yet, the occasion has pleasurably arisen and, I suppose, this event renders the first edition of VOICES an item which has now passed into Chicano history. At this juncture one can only hope that some Chicano historian in the year 2005 will grace us retrospectively with some kind comments and not be too harsh in his judgment of our efforts in 1971, and of our efforts in this revision of 1973.

The articles that have been selected for inclusion in this revised edition of VOICES deal with social science concepts and methodology, with bibliographies, history, education, and the modern state, as these subjects relate to the existence of the Chicano population. Just as in the first edition, the following articles originally appeared in the pages of the journal EL GRITO, and they represent the GRITO articles which have had most response since their publication between the years 1967 to 1973.* If I might say so, this is no small matter in light of the fact that the journal EL GRITO has achieved a very favorable international reputation, a fact that most certainly reflects the quality of the Chicano authors whose works have appeared in this quarterly publication.

In addition, the following articles have certain features in common:

1. Each article exhibits a profound and serious concern for the Chicano population.
2. These articles are uniformly devoid of negative stereotypes (traditional culture, fatalism, disadvantaged, culturally deprived, deviant, etc.) and their closely related glib slogans (emerging, awakening, stirring, search for identity, etc.) by which the Chicano population has been and still is commonly characterized.
3. These articles exhibit a forthright and incisive meeting of the issues with which they deal, whether these issues are theoretical, historical, educational, or relative to the modern state.
4. As a matter of considerable importance, the following articles also present an enormous wealth of material and information that has been absent in past writings about Chicanos in the fields of anthropology, sociology, psychology, social welfare, history,

education, etc., an absence that was brought about either by ignorance or by sloth.

With these considerations in mind, then, the contributions in this volume provide a myriad of multiple dimensions which can be utilized in order to gain some views regarding the Chicano past, the present, and the Chicano future, whether or not these views are primarily for research, for curriculum development, for program development, or simply for the informative scope of the contents.

A final comment. One overall impact can be discerned from the totality of the writings in this volume, an impact that bears strongly upon the so-called "loss of identity crisis" among Chicanos. After reading and re-reading these articles several times each, it appears that the so-called "loss of identity crisis" has been primarily a figment of some academic imaginations and/or the journalistic rhetoric of misguided liberals, militant and otherwise. The "loss of identity crisis," of course, is the contemporary version of the "marginal man" concept that was so popular in the early days of American sociology. But be that as it may, it seems clear now that had the so-called "loss of identity" really happened, as some would have us believe, then obviously this volume would not have been possible.

*The only exception is the article on the "Penal Population of California" which was written by Mr. Pinal especially for this issue of VOICES.

Octavio Ignacio-Romano-V.
Berkeley, Califas
20 de Febrero, 1973

Introduction

First Edition — 1971

When speaking of ethnically identifiable people-pools which exist within a broader national entity, of cultural enclaves, or even of ethno-religious-political self-identification within national borders, the extensive use of the terms "minority" or "minority peoples" at all levels of communications seems to be singular American coin. But the phenomenon of intra-national "minorities" itself is neither uniquely American nor even uniquely European. For it is true that virtually all nations in the world contain such groupings within their geographic and administrative boundaries. Thus, to begin with one example, Australia has the indigenous population in addition to more recent albeit controlled immigrant peoples from the United Kingdom, Italy, Germany, Holland, Greece, Austria, Finland, Yugoslavia, Poland, Hungary, and other European as well as non-European countries.[1]

This situation is common. Briefly, Japan has the Ainu, Viet Nam the Montagnards. Canada has its French enclaves, numerous Indian groups, in addition to the fact that today, "More than one in five Canadians are of foreign descent," and, ". . . immigrants constitute more than 13% of the Canadian labor force."[2] Mexico is a land of many "minorities," as is Peru, Chile, Brazil, Argentina, and Venezuela. East Indians, Pakistanis, Irish, Welsh, and a sprinkling of other peoples presently live in England. Spain would not be Spain without the Basques. Algerian-French, Hispanic-French, Italo-French, and other groups such as Germans and Poles all form an integral part of national France. Russia, Yugoslavia, Egypt, Israel, South Africa, Rhodesia, and a host of other nations all have their "minority" peoples. Therefore, throughout the world, within particular national boundaries it is the normal condition of national man to exhibit multi-ethnic peoples who have experienced multi-histories.

The actual scope of this condition, *pues,* is vast, as witness the seemingly countless numbers of indigenous peoples that still exist throughout the world. It is vast also because of the equally countless number of peoples who have migrated from one nation-state to another. It is a well-known fact, of course, that from Europe alone, "The overseas migration . . . from the great Age of Discovery until the eve of World War II totaled about 60,000,000."[3]

17

Perhaps not so well known is the fact that such massive shifts of people decidedly did not end with World War II, but rather the migrations largely changed in character. In the words of Brinley Thomas,

> A grim feature of the 20th Century is that *free international movement of people has been completely overshadowed by forced migrations.* After World War II, the partition of India and Pakistan uprooted 18,000,000 people; the Federal Republic of Germany took in 12,000,000 refugees; Japan 6,300,000; southern Korea 4,000,000; Hong Kong 1,300,000; Israel 1,000,000; and Arab refugees from Palestine numbered more than 1,000,000. The Intergovernmental Committee for European Migration settled 1,300,000 refugees overseas. This leaves out entirely what happened within the Soviet and Chinese areas, but even this limited survey gives a total of *45,000,000 forced migrants. Thus in one decade the number of people compelled by governments to move across frontiers was equal to the entire traffic of free migrants across the Atlantic ocean in the century ending in 1913.* [4]

This condition of vast shifts in populations with consequent intra-national multiplicity prevails not only the world over today, but it has been so through historic time. Very often such large shifts of peoples have been systematically accompanied by equally massive efforts by some peoples to somehow affect the life-styles of others in order to bring about particular and preplanned ends. In a classic example close to home, the Indian tribes of the Southwest have been subjected to "assimilation" programs for more than 400 years by the governments of Spain, Mexico, and the United States. Yet, as Edward H. Spicer has notably observed,

> In the middle of the twentieth century Navajos, Yaquis, Papagos, Seris, Hopis, Tarahumaras, and a score more of Indian groups had a vivid consciousness of themselves as distinct peoples from Mexicans and Anglo-Americans. The persistence of ethnic identification in the region seemed remarkable because of the smallness of the groups at the beginning of con-

tact, their military weakness, and the ultimate invasion of their territory in overwhelming numbers by
the European and European-derived peoples.[5]

In drawing world-wide comparisons through time, Spicer
also notes that in various parts of the world such a situation has
been neither unique nor exceptional. "The survival of native
groups in the face of successful conquests, followed by vigorous
programs for cultural assimilation, has been by no means exceptional in the course of human history. On the contrary it is
probably the most common result."[6] Then he goes on to add
specifically that,

> The Romanization of western European tribes,
> which never was completed, took place over periods
> of four to five hundred years. The spread of Arab
> civilization attendant on conquests beginning in the
> 700's went on for five hundred years in the vast area
> from Spain to the Philippines; and Moslemization
> like Romanization left a great variety of independent
> and unevenly influenced groups in its wake. The Hin-
> duization of tribes in southern Asia has been going
> on for two thousand years. The Europeanization of
> peoples in Africa and Oceania has likewise been in
> process for more than four hundred years. These
> processes of cultural assimilation based on conquest
> and rarely resulting in the complete assimilation of
> any people have gone on at markedly different
> rates.[7]

In light of this brief historic overview, among the peoples of
the world the case of the world's gypsies stands out in very bold
relief. For sheer migrating, of wandering and seemingly belonging nowhere, and for sustaining a self-identity for vast periods
of time, the gypsies hold the world record hands down.

Pues, En Esta Luz Mundial

In view of the foregoing, the current Chicano/Mexican-
American emphasis on self-ethno-cultural longevity has many
antecedents in history as well as numerous ethnic counterparts
in today's world. This condition runs strikingly counter to the
prevailng anthropological and sociological writings about Mexican-Americans, writings which overwhelmingly assume a rela-

tively simplistic assimilationist-ideological posture rather than
an analytical framework based on empirical realities and/or historical parallels. Such mini-theory as has been characteristic of
studies of Mexican-Americans (*o mejor dicho la falta de la
teoría*) bears some discussion.

The principal interpretive framework utilized in studies of
Chicanos has been Disintegrationist Theory, i.e., the disintegra-
tion of one life-style. The cornerstone of this interpretive approach has been the theory of acculturation, i.e., a bi-polar
model of unidirectional cultural and social change accompanied
by the ultimate and total disappearance of one of the poles, in
this case the Mexican-American population.

En Esa Luz Parroquial

Quite in keeping with this traditional interpretive approach
used in studies of Mexican-Americans, there has arisen an extensive vocabulary which lumps together virtually all Mexican-
Americans who do not embrace as their one and only life-style
this unidirectional process of change (lumping proletariat). Thus
such people who are "resistant to change" are said to be "fatalistic, resigned, apathetic, traditional, tradition bound, emotional, impetuous, volatile, affective, non-goal oriented, uncivilized, unacculturated, non-rational, irrational, primitive, unorganized, uncompetitive, retarded, slow learners, underachievers,
underdeveloped, or just plain lazy."[8] This vocabulary, and
variants thereof, has been the stock-in-trade of such writers on
the Mexican-American scene as Lyle Saunders, Florence Kluckhohn, Margaret Mead, Munroe Edmunson, Sam Schulman, William Madsen, Arthur Rubel, Julian Zamora, and Celia Heller.
Sometimes these words used to characterize Mexican-Americans
appear in combinations, as when Celia Heller writes, "The combination of stress on work and rational use of time . . . forms
little or no part of the Mexican-American socialization process."[9] Only recently has there been added a new dimension to
this vocabulary: sado-masochism. As William Madsen, an anthropologist, writes, "The Mexican-American wife who irritates
her husband may be beaten. *She should accept this punishment
as deserved.* Some wives assert that they are grateful for punishment at the hands of their husbands for such concern with
shortcomings indicates profound love."[10]

These views of Mexican-Americans, and the extensive vocabulary outlined above, have been widely adopted by agencies

which deal with Chicanos, ranging from educational institutions to health programs, to social welfare and the like. The net effect from the insistent use of this vocabulary has been the *polarization of the agency world view* vis-a-vis the Chicanos. As a consequence, it has come to pass that the governing philosophy of social services (no matter how humanistic sounding the rhetoric) also has been polarized, much in the same manner that the theory of acculturation has polarized the anthropological and sociological conceptualization of cultural and social change by the over-use of a bi-polar model analagous to a one-way street. In short, for some time now there has existed a comfortable wedding between social science rhetoric and the agencies' world view, the latter of which tends predominantly to determine the manner in which to "properly" deal with the Mexican-American population.

An excellent case in point of this polarization between agency and citizenry is the "joining of hands" between public school educators and social scientists in order to test Spanish-speaking children for I.Q., to administer all tests in English, and then proceed to classify thousands (20,000 in California alone) as *mentally retarded* because of their low performance in an unknown tongue. This practice dates back to the early Twenties and has been common ever since.[11] The additional and brutal truth of this matter is the fact that thus far the educational and the social science professional associations have remained totally mute toward this practice both at the policy level as well as in their respective postures concerning the ethics of such practices. Consequently, in the absence of any policy or real action on the part of the involved professional associations, a court action was instituted recently in San Francisco in which the Superior Court ruled this practice unconditionally illegal. Soon after, the California state legislature followed suit.

In ruling against this malpractice, the Superior Court in San Francisco articulated in legal form a protest which has had a long and bitter history, one which began in Chicano communities well over forty or fifty years ago in Texas, New Mexico, and California. The works of the eminent Dr. George Sánchez of New Mexico and Texas amply attest to this fact. The Federal Courts have finally caught up with the brilliantly innovative works of Professor George Sánchez. One cannot but wonder how much more time will pass before the involved professional associations also catch up. In the meanwhile, more than forty years, if not more, have passed and thousands upon thousands of Mexican-American children have passed through the public schools, have been similarly tested, and similarly labeled. The bi-polar model of acculturation with its counterpart of the unacculturated has largely tended to obscure such massive problems as those exemplified by its first cousin, I.Q. testing.

Other bi-polar Models

But Chicanos are not done with such Hegelianesque bi-polar models—more are in the offing, i.e., deviance and non-deviance, affluence and the "culture of poverty," the rational and the charismatic, the colonizer and the colonized, the so-called Third World Peoples in "White" America, etc. All of these dualistic schemes create the tendency to deal with entire populations in monolithic terms, as totally isolable and separable. In the context of the Mexican-American population, this means that the historically pluralistic nature of these people is brusquely turned aside, and the pluralistic antecedents plus the pluralistic directions of change experienced by Chicanos never constitute either a theoretical or an analytical baseline for study or interpretation.

More important, since such people are dealt with as separable, *ergo,* their thought processes must also be separable, i.e., different. This mode of thinking invariably leads to a view that Chicanos never think of things other than Chicano, and hence they are seldom seen as individuals who ponder questions which have to do with the philosophy of social welfare, with ideology and social science, theoretical constructs, world history, war and peace. After all, how could Chicanos think of such things when the sociologist Celia Heller has informed the world that, "...few Mexican-American homes stress higher education or *intellectual effort.*"[12]

A Pluralistic People in a Pluralistic Society

The pluralistic nature of the Mexican-American population has its roots in history as well as in many contemporary empirical manifestations throughout the Southwest, in the Midwest, now rapidly expanding in the Northwestern portion of the United States as well as growing in the Northeast. This pluralism has been documented in countless forms outside of the social sciences. Such documentation can be found in the Spanish language and bi-lingual newspapers published by Chicanos in the past and present (well over 500 between 1850 and 1950).[13] Such documentation can also be found in the by-laws and the constitutions of a myriad of formal organizations from mutualist and cooperative societies to labor unions, in countless individual as well as family histories, in the past and present composition of the populations in the *barrios,* as well as in many other forms. (Today in the popular mind the word *barrio* has been used interchangeably with the Italian word *ghetto,* but it is not synonymous with the Italian word.)

Historically, discriminatory hiring practices relegated Mexican-Americans largely to agricultural work in the fields, hence the popular notion that this population is overwhelmingly rural and agrarian. It remains for some future historian, therefore, to correct this view, bring it into some correspondence with history, and thereby compliment the classic work of Manuel Gamio, *The Mexican Immigrant: His Life Story.* In this work the Mexican anthropologist approached this population from the standpoint of multiplicity rather than a superimposed rural homogeniety with an ideological bent.

A note of caution. Such a proposed documentation of the pluralistic nature of Chicano existence must be careful not to overly rely upon contemporary statements concerning pluralism in the United States, either cultural or structural. Such statements which exist today largely appear to be mere rationales for ethno-class social structure and the corresponding category, ethno-cultural hierarchies. In their interpretive approach these studies (notably, Milton Gordon and Nathan Glazer, Patrick Moynihan)[14,15] have heavily relied upon the concept of unihistory (i.e., diverse groups of people undergo similar and sequential stages of development). This is merely micro-evolutionary social theory in a domestic garment. Its principal conceptual tool remains the monolithic concept of cultural and social groups, and, in substance therefore, differs but very little from traditional acculturation theory.

En Fin

The case of the Mexican-American raises interesting questions in light of the vast migrations and pre-planned programs throughout the world. It also raises questions regarding the Chicano's actual history, both as migrants as well as "native" to the Southwest prior to conquest. The case raises questions concerning views of them held by non-Chicanos vis-a-vis their historical role. It is with these questions in mind that the following selections of literature by Chicanos have been made. The writings are contemporary. The views contained therein diverse. They reflect what has been ignored in past studies, the intellectual spectrum of Mexican-American life.

The articles contained in this book have been gleaned from the pages of *El Grito: A Journal of Contemporary Mexican-American Thought.* They are, in effect, statements which themselves have become historical documents outlining the major concerns of Mexican-American writers during the period from the founding of *El Grito* in 1967 to the present. Judging from the commentaries and communications received in the editorial offices of Quinto Sol Publications, they also represent those articles from *El Grito* which have had the largest impact upon the readers of the journal, both among individuals as well as in Chicano Studies Programs, sociology and history classes, and extension courses in universities, colleges, and junior colleges. Thus, not only do the articles contained in this volume depict some of Chicano history, they are historical documents themselves. Undoubtedly, for many people, they will constitute baselines and provide leads for research and writings which take a Chicano perspective. In this manner, they become not only a key into the past, but indicators of the future as well.

NOTES

1. Bouscaren, Anthony T., *International Migrations Since 1945,* Frederick A. Praeger, Publisher. New York, 1963. p. 106.
2. *Ibid.* p. 144.
3. Thomas, Brinley, "Migration," *Encyclopaedia Britannica,* Vol. 15. p. 421.
4. *Ibid.* p. 422. See also Brinley Thomas, *International Migration and Economic Development,* UNESCO, Paris, France. 1961. (Emphasis mine)
5. Spicer, Edward H., *Cycles of Conquest: The Impact of Spain, Mexico, and the United States on the Indians of the Southwest, 1533-1960.* University of Arizona Press, Tucson, Arizona. p. 576.
6. *Ibid.* p. 567.
7. *Ibid.* p. 569.
8. Romano-V., Octavio Ignacio, "Minorities, History, and the Cultural Mystique," *El Grito: A Journal of Contemporary Mexican-American Thought.* Vol. I, No. 1, Fall 1967. p. 7. (Emphasis mine)

9. As quoted in Romano-V., Octavio Ignacio, "The Anthropology and Sociology of the Mexican-Americans: The Distortion of Mexican-American History," *El Grito,* Vol. II, No. 1, Fall 1968. p. 21.

10. *Ibid.* p. 19 (Emphasis mine)

11. For an excellent historical and analytical discussion of the testing of Mexican-American children see Nick C. Vaca, "The Mexican-American in the Social Sciences: 1912-1970. Part I: 1912-1935," *El Grito,* Vol. III, No. 3, Spring 1970. p. 3-24.

12. As quoted in Romano-V., Octavio Ignacio, "The Anthropology and Sociology of the Mexican-Americans: The Distortion of Mexican-American History," *El Grito,* Vol. II, No. 1, Fall 1968. p. 22.

13. Communication from Mr. Herminio Rios and Miss Lupe Castillo whose present research is rapidly exploding the non-Chicano myth of the non-literate Mexican-American population, and whose preliminary findings appear in *El Grito,* Vol. III, No. 4, Summer 1970.

14. Gordon, Milton M., *Assimilation in American Life,* Oxford University Press, 1964.

15. Glazer, Nathan and Patrick Moynihan, *Beyond the Melting Pot,* M.I.T. and Harvard University Press, 1963.

Octavio I. Romano - V.

PART I
CUESTIONES SOCIOLOGICAS

INTRODUCTION

A critical stance toward the methods and concepts of the social sciences still remains the most fundamental and important aspect of the total activities which we call social science. This has always been the case, as anyone who has been in anthropology, history, psychology, or sociology well knows. This has been true regardless of content, methodological or conceptual considerations, or if one is talking about cultural evolution, functionalism, statistical inference, symbolic interaction, diffusion, cognition, positivism, neo-positivism, human ecology, social system theory, behaviorism, phenomenology, the super organic, folk-urban dichotomies, mathematical models, etc. Yet, for some reason or another, there has been remarkably little *critical* analysis of social science studies that have dealt with the Chicano population.

This strange situation is now changing, not so much because of a commonality of intra-disciplinary sensitivities, but rather due to the fact that Chicano social scientists are injecting alternative perspectives into a tradition-bound social science area. This introductory section to VOICES presents some of these alternative views.

The first article deals with the basic concept of objectivity, discussing how the concept has been under criticism within the major social science fields themselves. An effort is made to relate these criticisms to studies of the Chicano experience.

The second article, "The Anthropology and Sociology of Mexican-Americans" then addresses itself to the fact that stereotypes, if repeated often enough, tend to become sociological gospel. Soon after its original publication in 1968, over 17,000 reprints were requested by individuals from throughout the nation. Interest in this article continues to this date and, since it is no longer available in reprint form, it is included here for that reason.

Following this article, Miguel Montiel then focuses upon the concept of "machismo," and he goes on to demonstrate how this concept has been used in order to classify entire populations as pathological.

In "The Anthropology and Sociology . . ." article it was asserted that more and more social science was being used to "explain" history. As Mr. Raymond V. Padilla in "A Critique of Pittian History" has so competently demonstrated, this is precisely the conceptual tactic used by Leonard Pitt to "explain" Californio history. As Mr. Padilla points out, Leonard Pitt used a 1961 social science study in order to "explain"

Californios in 1861!! Padilla correctly points out that this is indeed a questionable procedure. There are other shortcomings. For example, his decline thesis bears a remarkable resemblance to the "declining Aztecs" thesis of so many works on this subject. This fallen tribes notion, of course, for anyone familiar with Western history, also bears a striking similarity to those statements in the past that held that some people or peoples had "fallen from Grace," i.e., declined. In this manner, we see something of the theological underpinnings of social theory, as well as in the interpretation of history.

All of this, of course, is intimately related to the question of who precisely is defining whom, the subject matter in Armand Sánchez' article, "The Definers and the Defined." Although Mr. Sánchez restricts his discussion to the field of mental health, it seems readily apparent that his articulation on the subject just as well applies to many other fields of inquiry.

Thus, in this section, we see the introduction of some Chicano views regarding the foundations of the social sciences, stereotypes used as analytical categories, excessive psychologizing, the confusion of social science with history, and some implications in mental health that can be pondered in relationship to other disciplines.

Social Science, Objectivity, and The Chicanos

Octavio Ignacio Romano-V., Ph.D.

Western theology is based on the belief that within the human body is a separable entity, *ergo*, the concept of the soul. Like Western theology, Western science is also based on the idea that within the human body is a separable entity, hence the belief in the separability of the mind from the body.

Plato has often been credited with the origin of the belief in the separability of mind and body. This dualism, however, was not Platonic in origin. Instead, the ultimate origin of the distinction between mind and matter was in Greek Orphic mystery religion. A somewhat refined version of this Orphic dualism was developed by the philosopher Pythagoras who died early in the 5th century B.C. "The metaphysical dualism of the Pythagorean philosophy . . . was accepted by Plato, and conveyed by his teaching to the era in which we now live."[1] Thus, the belief in the dualistic nature of man, i.e., the separation of mind and body, is traceable to Greek Orphic mysticism.

It was not until the 17th and 18th centuries, during the Age of Reason, the Enlightenment, and the times of the Empiricists and Rationalists of Europe that this belief became a dominant theme of major developmental proportions and historical effects. As a part of this historical process, there followed a renewed exploration into the concept of objectivity. As generally defined in Western thought, the concept of objectivity is impossible without a corresponding belief in man's ability to separate his mind not only from his body, *but also from all of his ecological surroundings, whether or not*

30

these ecological surroundings are human or physical. It is in this manner that the mind, when believed to be in its objective state, has come to be viewed as separable in Western science just as the soul has been seen as separable in traditional Western theology.

From the standpoint of known history, the idea of a dualism between mind and matter appears to have served the physical sciences rather adequately, especially insofar as it has concerned the separation of the mind from pre-existent theological notions about objective reality, and particularly with respect to the evolution of that reality. Western man, then, in his quest for a pure objective reality (that is, to be objective) began to consider events, phenomena, and ideas as apart from personal self-consciosuness, to be dealt with ideally in a detached, impersonal, and unprejudiced manner.

Within this climate of thought the social sciences themselves instituted major efforts to emulate the relatively successful postures and methods of the physical sciences. They followed this course of action for two major reasons. First, the social scientists joined in an effort to seek out a corresponding empirical reality in human behavior, the world out there, so to speak, which paralleled or equalled the findings of the physical sciences. Second, the effort simultaneously constituted a move toward the achievement of methodological and conceptual legitimacy in the eyes of the scientific community. Gravitating in this direction, the social sciences began to adopt the descriptive and methodological terminology of the physical sciences and to borrow heavily from their theoretical constructs for use in the study of human behavior. The sociologist Helmut Wagner has labeled this basic orientation in the social sciences as Natural Materialism.[2] It is from such efforts to parallel the physical sciences that today we have the basically biological notion of instinct translated into a bio-psychological theory of human behavior as manifested in Freudian psychology. In a similar vein, we have the biological-geographical ideas of the plant and animal ecologists translated into studies of human demography. From physiology and morphology we have the sociological version of societal structure and function with a borrowed vocabulary that includes such physiological terms as homeostasis, function, dysfunction, equilibrium, and other similar words that are used in what has been called the organic analogy in the social sciences. From studies of animal behavior we have inherited the stimulus-response orientation of social and psychological behaviorism. And the dominant model of mental illness has been borrowed from the medical world. Studies in the physical evolution of man, as well as variants in social Darwinism and cultural evolution, also have their antecedents in the physical sciences. All of these approaches stress one major idea, that there is a unity between the laws governing the physical universe and those which govern man's behavior, for both, ostensibly, can be studied by *similar if not identical* methods.

At the same time, another approach (called Interpretive Sociology by Helmut Wagner) has evolved in the social sciences that stresses the uniqueness of human behavior in the physical universe. From this basic orientation of man's uniqueness have emerged national character studies, modal personality studies, cultural linguistics, cultural configurations, culturology, social phenomenology, symbolic interaction, and other similar approaches found today in anthropology, sociology, and psychology.

Both of these major orientations (Natural Materialism and Interpretive Sociology) still lay fundamental claim to the Platonic idea of an objective reality in human behavior as observed through a "value free" social science. As a product of historical antecedents, today the traditional concept of objectivity and the related belief in the detachability of the investigator from the universe studied forms the core of social research.

Yet, despite major efforts to emulate the physical sciences, despite more and more efforts to achieve an objective state of mind in the study of human behavior, from an international as well as an historical perspective certain inconsistencies appear concerning the notion of pure objectivity within the social sciences. It has become increasingly evident that some of the major postures of social science may vary from nation to nation and according to time and place. This being the case, differences between the social science of one nation and another have led some writers to suggest the term "national social science" rather than the more generic term "social science." In part, the reasons for this spring from differences such as those between the behaviorism of Russian psychology with its assumptions of rational/responsible man in contradistinction to the American notion of cultural and subconscious man. Similarly, the idea of acculturating man in American anthropology and sociology is considerably different from its corresponding category of *transculturating man* in Mexican anthropology. Other similar differences at the national social science level exist throughout the world.

In 1964, a Unesco sponsored meeting took place in Paris in which the questions concerning these problems were discussed at length. Papers were presented by Julian Hochfeld (Sociology, Poland); Pierre Auger (Physicist, France); K. O. Dike (History, Nigeria); Daya Krishna (Philosophy, India); Oskar Lange (Economics, Poland); Paul Lazarsfeld (Sociology, United States); Claude Lévi-Strauss (Anthropology, France); Jean Piaget (Psychology, Switzerland); José Luis Romero (Philosophy, Argentina); A. A. Zvorykin (Philosophy, Russia). In the papers presented there was a recurrent theme which questioned the existence of a culture-free, or even a tradition-free, social science. From this, it follows, that the objectivity of the social scientists tends largely to be influenced by time, place, and culture (nationality).[3]

In itself, this is not a new idea. For example, quite some time ago Karl Mannheim made a parallel assertion when he asserted that there was no such thing as a timeless objectivity, but rather that the findings of the social sciences were always colored by the time, place, and culture in which they appear.[4] More recently, for example, Pietro Rossi, a Sardinian philosopher, advanced the notion that social science needs to drop the idea of a "neutral" social science. He added that, ". . . exclusion of value judgments from the social sciences is not alone sufficient to free those sciences from value hypotheses."[5]

Karl Mannheim, the Unesco commentaries, the philosopher Rossi, as well as others, all have had their philosophical and methodological counterparts in recent American social science writings that have emanated from the fields of anthropology, psychology, and sociology. On occasion, American social scientists have been critical of certain sub-segments of their respective disciplines, and on other occasions they have been equally critical of the fundamental foundations upon which their discipline rests. But whatever their frame of reference, they have been critical of the notion of objectivity as utilized in social science today, pointing to certain inconsistencies that exist.

The anthropologist Gerald Berreman, for example, has asserted that many anthropologists have succumbed to an over-preoccupation with quantification, with abstract models and simulation which produce lifeless descriptions of human life that are grimly pretentious.[6] Such over-emphasis upon tools and method has been called "scientism" by the philosopher Abraham Kaplan who observed recently that scientific policy today must be formulated with the help of charts, graphs, equations, and computers. Then he adds force-fully, "To acknowledge imponderables as the locus of important values comes to be seen as unscientific and even obscurantist. It is not only the law of the instrument which is at work here, but also a belief in the magic of symbols, and perhaps even a trace of the infantile delusion of omnipotence."[7]

Not only does the "law of the instrument" strongly color certain aspects of contemporary anthropology, the continuing use of obso-lete terminology also tends to predetermine the results of present research as pointed out by the anthropologist Francis Hsu. "If there is one term that is consistently identified with anthropology," he writes, "it is 'primitive,'"[8] as in primitive science, primitive religion, primitive economics, primitive mentality, primitive peoples, socie-ties, and cultures. "There is no doubt," Hsu concludes, "that the idea of being 'inferior' was what E. B. Taylor had in mind when he used the word in 1871."[9] Still, the word continues to be used in anthropology today despite the fact that it is ". . . ambiguous, inconsistent, and scientifically meaningless."[10]

The use of the word "culture" in a manner that rules out the individual also has come under fire by anthropologist Morris Opler. He has said that, "In this doctrine of a (cultural) order external to man, which nevertheless rules the affairs of man, we anthro-pologists meet two very old acquaintances, animism and animatism. It does not disguise them too much to give them sonorous scientific labels now."[11] And looking over the general state of the discipline, in 1964 Leslie White observed that ". . . we have reached the point in many quarters where we have little but trivialities to offer . . ."[12] Addressing himself to these problems, John L. Sorensen concluded that, "Our own experience in the field should warn us that we anthropologists may be the last to understand much about our-selves, at least from an anthropological view."[13] Then he added, *"If behavior is strongly shaped by societal or cultural forces as we maintain, how can we escape the realization that our activities as anthropologists also are so controlled?"*[14]

In the field of psychology similar statements have been made in recent years. J. F. T. Bugental, for example, criticized psychol-ogy for borrowing the Model of Science from physics, and the Model of a Practitioner from medicine. He added that, "Despite increasing elaboration of statistical methodologists, despite greater and greater refinement of laboratory procedure, the product of years of conscientious effort has not been such as to warrant confidence that we will eventually arrive at a genuine understanding of human behavior by this route."[15]

Kenneth B. Clark echoes this view when he says that, "Most social psychology is still primarily concerned with the investigation of isolated, trivial, and convenient problems . . ." adding that ". . . social scientists . . . are not more immune to social and intellectual inertia and resistance to change . . ." than are other members of society.[16] He sums up his views by saying that there exists in psychology a constricted concept of scientific objectivity which ". . . produces academic pedantry, qualified trivia and sterile objectivity."[17]

Theodore Kahn, another psychologist himself, is of the belief that, "One of the reasons for the shallowness of present day psychological research literature stems from the fact that psychologists are attempting to untangle the behavioral aspects of reality without any grasp of reality's philosophical implications."[18] In Kahn's opinion, every good psychologist must be a philosopher first. Without that quality, he is merely a technician.

Robert T. MacLeod has claimed that he is ". . . honestly in doubt as to whether much of what we teach as psychology is really worth teaching."[19] He elaborates by saying that, "My own impression, based on my observation of a good many generations of students, is that the conventional undergraduate curriculum in psychology is about as culture-bound as any curriculum could be."[20] He adds wryly that, "The favorite delusion of the experimental psychologist is that psychology is a science. . . ."[21]

Psychiatry does not escape from this onslaught against unquestioned scientism. Bert Kaplan, for one example, has asserted that psychiatry suffers from an over-reliance on the scientific and medical traditions from which it has borrowed heavily. He observes that psychiatry has taken for its own side science, medicine, understanding and care. On the other side, on the side of the patient, "What the patient experiences is tied to illness and unreality, to perverseness and distortion."[22] In a similar vein, Thomas Szasz has stated that mental illness is a convenient myth which has become a familiar theory. Familiar theories, he goes on to say, have a habit of posing sooner or later as objective truths.[23]

The foregoing has concerned anthropology and psychology. In addition, sociology can be included in such introspective and critical efforts. One such example comes from the writings of Ralf Dahrendorf who has said that, "Much of the theoretical discussion in contemporary sociology reminds me of a Platonic dialogue. Both share an atmosphere of unrealism, lack of controversy and irrelevance."[24] Similarly, Harold Garfinkle has said that, "Social science theorists (social psychiatrists, social psychologists, anthropologists and sociologists) have used the fact of standardization to conceive the character of human actions.[25] This, he adds, has largely contributed to making man out to be a "judgmental dope." Alvin Gouldner enters the fray by calling "value-free" sociology a myth, and an absurd one at that.[26] Irving Horowitz points to a sister discipline when, in comparison to sociology, he believes that contemporary anthropology is still in a state of methodological underdevelopment. "The science of culture," he has said, "makes only the vaguest distinction between objective facts and subjective opinions."[27] Everett C. Hughes displays similar views concerning sociology. Sociology is falling into the sin it named, that of ethnocentrism because (1) we study only one society and (2) we use those methods which are suitable only for a homogenous mass society.[28] Then, taking an interdisciplinary overview, he comes to the conclusion that, "We (sociologists) have become methodologically ethnocentric, the anthropologists have become eccentric."[29] And, finally, from the sociology of Dennis Wrong, "We must do better if we really wish to win credit outside of our ranks for a special understanding of man, that plausible creature whose wagging tongue so often hides the dispair and the darkness that is in his heart."[30]

From these statements by anthropologists, psychologists, and sociologists, it can be seen that indeed limitations are present which parallel the UNESCO conference, but in intra-national as well as international social science. This has a direct bearing on the concept of objectivity and the absence of emotion (i.e., the separation of mind and body), for it would appear that in the past many researchers have confused the absence of emotion with the achievement of truth and the precise identification of an empirical reality. But, merely because an individual researcher displays no *observable* emotion does not mean that in doing so his perceptive ability has been magically enhanced, nor does it mean that his cognitive and analytical power has become superior. All it means is that the researcher has displayed no observable emotion.

Evidently, in contemporary social science, two things appear to have happened that merit serious comment and very critical scrutiny by those who aspire to become researchers, as well as by those in other disciplines who utilize social science literature for one reason or another. First, as strongly indicated in the foregoing, an apparent lack of emotion on the part of a researcher has been accepted commonly as, *per se*, constituting a state of objectivity, therefore the achievement of the objective mind, thus the successful separation of mind and body. For the reasons cited above, this is a fallacy. In addition, it is a fallacy because it presupposes a total separability of the mind *as such* from emotion *as such*, and as a consequence *the ultimate locus, source, and cause of emotion has come to be seen as residing somewhere outside of the mind*. Emotion in the lives of men is thus relegated to a generic kinship with such forces as instinct, hunger, and the like, somewhat animalistic in nature, somewhat sub-human, a throwback or a contemporary survival of the pre-*Homo Sapiens* state of existence in the evolution of man.

Second, and much more important with reference to research methodology, quite often what has passed for objectivity has not been objectivity at all, but merely the relatively simple process of *objectification*. Objectification, of course, is the externalization and the systematic articulation of a thought or theoretical construct the parts of which are *seemingly* interrelated and *seemingly* cohesive. However, there is no automatic and ineluctable corerspondence between an exercise in objectification (articulation) and empirical reality. For, as we have seen, such constructs can be influenced, modified, and limited by forces that are extraneous to the theoretically pure process of objectification itself, forces which vary from person to person, from time to time, from place to place, and from nation to nation.

This brings us to the question of precisely how one may go about conducting social science studies of the Chicanos. Do the points of view advanced above doom us to an unending morass of relativism? Do we surrender to despair simply because of a realization that our objectifications are bound to enjoy but a limited temporal existence? Or must we, in turn, create yet another fiction, a counter-fiction if you will, to replace that of the separation of mind and body? True, some researchers may choose to select from the present array of sociological and anthropological theories, dress them up in up-to-date Space Age terminology, apply them to Chicanos and thus assume the mantle of contemporaniety before the uninitiated in social science theory. However, this avenue is but another way in which to *avoid the central issue* of objectivity and the question of the separation of the mind and body.

Elsewhere I have asserted that with reference to contemporary studies of Mexican-Americans such a theoretical separation (objectivity as such) does not exist.[31] This point of view has been further documented by Nick C. Vaca in his superb and comprehensive review of social science literature on Mexican-Americans,[32] by Miguel Montiel in his incisive critique of studies of the Mexican-American family and the concept of machismo,[33] by Samuel Alvidrez in his excellent and very revealing study of drug use in California,[34] and by Steve Moreno in his concise and critical review of psychological testing of bilinguals.[35] Currently these writers are addressing themselves to the question of objectivity. In fact, they have found the literature on the Mexican-Americans sadly and uniformly wanting, on occasion spurious, and in other instances out-and-out distorted for reasons unrevealed by the authors of such studies, but which are indicated by their Chicano critics.

This situation is unique in the annals of American social science. It is unique because a population heretofore studied is now studying the studiers. The final outcome of this venture is yet to be revealed. Nevertheless, it promises to introduce perspectives that are unique in social science, perspectives which have their origin within a previously studied population (Mexican-Americans) whose objectifications in the past have not been an accepted, explicit, and integral part of traditional social science thought. As such, these perspectives will introduce a *self-image* into the arena of rational thought. If this self-image is rejected by non-Chicano social scientists, then, in effect, they will have rejected summarily the rationality of the Chicano. In doing so, wittingly or unwittingly, it matters not, they will have opted to join the ranks of the traditionalists in social science who have passively accepted the traditional view of the totally non-rational Mexican-American as handed down from social science generation to social science generation since the early 1900's, and before, down to the present day. Should non-Chicano social scientists choose to follow this course, they will have become traditionalists rather than empiricists, and as such their writings will reflect traditional conservatism rather than open-ended inquiry.

Culture, History, and Self-Image

To introduce *Chicano self-image* into the arena of social science thought, certain preliminary steps are necessary the first of which is to discard the classic (classic in the sense of old) concept of culture, or to modify it to such a degree that it no longer bears a resemblance to the uses to which it has been put in studies of Mexican-Americans. This is necessary because, in its present usage, the concept of culture deals with Mexican-Americans *only as passive receptors and retainers* of whatever has transpired before them (unchanging traditional culture). Hence, the concept of culture has eliminated Chicanos as being generators of, and participants in, the historical process (a changing entity).[36] This is grossly naïve posture at best, and an ideological stance at its worst.

Having taken this first step, it follows secondly that the related concept of acculturation must similarly be dealt with, for basically it constitutes a simplistic, intellectually crude dichotomy the effect of which has been to distort Chicano history and therefore reality by placing all causes of change *outside* of Chicano existence.

For the present it is not necessary to replace the concepts of culture and acculturation with any other. It is sufficient merely to ignore them, for they serve no useful or necessary purpose toward the objectification of a self-image. All that is necessary at this point is an historical perspective and a paradigm by which to articulate that perspective. For the purposes outlined above, the eight point paradigm that follows seems most useful at present. Others are certain to follow.

First, from the standpoint of self-image, Chicanos do not view themselves as traditionally unchanging social vegetables (traditional culture), but rather as creators of systems in their own right, for they have created cooperatives, mutualist societies, political blocks, international networks of communications, and social networks, to name but a few examples.

Second, Chicanos view themselves as participants in the historical process, for they are inseparable from history.

Third, this population has been the creator and generator of social forms such as dialects, music, personal networks, creators of communities where none existed before, and they proclaim their Mestizaje and, as such, constitute a pluralistic people.

Fourth, Chicanos see in their historical existence a continuous engaging in social issues, the spurious concepts of "resignation" and "fatalism" notwithstanding. Two examples are the pioneering of the labor movement in the West, and the fifty-year or more struggle for bilingual education (not bilingual acculturation theory).

Fifth, the concept of the illiterate Mexican-American must go, for it is true that this population has published well over 500 newspapers in the Southwest from 1848 to 1950, to say nothing of countless posters, signs, newsletters, and the like.

Sixth, the Chicano must be viewed as capable of his own system of rationality, for without this faculty he could not have survived, establish philosophies of economics, politics, Chicano studies programs, and philosophies of human existence.

Seventh, intellectual activity has been part and parcel of Chicano existence as evidenced by speech patterns, bilingualism, and a highly sophisticated humor that relies heavily upon metaphors and satire. This activity requires of the participants a mastery of language in order to engage in this common practice.

And *eighth,* as a population whose antecedents are Mexican, the bulk of Chicano existence has been oriented to a symbiotic residence within ecosystems. For in Mexico, unlike the United States, no plant or animal has been rendered extinct in its five hundred year history. Thus Chicano history has for centuries practiced what only today is becoming a concern of modern science for the conservation of natural resources and a balance of nature. In other words, what in ignorance and crudeness has been called the Mexican *traditional subjugation to nature* by Saunders, Edmunson, Kluckhohn, Heller, Samora, and many other social scientists, in reality has been a conscious philosophy for the maintenance of ecological balance in an ecosystem.

This symbiotic relationship within the universe, that is the historical patrimony of Chicanos, revolves around a philosophical system about the nature of man and man, of man in nature, and man in the universe. In essence, this philosophy is non-Weberian, non-Hegelian, and it is very dissimilar to Greek ontology. The complexities of this philosophy remain to be adequately explored by contemporary Chicano social scientists and historians in their efforts toward the articulation of a self-image. But when this has been done, the cycle by which the studied become the studiers will have been completed, and still another new dimension to Chicano existence will have been added to a long, a complicated, and a very rewarding experience that is called Chicano history.

Berkeley, Califas.

NOTES AND REFERENCES

1. Doran, F. S. A., *Mind, A Social Phenomenon,* William Sloane Associates, Publishers. New York. 1952, p. 4.

2. Wagner, Helmut R., "Types of Sociological Theory, Toward a System of Classification," *American Sociological Review,* 1963, Vol. 28, Number 5, pp. 735-742.

3. "Problems of Surveying the Social Sciences and Humanities," *International Social Science Journal* (Unesco), Vol. XVI, Number 4, 1964 (special issue devoted to this subject matter).

4. Remmling, Gunter W., "Karl Mannheim: Revision of an Intellectual Portrait," *Social Forces,* 1961, Vol. 40, Number 1, p. 27.

5. Rossi, Pietro, "Scientific Objectivity and Value Hypotheses," *International Social Science Journal* (Unesco), 1965, Vol. XVII, Number 1, p. 68.

6. Berreman, Gerald D., "Anemic and Emetic Analysis in Social Anthropology," *American Anthropologist,* 1966, Vol. 68, Number 2, p. 350.

7. Kaplan, Abraham, *The Conduct of Inquiry: Methodology for Behavioral Science,* Chandler Publishing Co., San Francisco, California, 1964, p. 406.

8. Hsu, Francis L. K., "Rethinking the Concept 'Primitive,'" *Current Anthropology,* 1964, Vol. 5, Number 3, p. 169.

9. *Ibid.,* p. 169.

10. *Ibid.,* p. 170.

11. Opler, Morris E., "The Human Being in Culture History," *American Anthropologist,* 1964, Vol. 66, Number 3, p. 524.

12. White, Leslie A., "Anthropology 1964: Retrospect and Prospect," *American Anthropologist,* 1965, Vol. 67, Number 3, p. 630.

13. Sorenson, John L., "Some Field Notes on the Power Structure of the American Anthropological Association," *American Behavioral Scientist,* 1964, Vol. VII, No. 6, p. 8.

14. *Ibid.,* p. 8 (Emphasis mine)

15. Bugental, J. F. T., "Humanistic Psychology: A New Breakthrough," *American Psychologist,* 1963, Vol. 18, Number 8, p. 565.

16. Clarke, Kenneth B., "Problems of Power and Social Change: Toward a Relevant Social Psychology," *Journal of Social Issues,* 1965, Vol. XXI, No. 3, p. 5-6.

17. *Ibid.,* p. 8.

18. Kahn, Theodore C., "Evaluation of United States of America Psychology by the 'Four-years-Absent' Method," *American Psychologist,* 1962, Vol. 17, No. 10, p. 708.

19. MacLeod, Robert B., "The Teaching of Psychology and the Psychology We Teach," *American Psychologist*, 1965, Vol. 20, Number 5, p. 344.

20. *Ibid.*, p. 346.

21. *Ibid.*, p. 350.

22. Kaplan, Bert, "Introduction," in *The Inner World of Mental Illness*, Harper and Row, New York, 1964. (B. Kaplan, editor), p. vii.

23. Szasz, Thomas S., "The Myth of Mental Illness," *American Psychologist*, 1960, Vol. 15, Number 2, p. 113.

24. Dahrendorf, Ralf, "Out of Utopia: Toward a Reorientation of Sociological Analysis," *The American Journal of Sociology*, 1958, Vol. LXIV, Number 2, p. 118.

25. Garfinkle, Harold, "Studies of the Routine Grounds of Everyday Activities," *Social Problems*, 1964, Vol. 11, Number 3, p. 244.

26. Gouldner, Alvin W., "Anti-Minotaur: The Myth of a Value-Free Sociology," *Social Problems*, 1962, Vol. 9, Number 3, p. 199.

27. Horowitz, Irving Lewis (Book Review), "Anthropology for Sociologists: Cross Disciplinary Research as Scientific Humanism," *Social Problems*, 1963, Vol. 11, Number 2, p. 202.

28. Hughes, Everett C., "Ethnocentric Sociology," *Social Forces*, 1961, Vol. 40, Number 1, p. 1 (see abstract).

29. *Ibid.*, p. 3.

30. Wrong, Dennis H., "The Oversocialized Conception of Man in Modern Sociology," *American Sociological Review*, 1961, Vol. 26, Number 2, p. 193.

31. Romano-V., Octavio Ignacio, "The Anthropology and Sociology of Mexican-Americans: the Distortion of History," *El Grito*, 1968, Vol. II, Number 1, pp. 13-26.

32. Vaca, Nick C., "The Mexican-American in the Social Sciences, 1912-1970. Part I: 1912-1935," *El Grito*, 1970, Volume III, Number 3, pp. 3-24. (See also Part II in this issue of *El Grito*.)

33. Montiel, Miguel, "The Social Science Myth of the Mexican American Family," *El Grito*, 1970, Vol. III, Number 4, pp. 56-63.

34. Alvidrez, Samuel (See "Drug Use Trends in California," this issue of *El Grito*).

35. Moreno, Steve, "Problems Related to Present Testing Instruments," *El Grito*, 1970, Volume III, Number 3, pp. 25-29.

36. (See note 31 above.)

The Anthropology and Sociology of the Mexican-Americans:

THE DISTORTION OF MEXICAN-AMERICAN HISTORY

A Review Essay

OCTAVIO IGNACIO ROMANO—V.

Suppose that you are a traveler from outer space. You land on earth. Everything has been devastated by some final war. You wander about, looking. Finally you find a trap door leading down into the ground. There you find an underground library — left there for posterity. You are now that posterity.

Curious, you pull a book down from a shelf. The book you select is about Mexican-Americans, written by a social scientist. You begin to read. Interesting. Strange. Intrigued, you read more about Mexican-Americans, more books by social scientists from the same shelf. You read Tuck, Griffith, Saunders, Clark, Edmonson, Rubel, Heller, Madsen, Landes, Kluckhohn, and Samora. By the time you finish reading these books you have come to two conclusions: (1) Earthlings used social science to "explain" history, and, (2) Mexican-Americans had virtually no history to speak of, trapped as they were in their isolated Traditional Culture, an ahistorical process to begin with.

The first conclusion is correct. The second is not. Here's why.

The Concept of Traditional Culture

The social concept of Traditional Culture is a passive concept — scientifically, philosophically, and empirically equipped to deal with human beings only as passive containers and retainers of culture. In the United States, all social science studies of Mexican-Americans have blindly relied upon this totally passive concept of Traditional Culture in order to, (1) describe the foundations of Mexican-American culture, (2) to "explain" the existence of Mexican-Americans over time, and (3) to use the idea of Traditional Culture as a final cause of empirical life. For these reasons, social science studies have dealt with Mexican-Americans as an ahistoric people – with a place in history reserved for them only when they undergo some metamorphosis usually called acculturation. As a consequence, Mexican-Americans are never seen as participants in history, much less as generators of the historical process.

This stultified view of Mexican-Americans is clearly illustrated by the following statement by William Madsen, anthropologist.

> Mexican-Americans caught in the middle of the conflict between two cultures may react in one of several ways. Some retreat to the security of the conservative Mexican-American world. Some seek geographical escape by migrating to the larger cities of Texas or to California, Michigan, or Illinois. Some escape into the twilight zone of alcoholism. Some rebel and commit crimes or engage in antisocial behavior. As their numbers increase, more and more *acculturated* Mexican-Americans are trying to create for themselves a respected place embracing the best of both worlds. (p. 109, my emphasis)

According to Madsen, Mexican-American culture represents a retreat, whereas acculturation represents creativity and change. It is with bi-polar dichotomies such as this that the notion of the passive Traditional Culture is perpetuated.

Is this view historically accurate? Is it true that people of Mexican descent in the United States have waited to become acculturated before participating in history?

Mexican-Americans: An Historical Perspective

Contrary to the ahistorical views of anthropology and sociology, Mexican-Americans as well as Mexican immigrants have not simply wallowed passively in some teleological treadmill, awaiting the emergence of an acculturated third generation before joining in the historical process.[1] For example, in 1883 several hundred cowboys in the Panhandle went on strike, and this strike call was signed by a man named Juan Gomez. Aside from this signature, it is not known how many of these strikers were of Mexican descent. What is known, however, is that this event signaled the beginning of over seventy years of labor strife between Mexicans, Mexican-Americans, and their employers.[2] Then, in 1903, over 1,000 Mexican and Japanese sugar-beet workers went on strike in California. This was followed by a wave of strikes in Los Angeles, initiated by Mexican railway workers. In 1922 Mexican field workers sought to organize in Fresno; this effort was followed by the formation of a large union *La Confederación de Uniones Obreras* in southern California during 1927. This worker confederation organized twenty locals with over 3,000 members. Its first strike was called in the Imperial Valley in 1928. Scarcely two years later, in 1930, some 5,000 Mexican field workers were on strike in the Imperial Valley for the second time. Not long after that, in 1933, the largest agricultural workers' strike to date in California took place when 7,000 Mexican workers walked out of the onion, celery, and berry fields in Los Angeles County. Later, in the same year, Mexican workers were on strike in the southern area of the San Joaquin Valley. That was the same year in which Mexicans and Mexican-Americans struck for the third time in the Imperial Valley.

Only three more years had elapsed when, in 1936, 2,000 Mexican celery workers went on strike outside of Los Angeles. In this same year, 2,500 Mexican workers tied up for several weeks a $20,000,000 citrus crop in Orange County.

These upheavals, virtually continuous from the turn of the century until World War II, were only the major events which took place in California. These, however, were not the only efforts made by Mexicans and Mexican-Americans. During the thirties, for example, workers of Mexican descent were striking in Arizona, New Mexico, Texas, Idaho, Colorado, Washington, Michigan, as well as in California — that is, in eight different states of the Union.

These were only the agricultural strikes. Parallel efforts included the 1934 sheepherder strike in west Texas, a similar action by pecan shellers in San Antonio, as well as a protest in south Texas. Moreover, several thousand Mexican coal miners went on strike in New Mexico during the mid-thirties. Here, too, a union was organized. It was called *La Liga Obrera de Habla Española,* with a membership of 8,000 individuals.

In Arizona the story was much the same, with labor unrest beginning as early as 1915 with a strike involving 5,000 workers. This unrest has continued sporadically over the years.

The growing labor movement involving Mexicans and Mexican-Americans was met with massive military counter-action in order to break the strikes. Massive deportations followed, even though the unrest continued.

Then, in 1946, after decades of widespread and constant turmoil and upheavals followed by military action against demands for a better life, a sociologist named Ruth Tuck made the following incredible statement:

> For many years, the (Mexican) *immigrant and his sons made no effort to free themselves.* They burned with resentment over a thousand slights, *but they did so in pri-*

vate. . . . Perhaps this *passivity* is the mark of any minority which is just emerging. . . . (p. 198, emphasis mine)

Thus, in one semantic stroke, this sociologist wiped out the decades of strife in which Mexican immigrants and their sons fought to free themselves. In effect, Tuck wiped out history. In so doing, she set the stage for what was to follow in subsequent anthropological and sociological studies of Mexican-Americans.

Social Science, Mexican-Americans, and the Distortion of History

Ruth Tuck's opinion of a population that does nothing but "burn with resentment privately" became the dominant view of Mexican-American character in the literature of the social sciences. Scarcely eight years later, for example, the sociologist Lyle Saunders wrote,

> A closely related trait of the Spanish-speaking people is their somewhat greater readiness toward acceptance and resignation than is characteristic of the Anglo. Whereas it is the belief of the latter that man has an obligation to struggle against and if possible to master the problems and difficulties that beset him, the Spanish-speaking person is more likely to accept and resign himself to whatever destiny brings him. (p. 128)

And again from Saunders,

> The Spanish-speaking person, by contrast (to Anglos) is likely to meet difficulties by adjusting to them rather than by attempting to overcome them. Fate is somewhat inexorable, and there is nothing much to be gained by struggling against it. If the lot of man is hard — and it frequently is — such is the will of God, incomprehensible but just, and it is the obligation of man to accept it. . . . In the collective recollection of village life there is only the remembrance of men and women who were born, resigned themselves to suffering and hardship and occasional joys, and died when their time came. (p. 129)

In this manner, as Ruth Tuck before him, Lyle Saunders distorted history, essentially rewrote history, and perpetuated the concept of an ahistoric people, the "somnolent, passive Mexican" referred to in Vaca's article,[3] the Mexican lazily asleep under the cactus in the popular and ignorant mind.

Saunders' "study" was quickly followed by another equally distorted interpretation, Munro S. Edmonson's *Los Manitos*, a New Mexico study. Here the perverted litany continues when he states that ". . . fatalistic acceptance of things which 'just happen' are a source of wonder and despair to Anglo housewives with Mexicano

servants, but they are a *precise* expression of the Mexican attitude
. . ." (p. 60, emphasis mine) Edmonson goes on to say, "Hispanos
give a characteristic shrug of acceptance of death and illness as inevitable." (p. 60) In other words, Hispanos do not cry at funerals,
they just give a "characteristic shrug." These absurd statements are
not enough for Edmonson, he has more. Hispanos have no "individual responsibility" in sexual relations (p. 60), perhaps they are like
cats and dogs, whereas Anglo sexual practices provide "rational"
alternatives. In other words, not only is history distorted, but Hispanos are now sexually irresponsible and irrational. There is little
need to dwell upon such absurdities, except to point out that Hispanos are also said to be fatalistic about the "natural order of things"
due to their religion (p. 60), are willing "to live with failure," live
in "mañana land," are politically apathetic, and finally, ". . . where
Hispano culture is fatalistic, American culture is markedly activist."
(p. 61) In this simple little phrase, like Tuck and Saunders before
him, Edmonson cleanly wipes out history and simultaneously classifies these people of New Mexico as basically un-American. This is
a theme that is incessantly recurrent in all of the social science literature on Mexican-Americans. It is an ideological precursor to the
current un-American charges leveled against the Tijerina movement
in New Mexico today.

From Munro Edmonson's 1957 "study" it is an easy jump to Florence Rockwood Kluckhohn and Fred L. Strodbeck's 1961 report
that, conceptually, is the exact mirror image of the Edmonson publication. The Kluckhohn-Strodbeck section on Hispanos in New Mexico is based upon a sample of twenty-three in a community of 150
people. Then this minute sample is used to describe Mexican-American and New Mexican value orientations for the past 400 years! It
is important to keep this fact in mind in view of Celia Heller's subsequent study of Mexican-Americans which relies heavily on the
Kluckhohn sample of twenty-three, and also the Samora-Lamanna
Chicago study of Mexican-Americans which accepts the same views
without question.

The historically distorted studies of Tuck, Saunders, Edmonson,
and Kluckhohn-Strodbeck have been widely accepted in departments of anthropology and sociology throughout the United States.
These books have become *the* authoritative sources of information
about Mexican-Americans for a wide variety of institutional agencies, from schools of medicine, departments of social welfare, to departments of employment and other governmental agencies. In this
way, thousands upon thousands of people, many of them Mexican-
Americans themselves, have been indoctrinatd with the historically

perverted notion that Mexican-Americans are an ahistoric people who have had no history except that of a long and tedious siesta.

But, one might say, these are "old studies" — the latest of them published in 1961. Fortunately we live in a nation dedicated to "progress." Obviously, then, such stereotypes of Mexican-Americans have been corrected in the intervening years — thanks to science which is the handmaiden of progress. To see if this is so, let us turn to three widely circulated current studies of Mexican-Americans: *The Mexican-Americans of South Texas* by William Madsen (1964), *Mexican-American Youth: Forgotten Youth at the Crossroads* by Celia Stopnicka Heller (1968, third printing), and *Mexican-Americans in a Midwest Metropolis:A Study of East Chicago* by Julian Samora and Richard A. Lamanna (1967).

Today these books are used in the training of professionals as well as in race and ethnic relations courses in colleges and universities. Therefore, it is of importance to consider them in some detail.

William Madsen's Mexican-Americans

In *The Mexican-Americans of South Texas,* Madsen begins by saying,

> In our melting-pot process, there is a willingness to accept foreign holidays, foods, and some expressions of speech. However, it is assumed that every acculturated American shares certain core values with the rest of the population. His behavior must be comprehensible and predictable in most situations. Every American is expected to show maximum faith in America, science, and progress. (p. 1)

But apparently faith in progress and progress itself are two different things, for Madsen's volume reveals no significant change from the views of its predecessors. It, too, deals with Mexican-Americans as an ahistoric people. It, too, deals with this population as if it were composed of passive, anxiety-ridden receptors who must undergo a complete psychological, cultural, and personality metamorphosis before they can be considered fullfledged members of society. Madsen sees this total changeover as associated with acculturation and a simultaneous movement from the lower into the middle class. In his words, "By whatever criteria one judges successful acculturation among Mexican-Americans, it is generally a middle- or upper-class phenomenon." (p. 3) *Ergo,* lower class Mexican-Americans are not Americans at all. Once again we see the un-American theme which appeared in Edmonson's publication.

As it turns out, the creatures who inhabit Madsen's book are the same as those found in the works of Tuck, Saunders, Edmonson, and

Kluckhohn. For example, Madsen bases his study on his conceptualization of the traditional culture which allows him to say, "Fatalistic
philosophy produces an attitude of resignation which often con-
vinces the Anglo that the Latin lacks drive and determination. What
the Anglo tries to control, the Mexican-American tries to accept.
Misfortune is something the Anglo tries to overcome and the Latin
views as fate." (p. 16) Then he adds, "Acceptance and appreciation
of things as they are constitute primary values of La Raza." (p. 17)
In these comments once again we see Edmonson's "characteristic
shrug" and Saunders' passive people who are born, live, and die in
total and abject resignation. Here, too, we see Tuck's creatures who
make no effort whatever to free themselves. Once again these social
scientists want us to believe that Mexican-Americans accept hunger,
malnutrition, death, exploitation, oppression, and segregation with
characteristic shrugs, and, according to Madsen, with an "acceptance
and appreciation of things as they are." Once again the history, especially the history of non-acceptance, has been totally obliterated.

The obvious implication, of course, is that because Mexican-
Americans are so resigned, then all salvation must come from without.

In Madsen's world, not only are Mexican-Americans passively
fatalistic, their women are super-passively-fatalistic with a touch of
sado-masochism thrown in for good measure. For example, "The
Mexican-American wife who irritates her husband may be beaten.
She should accept this punishment as deserved. Some wives assert
that they are grateful for punishment at the hands of their husbands for such concern with shortcomings indicates profound love."
(p. 20)

There is more. Mexican-Americans ". . . regard envy as a destructive emotion and admit that it is a major barrier to the material
advancement of La Raza. Envy is felt to be such a powerful emotion
that it is difficult or impossible to suppress." (p. 22) "While the
Anglos try to keep up with the Joneses, the Latins try to keep the
Garcias down to their own level." (p. 22) They accomplish this
through gossip, ridicule, witchcraft, and fear. (p. 22-23)

What Madsen has said, of course, is that Mexican-Americans are
the generators of their own problems. Consequently, they are their
own worst enemies. This is all a part of their traditional culture
which they learn from their parents. Therefore, their parents are
their own worst enemies.

Let us delve a little more into what this author has said about
the family. "The family is the main focus of social stratification in
all classes of Mexican-American society." (p. 44) In addition, "An-

glos believe that equality in the home and self-advancement are necessary to maintain the American ideals of freedom, democracy, and progress. Mexican-Americans believe that putting family above self is necessary to fulfill the will of God." (p. 46) From this it follows that not only are Mexican-American parents their children's own worst enemies, they are also a potential threat to the American ideals of freedom, democracy, and progress. And, according to Madsen, going to college doesn't seem to help much either, for, "A good many of the Mexican-Americans who go to college don't seem to know what they want out of an education. This lack of purpose is particularly characteristic of Latins who are seeking a higher education than their parents received." (p. 108) All of this, of course, leads to a "characteristic lack of goal orientation," a modern euphemism for the Mexican slumbering under the cactus.

To summarize Madsen's views, due to their own culture Mexican-Americans are the generators of their own problems. This impedes their material advancement. Therefore, today they are just as they have always been, and they will not progress until they change completely. Thus, *Madsen has equated economic determinism with cultural determinism,* just as Oscar Lewis has done.[4] Finally, Madsen has made Mexican-American culture the final cause of all of the problems that Mexican-Americans have encountered throughout history.

Celia S. Heller's Mexican-Americans

Celia Stopnicka Heller opens her book with the following introductory statement:

> The Mexican-American minority has received little attention from the mass media of communication and, outside the Southwest, there is hardly any awareness of its existence. . . . Moreover, in those southwestern states, where they are concentrated, an awareness exists but there is no corresponding knowledge about them. Of course, few people in those states would admit ignorance and more would vouch that they "know all there is to know" about Mexican-Americans. The "all" very often consists of a stereotypic image of Mexican-Americans that is widespread. I have heard numerous comments which reflect it. The comments about Mexican-American youth in particular — made even by individuals having contact with them, such as teachers, school administrators, and social workers — run something like this: How "Mexican" the young people are in their ways, how lacking in ambition, how prone to delinquent behavior.

> Even for the person who is not satisfied with those stereo-
> types it is not easy to obtain factual information. (p. 3-4)

As we shall see, Celia Heller is more than well satisfied with
"those stereotypes," almost exhuberant — adding some of her own to
boot. Her starting point, as in other such books, is the traditional
culture of the Mexican-Americans. From such a notion she proceeds
to construct the following image of Mexican-Americans. First, Mexican-Americans are not quite Americans, or, in her words, "among
the least Americanized." (p. 4) In this one phrase she suggests that
there are immutable and incontrovertible criteria that define what
an American is, which, as it turns out, is something that Mexican-
Americans are not. If, then, Mexican-Americans are not Americans,
what are they? This question poses absolutely no problem to Miss
Heller for, wouldn't you know, Mexican-Americans are really all
alike. Know one and you know them all, as we say. Or, to put it in
her own words, Mexican-Americans exhibit a "marked lack of internal differentiation" and therefore constitute an "unusually homogenous ethnic group." (p. 15)

Mexican-Americans, she goes on to say, have a language problem with a "foreign" accent often persisting to the third generation
(p. 30), their progress is retarded because of their large families
(p. 33), and they manifest an unusual persistence in traditional
forms. (p. 34) All of this makes for a socialization process in Mexican-American families that is not conducive to advancement." (p.
34) This is especially true since "parental indulgence hampers the
son's need for achievement." (p. 37) Then she sums it up by saying,
"This lack of emphasis upon 'making good' in conventional terms is
consistent with the themes of fatalism and resignation which run
through Mexican-American culture." (p. 38)

In less than forty pages, then, this sociologist has said that Mexican-Americans are not Americans, that they are all virtually alike,
that they tend to speak with a foreign accent, that they are held
down by their own families, that their sons are helpless victims of
parental indulgence which retards them, and that they are fatalistically resigned to this cultural miasma. Miss Heller is just warming
up. She then goes on to add that Mexican-Americans are also char-
acteristically lazy and somewhat irrational about it all. In her own
words, "The combination of stress on work and rational use of time
. . . forms little or no part of the Mexican-American socialization
process." (p. 38) Due to their parents' and their parental culture,
therefore, Mexican-Americans learn "lax habits," have no "habits of
self-discipline," because they are "vigorously trained to be depend-

ent" people. (p. 39) All of this would not be so bad if only Mexican-Americans would only try to think for themselves. But, this is not the case for "few Mexican-American homes stress higher education." (p. 39) In fact, they don't even stress "intellectual effort." (p. 39)

What is a major consequence of all this Mexican-American cultural persistence? CRIMINAL BEHAVIOR!! Let Cecial Stopnicka Heller tell us in her own words:

> ". . . it may be suggested that the excess of juvenile delinquents among Mexican-Americans . . . is not composed of deviants from the cultural pattern of the Mexican-American population but rather of *boys who over-conform to this pattern.*" (p. 76, emphasis mine)

In summary, Celia S. Heller believes that virtually all Mexican-Americans are the same, that they behave like foreigners, that the parents are their children's own worst enemies, and that they are fatalistically resigned to all of this. In addition, Mexican-Americans do not stress work or even rationality, they have lax habits, they are undisciplined, have no initiative and even less ambition — all because of their traditional culture, which breeds excessive crime.

You will recall Heller's introductory comments in which she decried the stereotypes about Mexican-Americans held by teachers, school administrators, and social workers. This disclaimer did little, if anything, to conceal the fact that she actually expanded the existent stereotypes to the lazy, ahistoric, somnolent, childish, and criminally intent Mexican — giving such dehumanizing views a spurious legitimization by calling them socal science. But neither the crocodile tears of her disclaimers, nor the false mask of scientific procedure, conceal the fact that Heller's book is one of the most vicious in existence today. It is vicious because it classifies millions and millions of people as being virtually all alike, just as Adolf Hitler classified millions of people twenty-eight years ago as being all the same — calling them the progenitors of all of their own problems — problems which were said to be the direct *consequence of their own history,* a history which, in Hitler's eyes, was also a Traditional Culture.

Julian Samora and Richard A. Lamanna's Mexican-Americans

The volume titled *Mexican-Americans in a Midwest Metropolis* by Samora and Lamanna perpetuates the same spurious fiction of its predecessors. For example,

> The very nature of some of the value orientations of the Mexican-Americans presents a barrier to their rapid as-

similation. There is a note of fatalism and resignation in the attitudes and behavior of the residents and an orientation to the present (not unlike that described by Kluckhohn in connection with the Southwest) that would have to change somewhat before they could be expected to achieve significant changes in their social situation. (p. 135)

Thus, Samora and Lamanna, like Heller, Madsen, and the others before them, place the final cause of social conditions upon the Mexican-Americans themselves. In doing so, they also commit the fallacy of equating economic determinism with cultural determinism. This is the modern version of the Protestant Ethic as described by Max Weber many years ago.

Social Science Fiction

What are these Mexican-Americans who have been created by social scientists?

First, they are masochistic, for, according to Tuck, they make no effort to free themselves from the social conditions in which they find themselves. Therefore, they are passive. This is primarily due to their religion according to Saunders. He then draws a picture of a world populated by vegetables which he chooses to call the Spanish-speaking people — people who are born, resign themselves to suffering, and then lay down and quietly die when their time comes. The same blobs are molded from the same semantic clay by Munro Edmonson. To him, these people behave as they do according to their religion, are somewhat irrational as well as irresponsible, live in mañana land, are politically apathetic and chacteristically fatalistic. In addition, they are un-American. Madsen elaborates on the un-American theme, then proceeds to elaborate on the social vegetable theme. These un-American social vegetables are produced by their own parents who follow their own traditional culture which, as it turns out, is the prime generator of all of the problems faced by these people. Taking her cue from her predecessors, quoting them profusely, Celia Heller zeroes in on the Mexican-American family as the principal cause of all that foreign behavior among Mexican-Americans, adding that this produces a population of people who are virtually all alike, resigned to their lot, basically lazy, irrational, lax in their habits, have no initiative, less ambition, and, as such, are criminally prone.

William Madsen asserted that to be "American" one must espouse a faith in progress. But, clearly, these studies represent no progress at all. Perhaps a peek into the past history of the United

States will clarify this apparent ambiguity. For example, some one-hundred years ago the New Mexico senator, Thaddeus Stevens, said that the native New Mexicans were "a hybrid race of Spanish and Indian origin, ignorant, degraded, demoralized, and priest-ridden."[5] The only difference between the rhetoric of Thaddeus Stevens and that of the social scientists is the jargonese. There is no difference in meaning. During these same American frontier days, many other writers depicted the "idle, thriftless" natives they encountered in the west. In the words of Carey McWilliams,

> Essentially this same impression was formed by a wide variety of observers: men and women; officers, miners, surveyors, trappers, mountainmen, sea captains, and journalists. Passed along to those who were about to leave for the borderlands, repeated by all observers, these stereotyped impressions were national currency during the Mexican-American war and the patriotic sanction long continued. (p. 131-2)

It is clear from these statements that contemporary social science views of Mexican-Americans are precisely those held by people during the days of the American frontier. In short, there has not been any significant change in views toward Mexican-Americans for the past 100 years. Certainly this is not progress at all. What we have, instead, are contemporary social scientists busily perpetuating the very same opinions of Mexican culture that were current during the Mexican-American War. These opinions were, and are, pernicious, vicious, misleading, degrading, and brainwashing in that they obilterate history and then re-write it in such a way as to eliminate the historical significance of Mexican-Americans, as well as to simultaneously question the legitimacy of their presence in contemporary society.

The Significance of Mexican-American History

Historically, Mexican-Americans have been, and continue to be, a pluralistic people. As such, they cannot be described according to a simplistic formula, despite the strident assertions made by social scientists, assertions that insist upon the antiquated idea of a bipolar process of change beginning at one point and leading all Mexican-Americans in the same direction, like sheep — from stagnant fatalism to assimilation and creativity.

But actual history itself reveals this formulation to be a grand hoax, a blatant lie. Witness the seemingly endless decades of labor conflict initiated by Mexicans and Mexican-Americans — briefly outlined at the beginning of this paper — conflict which involved literally tens of thousands of people of Mexican descent and which at one time spread to eight different states in the nation — conflict which was met with massive military counter-action. Social scientists have never asked themselves just why such massive military action was necessary in order to deal with a "resigned, passive, fatalistic, non-goal oriented people with lax habits and no plans for the future." To ask themselves this question would be to acknowledge history, a history of constant confrontations brought about by elements of the same "traditional culture" which they have repeatedly described as virtually stagnant and actionless. "Long charged with a lack of 'leadership' and talent for organization, they proved all too effectively that neither talent was lacking," wrote Carey McWilliams in 1949. (p. 193) Proof of this assertion is the fact that Mexicans and Mexican-Americans were the pioneers of the trade union movement in the American Southwest.

These organized confrontations led the same author to say that, "By 1930 the myth of the docility of Mexican labor had been thoroughly exploded. . . " (p. 193) since they were quick to rebel against the subordinate status imposed upon them. *But McWilliams did not count on either the semantic genius, or the frontier-expansionist mentality, of the social scientists who later came west to rewrite history* — to merge the myth of the docile Mexican with that of the fatalistic and non-goal oriented Mexican-American — which is no change at all, but only a latter-day repetition of the ideas that have been predominant since before the days of Manifest Destiny.

Confrontation With Life

If the "traditional culture" of Mexican-Americans is not that described by social scientists, then what is it? What are the origins of the historical movements and conflicts of the past? What are the roots of the movements and conflicts taking place today? Have Mexican-Americans simply been reacting blindly to external circumstances? Have they merely tried to imitate people of other cultures? Or has their historical confrontation with life come from elements within their historical culture, elements heretofore ignored in studies of Mexican-Americans.

These questions can be answered in two ways. First, the concept of the "traditional culture," as presently used by social scientists, must be totally dropped. Instead, the concept of the historical culture must be adopted. Second, the idea of the non-intellectual Mexican-American must be dropped also. Instead, in order to answer these questions, one must know something about the intellectual history of Mexican-Americans.

NOTES

[1]See Nick C. Vaca, 1967.
[2]This event, as well as the historical events that follow, is from Carey
McWilliams, 1949, pp. 195-209.

[3]See Nick C. Vaca, 1967.
[4]See Nick C. Vaca, 1968.
[5]McWilliams, 1949, p. 121.

BIBLIOGRAPHY

Edmonson, Munro S.
1957 *Los Manitos: A Study of Institutional Values,* Middle Ameri-
can Research Institute, Tulane University, New Orleans.
Heller, Celia S.
1968 *Mexican-American Youth: Forgotten Youth at the Crossroads,*
Random House, New York (Third Printing).
Kluckhohn, Florence Rockwood and Fred L. Strodbeck
1961 *Variations in Value Orientations,* Row, Peterson and Company,
New York.
Madsen, William
1964 *Mexican-Americans of South Texas,* Case Studies in Cultural
Anthropology, Holt, Rinehart and Winston, New York.
McWilliams, Carey
1949 *North From Mexico: The Spanish-Speaking People of the
United States,* The Peoples of America Series, J. B. Lippincott
Company, New York.
Samora, Julian and Richard A. Lamanna
1967 *Mexican-Americans in a Midwest Metropolis: A Study of East
Chicago,* Mexican-American Study Project, Division of Re-
search, Graduate School of Business, University of California,
Los Angeles.
Saunders, Lyle
1954 *Cultural Difference and Medical Care: The Case of the Spanish-Speaking People of the Southwest,* Russell Sage Foundation, New York.
Tuck, Ruth
1946 *Not With the Fist,* Harcourt, Brace and Company, New York.
Vaca, Nick C.
1967 "Message to the People," *Mexican-American Liberation Papers,* Quinto Sol Publications, Berkeley, California.
1968 "The Sociology of Being a Mexican-Russian," *El Grito,* Summer 1968, p. 39-40.

o   o   o

The Social Science Myth
of the
Mexican American Family

MIGUEL MONTIEL

There is an ideological, philosophical, and theoretical resemblance between studies of the *Mexican* family and their counterparts, studies of the *Mexican American* family. These similarities have generally been taken for granted, for such thinking has been based primarily on the assumed similarities between the value orientations of Mexicans and Mexican Americans. Such assumptions have had a considerable impact on the method of study used when dealing with this subject matter. For example, the sociologist Fernando Peñalosa has said that, ". . . the dynamice of Mexican family life as portrayed by Mexican scholars are *essential and relevant* for understanding the current changes in the Mexican American family."[1]

But the theories and concepts that have guided Mexican family studies have consistently lacked both methodological sophistication as well as empirical verification. Specifically, they have relied almost totally upon a psychoanalytic model in which there is an uncritical use of concepts like *machismo*. However, as used, this approach has relegated all explanations of Mexican family life to a pathological perspective.

An analysis of the literature will give us an understanding of psychoanalysis as it appears in Mexican social science and how it is related to the concept of *machismo*. This concept is the central device used to explain family roles in Mexican studies and subsequently in Mexican American studies. The careless use of *machismo* as an explanatory device has resulted in what is here called the myth of the Mexican American family.

Psychoanalysis: Inferiority and Machismo

The origin of psychoanalysis in Mexican philosophy and subsequently its diffusion into Mexican social science is an ironic historical occurrence indeed. Using Ortega's thesis — *Yo soy yo y mi circunstancia,* Samuel Ramos, pioneer in the philosophy of Mexican culture, framed a rationale for his philosophy. Ramos' principal objective was to ultimately define a perspective which revolved around the Mexican experience thus avoiding dependence on European thought.[2,28] Ramos believed that imitation by Mexicans of European thought had resulted in a feeling of inferiority among the Mexican people, and as a consequence the time had come for Mexicans to "adopt a living culture."[3] Noble as this cause may have been at the time of its initial proposal, it is an historic irony that Ramos himself was not true to his own ideal, for he ultimately relied upon Alfred Adler's individual psychology to "explain" the causes of Mexican "inferiority" as he saw it.[4]

Alfred Adler's theory postulates that children born with hereditary organic weaknesses are inclined to compensate both physically and emotionally in the direction of the defective function.[5] Furthermore, Adler's theory asserted that ". . . the whole human race is blessed with deficient organs," and thus there exists a continual resistance to the establishment of a harmonious life situation.[6] Specifically, he claimed that most individuals suffer from a "sense of female inferiority" and as a result "both sexes have derived an overstrained desire for masculinity." Adler called this the *masculine protest*.[7]

In much the same way, Samuel Ramos' historical interpretation of the evolution of the Mexican character concludes that the persistent domination of the Spaniards, first over the Indians and later over the Mexicans, created in the Mexican personality a sense of inferiority and resentment toward authority.[8,28] Correspondingly, Ramos' *pelado* becomes the essence of the Mexican character. This "nobody" in his lowly status and in his sense of worthlessness is then said to be revengeful and hostile toward those who threaten his virility which, supposedly, he has built up to support a deflated ego.[9,28]

Historically, the term inferiority is later substituted by insufficiency, but nevertheless the continual and persistent *external* domination is said to cause the Mexican to hide his feelings of inferiority.[10] Leopoldo Zea, for example, attributed the external force to the compromise of the Latin American ideal ". . . for the North American ideal of material comfort."[11] Octavio Paz provides the best example of a contemporary psychoanalytically oriented analysis of the Mexican character. In typical manner Paz states that he,

". . . agrees with Samuel Ramos that an inferiority complex influences our preference for analysis, and that the meagerness of our creative output was due not so much to the growth of our critical faculties at the expense of our creativity as it was to our instinctive doubts about our abilities."[12]

Octavio Paz becomes particularly important because his ideological explanation transcends national boundaries when he attempts to "analyze" the plight of the *pachuco*. Again alluding to
the inherent inferiority, he states:

> "The *Pachuco* tries to enter North American society in secret
> and daring ways, *but he impedes his own effort*. Having been
> cut off from his traditional culture, he asserts himself for a
> moment as a solitary and challenging figure. He denies both
> the society from which he originated and that of North Amer-
> ica. . . . The *Pachuco* is the prey of society, but instead of
> hiding he adorns himself to attract the hunter's attention."[13]
> *(emphasis mine)*

At this point the reader is probably wondering what these
"national character" studies have to do with the Mexican American or perhaps even the Mexican family. The fact of the matter
is that such studies have a way of appearing and reappearing in
many guises, like Octavio Paz' masks. For example, if it can be
said that there is a Mexican national character, then it must logically follow that the basic individual units of that national entity
must be a reflection of the national pattern. Not surprisingly, therefore, the central issue here is not only national character, but how
the national character manifests itself through individuals (traditional culture). In this manner, almost always the studies which
address themselves to the Mexican American family ultimately
evolve into a discussion of *machismo*: i.e., the national male character as it manifests itself through individual males over time.

It is around this concept that most "explanations" of family
structure evolve, including the Mexican American family, in spite
of the fact that the methodological transition required to jump
from the national character in general to the Mexican family in
particular is a hazardous enterprise indeed. In short, Ramos, Zea,
and Paz began with what can only be called essentially an aesthetic,
philosophical and psychoanalytically oriented exercise. In the following years their explorations have been accepted as the "true"
description of the Mexican character, the Mexican male, and ultimately the Mexican and Mexican American family. Their exercises
have been accepted uncritically by North American and Mexican
social scientists alike. Thus whatever reliability and validity these
studies might have had, has been predicated primarily upon philosophical emulation. *However, mere repetition of philosophical and
quasi-psychoanalytic postures does not per se constitute empirical
reality.*

Mexican Family Studies: Three Examples

An excellent example of the repetition of such postulates using *machismo* couched in psychoanalytic theory under the guise of "social science" is provided by Maria Bermudez in *La Vida Familiar Del Mexicano*.

The similarity between *machismo* and the inferiority which Ramos postulated provides the basic framework for Bermudez' theory. On the assumption that both factors (inferiority and *machismo*) originate from a common source, she then proceeds to outline the sequence of events that lead to the formation of the Mexican character — male and female.[14]

Briefly stated, Bermudez' basic argument is that the false concepts Mexicans have regarding masculinity and femininity impede Mexican males from being "candid and humane" and females from being "dignified and independent." Thus she declares that the characteristics of self-denial and self-inflicted suffering are mere products of ineptitude and nothing else among Mexican women. From this premise Bermudez builds a series of instances in which the Mexican is "deficient," ranging from excessive delinquency to underdeveloped industrialization.[15]

The writings of a well-known Mexican psychiatrist, Diaz-Guerrero, and a not-so-well known American psychiatrist, G. M. Gilbert, illustrate further their resemblance to the philosophical postulates of the Mexican cultural philosophers. Using a survey questionaire containing only ten structured questions, Diaz-Guerrero postulated that two propositions; (1) the unquestioned and absolute supremacy of the father, and (2) the necessary and absolute self-sacrifice of the mother, form the dominant Mexican family pattern.[16] On the basis of these ten questions he concluded that the inability of either partner — particularly the females — to fulfill their expectations created a tendency toward neurosis.[17]

Similarly, on the basis of talking to only *nine older adults*, G. M. Gilbert, in a study regarding sex differences in mental health in a Mexican village, found,

> ". . . a pronounced tendency to either severely constricted affect or to morbid-depressed-hypochondriacal types of responses among the older males . . . this may be indicative of increasing impotence and 'castration anxiety': as the males fail in the life-long struggle to live up to the demands of *machismo* . . .[18]

The "inferiority models" constructed by Bermudez, Diaz-Guerrero, and Gilbert — like those of Ramos, Zea, and Paz — lead to the same foregone conclusions regarding *machismo* and the Mexican character in general. Unlike the philosophers, however, the social scientists attempt to legitimize their observations "scientifically." For example, in her analysis of the Mexican population Bermudez' assumption that similarities outweigh differences justifies for her the methodological jump from the case to the class. In light of the evidence, this assumption must be viewed with suspicion. Such "legitimization" of philosophical postulates without serious attempts to validate them scientifically is illustrated also in Mexican American studies.

Mexican American Family Studies

In 1948, after a review of the literature pertaining to Mexicans in the United States, R. C. Jones assessed the situation regarding family studies in this way,

> Little of this material represents really basic or prolonged research but it is largely explanatory in character. A tremendous amount of duplication exists. References to family life are scattered and seldom documented.[19]

Twenty years later in 1968 Fernando Peñalosa stated this about Mexican American family studies,

> ". . . Mexican American family structure has not yet been subject to any systematic analysis. It may be said without exaggeration that neither the empirical data nor an adequate theoretical framework is yet available for the carrying out of this task.[20]

In 1944 Norman D. Humphrey conducted a study of the Detroit Mexican family. His findings closely parallel the generalizations in Mexico and set a framework for subsequent interpretations. Humphrey viewed the father's role as (1) food provider and (2) family judge and protector. The immigration of the Mexican family to the United States created "special" problems that would not be encountered had the family remained in Mexico. The failure of the father to provide adequately for his family created a decline in the status of the father and a lessening of the respect in the new culture.[21]

Twenty years later, William Madsen, an anthropologist, has some interesting comments relative to the status of the Mexican father in the United States:

> To a large extent, the supremacy of the male within his own home compensates for subservience he may have to demonstrate on the job or in the presence of a social superior.[22]

In discussing further the role of the Mexican American male he states that "The most convincing way of proving *machismo* and financial ability is to keep a mistress in the second household known as a *casa chica*.[23] In essence, Madsen, as did Humphrey twenty years before, depicts the role of the Mexican American father as insignificant and pathological.

A slightly different interpretation of the father's role in the Mexican family is provided by Robert Hayden who believes that supreme male dominance, individualism, pride, *wife beating*, aversion to contraceptives, and other traits traditionally attributed to the father are typical of Mexican American culture.[24] Hayden explains that these characteristics do not indicate either a neglect of responsibility or a break-up of family ties.[25] It is inconceivable to imagine, however, that there could exist any semblance of stability or close relationship in a family where behaviors described by Hayden are the norm.

In like manner, Celia Heller, sociologist and accepted "expert" on Mexican American youth, uses the *"enemy within"* notions of pathology to explain her belief in the lack of independence and achievement among Mexican American people. With reference to *machismo* she states:

> The kind of socialization that Mexican American children generally receive at home is not conducive to the development of the capacities needed for advancement by stressing values that hinder mobility — family ties, honor, masculinity, and living in the present — and by neglecting the values that are conducive to it . . .[26]

Summary

From the tremendous volume of literature that makes reference to the Mexican American family several generalizations emerge regarding their ideological, philosophical, and theoretical orientation.

First is the unquestioned acceptance of the "masculinity cult" to explain family roles. Unlike Mexican studies, however, *machismo* is not generally linked to what can be called a psychoanalytic orientation *per se*, but rather is arbitrarily interjected to explain family roles or concomitant problems *irrespective of the data available*. For instance, permeating the literature pertaining to the "problems of the Mexican American" is the idea that the nature of the family is best characterized by the cult of masculinity, which is said to be to blame for their problems. Secondly, this indiscriminate use of the concept of *machismo* coupled with the loose methodological approaches accounts for another characteristic of the literature — low level theoretical sophistication. Finally, the strong evidence of speculation (plus the patronizing and condescending sentiments of the writings) further make the findings and interpretations highly suspect.

Conclusion

The myth of the Mexican family has been created because of certain questionable assumptions that have dominated Mexican and Mexican American family studies. First and foremost is the concept social scientists have regarding *machismo,* as supposedly *the* underlying cause of Mexican and Mexican American problems. Secondly, it follows that this formulation is inherently incapable of defining normal behavior and thus automatically labels all Mexican and Mexican American people as sick — *only in degree of sickness do they vary.*

The seriousness of this fallacy can be brought to perspective only by examining concepts like ineptitude, irresponsibility, and inferiority that have been used to define *machismo.* Terms like *machismo* are abstract, value-laden concepts that lack the empirical referents necessary for construction of sound explanations. Accordingly, as long as research on the Mexican and Mexican American family is guided by anything other than sound operational definitions its findings, conclusions, and interpretations must be seen only as philosophical and ideological speculations — not as empirical truths.

NOTES

[1]Fernando Peñalosa, "Mexican Family Roles," *Marriage and the Family,* Vol. 30 (1968), p. 681.

[2]Patrick Romanell, *Making of the Mexican Mind,* (Lincoln, Nebraska: University of Nebraska Press, 1952), p. 164.

[3]*Ibid.,* p. 165.

[4]Alfred Adler, *Individual Psychology* (Paterson, New Jersey: Littlefield, Adams and Co., 1959). Alfred Adler was a famous Vienna physician who with Freud and Jung, has been so largely responsible for the widespread interest in psycho-analytic methods.

[5]Alfred Adler, "Individual Psychology" in *Theories of Personality,* Primary Sources and Research (New York: John Wiley and Sons, Inc., 1965), p. 99.

[6]*Ibid.*

[7]*Ibid.*

[8]G. W. Hewes, "Mexicans in Search of the 'Mexican': Notes on Mexican National Character Studies," *The American Journal of Economics and Sociology,* Vol. 2 (1954), p. 13.

[9]*Ibid.*

[10]*Ibid.*

[11]Romanell, *op. cit.,* p. 166.

[12]Octavio Paz, *The Labyrinth of Solitude: Life and Thought in Mexico* (New York: Grove Press, Inc., 1961), p. 10-11.

[13]*Ibid.*, p. 17.

[14]Maria Elvira Bermudez, *La Vida Familiar Del Mexicano* (Mexico: Antigua Libreria Robredo, 1955), p. 98.

[15]*Ibid.*

[16]Rogelio Diaz-Guerrero, "Neurosis and the Mexican Family Structure," *American Journal of Psychiatry*, Vol. CXII (1955), p. 411-417.

[17]*Ibid.*

[18]G. M. Gilbert, "Sex Differences in Mental Health in a Mexican Village," *The International Journal of Social Psychiatry*, Vol. 3 (1959), p. 212.

[19]R. C. Jones, "Ethnic Family Patterns: The Mexican Family in the United States," *The American Journal of Sociology*, Vol. 52 (1948), p. 450.

[20]Peñalosa, *op. cit.*, p. 680-681.

[21]Norman D. Humphrey, "The Changing Structure of the Detroit Mexican Family," *American Sociological Review*, Vol. 9, No. 6 (1944), p. 622-626.

[22]William Madsen, "The Mexican-Americans of South Texas" (New York: Holt, Rinehart, and Winston, 1964), p. 48.

[23]*Ibid.*, p. 49.

[24]Robert G. Hayden, "Spanish-Americans of the Southwest: Life Style Patterns and Their Implications," *Welfare In Review*, Vol. 4, No. 10 (April 1966), p. 20.

[25]*Ibid.*

[26]Celia S. Heller, *Mexican American Youth: Forgotten Youth at the Crossroads* (New York: Random House, 1966), p. 34.

A CRITIQUE OF PITTIAN HISTORY

Raymond V. Padilla

PROLOGO

Aquí curioso lector pongo en tus manos mi crítica de la historia pitista. Te la encargo con el acuerdo de que ni la elogies ni la desprecies —sólo quiero que pienses en ella. En aquello del Chicanismo todavía no hay quien haya escrito la última palabra sobre el tema. Y tú bien sabes que en realidad solamente unas cuantas palabras se han escrito.

Quizás esta condición nos produce menos mal. Porque la fuerza de nuestro pueblo está en que *vivimos* nuestro fenómeno chicano y en que llevamos nuestra experiencia chicana pegada entre las entrañas—no obstante que nos arrinconen en miserables cárceles o que nos suban hasta las más altas esferas de la torre de marfil.

Sin embargo, aunque todos tengamos los ojos abiertos, hay que cuidarnos de no cegar nuestro espíritu chicano. Y recuerda que la fuerza del espíritu también está en el pensamiento. Por eso hay que hacer el esfuerzo de también llevar nuestro fenómeno en la mente. No te apures del peso, que si pasas por buenos pensamientos todos quedaremos más livianos.

Octubre de 1972
En el antiguo rancho de
don Luis Peralta
California La Alta
Aztlán

INTRODUCTION

Several important questions confronted me as I began my analysis of Pitt's work. These questions related to the audience or audiences to which I was addressing my comments, the methods to be used to more effectively convey my thoughts and feelings, and the cultural and methodological assumptions I was accepting or rejecting. These and other questions were difficult for me to handle, yet I had to deal with them in some fashion in order to create a framework within which to present my critique.

Overall, I have deliberately avoided trying to write another history of the Californios as a rebuttal to the Pittian thesis. The task of re-writing history I leave to some committed historian who is willing to spend much time and energy—perhaps a lifetime of scholarship—rounding up materials and synthesizing a useful account of those vastly complicated people. Nor is my concern here to dispute this or that datum, or to challenge the historicity of some obscure or doubtful event, although in some cases where I recognize that the historical record has been violated flagrantly, I make an effort to highlight the discrepancies.

My objective is to write a critique which considers the problems and issues of historical thought: its logic and consistency; its biases and blind spots; its egocentric and ethnocentric pitfalls; in short, its theories and methods. I make special effort to show how cultural and attitudinal biases affect historical thinking and historical writing. Specifically, I bring these considerations to bear on Professor Pitt's work.

On a different level, another objective is to raise again as an issue the meaning and relevance which Gabacho[1] research has for the Chicano experience. More generally, I also want to challenge the Chicano to examine critically the generic concept of research and its implications for the Chicano. Assuming that one views research as an important fact of life in contemporary American society (and perhaps twentieth century man), then it is necessary for Chicanos to come to terms with it, just as they must come to terms with agri-business, the military, political powerlessness, inadequate education, poverty, prejudice, and a host of other issues.

A third objective is to "send a message" to those researchers—largely but not exclusively Gabachos—who have made a travesty of research, in its normative sense, by entering the Chicano world under the guise of "unbiased researchers," and who then proceed to exercise freely their cultural biases and hang-ups on their luckless Chicano subjects. "Studies" produced by these pseudo-researchers have often gone unchallenged by their supposedly more critical colleagues who perhaps share the same biases or who may have little interest in the subject.

For the Chicano, both as critic and as subject, such pseudo-researchers and their research products pose a particularly difficult problem. If the Chicano attempts to criticize either the researcher or his products within the framework of a mythical rationalism and objectivism (the domain of pseudo-researchers), he may well be doomed to failure because historically such researchers have often refused to recognize the irrationality and subjectivity of some or all of their methodologies and conclusions. When a researcher claims to be objective by virtue of his methods or his theories, then, in my view, he is already engaging in irrational behavior. Research conducted under such a presumption has a rather large component of subjectivity—perhaps even irrationality—even if it is technically well executed. Therefore the message for the pseudo-researcher is this: Pick up your toys and go elsewhere.

In carrying out these thoughts I have exposed myself to a number of criticisms, two of which I will answer directly. First, I may be criticized for doing "reactive research." The argument here is that Chicanos need not worry about tearing down every bad book that has been written about Chicanos. For if one were to follow that tactic, one could spend a lifetime merely writing rebuttals to ridiculous arguments and never get to the important task of *building* useful materials for the Chicano. I am swayed in favor of the healthy pragmatism contained in this argument. But I feel that its usefulness is largely a matter of application. Granted that one need not react to *every* bad account about the Chicano—for such accounts appear to be the rule rather than the exception—yet there is also a great need to react to *some* of them. Otherwise we would lose the positive contribution of the negative example. Philosophically, there is also some merit in knowing where we as Chicanos have been—or have been taken—in order to decide where we want to go. The issue, then, is one of judgment. I judge it important to criticize Pitt's work on several grounds. First, it deals with history and there is a great need for the Chicano to look critically at his history and his historical condition. Second, Pitt's book has received much favorable attention from both non-Chicanos and Chicanos. It has had considerable impact both in and outside of the Chicano community—at least in the academic segment of the former—and one might well profit by a skeptical reading of the work. Third, by taking a critical stance toward the work I believe that much positive knowledge can accrue to the Chicano. Only through such a critical stance can the Chicano pursue the positive construction of his own reality.

Those who challenge my critique on the basis that it is polemical *may not fully understand the polemical basis of Pitt's decline thesis.* They may also not fully understand the difficulties involved in devising a strategy for ridding oneself of exploitative researchers and their products.[2] For my part, I refuse to be intimidated or limited by rationalist mythology (and methodology).

The Chicano, both as critic and as subject of research, who is boxed-in by mythical rationalism and objectivism creates a dilemma for his own defense. If he limits his arguments to the "rules of the game," he will not communicate his message. If he is to communicate his message successfully, he must go beyond the rules of the game as set by the Gabacho researcher. It is not surprising, therefore, that a last ditch response left to such a boxed-in Chicano may be at the existential level. His response is fundamentally an act of self-assertion where the Chicano refuses to negotiate the authenticity of his own reality.[3] In operational terms this means that any Chicano (or any other human being for that matter) as subject of research has the inalienable right to tell any researcher to mind his own business.

These observations lead me to offer two propositions for Chicano research. First, Chicano research must be allowed to run its own course within the evolving Chicano perspective and its evolving criteria for validation; Chicano research should not be short-circuited by external validation criteria *unique* to the Gabacho perspective.

Secondly, the results of Chicano research, as of all good research, can be considered only as tentative conclusions and propositions. These conclusions and propositions can then be further tested and refined within the Chicano perspective.

These two propositions, combined with my earlier observations, are the basis upon which the following critique was written.

PART I
THE PITTIAN THESIS
AND ITS ELEMENTS

THE PITTIAN THESIS
THE ARCADIAN MYTH AND CALIFORNIO DECADENCE
STEREOTYPING AND "SOCIAL SCIENCE FICTION"
THE ABUSE AND MISUSE OF HISTORICAL RESEARCH

THE PITTIAN THESIS

The fundamental thesis underlying Professor Leonard Pitt's interpretation of Californio history is that Californios as a people and as a culture *declined*. The title of his book, *The Decline of the Californios*, is a succinct assertion of that thesis.

As a point of departure, I suggest that the word "decline" needs explication. I take "decline" to mean, in its nounal sense, "a falling off; a diminution."[4] The concept has even greater specificity if it is compared with various synonyms. These synonyms are "deterioration," "degeneration," and "decadence." The distinctions between these synonyms have been stated as follows:

> *Deterioration, degeneration, decadence, decline* mean the falling from a higher to a lower level as in quality, character, or the like. *Deterioration* implies impairment, as of vigor, usefulness, or the like; *degeneration* stresses retrogression physically, intellectually, or often morally; *decadence* presupposes a former reaching of the peak of development and implies a turn downward with a consequent loss in vitality, or the like; *decline* differs from decadence in suggesting more momentum, more obvious evidences of deterioration, and less hope of revivification.[5]

I will examine the meaning and the apparent assumptions of the Pittian thesis within the framework of these definitions and distinctions.

69

Professor Pitt appears to rest the decline thesis on the following assumptions: (1) that the Californios and Californio culture underwent a developmental process which peaked either at some period before, or at about the time of, the Gabacho invasion of California, (2) that Californios and Californio culture entered a decadent phase perhaps before, but certainly during and after the Gabacho invasion, and (3) that the decadence of the Californios was rooted in Californio culture itself. Moreover, since "decline" implies "less hope of revivification," Pitt's thesis infers bleak prospects for the descendents of the "decadent" Californios.[6]

Professor Pitt uses three main tactics to justify his assumptions and to support his thesis. These tactics are: (1) the creation of a myth, (2) the use of a social science stereotype, and (3) the abuse and misuse of standard Gabacho historical research methods. The purpose of this critique is to show that none of these tactics can withstand close scrutiny and therefore that the Pittian thesis is invalid.

THE ARCADIAN MYTH
AND CALIFORNIO DECADENCE

Pitt's fabrication is a kind of arcadian myth about Californio existence before the Gabacho invasion of the middle nineteenth century. The first chapter of his book is signally titled "Halcyon Days," and the author's message is clearly that Californios before the Gabacho invasion were living "high on the hog." But Pitt seems confused in describing precisely *how* the Californios were supposed to have lived their grand lifestyle. He presents two visions of the halcyon days which are competitive rather than complementary. On the one hand he presents Californios as hedonistic gentlemen farmers; on the other, he depicts a society of noble savages living from the goodness of Nature and Providence.

The picture of hedonistic gentlemen farmers arises from Pitt's transformation of California into a massive baronial estate where rancheros develop an ethic of conspicuous consumption. In this setting rancheros resemble wealthy planters from the South, or perhaps hacendados from across the Rio Grande. The business of the ranchero is to preside over a household of family, friends, guests, relations, servants, Indians, and an occasional Yankee adventurer who wanders across the sierras or around the Horn to find himself a guest of honor at a Californio table. These mythical Californios are a class of idle rich who enjoy idleness for its own sake. When they somehow bestir themselves to action, they spend their energies in amusement and entertainment. Their industry is therefore limited to horse racing, bear baiting, cock fighting, and gambling.

At the same time, Pitt's vision of Californios as noble savages depicts California as a fantasy land of pristine and quasi-civilized rancheros who bask in the good graces of nature and exhibit amoral and childlike qualities. In this scenario, Californios enjoy rural bliss within the confines of simple and commodious ranchos. Their existence is pastoral and serene, and California is a veritable land of milk and honey where indolence reigns supreme. Moreover, Californio society is structured to increase the individual's life of luxury and ease. Pitt dwells on the dances—the fandangos—the fiestas and celebrations, the quaint religious festivities, and the generally salubrious social climate of a "tradition bound," non-technological society. This romantic vision of California has deep roots within the writings of some Gabacho historians. While Pitt at times appears to debunk such historians, he simultaneously reifies their numerous fantasies by piling one denigrating Gabacho quote onto another as he spins the elaborate arcadian myth.

Pitt's fabrication of the halcyon days has a crucial function in the decline thesis. By engineering a Californio society composed of "grandees without a court" and "indolent natives," Pitt creates an *imaginary peak* of Californio culture from which the rancheros will tumble helplessly once they are confronted with the Gabacho invasion. Yankee Argonauts with self-proclaimed puritanical virtues will be disgusted by a society of gregarious ranchero-aristocrats who surround themselves with retinues of relations, foreigners, servants, and Indians. For the Gabacho, the ranchero's life is too easy. He raises his cattle but without great toil, plants his crops but without much passion for trade, and lives off of nature in a state of society only once removed from that of the Indians whose labor the ranchero exploits. Pitt thus elevates the Californio to ethereal levels of pastoral enchantment only to hurl him into decline and decadence with ever greater tragedy and pathos. Here Pitt's scenario becomes more histrionic than historical.

As a result, Pitt's mythological presentations leave us without a real sense of California's revolutionary transformations prior to the Gabacho invasion. Nueva España's long struggle for independence, the secularization of the missions, the political feuding for regional control, and the development of ranchos through liberal land grant policies are all aspects of California before the Gabacho invasion which Pitt fades into the background of his mythical arcadia. Nor can the incessant military activity endemic to California during the Mexican period—which coincides with Pitt's halcyon days—be understood within Pitt's vision of playful Californios eternally basking themselves in a land of perpetual sunshine.

Pitt's halcyon days are also contradicted by other Gabacho writers who take a different view of the period. Mervyn Miller's account of the secularization of the California missions depicts California before the invasion as no arcadian paradise or pastoral utopia.[7] Miller's ambitious Californios, eager to secure mission properties and governmental and military control of the territory, have no meaning in Pitt's mythology. Another writer, George Tays, recounts the political instability of California between 1822 and 1846—the period which Pitt designates as the "Halcyon Days." Tays calls this period "Revolutionary California."[8]

As an aside, I propose that California before the Gabacho invasion could have been most aptly characterized as transitional, undergoing quick changes and the constant internal and external power plays of ambitious Californios and expansionist foreign powers. The secularization of the missions marks a shift of economic and political power in California comparable to the subsequent shift of power from Californios to Yankees after the Gabacho invasion. By transforming mission properties, and occasionally the missions themselves, into ranchos and general civilian control, Californios effectively changed the basis of settlement of California. The change was mainly from a mission to a rancho-oriented society. Naturally both the philosophy and the strategy of the ranchero meant a radical departure from the missionary pattern of settlement. I seriously doubt, however, that the change was from a mission utopia to a rancho arcadia.*

Yet the "Halcyon Days" myth serves Pitt very well because his thesis presumes that Californio culture reached a "peak" of development. By placing the Californios on an imaginary pedestal of cultural and social development, Pitt lays the groundwork for his thesis of Californio decline. From that elevated point, Pitt launches three attacks to carry his argument. These are (1) an attack on the quality of Californio culture in general, (2) an indictment of rancho culture in particular, and (3) an attack on the morality of the Californio lower classes.

Pitt's general attack on Californio culture rests on observations and judgments made by Gabacho settlers and adventurers who moved into the region during the Mexican period. Often expressing tacit or outright agreement with these writers, seldom presenting contradicting evidence, only occasionally indicating the heavy Gabacho bias, Pitt is tireless in concatenating one calumny after another in a seemingly endless chain of Gabacho deprecations of Californio culture. Through such a style of presentation, Pitt creates a gruesome picture of Californio decadence and decline.

Los Angeles, for example, is a perfect picture of decrepitude and deterioration:

---

*This viewpoint is subject to historical research, and I hope that studious Chicanos, and perhaps others as well, will investigate the historical records and delineate precisely the activities of the Californios before the invasion. Whether or not such research confirms my perspective, I would contend that my hypotheses are a more suitable starting point for serious research than Pitt's fanciful arcadia.

The village's human aspect seemed "very ugly," even to some settlers.* Domesticated creatures ambled about freely even in the best homes, which were cold and dark. And over everything man-made hung the "antiquated and dilapidated air" of Mexico. The cliché of the day was that the pueblo of *Nuestra Senora de los Angeles* contained no angels, unless they be fallen ones.** (page 122)

Quoting the Reverend James Woods, who sermonizes about the degeneracy in the same city, Californio culture is reduced to decadency of biblical proportions:

Near his doorstep a neglected child was bawling for its mother, dogs were fighting, and one man was trying to run down another with his horse; "what a spectacle for a country laying claims to christianity . . ." The afternoon's main attraction, the horse races, are the "fruits of popery—the only form of religion known among the Spaniards of the region." The "horses are very fine and richly caparisoned. But the men are a dark complexioned set with darker minds and morals. I preached this morning upon the destruction of sodom and Gomorroh (sic) and had I wanted materials for supposed scenes in those cities I could have found them in the very scenes" before his eyes.***(page 222)

Arguing along similar lines, Pitt tries to show that the Californio family, religion, and general social structure were less than what the upright Yankees desired.[9]

The ranchero class is especially vulnerable to Pitt's charges of decadence and decay. This is because Pitt manages to place the rancheros at the apex of an imaginary aristocratic society, where their behavior is strangely one-dimensional and fantastic. Pitt's ranchero "aristocrats" totally lack a sense of proportion and refinement. Their activities appear to be all form and little content, while their lifestyle seems dominated by childlike concerns and patterns of behavior which mimic adult society. In short, Pitt turns the rancheros into motion picture characters of the worst sort.

Yet, in a bizarre way Pitt may appear to speak well of the rancheros. He does this by attributing to them all the trappings and pretensions of aristocrats in a royal court. One suspects that the living conditions in

---

*Mrs. Hayes, March 31, in Benjamin Hayes, Pioneer Notes . . . 1849-1875, ed. by Marjorie Tisdale Wolcott (Los Angeles, 1929), p. 93; John W. Audubon, "Diary," Nov. 6, 1849, in Valeska Bari, ed., *The Course of Empire . . . Accounts of the Gold Rush . . .* (New York, 1931), p. 127.

**Joseph Lancaster Brent, *The Lugo Case: A Personal Experience* (New Orleans, 1926), p. 3; Hayes, *op. cit.*, p. 92.

***Lindley Bynam, ed., "Los Angeles in 1854-1855: The Diary of Reverend James Woods," Historical Society of Southern California *Quarterly*, XXII (1941), 82-84.

the northern Mexican frontier were far from royal. However, the ultimate and cumulative effect of Pitt's manipulations is to effectively degrade the rancheros and thereby fit them more neatly into the decline thesis. It is through his power to dramatize and stylize that Pitt casts the rancheros first in the role of noble aristocrats, then in the part of *decadent* aristocrats.

I suggest that this kind of artificiality serves as the major basis for Pitt's decline thesis. Politically, for example, the rancheros are said to be a weak, pugnacious, and powerless bunch who reach out for foreign domination:

> Meantime, Californians were so hopelessly embroiled among themselves that the spring of 1846 found the province in a particularly jittery state. The northerners recently had fought the southerners to a standstill over control of the treasury, which they both meanwhile had drained dry; José Castro and Pio Pico were about to resume the struggle and were lining up troops and horses for that purpose; and the Indian depredations were increasing. Grasping at diplomatic straws, the northerners sought out the French consul with a request for a French protectorate, while the Angeleños, never to be outdone by the Montereños, went to the British consul with a similar entreaty. Both the British and the French officials dismissed the proposals as irrelevant, however.[10] (page 24)

Pitt, however, builds his strongest case against the rancheros around the notion of opulence and extravagance. He succeeds in transforming the mythical gentlemen-farmers-aristocrats into a class of idle rich thoroughly immersed in conspicuous consumption. Ordinary Californio festivities and diversions, under Pitt's flamboyant pen, turn into fabulous displays of opulence, indulgence, wealth and splendor. To the sober reader, Pitt's caricaturization becomes both ludicrous and unconvincing.[11]

For example, speaking of the southern rancheros during the booming cattle trade at the time of the Gold Rush, Pitt notes:

> If they had ever lacked the wherewithal to feel fulfilled as grandees, they now had it. Former poor men stuffed their pantries and wine cellars, bought goods from Yankee peddlers to their heart's content, gave generous handouts to friends, strangers, and servants, and generally spent—"wasted," as puritans clucked—their wealth freely. Don Antonio Lugo, son of a common soldier, owned a bridal outfit inlaid with $1,500 worth of silver and used it in his daily chores, even at a time when he was strapped for cash. Pablo de la Guerra in 1851 splurged $80 on a single chair for his father, even while expensive litigation got under way.* Rancheros snapped up

---

*José Antonio Menéndez to Pablo de la Guerra, March 4, 1851, MS, de la Guerra Collection, Owen Coy Room, University of Southern California (Los Angeles, Calif.).

costly European laces and silks for their wives to convert into *rebozos* and gowns that would be trailed about on clay floors in daily use. The variety and richness of personal effects were limited more by what Yankees imported than by what Californios would buy, for they bought almost anything. (page 128)

However, it appears that for Pitt the quintessence of ranchero decadence is best represented through their fiestas and celebrations. Describing what he considers a "typical" event, Pitt writes baroquely:

The regal Petra Pilar Sepúlveda required half a day for the drive from San Pedro and customarily migrated with an entourage of servants, trunks stuffed with gowns and jewels, and mattresses piled high for their stay at the wretched Bella Union Hotel. Her wedding in 1853 had lasted five days and nights, and its lavishness had made a deep impression on gringos. At the typical fiesta, dancing, singing, and eating proceeded all night and well into the following morning, perhaps even into the next evening, or at least until Juan Bandini, Antonio Maria Lugo, or Nicholas Den had finished competing at the *jota*, bolero, fandango, or waltz. (page 129)

And as if to add the finishing touch to his portrait, Pitt adds the following climactic end to the festivities:

At the climax of the fiesta came the flirtation called the *cascarón*. The object was to catch a victim unawares and crack open an eggshell filled with some harmless substance; he or she would then try to get even. Ordinarily, confetti or cologne water filled the egg, but in good years gold dust, even gold leaf, fluttered down on some heads. This delightful extravagance invariably made gringos gasp. (page 129)

The material extravagance which Pitt attributes to the ranchero class goes hand in hand with the moral laxity and criminality which he ascribes to all social classes, but especially to the Californio lower classes. Pitt devotes considerable space and attention to this subject, as if the key to "Californio decadence" is to be found in this archetypal theme of the cinema and television.

In fact, Pitt goes further than mere description of the Californio's criminality and attempts to establish the causes for such perverse behavior. He hints, for example, that race might be a significant factor:

The resulting proliferation of crime netted for Los Angeles one of the worst reputations of any gold rush town; northern detractors thought of it as a place combining jaded opulence with rampant drinking, murder, brutality—the kind of disorder associated with mixed breeds and the stagnant cow county culture. (page 154)

Although Pitt does not appear to subscribe to the "it's in their blood" argument, it seems that he places some credence in the "it's in their culture" thesis. He ascribes a disruptive role to Mexican convicts in California.[12] Later he strongly implies that Californio criminality had its roots in Mexican culture. Pitt observes:

> ... the bandido must be understood also as a product of social upheaval in Mexico. During the uncertain era that followed the revolutionary break with Spain, caudillos or banditlike chieftains roamed the countryside—a law unto themselves. Yankees who had fought them in the Mexican War recognized their special ferocity and learned, as Horace Bell put it, that south of the Rio Grande the line between "rebel and robber, pillager and patriot, was dimly defined." The resemblance of the California bandits to their Mexican counterparts was unmistakeable.* (page 75)

As an aside, one could just as well observe—using similar reasoning—that Bell and his cohorts learned their lessons well from the Mexican caudillos, for in the Gabacho invasion of the Southwest, it can be said, with perhaps greater verity, that among the Yankees one can hardly distinguish between "rebel and robber" and "pillager and patriot." One would certainly be hard pressed to defend the "squatters," the claim jumpers, and the *buitres negros*—the crooked lawyers—who invaded the southwest. In any case, it appears that Pitt's theory of Californio criminality lies somewhere between biological determinism and cultural determinism.[13]

In a sense, Pitt's treatment of the criminality theme is a replay of his ranchero mythology. He does not treat Californios as rational beings. Instead he makes sweeping generalizations and draws gratuitous conclusions, thereby transforming the Californios into two-dimensional bad guys not unlike those on celluloid filmstrip. When Pitt concludes that

> Mexicans engaged in numerous and brutal individual crimes, but their forte was highway robbery, stage holdups, and rustling, activities in which they continued to surpass all other nationalities, even after the gold rush. As late as 1875 the most notorious characters in the state still wore sombreros (page 256)

it seems that the only contribution he makes is to the mythology of Californio badmen, while adding nothing to our understanding of the Californios as a people. Were one inclined to argue along the same lines, the assertion could be made, probably with greater historicity, that in the "robbery" of real estate the Yankees far outstripped any other nationality in California.

Pitt's rendering of the criminality theme leads to absurd caricatures of some Californio "bandits" in particular and of all Californios in general. His "badmen" are alternately crafty and stupid, fierce and meek, ugly and dashing, lawless and penitent, and especially guilty and repentent. Crafty criminals like Pancho Daniel lose their wits in the end.

---

*Reminiscences of a Ranger ... (Santa Barbara, Calif., 1927), p. 100.

The last of the badmen, Pancho Daniel, managed to evade capture until March, 1858, when he stumbled into the hands of the law.* (page 173)

Or the criminal will blurt out confessions, especially to "white-heat" vigilantes, and then moralize to his Californio compatriots as he faces the gallows.[14] Pitt's peculiar mythology-as-history bias is perhaps best illustrated in the following passage where victims are criminals, criminals are victims, and "white-heat" lynchers turn into a white tornado that purges the fair California countryside of the degenerate Californios:

Next, the vigilantes went after José Antonio Garcia, the only available accomplice in the murder of Obiesa and Graciano. Taken into custody, Garcia wrote his mother in Mexico and dictated a confession detailing the crime and the extent of Jack Powers's leadership, but asserted that he regretted having participated in the killing. "To all appearances truly penitent, and exhorting his friends to take warning by his fate, and to avoid evil companions," Garcia was executed. Enlarged to 150 strong, the vigilantes set out that very night to hunt down several gang members hiding in a nearby wood. The brigade spread out and systematically tramped through the brush until they gunned down Linares and Blanco and captured Grijalva and others. The next day the town interred the dead bandidos and a martyred vigilante, and on the following day hanged yet another pair of badmen, both of whom confessed guilt, exhorting their countrymen to "keep away from bad company," and acknowledged the fairness of their captors. (page 177)

And so as the California golden sun sinks into the blue Pacific Ocean, the wretched Californio criminals receive their just desserts and sink into eternity.

STEREOTYPING AND
"SOCIAL SCIENCE FICTION"

For all its concern with Californio decadence, the Pittian thesis of Californio decline must be understood within a broader context than the mere ranchero class or even the Californios collectively. Pitt stresses this point when he confesses that

Despite my initial doubts . . . the longer I worked on this project . . . the more I became convinced that it touched at least tangentially some large and consequential themes of history. (page vii)

His message is even clearer when he says:

I see this study as an instance of the worldwide defeat of the relatively

---

*Los Angeles *Star,* March 27, 1859.

static, traditionalist societies by societies that were oriented to technology
and the ideal of progress. (page viii)

Hence, Pitt seems to conclude that though Californios were not especially important in themselves,[15] they may represent important global
themes not only of history, but, as seen in the last quote, of social
science as well.

On a different but related level, Pitt believes—and quite correctly—
that "... the role of California's contemporary Spanish-speaking minority is at once enormously misunderstood, and thus in need of elucida-
tion." (page viii) Moreover, he contends[16] that

> I show, in essence, that the current predicament of the Spanish-speaking
> has far deeper and older roots than might appear to those who reckon time
> from the Mexican Revolution of 1910, or World War I and the mass migra-
> tion northward which followed. (page viii)

Therefore, Pitt sees his history as "... at the very least ... an effort to
go back to first instances in order to shed light on a contemporary
issue." (page viii)

In the context of these remarks, the decline thesis acquires new
meaning and importance. What is of interest here is no longer merely
the defeated Californios, but their twentieth-century progeny and cultural heirs as well. By coupling history and social science to his decline
thesis, Pitt attempts to arrive at an explanation of the Chicano "predicament." In doing so Pitt makes a number of assumptions about the
nature of the Chicano and Chicano culture which, while they may
support his decline thesis, shed very little light on the contemporary
Chicano world. Nor do they help us to understand the Californio and
his culture.

Pitt's basic borrowing from social science is the notion that some
cultures are "traditional" while others are "progressive." A given culture is "traditional" or "progressive" depending upon the "cultural
values" of the people who make that culture. Cultural values are in turn
dependent upon the "value orientations" of a given people.

As a number of contemporary Chicano writers have observed,[17]
these notions have been popularized by some Gabacho social scientists
to create a cultural deterministic view of the Chicano. At its worst, this
view simply stereotypes both the Chicano and the Gabacho. The stereotypes are then used to justify existing social, economic, and political
relations in contemporary Gabacho society.

In reviewing the Gabacho treatment of Chicanos in the social sciences, Nick Vaca has summarized the opposing value systems which
impinge on the Chicano: at least as these value systems have been
posited by Gabacho social scientists. The values of the two systems are
essentially dichotomous and can be summarized as follows:

MEXICAN AMERICAN VALUE SYSTEM[18]	ANGLO (GABACHO) VALUE SYSTEM
Subjugation to nature	Mastery over nature
Present oriented	Future oriented
Immediate gratification	Deferred gratification
Complacent	Aggressive
Non-intellectual	Intellectual
Fatalistic	Non-fatalistic
Non-goal oriented	Goal oriented
Non-success oriented	Success oriented
Emotional	Rational
Dependent	Individualistic
Machismo*	Effeminacy*
Superstitious	Non-superstitious
Traditionalism	Progressive

In discussing this paradigm, Vaca concluded that the cultural determinism advocates have gained considerable following over the years because their approach explains "... the social ills of the Mexican American in the United States without indicting Anglo institutions."[19] By first assigning to the Chicano's culture inherently negative characteristics, Gabachos then can spin elaborate causal explanations for any number of Chicano phenomena. Thus it is through the Chicano's culture that the Gabacho has explained the Chicano's "... mental and public health rates, high delinquency rates, poor academic achievement, occupational levels, rates of income, high mortality rates, and a multitude of other social puzzles ..."[20] Among those social—or in this case historical—puzzles is the Californio decline thesis of Professor Leonard Pitt.

Through his use of cultural determinism, Pitt proclaims both the superiority of Gabacho culture and the inferiority and decadence of the Californio culture. The paradigm also allows him to sympathize with the "progressive conquerors" who are "bemused" as their victims "decline." (page vii) Within this context, Pitt's return to "first instances" for an explanation of the current Spanish-speaking "predicament" seems to be drenched with the ethnocentric bias of both Gabacho social science and history. His return to "first instances" acquires an ironic meaning in that Pitt uses history to show that Chicano culture, as portrayed by some Gabacho social scientists, is, in the first instance, based on a cultural legacy of a people who were conquered because they failed to cope with a superior Gabacho invader.

Cultural determinism has a profound and pervasive effect on Pitt's

---

*This and the Gabacho corresponding category were added by Vaca more-or-less tongue in cheek, one supposes.

history. Often the categories outlined by Vaca can be easily detected in Pitt's sentences and paragraphs. At other times, the effects are subtle and indirect, camouflaged through a bit of nostalgia or a piece of local color.

In either case, Pitt's affiliation with the cultural determinism paradigm of the social sciences can be easily established, for he can be quite explicit in indicating his position. His acceptance of the Chicano's alleged subjugation to nature, present orientation, immediate gratification syndrome, and complacency can be seen in the following excerpt. Note that opposite characteristics attributed to the Gabacho also surface.

> An orientation toward the present, not the past or the future, permeated the value system of the Californios. The "old mañana habit" . . . implied a satisfaction with what one had today. Men did not prepare for the future, as such. They did do hard work when necessary and did take pride in it, but more in anticipation of the fun that came right at the end of it, rather than for any anticipated distant need. Owing to a happy combination of good climate, ample land, and cheap Indian labor, the rancho order worked smoothly on the basis of this value system. Once these conditions worsened, however, the Californios had neither the necessary psychological nor economic reserves to fall back upon. The future, in short, would come as a shock to them, and the Anglo-Saxon's (Gabacho's) preoccupation with labor, profit, and savings for the future always remained something of a mystery to them. (pages 12-13)

Carrying the point further, Pitt argues that "The Californios exemplified the tendency of Latin Americans to make pleasure the chief end of work." (page 13) And as if to elaborate on what pleasure means to Latin Americans, Pitt remarks that on festive occasions ". . . they consumed heroic amounts of food and drink, clearly indulging in conspicuous consumption." (page 13) Here Pitt may be leaving historical research altogether and falling into a quagmire of "social science" speculation.

Moving beyond description, Pitt uses the cultural values paradigm to spin out diaphanous causal relationships. These causal relationships are imagined to substantiate the thesis of Californio decline. For example, in speculating about the "causes" of Californio banditry—presumably a symptom of Californio decadence—Pitt reverts to cultural explanations which are not only the province of Old Rangers—like Bell—but of some social scientists as well. In what he calls a "promising conjecture," he inclines toward Margaret Mead's ". . . comment that crime among the Spanish Americans of the United States is often related to the destruction of village life." (page 75) For additional insight Pitt refers to Florence Kluckhohn who

... speculates that the sadism of some Spanish-American men represents the breakdown of the all-important relationship of brother to brother and father to son which pervades the entire culture.* (page 75)

In analyzing the specific "causes" of Californio "decline," Pitt seriously entertains the notion of "culture conflict." He says:

> Culture conflict explains a great deal. Quite plainly, the Californian's economic naiveté and his penchant for conspicuous consumption led him to the brink of disaster. California after 1848 provides a classic instance of what David Riesman describes in another connection as the "inner-directed" society superimposing itself on one that is "tradition-directed." Margaret Mead's anthropological observations about the present-day New Mexicans shed clear light on the Californians of the nineteenth century: "It is still the present, the known and the sure, which has meaning ... (He) wants things as they are, not as they were or as they should be ... The persistence of this orientation to the present time in the face of equally persistent future orientation of Anglos is central to the whole process of Spanish American acculturation."** (page 283)

It seems that Pitt views the cultural values paradigm as appropriate for describing not only contemporary Chicanos, but also their immediate as well as their distant ancestors. His return to "first instances" is merely to show that today's Chicanos are the exact opposite of Gabachos because historically they have always been so. Since Gabachos have, and always have had, inherently superior characteristics, Chicanos necessarily have, and always have had, inferior ones. The proof for this contention is historically derived because Gabachos were triumphant over Californios during the 19th century invasion, and those Gabachos saw their victory as a function of their superior culture. The attempted proof is also scientific because a century after the invasion certain Gabacho social scientists have demonstrated that the descendents of the invaders (Gabachos) have a culture which is superior to the culture of the descendents of those who were invaded (Chicanos). Through nimble manipulation Pitt has gained a double-barrelled analytical weapon: He can use data gathered by *recent* social scientists to analyze *past* Californio culture and formulate facil explanations for its "decline," or he can explain the "decadent" condition of contemporary Chicanos by showing that they continue to exhibit the same dysfunctional cultural characteristics which he contends caused the "decline" of their ancestors as they faced the invaders. This parsimonious sequence of circular reasoning is satisfactory if all one is searching for is the face-lifting of an

---

* ... Florence Kluckhohn, in *Variations in Value Orientations* (Evanston, Ill., 1961), p. 198.

** *Cultural Patterns and Technical Change* (New York, 1855 (sic)), p. 175.

old and continuing mythology. For those with a serious interest in Chicano history, the ruse is tinged with methodological and intellectual ineptitude.

Because Pitt buys wholesale the cultural values paradigm, he is unable to guard himself from entering the world of mythology and stereotypes. Consequently his characterizations of both the Chicano and the Gabacho are far from convincing. Yet even more damaging to the Chicano is his lapse from the generalizations of the cultural values paradigm into grossly stereotypical characterizations of the Chicano. It seems that once the door is opened to stereotypes, there is no way of telling where they will lead. For example, non-intellectuality can quickly turn into stupidity, dependency becomes docility, and complacency turns into laziness.[21]

In Pitt's work stereotypes become so rampant that, perhaps before he even realizes it, he leaves the foul arena of the cultural values paradigm only to become mired in the rhetoric of biological determinists. Sonorans seem to be favorite targets for this physical degradation, although Mexicans in general, as well as Californios, are similarly treated. In a cross-cultural transposition of the Gabacho racism which imputes an ape-like degeneracy to Blacks, Pitt creates an absurd fiction of Chicano biological deformity and deterioration which transforms the Chicano into an almost subhuman animal.

For example, Pitt offers only the lamest contradictions to the following quotations and viewpoints:

> California's European roots were a source of pride to her people, but Farnham dwelt on "the Indian character" of the lower class, "the dull suspicious countenance, the small twinkling piercing eye, the laxness and filth of a free brute, using freedom as a mere means of animal enjoyment ... dancing and vomiting as occasion and inclination appear to require."* (page 16)

It is therefore not surprising that Sonorans assume ogre-like proportions even when they were considered the best miners in the fields.

> Where water was scarce and quartz plentiful, as in the southern mines, they (Sonorans) had the endurance to sit for hours and winnow dirt in their serapes, sometimes using their own gargantuan breath if the wind died down. (pages 54-55)

And completing the circle, such physical grotesqueness leads directly to an atrophied intellect and moral putrefaction:

> In the first (California) legislature, nativists (Gabachos) freely categorized

---

*Thomas Jefferson Farnham, *Travels in the Californias and in the Pacific Ocean* (New York, 1844), pp. 356-357.

the Pacific immigrants (Mexicans and South Americans) as a race whose morality and intelligence stood "but one degree above the beasts in the field." (page 58)

It is upon such evidence that Professor Pitt attempts to establish his decline thesis.

On the other side of the coin, the cultural values paradigm can also lead to stereotyped views of the Gabacho and Gabacho culture. Though most stereotypes represent popular prejudices and cultural myths, the stereotypes of the Gabacho which have been fabricated by Gabachos exalt their own values and culture. Professor Pitt appears to believe in the Gabacho's progressiveness, aggressiveness, rationality, individualism, as well as, among other things, his success and goal orientations. If Pitt's Chicanos appear as marginal and perhaps even subhuman, then his Gabachos exemplify a class of demigods. They are an army of blond-haired and blue-eyed Argonauts for whom no obstacle is too great or any design too grand to remain unfulfilled. They march through Pitt's pages as an unchallengeable force, impelled by the force of Manifest Destiny and the inevitable advance of progress.[22] They are superior to treaties, laws, customs, and conscience.[23] Their mission is to "advance civilization," and to place in the dustbin of history all those who might get in their way. In contrast to Chicanos who are heirs to a decadent race and culture, Yankees become the harbingers of a new order.[24] Within this framework, Pitt turns the Gabacho invasion of California into a holy crusade in the name of progress.

This attitude is perhaps best described in Pitt's view of the "Americanization" of southern California:

> The boom of the eighties contributed vastly to the ongoing process of "Americanization." The sheer volume of immigration brought to southern California the very transformation the northerners had witnessed a generation earlier. In two years or so the population of Los Angeles jumped 500 percent, automatically transforming the electorate into an Anglo-American one. The mores changed equally radically. The type of consumer goods advertised for sale, the tastes in food and dress, prevalence of English over Spanish in daily and official conversation, the Gilded Age recreations, and the style of commerce—all changed rapidly and irreversibly. While describing the changing ethos of real estate promotion and commerce, Professor Glenn S. Dumke notes that "From 1888 onward, the southern counties were imbued with Anglo-American aggressiveness."* What started out as a "semi-gringo" town and a cultural backwash became practically overnight a booming Yankee commercial center and the best-known place in the entire West. (pages 274-75)

---

*Op. cit., (The Boom of the 'Eighties in Southern California (San Marino, Calif.: Huntington Library, 1944)), p. 226.

As is the case with stereotypes of Chicanos, Pitt's use of Gabacho stereotypes leads him far astray. Transcending such abstract notions as "initiative," "progress," "goal and success fulfillment," etc., Pitt confers heroic qualities on his Gabacho protagonists. Seemingly, the invasion must be viewed in heroic terms lest one deny the Gabacho mythology of fearless lawmen, tough rangers, rugged squatters, and indefatigable pioneers who trek into the wilderness to blend into the sunset. So from the villainy, decay and cowardliness of the Chicano emerges, with histrionic commotion, the Gabacho hero. Whether it is politics, gambling, love, or war, the Gabacho is ready to perform masterful feats of skill and daring.[25] However, the greatest heroism of Gabachos is exemplified in the maintenance of "law and order." The following novelesque passage will illustrate Pitt's handling of the heroic theme:

> A sheriff now could succeed without vigilante aid, particularly if, like Alameda Sheriff Harry Morse, archenemy of bandidos, he possessed perseverence to match their bravado. So closely did Morse hound bandidos that they took him for a demon. Between 1864 and 1874 he trailed Bojorques mercilessly (but never laid eyes on him); killed Norrate Ponce (although killing was not his speciality); captured Tejada; and simply strode up to Procopio in a San Francisco dance hall, laid a hand on the bandido's shoulder, calmly declared, "Procopio, you're my man," and took him to jail.*
> For sheer drama nothing surpassed his single-handed showdown with Juan Soto, whom he began tracking after the badman had robbed and killed a Suñol shopkeeper in January, 1871. With customary aplomb Morse hiked directly into Soto's mountain fastness south of Gilroy, masquerading as a weary and lost traveler. His disguise gained Morse easy entry into Soto's casa for "a rest." When the bandit and his crew discovered the ruse, they began shooting it out with the Sheriff. A Mexican amazon momentarily pinioned Morse's arms, but he broke her grip and got safely outside. Finally the wounded Soto burst from the shack, "bareheaded, his long black hair streaming behind him, a cocked revolver in each hand," and flying suicidally at Morse. At this the Sheriff raised his rifle and shot Soto in the head.**
> (page 260)

Pitt's use of history, therefore, becomes the final component in an almost circular process of legitimizing racism and prejudice in the Gabacho culture. The persistence of 19th century Gabacho folk and popular prejudices against Mexico has been legitimized by some Gabacho social scientists through what Octavio Romano has called "social science fiction."[26] The cultural values paradigm is a product of these social science fiction writers. When a historian like Pitt makes use of it to

---

*Shinn, op. cit., p. 64.

**Jackson, op. cit., pp. 264-267.

explain the decline thesis and the Gabacho invasion of California, he is legitimizing these social scientists and their theoretical models. Through this circular process of legitimation, Gabacho prejudice is defended on the basis of a historical fiction based upon a social science fiction based upon folk prejudices and stereotypes, which in turn are constantly reaffirmed and legitimized by some social scientists and historians. Neither history nor social science seems to profit from this circularity. Nor does this process shed much light on the history of the Chicano.

THE ABUSE AND MISUSE
OF HISTORICAL RESEARCH

The use of myths and stereotypes is an inadequate means of substantiating the Pittian thesis of Californio decline. It goes without saying that they are totally inadequate as valid techniques of any historical research methodology premised on "objectivity." To repeat, these fraudulent techniques are useful mostly for engaging in circular arguments of self-affirmation. Yet, these and other equally invalid techniques are the basis upon which Pitt attempts to build his thesis.

In the brief discussion that follows, I will call attention to three inter-related areas of methodological weakness. These areas are: (1) the persistent bias in the use of language, (2) an intrusive editorial posture, and (3) the careful selection of quotes and references to exclude contradicting evidence.

As Billington *et al.* have noted, "Loaded language can be used to convert innocent sounding descriptions into instruments of propaganda."[27] Some careful readers may have already noted from the material quoted thus far that Pitt demonstrates a remarkable carelessness in his use of words and phrases. The decadent ranchero, the heroic Gabacho, and the criminally-prone lower class Californio are all in some measure constructed through the use of biased language. Some readers might contend that these caricatures are playful and harmless. However, when they are presented disguised as history, their effect is mainly propagandistic. Certainly they have no place in a meaningful history of the Chicano or of any other people.

I do not think it necessary to belabor the point of word bias. Any reader can draw his own conclusions by opening the book—almost at random—and reading Pitt's exposition. Keeping in mind Pitt's decline thesis, it will quickly become apparent to the reader the extent to which Pitt is loading the language. Some typical examples will serve to make the point here.[28] For instance, speaking about Henry A. Crabb, who had been accused of fomenting revolution, Pitt writes:

With little provocation, a *brutal* Mexican governor seized and executed him (Crabb) together with fifty-eight followers. This *savagery* called forth a violent storm of words against all the Spanish-speaking. (page 209, emphasis mine)

In another instance, Pitt creates the stereotype of the non-intellectual Chicano simply through the use of loaded words.

This bill of particulars (i.e., the Gabacho revolt) *mystified* the Californians; aware of their own *numerous shortcomings*, they yet saw none that would serve as provocation for the Yankee rebellion. (page 28, emphasis mine)

Finally, in describing the Californio's resistance to the Gabacho invasion, Pitt demeans the tactics, ethics, and professionalism of the Californios through the use of language:

Employing *bluster* and *trickery*, Flores and his men overwhelmed Gillespie's eighty dragoons and forced the captain to sign surrender terms. On October 4 the *guerrillas* lined the street and *gloated* while Gillespie's dejected men marched out of town . . .[29] (pages 33-34, emphasis mine)

This same technique is applied in reverse to the Gabachos. On one occasion Pitt says, "The real aggressors were not Benton, Gwin, or the Californians, but the *Yankee Argonauts bursting* with *explosive energies.*" (page 86) Many other similar examples could be cited.[30]

A different, but equally flagrant, bias results from Pitt's editorial posture. Now I am calling attention specifically to the way in which Pitt "packages" his book (although later in this section I call attention to the discrepancies between Pitt's book and doctoral dissertation). Pitt gives headline attention to his thesis by making it the book's title. As a result, the thesis does not appear to the reader as a *hypothesis* but as a *given.* Similarly, a number of chapter headings can lead a casual or uncritical reader to draw unwarranted conclusions.

For example, Chapter One is titled "Halcyon Days." Yet, as I have already suggested, the Californio "Halcyon Days" are more myth than reality. Pitt, however, effectively uses this lead-in to make a case for his thesis. Similarly, Chapter Two is called "Rain in the Sheepfold." The metaphor obviously refers to the Californios as a nation of bleating and timid inhabitants, thus scoring another point for the Pittian thesis through editorial manipulation.

" 'Greasers' in the Diggings . . ." is the title of Chapter Three. Here Pitt uses quotation marks around the word "greasers" but the repeated use of such words eventually has a tendency to restore their pejorative meaning. This title fits well with the degeneracy theme. Further, the notion of Californio criminality—an important component of the decline thesis—is given star billing in Chapter Ten: "Cow County Bandidos."

But perhaps the best example of Pitt's editorial intrusion into history is the last chapter which Pitt headlines "Schizoid Heritage." With this bold title Pitt relegates the contemporary Chicano to a rather feeble mental and cultural condition. "Schizoid Heritage" is Pitt's final verdict after having returned to "first instances" to "shed light" on the contemporary Chicano. This chapter title, as well as the decline thesis itself, unquestionably places Professor Pitt in the camp of those with a pathologic perspective of the Chicano.

The third bias is Pitt's apparent selection of sources to exclude evidence contradicting his thesis. Very early in his study he dismisses Californio sources because of "prejudice." He then builds his arguments largely from Gabacho sources—many of them newspapers and personal diaries. When he does incorporate Californio sources, they seem to speak against their own kind or in favor of the invader. For example, the beleaguered General Vallejo—who might have had second thoughts about his involvement with Gabachos—went to Washington to seek Congressional help in settling his disputed land claims. Pitt reports the following interview between Vallejo and Lincoln:

> "The Yankees are a wonderful people—wonderful!" Vallejo exclaimed, as he warmed to the occasion. "Where they go, they make improvements. If they were to emigrate in large numbers to hell itself they would irrigate it, plant trees and flower gardens, build reservoirs and fountains and make everything beautiful and pleasant, so that by the time we get there, we can sit at a marble top table and eat ice cream." (pages 240-41)

This anecdote, and others like it, generally help to perpetuate the image of progressive and "energetic" Gabachos; or they show the "shortcomings" of the Californios.[31] The assumption, it seems, is that the "evidence" is more convincing since it is coming from Californios themselves.

Perhaps a clearer statement of these methodological biases—and their effects—can be made through what I call a "test of consistency" between two related works of Professor Pitt. One is the text under discussion, and the other is Pitt's own doctoral dissertation from which is drawn much of the material in the book.[32] I note at the outset, however, that while the book draws heavily from the dissertation, there are also significant differences between the two works. Moreover, there is a great deal of bias in the dissertation itself. Yet, the comparison is still instructive because the distortions in the book are more systematic and apparently more formalized within the Pittian thesis.

In his dissertation, Pitt makes certain qualifying judgments which do not appear in the book. Generally these judgments are somewhat more favorable toward the Californios than toward the Gabacho: a situation seldom encountered in the book. For instance, regarding California before the invasion, Pitt observes:

Many Mexicans who were crushed spiritually and otherwise by the rapid changes of the 1850's had actually already experienced in the Mexican era a slower and more acceptable transformation of the primary institutions that had traditionally molded their fathers' lives. (page 4)

Pitt's judgment of Gabacho writers who condemned Californio culture does not appear in the book:

The 1840's (Gabacho) conception of California was molded by literary conventions derived from established works such as *Gil Blas*, by popular myths growing out of the hoary Black Legend of Spanish cruelty, by racial theories stemming from the South's current pre-occupation with miscegenation and by feverish sentiments against Mexicans, as the West remembered the Alamo. (page 35)

Similarly,

With ... (the) highest of all possible moral criteria the American tried to rationalize his forcible suppression of the Mexican. (page 36)

In the dissertation Pitt quotes many Gabacho writers, just as he does in the book. However, in the former work, as noted above, he sometimes tries to show the bias inherent in the material. After citing the wretched description of Juan Bandini given by Dana, Pitt suggests: "Of course, Dana was quite mistaken about the economic fortune of the Bandinis; the family was very solvent indeed." (page 10) He makes no such correction in the book, but instead leaves the uninformed reader to draw his own conclusions.

In fact, Pitt goes even further in the dissertation and presents a description, again from Dana's book, of a Yankee trader in California. It is an unflattering portrait which does not appear in the book. The Yankee trader was a

... fat, coarse, vulgar pretending fellow ... who was eating out the very vitals of the Bandinis, fattening upon their extravagance, grinding them into their poverty; having mortgages on their lands, forestalling their cattle and already making an inroad upon their jewels, which were their last hope. (page 11)

Certainly this is not a wholesome picture of Gabacho enterprise.

Pitt contradicts the notion of an opulent Californio aristocracy in the following quote—which does not appear in the book—from Alfred Robinson.

... A. M. Lugo "amused us by his stories and eccentricities." For all his wealth "he lives miserably poor, depriving himself of the comforts of life, yet he thinks nothing of squandering thousands upon others." (page 12)

Californios, who are generally two-dimensional characters in the book, at times appear more humanized in the dissertation. For example, Pitt recounts the following anecdote.

> According to an apocryphal story, when a native child reported excitedly to
> his parents that people from the 'States were coming along the road, his
> father mildly reprimanded, "Those are not people, those are gringos!" (page
> 105)

Whether apocryphal or authentic, no such stories appear in the book.

On the other hand, even while describing Californio dissensions, Pitt
makes the following observation which will not be found in the book:
"It cannot be said that the *Californios* lost the war or even a single
battle because of dissensions in their ranks; their losses came from more
fundamental causes." (page 63)

In the dissertation Pitt also draws a surprising conclusion about
Californio reaction to the Gabacho invasion. There is no easy way one
can come to a similar conclusion by reading the book alone. Pitt concludes:

> The Californios have been depicted as bewildered innocents who stood by
> helplessly watching the march of progress. But it is not altogether true that
> they were idle spectators to the decimation of their land. Up to and about
> 1851 or even 1852 many were adjusting satisfactorily to what was new in
> their lives. They were active participants and successfully met new chal-
> lenges with old responses. Even at their worst, they evaluated their struggle,
> fought back as best they could and appraised their losses carefully. (page
> 190)

Obviously such a conclusion is not in line with the decline thesis. It is
also noteworthy that 1851 is the year Congress passed the nefarious
Land Law.

Perhaps the greatest contrast between dissertation and book is most
clearly illustrated by quoting parallel passages from both works and
letting the reader draw his own conclusion. In describing the Sonoran's
mining skill, for instance, Pitt notes in the dissertation:

> The Sonoran seemed able to perform miracles by winnowing dirt in the
> breeze or even with the aid of his own breath. He could poke at the top soil
> with a knife and come up with a nugget the size of his fist. (page 102)

The equivalent passage in the book reads:

> Sonorans somehow could probe the topsoil with knives and bring up nug-
> gets, or work the *batea* (pan) to great advantage. Where water was scarce
> and quartz plentiful, as in the southern mines, they had the endurance to
> sit for hours and winnow dirt in their serapes, sometimes using their own
> gargantuan breath if the wind died down. (page 54)

In the dissertation Sonoran traders appear as a welcome sight to the
miners.

> The cries of the "skinners" and the clank of animal bells was welcome

music in the mines, for they signaled an increase in the supply of goods
even in the remotest camps (page 101)

In the book the traders are cheapened considerably.

... Yankee miners ... had come to associate Mexican mule bells with sa-
vory cooking odors and a few cheap comforts of life ... (page 57)

The Varela-Gillespie incident is a superb example of the way in
which Pitt manipulates words in the book. Californios naturally lose in
the transposition. The dissertation reads:

Memoirs of the Californios reveal a great deal of pride in the memory of
Varela. Saddled with a fine for a trivial offense, this young Mexican stirred
up about 15 or 20 boys and young men—"mere youths" and almost un-
armed, one ranchero boasted—went down to Gillespie's headquarters and
taunted him with shouts of *Viva Mexico!* An American officer of more
gentle temperament would have regarded this merely as a drunken carousel
of vagabonds and would have let it go at that, but Gillespie retaliated in a
panic. (page 63)

The subtle as well as the obvious shifts which occur in the book version
could serve as a lesson in distortion.

Fearful of a conspiracy, Gillespie searched several houses, confiscated arms,
and did everything in his power to intimidate the occupants. In response,
Servulio Varela, a young Mexican dabbler in rebellions, took a score of
drinking companions to Gillespie's quarters and taunted him with drum
rolls and shouts of "¡Viva Méjico!" In a panic, Gillespie fired his rifle into
the darkness and sent the intruders scurrying into the hills. (page 33)

Equally instructive, if not revolting from a Chicano viewpoint, is
Pitt's handling of the notorious Downieville incident where a Mexican
woman was lynched by Gabachos. In the dissertation Pitt seems to be
mildly judgmental.

Perhaps it was merely coincidence that the first woman lynched was dark-
skinned and her victim light-skinned, that she was a foreigner and he a
native, that she was a Mexican and he a gringo. But an American woman
might not have suffered this same fate had she committed the same crime
as the dark lady from Mexico. (page 160)

Professor Pitt's judgment in the book is on an entirely different level.
Referring to the pregnant victim, Pitt boasts:

In light of the preceding two years of trouble, it seems altogether fitting
that a *Mexican* woman should be so honored by gringos; if they had to
punish Eve, then so much the better if she were a "greaser." (page 74)

Describing the confrontation between Soto and Morse (which I have
previously quoted in detail) the dissertation reads:

> A Mexican sheepherder, trembling lest his treason be uncovered by Soto, led Morse into the edge of the *bandido's* mountain fastness, a day's ride south of Gilroy. There Morse put on one of his unbelievably phony disguises. Posing as a weary traveler he talked his way right into the Soto hideout. (page 286)

The revised version printed in the book is:

> With customary aplomb Morse hiked directly into Soto's mountain fastness south of Gilroy, masquerading as a weary and lost traveler. His disguise gained Morse easy entry into Soto's casa for "a rest." (page 260)

Finally, in the sanitation battle of Los Angeles, the dissertation reads:

> Lower-class women persisted in using the town's water supply—the *zanja* ditches—for drinking and washing and disposal, despite repeated ordinances by gringo water commissioners. One decree asked that the women at least wash clothing on the *edge* of the main zanja, but to no avail. The washing of the laundry was a local institution where gossip was transferred and the women resisted efforts to curtail it. (page 315)

In the book the explanation of local custom is deleted and the reader is left only with stupidity as a reason for the women's behavior.

> ... the Yankee town fathers tried to dissuade the Mexican women from washing clothes in the *zanja,* the town's chief source of water, or at least to do their washing on the *edge* of the ditch; but lectures on hygiene generally produced only blank stares. (page 124)

Note also how the book includes *all* Mexican women, while the dissertation speaks only of "lower class" women.

It is worthwhile to emphasize again that there is much distortion in the dissertation itself. But, as I have demonstrated, it is even worse in the book. Sometimes, however, the differences between the dissertation and the book are minimal. The dissertation chapter on bandidos, for example, is almost as distorted as its equivalent chapter in the book. For instance, Pitt's belief in the inherent criminality of Californio culture is already clear in the dissertation: ". . . Hispanos were fundamentally depraved and constituted a class of the most 'desperate characters,' composed of 'idle hangers on about the large Spanish ranchos.' " (page 236) Similarly,

> Among the very many cultural traits transported to California in Spanish or Mexican saddlebags, banditry was the most destructive. More than anything it was a product of Mexico's social revolutionary turmoil. (page 255)

Pitt appears to discount the possibility that banditry might just as well have been transported to California in covered wagons.

There are a great many other comparisons which could be made to show the differences between the dissertation and the book. Those which I have already given show that Pitt's book is an effort to develop systematically the thesis of Californio decline. Clearly the thesis is already present in the dissertation, yet it is not well integrated. The book represents an effort to remedy that weakness.

It is an irony that the kindest words one could have for either of Pitt's works are the very words which the author writes in the preface to his dissertation: "A synthesis of the Mexican (American), his past and present, is yet to be written." (page v) Notwithstanding Pitt's dissertation and book, or perhaps because of them, the same words can be said today with equal accuracy.

PART II
SOME THEORETICAL PITFALLS

A FALSE PARALLEL AND AN IMPORTANT OMISSION
THE CASE OF FOOTNOTE 20a
HISTORY VS SOCIAL SCIENCE DE PASADA
A POSTSCRIPT

A FALSE PARALLEL
AND AN IMPORTANT OMISSION

A singular aspect of Pitt's text is the intricate manner in which he combines historical distortion, shoddy social science, and opinion to compile an exhaustive defense of his decline thesis. His principal attacks on Californio culture have been described; and they form the major basis for his thesis. However, Pitt is adept at producing other distortions to bolster his position. Among these are his comparative distinctions between New Mexico and California. He appears to contend, although with little conviction and less documentation, that after the Gabacho invasion of the Southwest the Nuevo Mexicanos somehow fared better than the Californios. Or, saying it differently, he appears to suggest that the Californios were particularly decadent when compared to other Mexican groups in the Southwest.

I tend to believe that arguments about which Chicano groups fared better under the Gabacho onslaught are somewhat academic, since most Chicanos seem to have led a troubled existence under the new Gabacho scheme. Further, any comparative account of the Chicano in the Southwest would probably require a complex research design and a considerable expenditure of time and energy.

On the other hand, Pitt's spontaneous and disconnected comparative judgments between Nuevo Mexicanos and Californios seem muddled, gratuitous, and facile; and the reader may well ask why Pitt forces the comparisons. By way of explanation, I suggest that Pitt wanted to take advantage of contemporary studies carried out in New Mexico and apply them to California. Consequently, he felt obliged to construct some kind of nexus between the Californios and the Nuevo Mexicanos. Pitt's comparisons, it would seem, are an effort to draw parallels between two distinct regions in order to legitimize the use of data from one area for analyzing the problems of another. The result is that Pitt does an inadequate job on what might otherwise be an interesting, though difficult, topic.

Important omissions abound in Pitt's book. I have already suggested that his treatment of pre-invasion California leaves out much of the historical record. But most important is Pitt's failure to discuss the Treaty of Guadalupe Hidalgo. In the entire text, Pitt makes less than a dozen references to the treaty, and nowhere does he discuss it as a separate topic. I suspect that a more careful historian of the Californios or the Southwest would give considerable attention to the treaty and its effects on the Mexican inhabitants of the region. To study Chicano history without taking into account the Treaty of Guadalupe Hidalgo is a glaring omission in Pitt's work. On the other hand, I can imagine the difficulties one might encounter in trying to fit the treaty into the decline thesis.

THE CASE OF FOOTNOTE NUMBER 20a

The Pittian thesis was received well in several quarters when it first appeared in *The Decline of the Californios*. The first printing of the book received an award from the Commonwealth Club for "the best work on California history" in 1967. But an astute critic might have remarked that Pitt had failed not only in his attempt to shed light on the contemporary Spanish-speaking scene, but on the Chicano scenes of the past as well. And if indeed Professor Pitt was interested in searching the Chicano past in order to clarify the meaning of the present, why did he choose to straitjacket Californio history in his absurd decline thesis?

Nor can one excuse the Pittian thesis on the grounds that there is a scarcity of primary sources and data for a thorough scrutiny of Californio history. While data may be missing in certain areas and for completing some of the details, the general outline of Californio history can be amply documented. It is clear, for example, that the Californios fell victims to a Gabacho invasion. Professor Pitt seems to be well informed on this point, yet his interpretation of this event (through the decline thesis) is based largely on Gabacho sources which are heavily biased. From reading Pitt, one might conclude that the invasion was a godsend to the Californios who were decaying in a fetid cultural miasma.

It is quite baffling to see Pitt reach such a dismal conclusion even after he has handled a great many documents which could just as well point to contrary conclusions. A cynical reader might claim, with some justice, that Pitt chose to ignore a great deal of history in order to fabricate a small bit of historical fiction. Fortunately, while traditional historians were lauding Professor Pitt for his new insights into an old problem, energetic Chicanos were vigorously rejecting the Pittian thesis through their words and actions. The Chicano's message was, and is, that the Gabacho has consistently exploited the Chicano first through a political and military invasion, then through economic manipulation and social subjugation. This seems to be an inescapable fact of history and no amount of historical manipulation or of intellectual fantasizing can eradicate it from the real world.

While the signs of the times may have escaped Professor Pitt in 1967, they certainly did not fail to attract his attention in 1970 when the third printing of *The Decline of the Californios* came off the presses. By then Pitt had some misgivings about his decline thesis and, perhaps as an act of penitent self-absolution, appended footnote number 20a to the text which in part reads:

> In the final analysis the Californios were the victims of an imperial conquest, a fact of overriding importance which some Yankees, in their preoccupation with "Providence" or "moral factors," chose to ignore. Only when the pattern of conquest is understood can the decline of the Californios be entirely comprehended. Stating the pattern simply and in its boldest terms: the United States, which had long coveted California for its trade potential and strategic location, finally provoked a war to bring about the desired ownership. At the conclusion of fighting, it arranged to "purchase" the territory outright, and set about to colonize, by throwing open the gates to all comers. Yankee settlers then swept in by the tens of thousands, and in a matter of months and years overturned the old institutional framework, expropriated the land, imposed a new body of law, a new language, a new economy, and a new culture, and in the process exploited the labor of the local population whenever necessary. To certain members of the old ruling class these settlers awarded a token and symbolic prestige, at least temporarily; yet with that status went little genuine authority. In the long run Americans simply pushed aside the earlier ruling elite as being irrelevant. (page 296)

Thus at the *end* of 3rd printing of the book the astonished reader discovers that in one paragraph Pitt wipes out a large portion of the 296 page argument for the Pittian thesis. Some pundit might suggest that for all of his research and elaborate arguments Pitt finds it impossible to believe his own thesis. For this reason one might assert that the rightful place for this paragraph is in the prologue, not in the epilogue. In fact, with only slight modification this paragraph might be the preface for another more historically accurate account of the Californios.

Footnote 20a is noteworthy on another score. If paragraph one demonstrates Pitt's inconsistency, then the second paragraph (following below) is a notable example of Pitt's consistent tendency to dilute the importance of facts which appear favorable to the Chicano. Thus while Pitt concedes in the first paragraph that the Californios were fundamentally the victims of Gabacho imperialism, the second paragraph serves both as a palliative for the Gabacho conscience and as a way to muddle the issue. The second paragraph reads:

> To be sure, this imperial conquest was not the result of a closely co-ordinated federal government policy (such as was the case in Cuba or the Philippines after the Spanish-American war), nor was it the result of a program of genocide (as in the instance of the California Indians). Nor did every participant act out of personal malice; in fact the conquest aroused in some Yankees a sense of remorse and guilt for the worst excesses of their fellow countrymen. Yet this subjugation by local authority proceeded steadily and swiftly in the towns and farms, in the courtrooms and school-houses throughout the state, and it had irrevocable consequences. The imperialism of Everyman, while not so tidy as the imperialism of statesmen and generals, can be every bit as encompassing; such was the case in California. (page 296)

While Pitt is quite correct in suggesting that Gabacho imperialism is a key element in Californio history, he is mistaken in claiming that the Gabacho invasion was *not* the result of "a closely coordinated federal government policy." Other historians have arrived at the opposite conclusion. Gastón Garcia Cantú's *Las invasiones norteamericanas en México* recounts in some detail the Gabacho strategy to wrench from Mexico over fifty percent of its national territory.[33] From García Cantú's work it appears clear that the Gabacho policy of domination was very well coordinated at the diplomatic, military, and political level. Manuel Medina Castro's *El gran despojo,* while somewhat more partial than the previous work, is a scathing account of the Gabacho invasion of Mexican territory.[34] Like García Cantú, Medina Castro leaves no doubt whatever that, in his view, the American venture to capture Mexican territory was a coordinated plot hatched within the federal government over a period of several presidencies and consummated during the Polk administration.

Similarly, Pitt's fanciful notion of the "imperialism of Everyman" is a wide-eyed fabrication of little interest to Chicanos. It is about as useful in explaining the Gabacho invasion as the Pittian thesis is in explaining the "decline" of the Californios.

Having conceded that the imperialism thesis may provide a more historically viable interpretation of Californio history, one can raise several issues concerning the Chicano past as well as the implications of that past for the Chicano present and future. Clearly, if the Chicano is heir to a history of invasion, colonization, and exploitation, then the present task of the Chicano is not to minister to his "schizoid heritage" as the Pittian thesis would suggest, but to raise again the collective consciousness of an oppressed people. Similarly, Californio history could be examined from the perspective of Gabacho aggression, a perspective adopted by both García Cantú and Medina Castro (as noted above). And if one is interested in viewing the Californios from a sociopsychological perspective, then the observations of Frantz Fanon may provide useful insights.

On the other hand, the Pittian thesis could possibly have an application—but quite an ironic one. Few would argue, for example, that a colonialist conquest is ever made without the active participation of some of the native population. Furthermore, few conquests can be maintained without the continued collaboration of some native faction. California and the Southwest were no exception. In California men like Mariano Vallejo and Pablo de la Guerra, in Texas Lorenzo Zavala, played important roles in bringing California and the Southwest under Gabacho control. These political opportunists had much to gain by way of land speculation, increased commerce, and the hopes of political aggrandizement. They were men of influence and power who hoped to continue in privileged positions and even increase their power through a Gabacho hegemony. Unfortunately, the Gabacho destroyed them very quickly after the invasion through the use of many subterfuges, including the Foreign Miners' Tax and the Land Law. Mexican historians treat these collaborators somewhat gruffly,[35] and one might suggest that in some sense these Californios and Tejanos declined. Had they taken a strong anti-invasion position, today they might enjoy a prominent place in Chicano history. As it is, many Chicanos know about men such as Tiburcio Vasquez, Joaquín Murieta, and Juan Cortina, but very few know about men with names like Vallejo, Zavala and de la Guerra.

HISTORY VS SOCIAL SCIENCE DE PASADA

Part One of this critique deals, in part, with Pitt's use of mediocre Gabacho social science for interpreting Californio history. While I do not wish to discuss here the history vs social science debate, one theoretical point must at least be noted.[36] To what extent can a historian use social science theory and research in interpreting historical research? And if a historian chooses to combine social science and historical methods and theory, what responsibility does he have to insure that he is not merely using the methodological and theoretical weaknesses of one discipline to camouflage similar or different weaknesses in another discipline? Or what responsibility does the historian have to avoid legitimizing theoretical, methodological, and researcher prejudices which may be lurking in the social sciences?

One can conceive of mutual benefits which could accrue from a judicious combination of social science and history. Yet, Fischer has warned that,

> If sociological history and historical sociology are conceived as a combination of the conceptual sophistication of the best sociologists and the dogged if often undirected empiricism of the best historians, then the prospects are very bright indeed. But one might also imagine an interdisciplinary effort which combined the worst of both worlds—the stupidity of historians and the ignorance of sociologists.[37]

The Pittian thesis rests heavily on the assertion that Californio culture had dysfunctional traits. The primary defense for this assertion is the work of various social scientists which culminates in the cultural values paradigm. Since this paradigm is at best a compound stereotype, Pitt may have fallen victim to the ignorance of some social scientists. If this is the case, then Fischer's last sentence could be used as a terse summary of Pitt's fundamental methodological weakness in *The Decline of the Californios.*

A POSTSCRIPT

An important goal of this critique has been to challenge the Pittian thesis and to counteract the widespread support which it has received in the past several years. Pitt's book has been widely used in Chicano Studies courses and as an authoritative source on Chicano history. Yet few critics—Gabacho or otherwise—have challenged the basic assumptions and assertions of the work. On the contrary, much praise has come from a number of quarters. Navarro, for example, asserts that *The Decline of the Californios* is ". . . probably the most scholarly work on Mexican-American history."[38] Moses Rischin, who swallows the Pittian thesis with gusto, believes that:

> The book's major claim to originality is in the link that the author established between the bleak prospects of today's over two million Spanish-speaking Californians and the misfortunes of ten thousand nineteenth-century Californios.[39]

Rischin thus proves his considerable capacity to swallow Pitt's nonsensical thesis. Even more astounding is his conclusion that ". . . Pitt is dedicated to historical rehabilitation . . ." In fact, following Fischerian logic one could suggest that Rischin's review combines the stupidity of historians, the ignorance of sociologists, and the imbecility of reviewers. Otherwise it is difficult to explain a statement like:

In California as elsewhere, nineteenth-century individualist Anglo-Saxondom overwhelmed a communally oriented caballero culture rendering the *Californio* quixotic, picturesque, and pathetic with a finality that was not to be quite the lot of their numerous and more isolated fellow ethnics in New Mexico.[40]

Such is the extent to which Rischin internalizes the Pittian pendejada.

Even Meier and Rivera, who are certainly not biased against the Chicano, are in fundamental error when they claim that Pitt's book ". . . is an excellent pioneering monograph, one of the few written from a Mexican American viewpoint."[41]

Finally, the work of two anthropologists, currently used as a text in some university social science courses, accepts the Pittian thesis and presents it as a matter of fact.[42] Thus we have again come full circle and now we see that some social scientists are legitimizing the historian and reifying the Pittian thesis. Borrowing a currently popular concept, it seems that the Pittian thesis has been promptly recycled back to the social sciences, from where it came.

NOTES

1. *Gabacho* as used throughout this critique refers to the amorphous agglomeration of U.S. inhabitants who are either of European origin or of European extraction. The term comes from a Chicano universe of discourse and might be translated into the Gabacho idiom as "Euro-American."
2. For more commentary on this subject, see Eduardo Seda, "Ethnic Studies and Cultural Pluralism," *The Rican*, I (Fall, 1971), pp. 56-65.
3. Such a response, of course, is most often labeled as irrational and subjective by Gabacho researchers. An alternate strategy for such a boxed-in Chicano is to take a critical stance toward his own reality. Under these circumstances, Gabacho criticisms become irrelevant.
4. *Webster's New Collegiate Dictionary*, 6th ed., 1961, p. 214.
5. *Ibid.*, p. 226.
6. See especially Chapter XVI, "Schizoid Heritage." Note: unless otherwise stated, references to Leonard Pitt are based on the 1970 printing of *The Decline of the Californios* (Berkeley: University of California Press). Henceforth only page numbers are given.
7. Mervyn Miller, "A History of the Secularization of the Missions of California" (unpublished M.A. thesis, College of the Pacific, 1932).
8. George Tays, "Revolutionary California" (unpublished Ph.D. dissertation, University of California, Los Angeles, 1932).
9. For example, discussing Bouchard's attack on California, Pitt comments, "Family feeling and respect for age thus produced powerful sentiments whose weakening the Californians would later find especially painful." (page 12) Apparently, Pitt concludes that there was something weak about the Californio family as an institution.

Describing a religious scene, Pitt creates a semi-paganistic scenario:

The Assumption fiesta of August, 1857, lasting three days, included a bull-
fight, in which *el toro* gored a horse and killed a man.* On June 3, 1858,
Corpus Christi began with two morning Masses, which were followed by an
afternoon procession. When the laity and the clergy emerged from the
church, the hundred white-robed girls of the Catholic orphanage walked to
the cadence of a musical band and the escort of Twist's Southern Rifles and
the mounted California Lancers with swords drawn. They toured the plaza,
passing under flowering arches and pausing for benediction before be-
jeweled altars near the homes of Doña Benicia Sotelo, Ignacio del Valle, and
Agustín Olvera. (page 218)

Finally, speaking through second parties, Pitt observes:

The nativos valued their military prowess, but Clyman certified it as "weak,
imbecile and poorly organized and still less respected" . . . *The National
Intelligencer,* in April 1846, told the gringo nation that "the Spanish portion of the inhabitants are a thieving, cowardly, dancing, lewd people, and
generally indolent and faithless" . . . (page 16)

For an original source that makes vitriolic attacks on Californio religion, as well
as Californios in general, see Lansford W. Hastings, *The Emigrants' Guide to
Oregon and California* . . . (Cincinnati: George Conclin, 1845). Facsimile edition by Charles Henry Carey (Princeton: Princeton University Press, 1932).

10. The British and the French governments (especially the British) may have been
    more interested in gaining a foothold in California than Pitt suggests in this
    passage.
11. In one of Pitt's "sketches" which supposedly pictures Californio opulence, Pitt
    notes, "watermelon and other refreshments were available on call." (page 253)
    For me, at least, watermelons are not a particularly significant indicator of great
    wealth, regardless of the quantity consumed.
12. Pitt comments:

    Those convicts (from Mexico) usually arrived in a state of wretchedness
    exceeded only by that of the Indians. Bands of so-called *cholos* (scoundrels)
    would brawl drunkenly on the public streets and commit theft and other
    assorted misdeeds—even homicide—while the political prisoners among them
    organized rebellions. This state of affairs greatly distressed the more genteel
    settlers.**(page 6)

    On the same theme of Californio criminality, Pitt writes:

    It is, nevertheless, true that in the early Yankee years some Californios took
    to the highway and earned bad reputations entirely on their own hook.
    Disaffected youths found many reasons and opportunities to turn to
    crime . . . (page 149)

13. "Biological determinism" as a concept means that there is some genetic factor
    in the Californio which makes him, in this case, criminally prone. On the other

---

*Los Angeles *Star,* Aug. 22, 1857.

**Angustias de la Guerra Ord, *Occurences in Hispanic California* (Washington,
1956), pp. 54-55.

hand, "cultural determinism" means that there are elements in the Californio's culture which, when acquired by a person, will render that person criminally prone.

14. For example, "Reyes Felix also pleaded innocence, but so frantically that he confessed a previous crime." (page 157) Of course, Reyes was hanged anyway on his confession. In another instance, "A committee of public safety (i.e., vigilantes) . . . took the prisoner's confession in English and Spanish. The jury returned a verdict of first degree murder for Zavaleta and Rivas, and the next morning the town witnessed its first "grand" lynching. (page 156)

The final tableau for a number of Californio badmen is filled with heart-breaking pathos and cathartic repentance. In describing the Flores lynching, Pitt appears to vindicate Hollywood:

Flanked by two priests, Flores strode up the hill with firm steps, still looking "as composed as any one in the crowd . . . He was a young man . . . of pleasing countenance. There was nothing in his appearance to indicate the formidable criminal he had proved himself to be."* Through an interpreter, Flores told the crowd that he had committed many crimes, bore no ill will toward anyone, and was ready to die; . . . (page 171)

15. In the preface Pitt states,

. . . even in their heyday, the Spanish and Mexican Californians were numerically too small and culturally too backward to contribute to mankind much that was new or original. In the crowning phase of their evolution, the Yankees beat them badly and all but swept them into the dustbin of history. (page vii).

16. Carey McWilliams had already established this point in his *North from Mexico; The Spanish-speaking People of the United States* (Philadelphia: J. B. Lippincott Company, 1949).

17. See Octavio Romano-V., "The Anthropology and Sociology of the Mexican-Americans," in *Voices; Readings from El Grito*, edited by Octavio Romano-V. (Berkeley: Quinto Sol Publications, 1971), pp. 26-39; also Nick C. Vaca, "The Mexican-American in the Social Sciences," *El Grito*, IV (Fall, 1970), pp. 17-51.

18. Nick Vaca, "The Mexican-American in the Social Sciences," *El Grito*, IV (Fall, 1970), p. 45.

19. *Ibid.*

20. *Ibid.*, p. 46.

21. To illustrate this point, note the following passages:
    (a) Dullness of native women—

. . . the Yankee town fathers tried to dissuade the Mexican women from washing clothes in the zanja, the town's chief source of water, or at least to do their washing on the edge of the ditch; but lectures on hygiene generally produced only blank stares. (page 124)

    (b) Docility of Californios—

He (Thomas Larkin) promised to all Californians the benefits of free trade, representative government, public education, and agricultural progress, and

---

*Los Angeles *Star,* Feb. 21, 1857 . . .

to their government leaders, posts in the new government. Eventually he felt that he had them (Californios) "eating out of his hand" and was reasonably confident that no blood need be shed in converting California into a Yankee territory. (page 21)

(c) Californio laziness—

The Californians, in Clyman's eyes, were "a proud indolent people doing nothing but ride after herds from place to place without any apparent object."* "Nature doing everything, man doing nothing" was Simpson's summation of the (Californio) economy.** (page 16)

22. Pitt can be quite explicit on this point:

The first two phases of American annexation, rebellion and military conquest, have greatly appealed to the popular imagination. The final stage, military government, by comparison seems inconsequential—an irritating interruption in the inevitable progress from Spanish-American to Anglo-Saxon control. (page 35)

23. One of the few references which Pitt makes to the important Treaty of Guadalupe Hidalgo is presented in the following way:

They (some Californios) dismissed the news that a few Californios had been harried from their claims by fist-swinging Oregon Yankees, who refused to acknowledge that the Treaty of Guadalupe Hidalgo granted some Mexicans full citizenship . . . (page 50)

24. Note the peculiar Freudian overtones to the way in which Pitt presents the "wave of the future" concept:

Zealous advocates of the new business ethos, Couts, Brinley, and Johnson represented the wave of the future in the cow counties. . . . Their Puritan ethic of labor and profit contributed to the emasculation of the local manhood. (page 115)

25. As noted in footnote 18, it seems that one Gabacho alone could engineer a diplomatic coup of California. Transferring this prowess from politics to romance, Pitt declares, "Curiously, many California women seem to have been more favorably disposed toward the Yankees than were their men." (page 23) Pitt then goes on to say why he thinks this is a reasonable conclusion. His evidence is the following stanza from a Yankee war song:

Already the señoritas
Speak English with finesse.
"Kiss me! say the Yankees,
The girls all answer "Yes!"
(page 23)

I tend to believe that such delusions are common to men at war, but of little value for Pitt's argument.

Finally, Pitt draws the following conclusion about gambling:

---

*Camp, loc. cit., p. 29.

**Simpson, op. cit., p. 29.

> Whether the (Gabacho) gamblers cheated or played straight, they usually beat the local novices hands down. One young Bandini lost as much as $10,000 while "locked up along with those men." (page 108)

26. Octavio Romano-V., "The Anthropology and Sociology of the Mexican-American," in *Voices; Readings from El Grito,* edited by Octavio Romano-V. (Berkeley: Quinto Sol Publications, 1971), p. 36.
27. Ray Allen Billington, *et. al., The Historian's Contribution to Anglo-American Misunderstanding* (New York: Hobbs, Dorman & Co., Inc., 1966), p. 11.
28. Other examples include the following:
    (a) The non-intellectual Chicano—

    > The Californians now simply reverted to their *customary circular logic,* which held that evil came from outsiders, that outsiders were mostly evil, and that evil mothered evil. (page 52, emphasis mine)

The xenophobia which Pitt attributes to the Californios in the quote above is a ridiculous Pittian fabrication. Californios had been trading with foreigners, especially Yankees, since Mexican Independence. Even the missions engaged in some trade with foreigners after hostilities broke out between Mexico and Spain.
    (b) The present orientation syndrome is shown in the following passage—

    > Just as the Spaniard's *eccentric work habits* could be turned to the operator's profit, so could his *spendthrift tendencies* be turned to the advantage of the merchant." (page 59, emphasis mine)

It is noteworthy that in the above passage Pitt equates Spaniards with Indians, Mestizos, Mexicans, Sonorans, and Californios.
    (c) The irrational-emotional Chicano comes out in this excerpt—

    > The ranchero *never understood,* much less accepted, the gringo's concept of land tenure. The Land Law, preemption and occupancy rights, and the "jungle thickets" of land litigation made him not only *violently angry* but also *mystified him.* (page 89, emphasis mine)

It seems doubtful, however, that Californios did not understand that Gabachos were robbing them out of house and home. It is true, of course, that they refused to accept the Land Law without a struggle. They fought as best they could through the courts and through political influence. Vallejo went to Washington to fight for his land titles. See the excerpt from a de la Guerra speech to the California legislature which shows how some of the Californios felt about their situation, *El Grito,* V (Fall, 1971), p. 19.
29. In the only significant battle of the war fought in California, the Californios, though outnumbered, also defeated Kearny's forces.   ·
30. The success orientation of the Gabacho is portrayed as follows:

    > General Riley discovered that "Americans, by their *superior intelligence* and *shrewdness* in business, generally contrived to turn to their own benefit the earnings of Mexicans, Chileans and Peruvians." (page 59, emphasis mine)

On another occasion Pitt notes: "For the *creative economic energy* of the Yankees, Californians had both admiration and criticism." (page 23, emphasis mine)

31. On a number of occasions Pitt manipulates the Californios so that they either praise the invaders or criticize their countrymen. An anecdote by Ygnacio del Valle is recorded as follows:

> On arriving at the plaza of the government house, Senator del Valle suddenly saw "how far these demons, the Yankees, have gone" in dominating the Californians. Among the boys milling around, eating sweets, and selling newspapers, one small Yankee, perhaps nine years old, sacrificed half of his tin of molasses for a newspaper. He promptly unfolded the massive sheets and disappeared behind them to digest the latest news. This display of Yankee precocity contrasted horribly with the backwardness of native-born youngsters. "No wonder they eat us alive!" Don Ygnacio exclaimed. (pages 141-42)

Along the same lines, see Pitt's discussion of Francisco Ramirez on page 190.

32. "Submergence of the Mexicans in California, 1846-1890: A History of Culture Conflict and Acculturation" (unpublished Ph.D. dissertation, University of California, Los Angeles, 1958).

33. Gastón García Cantú, *Las invasiones norteamericanas en México* (México: Ediciones Era, 1971).

34. Manuel Medina Castro, *El gran despojo* (México: Editorial Diógenes, 1971).

35. In discussing Texas' declaration of independence, Medina Castro observes:

> En seguida las firmas. 48 norteamericanos, 10 europeos, 3 traidores: Lorenzo de Zavala, ex ministro, ex gobernador, etc., y gran concesionario de tierras en Texas, J. Antonio Navarro y Francisco Ruiz.

36. The debate has also affected the Chicano. See for example Joseph Navarro's "The Condition of Mexican-American History," *The Journal of Mexican American History*, I (Fall, 1970), pp. 25-52.

37. David H. Fischer, *Historians' Fallacies; Toward a Logic of Historical Thought* (New York: Harper and Row, 1970), p. 37.

38. Navarro, p. 34.

39. Moses Rischin's review of *The Decline of the Californios* in *American Historical Review*, LXII, (April, 1967), p. 1089.

40. *Ibid.*

41. Matt S. Meier and Feliciano Rivera, *The Chicanos; A History of Mexican Americans* (New York: Hill and Wang, 1972), p. 288.

42. Robert F. Heizer and Alan J. Almquist, *The Other Californians* (Berkeley: University of California Press, 1971). See especially Chapter VI.

BIBLIOGRAPHY

BOOKS

Billington, Ray Allen, *et al. The Historian's Contribution to Anglo-American Misunderstanding.* New York: Hobbs, Dorman & Co., Inc., 1966.

Fanon, Frantz. *The Wretched of the Earth.* New York: Grove Press, 1968.

Fischer, David H. *Historians' Fallacies; Toward a Logic of Historical Thought.* New York: Harper and Row, 1970.

García Cantú, Gastón. *Las invasiones norteamericanas en México.* México: Ediciones Era, 1971.

Hastings, Lansford W. *The Emigrants' Guide to Oregon and California* . . . Cincinnati: George Conclin, 1845. Facsimile edition by Charles Henry Carey, Princeton: Princeton University Press, 1932.

Heizer, Robert F. and Almquist, Alan J. *The Other Californians; Prejudice and Discrimination Under Spain, Mexico, and the United States to 1920.* Berkeley: University of California Press, 1971.

Medina Castro, Manuel. *El gran despojo.* México: Editorial Diógenes, 1971.

Meier, Matt S. and Rivera Feliciano. *The Chicanos: A History of Mexican Americans.* New York: Hill and Wang, 1972.

Pitt, Leonard M. *The Decline of the Californios; A Social History of the Spanish-Speaking Californians, 1846-1890.* Berkeley: University of California Press, 1966. Third Printing, 1970. All references in this critique are based on the 1970 printing.

Romano-V., Octavio, ed. *Voices; Readings From El Grito.* Berkeley: Quinto Sol Publications, 1971.

ARTICLES

Navarro, Joseph. "The Condition of Mexican-American History." *The Journal of Mexican American History,* I (Fall, 1970), 25-52.

Rischin, Moses. Review of *The Decline of the Californios* in the *American Historical Review,* LXII, (April, 1967), 1089.

Seda, Eduardo. "Ethnic Studies and Cultural Pluralism." *The Rican,* I (Fall, 1971), 56-65.

Vaca, Nick. "The Mexican-American in the Social Sciences." *El Grito,* IV (Fall, 1970), 17-51.

UNPUBLISHED WORKS

Kenny, William R. "History of the Sonora Mining Region of California, 1848-1860." Unpublished Ph.D. dissertation, University of California, Berkeley, 1955.

Lederer, Lillian. "A Study of Anglo-American Settlers in Los Angeles County Previous to the Admission of California to the Union." Unpublished M.A. thesis, University of Southern California, 1927.

McGinty, Ruth M. "Spanish and Mexican Ranchos in the San Francisco Bay Region." Unpublished M.A. thesis, University of California, Berkeley, 1921.

Miller, Mervyn. "A History of the Secularization of the Missions of California." Unpublished M.A. thesis, College of the Pacific, 1932.

Miller, Robert R. "Mexican Secret Agents in the United States, 1861-67." Unpublished Ph.D. dissertation, University of California, Berkeley, 1960.

Pitt, Leonard M. 'The Foreign Miners' Tax of 1850: A Study of Nativism and Antinativism in Gold Rush California." M.A. thesis, University of California, Los Angeles, 1955.

Pitt, Leonard M. "Submergence of the Mexicans in California, 1846-1890: A History of Culture Conflict and Acculturation." Unpublished Ph.D. dissertation, University of California, Los Angeles, 1958.

Robertson, James R. "From Alcalde to Mayor: A History of the Changes from the Mexican to the American local Institutions in California." Unpublished Ph.D. dissertation, University of California, Berkeley, 1908.

Ruby, Carrie L. "Attitudes Toward Latin Americans as Revealed in Southwestern Literature." Unpublished M.A. thesis, University of Texas, Austin, 1953.

Tays, George. "Revolutionary California." Unpublished Ph.D. dissertation, University of California, Los Angeles, 1932.

THE DEFINERS AND THE DEFINED
A Mental Health Issue
Armand J. Sanchez

"We have passed the point of no return in our long journey from a helter-skelter system of mental health services divorced from community life," concluded Robert H. Felix, chief architect of the community mental health program.[1] These words, auspicious and monumental in implication, were enunciated about two years ago and presumably ushered in a new era in the mental health field. And notwithstanding the auspiciousness of the words, the concepts of mental health and mental illness continue to be used and implemented programatically in the old and traditional way. According to Dr. Jahoda, "As far as we can discover, there exists no psychologically meaningful and, from the point of view of research, operationally useful description of what is commonly understood to constitute mental health. Yet the establishment of some criteria by which the degree of mental health of an individual can be judged is essential if one wishes to identify social conditions conducive to the attainment of mental health."[2]

However, recent articles have pointed out the irrelevancy of mental health services, specifically as they concern the Chicano community. Dr. E. Fuller Torrey, M.D., in a paper delivered at the meeting of the American Orthopsychiatry Association, which paper is appropriately titled "The Irrelevancy of Traditional Mental Health Services for Urban Mexican-Americans," states: "The irrelevancy began at a higher level. It began at the very conceptualization of the Community Mental Health Centers. It began when the architects of the Act unconsciously and ethnocentrically perpetuated the dominant-class, dominant-culture, dominant-caste model of mental health services as The Model."[3] Obviously the concepts of mental health and mental illness have been very elusive, engendering tautological wheelspinning at every level, particularly at the administrative level.

107

Addressing himself to the relevancy of mental health services specifically as they concern the Chicano community, Dr.
Torrey gives six reasons for their irrelevancy. He also makes
two cogent and significant suggestions: a) "The control and
money for mental health services should be firmly in the
hands of a board from the Mexican-American community;"
and b) "The services should be delivered by those capable of
doing it, not by someone with a certain number of degrees."[4]
Dr. Torrey aptly concludes: "The services will be used when
they are relevant, and they will be relevant only when they
are set up by the Mexican-Americans themselves."[5]

In another article titled "Perception of Mental Health Illness in a Mexican-American Community," Dr. Karno and Dr.
Edgerton attempt to explain an "epidemiological paradox"—
the expected high incidence of mental illness in the Mexican-
American population and yet the striking underrepresentation
of Mexican-Americans as psychiatric patients in public outpatient and inpatient facilities throughout California. Drs.
Karno and Edgerton conclude that, "The underutilization of
psychiatric facilities by Mexican-Americans (at least those that
reside in East Los Angeles) is not to be accounted for by the
fact that they share a cultural tradition which causes them to
perceive and define mental illness in significantly different
ways than do Anglos."[6] Aside from a questionable methodology, their starting assumption is defective, namely, that
Mexican-Americans share *a* cultural tradition. They fail to
specify what that "cultural tradition" is, but it seems that
they have bought without question the *gospel* of social scientists.* In brief, culture is interpreted in terms of identifiable
traits—a static, passive, stereotypic interpretation of culture.
En precis, Drs. Karno and Edgerton seem to be begging the
question. Although the term "mental health" was not defined
by them, it seems that their definition is predictably limited
to individual pathology—thus again interpreting behavior in
intrapsychic terms, the traditional approach. It seems that
Drs. Karno and Edgerton postulate internal causation—in
essence assuming that "culture" causes mental illness among
Chicanos.

---

*Cf. Octavio I. Romano, "The Anthropology and Sociology of the
Mexican-American," *El Grito,* Vol. II, No. 1 (Berkeley: Quinto Sol Publications, Inc., 1968) Fall., & Nick C. Vaca, "The Mexican-American in
the Social Sciences 1912-1970, Part I: 1912-1935, *El Grito,* Vol. III,
No. 3 (Berkeley: Quinto Sol Publications, Inc., 1970) Spring.

In another article, "The Enigma of Ethnicity in a Psychiatric Clinic," Dr. Karno again bases his study on the major assumption that Mexican-Americans share *a* cultural tradition. He cites Saunders, Madsen, and Clark in support of this assumption. Dr. Karno concludes: "In addition to avoidance of ethnicity (by clinic personnel), there is another factor operative in the clinic which may significantly contribute to therapeutic failure with ethnic patients. This is the pervasive use of and reliance upon a model for the psychiatric historical interview which derives directly from the classical medical history. This is an information retrieving process which, to a remarkable extent, systematically ignores the socio-cultural context of the patient's life."[7] It is imperative to note that cultural context means cultural tradition.

In another article titled "Successful and Unsuccessful Approaches of Mental Health Services for an Urban Hispano American Population" M. J. Philippus, Ph.D., relates success and lack of success to utilization of services. The entire point of his article is that the formal traditional, bureaucratic way of delivering mental health services to the Spanish speaking population must be eliminated and an informal, personal approach with heavy emphasis on utilization of neighborhood personnel initiated. Dr. Philippus' point is that the delivery system needs to be changed but he does not address himself to the effectiveness or lack of effectiveness with respect to the psychoanalytic model. Implicitly he is saying that adjustment is the goal to strive for since his assumption is that assimilation into the majority way of life is the ultimate goal of the Mexican-American community.

In summary, although the authors of the articles mentioned above make commendable attempts to address themselves to the problem of "mental health," they fail to address themselves to the issue of mental health itself.

The authors of the articles cited above concur that Mexican-Americans underutilize mental health services. However, in another article Mr. Armando Morales takes the opposite stance. He concludes: "With regard to the existing notion that mental health problems are not as severe in the Mexican-American community as in the dominant society, direct psychiatric clinical experience in the East Los Angeles Mental Health Service Clinic is clearly disproving this notion. While the major diagnosis reported by twenty-five county health districts is 18% 'schizophrenic' and 'other psychoses,' East Los Angeles Mental Health Service staff estimated thirty to forty percent in this category."[8] The other point that Mr. Morales makes is that "Contrary to the belief that Mexican-Americans would be hesitant in utilizing mental health services because of cultural factors, recent statistics reveal that while 'whites' had 23% self and family referrals and 'Negroes' 30%, 'Mexican-Americans' accounted for 50%."[9] Mr. Morales' entire assumption is that because East Los Angeles Mental Health services has twenty-one out of twenty-two bilingual personnel, therefore mental health for the Chicano community can be explained in terms of utilization of services through bi-lingual personnel, referrals, and a more severe diagnosis. But, to transfer mental health rhetoric from one language to another is no solution at all, for it makes very little difference whether the root assumptions are expressed in Spanish, English, Japanese, or Zulu. Therefore, *the posture to integrate Spanish-speaking personnel with no change in philosophy is assimilative in nature and avoids the central issue of what is mental health.* It is patently obvious that the application of the psychoanalytic model to a culture whose underlying philosophy is humanism will result in a high incidence of mental illness as well as a pronounced severity among the Chicano population.

In preparation for a recent Chicano Conference on Mental Health, a questionnaire was developed by Mr. Ernest Solano, M.S.W., to assess mental health resources. Although responses were not received from all counties contacted, the results were significant in pointing out the inadequacy of services, lack of bi-*cultural* staff, and the almost non-utilization of mental health facilities.

In short, although studies regarding the utilization of mental health services by the Chicano community are not extensive, it seems safe to conclude on the basis of Mr. Solano's questionnaire, that Chicanos do not use mental health services. Various reasons for this lack of utilization have been advanced. The sociologist, E. G. Jaco, concluded that Mexican-Americans suffer from less mental illness than Anglo-Americans on the basis that the existence of a cultural pattern of warm, supportive, extended family with strong values of mutual acceptance, care, and responsibility tend to protect Mexican-Americans against the development of major mental illnesses.[10] Others have asserted that Mexican-

Americans view mental health problems negatively and hence tend to tolerate them rather than seek assistance.

The major assumption in studies of utilization of services and severity of mental illness, however, is that the psychoanalytic model works with the Chicano community. *A second assumption is that the Chicano community perceives mental illness in exactly the same way that the dominant society perceives mental illness.* It must be noted that the psychoanalytic model has its basis in the sociological assimilation model which has been operative unilaterally vis-a-vis the Chicano community. Agencies and personnel still operate on the assumption that assimilation into the melting pot is the goal. Moreover, agencies are always assumed to be non-causal. Politically, the medical model lends itself well to retention of a colonialist posture, for it establishes the definer and the defined—the manipulator and the manipulated. Philosophically, the medical model assumes that it is possible to jump from the logical to the ontological; *ab posse ad esse non valet illatio.*

In the final analysis, the Chicano predicament is a problem caused by social, political and economic conditions: to force these conditions into the innerpsyche of the Chicano is detrimental to and destructive of a distinctive way of life. The result, obviously, is an intensification of social problems and "mental" problems—stress and strains in the life style of the Chicano community. It makes little sense to talk about mental health without social health. To treat the problems and neglect the issues is a disservice to the Chicano community and to society. "The concepts of mental health and mental illness are increasingly used ambiguously to include a wide range of social problems. These psychiatric definitions implicitly suggest that the individual is at fault . . ."[11]

Mental health for the Chicano community consists in the full awareness of itself as a distinct ontological entity with its philosophy of man, nature, and the universe. A corollary of the full awareness is the full realization of its power of self determination. Hence it is imperative for Chicanos to sustain and/or enlarge their human interrelational community services. A "system" already exists within the Chicano community. Hence the diagnosing and defining of mental illness is already done within the framework of the Chicano way of life and view of man, nature and the universe. A particular behavior is reflective of that community's philosophy of life. At no time have "mental health services" been developed to reflect this aspect of the Chicano barrio. Hence "mental health" concepts must be developed out of the Chicano philosophy of life. However, "The fiestas patrias, the characteristic foods, the music, the sociedades mutualistas, and all of the other by-products of culture that people write about, are simply appurtenances to more profound conceptualizations regarding the nature and the existence of man."[12]

The starting point suggested for human development services is the assessment of a barrio's existing total human health, *for problem solving in the Chicano community is related to the Chicano community rather than to an agency.* The health of an individual and community does not exist in a vacuum; rather, it is related not only to the total environment but also to other individuals and the network of inter-relationships that give life as well as a specific, unique character to a community. Hence the well being of an individual and community must be studied from within the barrio with its complex network of relationships, for, when all is said and done, the barrio is a social institution.

It is a basic concept of human well-being that a person is much "healthier" if he accepts what he is and values himself and background. Hence, again it is not basically a problem of non-utilization of "mental health" services of the Chicanos; rather, the non-utilization is the result of the failure of "mental health" agencies to acknowledge and accept the Chicano way of life as a valid, viable and dynamic expression of a philosophy of man and his existence together with a view of nature and the universe, which philosophy must form the framework for a definition of well being for Chicanos.*

In summary, I would add that the major premise on which a policy vis-a-vis Chicano well-being and the Chicano community must be based is that of a pluralistic society founded on mutual respect, appreciation, and understanding with an increase in mutual experiences for Anglos and Chicanos. The impact of the barrio way of life on the individual and barrio, an etiological question, underlies epidemiological

---

*This is not to negate the fact that an added dimension to well-being for Chicanos must be the impact, and influence that the majority way of life has on Chicanos but it is an added dimension.

results. The first problem, therefore, is to indicate the barrio way of life in its possible relation to the individual's well-being.

To do otherwise, of course, is to perpetuate the artificial dichotomy of the defined and the definers.

Notes

1. Connery, Robert H. *The Politics of Mental Health.* (Columbia University Press, New York, 1968) pg. 469.

2. Kotinsky, Ralph & Witmer, Helen L. (eds.) *Community Program for Mental Health.* (Cambridge: Harvard University Press, 1955) p. 298.

3. Torrey, E. Fuller, M.D. "The Irrelevancy of Traditional Mental Health Services for Urban Mexican-Americans." Paper presented at American Orthpsychiatry Association, San Francisco, March, 1970.

4. *Ibid.*, p. 16.

5. *Ibid.*, p. 17.

6. Karno, Marvin, M.D. & Edgerton, Robert B., Ph.D. "Perception of Mental Illness in a Mexican-American Community," *Archives of General Psychiatry,* pp. 233-238, Feb., 1969.

7. Karno, Marvin, "The Enigma of Ethnicity in a Psychiatric Clinic," *Archives of General Psychiatry,* pp. 516-520, May, 1966.

8. Armando Morales, "Mental Health and Public Health Issues: The Case of the Mexican Americans in Los Angeles," *El Grito,* Vol. III, No. 2 (Berkeley, Quinto Sol Publications, Irrc., 1970) Winter.

9. *Ibid.*

10. Jaco, E. Gartley, "Mental Health of the Spanish-American in Texas." *Culture and Mental Health,* Marvin K. Opler, ed. (New York: The Macmillan Co., 1959).

11. Mechanic, David *Mental Health and Social Policy.* (Prentice-Hall, Inc., New Jersey, 1969) pp. 31 & 33.

12. Romano, Octavio. "The Historical and Intellectual Presence of Mexican-Americans." *El Grito,* Quinto Sol Publications, Inc., Berkeley, Vol. II, No. 2, Winter, 1969.

BIBLIOGRAPHY

Books

Connery, Robert H. *The Politics of Mental Health.* New York: Columbia University Press, 1968.

Casanova, Pablo Gonzales. *Sociologia de la Explotacion.* Mexico: Sigle XXI Editores, 1969.

Kotinsky, Ralph & Witmer, Helen L. (eds.) *Community Program for Mental Health.* Cambridge: Harvard University Press, 1955.

Mechanic, David. *Mental Health and Social Policy.* New Jersey: Prentice-Hall, 1969.

Opler, Marvin K. ed. *Culture and Mental Health.* New York: The Macmillan Co., 1959.

Valentine, Charles. *The Culture of Poverty.*

Articles

Karno, Marvin. "The Enigma of Ethnicity in a Psychiatric Clinic," *Archives of General Psychiatry.* May, 1966.

Karno, Marvin & Edgerton, Robert H. "Perception of Mental Illness in a Mexican-American Community," *Archives of General Psychiatry.* Feb., 1969.

Morales, Armand. "Mental Health and Public Health Issues: The Case of the Mexican-Americans in Los Angeles," *El Grito,* Quinto Sol Publications, Inc., Berkeley, Vol. III, No. 2, Winter, 1970.

Phillipus, M. J., Ph.D. "Successful and Unsuccessful Approaches of Mental Health Services for an Urban Hispano American Population." Department of Health and Hospitals, Division of Psychiatric Services, Westside Neighborhood Health Center, Denver, Colorado, February, 1970.

Romano, Octavio. "The Historical and Intellectual Presence of Mexican-Americans," *El Grito,* Quinto Sol Publications, Inc., Berkeley, Vol. II, No. 2, Winter, 1969.

Torrey, E. Fuller, M.D. "The Irrelevancy of Traditional Mental Health Services for Urban Mexican-Americans." Paper presented at the American Orthopsychiatry Association, San Francisco, California, March, 1970.

PART II
CUESTIONES BIBLIOGRAFICAS

INTRODUCTION

This work, without question, is the single most extensive, thoughtful, and thought-provoking study ever to be published from the standpoint of a Chicano perspective toward bibliographies of materials that relate in one way or another to Chicano existence. This is a heretofore little explored area of scholarly inquiry.

Mr. Padilla's clearly demonstrated competence in dealing with his subject matter forcefully reminds us once again of that vital difference that always exists between (1) a scholar, and (2) a technician garbed as a scholar. His approach is comprehensive, diligent, insightful, and forthright, producing a work that is refreshingly devoid of puerile semantic vortices and pedantic circumlocutions. He proceeds far beyond the technical gathering of data in order to develop his subject matter to the peripheries of dimensions that simultaneously elucidate the past and indicate the future. In this sense, Mr. Padilla delves deeply into history. In doing so, at the same time his work promises to become an historical landmark in the annals of Chicano scholarship.

In the future, certainly, no one who has read Mr. Padilla's study can ever again look at a bibliography with an uncritical eye, for bibliographies are, too, as are other documents, subject to the currents, biases, and the interests of the time, the place, and the source from which they originate.

Apuntes
Para La Documentación
De La Cultura Chicana

Ray Padilla

The output of self-proclaimed "Chicano" bibliographies during recent years has made manifest such a diversity of style, content, and usefulness on the one hand, and an absence of serious or scholarly criticism on the other, that the more careful student of Chicano culture finds himself bewildered when searching to select materials for his general or scholarly interests. Most difficulties result from the lack of serious criticism about alleged Chicano materials. Symptomatic of these problems is that, either through ignorance or misunderstanding, materials both relevant and irrelevant to Chicanos are often included under the same "Chicano" cover. A further complication arises from the failure of bibliographers to discriminate between those items which are valuable to Chicano culture and those which are not. Much is labeled "Chicano" which has only the remotest connection with the Chicano world. All in all, the most salient feature of recent bibliographies has been a lack of serious criticism of the materials which they catalogue.

This study will offer a tentative evaluation of Chicano bibliographies. The intent is to promote some serious Chicano criticism of previous bibliographies and to suggest some guidelines for the preparation of future, perhaps more useful, compilations. Our task will be to provide some criteria with which to judge previous bibliographies, and to review, from a historical perspective, those bibliographies which fall within our purview.

The Chicano world can be defined as the interaction of the Gabacho and Raza Universes. Within this world several groups can be discerned, for example, the Chicano Boricua, Cubano, or Aztlanense. This study focuses only on the Chicano Aztlanense. Such a restriction has been imposed not to diminish the importance of other Chicano groups, but to make the present task manageable within the limits of bibliographic

117

materials available to the author, and to stay within the author's area of competency.

The very definition of the Chicano Aztlanense implies the confluence of distinct cultural and racial groups, both from the Raza and Gabacho Universes. In this conceptual sense one could include bibliographic materials from both the purely Gabacho or the purely Raza Universes and designate them as Chicano materials. Methodologically, however, it is best to designate such materials as either Gabacho or Raza, and to consider as specifically "Chicano Aztlanense" only those materials which belong to the historical period of this group.

The historical beginning of the Chicano Aztlanense has yet to be agreed upon, but for discussion purposes one could propose 1836 (secession of Texas) or 1848 (Treaty of Guadalupe-Hidalgo) as the birth of the Chicano Aztlanense. For this study, 1848 is arbitrarily chosen to mark the beginning of the Chicano Aztlanense period. Thus all works prior to 1848 can be treated as pre-Chicano Aztlanense materials. These works are largely Gabacho and Raza studies. After 1848 we find Raza, Gabacho, and Chicano Aztlanense materials. These should be labeled and critically analyzed accordingly.

The proposed typology of Raza, Gabacho, and Chicano Aztlanense has the dual advantage of providing the reader with an opportunity to assess both the relevance and the potential bias in the materials. It is within this framework that we will review the publication of bibliographies during the Chicano Aztlanense period.

First Period (1848-1919)

The first bibliographers of the Chicano world were either from the Raza or the Gabacho Universes and they wrote primarily for readers of their own kind. Most of these compilers were either vocational or avocational historians, with Gabacho historians having strong input in the field. These works are ponderous, academic, and they reflect the biases and concerns of the authors' periods and constituencies. The authors were not particularly concerned with mass audiences, and one can detect a certain air of antiquarianism in their tomes.

The contemporary Chicano Aztlanense might well ponder why Gabachos so soon became such diligent investigators of the Raza they had conquered. It is clear from their initial contact with the Raza population of the Southwest or Aztlán that Gabachos held Raza in great contempt and could hardly restrain themselves from a genocidal attack on these people.[1] It seems strange indeed that less than half a century after the conquest, Gabachos became fascinated with the history of a people whom they had so ruthlessly subjugated. Such is the irony of history that the very people who overwhelmed and decimated La Raza became the energetic architects who wanted to reconstruct Raza history.* We do not intend to deal with these issues in the present study. Suffice it to say that, for the historian who wishes to concern himself with this paradox, he should consider that most of these Gabacho works were written under the sponsorship of individual state or United States histories.

One of the earliest works of this period is Cadwell Walton Raine's *A Bibliography of Texas* (Austin: Gammel Book Co., 1896). Under the ponderous subtitle of *Being a Descriptive List of Books, Pamphlets, and Documents Relating to Texas in Print and Manuscript Since 1536, Including a Complete Collation of the Laws; With an Introductory Essay on the Materials of Early Texas History,* Raines attempts to catalogue a comprehensive list of materials for the writing of Texas history, as well as the history of neighboring areas like northern México, New Mexico and adjacent southern states. The emphasis, quite naturally, is on Texas itself. Raines, an educator, judge and state librarian, gains strength from his ready access to the wealth of information within the state library and archives.

Unfortunately, Raines is a Gabacho who is writing primarily for Gabachos, with the result that he has a tendency to bias both his selection of materials (notwithstanding the full title, his selections emphasize the period after 1836) and the criticisms of the materials he does include. Perhaps Raines's orientation and constituency can be understood best from his dedication: "To the Daughters of the Republic of Texas whose loving purpose is to keep alive the memory of the Texans who won an empire *from the wilderness,* and consecrated it *to liberty and civilization.*" (my italics) It is patently clear that, according to Raines, the Raza who lived in Texas before the Gabacho arrived were both wild and uncivilized. Such is the extremely short memory of the conqueror who forgets that many of the defenders of the Alamo were Raza. Chicanos who utilize this bibliography should use it simply as a first and certainly not the last word on the subject.

For those Chicanos who wish to research early Raza history, the work of the great Chilean bibliographer José Toribio Medina should be useful. Medina wrote extensively about early Raza publications in most parts of the Raza world, including in some instances the lands of

---

*The history of American ethnology, and the preoccupation with the American Indians by anthropologists, is an historical parallel to the Chicano experience. For decades, the reconstruction of the Indian past was the main thrust of American anthropology. —*Editor*

Aztlán. A typical example is his *Notas bibliográficas referente a las primeras producciones de la imprenta en algunas ciudades de la América española* ... 1764-1822 (Santiago de Chile: Imprenta Elzeviriana, 1904). This particular work includes, among others, notes on Raza publications in New Orleans, Puerto Rico, Cuba, and various places in México. As the title indicates, this volume is most useful for the late 18th and early 19th centuries. Because of the period covered and the nature of the Raza press at that time, Medina's notes deal largely with newspapers,* official and ecclesiastic bulletins, announcements, orders, decrees, etc. Chicanos interested in reconstructing Raza history from original sources might well consult Medina's prolific works as a first step. His work is scholarly, and, it is Raza writing for Raza.

The intimate cultural and historical interaction between Nueva España, or México, and the lands of Aztlán makes it especially profitable for Chicanos to study materials pertaining to this region. Medina's classic eight volumes on *La imprenta en México—1539-1821* (Santiago de Chile: Casa del Autor, 1907-1912) is a critical work on Raza literature which may be useful to Chicanos. Medina's meticulously annotated entries are further strengthened by his comprehensive knowledge of the subject, including data on publishers, printing houses, bio-bibliographical criticism, laws regarding the press, etc. Moreover, Medina himself supervised the printing of the eight massive volumes, scrutinizing the galleys to ensure that errors would be eliminated.

Mexicans themselves have a long history of bibliographic inquiry. In the 19th Century Joaquín García Icazbalceta produced his *Bibliografía mexicana del siglo XVI* (1886). This erudite Mexican scholar collected enormous quantities of printed materials pertaining to the Spanish colonial period. His collection was ultimately purchased by the University of Texas where it can be found today. Texas Chicanos might well investigate this collection for reconstructing Aztlanense history. García Icazbalceta was, quite naturally, writing primarily for a Raza reading public.

Another Mexican, Vicente de P. Andrade, continued García Icazbalceta's work with the publication of (the former's) *Ensayo bibliográfico mexicano del siglo XVII* (México: Imprenta del Museo Nacional, 1899). This volume is a "second edition" of earlier materials published in the *Boletín* of the Sociedad Alzate and later incorporated into the 1899 volume. The original material (published in the *Boletín*) covered only up to 1624. The introduction to this work has useful notes on Mexican bibliographic history and specifically mentions the names of several early Mexican bibliographers. The volume has a good index plus a tabulation of the number of publications per year during the seventeenth century. It includes a list of printers and the years they operated. This work is especially useful for printed matter relating to religious and administrative directives and records of the secular administration. The volume is amply annotated.

Contemporary with Andrade's work is the slim volume of Nicolás León, *La imprenta en méxico: ensayo histórico y bibliográfico* (México: Tipografía de "El Tiempo," 1900). This booklet is a listing of the press output in Mexico, mostly during the 19th Century. A few border states of northern Mexico are included. These citations may be useful to Chicanos doing research on the conquest of Aztlán.

A much more ambitious work by the same author is his *Bibliografía mexicana del siglo XVIII* (México: Imprenta de Francisco Díaz de León, 1902) which attempted to complete the works of both García Icazbalceta and Andrade with respect to Raza publications of the first three centuries. This multi-volume effort, however, is incomplete. Some of the material included in this work had already been published in the *Anales del museo michoacano* in the 1890's. León's work is strong on clerical items, mostly because he worked from libraries belonging to religious organizations and because of the heavy influence of religious life in 18th century Nueva España. León included both biographical and bibliographical data, as well as excerpts from some of the documents. His work is strictly Raza for Raza. Chicanos may find this work useful because of the strong influence of religious orders in Aztlán during the colonial period.

Beginning with the second decade of the twentieth century, Gabacho historians began to develop an ardent interest in the history of Aztlán during the Spanish colonial period. Their task was to seek documents for the purpose of writing various state and U.S. histories. With a mixture of surprise and naïveté, these historians asked why their predecessors had not searched the archival remains entombed in Latin America and Spain for materials pertinent to U.S. history. The obvious fact that the U.S. prior to 1848 and east of Aztlán had no need for Raza history appears to have eluded these gentlemen. At any rate, a cadre of U.S. historians invaded the archival depositories of México, Cuba, Spain, France and a host of other places. These zealous gentlemen ransacked the dusty piles of colonial bureaucratic records, made catalogues and calendars of their contents and sorted useful from useless documents. Naturally they established their own criteria about what was useful and what was not. Since they were interested in writing U.S. or state histories, their selections necessarily reflected this prejudice. Ironically, these tireless scholars thought themselves lucky to have found such "gold mines" in Spanish archival depositories. Hardly more than a generation before, their parents had secured gold mines and other properties by destroying these same types of documents in Aztlán. Such is the irony of the conquest that what the parents considered mere wrapping paper, their sons considered invaluable documents.[2]

Herbert Eugene Bolton spent considerable time in México and finally published his *Guide to the Materials for the History of the United States in the Principal Archives of Mexico* (Washington: Carnegie Institution, 1913). This work is geared to the historical and focuses on the lands of northern México or Aztlán. It is especially strong on 18th and 19th century documents. Since the author is a Gabacho writing for a Gabacho audience, the Chicano reader should be aware that documents of interest to Chicanos may have been overlooked and omitted from the volume. The main criterion for including items in this volume is relevance to U.S. history. Chicanos may find this volume useful in gaining some idea about the kinds of documents available in archival depositories in México. Serious researchers should consult the archives themselves. One suspects that a number of documents in the Mexican archives may not lend themselves readily to incorporation into an ordinary history of the U.S.

Shortly after Bolton's volume left the presses, a similar work was published by a New Mexican lawyer who, though lacking the expert training of Bolton, compiled a massive two volume catalogue of the Spanish-Mexican archives of New Mexico. Ralph Emerson Twitchell's *The Spanish Archives of New Mexico; Annotated and Chronologically Arranged with Historical, Geneological, Geographical and Other Annotations* (Cedar Rapids, Iowa: Torch Press, 1914) are plainly directed at the general reader, as the author vehemently proclaims. The first volume catalogues the archives at the Surveyor-General's Office in Santa Fe, and the second deals with the archives removed to Washington, D.C. (now in the Library of Congress) in 1903 under very complicated and not altogether clear circumstances. Perhaps the most interesting part of Twitchell's work is his introductory remarks where he discusses the rather turbulent history of the archives. As many Chicanos know, Gabachos did not take kindly to the all too accurate records of the Spaniards and Mexicans, especially when those records related to land titles and land grants. It is therefore not surprising that many of these documents were misplaced, lost, or destroyed by Gabachos who had them under their custody. Forgeries were not uncommon during that time.

Yet the New Mexican archives are potentially the most important documents for Chicanos. Millions of acres of land have been disputed on the basis of ancient land grants. Naturally the difficulty was (and is) that the archives have been under Gabacho jurisdiction since the conquest. Thus the serious Chicano researcher of land grant claims should search for alternate sources of documentation. Perhaps México City, Guadalajara, or Sevilla would be better hunting grounds for locating duplicates of misplaced or stolen New Mexican land grant documents.

Twitchell's work from the existing documents is filled with ample local color, inasmuch as wills, testimonies, laws, prayers, etc. were quite abundant during the Spanish colonial administration. These are dutifully catalogued and noted in Twitchell's work. Chicanos can use Twitchell's work for whatever they can glean from it, and proceed to archival depositories which have suffered less tampering. Perhaps some ambitious Chicano historian will take it upon himself to write a critical history of the New Mexican archives.

The indefatigable Henry Raup Wagner produced a small volume during the early part of his career, *Bibliography of Printed Works Relating to Those Portions of the U.S. Which Formerly Belonged to Mexico* (Santiago de Chile: La Imprenta Diener, 1917), much along the lines of the authors discussed thus far. Unfortunately, one gets the impression from this preliminary work that Wagner merely went through Medina's list of bibliographic items, extracted those which he felt were relevant to his interest, and signed his name to the volume. The serious student should naturally consult the full Medina bibliographies and decide which items are relevant to Aztlán history, thus saving himself the dubious assistance (in this case) of an intermediary. Wagner was writing for Gabachos, and a Chicano cannot assume that Wagner's choices are the only ones in Medina's work relevant to Chicano history.

What Bolton started in México, Charles Edward Chapman consumated in Spain where he compiled his *Catalogue of Materials in the Archivo General de Indias for the History of the Pacific Coast and the American Southwest* (Berkeley: University of California, Publications in History, v. 8, 1919). Unfortunately, the Archivo General in Sevilla contains thousands of documents with more or less minimal indexing. The most dedicated and persistent scholar would find it nearly impossible to find his way through such a papyrus jungle. Perhaps it is to the credit of Chapman that he attempted the task. At any rate, Chapman was limited by time, resources, and the narrowness of his topic. Although the title implies that a search was made for documents concerning the history of the Southwest, Chapman's perspective may not have been the same as a Chicano's. Consequently, the serious Chicano student should view this work as tentative and search for his own materials in the Archivo General. Since Chapman was charged to search specifically for materials relevant to California history, students should view his selections accordingly. His materials cover up to 1821.

SUMMARY

The first period of Chicano Aztlanense bibliographies can be characterized as leaning heavily on the side of historians and bibliophiles who were trying to write either U.S. history or Raza history. These bibliographies therefore were written largely by Gabachos for a Gabacho reading public, or by Raza. The Chicano can hardly expect to find the stamp of Chicanismo in these works. These bibliographies can be useful as introductory works, or as first steps for Chicanos who wish to reconstruct Raza history through Raza documents. Naturally the Chicano scholar ultimately must handle the original documents to make his own evaluation of the Raza Universe.

Alternatively, these bibliographies, at least those produced by Gabachos, can also provide an important window through which the Chicano can view the Gabacho's perspective of the Chicano and Raza worlds. Valuable insights can be gained about the Gabacho's outlook if one analyzes how he chose to reconstruct the Raza Universe. What is more important, these works allow the Chicano to study the Gabacho's perception of the Raza-Gabacho interaction and conflict.

Second Period (1920-1959)

If historical interest describes the first period, then the notable characteristic of the second period is interest in the Chicano as a "problem." To be sure, the historical interests of both Gabachos and Raza continue, and even increase, during the second period, but the 1920's also bring a Gabacho awakening of the Chicano as an enduring social reality. The Gabacho is not only cognizant of the Chicano's presence, but he perceives the Chicano as a foreigner, an alien, and, ultimately, as a social problem.

At least two important factors can be related to the Gabacho's attitude toward the Chicano. First is the increase of Chicano population through Mexican immigration. Millions of Mexicans emigrated from Mexico during the turbulent years of the Mexican Revolution. Expanding economic conditions in agriculture and railroads offered displaced Mexicans an opportunity to head north and bypass the ravages of civil war. Expansion in automobile factories, steel foundries, and packing houses, offered opportunities for Mexicans in cities as far north as Chicago and Detroit. In the Southwest, Mexicans could find respite from the turmoil of the homeland by settling in Chicano communities

similar in life style to the villages, towns, and cities from which they
had emigrated.

Secondly, Gabachos had exhibited considerable anti-immigration
feeling since the 19th century, and the 20th century saw these feelings
crystalize in the enactment of a quota system during the 1920's.[3] Although Mexican immigration was exempted from the quota system, the
Gabacho was clearly no longer interested in an open door policy for all
immigrants. Thus the combination of Gabacho industrial and agricultural expansion and a Mexican immigrant labor supply did not stabilize
into a durable working relationship. Instead, the fragile working arrangement between Mexican immigration and the demand for a supply
of cheap labor in an expanding war economy gradually deteriorated
until, in the 1930's, the Gabacho viewed the Chicano more as a liability
than as an asset. The view was strong enough to permit mass deportations of Chicanos during the 1930's.

The yearly increase of Mexican immigrants in the U.S. elicited an
ever growing body of literature concerned with the "Mexican problem." The bulk of this material came from social workers, government,
community, religious and welfare agencies. Interestingly enough, the
"problem" oriented materials took their place alongside the historically
oriented studies of the first period which continued to grow through
the second period. *To a contemporary Chicano, the most singular aspect about these two types of materials is how little one took the other
into account. The historians failed to relate their studies to the contemporary Chicano works, and the "problem" oriented writers failed to
see the Chicano within a historical context.*

An important aspect of the second period is the production of bibliographies by Chicanos. Whereas Raza and Gabachos monopolized the
first period, the 1930's and 40's saw an ever growing number of Chicanos enter the field, among them Castañeda, Campa, Espinosa, Rael,
and Sanchez. More importantly, bibliographies began to treat aspects of
the Chicano which Chicanos themselves thought important: education,
literature, music, folklore, as well as history. Some of these bibliographies are the first to treat Chicanos as a contemporary people, rather
than as a quaint group of conquistadores and padres.

During the Second World War, much attention was officially be-
stowed on Latin America as part of the war effort. At a time when
allies were at a premium, Gabachos found themselves virtually ignorant
about the culture and history of the Latin American people. It then
became a matter of policy to woo the confidence and friendship of
these new found friends. The vehicle engineered for this purpose was
the Good Neighbor Policy. While it is not entirely clear that there ever
was a Bad Neighbor Policy, wiley Latins had an old saying: "Poor
Mexico, so far from God and so close to the United States." At any

rate, the self interest of Gabachos in promoting good relations with Latin America produced, as a side effect, at least a lukewarm attitude toward "Latin Americans" in the U.S. Unfortunately, it was easier to woo Latin Americans in Latin America than to grant equal rights to "Latin Americans" in the U.S. The notorious "Zoot-Suit Riots" of Los Angeles in 1943 poignantly demonstrated the hypocrisy with which Gabachos treated their "Latin Friends." Like the unstable relationship between Mexican immigration and labor shortage in the U.S., the wooing of "Latin American" friendship in the 1940's was emotionally ambivalent for the Gabacho. In both cases there was a great need to treat the Chicano with decency, but in both cases the Gabacho failed to combat his deeply ingrained prejudices.

The decade of the fifties marked a significant decline in the production of bibliographic materials. With the war over, Gabachos no longer felt pressured to woo Latin America. For the Gabacho, the Cold War neatly froze over the "Chicano problem." The cooling off, however, did not prevent the production of several significant works. By and large, though, Gabacho interest in the Chicano waned considerably.

.   .   .

We have noted that the historical trend continued during the 1920's. Nicolás León, now Dean of the Museo Nacional de México, published a small volume, *Bibliografía Bibliográfica Mexicana* (México: Talleres Gráficos del Museo Nacional de Arqueología, Historia y Etnografía, 1923) which is basically a bibliography of bibliographies and includes citations gathered from several languages and briefly annotated. This volume marks a resurgence of Mexican bibliography, since the Mexican Revolution caused a significant decline in bibliographic works during the second decade of the twentieth century. A work directed primarily at a Raza reading public, this volume has a useful introduction which provides information on early Mexican bibliographers.

We have already cited Henry Raup Wagner's bibliography published in 1917. Seven years later Wagner updated and expanded his work in a new publication, *The Spanish Southwest, 1542-1794; An Annotated Bibliography* (Berkeley: James J. Gillick, 1924). This work is critically annotated and quite useful for those Chicanos who wish to tackle early Raza history from primary sources. Although limited to a relatively small number of documents, Wagner includes careful annotation of each item. Unfortunately, only one hundred copies of this edition were printed, and the student with scarce library resources will find it difficult to procure a copy of this work. While not especially prepared with Raza in mind, this work can be useful to Chicanos if for no other reason than to demonstrate the tremendous care and research necessary to critically annotate a bibliography.

As mentioned above, the 1920's saw a resumption of Mexican

bibliographic inquiry. An early work by Vito Alessio Robles exemplifies the renewed interest on the subject. His *Bibliografía de Coahuila: historia y geografía* (México: Imprenta de la Secretaría de Relaciones Exteriores, 1927) is a Raza work especially useful for Texas history. Unfortunately, Alessio Robles's volume depends on the works of Bolton (already cited). Still, the volume is a good starting point for those Chicanos interested in developing a comprehensive history of Aztlán. Moreover, this work provides a useful introduction to the prolific writings of Alessio Robles (1879-1957), and to the massive bibliographic compilation of the series *Monografías Bibliográficas Mexicanas* of which Alessio Robles's volume is number 10. The *Monografías* series originated from an executive mandate of 1925. Other important volumes in this series will be mentioned later.

The Pan American Union has a long history of bibliographic interest in Latin America. Even by 1928 it had produced enough bibliographic materials to compile its *Bibliographies Pertaining to Latin America in the Columbus Memorial Library* (Washington: Pan American Union, 1928). This annotated bibliography of bibliographies is only tangentially useful to Chicanos, with the section on Mexico perhaps the most useful. The bibliography is easy to use, listing bibliographies by country. Needless to say, the material is quite dated by now, and its prime value would be in the reconstruction of Chicano history. Materials from the Pan American Union are oriented both to the Gabacho and Raza, but not necessarily to the Chicano.

Continuing in the historical vein, the University of California published a two volume compilation of its holdings relevant to Raza history. The first volume, *Spain and Spanish-America in the Libraries of the University of California; A Catalogue of Books . . . v.1: The General and Departmental Libraries* (Berkeley: University of California Press, 1928) was compiled by Alice Lyser and consists of 15,000 titles. The catalogue includes holdings up to January 1, 1927. This should alert the student to at least the temporal limitations of this work. The volume is well indexed and can be useful for Raza history.

Two years later Eleanor Ashby completed the second volume of the catalogue, *Spain and Spanish-America in the Libraries of the University of California . . . v.2; The Bancroft Library* (Berkeley: University of California Press, 1930). For the contemporary reader the second volume has the same temporal limitations as the first one. Moreover, the Chicano looking for materials with a distinctive Chicano stamp will not find them in either volume. As Ashby says, "Books on areas once Spanish but now within the U.S. are excluded unless they treat of the Spanish or Mexican occupation." In other words, the uniquely Chicano is excluded. Nevertheless, the work is strong on Raza history and has a wealth of information on California history. It is a well-known fact that the Bancroft Library has one of the world's finest collections of documents on Aztlán under Spanish rule as well as on Raza history. Were it also to include Chicano materials, it would indeed become a rarity worthy of universal admiration.

The two volume work compiled by Lyser and Ashby is known as the Cebrian catalogue, so called after Juan C. Cebrian. Cebrian was a wealthy San Franciscan who had emigrated from Spain in 1870 and wanted to insure that the Spanish influence in the Americas would not be forgotten. His financial support permitted the compilation of the catalogue. One suspects that in times past there may have been a real danger of extinction for all Indo-hispanic history and artifacts in Aztlán. The Bancroft Library is a prime example of the persistence of Raza artifacts. The physical presence of the Chicano, however, is an indisputable example of the continuity of the Raza world itself.

Emory Stephen Bogardus's volume *The Mexican Immigrant—An Annotated Bibliography* (Los Angeles: Council on International Relations, 1929) is a landmark in the history of Chicano bibliographies. This bibliography is one of the first to focus on the Chicano Aztlanense world and not just cn Raza history. In style, content, and approach, this bibliography marked the beginning of a type that would not be challenged or surpassed until the late 1960's and 70's.

It has been mentioned that the rise of the "problem" approach to Chicanos by Gabacho writers occurred during the 1920's. Thus Bogardus's volume is both a documentation of materials concerned with Chicanos and, more importantly, of the attitude of Gabachos toward Chicanos. It should be clearly understood that Bogardus's work is not intended for Chicanos. His position is clear from the introduction: "Since this annotated bibliography is prepared for the use of Americans, the references are limited to those found in English" (page 3). Bogardus's work thus gains tremendous value for Chicanos who wish to trace the history of the Gabacho's attitude toward Chicanos.

Bogardus divides his topic into three areas: (1) Culture, (2) Studies, and (3) Interracial Adjustments. As the author notes, "Most of these studies emanate from social and civic welfare workers as well as from religious sources" (page 11). Within the three general categories the author includes materials on such topics as labor, education, intelligence, poverty, assimilation, immigration and a host of other issues all too familiar to Chicanos. This bibliography is therefore crucial for Chicanos investigating the genesis of the "problem" approach to Chicanos. It should be clear that this volume has a strong bias toward the Gabacho view of the Chicano, but this in itself has a certain usefulness for Chicanos. It is also one of the first bibliographies to recognize the Chicano as a contemporary reality and shift the emphasis in materials from the historical to the social scientific.

. . .

The decade of the thirties ushered further diversification in the production of Chicano bibliographies. Arthur León Campa was one of the first Spanish surnamed bibliographers to concern himself with a hitherto relatively uninvestigated field of Chicano culture. His short volume, *A Bibliography of Spanish Folk-Lore in New Mexico* (Albuquerque: University of New Mexico Bulletin, Language Series, v.2, no. 3, September, 1930) includes poetry, songs, tales and other items of a basically traditional and oral nature. This work is important because it opens an area of purely Chicano interest. Chicano culture as such has been largely ignored by the Gabacho public, save for a few folklorists and ethnographers. This work should receive wider circulation if for no other reason than to stimulate systematic inquiry into Chicano folk culture which today continues to change rapidly.

Historical bibliographies have a significant role in the 30's, especially with the increased activities of Mexican bibliographers. Juan B. Iguiniz, a member of the Real Academia de la Historia, published his *Bibliografía biográfica mexicana* (México: Imprenta de la Secretaría de Relaciones Exteriores, 1930) which is a compilation of 18th, 19th, and 20th century biographical items. It has greater strength in the late 19th and early 20th centuries. The work is generally for Raza and covers only México. It has an index of individuals covered in the biographies, and may be useful for Chicanos studying Mexican historical personalities who influenced events in Aztlán.

On another Mexican topic, Roberto Ramos published his *Bibliografía de la revolución Mexicana* (México: vols. I and II, Imprenta de la Secretaría de Relaciones Exteriores, 1931, 1935; vol. III, Imprenta de la Secretaría de Educación Pública, 1940) which, more or less, occupied a full decade in preparation. Ramos was the librarian of the Biblioteca Nacional de México and therefore had the resources to undertake and endure such a monolithic endeavor. The Mexican Revolution had a profound impact on the Chicano Aztlanense and should be the object of careful study by Chicano historians. Ramos' work may be a useful beginning for Chicanos because he interprets his subject in a general way. He openly declares: "Mi propósito ha sido reunir el mayor número de obras y folletos relacionados directamente o indirectamente con los movimientos revolucionarios de 1910 a 1929. Así habrá temas cuya relación será clara y precisa, y otros parecerán extraños . . ." (page x).

The diversification of bibliographies can be further exemplified by the work of Everett Eugene Edwards, *Agriculture of the American Indian: A Classified List of Annotated Historical References with an Introduction* (Washington: U.S. Department of Agriculture Library, Bibliographical Contributions, No. 23, Edition 2, June, 1932). This work is useful to the Chicano because it reviews significant Indian contributions to agriculture. Since Indian culture is an important part of the Chicano's world, this volume provides interested Chicanos with information on one aspect of the Indian's culture. The material is well organized into geographic areas, crops, and tribes. Indians from both Aztlán and middle America are included. This volume leaves one with the impression that the Gabacho has absorbed more from the Indian than the Gabacho openly recognizes or admits.

A short monograph by Katherine Margaret Cook and Florence E. Reynolds, *The Education of Native and Minority Groups; A Bibliography,* 1923-32 (Washington: United States Department of the Interior, Office of Education, Bulletin 12, GPO, 1933), is most notable for the conspicuous absence of Chicano Aztlanense items. The work is included here because it deals with education, a topic of great importance and grave concern to Aztlanenses, and because it devotes some attention to Puerto Rican education as well. The volume is also useful for studying the Gabacho's attitude toward the Aztlanense. From this work at least, it would appear that the Aztlanense's education is no great concern to the Gabacho.

The volume by W. Ralph Janeway, *Bibliography of Immigration in the United States, 1900-1930* (Columbus, Ohio: H. L. Hedrick, 1934), has the novelty that "Mexicans" now find their way into immigration bibliographies.[4] Whereas other bibliographies on immigration had not taken the Chicano into account, this bibliography is already in the "Mexican problem" vein. The work is basically directed to Gabacho undergraduates, but it can be useful for Chicanos interested in studying the history of Chicano immigration. The volume has a good organizational scheme, devoting a separate section to each nationality as well as having a topical arrangement.

In still another area, George Herzog's *Research in Primitive and Folk Music in the United States* (Washington: American Council of Learned Societies, Bulletin 24, April 1936) is important because it might provide useful ideas for the study of Chicano music despite the obnoxious and pernicious use of the word "primitive" in the title. The number of entries on Chicanos is limited, but it does point the way to further research by Chicanos in an area which needs much more attention than has previously been given to it. There is a considerably stronger treatment of Indian music (including Mexico), though the work is very much oriented towards the Gabacho.

On the historical side, Henry Raup Wagner's 1924 volume, *The Spanish Southwest, 1542-1794: An Annotated Bibliography* (previously cited), was reprinted by the Quivira Society in 2 volumes (Albuquerque, 1937). Four hundred and one copies of this edition were printed. Those students interested in the work may find this edition slightly more accessible than the first one.

On a similar topic, the Mexican bibliographer Joaquín Díaz Mercado published his *Bibliografía sumaria de la Baja California* (México: Departmento Autónomo de Prensa y Publicidad, 1937). This volume uses an alphabetical arrangement and includes many Gabacho entries. It includes a list of newspapers and a topical index of more or less limited usefulness. This is a Raza work with some Gabacho influence: For those who want to get beyond Tijuana.

An annotated bibliography by Mary Tucker, *Books of the Southwest; A General Bibliography* (New York: J. J. Augustin, 1937), is heavily biased toward the Gabacho's view of the Southwest. It places heavy emphasis on the twentieth century, although it does include considerable information on the Indian as well as the "pioneers and conquest." The greatest value of this work is that it demonstrates to Chicanos the Gabacho's view of the Southwest.

Another bibliography of the "Chicano problem" variety is Ann L. Baden's *Immigration and its Restrictions in the United States: A Selected List of Recent Writings* (Washington: Library of Congress, Division of Bibliography, 1937). This annotated bibliography is definitely intended for Gabachos. However, Chicanos will find it useful as a tool for researching some of the social conflicts of the Chicano in the 1920's and 30's.

We have already mentioned the series *Monografías Bibliográficas Mexicanas*. A four volume work in this series, *Indice de documentos de Nueva España existentes en el Archivo de Indias de Sevilla* (México: Imprenta de la Secretaría de Relaciones Exteriores, 1938, v.1), may be useful for Chicanos interested in the Archivo de Indias as it relates to México and Aztlán. Some interesting comparisons might be made between this work and the work of Chapman already cited. The entries are chronologically arranged from 1524 to 1754. Some of the original research for this work was done by Francisco del Paso y Troncoso, probably in the 1890's. The work contains an introduction by Genaro Estrada who was the director of the *Monografías* project. This work is significant if for no other reason than the point highlighted by Estrada: "Si se tiene en consideración que fuera de las incompletas listas que se encuentran en los catálogos del Archivo de Indias y de los cedularios publicados por universidades norteamericanas, en donde se hallan varias referencias a México, no hay ninguna otra guía acerca de los documentos sobre Nueva España en el Archivo de Sevilla, la publicación del presente catálogo vendrá a llenar una importante necesidad de la historia Mexicana" (page XI).

Further north Carlos Eduardo Castañeda and Jack Autrey Dabb published their *Guide to the Latin American Manuscripts in the University of Texas Library* (Cambridge: Harvard University Press, 1939). Listed by geographic area, including Texas, California, and New

Mexico, some 2098 entries are made. This historically oriented volume was probably directed more at the Gabacho than the Chicano. It has a useful index and may be quite helpful to Chicanos interested in investigating the holdings of the University of Texas. In certain respects, however, the work is now somewhat dated.[5]

A literary bibliography by Levette Jay Davidson and Prudence Bostwick, *The Literature of the Rocky Mountain West, 1803-1903* (Caldwell, Idaho: The Caxton Printers, 1939), is most noteworthy for its ethnocentric view of the subject. The area covered includes Wyoming, Colorado, Montana, Idaho, Utah, and northern New Mexico. This work is both an anthology and a bibliography. It is of little value to the Chicano, except as it communicates the Gabacho's view of the world.

On the folk scene, Ralph Steele Boggs produced his *Bibliografía del folklore mexicano* (México: Instituto Panamericano de Geografía e Historia, 1939), which has the distinction of being one of the few Gabacho bibliographies intended mainly for Raza. The volume contains over 1300 entries which cover Indian mythology, cuentos, poetry, music, danzas, refranes, adivinanzas, popular culture, language, etc. This annotated bibliography can be quite useful for those Chicanos interested in exploring the rich and relatively unexplored area of Chicano folk culture.

.   .   .

As we have indicated above, the exigencies of war during the 1940's spurred Gabacho interest in Latin America. An early publication of this type is Anita Ker's *Mexican Government Publications: A Guide to the More Important Publications of the National Government of Mexico, 1821-1936* (Washington: GPO, 1940). In the author's words: "This is a guide to selected official publications of the Mexican national government from 1821-1936, inclusive." About a year's time was spent in compiling the volume from the Library of Congress as well as other libraries in the United States and Mexico. This annotated work is directed primarily at Gabachos, although it does include a bilingual introduction—a great rarity in Gabacho bibliographic work. The material is arranged by governmental divisions, i.e., Executive, Legislative, Judicial, and autonomous departments; it includes the official Gazette from 1821-1936. The *Guide* is useful to Chicanos as an introduction to research in this area.

A more ambitious work, at least in terms of geographic area, is Madaline Wallis Nichol's *A Bibliographic Guide to Materials on American Spanish* (Committee on Latin American Studies, American Council of Learned Societies, Miscellaneous Publications No. 2, 1941). Supported by an advisory committee of such notables as Amado Alonso, Hayward Keniston, and Tomás Navarro Tomás, the material is listed by country and even includes a very small section on the U.S. Although departments of Spanish in the U.S. have traditionally ignored and even looked down on Chicano Spanish, the topic is extremely vital to the survival and development of Chicano culture. For Chicanos, this work may at least be suggestive of what can and needs to be done in the uncharted area of Chicano Spanish.

The work of George Peter Murdock, *Ethnographic Bibliography of North America* (New Haven: Yale University Press, 1941), has limited application for Chicanos, but may be useful to Chicanos exploring the Indian part of mestizaje. The work is anthropologically oriented and does not deal with the Indians of Mexico.

Through its Historical Records Survey Project, the Works Project Administration produced a volume, *Inventory of the State Archives of California: Department of Industrial Relations, Division of Immigration and Housing* (San Francisco: The Northern California Historical Records Survey Project, 1941, mimeo), which may provide much information to Chicanos researching Chicano conditions in California during the 1920's and 30's. Although the title is somewhat obscure, the bibliography concerns only the Division of Immigration and Housing. Noteworthy aspects of this work include (1) the absence of Chicanos in the staff which put the report together, and (2) the introduction by Carey McWilliams, then Chief of the Division. The bibliography contains references to labor camps (including licensing), labor activities (strikes), education, housing, aid to immigrants, and information on newspaper clipping files in the division. Chicanos doing research in immigration and housing may find many useful references in this work.

On the same topic the Pan American Council published its *Suggested References on the Mexican Immigrants in the United States* (Chicago: Pan American Council, 1942), which is unavailable to the author for first-hand inspection. However, the *Bulletin* of the Council has been reviewed from 1941 to 1944 where considerable "Suggested Reading" lists are found. The Council was a super Good Neighbor Policy advocate and treated Latin Americans (from Latin America, of course) with almost maniacal deference. Though the activities of this organization may seem somewhat strange to the contemporary Chicano, researchers may find its publications useful for studying the Gabacho's attitude toward the Chicano during the Second World War.

Robert C. Jones's *Mexicans in the United States: A Bibliography* (Washington: Pan American Union, Columbus Memorial Library, Bibliographic Series No. 27, 1942) can be useful for the Chicano researcher, though it has a tendency to take the "problem" approach. With an introduction by Ernesto Galarza, the volume provides a useful summary of academic work done on Chicanos during the 1920's and 30's. Useful for finding early items on education, migrants, health, language, culture, etc.

On another Latin American topic, the work of Gilbert Chase is quite useful. Starting out with his annotated volume, *Bibliography of Latin American Folk Music* (Washington: Library of Congress, Division of Music, 1942), he transforms the volume into a much more useful work, *A Guide to Latin American Music* (Washington: Library of Congress, Division of Music, 1942). The material in both volumes is arranged by country, including a small segment on the U.S. Most of the latter entries are from Works Progress Administration (WPA) projects or a handful of folklorists. A number of Chicano authors appear, among them Espinosa, Campa, González, and Rael. The *Guide* was reprinted by the Library of Congress in 1945, with a considerable increase in the number of entries. The 1945 edition is recommended for those who wish to get to the heart of the matter. Entries are generally limited to items found in the Library of Congress. The 1945 edition contains some 2699 items, including some on folklore. The Mexican section is extensive. This work is useful for those interested in the Chicano oral and folk histories.

On the historical, Francis Borgia Steck's *A Tentative Guide to Historical Materials on the Spanish Borderlands* (Philadelphia: Catholic Historical Society, 1943), is based on a plea for more exposure to the Spanish history of the Southwest. This volume is probably the prototype of the "we're-interested-in-the-subject-but-we-don't-know-where-to-find-the-materials" works which are to proliferate some thirty years later. Intended for Gabachos, the work can provide an introduction for Chicano students to the major Raza and Gabacho historians up to that time. The volume is partially annotated and includes a large number of periodical entries. Items up to 1942 are included in a state by state arrangement.

More related to the Chicano, at least in topic, is the work of Lyle Saunders, *Spanish-Speaking Americans and Mexican-Americans in the United States; A Selected Bibliography* (New York: Bureau for Intercultural Education, 1944). Reprinted in 1945, this work is similar to the volume of Bogardus already cited. Entries are topically arranged and cover a wide range of subjects including migrants, education, history, folklore, architecture, health, music, bibliographies, and unpublished studies. This is one of the first bibliographies to use the terms "Spanish-Speaking Americans" and "Mexican-Americans" in its title.

Saunders's main work, however, is *A Guide to Materials Bearing on Cultural Relations in New Mexico* (Albuquerque: University of New Mexico Press, 1944). The *Guide* is conceptualized along instrumental and propagandistic lines. First, the *Guide* is to serve the needs of researchers, government agencies, etc. Secondly, "The guide would furthermore serve the purpose of bringing to the attention of our friends in Latin America the fact that, though the situation [in race relations] is far from perfect, a great deal of thought and effort has been devoted to it by earnest students and governmental and private agencies." In fact, continues the writer, "As practically all these studies of acculturation are sympathetic to the Indians and the Spanish-speaking people, they should somewhat neutralize the widespread impression in Latin America that our minorities have been neglected."

Unfortunately, these words come from the general editor, J. Ortega, who should have known quite clearly that the riots in Los Angeles in 1943 were not exactly for the benefit of the Chicanos. Instead he blindly goes on to say, "Naturally the inter-relationships of the different ethnic groups must be considered, but they will not be particularly emphasized, for we believe that the harmonious solution of certain social and economic problems will inevitably improve human relations without the necessity of making any distinct issue of them." Thus wrote Mr. Ortega in 1944.

Whatever Saunder's and Ortega's sins may be (and they may be many), the volume deserves the Chicano's attention because it includes a large number of items which may be useful to the Chicano. Although unannotated, some 5335 entries are topically arranged, with a handy dictionary-guide for those who need such an instrument. The most useful section is probably "Spanish-Americans and Mexicans." A handy bibliography of bibliographies is included. Unfortunately, many of the entries are by Gabachos who often have the tendency to regard the Chicano as quaint and curious. This can be a useful work, but it must be used with great care.

A work by Sylvia Pollack Bernstein for the Pan American Union, *Bibliography on Labor and Social Welfare in Latin America* (Washington: Pan American Union, 1940 - revised 1944), is a ". . . selected list of materials in English published from 1930 through December 1943" which can have some value for Chicanos interested in this aspect of Raza history. Arranged topically and by country, Chicanos may find the section on México most relevant. Education is included as a topic. The value of the entries is mostly historical, since they now appear quite dated.

Much along the same lines is the work of Eugene D. Owen, *Index to Publications and Articles on Latin America Issued by the U.S. Bureau of Labor Statistics, 1902-1943* (Washington: Pan American Union, 1945). This index covers 19 bulletins in 739 entries from the U.S. Bureau of Labor Statistics. Arranged by country and indexed geographically and by topic, few citations are directly relevant to Chicanos. However, those researchers interested in the labor agreements between Mexico and the United States may find some useful items in this work.

On the literary side, the work of Mabel Major, Rebecca Smith and T. M. Pearce, *Southwest Heritage: A Literary History with Bibliography* (Albuquerque: University of New Mexico Press, 1948 - first edition

1938), is notable on several points. The volume consists of a three part essay plus a bibliography of 750 titles. The first part is devoted to literature before "the coming of the Anglo." Part Two covers "Anglo-American adventurers and settlers." Part Three reviews literature to the contemporary period. The authors communicate an awareness of the multi-cultural elements in the Southwest. They proclaim: "Moreover, we shall frankly relate all other [than Anglo] cultures in the southwestern scene to our contemporary American life." However, they appear to detect no contradiction when they propose to limit themselves to works available in English or English translation! Even more devastating is their conclusion that "inevitably . . . we adopt America in the Southwest as a focal point." If Chicanos can fight through the assimilationist tendencies of the work, they may find useful items in this volume. The work has some redeeming qualities.

Jesse Lee Rader's *South of Forty, From the Mississippi to the Rio Grande; A Bibliography* (Norman: University of Oklahoma Press, 1947) is an annotated bibliography which lists some 3793 entries in an alphabetical arrangement. Some early Spanish works are included in this volume which leans toward the historical. For Chicanos, the items on Texas may be most relevant, with the treaty items perhaps worthy of notice. Basically, however, the work is oriented toward the Gabacho.

A volume published by the American Council on Race Relations, *Mexican Americans; A Selected Bibliography* (Chicago: The Council, 1949), is most noteworthy for the rare items it includes on early Chicano education and on the Midwest, especially Chicago. This work is most useful for those tracing Chicano history and development through the 1930's and 40's.

. . .

We have indicated that the decade of the fifties suffered not only the Cold War but a cooling of bibliographic activity as well. The bibliographies which were compiled during those years tended to lean on the literary or the historical.

An important work of this kind is by Marjorie F. Tully and Juan B. Rael, *An Annotated Bibliography of Spanish Folklore in New Mexico and Southern Colorado* (Albuquerque: University of New Mexico Press, 1950). This publication is Rael's expansion of Tully's master's thesis which the latter had compiled as Rael's student. Titles are briefly annotated and extend to December, 1948. As Rael puts it, "Except for manuscripts available to the general public, only published books and articles have been included." The manuscript material refers to W.P.A. sponsored studies then held in Santa Fe. These manuscripts were not handled first hand but taken from the *Guide* of Saunders already cited. The work is basically a compilation of relevant holdings in the libraries of the University of California, Berkeley, and Stanford University. The

702 items included in this work are a significant contribution in an area (folklore) which Chicanos must explore more fully. Unfortunately, far too many of the items were written by Gabachos in a subject where Chicano preeminence might be expected. The greatest collection of Chicano folklore is still in the barrios and fields where the Chicano people live and work.

The *Revista interamericana de bibliografía/Review of Interamerican Bibliography* was first published by the Pan American Union in 1951. This review contains bilingual essays and critical reviews which may be useful to Chicanos doing research on general Raza history and culture. Regrettably, it does not focus on the Chicano, an all too common failing of Gabacho oriented publications.

A unique volume by Raymond R. MacCurdy is worthy of some attention by Chicanos. Divided into three parts, *A History and Bibliography of Spanish-Language Newspapers and Magazines in Louisiana 1808-1949* (Albuquerque: The University of New Mexico Press, 1951) will be a useful work for those Chicanos interested in the history of the Chicano press. Some 40 individual papers are listed, plus a brief historical essay. A third section discusses bibliographic sources used to prepare the study.

J. Frank Dobie's *Guide to Life and Literature of the Southwest* (Austin: University of Texas Press, 1952 - 2nd edition) has a small section on the Chicano ("Spanish-Mexican"), but Dobie's main preoccupation is with cowboys. The author's knowledge of certain aspects of Aztlanense folklore is well known. It is not clear why he chose to minimize this element in the *Guide.* The first edition of this work was published in 1943.

Stanley Vestal (writing under the name of Walter S. Campbell) first published in 1952, and reprinted in 1955, *The Book Lover's Southwest: A Guide to Good Reading* (Norman, Oklahoma: University of Oklahoma Press, 1952). Of course, what is good reading for Campbell may not be good for Chicanos. This Rockefeller Foundation backed project includes a usable index of authors and editors. Chicanos who can get beyond the "Anglo" breast-beating of Campbell, and who can find their way through the items on David Crocket, Texas Rangers and the Alamo, may gain useful insights into the Gabacho's perception of the Southwest. This volume is several notches below the work of Major et al.

On the historical side, John Parker Harrison's *Materials in the National Archives Relating to the Mexican States of Sonora, Sinaloa, and Baja California* (Washington: U.S. National Archives, Reference Information Papers, No. 42, GPO, 1952) may be useful for those Chicanos researching Uncle Sam's interest in this geographical area during the 19th century and the first third of the 20th. The work includes brief descriptions of general catalogues available in the archives relevant to the topic. Much of the material pertains to official government business.

Two Mexican bibliographers; Manual Germán Parra and Wigberto Jimenez Moreno, compiled *Bibliografía indigenista de México y Centroamérica, 1850-1950* (México: Ediciones del Instituto Nacional Indigenista, 1954). For Chicanos researching the Indian element of mestizaje, this work can be a useful tool. Parra's long introductory essay, "Las grandes tendencias de la evolución histórica de la política indigenista moderna en México," gives the work additional strength. Over 6400 entries are made, topically arranged into 31 sections, including a section on bibliographies. The volume is indexed by tribes, language groups, and alphabetically. Unfortunately, the work omits all colonial literature on the subject.

On an old topic, Lota May Spell's *Research Materials for the Study of Latin America at the University of Texas* (Austin: The University of Texas Press, 1954) provides updated information on this important university collection. The work also serves as a useful introduction to the collection in general. The volume is mostly a descriptive essay, arranged topically and including an index for those interested in individual items. Chicano bibliographers may be inspired by the section on bibliographies.

On a similar topic, Claude Elliot's *Theses on Texas History: A Check List of Theses and Dissertations in Texas History Produced in the Departments of History of Eighteen Texas Graduate Schools and Thirty-three Graduate Schools Outside of Texas, 1907-1952* (Austin: Texas State Historical Association, 1955) provides an alphabetical listing with abstracts. Some 652 items are entered, all but ten for the Master's degree. Naturally Chicano authors are scarce, though not altogether absent, and the Gabacho viewpoint exudes from the theses. Nevertheless, those interested in Texas's turbulent history may find useful as well as relatively unknown items.

Working with similar materials but on a different topic, Clyde Hull Cantrell's and Walton R. Patrick's *Southern Literary Culture: A Bibliography of Masters and Doctors Theses* (University of Alabama Press, 1955) provides some 2529 theses and dissertations encompassing 14 states and the District of Columbia. Items are selected from the beginning of graduate work to 1948, and encompass all graduate schools in the nation. Annotations are brief, but the volume is well indexed. There are a number of items relevant to Chicanos, for example number 900 by Fermina Guerra, *Mexican and Spanish Folklore and Incidents in Southwest Texas* (University of Texas, Master's Thesis, 1941). Though not intended for Chicanos, the volume can be useful in areas where it deals with Chicano topics. Its research value is increased because

theses and dissertations are generally obscure and have limited circulation.

Further west, Ellen C. Barrett's *Baja California, 1535-1956; A Bibliography of Historical, Geographical and Scientific Literature Relating to the Peninsula of Baja California and to the Adjacent Islands in
the Gulf of California and the Pacific Ocean* (Los Angeles: Bennett
and Marshall, 1957) is a collection of both significant and insignificant works depending upon the reader's likes and dislikes. Barrett
herself has no pretensions: "Because the work is planned to satisfy as
large a number of users as possible, it is neither selective nor critical."
And since Barrett was a librarian at the Los Angeles Public Library,
much material passed through her hands. On the other hand, perhaps
the very indiscriminate selection of entries may make this work more
useful to Chicanos. Many standard items cited in other bibliographies
are included in the volume.

In 1967 a second volume, published posthumously, extended from
1935-1964. Some two thousand new items are included in this work.
An added bonus is a chronological index for both volumes which lists
all publications from 1535-1964 on a yearly basis. Good prospecting
territory for those with a miner's instinct.

While the fifties entered with bibliographic production on the cool
side, they ended with the promising work of George Isidore Sanchez
and Howard Putnam, *Materials Relating to the Education of Spanish-
Speaking People in the United States; An Annotated Bibliography*
(Austin: University of Texas, Latin American Studies No. 97, 1959).
This bibliography is as close to a Chicano Aztlanense bibliography as
one will find prior to the present. Sanchez makes his intention clear:
"This bibliography is concerned primarily with the education of those
Spanish speaking people in the United States who are of Mexican
descent." Some 882 items are included, mostly the compilation of
graduate students, but judiciously selected by the dean of Chicano
studies. Though heavy on educational items, a great many other areas
are covered. The work includes a list of bibliographies as well as
unpublished theses and dissertations. The volume is a good introduction for Chicano researchers interested in a broad survey of Chicano
Aztlanense literature, especially those working in education.

.   .   .

SUMMARY

The second period marks the rise of the "problem" approach to
Chicano bibliographies, especially during the thirties. Though historical works remain a strong influence among bibliographers, other

areas, including education, folklore, music, immigration, literature, language, welfare, and culture command significant attention.

If during the thirties the "problem" aspects of the Chicano were emphasized, a cozy, if superficial, Good Neighbor approach took precedence during the forties. A cooling off occurred during the fifties. Yet, by the end of the decade, the work of Sanchez already pointed to the direction Chicanos would take during the sixties.

Third Period (1960-   )

We have indicated that history and social science were the hallmarks of the first and second periods, respectively. Historical interest in the hispanic past took precedence during the first period and the "problem approach" that derived from social science gained remarkable strength during the second period. The third period begins with the sixties where these same tendencies persist, although new variants emerge as well. Education thus becomes an important theme during the early sixties. New programs such as compensatory education, bilingual education, migrant education, headstart, education for the "disadvantaged," etc. gain considerable prominence, especially with the stimulus of federal monies. These new programs, however, have a common ancestry with earlier social scientific work, namely, their approach is pathologic or problem oriented. Of course, in view of the vast literature produced on Chicano education since the twenties, it would have been surprising indeed if educational programs had assumed a more positive approach during the sixties. *As it happened, educators merely turned to well-established social science "authorities" for educational schemes based upon "objective" information on the Chicano student.*

A second theme of the sixties is what might be called the "minorities melting pot" theory. Simply stated, this theory holds that all minorities are more or less the same. During the fifties and throughout the sixties, the Black movement caused a significant impact on virtually all aspects of American society—social, economic, political, military, penal, legal, educational, cultural, etc. Gabachos naturally focused attention on the "Negro Problem." In the minds of Gabachos, all other exploited groups—Chicanos, Indians, Orientals, and numerous other ethnic and non-ethnic minorities—had little or no significance. Minority came to be equated with Negro, and Gabachos concluded that settling the "Negro Problem" would also settle the minority problem. Programs created for "minorities" were in fact

Black programs. Even worse, when Gabachos finally conceded that different peoples were subsumed within the "minority" category, it was thought that the other "ethnic problems" were merely the "Negro Problem" in miniature. From this line of reasoning it was easy to conclude that the solutions suggested for the "Negro Problem" were to be applied equally to the "other minorities." Operationally, this meant that a few token Chicanos in Black programs would magically transform such programs into "minority programs." This approach obviously failed to consider the substance of the two periods which we have reviewed. In short, Gabachos obliterated history. In bibliographic terms, these Gabacho failings produced many volumes which are most noteworthy for their irrelevancy to Chicanos, even when the covers are boldly inscribed with "Chicano," "minorities," or similar words.

A third theme gains ascendency during the middle and late sixties. This theme is the vocal and mobilized Chicano reaction against the excesses of non-Chicano historians, social scientists, politicos, educators, social workers, lawyers, doctors, farmers, capitalists, immigration officers, artists, novelists, filmmakers, as well as schools, colleges, universities, churches, prisons, the draft, courts, housing projects, politics, agribusiness, unions, monolingualism, monoculturalism, majoritarianism, Democrats, Republicans, the Department of the Interior, Farm Labor Service, Michigan State Patrol, food stamps, planned poverty, discrimination, College Entrance Examination Board, Parents Confidential Statement, NEDA, Vietnam, Hollywood, the mass media, John Wayne, The University of Michigan, The University of California. Chicanos challenged the assumptions and stereotypes which the Gabacho had held since the Conquest. Angry young Chicanos felt a need to assert their culture of mestizaje and carnalismo. The barrio became La Nueva Patria and La Causa became the rallying cry. The gente de bronce began to push again, as in the past, for self-determination in the fields, the factories, the public schools, the government, and within the general Gabacho culture. In three or four years more Chicano oriented bibliographies were produced than in the previous three or four decades.

In bibliographic terms the three themes discussed above are woven in a complex pattern which mixes together social scientific, historical, cultural, critical, apologetic, ideological, political, educational, and numerous other orientations, depending upon the specific period of time and the interests of the compiler. Thus a rash of "Chicano bibliographies" appeared during 1969 and 1970 which purport to demonstrate the cultural contributions of the Chicano, his magnificent Spanish heritage, and optimism for the future. Most of these compilations are neither annotated nor critical. Many of them are mere listings of titles in the form of mimeographed handouts. Others are voluminous compilations of highly specialized materials, often espousing the Gabacho viewpoint. Certain bibliographies are simple adaptations or extractions from other bibliographies. A great number of them are redundant and add little or nothing to the bibliography of the Chicano.

Most bibliographic production during the decade of the 60's has clearly identifiable sources. Government at all levels, public schools, colleges and universities, public libraries, professional associations, foundations, welfare agencies, religious organizations, research laboratories, information centers, doctoral students, master's candidates, and even college seminars have all had a hand in producing Chicano bibliographies. In fact, the deluge of "Chicano bibliographies" almost drowned out the bibliographic production of Chicanos themselves. Fortunately, the Chicano asserted himself and towards the end of the decade said basta! Chicanos now claim the right to compile Chicano bibliographies. This Chicano act of assertion and criticism is the most notable aspect of the third period.

It would be extremely difficult, if not impossible, to review all of the bibliographic production for this period. Many bibliographies were printed for a local reading public, others were distributed at special meetings or workshops, some were used as instructional material for specific college courses. Bibliographies which seem promising by their title very often turn out to be irrelevant for Chicanos. Words such as minority, ethnic, disadvantaged and even Chicano have been much exploited during the sixties.

In the following pages a number of bibliographies will be reviewed. They do not represent a statistical sampling of the total bibliographic production for the period. Yet, the reader will see that the items included represent the various tendencies which we have described.

.   .   .

On an old topic is Charles Curtis Cumberland's *The United States-Mexican Border; A Selective Guide to the Literature of the Region* (Supplement to *Rural Sociology*, v. 25, No. 2, June, 1960). The volume has a highly readable essay format. Says Cumberland, "With few exceptions, and then only if the work is particularly applicable, the *Guide* includes materials dealing only with the period after Mexican Independence" (page 3). Citations are included up to 1958. Most of the titles are by non-Chicanos, and many citations reflect the Gabacho view of the borderlands. The diligent reader, however, may note that some of the entries present the Mexican view of U.S. aggression in the Southwest. These entries are a good beginning and should lead the student to further research in this important area.

Chapter IV is devoted to the "Spanish-Speaking" population of the United States and provides many of the standard items on the subject. All in all, the volume is useful as a summary of the Gabacho literature on both the Southwest and the Chicano. A compilation of Chicano materials on the same topic has yet to be made.

In a more restricted geographic and topical area, Mitchell Slobodek's *A Selective Bibliography of California Labor History* (Los Angeles: University of California, Institute of Industrial Relations, 1964) has a selection on agriculture which includes a few citations (four or five pages) on "Mexicans." There is even a sprinkling of authors with Chicano names, but mostly the Gabacho view of the migrant prevails. The work is topically arranged and has an author-title index. The volume was completed before the effective organizing campaign of Cesar Chavez and therefore omits much material that properly belongs in such a volume.

Further east, Alfred M. Potts, et al., compiled their monolithic *Knowing and Educating the Disadvantaged: An Annotated Bibliography* (Alamosa, Colorado: Adams State College, Center for Cultural Studies, 1965—also available through Educational Resources Information Center: ERIC). This Office of Education sponsored project epitomizes the Gabacho's socio-pathological approach to Chicano issues. Extensively annotated, the volume was compiled as an aid for planning research and demonstration projects related to the education of agricultural migratory adults. Unfortunately, Potts views his client population as economically and even spiritually deprived (see introduction). Therefore it is not surprising to Chicano readers that most of the entries portray a Gabacho perspective of the Chicano. In summary, the volume is an excellent record of what the Gabacho has done to the Chicano in the name of assistance.

In a related topic of the poverty industry, the serial publication *Poverty and Human Resources; Abstracts and Survey of Current Literature* (Ann Arbor: University of Michigan/Wayne State University Institute of Labor and Industrial Relations, 1966-   ) provides a bi-monthly publication of a general bibliographic character. The classification scheme includes the descriptor "Spanish American" under which are cited a few Chicano items. The poverty approach, however, overly restricts the types of entries made, and it also omits items in which Chicanos might very well be interested. *The volume is remarkably silent on migrant workers, even though Michigan's agribusiness drew hundreds of thousands of Chicanos, especially during the late fifties.*

Throughout the sixties a great deal of confusion occurred regarding the nature of the relationship between the Chicano and the Mexican. In some cases it was assumed that Mexican materials were equivalent to Chicano materials. Anna Angelini's pamphlet, *Mexico* (Stockton, California: Public Library, 1966 - supplement, 1970), is a case in point. Topically arranged and briefly annotated, this short list is intended for "better inter-cultural understanding." It is not clear whether the better understanding is expected between Mexicans and Gabachos or between Chicanos and Gabachos. Most of the entries concern Mexico.

On a strictly Mexican topic, Merlin Forster's *An Index to Mexican Literary Periodicals* (New York: Scarecrow Press, Inc., 1966) provides a summary of post revolutionary literature (1920-1960) as it appeared in 16 Mexican periodicals. The volume contains some 4036 entries in a two part arrangement: Items are listed by author in part one, and part two is an index. This work is not particularly useful to Chicanos, except for those interested in modern Mexican literary influences on Chicanos.

Back on the subject of Chicanos, Jack Forbes's *Mexican American: A Handbook for Educators* (Berkeley: Far West Laboratory for Educational Research, 1966 - also available through ERIC) provides a limited bibliography from a curricular perspective. Now largely outdated, the bibliography provides an early example of the typical "Chicano bibliography" which was later to flood the Chicano scene. Forbes's handbook is basically not a bibliography, but a brief and sympathetic historical description of the Chicano Aztlanense.

From a different perspective, Lois J. Farley's and Sam Shulman's *A Selected Bibliography: Health and Culture of Spanish Speaking Migrant Labor* (Ft. Collins: Colorado State University, Sociology-Anthropology Department, 1966) is another example of the social scientific-pathological Gabacho view of the Chicano and his culture. Some 180 citations are included in this mimeographed bibliography, mostly from the 1950's and 60's. This list is a handy summary of the Gabacho's social scientific meddling with Chicanos. Some general items (such as folklore) are included.

In the area of legal work, Betty Anne McCarthy compiled a short mimeographed bibliography called *Legal Services to the Poor: A Selected Bibliography* (Sacramento: California State Law Library, 1967 - reprinted in 1970). Though the citations are not specifically about Chicanos, the topic is of such importance that we have included the work here. The citations lean toward Office of Economic Opportunity (OEO) programs. Those interested in the delivery of legal services to poor Chicanos may find some useful references in this work.

A very short work (eight pages) by Martha Beauchamp, *Bilingualism with Reference to American Minority Groups (Especially Spanish Americans); Selected References* (Washington: Library of

Congress, Legislative Reference Service, 1967), provides items which are common to Chicanos, Puerto Riquenos and Aztlanenses. Many citations from periodicals are included. In general, the work is a mixed bag of the pathologic approach, enlightened reappraisal, and irrelevancies to bilingualism.

From the same quarter another mini-bibliography appeared, this one from the U.S. Department of Labor: *Mexican Americans; Selected References* (Washington: U.S. Department of Labor, 1967). This eight page bibliography is concerned almost exclusively with social scientific studies of the 1960's. The work takes a pathologic view and is of minimal value to Chicanos.

In more or less the same perspective is the work by Robert Edmond Booth, et al., *Culturally Disadvantaged; A Bibliography and Keyword Out of Context (KWOC) Index* (Detroit: Wayne State University, 1967). Some Chicano entries are made under various descriptors, such as migrant, Spanish-Speaking, bilingualism, etc. The technical production of this bibliography (Keyword out of context approach) is worthy of some attention. If criticism could be added to description, the system might be promising for Chicano use. The general content of the work is obvious from the title.

On the Mexican side of the border, the annual publication of the Centro de Estudios Históricos of the Colegio de México, *Bibliografía Histórica Mexicana* (México: El Colegio de México, 1967-   ), is worthy of note. For the Chicano Aztlanense, the usefulness of this publication lies in its antidotal effect for the bias in Gabacho publications. The work is annotated and includes thousands of entries in some 19 categories which are subdivided into numerous classifications. Both Mexican and Gabacho theses are included. History has a broad meaning in this publication, and many items in a wide number of fields are included. Unfortunately, the compilers have not yet discovered the Chicano as a subject for documentation.

On a strictly Chicano Aztlanense subject, Ralph C. Guzman's *Revised Bibliography* (Los Angeles: University of California, Mexican American Study Project, Advanced Report Number 3, 1967) is an important work because of its influence on subsequent Chicano bibliographic production, especially during the late sixties and early seventies. The work is severely weakened by omitting annotations, but the lists of books, pamphlets, journal articles, dissertations and unpublished materials is extensive. A partial compensation for the lack of annotations is Guzman's "The Search for Meaning: A Bibliographic Essay" in the same report. This essay is a precursor of the more definitive criticism by Romano, Vaca, Hernandez, and others.[6] Guzman's work is clearly a turning point in Chicano bibliographic production. Its most serious weakness is the failure to distinguish between Chicano, Gabacho, and Mexican materials, and to show the relationship between all three: A fault common to most Aztlanense bibliographies regardless of authorship. This bibliography also appears in *The Mexican-American People: The Nation's Second Largest Minority* (New York: Free Press, 1970) by Leo Grebler, et al.

. . .

Only a small number of works are available (at the present time) for inspection by the author from the numerous publications of 1968. In the state of Washington, the partially annotated volume *Preliminary List of Resource Materials on Minority Groups* (Olympia: Office of the Superintendent of Public Instruction, 1968) has only a sprinkling of citations on Chicanos. Most items are on Blacks and Indians. The work includes a list of publishers who produce "integrated education materials." Of minimal use to Chicanos, the work exemplifies the common misuse of the term "minorities." Perhaps the "final list" will include items on Chicanos.

Closer to México (at least geographically) is the master's thesis of Nora Ramírez González, *Familiarizing the Mexican American Student with his Culture Through Books: An Annotated Bibliography* (Denton: Texas Woman's University, Master's Thesis, 1968). The work is basically oriented toward public school students and includes innocuous annotations of works in history, literature, aand culture. Much material is included about Spain, and González appears to believe in the myth that Chicanos are Spaniards. A list of English books translated into Spanish is included. This work is strictly for "Latins."

Two other Texans, Owen L. Caskey and Jimmy Hodges, compiled *A Resource and Reference Bibliography on Teaching and Counseling the Bilingual Student* (Lubbock: Texas Technological College, School of Education, 1968). Some 733 unannotated entries are alphabetically arranged through 1967. Their approach is comparative, cross cultural and cross national. Much of the Gabacho dogma associated with Chicano bilingualism is included. The obvious escapes the authors, namely that the best counselor for the bilingual Chicano student is a bilingual-bicultural Chicano counselor.

By 1969 the Chicano movement had gained momentum and bibliographic production mushroomed. From California to Texas to Michigan and even further east, colleges, universities, public libraries and many government organizations put down in ink and paper their interest in the Chicano and his problems. Unfortunately, much of this effort resulted in slick title pages with little substance between covers.

A publication by the library of California State College, Fresno, *Afro- and Mexican-Americana; Books and Other Materials in the Library of Fresno State College Relating to the History, Culture, and*

Problems of Afro-Americans and Mexican-Americans (Fresno: California State College, The Library, 1969), is an unannotated list of library holdings. The work is divided into four categories, including government publications and theses. A topical arrangement then follows. Library holdings up to 1969 are included. The volume is more Afro than Mexican with authorship generally by "Americana."

As a result of MECHA (Movimiento Estudiantil Chicano de Aztlán) activity, the University of California, Davis published *Chicano Bibliography* (Davis: University of California, The Library, 1969) which was compiled under the general leadership of Ben Garza. The work is intended specifically for Chicano Aztlanenses. A topical arrangement is followed in this unannotated bibliography which includes both books and journal articles. Many of the entries represent standard items included in most Chicano bibliographies. A brief list of Chicano Aztlanense periodicals is included. The work is mainly a record of some of the holdings at the Davis campus library.

A mimeographed bibliography was published from the Berkeley campus of the same university: *Bibliography Relating to Mexican Americans* (Berkeley, University of California, School of Social Welfare, 1969). This unannotated list includes items on Blacks and Indians. Books, journal articles, and unpublished materials are included, generally in the areas of social science, history, and literature. The list can be useful if you know what you are looking for.

A short work (14 pages) from Los Angeles, *A Library Guide to Mexican-American Studies* (Los Angeles: California State College, J. F. Kennedy Memorial Library, 1969), is both unannotated and includes more or less standard items. The section on bibliographies is useful. One would think, however, that Los Angeles might provide more than fourteen pages on Chicano materials.

On the recurring theme of migrants and education we find *A Selected Bibliography Concerning the Education of Mexican American Migrant Children* (San Luis Obispo: California State Polytechnic College, Department of Education, 1969). This mini-bibliography (ten pages) proclaims somewhat murkily: "The contents of this publication have been carefully selected to assist you in your relevancy to compensatory education" (introduction). What the anonymous author fails to see is that compensatory education is irrelevant to the Chicano. The work is not annotated and contains materials from 1960-1969. For a more comprehensive treatment of the subject see the Potts work already cited.

On the bilingual front, Herb Ibarra, et al., compiled *Bibliography of ESL/Bilingual Teaching Materials* (San Diego: San Diego City Schools, 1969) which includes both English and Spanish texts. This curriculum materials guide is topically arranged y es para el que quiera hablar inglés.

Keith Revelle's *Chicano: A Selected Bibliography of Materials by and About Mexico and Mexican-Americans* (Oakland: Latin American Library of the Oakland Public Library, 1969 - addendum 1970) is intended for both Chicanos and Gabachos. It includes brief but un-critical annotations. This pamphlet contains mostly standard items from published books, journal articles and Chicano periodicals. The work has limited value for the serious researcher. Revelle's intro-ductory remarks may be of historical interest for the Chicano Azt-lanense.

Another publication from the same city, *The Mexican Americans: Books for Young People* (Oakland: Oakland Public Schools, Division of Instructional Media Library, 1969), has a section on "Mexican Americans" and another on "Mexicans." Each section is further sub-divided into fiction and non-fiction. The citations are annotated and graded according to their most appropriate use in the public schools. Greater emphasis is given to the Mexican section. Both sections em-phasize Gabacho writers, even in the "Mexican Fiction" category. For example, together with Azuela, Fuentes, and Rulfo, one can find Baker, Carr, and Steinbeck. This 27 page document is probably in-dicative of what Chicanos can expect to find in public school li-uraries.

A 31 page mimeographed bibliography by Anthony J. Salamanca and Mack E. Ford is an adaptation of an unidentified Ford bibliog-raphy. *Americans of Mexican Descent; A Selected Bibliography . . .* (San Francisco: San Francisco State College, History Course 104 Exp., 1969) is unevenly annotated. It is composed of three sections, including one on education. This bibliography is intended for Chi-canos and is useful as an introductory bibliography, especially where citations are critically annotated.

From the nation's capital we have *Not Just Some of Us; A Lim-ited Bibliography on Minority Group Relations* (Washington: Social Security Administration, GPO, 1968 - 2d edition, 1969). The main limitation of this work is that it tries to cover too much in its 42 pages and imbues everything with a Gabacho perspective. It includes briefly annotated citations on Chicano Aztlanenses and Puerto Ri-queños, Blacks, Indians, Jews, and Chinese. El que mucho abarca poco aprieta. Most entries on Chicanos have a social scientific bent. This work is no gold mine for the Chicano.

A much more noteworthy volume from the same quarter is *The Mexican American; A New Focus on Opportunity: A Guide to Ma-terials Relating to Persons of Mexican Heritage in the United States* (Washington: Inter-Agency Committee on Mexican American Affairs,

GPO, 1969). This unannotated volume arranges material into nine categories, and is intended both for Gabachos and Chicanos. A useful section on bibliographies is included, as well as unusual listings of Chicano periodicals, Chicano Spanish language radio and TV stations, government reports, and records of hearings and other official proceedings. Though not actually a guide, this extensive listing of materials has influenced many subsequent bibliographic works.

From the Midwest comes *A Bibliography of Books and Audio Visual Materials on Mexican Americans and Other Minorities* (Toledo: Mexican American Leadership Training Program, 1933 Spielbusch Ave., 1969?) with the blessings of the Catholic church. A concoction of books (elementary, high school, and adult), newspapers, teaching materials, and list of publishers, the only significance of this work is that it exemplifies the wide geographic breadth of the Chicano movement in the United States. It is widely assumed that only the Southwest has Chicano activity.

On the scholarly level is E. G. Navarro's *Annotated Bibliography of Materials on Mexican Americans* (Austin: University of Texas, School of Social Work, mimeo., 1969; published in New York: *The Chicano Community*, Council on Social Work Education, 1971). Navarro's main purpose ". . . is to locate, critically examine and annotate available literature and films in the various fields of social science and related disciplines which reflect on the Mexican-American experience" (introduction). The work is oriented toward social work courses, and though extensively annotated tends to be more descriptive than critical. The introductory essay "Mexican-Americans of the Southwest—Some Basic Misconceptions," includes a discussion of McWilliams, Kibbe, Simmons, Heller, Madsen, etc. Navarro, however, does a relatively weak job of dispelling some of the historical misconceptions and stereotypes held by Gabachos. All citations relate to the Chicano Aztlanense, but there are far too many Gabacho entries, mostly from the social sciences. The volume is alphabetically arranged and is a handy summary of standard Gabacho materials on the Chicano.

Another Chicano Aztlanense work comes from Arizona: *Bibliography* (Phoenix: Southwest Council of La Raza, 1969?). The author (or authors) is well aware of the volume's shortcomings. "This list is not complete, has not been annotated, and has not been edited for validity or relevancy to the Mexican American community" (introduction). The strength of this work is that it recognizes the need for materials that are truly relevant to the Chicano, even if it does not meet that need completely. Entries are topically arranged and include a number of disciplines. The good, the bad, and the irrelevant are indiscriminately put under one cover. The spirit of the volume is excellent; the usefulness of the bibliographic content is self-consciously limited.

On the rudimentary level are two micro-bibliographies (two pages each) from Oklahoma—*Mexican Americans: Some Recommended Titles for Elementary Schools,* and *Mexican Americans: Some Recommended Titles for Secondary Schools* (Oklahoma City: Oklahoma State Department of Education, Library Resources Division, 1968 and 1969 respectively). Neither list is annotated, nor are they worth recommending. They are cited to indicate the geographic spread of "Chicano" bibliographies.

Another work which is included for illustrative purposes only is *A List of Books on the History of Negroes and Other Minorities* (Lansing: Michigan Department of Education, Bureau of Library Services, 1969). Though Michigan has the tenth largest Chicano population in the nation, the bibliography has fewer Chicano entries than there are letters in the word "minorities." In the last few years, however, the Chicano movement has gained considerable momentum in Michigan, and one can expect more substantial contributions from this area.

Nancy Saldaña's *Mexican Americans in the Midwest: An Annotated Bibliography* (East Lansing: Michigan State University, Rural Manpower Center, 1969) provides an example of what can be expected from the Midwest. This volume is really a guide to social science literature on the Chicano. It includes items from outside of the Midwest. The introductory essay is useful because of Saldaña's ideas on the periodization of Chicano materials. Saldaña's strength is that she approaches the topic professionally; her weakness is that she tends to be less critical of the material than Chicanos can afford to be. All in all, however, the work is commendable.

Another important annotated work, this one from the west coast, is *The Mexican American; A Selected and Annotated Bibliography* (Stanford: Center for Latin American Studies, 1969; 2nd edition, 1971). The volume has a multiple authorship which includes graduate students. "Quite intentionally, the bibliography focuses upon the contemporary interests and concerns of the Mexican-American community . . ." (introduction). The importance of this work is that it clearly attempts to include only materials on the Chicano Aztlanense, though the definition of the Aztlanense is awkward and incomplete (see "Notes on Terminology," page vii). The volume includes a list of bibliographies but generally leans toward the social sciences. Some 274 entries are extensively annotated, though the reviewers tend to be more descriptive than critical. Moreover, the reviews have an obvious Gabacho perspective and fail to arrive at a rigorous criticism of Gabacho social science.

The second edition of this work is enlarged to include dissertations as well as more Chicanos among the compilers. Consequently there is a general improvement in the usefulness of the selections, even though there is no marked improvement in criticism. The second edition is preferable over the first.

On an entirely different level is the *Catalogue of the Latin American Collection of the University of Texas Library* (Boston: G. K. Hall and Co., 1969). This is an important reference work for those interested in the Texas collection but who have no easy access to it. The card catalogue is neatly fitted into thirty-one large volumes.

. . .

The deluge of bibliographic materials continues into 1970. The west coast appears to be especially prolific. From Long Beach we have *Chicano Bibliography: A Selected List of Books on the Culture, History and Socio-economic Conditions of the Mexican-American* (Long Beach: California State College, The Library, 1970). Annotated and arranged by subject according to the Library of Congress system, this booklet lists some of the holdings of the Long Beach State College Library. Most items are quite standard, but the work is worth thumbing through because so many subjects are covered.

The Los Angeles Public Library's *De Aztlán a Hoy; Mexican American Culture and History* (Los Angeles: 1970) boldly announces: "This is a major bibliography of English and Spanish language materials dedicated to Mexican-Americans" (introduction). This bilingual and annotated bibliography promises much more than it delivers in its twelve pages, perhaps due to the proximity of Hollywood. The only citations worth noticing are the half dozen entries listed under "Old and Rare." We suspect that El Pueblo de Nuestra Señora La Reina de Los Angeles can do much better (cf. Barrett's work already cited).

A Chicano from the same city, Juan Gomez-Q, compiled *Selected Materials on the Chicano* (Los Angeles: University of California, Mexican American Cultural Center, 1970) which is intended for Chicanos. This topically arranged *unannotated* work is an introductory list to the good and the bad in current Chicano materials. The purpose of the work was undoubtedly pedagogical.

In northern California, Lorna Flesher compiled a seven page pamphlet, *American Minorities: A Checklist of Bibliographies Published by Government Agencies, 1960-1970* (Sacramento: California State Library, 1970). This document is basically a bibliography of bibliographies which includes briefly annotated citations on Chicanos, Blacks, Orientals, and Indians. The list is handy if you are starting from zero.

A mini-bibliography from San Diego is *Chicano: A Selected List* (San Diego: San Diego Public Library, 1970). The list is topically arranged and has no particular significance, except perhaps to demonstrate the paucity of Chicano materials in public libraries (at least as exemplified by their bibliographies) which are almost contiguous with the Mexican border.

Brief annotations on items of general interest is the main characteristic of *Chicano; Mexican-American Bibliography* (San Diego: Sierra Regional Library System, Imperial Valley Public Library, 1970). This eighteen page pamphlet has an alphabetical arrangement and leans somewhat towards history.

A useful reference work is the thirteen page mimeographed list by Steven Tash, *Selected Bibliography of Resources for Chicano Studies* (Northridge, California: San Fernando Valley State College Library, 1970). This list is topically arranged and is actually a bibliography of bibliographies. Those who want to know where to start will find it most useful.

The six page leaflet *Chicanos—Relevance Now: A Mexican-American Bibliography* (Cupertino, California: De Anza College Library, 1970) is an unannotated alphabetical list of no particular significance. It has no research value and is included here to demonstrate the mushrooming of "Chicano" bibliographies, and the misleading journalistic use of titles.

A much more complete work is Linda Fowler Schramko's *Chicano Bibliography, Selected Materials on Americans of Mexican Descent* (Sacramento: Sacramento State College Library, Bibliographic Series No. 1, 1970 - 1st edition, 1969). Some 1000 entries are topically arranged (includes a section on education) and basically represent relevant library holdings to the spring of 1969. The volume includes journal articles and a considerable number of ERIC items. The work also contains an index and a list of Chicano journals. The section "Guide to Further Information" points to further sources, mainly by Gabachos.

The Minority Experience; A Basic Bibliography of American Ethnic Studies (Santa Rosa, California: Sonoma County Office of Education, 1970) by Ron Caselli, et al., is an alphabetical listing, largely of standard items, concerning Chicanos, Blacks and Indians. This colorfully assembled document has limited usefulness for serious work.

From the more prestigious University of California, Berkeley comes *Bibliography on Minorities; Black and Mexican American Studies and Literature* (Berkeley: School of Social Welfare, 1970). This 25 page mimeographed bibliography is an unannotated list of more or less standard books and journal articles. It leans to the Black side.

Another mimeo, this one by and for the Chicano Aztlanense, is *Chicano Bibliography* (East Los Angeles: Los Trabajadores de La Raza, 512 S. Indiana Street, 1970). The reader is warned, "You will be highly pleased with some of the enclosed selections. You will be outraged by others" (introduction). Since the list is not annotated, the reader's potential for pleasure or rage is maximized. The topical arrangement includes such unconventional categories as "Stereotyping of the Chicano," and "Critiques of Myths and Stereotypes." Most titles are quite standard; many paperbacks are listed.

A collection of bibliographies, *Bilingual-Bicultural Materials available in the Anita Osuña Carr Collection* (Albuquerque: University of New Mexico, College of Education, 1970), represent textbook holdings in both Spanish and English. The work is unannotated and contains bibliographies on language arts (Spanish and English), science, filmstrips, social studies aand other areas. The catalogue is most useful for those interested in bilingual education.

An annotated work by Kenneth Hedman and Patsy McNiel, *Mexican American Bibliography: A Guide to the Resources of the Library at the University of Texas at El Paso* (El Paso: University of Texas, The Library, 1970) is topically arranged and includes sections on education and bibliographies. As the title implies, this 24 page pamphlet basically describes some holdings of the UTEP library. Mostly standard items are included, but a few uncommon citations make it worthwhile to at least thumb through this bibliography. The introduction promises that the work will be updated. Hopefully the new edition will reflect more fully the library's holdings on Chicanos.

Holdings of the Denver Public Library are reflected in *Mexican Heritage* (Denver: Public Library, 1970?). The 34 page list is annotated and is "Planned as a popular book list for the use of many readers ..." (introduction). Materials for children and adults are topically arranged; a list of films and recordings is included. The work has little merit for serious work.

From Saginaw's Mexican American Cultural Materials Center we have a seven page mimeo, *A List of Materials Available at the Center* (Saginaw, Michigan: Diocese of Saginaw, Mexican American Cultural Materials Center). The holdings include some 50 filmstrips, 15 records, and 400 books, periodicals and pamphlets. The list is not annotated. An augmented version of this list was mimeographed as *Bibliography for and About Spanish-Speaking Americans* (1970?). Both items are cited here mostly to illustrate the dispersion of the Chicano movement.

In the same vein we find the short mimeo *Latin American History and Culture Center* (Detroit: Archdiocese of Detroit, Latin American Secretariat, 1970?) which is a list of materials available at the center. Items cited are maps, records, slides, films, filmstrips, books, texts, etc. There are no annotations.

On a more professional level is the Chicano authored work

Chicano Resource Materials; Prepared for the Chicano Studies Institutes to be held in Summer, 1970 in Aztlan (Washington: Montal Systems, Inc., 1970). "This information was gathered from educational laboratories, libraries, distribution centers and Chicano Studies programs" (introduction). Mostly unannotated (except for ERIC citations), the volume is topically arranged and includes a list of over a dozen bibliographies. Standard items predominate, but the section "Chicano Studies Graduate Program" may be useful for those concerned with the curricular aspects of this subject.

The *Catalog of Primary Descriptors* (Albuquerque: Southwest Cooperative Educational Laboratory, Clearinghouse on Mexican American Adult Basic Education, 1970?) is the clearinghouse's tally of the number of abstracts listed under each descriptor. A descriptor represents a subject under which materials are classified, for example, "migrant." Some descriptors list two abstracts, others list several hundred. Materials are available from the clearinghouse. The catalog provides no detailed information.

From the same state we have *Bibliography of Materials on Bilingualism* (Las Cruces: New Mexico State University, Educational Resources Information Center [ERIC] —Center for Rural Education and Small Schools [CRESS], 1970?), which is an unannotated alphabetical listing of educational items drawn largely from the late sixties. This eleven page mimeo represents ERIC holdings and has greater relevance for educators. The bulk of materials from this and other "centers" usually conveys the Gabacho perspective.

David M. Altus's *Bilingual Education, A Selected Bibliography* (Las Cruces: New Mexico State University, ERIC-CRESS, 1970) is a compendium of citations from *Research in Education* through June, 1970. The standard ERIC format is followed, which means that abstracts are included. Most citations are from the research of the sixties. A subject index is included. The abstracts, of course, make no critical judgments. This work is useful for those who want to know what the Gabacho has done in the field of bilingual education during the sixties.

A work by Manuel Romero, under the guidance of William Raat, is not annotated and includes book as well as journal items. The book section leans toward the historical; the journal articles emphasize the farm worker. *The Mexican American: A Selected Bibliography* (Moorhead, Minnesota: Moorhead State College, 1970) is somewhat stronger on journal articles than on books.

The recent bibliographic production is mixed, but there is increasing Chicano demand and interest in more rigorous compilations (cf. the 1971 edition of the Stanford work already cited). On the other hand, *Mexican American Bibliography; A List of Library Materials*

Relating to the History of Mexico and Mexican-Americans (Hayward, California: Chabot College Library, 1969 - revised 1971) is a mediocre pamphlet of 24 pages. Material is topically arranged and includes audio-visual items. Mostly library holdings are listed.

Helena Quintana's *La Raza at UNM; A Selected Bibliography in Education* (Albuquerque: University of New Mexico, Zimmerman Library, 1971) is basically a leaflet which can be loosely called a bibliography. This short and unannotated list is almost trivial. New Mexico can do better.

Juliette S. Ruiz's *A Selected Bibliography: Socialcultural and Psychocultural Perspectives of Human Behaviour* (Tempe: Arizona State University, Graduate School of Social Service Administration, 1970-71) is considerably better, at least quantitatively. Ruiz takes an intercultural relations approach and suggests that ". . . the materials have been selected especially for social work practice" (introduction). The work is unannotated and divided into five sections, each containing entries on Chicanos, Blacks, Indians, and Japanese. A list of Chicano newspapers and journals is included, as well as a bibliography of bibliographies. The author is certainly concerned with multi-ethnic relations, but the work is a bit overly ambitious. The quote above speaks for the general content of the work.

A three page leaflet, *Michigan's Deprived: A Selected Bibliography* (Lansing: Michigan Department of Education, Bureau of Library Services, 1971), is "A partial bibliography of books, documents and periodical articles on economically, socially, historically and educationally deprived people in Michigan . . ." (introduction). It is plain enough that a three page leaflet has limited selections. From a bibliographic point of view, this Michigan Department of Education effort is economically, historically, and educationally deprived. Ironically, this micro-bibliography contains about half a dozen Chicano items which are rarely cited elsewhere. The list is not annotated.

Chicano Bibliography (Salt Lake City: University of Utah Libraries, 1971) contains mostly items from the Marriott Library of the University of Utah. "The term 'Chicano' is used in this bibliography to bring together materials about Spanish Americans, American Indians, Cubans, Puerto Ricans and Eskimos who reside in the United States" (introduction). The arrangement is topical and includes journal articles, books, films, ERIC items, and citations from the Human Relations Area Files. It also lists Chicano newspapers and magazines. The work is not annotated, except for the ERIC entries. The above quote aptly characterizes the orientation of the contents.

A useful guide is titled *Manual for Providing Library Services to Indians and Mexican Americans* (Las Cruces: New Mexico State University, ERIC-CRESS, 1971). The work is more than a bibliography, but the bibliography is the most useful section. The citation is included here mainly because of the importance of the topic: Library services for Chicanos. This is an area which Chicanos must explore much more systematically than in the past.

Finally, but importantly, the tone of the future is set by *Bibliografía de Aztlán; An Annotated Chicano Bibliography* (San Diego State College, Centro de Estudios Chicanos, 1971) by Ernie Barrios et al. "The purpose of this annotated bibliography is to objectively review the literature that has been written on the second largest minority, the Chicano. This literature has been (1) biased and has perpetuated long standing negative stereotypes of the Chicano that have in no way aided American [Gabacho] society to better understand the problem nor aided the Mexican American to solve it, (2) or, it has been of such paternalistic and apologetic nature that it has inadvertently reinforced the negative stereotypes and worsened the problem" (page xvi). The volume is topically arranged and annotated by a diversified group of capable Chicano intellectual leaders, many of them college professors. There are sections on Chicano and Southwest history. The entire volume is indexed by author and title.

This is one of the best annotated Chicano bibliographies available, though it is not consistent in the quality of its criticism—perhaps an inherent problem of multiple authorship. Many reviews are critical and incisive as well as insightful, others are essentially descriptive. The review of Leonard Pitt's *Decline of the Californios,* for example, is quite weak. Pitt's heavy biases are not mentioned. On the whole, however, this volume is several notches above most of the literature reviewed in this study.

· · · ·

SUMMARY

The essential features of the third period are (1) the tremendous increase in bibliographic output, and (2) the Chicano awareness that bibliographies must be relevant to the specific needs of Chicanos.

Many compilations which are labeled "Chicano' are embarrassingly half-baked and add little or nothing to the Chicano's awareness of himself, his history, or his culture. The Gabacho perspective continues to predominate. The *Bibliografía de Aztlán* from the Centro de Estudios Chicanos at San Diego State College points toward the proper scholarly direction, for this compilation is more comparable to the competence demonstrated by the Chilean José Torribio Medina (1904), the Mexicans Joaquín García Icazbalceta (1886) and Vicente de P. Andrade (1899), mentioned at the beginning of this study. It remains now for a Chicano to write a true Chicano Aztlanense bibliography.

NOTES

1. McWilliams, Carey. *North from Mexico: The Spanish-Speaking People of the United States* (New York: Greenwood Press, 1968).

2. See introduction to Ralph Emerson Twitchell's *The Spanish Archives of New Mexico; Annotated and Chronologically Arranged with Historical, Geneological, Geographical, and Other Annotations* (Cedar Rapids, Iowa: Torch Press, 1914).

3. Relevant literature for this period can be found in *A List of Books on Immigration* (Washington: Library of Congress, 1904). This list is especially good for periodical entries and government documents.

4. There are no references to Chicano immigration in the bibliography listed above (note 3), or in *Deportation of Aliens: A Bibliographical List* (Washington: Library of Congress, Division of Bibliography, 1931).

5. A discussion of this work can be found in Lota May Spell's *Research Materials for the Study of Latin America at the University of Texas* (Austin: The University of Texas Press, 1954).

6. Romano, Octavio I. "The Anthropology and Sociology of the Mexican-American: The Distortion of Mexican-American History—A Review Essay," *El Grito*, II:1 (Fall 1968); Vaca, Nick C. "The Mexican-American in the Social Sciences, 1912-1970; Part II: 1936-1970," *El Grito* IV:1 (Fall 1970); Hernandez, Deluvina. *Mexican American Challenge to a Sacred Cow* (Los Angeles: Mexican American Cultural Center, Monograph No. 1, 1970).

Editor's Note: Mr. Padilla included a large number of bibliographies of bibliographies to accompany his article. Those that have been included in the bibliography of Clark Moreno that follows have been deleted, leaving only those that constitute an additional number to Clark Moreno's listing. This brings the total number of bibliographies relating to Chicanos to 513, as listed in this issue of EL GRITO.

A Concise Bibliographic Guide on Mexicans and Mexican-Americans (Austin: Hispanic American Institute, 1970)

Babin, Patrick. *Bilingualism: A Bibliography* (1968). ERIC no. ED 023-097.

Black Brown Bibliography (Northridge, California: San Fernando Valley State College Library, 1969)

Black and Brown Bibliography: Volume 1, History (San Bernardino: California State College Library, 1970)

Black and Brown Bibliography: Volume 2, Literature, Art, Music and Theater (San Bernardino: California State College Library, 1970)

Campbell, Vera. *Myths and Legends of Colorado: A Bibliography* (Greeley: Colorado State Teachers College, 1924)

Carroll, Bailey. "Texas County Histories," *Southwestern Historical Quarterly*, 45 (1941-42): 74-98, 164-187, 260-275, 341-361

Charles, Edgar. *Mexican American Education: A Bibliography* (1968). Available through ERIC.

Chicano Bibliography (Northridge, California: San Fernando Valley State College Library, 1969)

Children's Books About Mexican Americans and Children in Mexico (Oakland: Latin American Library of the Oakland Public Library, 1968)

Cortez, Ruben and Joseph Navarro. *Mexican-American History: A Critical Selective Bibliography* (Santa Barbara: Mexican-American Historical Society, 1969). Republished in *The Journal of Mexican American History* v. 1, Fall 1970.

Dean, Frances. *Programa de Educacion Interamericana* (Austin: University of Texas, Intercultural Education Series, Monograph No. 2, 1967)

Degoyler, E. L. "Compleat Collector: New Mexicana," *Saturday Review of Literature* 25 (May 16, 1942) 29-30

Dobie, J. Frank. *Guide to Life and Literature of the Southwest* (Austin: University of Texas Press, 1943). See citation under 1952 edition.

Dorn, Georgette. *Latin America* (Washington: Hispanic Foundation Bibliographic Series No. 11, GPO, 1967)

"Easy Material for the Spanish Speaking," *Booklist and Subscription Books Bulletin*, (July 15, 1968): 1266-77.

Foik, Paul J. "Survey of Source Materials for the Catholic History of the Southwest," *Catholic Historical Review*, 9 (1929): 275-281

Gerez, Toni de. "Books for Miguel," *Library Journal* (December 15, 1967): 4585-7

Grimes, Larry J. *A Bibliography of the Uto-Aztean Languages* (1966). ERIC number ED 011 662

Hammond, George. "Manuscript Collections in the Bancroft Library," *American Archivist*, 13 (1950): 15-26

Harrigan, Joan. *More Materiales Tocante Los Latinos: A Bibliography of Materials on the Spanish-American* (Denver: Colorado State Department of Education, 1969). Also available through ERIC.

Harwood, T. F. "Review of the Work of the Texas State Historical Commission," *Southwestern Historical Quarterly*, 31 (1927-28): 1-32.

Hispanic Heritage (Denver: Denver Public Library, 1969)

"In the Interest of Understanding: Some Recent Studies Concerned with Education of Minority Groups." *Education for Victory,* 1 (September 1, 1943): 18-20

Jones, Robert C. *Selected References on Labor Importation Program Between Mexico and the U.S.* (Washington: Pan American Union, 1948)

Los Angeles County Board of Education. *Bibliography on Mexico* (1935)

Los Angeles County Board of Education. *Bibliography on Mexico* (Los Angeles: 1940)

"Mas de cuatrocientos periodicos en Espanol se han editado en Los Estados Unidos," *La Prensa* (San Antonia): February 13, 1938

Mexican-Americans: A Selective Guide to Materials (Santa Barbara: University of California, The Library, 1969)

Mexican-American Bibliography (Redlands, California: University of Redlands, Armacost Library, Department of Special Collections, 1970)

Mexico and Mexican Americans (Whittier, California: Whittier College, Prepared by participants in the Seminar on Mexican Americans, 1968)

"Multi-ethnic Media: Selected Bibliographies," *School Libraries,* (Summer 1970): 44-7

Pane, Remigio U. "A Selected Bibliography of Latin American Literatures in English Translation," *Modern Language Journal,* v. 26 (February, 1942) 116-122

Pesqueira, Fernando. "La introduccion de la primera imprenta de Sonora," *El Imparcial* (Hermosillo, Sonora): February 15, 1942

Rael, Juan B. "New Mexico Folklore Bibliography," *New Mexico Folklore Record,* III (1948-49): 38-39

Reindorp, Reginald D., et al. *References for Teachers of English as a Foreign Language: A Bibliography* (Austin: University of Texas, Inter-American Education, Occasional Papers, IV, 1949)

Ríos, Herminio and Lupe Castillo. "Toward a True Chicano Bibliography; Mexican American Newspapers: 1848-1942," *El Grito,* III:4 (Summer 1970): 17-24

Rocha, Jose G. "La Imprenta y el Periodismo en Parral, 1856-1939," *Boletin de la Sociedad Chihuahuense de Estadios Historicos,* 1 (1938-39): 285-288, 356-358, 360

Rousseau, Manuel Estrada. "El Cuarto Poder en el Estado de Sinaloa," *El Nacional* (Mexico: May 27, 1931. List of newspapers of Sinaloa, 1900-1930

Saunders, Lyle. "A Guide to the Literature of the Southwest." Regular feature in *New Mexico Quarterly Review* from January 1, 1942 to 1955

Seelye, H. N. *A Handbook on Latin America for Teachers: Methodology and Annotated Bibliography* (DeKalb: Northern Illinois University, 1968)

Segura, David. *El mercurio en Mexico* (Mexico: 1941 - mimeo)

Shelton, Wilma Loy. "Checklist of New Mexico Publications," *New Mexico Historical Review*, 25 (1950): 57-72, 136-161, 222-241, *NMHR* 26 (1951): 64-67, 137-147, 225-241, 325-331, *NMHR*, 27 (1952): 51-63; *NMHR* 29 (1954): 58-70, 124-153

"Some Materials for Teaching English as a Second Language in the Elementary School," *Elementary English*, XLVI (October, 1969): 803

Thorne, Kathleen, et al. *Minorities in America* (San Jose: San Jose State College Library, Bibliography Series No. 2, 1969)

Trejo, A. D. "Bicultural Americans with an Hispanic Tradition," *Wilson Library Bulletin* (March 1970): 716-20

Troike, Rudolph C. *Bibliographies of American Indian Languages* (Austin: University of Texas Press, 1967). ERIC number ED 016 200.

Turner, Pearl, Ken Karr and Gloria Jameson. *The Education of Mexican American Children and Teaching English as a Second Language* (San Luis Obispo, California: California State College Library, 1969)

United States Bureau of Labor Standards, *Selected References on Domestic Agricultural Workers, Their Families, Problems and Programs, 1955-1960* (Washington: Bulletin No. 225, 1961)

Valle, Rafael Hilidoro, "Mexico en la prensa de habla inglesa," *Libro y Pueblo*, 13 (1935): 33-68, 134-139. Also *Hispanic American Historical Review*, 15 (1935): 1-40

Villa, Eduardo, "El periodismo en Sonora," *Divulgacion Historica*, 3 (1942): 371-373

Wagner, Henry R. "New Mexico Spanish Press," *New Mexico Historical Review*, 12 (1937): 1-40

Wallace, William S. "Bibliography of Published Bibliographies on the History of Eleven Western States, 1941-47," *New Mexico Historical Review*, 29 (1954): 224-233

Wallace, William S. "A Checklist of Western Newspapers in the Mills Collection." *New Mexico Historical Review*, 30 (1955): 136-152

Wilkerson, D. A. "Bibliography on the Education of Socially Disadvantaged Children and Youth," *Journal of Negro Education*, 33 (Summer 1964): 358-66

W.P.A. of Texas. Division of Professional and Service Projects, Historical Records Survey Program. *Texas Newspapers, 1913-1939: A Union List of Newspaper Files Available in Offices of Publishers, Libraries and a Number of Private Collections* (Houston: San Jacinto Museum of History Association, 1941).

PART III
LA HISTORIA

INTRODUCTION

To whom does a people's history belong?

With the advent of contemporary professionalism and its related compartmentalization of knowledge, there has developed in some quarters a strong tendency to treat history itself as if it were the real and private property of professional historians. Yet, in an ultimate sense that supersedes the boundaries of professional parochialism, a people's history belongs to those people who made it and experienced it. This places a burden upon those who choose to write about historical events. In short, the writers of history must be the servants of those about whom they write. Only in this sense can historical writing be truly empirical.

It is with this in mind that the following selections have been included in this volume of readings. They have also been included because they raise major questions about the nature of historical discourse. As one reads through the selections in this section two things will become clear: First, they contain information that has not been current or dealt with in other writings about Chicano history. Secondly, each article highlights an influence or influences which Raza has had upon American history.

The first article, "The Historical and Intellectual Presence of Mexican-Americans," provides the temporal setting for the profound influence that Chicanos have had upon bilingual and bicultural education in the United States, and some of the closely related factors.

This article is then followed by the Rodriguez' account of Santa Teresita and the influence she had in healing circles in Arizona, California, and New York. Equally important is the fact that Teresa Urrea is dealt with within a comprehensive historical and social setting. This alone makes the Rodriguez' account outstanding among writings about healers who, more often than not, have been arbitrarily divorced from their history.

"La Raza Influence on Jazz" by Ronald D. Arroyo is also innovative in that it deals, to the best of my knowledge for the first time, with an influence that continues to this day but heretofore has not been the subject matter of research. Our picture about jazz should change with the knowledge provided by Mr. Arroyo which removes the stereotypes that have surrounded this musical form. Today, Raza influence on jazz continues with musicians such as Luis Gasca, Carmelo García, Carlos and Jorge Santana, Chepito Arias, Coke and Pete Escovedo, Victor Pantoja, and many others.

Providing still another historical perspective is the article by Salvador Alvarez on community organizations. The significance of Mr. Alvarez' historical probe lies in the fact that the organizations about which he writes were the precursors of present farm labor struggles. Historically, these organizations greatly affected the history of agriculture in California.

The now classic article by César Chávez, "Huelga and the Church," is well known for the influence it has had, and continues to have, upon the thinking of those who write about La Huelga, as well as upon many individuals who are members of various religious groups. Perhaps the best evidence of the impact of this article and subsequent events lies in the fact that recently at a rally sponsored by the Union in attendance were two Catholic bishops.

The article by César Chávez is then followed by the thoroughly documented work on "The Legal and Legislative Struggle of Farm Workers" by Salvador Alvarez. That such a struggle has had an influence upon contemporary American history goes without saying. It only remains to be said that the scholarly perseverence and thoroughness exhibited by Alvarez certainly rates his work as a landmark in Chicano studies in history.

Of course, these articles do not exhaust the subject of Chicano history. For such a task one would need several large volumes. However, to repeat, they do highlight influences that Raza has had on American history. These influences began in the mid-1800's with the Mexican invention of the *batea* sometime before. The *batea*, or gold-mining pan, was later used by miners during the gold rush. Also borrowed from the Mexicans were the techniques of quartz mining, the fundamentals of the cattle industry, the practice of branding, irrigation, and the technique of horsebreaking as practiced by the American cowboy. This was borrowed directly from the *domador,* or professional Mexican horsebreaker. There are many other similar examples.

Now, with the information contained in the following articles, it can readily be seen that the Chicano population not only has, but continues to influence American history.

A final note. The word *influence*, rather than *contributions*, has been used here advisedly. The word *contribution* has the tendency of making the contributor a passive agent, rather than an agent that is active in the processes of history. Therefore the word *influence* for the simple reason that its connotation is that of active participation in history which, it seems to me, is more historically accurate insofar as Chicanos are concerned.

The Historical and Intellectual Presence of Mexican-Americans

Octavio Ignacio Romano—V.

— Muchos murieron, otros se fueron —

During and following the Mexican Revolution of 1910, it is estimated that one of every ten people left the country. Some went to Spain, some to France, some went to Cuba, to Guatemala, but most went north to the United States. Among those who went to the north were printers, poets, civil servants, merchants, farmers, school teachers, campesinos, musicians, bartenders, blacksmiths, jewelers, carpenters, cowboys, mestizos, village Indians, religious people, atheists, infants, mothers, Masons, counter-revolutionaries, philosophers.

Among those who went north was José Vasconcelos who later became Secretary of Education in Mexico. So did Martín Luis Guzmán, author of the classic novel of the Revolution, *El Aguila y la Serpiente*. Adolfo de la Huerta started the rebellion in northwest Mexico, was Provisional President(1920), and persuaded Pancho Villa to settle on the Canutillo Ranch. Huerta finally fled to Los Angeles, California, worked there as a singing instructor, and later returned to Mexico. Another northern migrant was José María Maytorena, governor of Sonora, supporter of Madero, follower of Villa, who finally ended up in California. Ramón Puente was a doctor, teacher, journalist and writer in the Villa army. Following Villa's defeat, Puente left for the United States. Along with the others, these men were among the great number of people who became the "immigrants" and "refugees" from the Mexican Revolution. In the words of Ernesto Galarza:

> As civil war spread over the republic after 1911 a major exodus from the countryside began. Landowners fled to the large cities, principally the capital, followed by hundreds of thousands of refugees who could find no work. This was one of the two great shifts that were to change radically the population patterns, until then overwhelmingly rural. The other current was in the direction of the United States, now accessible by rail. It moved in the dilapidated coaches with which the Mexican lines had been equipped by their foreign builders, in cabooses fitted with scant privacy, on engine tenders and on flat cars for the steerage trade. "A la capital o al norte" (to Mexico City or to the border) became the alternatives for the refugees from the cross-fires of revolution.[1]

In the north they worked on the railroad, in the clearing of mesquite, in fish canneries, tomato fields, irrigation, and all other such work that became so drearily familiar to the people living in the colonias. At the same time, for many, the Revolution continued to be fought in the barrios in the United States, as decribed by José Antonio Villareal in his novel, *Pocho*.

> The man who died under the bridge that night had no name. Who he was, where he came from, how he lived — these things did not matter, for there were thousands like him at this time. This particular man had fought in the army of General Carrillo, who, in turn, was one of the many generals in the Revolution. And, like thousands of unknown soldiers before and after him, this man did not reason, did not know, had but a vague idea of his battle. Eventually there was peace, or a lull in the fighting, and he escaped with his wife and children and crossed the border to the north.[2]

Not only did an attenuated version of the Revolution continue in the north, with plot and counterplot, avoidance and memories of hate, but there also continued the ideas, the intellectualizations, and the philosophies of the day. In the northern colonias, as was happening in Mexico, people still discussed and argued over the relative merits of Indianist philosophies, of Historical Experience and Confrontations, and about the philosophical and historical significance of the Mestizo. These relevant philosophies became a part of the common poetry readings of those days in the barrios. They also appeared in the colonia newspapers of the day, in stage and other dramatic presentations, in the music of the trumpet and guitars, in schools of Mexican culture, in the rationales and goals of the autonomous labor unions as well as in the constitutions and by-laws of the sociedades mutualistas. In some cases, the ideas had been transplanted from Mexico. In others, they were merged with pre-existent philosophies among the Mexican descended people already in the United States. And through it all, there continued the human quest and the conflict between Nationalistic Man and Universal Man, between Activist Man and Existential Man, Cleric and Anti-Cleric, Mutualist, Classical Anarchist,[3] Nihilist Man, Agrarian and Urban Man, Indian Man and Mestizo.

These are the principal historical *currents of thought* that have gone into the making of the mind of el Mexicano, the "refugee," el cholo, the Pocho, the Chicano, Pachuco, the Mexican-American. They have their roots in history and currently appear in three mainstreams of thought — Indianist Philosophy, Historical Confrontation, and the philosophically transcendant idea of the Mestizo in the form of Cultural Nationalism. These are philosophies, styles of thought, ideas as they persist over time. At times they coincide with actual historical occurrences. Other times they lie relatively dormant, or appear in a poetic metaphor, a song, a short story told to children, or in a marriage pattern. These philosophies were articulated in the post-Diaz days in Mexico and in the days of the Revolution.

— En aquéllos dias —

The ideologies and philosophies that gave air to the smoldering fires of the Mexican Revolution of 1910 were pluralistic, reflecting the composition of Mexico at that time. Many world views, numerous projected plans, desires for power, and historical precedents all contributed to this fiery outburst that led to untold human agonies, an attempted reconstruction, and a massive exodus. In the *Labyrinth of Solitude*, the philosopher-poet Octavio Paz attempted bravely to deal with these criss-cross currents in their historical relation to the present. His published effort resulted in a somewhat Quixotic quest for *THE* Mexican — El Puro Mexicano — a quest that fluttered between the two extremes of National Man and Universal Man. What emerged from his search were NOT many masks, as Octavio Paz insisted in the Freudianesque overtones of his work. Instead, what emerged from his search were but different life styles which represented different historical trends, a variety of individual experiences, and multiple intellectual currents — in short, Many Mexicans, just as today there are Many Mexican-Americans. Quite often, this seemingly endless multiplicity represents many men. Equally often, it represents every man.

— Cada loco con su tema — dicho

In 1926, José Vasconcelos, former Secretary of Education in Mexico, wrote, "The struggle of the Latin-American revolutionist is the struggle of democratic European ideas to impose themselves upon the Oriental indigenous type of despotism."[4] Vasconcelos condensed his notions into the "philosophy of the Ibero-american race," having its origins in an ethnically pluralistic Spain, transplanted to an equally pluralistic Mexico, reinforced by the universalistic components of the Catholc faith, and ultimately manifested in the Mestizo — genetic assimilation with European ideology integrated into the contemporary Mexico of his day.[5] The heart of his argument, of course, was that ideas invariably supercede the biological imperatives of miscegenation. Therefore, if miscegenation was the best vehicle for advancing pre-existent ideas, then such a course was desirable for Mexico. In all this process he envisioned ". . . the hope that the mestizo will produce a civilization more universal in its tendency than any other race of the past."[6]

This was not the only view that depicted the thought currents of the time. For example, Octavio Paz has written, "The Revolution had antecedents, causes and motives, but in a profound sense it lacked precursors. . . . The Revolution began as a demand for truth and honesty in the government, as can be seen from the Plan of San Luis (Oct. 5, 1910). Gradually the movement found and defined itself, in the midst of battle and later when in power. Its lack of a set program gave it popular authenticity and originality. This fact accounts for both its greatness and its weaknesses."[7] Then, "The Revolution, without any doctrines (whether imported or its own) to guide it, was an explosion of reality and a groping search for the universal doctrine that would justify it and give it a place in the history of America and the world."[8] Finally, "Our movement was distinguished by a lack of any previous ideological system and by a hunger for land."[9]

The views of Joé Vasconcelos and those of Octavio Paz reflect two major trends of thought at the time of the Revolution. First, there was the articulation of the desire to emulate pre-existent ideologies, i.e., el Mestisaje. Second, there was the desire to do autonomously, to confront, and then to articulate. Both ultimately envisioned something uniquely Mexican in its final outcome, a new synthesis. There was a third trend, the Zapata movement. This movement was a form of Indianism as intellectualized largely by the school teacher Montaño, a pure Indian. According to Vasconcelos, "There was a time when the European dress was not allowed in the Zapata territory; and those Mexicans of white Spanish skin that happened to join the Zapata armies had to adopt the dress and the manner of the Indian, in a certain way had to become indianized before they could be accepted."[10] As Paz describes it, "The Zapatistas did not conceive of Mexico as a future to be realized but as a return to origins."[11] It seemed almost as if a star had exploded long before, and only now could they see its light.

The Zapatista-Indianist philosophy, the Historical Confrontation, and the philosophy of the Mestizo were the three dominant philosophies of Revolutionary Mexico. Sometimes elements of one trend of thought would blend with another, as did the Indianist with Historical Confrontation. But when this took place it was in a complementary fashion, and not at the expense of the ideological premises that were guiding each chain of thought. In the same manner, any given individual could ally himself with any of the three philosophies in the course of his life, or shift from one to the other depending on surrounding circumstances, just as was the case with the "whites" who joined the Zapatista Indian forces. In short, the three ideological currents actually gave individuals alternatives from which to choose. These alternatives, in turn, represented relatively new historical manifestations at the turn of the century — cumulative changes that had been taking place in Mexico. They represented, therefore, the historical development of thought and not the rigid, unbending, and unchanging Traditional Culture so commonly and uncritically accepted in current sociological treatises that deal with people of Mexican descent. At the same time, *these three alternatives also made it possible for individual people, even families, to be living three histories at once*, a fact that escaped Octavio Paz when he accepted the notion of the Freudianesque masks.

In any event, when the time came for people to change locale and move to the United States, this was but another in a long series of changes that had been taking place.

— Cada cabeza un mundo — dicho

It is this complexity of thought and its many individual manifestations that made so popular the saying, "Each head a world in itself." For multiple histories could hardly have done other than breed complex people and equally complex families. It is this complexity, actually pluralism, that was transferred with the "refugees" and the "immigrants" to the north and which appeared in the colonias and barrios. This complexity was condensed in the recent poem by Rodolfo Gonzales of Denver, Colorado, titled "*I am Joaquin.*" Just who is this Joaquin? Joaquin is Cuahtemoc, Cortez, Nezahualcoyotl of the Chichimecas. Joaquin is Spaniard, Indian, Mestizo, the village priest Hidalgo, Morelos, Guerrero, Don Benito Juarez, Zapata, Yaqui, Chamula, Tarahumara, Diaz, Huerta, Francisco Madero, Juan Diego, Alfego Baca, the Espinoza brothers, Murietta. Joaquin is slave. Joaquin is master. Joaquin is exploiter, and he is the exploited. Joaquin is corridos, Latino, Hispano, Chicano. Joaquin is in the fields, surburbs, mines, and prisons. Joaquin's body lies under the ground in Mexico. His body lies under the ground in the United States, and in the "hills of the Alaskan Isles, on the corpse-strewn beach of Normandy, the foreign land of Korea, and now, Viet Nam."[18] Joaquin is many men. Joaquin is every man.

The ideas that were, and are, present wherever people of Mexican descent live involve the Indianist philosophy, Historical Confrontation, and Cultural Nationalism. Now, to the three currents of thought manifested historically there was added a fourth, The Immigrant Experience.

— Indianism —

Indianism has never been a focus or a rallying cry for action among Mexican-Americans as was Indigenismo during the War for Independence and the Revolution in México: Yet, symbolically, the Indian penetrates throughout, and permeates, major aspects of Mexican-American life, and hardly a barrio exists that does not have someone who is nicknamed "El Indio," or "Los Indios." For decades, Mexican-American youth have felt a particularly keen resentment at the depiction of Indians in American movies, while Indian themes consistently have been common subject matter for the neighborhoods' amateur artists, a fact that may be called an anachronism by some or the dislodging of history by others. On occasion, los Matachines still make their Indian appearance in churches, and Aztec legends still pictorially tell and retell their stories in barrio living rooms, in kitchens, in bars, restaurants, tortillerias, and Chicano newspapers. The stern face of Don Benito Juarez still peers out of books, still surveys living rooms, and still takes a place of prominence in many Sociedad Mutualista halls and in the minds of men throughout the Southwest. Small wonder, then, that several hundred years after the totally indigenous existence of Mexico reference is still made to these roots and origins in the Mexican-American community. Small wonder, also, that thousands of miles away from the Valley of Mexico, in contemporary Denver, Colorado, Señor Rodolfo Gonzales utilizes recurrent Indian themes in his poetic work. At the same time, such is found in the wall paintings at the Teatro Campesino center in Del Rey, California, and Indian art and life are common subject matter in such newspapers as *Bronze, La Raza, El Gallo,* as well as others. One should not be surprised, therefore, that the poet Alurista wrote in 1968:

> Unexpectedly
>   my night gloom came
> injusta capa fúnebre
> . . . .
> y corrí hacia el sol
>   el de mis padres
> the one that printed
>   on my sarape
> fantastic colors
>   through the prism
>   — la pirámide del sol
> at the sacrificial Teocatl
> my fathers wore their plumage
>   to listen
> and soplaron vida con sus solares rayos
> en mi raza[14]

Chichimeca, Azteca, Indio, Don Bento Juarez, Emiliano Zapata y Montaño; in art, prose, poetry, religion, and in Mexican-American study programs initiated by Mexican-Americans themselves in colleges, universities, and high schools, the presence of the Indian is manifested. It hardly need be added that the Indian is also manifested in the faces of so many Mexican-Americans. The Indian is root and origin, past and present, virtually timeless in his barrio manifestations — a timeless symbol of opposition to cultural imperialism.

— Historical Confrontation —

The philosophy of confrontations has had thousands of manifestations, from the retelling in an isolated corrido to protest demonstrations by thousands of people of Mexican descent in the United States. It, too, has an old history which in the north began with personages such as Joaquin Murietta, Alfego Baca, the Espinoza brothers, and Pancho Villa. Memories of these manifestations spread widely, as attested to by Enrique Hank Lopez when he wrote about his childhood in the United States:

> . . . Pancho Villa's exploits were a constant topic of conversation in our household. My entire childhood seems to be shadowed by his presence. At our dinner table, almost every night, we would listen to endlessly repeated accounts of this battle, that strategem, or some great act of Robin Hood kindness by *el centenauro del norte*. I remember how angry my parents were when they saw Wallace Beery in *Viva Villa!* 'Garbage by stupid Gringos' they called it. They were particularly offended by the sweaty, unshaven sloppiness of Beery's portrayal.[15]

Confrontationist philosophy continued with the labor protest movement among people of Mexican descent in the United States, which at one time became manifest in eight different states and which now has lasted for over eighty-five years. It also has taken other forms, such as the Pachuco who extended the notion of confrontation to a perpetual and daily activity with his own uniform and his own language. *The Pachuco movement was one of the few truly separatist movements in American History.* Even then, it was singularly unique among separatist movements in that it did not seek or even attempt a return to roots and origins. The Pachuco indulged in a *self-separation from history,* created his own reality as he went along even to the extent of creating his own language. This is the main reason why Octavio Paz, digging as he did into history in search for the "true Mexican," felt it necessary to "put down" the Pachuco. By digging into history for answers, Octavio Paz was forced to exclude people who had separated themselves from history, especially Mexican history. Thus, in denying the Mexicaness of the Pachuco, Octavio Paz denied the Mexican aspect of the processes that went into his creation. That is why Paz ended up by making the Pachuco into a caricature akin to a societal clown, for it was only by doing so that he could enhance the notion of el puro Mexicano in his own mind.

It is unfortunate that Octavio Paz chose to ignore the trend of thought represented by the famous, disillusioned, existential poet of Mexico, Antonio Plaza, who wrote in typical fashion, "Es la vida un enjambre de ilusiones / a cuyo extremo están los desengaños."[16] Had Paz chosen to acknowledge Antonio Plaza, and the philosophical trend he represented in his Mexican, existential, self-separation from history, then perhaps he would have understood a little about the Pachuco. For the Pachuco, too, separated himself from history, and in doing so became transformed into Existential Man. And, like existential man everywhere, he too was brutally beaten down.

The language of the confrontationist philosophy has been Spanish, English, Pocho, or Pachuco. Almost always, it has addressed itself to an immediate situation spanning the social environment from rural to urban. Normally, it has been regional or local in its manifestations. On different occasions, the confrontationist philosophy has been self-deterministic, protectionist, nationalistic, reacting to surrounding circumstances, and existentialist. The present Chicano movement has incorporated all of these alternatives in its various contemporary manifestations, making it one of the most complex movements in the history of Mexican-Americans.

Having been a recurrent theme in Mexican-American history, like that of Indianism, the confrontationist philosophy also makes up a part of study programs initiated by Mexican-Americans in colleges, universities, and high schools. Like Indianism, it is a history that has yet to be written in its entirety.

— Cultural Nationalism —

Vine a Comala porque me dijeron que acá
vivía mi padre, un tal Pedro Páramo.[17]

In Texas, New Mexico, Arizona, Colorado, California, Oregon, Washington, Idaho, Nevada, Utah, Oklahoma, Kansas, Arkansas, Ohio, Missouri, Ilinois, Michigan, New York, and other states, symbols of Mexican and Mexican-American culture can be seen. Invariably, in one way or another, these symbols are associated with the Mestizos — present descendants of untold Mexican antecedents and reduplicated in an ever-expanding northern arc. Different people have known them as Mexicanos, Cholos, Pochos, México-Norteamericanos, Chicanos, Mexican-Americans. Viewed as a group, they comprise a pluralistic minority within a pluralistically divided nation. They speak Spanish, or English, or both in a great variety of combinations.

The Mestizo-based notion of Cultural Nationalism is prominent among them. But this cultural nationalism is of a very particular kind, unamerican in a sense, and considerably unlike the rampant ethnocentrism with its traditional xenophobia (commonly called self-interest) that has been so characteristic of ethnic groups in the United States.

The fiestas patrias, the characteristic foods, the music, the sociedades mutualistas, and all of the other by-products of culture that people write about, are simply appurtenances to more profound conceptualizations regarding the nature and the existence of man. Generally, as a group, Mexican-Americans have been virtually the only ethnic group in the United States that still systematically proclaims its Mestizaje — multiple genetic and cultural origins exhibiting multiplicity rather than seeking purity. Philosophically and historically this has manifested itself in a trend toward Humanistic Universalism, Behavioral Relativism, and a recurrent form of Existentialism, this last of which is often naïvely and erroneously interpreted as fatalism.

The Indianist views, the Confrontationist Philosophy, and Cultural Nationalism with its Mestizaje-based Humanist Universalism, Behavioral Relativism, and Existentialism, when related to the types of people who have immigrated from Mexico, those born in the United States, as well as people of Mexican descent who were residents in conquered western lands, all give some glimmer of the complexity of this population, especially when one views it internally from the perspectives of multiple philosophies regarding the existence and nature of Mexican-American man. For, in truth, just as "el puro Mexicano" does not exist, neither does "the pure Mexican-American," despite the massive efforts by social scientists to fabricate such a mythical being under the monolithic label of the "Traditional Culture," rather than the more realistic concept of multiple histories and philosophies.

This multiplicity of historical philosophies, to a considerable degree, represents a continuation of the pluralism that existed in Mexico during the Revolution, undergoing modifications and shifts in emphasis. At the same time, it can be said that the philosophies of Indianism, Historical Confrontation, and Cultural Nationalism to this day represent the most salient views of human existence

within the Mexican-American population. To these there has been
added the immigrant dimension.

— The Immigrant Experience —

I'm sitting in my history class,
The instructor commences rapping,
I'm in my U. S. History class,
And I'm on the verge of napping.

The Mayflower landed on Plymouth Rock.
Tell me more! Tell me more!
Thirteen colonies were settled.
I've heard it all before.

What did he say?
Dare I ask him to reiterate?
Oh why bother
It sounded like he said,
George Washington's my father.

I'm reluctant to believe it,
I suddenly raise my mano.
If George Washington's my father,
Why wasn't he Chicano?

— Richard Olivas[18]

Just as could be expected from a pluralistic population exhibiting multiple histories, people of Mexican descent have adjusted to
life in the United States in many different ways, including the
Pachuco's self-separation from history, the organizers of labor unions, the publishing of bi-lingual newspapers, and the increasingly
militant student population. By and large, these adjustments mostly
fall into four broad categories: Anglo-Saxon Conformity, Stabilized
Differences, Realigned Pluralism, and Bi-Culturalism.

Anglo-Saxon Conformity. A number of people of Mexican descent have eschewed virtually all identity with their cultural past,
no longer speak Spanish, and possibly they have changed their name
and anglicized it. Most, if not all, of these people can be said to
have been acculturated, which, generally, is the process by which
people exchange one set of problems for another.

Stabilized Differences. Since 1921 there have been well over
1,000,000 immigrants from Mexico. In various communities they

have found pockets of people who have sustained the basic Mexican way of life, along with its multiple histories and philosophies. These pockets vary somewhat as one travels from Brownsville, Texas, to El Paso, to Albuquerque, New Mexico to Tucson, Arizona and through California and over to Colorado. Throughout this area one still hears the respect titles of Don and Doña, the formal Usted, as well as a variety of dialects of the Spanish language. This population comprises the heart of the sociedades mutualistas, the fiestas patrias, the music, food, and the other by-products of culture mentioned elsewhere in this paper.

Realigned Pluralism. It has been the experience of many immigrant groups to take on the general ways of the surrounding society, only to discover that despite their efforts they are still excluded from the main currents for one reason or another. Such has also happened to Mexican-Americans. As a result, those who have participated in such behavior often tend to establish ethnically oriented and parallel activities and institutions, principally organizational, such as ball clubs, gangs, etc. In addition, other organizational activities include scholarship oriented organizations, those that are charity oriented, commuuity service oriented, as well as political organizations. Within this sphere one also finds the common phenomenon of the "third generation return." That is, quite often members of the third generation return to identify themselves with their own ethnic group after having undergone the process of "assimilation."

Bi-Culturalism. Despite the merciless educational pressures to stamp out bi-culturalism and bi-lingualism among Mexican-Americans in schools and colleges, it still persists in many varied and developing forms. It exists, for example, all along the border areas among those entrepreneurs who operate equally well on both sides of the international border. It also exists among the untold number of Mexican-Americans who are interpreters, either on a professional or voluntary basis. There are many others who can deal with a bi-cultural universe, such as owners of Mexican restaurants, bookstores, gift shops, musicians and the like.

More recently a new phenomenon has begun to appear in increasing numbers. Specifically, more and more Mexican-American students are going to college. Many of them come from impoverished homes where reading resources were unnecessarily limited. Some of these students, attending college, gravitate toward Spanish or Latin-American majors. As a consequence, they begin to read Juán Rulfo, Martín Luis Guzmán, Gabriela Mistral, Pablo Neruda,

Gabriel García Márquez, and they hear the classical music of Chavez, Villalobos, Revueltas; or they see the art of Tamayo, Cuevas, Esteban Villa, Salvador Roberto Torres, Rene Yañez. As a consequence, such students eschew not their cultural past but rather reintegrate into it at the professional and intellectual level and they are well on their way toward bi-culturalism at another dimension.

The recent Mexican-American study programs in colleges and universities are certain to enhance and accelerate this process, especially if they adhere to the bi-lingual base. Therefore, in the near future it will become more and more possible for Mexican-American students to avoid the assimilative fallacies and pitfalls of the past and join in the truly exciting and challenging universe of bi-culturalism. In this way, not only will they participate in significant innovations in higher education, but they will also take a big step toward realizing one of the promises contained in the Treaty of Guadalupe Hidalgo.

— Many Mexican-Americans —

Yo. señor, no soy malo, aunque no me faltarían motivos para serlo. Los mismos cueros tenemos todos los mortales al nacer y sin embargo, cuando vamos creciendo, el destino se complace en variarnos como si fuésemos de cera y destinarnos por sendas diferentes al mismo fin: la muerte. Hay hombres a quienes se les ordena marchar por el camino de las flores, y hombres a quienes se les manda tirar por el camino de los cardos y de las chumberas. Aquéllos gozan de un mirar sereno y al aroma de su felicidad sonríen con la cara inocente; estos otros sufren del sol violento de la llanura y arrugan el ceño como las alimañas por defenderse. Hay mucha diferencia entre adornarse las carnes con arrebol y colonia, y hacerlo con tatuajes que después nadie ha de borrar ya . . .[19]

Indianist philosophy, Confrontationist, Cultural Nationalism based on Mestizaje with trends toward Humanistic Universalism, Behavioral Relativism, and Existentialism. Assimilation, Mexicanism, Realigned Pluralism, and Bi-Culturalism. Cholos, Pochos, Pachucos, Chicanos, Mexicanos, Hispanos, Spanish-surnamed people, Mexican-Americans. Many labels. Because this is such a complex population, it is difficult to give one label to them all. And probably the first to resist such an effort would be these people themselves, for such a monolithic treatment would violate the very pluralistic foundations upon which their historical philosophies have been based.

There is another dimension to this complexity, one involving the family. Traditionally, in the United States, the Mexican family has been dealt with as if it were monolithic, authoritarian, and uni-dimensional. This is a gross oversimplification based on sheer ignorance. The truth of the matter is that virtually every Mexican-American family takes several forms and includes many types of people, from assimilationist to Chicano, to cultural nationalist, and through all varieties including "un Español" thrown in every now and then for good measure. Mexican-American families have individuals who no longer speak Spanish, who speak only Spanish, or who speak a combination of both. In short, the same complexity that is found in the general Mexican-American population is also found in the family of virtually every Mexican-American.

If the day should ever come when all of these people are willingly subsumed under one label or banner, when they align themselves only under one philosophy, on that day, finally, they will have become totally and irrevocably Americanized. On that day, their historical alternatives and freedoms in personal choice of life-styles, and their diversity, will have been permanently entombed in the histories of the past.

Berkeley, Califa

NOTES

1. Galarza, Ernesto. 1964. *Merchants of Labor*, McNally & Loftin, Charlotte, Santa Barbara, page 28.
2. Villareal, José Antonio. 1959. *Pocho*, Doubleday & Co., Garden City, New York, page 29.
3. Classical anarchism as used here refers to the original anarchist movement promoting the decentralization of power, the opposition of dictatorships in any form, co-operative movements, and not the "mad bomb plot and madman" stereotype of later years.
4. Vasconcelos, José and Manuel Gamio. 1926. *Aspects of Mexican Civilization*, University of Chicago Press, pages 51-52.
5. Vasconcelos, José. 1926. see above, pages 90-102.
6. Vasconcelos, José. 1926. see above, page 92.

7. Paz, Octavio. 1961. *The Labyrinth of Solitude,* Grove Press, Inc., New York, page 136.

8. Paz, Octavio. 1961. see above, page 140.

9. Paz, Octavio. 1961. see above, page 141.

10. Vasconcelos, José. 1926. see above, page 90.

11. Paz, Octavio. 1961. see above, page 144.

12. Gonzales, Rodolfo. 1967. *I Am Joaquin,* Denver, Colorado.

13. Gonzales, Rodolfo. 1967. see above, page 15.

14. Alurista. 1968. "The Poetry of Alurista," *El Grito,* Quinto Sol Publications, Berkeley, California, page 11.

15. Lopez, Enrique Hank. 1967. "Back to Bachimba," *Horizon,* Winter, Vol. IX, No. 1, page 81.

16. Plaza, Antonio. (Book of Poetry, published in Mexico, handed down for decades and publisher page gone. Courtesy of Mr. Rudy Espinosa, San Francisco, California, whose grandfather used to read from this book after dinner each evening.)

17. Rulfo, Juan. 1968. *Pedro Páramo,* Fondo de Cultura Económica, México, D.F., (Novena edición), pagina 7.

18. Olivas, Richard. 1968. *Bronze,* Chicano Newspaper, page 8. (Señor Olivas is a student at San Jose State College.)

19. Cela, Camilo José. 1961. *La Familia de Pascual Duarte,* Appleton-Century-Crofts, Inc., page 11.

Teresa Urrea, "La Santa Teresa de Cabora," was not a revolutionary leader nor a conspirator. All she did was to devote her life to the healing of people. Her part in the history of Aztlán should be known, and that is our goal in writing the following account.

TERESA URREA
HER LIFE, AS IT AFFECTED
THE MEXICAN-U.S. FRONTIER

Richard and Gloria L. Rodriguez

EL ALBA

Díaz

The mid-1870's marked the beginning of a new era for México, the beginning of the regime of General José De La Cruz Porfirio Díaz. The populace believed that Don Porfirio would lead the nation out of troubled times, and into a more sedate and progressive future. However, in 1877, under Lerdo de Tejada, a rebellion began in northern México. The northern beginnings were led by Coronel Pedro Valdez and General Mariano Escobedo.[1] The following year, in Jalapa, Lorenzo Hernández and his followers joined in the rebellion against Díaz. Subsequently, Javier Espino and his men rebelled in the town of Tlapacoyán. In 1879 the rebellion continued, and on June 2, in Tepozotlán, Lieutenant Miguel Negrete, son of the hero of the Cinco de Mayo, joined the revolt against the government. The Lieutenant's father, General Miguel Negrete, labelled his son's movement subversive. Nevertheless, the movement continued to spread to other regions within the states of Veracruz and Puebla.

For a time, the Díaz government believed that the revolt had been crushed by General Luis Mier y Terán in Veracruz, since the plot had been discovered. Mier captured most of the conspirators, but many others managed to escape. Those who had been captured were executed on the 25th of June, 1879. These executions inspired other revolts in Sinaloa. One such revolt was led by General Jesús Ramírez Terrón, followed by still another in the Sierra Madre led by Heraclio Bernal. Two other uprisings were put down by the government; one in 1886 in Zacatecas led by General Trinidad García de la Cadena, and the other in 1890 on the border led by General Francisco Ruiz Sandoval. Nevertheless, despite the setbacks, the rebellions continued. In one way or another, these historical events, and those that followed, touched the life of Teresa Urrea.

Don Tomás

In Ocoroni, Sinaloa, México, on the 15th of October of 1872 or 1873 (our sources are not in agreement), Teresa was born of Cayetana Chávez, a poor Yaqui Indian woman, and Don Tomás Urrea, a Mexican patrón of the ranch at which Cayetana was living. The parents were not married.

> Her mother was only fourteen when she gave birth to Teresa. Her father had a total of eighteen children and her mother had four, but not one of them was a full brother or sister of Teresa's. Teresa and her mother lived in the dirt floor shack of Cayetana's sister.[2]

Don Tomás Urrea was a well-to-do rancher, active in the political affairs of México, and who considered himself a liberal. In 1876 he supported Sebastián Lerdo de Tejada, also a liberal, who was running for reelection as President of México against the conservative, autocratic, General Porfirio Díaz. The election never took place. Díaz executed a military coup; declared himself "elected," and seized power. Lerdo fled into exile. Thereupon Díaz began to liquidate the opposition, that is, the supporters of Lerdo. Don Tomás then realized that he must either support Díaz or leave the state of Sinaloa.

By now Don Tomás had married his first cousin, Doña Loreto Esceberri. Their uncle, Miguel Urrea, who owned silver mines in Alamos, Sonora and Chinipas, Chihuahua, as well as several cattle ranches in Sonora, gave them one of his ranches called Cabora as a wedding present. Don Tomás decided to leave Sinaloa and move to the ranch of Cabora in Sonora. First he went to Alamos and conferred with his Uncle Miguel who encouraged him to make the change, in addition offering to give him and Doña Loreto a large house in Alamos and to sell them at a low price two other ranches adjoining Cabora. The latter were the ranches of Aquihuiquichi and Santa María. The three ranches were situated about halfway between Alamos and the present city of Obregón.

Rancho Cabora

The arrangements to move completed, in 1880 Don Tomás returned to Sinaloa to bring his family and retainers to the new location. The result was an exodus of vaqueros, field workers, and domestic servants, herds and flocks, bullcarts, horses, mules and donkeys. Teresa and her

mother went along with the family of Cayetana's sister. There is no evidence that Doña Loreto knew of the identity of Teresa at this time.

Don Tomás left Doña Loreto and her children and attendants in a large house called "La Capilla," at the edge of Alamos. With his workmen and herds, he then moved on to the ranch of Santa María, which was nearest to Alamos. The ranch at Cabora was in need of repair due to damage done by Yaqui Indians two or three years earlier. Don Tomás used Santa María as a base while he made improvements at Cabora. When the improvements at Cabora were finished and several hundred acres of irrigated farm land had been put to cultivation, Don Tomás installed a beautiful teenage girl, Gabriela Cantúa, as mistress of Cabora. She later became his common-law wife. Doña Loreto and her troupe continued to live at La Capilla in Alamos. During these years, from 1880 to 1888, it is not certain where Teresa and her mother lived. It could have been at Alamos, at Santa María, or at Aquihuiquichi.[3] However, Teresa has been reported as saying, "When I was sixteen my father sent for me to come to his home. I went to his hacienda at Cabora."[4]

At that time the condition of the Indians was one of rampant poverty, with the government doing nothing to alleviate the problem. Instead, the Díaz regime sent engineers who built bridges and irrigation ditches so that large land owners could have water for their crops.

La Santa

Don Tomás had in his employ an old Indian servant named María Sonora. Research reveals varying accounts concerning the role María played in influencing Teresa Urrea's life. One such account recorded María as a practicing curandera and that Teresa became her understudy, learning thereby the names of over one-hundred herbs and what they might cure.[5] Other accounts relate that María taught Teresa to read, and that she suffered from a paralysis which Teresa cured "by rubbing her gently with her hands."[6]

Teresa's healing power was a result of a cataleptic state she experienced during her first few months at Cabora. It lasted three months and eighteen days. During the first fourteen days in the trance, Teresa's heartbeat became fainter and fainter until it seemed to cease altogether. Believing her dead, her family began preparations for her burial. An all night wake was held and late that night, as the women knelt around her saying their prayers and fingering their rosaries, Teresa revived, raised herself up, and inquired as to what was going on. For the three months following that occurence Teresa was in a state of abstraction. It is reported that Teresa said, "For three months and eighteen days, I was in a trance. I know nothing of what I did during that time. They told

me, those who saw, that I could move about but they had to feed me;
that I talked strange things about God and religion, that people came to
me from all (over) the country, and if they were sick or crippled, I put
my hands on them and they got well. Of this I remember nothing, but
when I came to myself I saw they were well."[7]

The news of the girl of Cabora who could cure all illnesses spread
rapidly and soon the roads leading to Cabora were filled with the sick
and crippled. Her curing power continued, and the crowds grew to
enormous proportions. A reporter from a newspaper in Las Cruces,
New Mexico, reported the number of people on the day he was there at
five-thousand.

With the ever-increasing numbers of people coming to see Santa
Teresa, as her followers now called her, the problem of housing and
feeding them, as most of them were the poor and the downtrodden,
became apparent to Don Tomás. At first he was not a believer in
Teresa's power, but he could not influence her to turn her patients
away. Therefore he resigned himself to digging more wells and opening
a commissary that sold food to those who could pay and giving food to
those who could not. He also gave Teresa a house of her own in which
she could receive her patients without having to bring them into his
own home. The majority of Santa Teresa's followers were the poor, and
predominant among them were Indians, especially the Yaquis and
Mayos of Sonora, the Gusaves of Sinaloa, and the Tarahumaras from
Chihuahua. It is interesting that such a vast number of people could
actually visit one person, see that person as a healer and a saint, and still
return home believers. One such group of believers were the Tarahumara Indians from the village of Tomochi.

MEDIODIA

Tomochi

In the year 1891 the Governor of Chihuahua, Lauro Carrillo, decided to travel through his large state. While visiting Tomochi, a small
village in the sierra of Chihuahua, he discovered a beautiful portrait of
the Virgen de Guadalupe. Upon his return to the capitol he ordered the
jefe político of Tomochi to take the painting and submit it to the State.
The Indians of Tomochi protested with such vigor that the Governor
felt obligated to return the painting.

Governor Carrillo never forgave the people of Tomochi for this
"discourtesy." Thereupon, Joaquín Chávez, a powerful regional political chief, took advantage of the Governor's antipathy toward the Tarahumaras of Tomochi. Chávez conspired with his brother Juan Ignacio
and their brother-in-law, Reyes Domínguez, to rid the town of

Tarahumaras. These three conspirators operated the British-owned mines of Pinos Altos and Ocampo of the Rayón District. In addition, it was rumored that Díaz himself had his eye on Tomochi because of its pine and fir tree covered mountains. Similarly, José Ives Limantour, the up-and-coming Secretary of the Treasury, exchanged valueless land in Baja California and some offshore islands for 170,000 hectares of this beautiful mountain forest area.[9] Tomochi was valuable. But it was valuable only to the people who had the money to develop it. The Tarahumaras had no money, nor knowledge of the economic value of the forest that surrounded their villages.

The only people who resisted the Chávez brothers, Joaquín and Juan Ignacio, and their brother-in-law Reyes Domínguez, were Cruz and Manuel Chávez. Cruz was known to have punished Reyes for taking advantage of some impoverished Indians. Having worked for such little pay for Reyes, the Indians now began to work at other mines or sawmills. There they discovered that they could earn more money. Thus, more and more Indians left the Pinos Altos mine.

False messages of uprisings went out from Joaquín, Juan, and Reyes. Joaquín Chávez, through his influence with the jefe político of Ciudad Guerrero, had one such message transmitted to Governor Carrillo. The Governor, in turn, forwarded the message to General Porfirio Díaz. The government responded by drafting all the young men who refused to work at the Pinos Altos mine.

After the conscription of the young men, Joaquín would no longer enter the village of Tomochi. The Indians had learned that it was he who had sent the fabricated message to the Governor, and that he was thus principally responsible for the legal kidnapping of their young men. The power that Joaquín had in the government now became evident. He openly laid seige on the house of Jorge Ortiz, ostensibly for no other reason than to take the land for himself.

Cruz and Manuel Chávez then decided that they could no longer stand aside while such injustices were committed on their people. Some nights after the takeover of the Ortiz house, the Tarahumaras met at the house of José Dolores Rodríguez. Thirty-three men attended and they decided to organize militarily. Cruz was elected Captain and Manuel was to be his second in command.

Some of the residents of Tomochi had visited Teresa, and perhaps some of these thirty-three men had seen her. But the military organization itself was neither inspired nor directed by Teresa Urrea. Nonetheless, she had probably spoken of the injustices by the government while the Church remained passive.

On December 5, 1891, formal accusations were brought on the people of Tomochi. A telegram from the jefe político of Ciudad de Guerrero to Carrillo, the Governor of Sonora, read,

> Just this moment I have been notified by Captain Joaquín Chávez, that there are forty armed rebels in Tomochi, that will not recognize authority. I am recruiting an army to march on said village and require the assistance of Captain Chávez, and a detachment from the 110 Battalion that is stationed here.[10]

On the same day, the Governor received another telegram from Captain Chávez (he had the rank of Captain in the National Guard). It read,

> Since the 25th of November about forty armed men had been encountered in Tomochi, according to information from the village President, with the purpose of becoming independent from the government. Today the jefe político wants me to accompany him with an escort to Tomochi. I am presently in command of three companies that I cannot leave; but if you order it, I will leave with the jefe político.[11]

On the 25th of November of 1891 the house of Jorge Ortiz had been seized by Captain Chávez. The meeting at Rodríguez' house with the Chávez and their followers had not taken place until the 30th of November. Joaquín Chávez, in his telegram, had informed the Governor that since the 25th of November forty armed men were to be found in Tomochi. The governor did not trouble himself to investigate these accusations. He accepted them without question. His reply to the jefe político was,

> You are ordered to go to Tomochi with the detachments from the 110 Battalion and to help the people of said village in whatever measures are adequate in the restoration of tranquility.[12]

The destruction of the small village of about three-hundred people was in progress. The Tomochis met the first detachment of federal troops at the outskirts of the village. Due to a shortage of ammunition, the Tarahumaras had to fall back. They retreated to the mountains and the federal troops did not pursue them. Instead, the soldiers, led by Joaquín Chávez, took over the village of Tomochi. Other detachments were sent for to join in the search for the rebellious Tarahumaras.

While the new detachment searched for the rebels, Don Silviano González along with Joaquín and Juan Ignacio Chávez, and Reyes Domínguez took over Tomochi. Martial law was declared. The people who lived on the best lands mysteriously disappeared at night and were never heard from again. Because of the reign of terror in the town, the majority of the villagers abandoned their homes.

The defeated Tarahumaras, led by Cruz and Manuel, at this juncture decided to go to Sonora and see Teresa Urrea. The trip from the sierras of Chihuahua to Cabora took many days. After crossing into the State of Sonora, they went directly to the Urrea rancho at Cabora. They did not find Teresa there so they decided to wait. When several days had elapsed with no success in their mission, they decided to return to their sierra. They left their younger brother, Jesús José Chávez, behind. He had been suffering from a high fever for several days. The older brothers left Cabora, knowing that the federales of Sonora had been notified of the uprising in Tomochi and that it would be dangerous to remain there any longer.

The National Guard of Sonora had been alerted about the Tarahumaras. They realized that the Tarahumaras were somewhere in the state, but they did not suspect any connection between the rebels' presence and Teresita. Somewhat later, a detachment of federal soldiers came upon a group of Indians who had stopped briefly to drink water at the small river of el Alamo de Palomares which ran through the Rancho del Alamo. This ranch was owned by Don Miguel Urrea, the uncle of Don Tomás Urrea. The military detachment was led by Captain Emilio Enríquez who thereupon laid seige upon the group of Indians. A short battle ensued. Captain Enríquez and some officers and men lost their lives. This event led the Tomochis to decide that it would be too dangerous to return to their village. They decided to remain in the mountains, only coming down to steal cattle and arms from the outlying ranchos. According to Francisco P. Troncoso's *Las Guerras Con Las Tribus Yaqui y Mayo Del Estado De Sonora,* the soldiers who patroled the sierras at that time reported considerable organized Indian activity in the vicinity. At the same time, the Yaquis were also in arms against the government. The Yaquis were led by Juan Maldonado, known as Tetabiate.

It was not until August of 1892 that the Tarahumaras returned to Chihuahua. 1892 was a bloody year for the State of Sonora. While the Yaquis continued their guerrilla attacks against federal troops, the Mayo Indians of Navajoa took over that town to the cry of, "VIVA LA SANTA DE CABORA." Almost immediately this uprising was put down by Lieutenant Coronel Severiano Talamante. Although the Mayos had succeeded in killing the jefe político and other prominent citizens, they themselves were almost annihilated by Talamante and reinforcements.[13]

Upon their return to Tomochi, the Tarahumaras slipped into the village unnoticed and found refuge in the homes of sympathizers. There they learned of what had happened during their absence. Now the small group of Indians increased from thirty-five to sixty men. Also supporting them were people in the outlying villages.

The jefe político of Ciudad de Guerrero learned of the Indians' return, and he informed the governor. Indecisive, the governor wired General Díaz. Subsequently General Díaz personally supervised the attack on Tomochi from México City. Two-hundred men were sent from Ciudad de Guerrero. The Tomochis waited for the soldiers in the valley just outside of their village. The third battle ensued, and the Tarahumaras were victorious. The commander of the federal forces was Lieutenant Coronel José María Ramírez who was taken prisoner. In addition, the Tomochis gained considerable booty from their victory. When the report of this defeat reached the capitol, General Porfirio Díaz is said to have become furious. He sent more reinforcements from Chihuahua and Sonora to deal with the situation.[14]

The last battle at Tomochi was the most furious. The first wave of attacking soldiers numbered about six-hundred, under the command of General José María Rangel. The men of Tomochi numbered about one-hundred, counting some boys of about fourteen. The battle began on October 29, 1892 around 8 o'clock in the morning, and the first encounter lasted two hours. The Tomochis would attack and fall back repeatedly throughout the day of the 20th. On the night of the 20th they picked up their wounded, the arms and munitions of the dead, and fell back once again. On the 21st nothing occurred since General Rangel had suffered heavy casualties and was awaiting reinforcements. On the 22nd artillery arrived. But the cannon was too light, and could not reach the buildings of the village where the people had taken refuge. The battle lasted two days, but its destruction would last forever. The government had lost more than seven-hundred men, dead and wounded. The village was leveled and burned. Only a few walls were left standing. Tomochi had been destroyed.

Tomasachi

On the 4th of April of 1893 two brothers named Celso and Simón Anaya led another village, Tomasachi, in rebellion against the Díaz government. It was said that the brothers Anaya had been sent to Tomasachi by Cruz Chávez to avenge the destruction of the village of Tomochi. The brothers brought with them what was now the battlecry: VIVA EL GRAN PODER DE DIOS—VIVA LA SANTA DE CABORA. The brothers enlisted four-hundred Tomasachios to lay siege to Ciudad de Guerrero. The 90th Battalion was sent to stop them, and the Battle of Casa Blanca was fought. The 90th suffered heavy losses and reinforcements had to be summoned. The newspapers of the day reported the rebels to number five-thousand, and that three-thousand of these were Yaqui and Mayo Indians. This account appears to be a gross exaggeration. Nevertheless, the rebels captured Ciudad de Guerrero on or about the 20th of April. Once again reinforcements were ordered to

Chihuahua from Sonora, and in May of 1893 the Tomasachios abandoned Ciudad de Guerrero and returned to their village.

Exile

No evidence has ever been uncovered to the effect that either Teresa
or Don Tomás inspired these rebellions, even though delegations from
the Tarahumaras, Mayos, and Yaquis visited and sought her approval.
To their inquiries, Teresa would only answer, "God intended for you to
have the lands, or He would not have given them to you."[16] Thus, the
Mexican government concluded that Teresa was a threat and decided to
take measures to "subdue" the young lady.

Even before the Tomasachio capture of Ciudad de Guerrero, therefore, on May 19, 1892, General Abraham Bandala arrived at Rancho
Cabora, ordered Don Tomás and Teresa arrested, and had them sent to
Cocorit, Sonora. The general had them detained because he had dis-
covered that the Rancho de Cabora was the nucleus of all the Indian
uprisings. He ascertained that the Urreas could no longer remain in the
area. From Cocorit he ordered the Urreas transferred to Guaymas,
along with whatever evidence he had that led to their arrest. But the
Governor of Sonora did not know what to do with Don Tomás and
Teresa, so he wired Porfirio Díaz who in turn ordered them deported.
Teresa and her father crossed the border into the United States at
Nogales, Arizona, in the year 1892[18] where they were provided with a
small furnished house by the citizens of Nogales.[19] When Gabriela, the
common-law wife of Don Tomás, and her children along with a company of aides joined the two in Arizona it became necessary to move to
a more spacious location. They moved to El Bosque, located several
miles north of Nogales.

> This place became the mecca for pilgrims seeking cures from
> as far away as Sinaloa. Not only the sick and crippled came, but
> political refugees as well. Nogales and El Bosque became the
> rendezvous for revolutionaries plotting the overthrow of the
> Díaz government. Their main recruiting source was from among
> the throngs of people streaming out of México to see Teresita.
> The agitators were collecting arms and ammunition. Don Tomás
> realized the revolutionists were anxious to exploit Teresita's in-
> fluence over the Indians and the Mexican peons.[20]

The Urrea family stayed at El Bosque for three years until an invita-
tion for them to move was offered by the people of Solomonville in
eastern Arizona. Realizing the necessity to move further away from the
border, and the conspiracies initiating there, Don Tomás made the decision to move. Thereupon the town of Solomonville sent a caravan of

twenty-five wagons to move the household. However, some eight months later, in June, 1896, the family moved again, this time to El Paso, Texas. The reason for this move is not clear, but of primary influence was a man named Lauro Aguirre, a Mexican newspaperman. Also in exile from México, due to his publication of anti-Díaz literature, by 1896 Aguirre had established three newspapers in the United States: *El Independiente*[21] and *El Progresista*[22] published in El Paso, and *El Independiente* published in Nogales.[23] The nature of his influence on Don Tomás to move to El Paso is not known, but it is reasonable to assume that it could not have been to assist in starting a revolution since that precisely was the principal reason that caused Don Tomás to move his family from Nogales.

Nogales

It had been hardly more than a month since Teresa had settled in El Paso when the Mexican customs house at Nogales, Sonora, was attacked by "a band of Santa Teresa fanatics." On the morning of Wednesday, August 12, 1896, at approximately 4:00 a.m., a group of sixty or seventy Indians, said to be Yaqui and Tomochi (Tarahumaras), rode in from the American side of the border armed with a variety of weapons; rifles, pistols, knives, bows and arrows. The citizens from both sides of the border (only a narrow street separates Nogales, México from Nogales, Arizona) were awakened by the shots and yells of VIVA LA SANTA DE CABORA. "Many on the American side, securing arms of the local Arizona National Guard company, crossed over the line and joined their Mexican neighbors in expelling their Yaqui assailants."[24] The battle lasted three hours, resulting in the death of ten Indians, one prisoner taken, four Mexican guards killed and two wounded.[25] No casualties among the Americans were reported. The attacking Indians succeeded in securing arms and ammunition from the customs house, but they failed to obtain $20,000 stored inside. Then they retreated across the border to Arizona, heading toward Tubac. Letters and newspaper articles found on the dead Indians left behind revealed that the band had organized a week earlier at Huevavi, on the American side, eight miles north of Nogales. The following account was printed in the *Arizona Daily Star.*

> The indians seem to be crazy on account of the fanatical worship of Santa Teresa de Cabora. On the body of a leader was found a picture of the saint and a half dozen copies of 'El Independent'; published at Nogales by Lauro Aguirre, who undoubtedly is the cause of inciting the rebellion; also several letters containing plans for an attack on the night of August 11th.[27]

The *New York Times* also showed an interest in these events.

> Copies of 'The Independence', Lauro Aguirre's paper pub-
> lished at El Paso, Texas, were found on the dead Yaquis. The
> papers were dated June 8 and July 25, 1896, and were special
> editions, containing nothing but revolutionary matter against the
> Mexican government. Some people think Lauro Aguirre was with
> the raiders, but no one seems to have recognized him.[28]

Within ten hours following the attack at Nogales a train from Magdalena brought the famed Colonel Emilio Kosterlitzky and his gen-
darmería to protect the Mexican side of Nogales. Shortly thereafter two
companies of U.S. infantry were sent by rail to Nogales, Arizona, under
the command of Colonel John Back of Fort Huachuca, Arizona. They
were to protect the American citizens from further attacks and to assist
the Mexican army in tracking down the insurrectionists.

On the Sonora side of the line there are four prisoners in jail.
One of them, named Francisco Vásquez, has outlined a history
of the movement and the intentions of the leaders. He says
Arvizu came to Greaterville, where Vásquez was at work, on the
9th, and enlisted nineteen Yaquis there. They moved to Huevavi
on the eleventh, and were there joined by twenty-five others.
Before daylight of the twelfth they attacked the custom house
and were successful. But for Lieutenant Piper's (of the Arizona
National Guard) prompt action in turning his guns loose upon
them they would have carried out the next steps in the pro-
gramme—get the money out of the vaults of the custom house,
loot the town, and move on Magdalena. The plan was to reach
Magdalena on the sixteenth. At that place they were to be joined
by a force from the Yaqui river. Col. Kosterlitzky is officially
informed that a band of armed Yaquis was seen near Magdalena
on the fourteenth. With failure on the attack on Nogales they
retired. Magdalena captured and looted the plan was then to
move on Hermosillo, gathering arms and adherents on route, and
appear at the Sonora capital with more than 1,000 armed men.
The rest of the plan involved a movement to the Yaqui river
from Hermosillo, after the capture of that place, junction with
the fighting Yaquis there, and an expulsion of all Mexicans—
whether soldiers or citizens—from that valley, with a complete
overturning of the present constituted authority in the State of
Sonora. How far they could have carried that plan is a matter of
conjecture only.[29]

Mrs. Carrillo, of this city, has received a letter from a son who is in Agua Cerca, Sonora, in which he relates an experience which he and two companions had recently with a band of Santa Teresa fanatics.

He and his companions were quietly in the pursuit of their avocations when a crowd of the worshippers came up, seized and bound them and threatened them with death. When the three discovered the character of their assailants they set up a lusty shout of "Viva Santa Teresa de Cabora" and were at once released. The fanatics relieved them of guns and other articles of which they were in need and went on their way rejoicing.[30]

Nogales, Arizona, August 18, 1896—Word has been received here that the Yaquis, numbering about 1,000 employed in placer mining in the Altar District of Sonora, Cirnega, eighty miles southwest of Nogales, have risen in sympathy with the recent revolutionary movement in this place.[31]

Nogales, Arizona, August 19, 1896—The Indian José Salcedo, who was brought in Sunday, is on the list of the original nineteen rebels and has been identified as one of those engaged in the fight on the morning of the 12th. All the prisoners were given a hearing yesterday before United States Court Commissioner Taylor and pleaded not guilty. Much speculation as to whether they can be turned over to the Mexican Government exists. Once across the line, short work would be made of all of them. It is reported here that the Mexican Government has already made a requisition on the United States for Lauro Aguirre and Teresa de Cabora, and her father, who is with her at El Paso.

The indian prisoners say her father is more to blame than she, as the girl does about as he wants her to. Aguirre is the worst, they say, as he has complete control over Teresa's father.

Aguirre is a highly educated man in his language, but is said to be dissipated. It is estimated by the Mexican officials here that he and Santa Teresa, by their influence, have caused the death of more than 1,000 people in the last six or seven years.

None of the Yaquis who quit work on the railway and who were around town yesterday before the attack on Nogales, have returned to work or applied for their pay.[32]

Despite these events, responsibility for the attack on Nogales was not directly ascribed to Teresa. For example, in the U.S. Secretary of War Report for 1896, mention of her was as follows: "Those engaged in the attack on the Mexican customhouse were undoubtedly followers of the so-called St. Teresa, styled from her birthplace Santa Teresa de

Caborda (*sic*). Her teachings, however, do not appear to be of a political or revolutionary character."

Mrs. Marguerite Peck, wife of the editor of the Nogales Border Vidette, recalled an article of August 14, 1896 which stated, "The insurrection, for it is nothing less, is undoubtedly the result of the revolutionary articles printed in El Independiente, published in El Paso, by Lauro Aguirre."[33]

Apparently Lauro Aguirre was very much sought after by the Mexican government, for ten years later an article appeared in the Arizona Daily Citizen regarding this interest:

> Lauro Aguirre, editor of "La Reforma Social" of El Paso, is again a free man. For 38 days he was kept in jail without a hearing while Federal Officials connected with the Immigration Department hunted high and low for evidence against him. They failed to find a single thing against him and he was released today.[34]

Teresa herself refused publicly to have any part in the affairs of México. On September 11, 1896, she issued a statement printed in the El Paso Herald. This open letter is of significance even today in that it is one of only three documents in existence that contain direct quotations by her. She wrote as follows,

> The press generally in these days has occupied itself with my humble person in terms unfavorable in the highest degree, since in a fashion most unjust—the fashion in the Republic of México; they refer to me as participating in political matters; they connect me to the events that have happened in Nogales, Sonora, Coyame and Presidio del Norte, Chihuahua, where people have risen in arms against the government of Sr. General Don Porfirio Díaz.
>
> I am not one who encourages such uprisings, nor one who in any way mixes up with them and I protest once, and as many times as may be necessary, against the imputations of my enemies.
>
> In the month of October of the past year, I went out from a point called El Bosque, sixteen miles from Nogales, Arizona, where I remained with my parents three years and three months, giving my attention exclusively to thousands of sick people who were constantly coming to that place from all over the world in search of my services. I arrived at Solomonville the last of October of the same year, and remained there seven months, or until June of the present year when I came to this city; that is to say,

three months have I resided here, and all this time have I given to my numerous patients, to whom, notwithstanding that I gave them all my attentions, I was unable to fully attend; the smallest number I have cared for in one day being one hundred and eighty, although generally the number was placed at two hundred.

I should note that the local authorities of each place where I have resided, in view of my entirely peaceful and orderly conduct, have been pleased to issue me credentials of very satisfactory character which may be seen by persons in this community having occasion to look at them. My neighbors generally in this hospitable town also can testify to my good conduct. Very honorable persons in this community have thought it worthwhile to offer me their kindly offices in defending me; and as for me, my conscience is at rest in that I have never committed any misdeed. I extend to those kind people my grateful acknowledgements.

I have noticed with much pain that the persons who have taken up arms in Mexican territory have invoked my name in aid of the schemes they are carrying through. But I repeat I am not one who authorizes or at the same time interferes with these proceedings. Decidedly I am a victim since in a most unjust way have I been expatriated from my country since May 19, 1892. It is now over four years, and this expatriation was announced to my father and myself through General Abraham Bandals and José Tiburcio Otero, as being ordered by the president of the republic, Don Porfirio Díaz, by telegraph. Without doubt the haste with which he acted was inspired of my enemies; but I ask, would it not have been more just in this case, if General Díaz, instead of ordering me expelled, has consented to order a judicial investigation before the authorities of my place of residence that the tribunal might judge whether or not I was guilty of wrong doing? Nothing was done beyond expelling me, but this was in such a way that I and my family were forced to hunt in a foreign country the guarantees which our own country denied us. Oh, that heaven may pardon this ingratitude of which I have been made the victim by the president of the Republic of México, with whom I condole with all my heart for being misled.

In conclusion I will state that if in the future more uprisings follow in the Republic of México, and as, even now, it has been said by my enemies that I am the kind of a person to start these movements, I will say once more that I am taking no part in them. Am I to blame because my offending compatriots demand of the government justice for me? I think not, and appeal to the judgement of every sensible person.

TERESA URREA
El Paso, Texas
September 8, 1896[35]

LA PUESTA

— Clifton —

With all of the turmoil concerning Teresa, at this time Don Tomás decided to move his family to Clifton, Arizona, a mining town as remote and isolated as he could find without living too distant from his properties in Sonora and Sinaloa. But before they left El Paso, Teresa and Lauro Aguirre wrote and published a book in Spanish titled *Tomochic.*

Clifton was a small copper-mining town, and the lives of the residents was slow-paced and uneventful. Upon arriving at Clifton, Teresa was warmly received by the townspeople and due to the remoteness of the location she found few pressures or demands made upon her. A local physician, Dr. L. A. W. Burtch became interested in her work with the families of the workers, and he visited her home frequently where he observed her methods of treatment. And in some of his own patients whom he had been unable to help he saw improvements. He had no medical answers for the phenomenon, but nevertheless he continued to refer cases to her. A deep friendship developed between this doctor and Teresa. It was through him that other wealthy Americans learned of her, such as the manager of the First National Bank, Charles P. Rosencrans. The bank manager had a daughter whom the doctors had said could not be cured. Thereupon he took the girl to Santa Teresa who soon cured the girl.

In 1899, Teresa and a Yaqui worker from the mines, Guadalupe Rodríguez, became interested in each other. But, "Lupe" was not looked upon favorably by Don Tomás. Nevertheless, against the wishes of her father, on June 22, 1900, Lupe Rodríguez and Teresa Urrea were married. The union lasted but a brief time, for the following morning Lupe armed himself and began acting somewhat violently. He was disarmed by some Mexican workers who were furious about his marriage to their "saint." Lupe was placed in jail and tried. Found insane, he was sent to an asylum.

— El Viaje —

It was after this episode in Teresa's life that Charles Rosencrans persuaded her to go to San Francisco.[36] In that California city Teresa

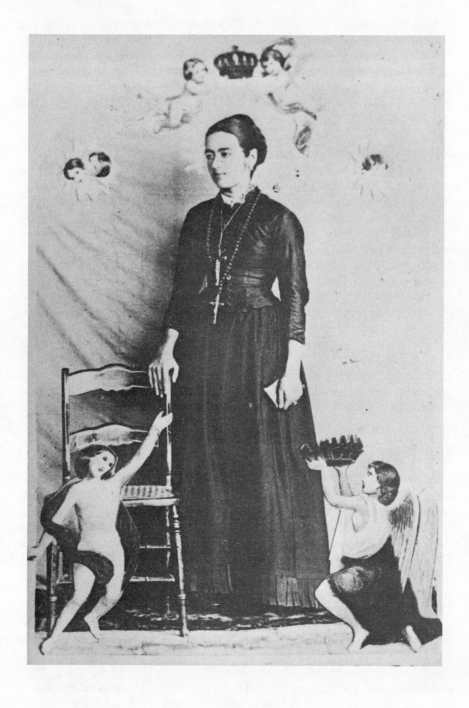

helped the daughter of Mrs. A. C. Fessler of nearby San Jose. The newspapers learned of this occasion and became interested in the story. The *San Francisco Examiner,* the *San Francisco Chronicle,* and the *Call* sent their reporters to interview Teresa.

Somewhat later, some scheming promoters induced Teresa to join them in forming a medical company that would tour the United States on a "Curing Crusade." She was promised the sum of ten-thousand dollars for her services. Teresa agreed on the condition that none of her patients would be charged for her help. It was her understanding that the venture was philanthropic, financed by wealthy people. However, she did not know that a substantial fee would be charged to all clients. After a few months in San Francisco, in January of 1901, the Medical Company moved to St. Louis for several months. While there, Teresa wrote a letter to her friend, Mrs. Juana Van Order, in Solomonville, Arizona, asking her to send one of her children to act as an interpreter. Teresa had met the Van Orders in 1895 when the Urrea family had moved from El Bosque to Solomonville. Juana Van Order sent her second oldest son, John, who was bilingual and four or five years younger than Teresa. Teresa was very pleased with John and soon thereafter she became his wife.

The Medical Company moved on to New York City. While there, news arrived that Don Tomás was seriously ill with typhoid. Teresa, in advanced pregnancy, was unable to return to Clifton. Don Tomás died on September 22, 1902. A few days later Teresa's first child was born in New York City. It was a girl.

— Return to Clifton —

Little is known of what Teresa did in New York. For publicity purposes, the Medical Company entered her in a beauty contest, and she was elected Queen of something-or-other. However, the Company was not a total success in New York, and in December of 1902 left for Los Angeles. In 1904, Teresa finally became totally disillusioned with the Medical Company and employed a lawyer who found justifiable grounds for her to terminate her contract. By this time she was pregnant with her second child. She arrived back in Solomonville in time for the birth of her second daughter, on June 29, 1904, at the home of Juana Van Order.[37]

She then returned once again to Clifton. With such money as she had earned on tour she had a two-story house erected where she hoped to "nurse the sick to health and heal the wounds of the injured."

During December, 1905, the San Francisco River flooded Clifton, overflowing its channel and sweeping away many houses. Teresa was in the cold rain and water for hours, rescuing people and their possessions.

From the *Reminiscences of Ignacio Calvillo* a story is told of this incident: "At one time she was caught in a big flood. The man with her and his mule were doomed. The following night people saw a supernatural light in the mountains and going to it found Santa Teresa lodged in a tree."[38]

She contracted a critical bronchial condition which put her in bed for days. A short while later (eighteen months after her return to Clifton), in January of 1906[39] Teresa died peacefully. Dr. Burtch's records show she died of consumption, but the family and the Mexicans said that she had worn out her spirit in the service of her people.[40]

FOOTNOTES

1. Gill, "Teresa Urrea, La Santa De Cabora," p. 626.
2. Putnam, "Teresa Urrea, The Saint of Cabora," p. 247.
3. Ibid., p. 248.
4. *San Francisco Examiner*, July 27, 1900.
5. Putnam, p. 248.
6. Patton, *History of Clifton*, p. 205. and Ridgway, *Saint or Nurse*, p. 22.
7. Putnam, p. 249.
8. Ibid., p. 250.
9. Lister, *Chihuahua—Storehouse of Storms*, p. 179.
10. Chávez Calderón, *La Defensa de Tomochi*, pp. 16-17.
11. Ibid., p. 17.
12. Ibid.
13. Troncoso, *Las Guerras Con Las Tribus Yaqui Y Mayo Del Estado De Sonora*, p. 196.
14. Lister, p. 185.
15. Gill, p. 642.
16. Putnam, p. 253.
17. Troncoso, p. 196.
18. Berber, *Nociones De Historia De Sonora*, p. 268.
19. Putnam, p. 254.
20. Ibid.
21. *New York Times*, August 14, 1896.
22. Putnam, p. 255.
23. *Arizona Daily Star*, August 12, 1896.
24. Report of the Secretary of War, 1896, *House Documents*, p. 146.
25. Western Union Telegram, August 12, 1896.
26. Report of the Secretary of War, 1896, *House Documents*, p. 146.
27. *Arizona Daily Star*, August 13, 1896.
28. *New York Times*, August 14, 1896.
29. *The Oasis*, August 22, 1896.
30. *Arizona Daily Citizen*, August 18, 1896.
31. *New York Times*, August 19, 1896.
32. *New York Times*, August 20, 1896.
33. Peck, *In The Memory Of A Man*, p. 374.

34. *Arizona Daily Citizen,* December 22, 1906.
35. Putnam, pp. 256-257.
36. Patton, p. 208.
37. Putnam, p. 263.
38. Calvillo, *Reminiscences of Ignacio Calvillo.*
39. Patton, p. 208.
40. Putnam, p. 264.

BIBLIOGRAPHY

Primary Sources:
"Fighting Rebels in Sonora," *The New York Times* (September 12, 1892), p. 5, col. 4.
"No Revolution in Mexico," *The New York Times* (September 19, 1892), p. 4, col. 7.
Long, R. Hughes, "Telegram" to W. W. Rockhill, Assistant Secretary of State, August 12, 1896, from Nogales Microfilm #M-283, Despatches from United States Consuls in Nogales, Sonora, Mexico, 1889-1906, Roll 2.
"Nogales," *The Arizona Daily Citizen* (August 12, 1896), p. 1.
"Insurrection At Nogales," *The Arizona Daily Star* (August 13, 1896), p. 1, col. 3.
"Sixty Indians Attack A Town," *The New York Times* (August 13, 1896), p. 1, col. 2.
"Yaquis On The War Path," *The Riverside Daily Press* (August 13, 1896), p. 2.
Long, R. Hughes, Report To The Department Of State On The Raid Of The Customs House, August 14, 1896, from Nogales Microfilm #M-283, Despatches from United States Consuls in Nogales, Sonora, Mexico, 1889-1906, Roll 2.
"Yaquis Defeat Pursuers," *The New York Times* (August 14, 1896), p. 1, col. 2.
"Two Nations Join In The Hunt," *The New York Times* (August 15, 1896), p. 1, col. 3.
"Yaqui Trail Wiped Out By Rain," *The New York Times* (August 18, 1896), p. 1, col. 2.
"Viva Santa Teresa," *The Arizona Daily Citizen* (August 18, 1896), p. 1.
"Brisk Fight With The Yaquis," *The New York Times* (August 19, 1896), p. 1, col. 2.
"Would Try The Girl Saint," *The New York Times* (August 20, 1896), p. 1., col. 2.
"The Insurrectionists," *The Nogales Oasis* (August 22, 1896), p. 1.
Letter #152 from W. W. Rockhill, Acting Secretary of State, to Matías Romero, Mexican Consul to the United States. U. S. State Department, Microfilm #M-99, Roll 73, Notes to Foreign Legations in the United States from the Department of State, 1834-1906.
Letter #165 from W. W. Rockhill, Acting Secretary of State, to Matías Romero, Mexican Consul to the United States. U. S. State Department, Microfilm #M-99, Roll 73, Notes to Foreign Legations in the United States from the Department of State, 1834-1906.
Letter from Edward Schwartz, Adjutant General, to B. J. Franklin, Governor of Arizona, October 6, 1896, A Report of the Attack of Yaqui and Temochi Indians upon the Customs House at Nogales, Sonora, 1896, The Arizona (Territory) Adjutant General's Office.

House Documents, Volume 2, Number 2, Report of the Secretary of War—1896, Volume 1, 54th Congress, 2nd Session, Document 2, Volume 1, pp. 145-147.

Woodridge, Bradford. "Santa Teresa," *The Overland Monthly* (July-December, 1896), pp. 422-426.

Troncoso, Francisco P. *Las Guerras Con Las Tribus Yaqui Y Mayo Del Estado De Sonora*, México: Tipografía Del Estado Mayor, 1905.

"Sainted Girl of Sonora Recalled," *The Arizona Daily Citizen* (December 22, 1906), p. 1.

Frías, Heriberto. *Tomochi*, México: Librería de La Viuda de Ch. Bouret, 1911.

Calvillo, Ignacio. *Reminiscences of Ignacio Calvillo—1936*, from Arizona Historical Society Library, 1971, Tucson, Arizona.

Ridgway, William R. "Saint or Nurse," *Arizona Days and Ways* (September 27, 1953), pp. 22-23.

Willson, R. G. "Deluded Yaquis Invade Town Under Order of the Witch," *Arizona Days and Ways* (March 10, 1957), pp. 22-23.

Berber, Laureano Calvo. *Nociones De Historia De Sonora*, México: Librería de Manuel Porrua, 1958.

Chávez Calderón, Placido. *La Defensa De Tomochi*, México: Editorial Jus., 1964.

Peck, A. M. *In The Memory Of A Man*, Collected between 1937 and 1966, from the Special Collections Division, University of Arizona, Tucson.

Lister, Florence and Robert. *Chihuahua—Storehouse of Storms*, New Mexico: The University of New Mexico Press, 1966.

Secondary Sources:

McClintock, John. *Arizona—The Youngest State*, Chicago: The S. J. Clark Publishing Company.

Enriquez, Rafael De Zayas. *Porfirio Díaz*, New York: D. Appleton and Company, 1908.

Turner, John K. *Barbarous Mexico*, Chicago, 1910.

Beals, Carleton. *Porfirio Díaz—Dictator of Mexico*, Philadelphia and London: J. B. Lippincot Company, 1932.

Gregg, Robert D. *The Influence of Border Troubles on Relations Between the United States and Mexico*, Baltimore: The John Hopkins Press, 1937.

Patton, James Monroe. *The History of Clifton*, M. A. Thesis, University of Arizona, Tucson, 1945.

Gill, Mario. "Teresa Urrea, La Santa De Cabora," *Historia Mexicana*, Volume VI: July, 1956 - June, 1957, Published by El Colegio de México.

Gill, Mario. *Nuestros Buenos Vecinos*, Mexico City, 1959.

Putnam, Frank Bishop. "Teresa Urrea, The Saint of Cabora," *The Southern California Quarterly*, The Publication of the Historical Society of Southern California, Vol. XLV, Number 3, Anderson, Ritchie and Simon, September 1963.

McWilliams, Carey. *North From Mexico*, New York: Greenwood Press, 1968.

NOTE: Photography courtesy of Arizona Historical Society Library.

LA RAZA INFLUENCE IN JAZZ

Ronald D. Arroyo

During the late 30's, a coterie of La Raza became evident by their mode of dress, talk and non-conformist habits. The emergent phenomena was the pachuco. An integral part of the pachuco scene was jazz. The pachuco, whom Ruben Salazar later elevated to the status of folk-hero, walked the jazz scene digging the sounds of the big bands of Woody Herman, Count Basie, Stan Kenton, Duke Ellington and the others. He dressed in wide brimmed hat, knee length coat with the reet-pleat pants waist high, broad tie, pointed shoes with a high shine. The pachuca who accompanied him wore her hair high on her head, much makeup, heavy lipstick, large round earrings, a suit jacket resembling the pachuco's with padded shoulders, above-the-knee tight skirts, net stockings, and high heels with straps around the ankle. When they went stepping, they dug jazz at the Avalon, the Palladium, the Civic Auditorium, the Paramount. Dancing the swing or the dirty boogie or sitting quietly at Town Hall, they dug the sounds which were ethnic in origin and bicultural in composition. The pachucos did not realize, as they dug the sounds, the deep influences of La Raza on Jazz music.

Jazz in the late 40's began to emerge, from ghettos where it was born and nurtured, to other communities through the media of radio and records. Jazz began to be accepted and enjoyed by a larger population. The big jazz bands brought jazz to the forefront of popular music. A parallel rise in the popularity of Latin bands predicted an inevitable fusion. The bands of Miguelito, Valdes, Desi Arnaz, Noro Morales and others brought the multi-variety of Latin music to popularity. The sophisticated angloized sounds of Vincent Lopez and Xavier Cugat were replaced by the more ethnic beats of Valdes, Arnaz and Morales. Valdes and Arnaz also brought to prominence the conga drum, the primary instrument responsible for the percussive infusion of Raza music to jazz.

As the 40's ended and the 50's began, the pachuco had put away his zoot suit having felt the wrath of prejudice erupt into the violence of the Pachuco War of 1943 with the continuing battles of the late 40's. The bopsters appeared, with young Chicanos and Puerto Ricans getting caught up in an acculturation wave that drowned their ethnicity. In place of the zoot suit, young batos were picking up on one button roll suits, white shirts with Mr. B collars, knit suspenders and matching tie, and Marine Cordovan dyed shoes. Their chicks kept their hair high, but put aside the suits for black sweaters and black skirts sometimes split on the side, a gold or silver cross decorated their breasts, bobby socks and low saddle shoes replaced the high heels. These cool pairs dug jazz now called bop.

The big bands kept swinging but the sidemen began migrating to small groups in small clubs on 51st Street in New York, Rush Street in Chicago, Sunset Boulevard in Los Angeles and the Tenderloin in San Francisco. A tradition began with the small band migration which gave the sidemen of the Latin bands a chance to explore their unique talents within jazz music. The jam session seemed to prove that the African beat of jazz could be complemented by the Latin beat. Jazz critics proclaimed the fusion as unique, but some critics wondered about the easy amalgamation of the two. Jazz had always been regarded as the music of the Blacks. Now some researchers began to look closely at the influence of Creole music to jazz with the implications of Latin Music as a primary source. What these theorists, led by Ernest Borneman, discovered was that jazz was spawned from a mixture of African and Spanish influences in the West Indies and Carribean Islands. The Carribean and West Indies were used by slave traders as stopovers between Africa and the American South. The Blacks who landed in these islands rediscovered a music with a familiarity they could assimilate easily.

As early as the Middle Ages, African music received a strong influence of Arab music. The Arabic music in turn had been imbued with Spanish music during the Moorish period and vice versa. Borneman felt there were all kinds of African strains in the music of Spain which the Black slaves then recognized "as a sort of musical second cousin." While other critics, like Schuller, disputed this theory, Schuller did admit it might be fruitful "to investigate further the notion that, with nearly eight hundred years of domination of Northern Africa and Spain by the Arabs, certain Islamic influences eventually found their way to the New World via the Spanish and Portugese settlers, and these found acceptance among the African slaves, not because they recognized any African strains therein but because specific musical elements were discovered to be identical with those in their own tradition." The influence of Spanish music which had become Latin music in the New World thus was a prime catalyst in the formation of jazz music. The Blacks discovering the elements of a new music were fusing the Latin music to their own long before the jazz musician of the 40's and 50's rediscovered this second cousin influence.

The other integral part of jazz spawned by the works of Bessie Smith, Ma Rainey and Leadbelly was the blues. Again the relationship between Andalusion flamenco music, especially the Cante Hondo, and the blues is a workable theory. Hondo (or jondo) is said by philologists to mean "soul" in Sindhi language, one of the Mohammedan people of India. So the web of evidence spreads to conclusions which are difficult at best to dispute. Following this course of evidence, jazz music is the music of two cultures (Latin and Black) rather than one (Black).

While theories are arguable, clearly the Latino musician has been a vital part of the jazz scene. In the late 40's and early 50's the Latino musicians came out of the Latin bands which were predominantly Cuban and began to join jazz groups. Through the jam sessions, the Latinos proved again that jazz could accept the Latin rhythms. The music that emerged from the recombining of Black and Raza music was named Afro-Cuban by gavacho writers who lacked an understanding of the ethnic differences within La Raza. The music was not strictly Cubano. Moreover, the impact was immediate and dynamic.

Again the assumption was that this was the first impact by Latin musicians on the jazz scene. The truth was that Latin musicians were among the pioneers of jazz music. When jazz music moved from the minstrel shows to its own entity, one of the early jazz bands was led by "Papa" Laine. Making up his band were a cornetist named Lawrence Vega, a Mexican guitarist by the unlikely name of Morton Abraham, and a clarinetist who was to have a great impact on jazz named Alcide "Yellow" Nuñez. This same Nuñez later formed the original Dixieland Jazz Band. However, the first group to use the word jazz and take it out of its ghetto connotation was Brown's Dixieland Jaass Band which featured Ray Lopez on cornet and Arnold Loyocano on bass and piano. The actual word "jazz" was then first used by the Original Dixieland Jazz Band which was also the first band to record jazz music. "Yellow" Nuñez, certainly so nicknamed because he was not Black but like many musicians of that time, Latin, claimed the copyright of *Livery Stable Blues,* the first jazz hit recording. He then started his own group, "The Louisiana Five." In 1919 he recorded some forty sides. One of them, *Yelping Howard Blues,* was the most popular jazz hit of its day. Nuñez was also one of the pioneers of improvisation. The Latin musician was then not only an early influence on the Black jazz but also responsible for the white off-shoot which has been termed Dixieland.

Not only was the musical past of jazz influenced so heavily by Raza musicians, but since jazz was a culture which encompassed music, dress, and also language, some of the most important jazz pieces were *en español.* Without realizing that he was reading and speaking Spanish, the jazz buff listened to *Manteca* by Dizzy Gillespie, *Un Poco Loco* by Bud Powell, or the jazz classic *Perdido* recorded by almost every group.

The most influential impact of La Raza musicians on jazz was in the rhythm section. The standard rhythm section for jazz groups and bands were drums, bass and piano with sometimes a guitar. Into this standard grouping first came the conga drum, then bongos and later the other instruments peculiar to Latin music. What this instrumentacion accorded to jazz was a return to the native instruments forsaken in the acculturation of jazz. The Latin beat was a native beat which took jazz back to its roots in the Carribean and Indies. Because it was so elementary for jazz, and the Latin beat was so influential, Stan Kenton once exclaimed in an interview that it threatened to take over all jazz.

The different varieties of music which the Latin world offered also made an impact. Jazz musicians began to experiment with the different structures offered by the mambo, tango, samba, canción, etc. In the earliest days of jazz, Marshall Stearns told in his *Story of Jazz,* Creole ('signifyin') songs in New Orleans used a rhumba rhythm and Jelly Roll Morton incorporated a tango rhythm in his playing which he called 'The Spanish Tinge.' Even W. C. Handy, the father of the Blues used a tango rhythm in *Memphis Blues* and also in the very popular *St. Louis Blues.* Experimentation with Latin Music began as early as the 30's. Cab Calloway recorded *Doin' the Rhumba* in 1931 and later with the assistance of Mario Bauza produced many Cuban-flavored jazz records—one of which had the innocuous title of *Chile Con Conga.* At the same time, Puerto Rican trombonist, Juan Tizol, began recording with Duke Ellington such tunes as *Caravan, Conga Bravo* and *Bakiff.* He also brought the valve trombone into prominence.

So Raza musicians throughout the history of jazz music were integrally influential. Like the music itself, a fusion of Black and Raza, the musicians came from mixed cultures having names like Chico O'Farrill, Chico Hamilton, Paul Gonzalves and Roger King Mozian.

The most influential reunion of Latin and Black music was seen in the rhythm section with Chano Pozo, Machito and Humberto Morales— later Willie Bobo, Potato, and Mongo Santamaria. But other musicians emerged on the front line. Laurindo Almeida did double duty as one of the foremost Latin classical guitarists, and a sideman with Stan Kenton. Later Almeida combined with Bud Shank and still later with the Modern Jazz Quartet for some jazz masterpieces. Composers Chico O'Farrill, Mario Bouza and Russ Garcia helped fuse the unique sounds of Latin music to jazz structures. O'Farrill with Machito's band cemented the melding of Latin sounds to modern jazz. Garcia moved out of the Latin influences and became influential strictly as a jazz composer-arranger.

Two jazz vocalists were extremely influential with their unique styles. Babs Gonzalves is credited with being the first scat or bop singer to use his voice as an instrument. Diminutive Damita Jo became influential with rock singers of a later generation.

The bright moments of La Raza in jazz were Jazz at the Philharmonic playing *Perdido,* Juan Tizol's soft solos with Duke Ellington, Machito included in Norman Granz's 500 releases only album *The*

Jazz Scene, the Lighthouse at Hermosa Beach swinging to the Shelley Manne solos with *Viva Zapata!* originally written by Shorty Rogers as *Mambo Del Crow,* Paul Smith's amazingly rapid rendition of *Cumbanchero,* Chano Pozo with Dizzy Gillespie at Town Hall, Jackie and Roy's bop vocal with Charlie Ventura in what was called a bop rhumba *Piña Colada.* The Easter Sunday "Tico Tico" dance at the Manhattan Center, which featured five Afro-Cuban bands (Hose Budet, Alberto Iznaga, El Boy, Louis Del Campo and Machito) lasted from one o'clock in the afternoon to one o'clock the next day. Two hours after the start of the concert, the Fire Department closed the door on a mob of 5000 aficionados.

Other bright moments of La Raza in jazz were Machito's rhythm section making Stan Kenton a hit with *The Peanut Vendor,* these same drummers walking into a radio station and sitting in with Will Bradley's Dixieland Jazz Band featuring Ella Fitzgerald, Tito Puente's popularity at the jazz corner of the world, Birdland, causing his inclusion in the Birdland Hall of Fame paintings, Ernie Caceres with the Metronome All Star Band, young Virgil Gonzales at the Monterey Jazz Festival and four years later an older Bola Sete in the same scene playing solo with Dizzy Gillespie, Stan Getz's poignant sound enhanced by the bossa nova of Antonio Carlos Jobim and Joao Gilberto, later the fusion of Getz's soft tone and Astrud Gilberto's soft voice in the popular *Girl From Ipanema,* Willie Correa being named Willie Bobo by the foremost woman jazz pianist, Mary Lou Williams, Mongo Santamaria performing Herbie Hancock's *Watermelon Man,* the classical albums of Charlie Parker with Machito, the all-Cuban jazz album produced by Norman Granz. And finally, but most important, modern guitarists can thank Nick Esposito for the design of their instruments.

The influences of La Raza were lasting because these influences began in its formation and continued through its growth. The influence has spread to the stepchild of jazz, rock music with the sounds of Santana, Malo, Jerry Garcia and El Chicano. Influence on jazz music is perhaps a misnomer since La Raza was an integral and rooted entity of jazz. Jazz is not Black, perhaps it is not even a fusion of Black and Raza. Perhaps jazz is the music of the people because it stems from many cultures and has been accepted by so many other cultures.

Bibliography

Feather, Leonard. The Encyclopedia of Jazz in the Sixties, New York, Horizon Press, 1966.

Feather, Leonard. *The Encyclopedia of Jazz.* New York, Horizon Press, 1960.

Schuller, Gunther. *Early Jazz: Its Roots and Musical Development,* New York, Oxford University Press, 1968.

Stearns, Marshall W. *The Story of Jazz,* New York, Oxford University Press, 1956.

Ulanov, Barry. *A History of Jazz in America,* New York, The Viking Press, 1959.

Mexican-American Community Organizations

SALVADOR ALVAREZ

The cause of the low socio-economic conditions among Mexican-Americans has been systematically subjected to a multitude of "explanations." There are two major sources for these explanations: (1) social science studies of Mexican-Americans, or journalistic quasi-literary efforts, and (2) Mexican-Americans themselves.

Social Science Explanations

The major assumption set forth by social science studies of Mexican-Americans is that they themselves, their culture and its values, are the ultimate or final cause of their low socio-economic status, i.e., internal cause of social conditions among Mexican-Americans and its counterpart, external cause of solutions. The most common solutions are, of course, acculturation, integration, and assimilation.

The "explanatory" orientations of internal cause and external solutions have consistently led to the assumption that Chicano culture socializes individuals to become lazy, resigned, passive, fatalistic, non-goal oriented, docile, shy, infantile, criminally prone, irrational, emotional, authoritarian, unreliable, limited in cognitive ability, untrustworthy, lax, priest-ridden, and above all, unorganized.

Variants of these stereotypes can be found in the works of social scientists, among whom one can list Bryan,[1] a sociologist (1912); Young,[2] a psychologist (1922); Garth,[3] a psychologist (1923); Sullenberg,[4] a sociologist (1924); Garretson,[5] a psychologist (1928); Walker,[6] a sociologist (1928); Haught,[7] a psychologist (1931); Humphrey,[8] a sociologist (1944); Tuck,[9] a sociologist (1946); Griffith,[10] a psychologist (1948); Saunders,[11] a sociologist (1954); Edmunson,[12] an anthropologist (1957); Clark,[13] an anthropologist (1959); Kluckhohn,[14] an anthropologist (1961); Landes,[15] a sociologist (1965); Samora,[16] a sociologist (1965); Rubel,[17] an anthropologist (1966); and Heller,[18] a sociologist (1968). Journalistic, quasi-literary efforts that reach toward the same explanatory frameworks can also be included, such as Novokov[19] (1969), Matthiessen[20] (1969), and Steiner[21] (1969).

As such, social science studies with their heavy reliance on culture, or the notion of culture, have presented a particular conception of Mexican-Americans which, in its total effect, has rendered this large group to an historical limbo out of which it must first emerge (and awaken) in order to engage in the currents of the American "mainstream." However, Vaca,[22] Romano,[23] Montiel,[24] Alvidrez,[25] Moreno,[26] have pointed out that the bulk of social science studies of Mexican-Americans have systematically stereotyped Mexican-American communities to the extent that differential cultural patterns among the population have been reduced to singular, monolithic concepts such as "The Mexican-American," "The Mexican-American Family," "The Mexican-American Community," "The Mexican-American Culture," and "The Mexican-American Value System," leaving the impression that all Mexican-Americans are virtually alike, have been a part of the same family structure and ethos, and have lived in exactly identical communities.

Chicano writers are presently refuting the view that the final cause of social conditions among Mexican-Americans lies within their communities or their cultural patterns. Romano, for example, has pointed out that the bulk of theory, or lack of it, for social science studies of Mexican-Americans has been based on the over-used concept of "traditional culture," as a result of which ". . . Mexican-Americans are never seen as participants in history, much less as generators of the historical process."[27] He concludes that "Thus, Samora and Lamana, like Heller, Madsen and others before them, place the final cause of social conditions upon the Mexican-Americans themselves. In doing so, they also commit the fallacy of equating economic determinism with cultural determinism."[28]

Another ramification of social science studies of Mexican-Americans lies in their insistent assertion that Mexican-Americans presently are, and have been, divided and unorganized. Therefore, major studies have concluded that there are no significant formal organizations among Mexican-Americans that can deal with social conditions, or, when formal organizations have appeared they tend to be rapidly broken down from within. This "lack of ability to organize" large formal structures is often said to result from family patterns which do not allow formal ties beyond the extended family. For example, in *Across*

the Tracks: Mexican-Americans in a Texas City, Arthur Rubel
states that,

> Mexican-Americans in Mexiquito, *and elsewhere,* tend
> not to organize corporate instrumental groups, al-
> though a few are found scattered in the history of the
> neighborhood. Moreover, when chicanos do join such
> voluntary associations this participation is short lived
> and discomforting. Unlike their Anglo-American
> counterparts, chicanos participate in secondary asso-
> ciations as if they were of a primary nature (familial).
> (Emphasis mine)[29]

To assist him in his "explanation," Rubel cites Paul Lin's
material from Kansas City, and Macklin's discussion of Chicano
participation in formal associations in Toledo, Ohio, i.e.,
Chicanos are the same all over. Rubel concludes by stating the
following with regard to two mutual aid societies.

> Anglo society across the tracks from Mexiquito, to
> which upwardly mobile chicanos aspire, organizes its
> membership in secondary associations of a formal
> character. Until chicanos learn to organize their social
> behavior in this way also, they cannot expect to par-
> ticipate in the segment which effectively controls the
> social, economic, and political system of the total
> society, in which Mexiquito is enmeshed. So long as
> chicanos continue to act as if the larger society was
> organized on the basis of small family units and as if
> Anglos engaged one another in personal dyadic rela-
> tions, they will continue to be frustrated in their at-
> tempts to secure some medium of predictable control
> over the social environment beyond the bound of
> their family.[30]

In this manner, like so many before him, Rubel reveals no
improvement over the studies of Mexican-Americans of the
1920's, for he too places the *final cause of social conditions*
within the Mexican-American individuals and their families.

Another study, by Paul M. Sheldon, insistently echoes this
same conclusion. The study appears in *La Raza: Forgotten
Americans.* Sheldon begins his work by stating that,

> Heterogeniety is a major factor in their ability to get
> together, to develop strong leadership, and to form

organizations through which this large group may express its needs and desires and make itself felt in the political, economic, and social life of the broader community.[31]

Sheldon then adds to this view with a discussion of the "Mexican Tradition of Individualism." In his words,

Individualism is a major characteristic of Mexican culture. . . . Where individual worth is held to be almost sacred . . . and admitted conformity to the group, any group outside the family, a cardinal sin . . . it is not surprising that Mexican-Americans have been unable to put to effective use the tool of the mass voice to promote the common good of their group. They are in fact not a group; they do not speak with a common voice; they do not have mutual agreement; they are fragmented first by their heterogeniety and second by the tradition of individualism.[32]

Thus Sheldon, like Rubel before him, also places final cause within the "tradition" and the "cultural values" that he believes are characteristic of Mexican-Americans. In the same volume, this same view is perpetuated by John Martinez when he says that,

The political potential of the Spanish-speaking is *only in its initial stages* . . . for the Spanish-speaking this is particularly difficult because of the individualistic nature of Hispanic peoples which vitiates against group action. . . . This, of course, is a manifestation of the underlying sense of inferiority imposed by a color and culture conscious society in the United States. . . . *The remarkable aspect of this situation is that the will to overcome this status has taken so long to assert itself.*[33] (emphases mine)

Martinez goes on to suggest that this sense of inferiority has to some extent been overcome, and he points out that there have been several factors leading up to an *awakening* which has, in turn, led to recent interest in political activities by Mexican-Americans. The "awakening" is then attributed to the Negro Movement in the United States.[34] These views, of course, are quite repetitive and quite familiar, for they represent no significant departure from the writings of Zamora, Lyle Saunders, William Madsen, and a host of other writers, virtually all of whom have repeatedly asserted that (1) Mexican-Americans have no history of organizing, (2) have virtually no knowledge of formal organizations, (3) and that this is ostensibly true because of their "traditional culture," their values, and their families, which, however, is now changing because Mexican-Americans are now "emerging," "awakening," or just simply now "asserting" themselves for the first time. The impetus for all this, of course, is said to come from forces external to the Chicanos themselves, such as the Negro Movement, (as John Martinez would have us believe), acculturation, or Fred Ross. Such distorted views, clearly, come from the essentially ahistorical methodology and ideology of the social sciences in the United States today.

But even the most cursory glance at history reveals otherwise, as witness the following sampling of Mexican-American formal organizations which have existed in the past and which continue to exist in a variety of forms in the present.

Date	State	Formal Organizations
1880's	New Mexico	Penitente Order
1890's	New Mexico	Mano Negra
1914	California	International Institute of Los Angeles
1915	California	Agricultural Workers Organization
1922	Colorado	Sociedad Mutualista Ignacio Zaragoza
1927	California	La Confederación de Uniones Obreras Mexicanas
1928	California	Sociedad Guadalupana
1929	Texas	League of United Latin American Citizens
1933	Indiana	Sociedad Mutualista Mexico
1933	Texas	Associacion de Jornaleros
1933	California	Club Latino Americano de Long Beach y Signal Hall
1933	California	Cannery and Agricultural Workers Industrial Union
1935	New Mexico	Liga Obrera de Habla Espanola
1936	Ohio	Sociedad Mutualista Mexicana
1937	California	Sinarquista Movement
1939	Colorado	Spanish Speaking Congress
1940	California	Unity Leagues
1946	Texas	San Antonio Council for the Spanish-Speaking
1947	California	National Farm Workers Union

1943	Texas	Pan American Student Forum of Texas
1951	Illinois	Club Latino Americano
1956	Washington	National Latin American Federación (Seattle)
1959	Illinois	Association Pro-Derechos Obreros
1959	California	Agricultural Workers Organizing Committee
1947	California	Community Service Organization
1948	Texas	American G.I. Forum
1960	California	Mexican American Political Association
1963	Colorado	Crusade for Justice
1963	New Mexico	Alianza Federal de las Mercedes
1961	California	National Farm Workers Association
1966	California	United Farm Workers Organizing Committee
1967	Texas	Mexican American Youth Organization
1968	California	Movimiento Estudiantil Chicano de Aztlán

This partial list is representative of a significant history of organizing efforts by Mexican-Americans in the Southwest. In essence, it reflects the process of organizing that continues even to today in eastern states where the Chicano population is presently growing. In June, 1970, the *Directory of Spanish-Speaking Community Organizations,* published by the Cabinet Committee on Opportunity for the Spanish-Speaking, listed some 800 organizations (principally Mexican-American), with information on about 207 such organizations. That this number represents a minimal estimate is indisputable, as acknowledged by the Committee itself.

It has been stated above that formal organizations among Mexican-Americans have never been considered seriously in social science studies of this population, but rather they have been summarily dismissed as having no social significance whatsoever. This preconceived and subjective predilection has even been reflected by some Mexican-American social scientists in recent years. Therefore, for relevant information concerning such organizations one must look elsewhere. At present, two major sources for such information are studies of Mexican-American labor union organizations. The first was compiled in 1930 by Governor Young's Mexican Fact Finding Committee in California, and it constitutes an investigation concerning labor unions among Mexicans and Mexican-Americans, principally La Confederación de Uniones Obreras Mexicanas. The second study was written by Ernesto Galarza, and it concerns the National Farm Workers Union. This was published under the title *Spiders in the House and Workers in the Field,* in 1970. Both of these sources reveal considerable organizing efforts and abilities among Mexican-Americans. For example, in 1928 the Confederation held its first general convention in May of that year. Delegates were sent from the following unions:[35]

Union number 1, Los Angeles
Union number 2, El Modena
Union number 3, Garden Grove
Union number 4, Palo Verde
Union number 5, Orange
Union number 6, Attwood
Union number 7, Stanton
Union number 8, Santa Ana
Union number 9, Talbert, Santa Ana
Union number 10, San Fernando

Union number 11, Anaheim
Union number 12, Gloryetta
Union number 13, Santa Monica
Union number 14, Placentia
Union number 15, Buena Park
Union number 16, Moor Park
Union number 17, La Jolla, Anaheim
Union number 18, Corona
Union number 19, Fullerton
Union number 20, San Bernardino
Union number 21, Colton

In addition to the delegations from these unions, representatives from the Mutual Aid Societies also attended.

In the second study, Galarza has the following to say,

". . . farm labor locals set up a resistance the length and breadth of California. They struck in the tomato, the peach, the melon, the cotton and the potato harvests. In a decade of lost engagements of this type, the Union forced the great ranches to the picket lines. The results were always the same—small wage gains for the harvesters, the adamant refusal of growers to recognize the Union. . . ."[36]

The major organizing effort by the Confederation took place during the 1920's and 1930's. The major organizing effort by the National Farm Workers Union took place during the 1940's and 1950's. They can be compared to the organizing effort of the United Farm Workers Organizing Committee during the 1960's and 1970's, thus revealing organizing activities among Mexican-Americans for a period of more than fifty years in one area alone, farm labor.

The question as to whether or not these organizing efforts have been successful or have resulted in failures has received much informal attention. It seems clear that, in view of the fact that there is a continuous history of organized activities culminating in today's hundreds of organizations, the social science views of Mexican-American organizing abilities is vastly distorted. For the significance of these efforts, therefore, one must look elsewhere again in order to achieve an understanding of the processes involved in Mexican-American organizations. In the first place, formal organizations invariably have two facets. First, they are organized to achieve certain projected goals. Second, *they provide a vehicle for the expression of the broader boundaries of the communities in which they exist.* For the present, it is hypothesized that the formal organizations among Mexican-Americans have performed certain functions that have been central for the on-going survival and existence of their communities. Primarily, they have functioned for the preservation of the general Mexican-American way of life in that quite often they have constituted the central hub of Mexican-American activities over and above the projected goals. Such activities involved celebrations, social events, and the provision of facilities for these events. In addition, they provided a series of alternatives for the population in that a variety of organizations have existed. The formal organizations also provided informational and communication networks. And finally, they have sustained, by and large, the core of the philosophy that encompasses bicultural and bilingual existence.

In the final analysis one thing is clear. Had these organizations been the failures that so many have claimed, then why do they persist to this day, and how is it that we are here today. What I am suggesting, of course, is that the significance of the formal organizations has all too often been studied from the standpoint of external criteria, and there has yet to be compiled a study that focuses upon the criteria as viewed by the memberships. To simply say, as Rubel has done, that Mexican-American organizations fail because they are not like us white folks is not to analyze the social forces involved, but it is merely a roundabout way of patting himself on the back. Rubel, like so many other social scientists before him, it seems, was so busy patting himself on the back that he failed to see what was before him. It is to be fervently hoped that Chicano social scientists themselves do not succumb to this malady.

REFERENCES

1. Bryan, Samuel, "Mexican Immigrants in the United States," *Survey,* 28:726-730.
2. Young, Kimball, "Mental Differences in Certain Immigrant Groups," University of Oregon Publications, Vol., No. 11, 1922.

3. Garth, Thomas R., "A Comparison of the Intelligence of Mexican and Mixed and Full Blood Indian Children," *Psychological Review* 30:388-401.

4. Sullenberg, Earl T., "Mexican Population of Omaha," *Journal of Applied Sociology*, May-June, 1924.

5. Garretson, O. K., "A Study of Causes of Retardation Among Mexican Children in a Small Public School System in Arizona," *Journal of Educational Psychology*, 19:31-40.

6. Walker, Helen, "Mexican Immigrants as Laborers," *Sociology and Social Research*, 13:55-62.

7. Haught, B. F., "The Language Difficulty of Spanish-American Children," *Journal of Applied Psychology*, 15:92-95.

8. Humphrey, Norma D., "The Changing Structure of the Detroit Mexican Family," *American Sociological Review*, Vol. 9, No. 6, 1944.

9. Tuck, Ruth, *Not with the Fist*, New York: Harcourt, Brace and Company, 1946.

10. Griffith, Beatrice, *American Me*, Boston: Houghton, Mifflin Company, 1948.

11. Saunders, Lyle, *Cultural Differences and Medical Care: The Case of the Spanish-Speaking People of the Southwest*, New York: Russel Sage Foundation, 1954.

12. Edmonson, Munro S., *Los Manitos: A Study of Institutional Values*, New Orleans: Tulane University, 1957.

13. Clark, Margaret, *Health in the Mexican American Culture*, Berkeley and Los Angeles: University of California Press, 1959.

14. Kluckhohn, Florence Beckwood and Fred L. Strodbeck, *Variations in Value Orientations*, New York: Row, Peterson and Company, 1961.

15. Landes, Ruth, *Latin Americans of the Southwest*, Saint Louis: McGraw-Hill, 1965.

16. Samora, Julian and Richard A. Lamanna, *Mexican Americans in a Midwest Metropolis: A Study of East Chicago*, Mexican American Study Project, Division of Research, Graduate School of Business, University of California, Los Angeles, 1967.

17. Rubel, Arthur J., *Across the Tracks: Mexican Americans in a Texas City*, Hogg Foundation for Mental Health, Austin and London: University of Texas Press, 1966.

18. Heller, Celia S., *The Mexican American Youth: Forgotten Youth at the Crossroads*, New York: Random House, 1968. (Third Printing).

19. Nobokov, Peter, *Tijerina and the Courthouse Raid*, Albuquerque: University of New Mexico, 1969.

20. Matthiessen, Peter, *Sal Si Puedes: Cesar Chavez and the New American Revolution*, New York: Random House, 1969.

21. Steiner, Stan, *La Raza: The Mexican Americans*, New York: Harper Row, 1969.

22. Vaca, Nick C., "The Mexican American in the Social Sciences: 1912-1970; Part I: 1912-1935," *El Grito*, Vol. 3, No. 3, Spring 1970, Quinto Sol Publications, Inc., Berkeley, California.

23. Romano-V., Octavio I., "The Anthropology and Sociology of the Mexican-Americans: The Distortion of Mexican American History," *El Grito,* Vol. II, No. 1, Fall 1968, Quinto Sol Publications, Inc., Berkeley, California.

24. Montiel, Miguel, "The Social Science Myth of the Mexican-American Family," *El Grito,* Vol. III, No. 4, Summer 1970, Quinto Sol Publications, Inc., Berkeley, California.

25. Alvidrez, Samuel R., "Drug Use Trends in California," *El Grito,* Vol. IV, No. 1, Fall 1970, Quinto Sol Publications, Inc., Berkeley, California.

26. Moreno, Steve, "Problems Related to Present Testing Instruments," *El Grito,* Vol. III, No. 3, Spring 1970, Quinto Sol Publications, Inc., Berkeley, California.

27. Romano-V., Octavio I., *Ibid.,* p. 13.

28. *Ibid.,* p. 13.

29. Rubel, Arthur J., *Ibid.,* p. 140.

30. *Ibid.,* p. 154.

31. Sheldon, Paul M., "Community Participation and the Emerging Middle Class," *La Raza: Forgotten Americans,* University of Notre Dame Press, 1966, p. 125.

32. *Ibid.,* p. 127.

33. Martinez, John, "Leadership and Politics," *La Raza: Forgotten Americans,* University of Notre Dame Press, 1966, p. 48.

34. *Ibid.,* p. 49.

35. _____ , "Mexicans in California: Report of Governor C. C. Young's Mexican Fact-Finding Committee," State Building, San Francisco, California, October, 1930, pp. 126-127.

36. Galarza, Ernesto, "Spiders in the House and Workers in the Field," University of Notre Dame Press, Notre Dame, 1970, p. 4.

The Mexican-American and the Church

CÉSAR E. CHAVEZ

The following article was prepared by Mr. Chavez during his 25-day "spiritual fast" and was presented to a meeting on "Mexican-Americans and the Church" at the Second Annual Mexican-American Conference in Sacramento, California on March 8-10, 1968.

The place to begin is with our own experience with the Church in the strike which has gone on for thirty-one months in Delano. For in Delano the Church has been involved with the poor in a unique way which should stand as a symbol to other communities. Of course, when we refer to the Church we should define the word a little. We mean the whole Church, the Church as an ecumenical body spread around the world, and not just its particular form in a parish in a local community. The Church we are talking about is a tremendously powerful institution in our society, and in the world. That Church is one form of the Presence of God on Earth, and so naturally it is powerful. It is powerful by definition. It is a powerful moral and spiritual force which cannot be ignored by any movement. Furthermore, it is an organization with tremendous wealth. Since the Church is to be servant to the poor, it is *our* fault if that wealth is not channeled to help the poor in our world.

In a small way we have been able, in the Delano strike, to work together with the Church in such a way as to bring some of its moral and economic power to bear on those who want to maintain the status quo, keeping farm workers in virtual enslavement. In brief, here is what happened in Delano.

Some years ago, when some of us were working with the Community Service Organization, we began to realize the powerful effect which the Church can have on the conscience of the opposition. In scattered instances, in San Jose, Sacramento, Oakland, Los Angeles and other places, priests would speak out loudly and clearly against specific instances of oppression, and in some cases, stand with the people who were being hurt. Furthermore, a small group of priests, Frs. McDonald, McCollough, Duggan and others, began

215

to pinpoint attention on the terrible situation of the farm workers in our state.

At about that same time, we began to run into the California Migrant Ministry in the camps and fields. They were about the only ones there, and a lot of us were very suspicious, since we were Catholics and they were Protestants. However, they had developed a very clear conception of the Church. It was called to serve, to be at the mercy of the poor, and not to try to use them. After a while this made a lot of sense to us, and we began to find ourselves working side by side with them. In fact, it forced us to raise the question why OUR Church was not doing the same. We would ask, "Why do the Protestants come out here and help the people, demand nothing, and give all their time to serving farm workers, while our own parish priests stay in their churches, where only a few people come, and usually feel uncomfortable?"

It was not until some of us moved to Delano and began working to build the National Farm Workers Association that we really saw how far removed from the people the parish Church was. In fact, we could not get any help at all from the priests of Delano. When the strike began, they told us we could not even use the Church's auditorium for the meetings. The farm workers' money helped build that auditorium! But the Protestants were there again, in the form of the California Migrant Ministry, and they began to help in little ways, here and there.

When the strike started in 1965, most of our "friends" forsook us for a while. They ran — or were just too busy to help. But the California Migrant Ministry held a meeting with its staff and decided that the strike was a matter of life or death for farm workers everywhere, and that even if it meant the end of the Migrant Ministry they would turn over their resources to the strikers. The political pressure on the Protestant Churches was tremendous and the Migrant Ministry lost a lot of money. But they stuck it out, and they began to point the way to the rest of the Church. In fact, when 30 of the strikers were arrested for shouting Huelga, 11 ministers went to jail with them. They were in Delano that day at the request of Chris Hartmire, director of the California Migrant Ministry.

Then the workers began to raise the question: "Why ministers? Why not priests? What does the Bishop say?" But the Bishop said nothing. But slowly the pressure of the people grew and grew, until finally we have in Delano a priest sent by the new Bishop, Timothy Manning, who is there to help minister to the needs of farm workers. His name is Father Mark Day and he is the Union's chaplain.

Finally, our own Catholic Church has decided to recognize that we have our own peculiar needs, just as the growers have theirs.

But outside of the local diocese, the pressure built up on growers to negotiate was tremendous. Though we were not allowed to have our own priest, the power of the ecumenical body of the Church was tremendous. The work of the Church, for example, in the Schenley, Di Giorgio, Perelli-Minetti strikes was fantastic. They applied pressure — and they mediated.

When poor people get involved in a long conflict, such as a strike, or a civil rights drive, and the pressure increases each day, there is a deep need for spiritual advice. Without it we see families crumble, leadership weaken, and hard workers grow tired. And in such a situation the spiritual advice must be given by a *friend,* not by the opposition. What sense does it make to go to Mass on Sunday and reach out for spiritual help, and instead get sermons about the wickedness of your cause? That only drives one to question and to despair. The growers in Delano have their spiritual problems . . . we do not deny that. They have every right to have priests and ministers who serve their needs. BUT WE HAVE DIFFERENT NEEDS, AND SO WE NEEDED A FRIENDLY SPIRITUAL GUIDE. And this is true in every community in this state where the poor face tremendous problems.

But the opposition raises a tremendous howl about this. They don't want us to have our spiritual advisors, friendly to our needs. Why is this? Why indeed except that THERE IS TREMENDOUS SPIRITUAL AND ECONOMIC POWER IN THE CHURCH. The rich know it, and for that reason they choose to keep it from the people.

The leadership of the Mexican-American Community must admit that we have fallen far short in our task of helping provide spiritual guidance for our people. We may say, "I don't feel any such need. I can get along." But that is a poor excuse for not helping provide such help for others. For we can also say, "I don't need any welfare help. I can take care of my own problems." But we are all willing to fight like hell for welfare aid for those who truly need it, who would starve without it. Likewise we may have gotten an education and not care about scholarship money for ourselves, or our children. But we would, we should, fight like hell to see to it that our state provides aid for any child needing it so that he can get the education he desires. LIKEWISE WE CAN SAY WE DON'T NEED THE CHURCH. THAT IS OUR BUSINESS. BUT THERE ARE HUNDREDS OF THOUSANDS OF OUR PEOPLE WHO DES-

PERATELY NEED SOME HELP FROM THAT POWERFUL
INSTITUTION, THE CHURCH, AND WE ARE FOOLISH NOT
TO HELP THEM GET IT.

For example, the Catholic Charities agencies of the Catholic
Church has millions of dollars earmarked for the poor. But often
the money is spent for food baskets for the needy instead of for
effective action to eradicate the causes of poverty. The men and
women who administer this money sincerely want to help their
brothers. It should be our duty to help direct the attention to the
basic needs of the Mexican-Americans in our society . . . needs
which cannot be satisfied with baskets of food, but rather with effective organizing at the grass roots level.

Therefore, I am calling for Mexican-American groups to stop
ignoring this source of power. It is not just our right to appeal to
the Church to use its power effectively for the poor, it is our duty to
do so. It should be as natural as appealing to government . . . and
we do that often enough.

Furthermore, we should be prepared to come to the defense of
that priest, rabbi, minister, or layman of the Church, who out of
commitment to truth and justice gets into a tight place with his
pastor or bishop. It behooves us to stand with that man and help
him see his trial through. It is our duty to see to it that his rights
of conscience are respected and that no bishop, pastor or other
higher body takes that God-given, human right away.

Finally, in a nutshell, what do we want the Church to do? We
don't ask for more cathedrals. We don't ask for bigger churches or
fine gifts. We ask for its presence with us, beside us, as Christ
among us. We ask the Church to *sacrifice with the people* for social
change, for justice, and for love of brother. We don't ask for words.
We ask for deeds. We don't ask for paternalism. We ask for
servanthood.

THE LEGAL AND LEGISLATIVE STRUGGLE OF THE FARMWORKER$

1965 – 1972

PART I: The Legal Struggle

PART II: The Legislative Struggle

Salvador Enrique Alvarez

THE LEGAL AND LEGISLATIVE STRUGGLE
OF THE FARMWORKERS
1965   -   1972

PART I: The Legal Struggle

INTRODUCTION

Legal struggles by farmworkers, either as individuals or in organized fashion, date virtually as far back as farm labor itself. Similarly, for centuries landlords have made use of legal authority in order to sustain or to expand their control over slaves, indigents, sharecroppers, migrants, and other farmworkers in general. This legal struggle and counter-struggle continues through this twentieth century, as attested to by the following examples:

". . . 1917 . . . IWW's Agricultural Workers Organization . . . charged with violation of the Espionage Act, and after the war they were prosecuted under the syndicalist laws passed during the war years."[1]

". . . 1929 . . . The Mexican Mutual Aid Society of Imperial Valley, Inc., . . . Sheriff Gillet . . . the first outbreak of any kind as a result of the movement now afoot, a general deportation movement of all Mexican laborers employed in the valley would begin . . . the sheriff made it clear that those abiding by the laws and not taking part in the strike movement would not be molested in any way."[2]

". . . 1935, when it was learned that only Southern Tenant Farmers Union members were being evicted from the huge Norcross plantation. STFU leaders decided to file for a court decision . . . the suit was eventually lost . . ."[3]

". . . 1939 . . . the Filipino Agricultural Labor Association . . . 258 asparagus growers signed agreements with FALA . . . members voted to affiliate with the AFL. The drive became bogged down in legal disputes . . . The coup de grâce was given FALA by Japan's invasion of the Philippines."[4]

". . . 1947 . . . Picket lines were maintained for nine months around twenty miles of DiGiorgio property. These lines were prohibited after the courts ruled they were boycotts and illegal under the National Labor Relations Act . . . strikers argued that since they were excluded from the protection of NLRA, they could not be subject to its provisions. The National Labor Relations Board finally reviewed their case and upheld their position, but by that time the strike had been lost . . ."[5]

". . . 1950 . . . National Farm Labor Union . . . the DiGiorgio Fruit Corporation filed suit for libel against the NFLU and the producers of the Union motion picture . . . the strike collapsed rapidly."[6]

"In 1952 NFLU became the National Agricultural Workers Union. An NAWU organizing effort in 1953 among Louisiana sugar cane workers culminated in a strike. The Louisiana courts issued anti-strike injunctions, which crippled Union activities. The Supreme Court later declared the injunctions illegal, but the damage had been done and the strike was dead."[7]

". . . 1959 . . . Someone on the staff of AWOC borrowed a surviving print of Poverty in the Valley of Plenty. It was shown in various parts of the Central Valley, in ignorance of the ban of 1950. Word of the showing reached the officers of DiGiorgio. Within ten days, the Corporation filed suit of defamation . . . a judge found the film libelous . . ."[8]

". . . 1961 . . . AWOC led two principal strikes . . . insisted that the Department of Labor enforce the law, and remove braceros from the struck area. It did not do so. The lettuce harvest was completed by braceros and the strike was broken."[9]

Thus, the farm workers' legal struggle prior to 1962, when César Chávez began to organize farm workers, had in part involved charges of espionage, violation of syndicalist laws, arrests for striking and picketing, deportations, anti-striking and picketing injunctions, libel suits, and lack of enforcement of laws against strike-breakers by the government. The most noted study of the farm workers' legal struggle prior to 1960 is found in Dr. Ernesto Galarza's recent book titled *Spiders in the House and Workers in the Field.* Here, Galarza asserts that during the 1950's California farm labor efforts to organize ultimately were destroyed both by court actions and by the Congress. About Galarza's study, another historian of farm labor problems, Carey McWilliams has said,

"In a sense, it is the pre-Chávez, pre-Delano phase of the story with which this work deals. Apart from its inherent interest and social and historical importance, *it has special theoretical significance as a study of how institutional power as represented in the courts and committees of the Congress* can be used on occasion to block the legitimate aspirations of impoverished farm workers to achieve self-organization."[10] (emphasis mine)

Aside from the personal documentary work by Ernesto Galarza which deals with the 1940's and 1950's, it can be said that the legal struggles by farmworkers prior to the 1940's, during the 1960's, and into the early 1970's have been neither described, documented, nor analyzed. Yet, clearly, in order to achieve a full understanding of the major forces that farm workers have had to cope with in their efforts to organize, then the social, economic, and theoretical importance of legal actions and counter-actions cannot continue to be ignored with any justification whatsoever. For to ignore this major aspect of farm labor activities is to contribute to the distortion of the total empirical and historical reality. Nevertheless, ignored it has been, particularly by social scientists. This fact poses the interesting possibility that insofar as farm labor is concerned, social scientists have strongly tended to develop theory by the process of omitting significantly relevant data, a peculiar methodological situation.

The following survey concerning the legal struggles by the farm-worker organization, UFW, from 1965 to 1972 constitutes a first step toward filling this vacuum in our knowledge relative to farm labor and legal actions. As the total picture develops, hopefully, the reader will realize that herein lies an extremely significant aspect of contemporary history and farm labor. In the same manner, how such legal actions are inextricably interwoven with other aspects of farm worker activities will be clarified. If such is the result, then the case of farmworker activities can no longer be dealt with in a unidimensional manner. Thus, our knowledge of this bit of contemporary history will be seen in a more accurate light and in a perspective that more properly relates to other aspects of farm labor organization efforts.

The dates are arranged in chronological order by year. This is a relatively arbitrary arrangement dictated largely by the need to present clearly such a massive amount of information in a form that is comprehensible to readers who may not be acquainted with this aspect of the farm labor movement in the United States. This account begins in 1965, when the Chávez union was known as the National Farm Workers' Association (NFWA), and proceeds through 1966 when the organizational name was changed to the National Farm Workers Organizing Committee (UFWOC), and into 1972. The name has since been changed again to the United Farm Workers (UFW). During this period, the Union's activities shifted from regional to national, and its headquarters was moved from Delano to Keene, California.

From 1962 to 1964, legal cases dealt primarily with family problems such as evictions, welfare appeals, contracts of sale, etc. These cases cannot be documented at this time for lack of sources and information. Such family and individual cases, however, continue today to comprise the bulk of legal activity for the Union.

In the same vein, the final outcome of every case presented in this historical summary is not available except insofar as a researcher is able to travel to the many courts of law where the cases transpired. This, clearly, has been impossible due to limited resources and time. Nevertheless, the outcome of a number of cases is noted in sufficient numbers as to provide data for the central thrust of this study.

From the following account, it will be readily evident that the legal struggle of the farmworkers' union has not been static. In fact, it appears that the United Farm Workers, AFL-CIO had some knowledge of history, particularly previous legal struggles, relating to farm workers. As a consequence, from its very inception it set forth its own legal strategy. In addition, the communications media of the Union focused considerable effort toward the understanding of such past legal history.

With this historical perspective upon which to base contemporary activities, the Union instituted its own legal department within its developing and complex organizational structure. The development of its own legal institution, ultimately controlled by farmworkers over a period of time, has provided the Union and its membership with both a protective legal arm and a forum for a sustained and progressive legal thrust oriented toward establishing new legal grounds relating to farm workers and the law. With this orientation, the membership has now been provided with a voice in an arena that heretofore had been neglected.

The progressive thrust of this legal struggle has been such that the United Farm Workers union, led by César Chávez, has been able to develop institutions long sought by farm workers all over the world. In other words, a wide range of legal services not traditionally available to farmworkers became more and more a reality. Additionally, the legal arm of the Union sought further changes in the National Labor Relations Act, unemployment insurance, pesticide control, progressive contracts, while simultaneously aiding the development of the Union's own cooperative institutions.

This aid to its own developing institutions includes legal support for the central facets of the Union's cooperative organizational structure: that is, legal support for the medical clinics, the medical plan, coop garage, credit union, retirement village, service centers, death benefit plan, hiring halls, ranch committees, farm workers press, organizing department, contracts, research department, accounting department, strike fund, economic development fund, legal defense fund, strike kitchens, boycott offices, huelga school, child care nursery, strike store, non-violent training center, and most importantly, the families of the membership.

Regarding assistance to families of the membership, from the very beginning and throughout the intervening years, the primary focus of the legal arm of the U.F.W. has been service to the workers. As such, it has primarily dealt with family problems, evictions, welfare appeals, contracts of sale, etc. Such casework continues to comprise the bulk of the legal activity of the Union. This fact, alone, is a considerably noteworthy achievement not only for the N.F.W., but also in the annals of the American labor movement. In other words, the N.F.W. has broken new ground in the area of the social responsibilities of labor unions toward their membership. Should the N.F.W. legal arm have done nothing else but this, it would have been sufficient, it seems to me, to qualify the N.F.W. for a position at the forefront of unionism today. Perhaps other unions will follow the N.F.W. example and re-orient their legal staffs more toward an orientation of service to the workers.

This, then, is the context within which the following account should be read, i.e., primary service to the workers, legal support for the cooperative structure, legal defense, and progressive efforts toward changing laws and labor conditions. As the reader will readily see, the task has not been small, but neither have the people who have pushed the overall effort forward.

The Legal and Legislative Struggle

AN OVERVIEW

Legal	Legislative
1965	**1965**
Complaints against labor contractors	Minimum wages
Rent strike in Visalia	Braceros
Complaints against illegal aliens	Unemployment insurance
Rancher charged with assault	Agricultural Hearings
Complaints against growers and police	Working conditions
The NFWA grape strike	Living conditions
	Small Farmer Price Support
	Land Taxation: Williamson Act
	Sections 14(b), Taft-Hartley Act
1966	**1966**
DiGiorgio sues UFWOC for $300,000	Minimum wages
Tulare Housing Authority tenants sue	Foreign labor
UFWOC sues DiGiorgio for $640,000	Section 14(b), Taft-Hartley Act
Charges against two strikers dropped	Unemployment insurance
DiGiorgio attempts picketing injunction	U.S. Senate Hearings
UFWOC charged with transgression by L&O	Calif. Senate Hearings
Chávez, priests, unionists arrested	National Labor Relations Act
UFWOC member charged with violence	Fringe benefits
El Malcriado sued for $1,010,000	Delano labor hearings
	State survey of farm labor
	Hawaiian farm labor
	National Agricultural Work Plan
1967	**1967**
Second complaint against *El Malcriado*	Collective bargaining
Boycotters arrested in San Francisco	Increased wage rate
UFWOC members arrested in Texas	Unemployment insurance
More members arrested in Texas	U.S. Reclamation Law
Teamsters clash with boycotters in S.F.	Green-card workers
Farm Workers Service Center protests	New bureau of employment agencies
Libel suit of $6,000,000 against UFWOC	Weakened protection for women
	Use of braceros
	Newly accepted 40 hour week

Legal (continued)

UFWOC officer sues John Birch Society
Texas Rangers arrest 60 UFWOC members
Judge declares Texas strike illegal
Rent strike in Visalia in 106th week
DiGiorgio and UFWOC clash in Yuba City
Foreman arrested for assault
Bakersfield judge limits UFWOC pickets
AFL-CIO sues to ban use of convict labor

1968
Anti-picketing injunctions and arrests
Illegal use of green-card workers
Chávez taken to court during fast
Fired worker has right to sue employer
Trial of 12 Texans
UFWOC organizer awarded $2,500
Growers sue New York Unions for 25 million
Damages claimed for boycott pickets
UFWOC suit on sanitary conditions
UFWOC denied pesticide records
Farm worker wins right to wear button
UFWOC challenges jury selection
UFWOC sues city of Delano
UFWOC sues growers for $650,000
UFWOC members interrupt Sen. Tunney
Show cause issued on pesticide files
UFWOC sues growers for $50,000,000
UFWOC sues growers for $125,000
Growers sue UFWOC for $75,000,000
Minimum wages granted by court
Pickets restrained in San Francisco
UFWOC sues AWFWA
UFWOC sues Agricultural Commissioner

1969
Hospitals refuse UFWOC members

Legislative (continued)

Illegal use of convict labor
Landrum-Griffin Act study

1968
New national farm worker lobby
NLRA coverage proposed
Calif. Land Conservation Act
Unemployment insurance
Illegal aliens and green-carders
Sen. Kennedy bill on green-carders
Federal Reclamation Law Subsidies
Minimum wages for minors

1969
Employment insurance

Legal (continued)

UFWOC demands pesticide records
UFWOC sues Coachella growers
G.E. ordered to allow gate funds
UFWOC charged with conspiracy
Growers sue UFWOC for $75,000,000
Jobless file for unemployment
Growers ordered to pay back wages
UFWOC sues labor contractors
UFWOC sues Bank of America
UFWOC sues AWFWA for $10,000,000

1970
UFWOC sues growers for $115,000,000
UFWOC sues to outlaw DDT
UFWOC sues for sanitary facilities
NLRB complaint against UFWOC
UFWOC sues Farm Labor Service
Injunctions issued for picketing
UFWOC sues Teamsters and growers
UFWOC sues Teamsters for $51,000,000
Restraining order against pickets
Strikers protected from evictions
Cel-A-Pak sues UFWOC and Teamsters
UFWOC sues Salinas growers
UFWOC strike ruled jurisdictional
NLRB refuses complaint against UFWOC
UFWOC files $5,000,000 pesticide suit
Chávez ordered to jail
State Supreme Court releases Chávez
Picketing limited with injunction

1971
UFWOC complaint against Defense Dept.
UFWOC members found guilty of assault
Growers sue UFWOC for $10,200,000
UFWOC chaplain in court suit

Legislative (continued)

Pesticides
Taft-Hartley Act
Illegal aliens
Anti-secondary boycotts
Right-to-work
Agricultural Conciliation Service
Nixon Farm Worker Plan
Immigration and Nationalist Act
NLRA coverage for farm workers
Labor contractors
Green-card workers
Farm subsidies
Sanitary facilities
Sen. Murphy's labor relations bill
Fair Employment Practice Act
Calif. Assembly Agriculture study

1970
Pesticide study
Consumer Agricultural Act
Congressional record on subsidies
Governor Reagan's Plan for farmworkers
State Conciliation Service
Economic Poison Safety Act of 1970
Farm Act of 1973

1971
Secret ballot elections proposals
Amendments to NLRB
Consumer Agricultural Act
Farm Workers Bill of Rights Act
Farm Workers Collective Bargaining Act

Legal (continued)

UFWOC sues Laird and Hamilton
UFWOC pesticide suit dismissed
Growers win case in court
State Supreme Court and Chávez case
UFWOC seeks injunctions against Laird
UFWOC fines suspended
Judge dismisses $240,000,000 suit
Egger-Ghio asks $350,000 damages
UFWOC sues Labor Department
Salinas sues UFWOC
UFWOC charges discrimination
UFWOC chaplain appeal denied
Restraining order against mass pickets
Discrimination case dismissed
Hearings for injunction dropped
Trespassing charges dropped

1972
Farm workers sue tomato shippers
Lettuce industry charged on practices
La Posada families challenge state
NLRB seeks injunction against UFWOC
NLRB sues UFWOC
Injunctions reviewed by judge
Pic 'N Pac wins right to evict families
UFWOC suspends wine boycott
Injunctions appealed to State Supreme Court
Suit against Arizona farm labor law by UFW
Proposition 22 investigated
UFW and AFL-CIO sue against Proposition 22
State sues to remove Proposition 22 from ballot
UFW picket sheriff's office
Farm Workers sue to end short handle hoe
Seventy pickets arrested
Two-hundred members arrested
UFWOC charges laxity on part of police
Calif. Supreme Court rules in favor of UFWOC

Legislative (continued)

Bans on secondary boycotts
Bans on strikes
Unemployment insurance
Calif. Ag. Labor Relations Act
Farm worker housing
Illegal aliens: Dixon Arnett bill
Oregon farm labor law veto
National Farm Labor Relations Act
Workmen's compensation
National Agricultural Bargaining Board
Farm Labor Secret Ballot Initiative

1972
California Labor Relations Act
U.S. Senate Hearings on farm labor
Unemployment insurance
Illegal aliens: Brophy and Arnett
National Labor Relations Board
National Ag. Labor Relations Act
Pesticide bill
Minimum wages
Idaho Agriculture Labor Act
Kansas farm labor bill
Arizona farm labor bill
Proposition 22

1965

Complaints against labor contractors
Rent strike in Visalia
Complaints against use of illegal aliens
Rancher charged with assault
Complaints against growers and police
The NFWA grape strike

Early in 1965, the National Farm Workers Association focused complaints against farm labor contractors before various labor commissions. The following is an example. A Delano contractor was taken before the Labor Commissioner in Visalia on charges that he had violated state law. At the hearing the contractor's attorney testified that workers were earning five dollars an hour. The workers represented by the Association, however, declared the workers' right to a minimum wage, saying that 50¢ per hour was illegal, and that the labor contractor should be made to pay a minimum wage.[11]

In Corcoran, California, another contractor was fined fifty-six dollars for refusing to reveal how much he was receiving from the grower and the salary he was paying workers. A new law was brought to the attention of the Association's members that declared that such information was public, and that the contractor had to provide the information if requested by a worker.[12]

Then, the Association's first major confrontation took place. Hundreds of farm workers in Linnell, and Woodville, California, stopped paying their rent. This action resulted from a rise in rents from eighteen to twenty-five dollars for those in "tin houses," which, according to the Association, were not worth sixteen dollars a month at the most. The workers were led by the Association's vice-president Gilbert Padilla. It was decided not to pay any rent until the authorities lowered the rent to eighteen dollars or less. An investigation to determine if there was fraud was begun by county officials. Subsequently, the rent strike was determined to be legal.

"The California State Civil Code, since 1941, says that if the proprietors do not keep up the houses at a minimum sanitation level against fires and fulfill all the code requisites of human habitation, therefore, the renters have the right under the law to withhold payment of rent."[13]

Meanwhile, a contractor from Tulare went before the Labor Com-

missioner in Visalia as a result of the Association's charges that he
falsified pay records. The grower then went to court to defend the
contractor. "The contractor's defense was cut to pieces by the Association's representative Gilbert Padilla. The contractor and the 'Patroncito'
lost the case. The labor Commissioner ordered the 'Patroncito' to pay
the workers immediately."[14]

In another case, a 56 year old member of the Association from
Corcoran was wounded by a contractor, Quiñones.

"In accordance with Olea's report he had gone to get paid. At the time Olea asked
the contractor how much the company was paying him. Quiñones became infuri-
ated and attacked him . . . The Sheriff's Officers of Kings County did not take any
action to arrest contractor Quiñones. . . . Moreover, Quiñones was taken to court
before the Labor Commissioner in Visalia on serious charges of violating the new
law. The law requires that the contractor reveal his earnings. Charges have been
pending for almost a year. The Association will demand that they take his license
away. The contractor has threatened the Association the last weeks. Publicly he
said he was going to fix Mr. Gilbert Padilla, who is working on this case for the
Association."[15]

A demand for $15,000 was made against contractor Manuel Quiño-
nes of Corcoran by Mr. Reynaldo Olea, who accused him of assault
with bad intent.[16] The District Attorney's office launched an investigation. Elsewhere, the Association filed complaints in Stockton against
growers who were employing illegal aliens. The immigration picked up
eighty-five illegal aliens (wetbacks) who were working on Mandeville
Island in Stockton. When investigated, the grower, Alfred Zuckerman,
said he did not know they were there.

"The only way to arrive on this island is by boat and no one is permitted on the
island without Zuckerman's permission. This is another example of how the big
ranchers feel that they are more important than the law."[17]

By August, the Visalia rent strikers were visited by eight health
inspectors from Tulare. They began investigating the charges of violations against sanitation laws by the housing commission.[18] Health officials later issued an order that the camps would be condemned if not
repaired. The county inspectors found fifty-one violations of the health
and housing laws. At the same time, another contractor from Corcoran
was called to court by the Labor Commissioner due to a complaint
made by the Association. The charges against the contractor consisted
of not having given receipts to a family on the deductions made from
their wages. The Commission fined the contractor, and money was
provided to the family in order to compensate them for lost time.

On September 1, a Buttonwillow, California judge signed a criminal
complaint against Bud Buerkle, a rancher accused of beating Ramiro
Villareal, age five years. The Association demanded that civil and criminal charges be made.

"The judge kept them there for more than an hour using such excuses as having forgotten the name of the person they were filing the complaint against, and other means of making the proceedings difficult. For these reasons, the Association feels that justice in a Buttonwillow court will not be met and possibly it will be requested that they will ask to take this to another court . . . Now Mr. Berkle, who is accused of beating the child without reason in the beginning of July, has two complaints against him—civil and criminal."[19]

Then, the Association filed complaints against Exeter Dehydration, a grower who fired twelve employees. The Federal Government investigated regarding wages and the improvement of working conditions.[20] Elsewhere a police officer from Hanford, California, was charged with assaulting two members of the Association. The two workers sued the officer in civil court for $100,000.[21]

The NFWA went on strike against the Delano grape growers on September 16, 1965. NFWA immediately charged that laws were not equally being applied to growers and strikers in Kern County, Tulare County, and the City of Delano.

"Strikers seeking justice or making complaints have been harassed and forced to face many delays . . . V. G. McElhancy, special agent of the Bureau of Investigation, Department of Justice was sent to Delano on a special mission . . .

"In Tulare County Eugene Nelson was shoved violently several times by Charlie Dispoto in front of four witnesses. Mr. Nelson reported the incident to the Sheriff on the spot. When he sought to file a complaint with the assistant D.A. in Portersville he was unable to meet with the official for sometime . . . The D.A. told Mr. Nelson that the complaint was stale, that the Sheriff's department was working 12 hours a day and didn't have enough men to investigate every complaint . . .

"In Delano, Milan Caratan knocked down a picketor, Israel Garza, in front of many witnesses. A police report was made by officers . . . when Mr. Garza sought to make a complaint against Caratan, the D.A. proved so uncooperative that Mr. Garza had to go to the judge. Also, in Delano, Hector Abeytia of AWOC was beaten by Charlie Dispoto, in front of witnesses. The police who made the report referred to Mr. Dispoto as 'assaultant unknown.' They ignored the testimony of Abeytia . . . Mr. Abeytia's complaint has still not been accepted."[22]

In October, a large group of workers decided to walk off the A. Caratan Ranch after hearing about the strike. Dolores Huerta, vice-president of NFWA, was charged with 'trespassing' on one of the ranches. A complaint was signed. She pleaded innocent and requested a jury trial. The trail was to be held in Pixley.[23] Meanwhile, many others were arrested and taken to the Bakersfield jail. They were in jail three days, while bail money was being raised. One minister was arrested for reading in a loud speaker "the definition of a scab."[24]

At the same time, the rent strikers of Linnell and Woodville won a victory when Judge Paul Eyman declared that the raised rent prices in the camps were illegal. The renters agreed to pay the back rent at eighteen dollars per month.[25] Shortly after, a state investigation looking into the problems of housing for farm workers was held in Visalia.[26]

Finally, NFWA's complaints against labor contractors were depicted by *El Malcriado* as follows:

"The most famous case was that of Jim Hronis, rich and powerful Delano contractor . . . A series of dramatic hearings were held in Visalia . . . Hronis took the first steps in a libel action against *El Malcriado* but he abandoned the charges when this paper continued to attack him with the truth.

"Charges were sought against many other contractors and growers for violations of the law. In one Corcoran case, contractor Lupe Martinez was fined $158 and this was given directly to the Alafa family."[27]

1966

DiGiorgio sues UFWOC for $300,000
Tulare County Housing Authority tenants go to court
USWOC sues DiGiorgio for $640,000
Charges against two strikers dropped
DiGiorgio attempts to obtain injunction against picketing
UFWOC charged with transgression by L&O
Chávez, priests, unionists charged with trespassing
UFWOC member charged with violence
El Malcriado sued for $1,010,000

After the grape strike started in September 1965, legal cases for the most part involved the strike efforts. NFWA and AWOC-AFL-CIO had great demands for attorneys to protect their rights. On February 12, 1966, the DiGiorgio Fruit Corporation claimed that the strike had not hurt it too much, but at the same time it wanted to sue the unions for about $300,000 it claimed to have lost since December. It demanded that the courts outlaw all picketing of their grapes at the docks. The lawyers for AWOC and the NFWA went to work on the case. A judge in Visalia studied the evidence and ruled that the farmworkers could picket the grapes in Delano, in San Francisco, Los Angeles, New York, in the vineyards, or on the docks. The judge dismissed DiGiorgio's lawsuits, saying that DiGiorgio should expect to lose money since there was a strike on, and the Corporation was ordered not to interfere with the legal picketing of the docks.[28]

At the same time, the Tulare County Housing Authority, facing legal action as tenants who were members of NFWA obtained a court restraining order to prevent evictions, began a public investigation of the "bureaucrats."[29]

In May, UFWOC (formerly NFWA and AWOC) sued DiGiorgio for

$640,000 for an attack by DiGiorgio security guards against their strikers.

"Nunes took out a loaded gun and pointed it at Miss Ida Cousino (a teacher) and five other persons who were not armed, and threatened to kill them. When Miss Cousino protested and tried to reprimand him she was attacked and thrown to the floor. Mr. Manuel Rosas stepped in to help he: and was struck and his head opened. He needed 13 stitches. DiGiorgio's gunman also hit and threatened Mr. Manuel Vasquez of Earlimart . . . Rosas is demanding $90,000 from DiGiorgio for the attack and pressed charges last week. Miss Cousino and the other strikers are suing for a total of $550,000 in their legal charges against DiGiorgio."[30]

On May 19, two striking grape pickers (Vincent Rivera, 22 and Pablo Ruiz, 55) who were charged with "slashing tires and breaking windows" of a contractor's bus at the M. Caratan "Hacienda" the previous January, pleaded not guilty in a Pixley, California court. The growers case against them was so weak that the judge and district attorney dismissed the case.[31]

By June, DiGiorgio was demanding that the Tulare County courts outlaw all picketing at the DiGiorgio ranch, and that policemen help them to break the strike. In addition to demanding that all strikers be arrested, if more than six of them were picketing together near the 4,700 acres of vineyards or 206 entrances to the Sierra Vista Ranch, they also demanded that the courts outlaw shouting by strikers who were trying to talk to "scabs" in the vineyards.

"All the DiGiorgio demands are contained in a complicated legal form called an injunction. DiGiorgio wants the Tulare County judges to make this injunction part of the law . . . The lawyers for the farm workers, including Alex Hoffmand and Abraham Lincoln Wiren, will ask the judges to throw the whole injunction into the garbage can where it belongs."[32]

In another case, Mr. Pablo Izquierdo, who worked at the L&O Growers Association of Santa Paula, was arrested and taken to court. The judge asked him if he pleaded guilty. He, in turn, asked for the charges against him. The judge answered that he was not to direct any questions to him, and that if he was not at fault, then he should get an attorney to represent him. He was accused of transgression. He denied the accusation, since he was already an employee of the company and had only asked for his check. On the 24th of June the county prosecutor announced that he was dropping the charges, based on a complete investigation and concluded that it would be unjust to blame Mr. Izquierdo since it was all a bad misunderstanding.[33]

Then on July 12, the first part of the trial of eight farm workers, a Catholic priest, a Protestant minister and César Chávez, took place in Ramona. The charge was trespassing. The charges against the workers were dismissed. But the jury concluded that the priests and Mr. Chávez were guilty. The conviction of Father Salandini, Reverend Hartmire, and Sr. Chávez were appealed.[34]

Meanwhile the union, UFWOC, charged injustice following the court decision made on October 12. The Pixley Court sentenced Manuel Rosas, a striker and longtime member of the union, to eight months in jail.

"After the attack, the cops rushed in and tried to arrest Rosas! But the other strikers grabbed Rosas away (he was dazed and bleeding profusely by this time) and rushed him to the hospital . . . Rosas actually pleaded guilty, since he had gone to the hospital after the battle, instead of going to jail . . . But Judge Del Rey closed his eyes to any kind of fairness, and sentenced Rosas to 240 days in jail.[35]

Then on November 4, a lawsuit was filed in the superior court of Kern County for $1,010,000.00 against *El Malcriado: The Voice of the Farm Workers*. The action was taken by Bud Antle, a large lettuce grower. *El Malcriado* had said that the contract signed between the Teamsters and Bud Antle, Inc., put the farm workers in "more slavery than ever."[36]

1967

Second complaint against *El Malcriado*
Boycotters arrested in San Francisco
UFWOC members arrested in Texas
More members arrested in Texas
Teamsters clash with boycotters in San Francisco
Farm Workers Service Center protests Century Home Products
Libel suit of $6,000,000 against UFWOC
IFWPC vice-president sues John Birch Society
Texas Rangers arrest 60 UFWOC members
Judge declares Texas strike illegal
Rent strike in Visalia in 106th week
DiGiorgio and UFWOC clash in Yuba City
Foreman arrested for assault on UFWOC member in Texas
Bakersfield judge limits UFWOC pickets
California AFL-CIO sues to ban use of convict labor

In January 1967 the Superior Court of Bakersfield threw out a second complaint by Bud Antle, Inc. against *El Malcriado* in the $1,100,000 lawsuit for libel. The newspaper's lawyer, Arthur Brunwasser of San Francisco, stated that there were not enough facts in Antle's complaint to bring an action against the paper.[37] Meanwhile, boycotters were arrested in San Francisco while protesting the sale of Perelli-Minetti products. And, four farmworkers were arrested at Trophy Farms on charges of using abusive language with a loud speaker system. The strikers were talking to the strike-breakers in the field and criticizing the unsanitary conditions in the fields.

". . . Rev. Jim Drake led the group in prayer at least sixty feet away from the building. During the ceremony Gilbert Padilla and Rev. Drake were arrested for disturbing the peace: The complaint was filed by the janitor who, at the time, was cleaning on the third floor of the court house."[38]

In Texas, more than 100 arrests of farm workers were made for picketing at La Casita Farms. As a result of the arrests by Sheriff Albert Peña of Starr County the FBI began an investigation of civil rights violations.

"The last straw that has brought about the FBI investigation was the arbitrary and illegal arrest of three Catholic priests who have been helping the strikers of Rio Grande City. Five priests arrested in Lanuby for appearing in Rio Grande City in support of the strikers were released from disciplinary action by their bishop."[39]

In March, a San Francisco boycotter and picket captain were attacked by four Teamster union members in front of the Purity Market in the Mission District. Three teamsters and two boycotters were arrested. The boycotters were picketing "scab" products of Perelli-Minetti & Sons.

"Police were reluctant to book the trio, but finally did when Shroyer (boycotter), who sped to police headquarters from the hospital, said that if they were not booked, UFWOC would make citizen's arrests."[40]

In April, the Teamsters arrested at Purity Market were tried and convicted. In sentencing them Judge Joseph Kennedy said:

". . . while the labor movement is definitely indispensible to this country, these labor people did not act in a civilized manner, and we cannot condone this uncivilized violence."[41]

The Farm Workers Service Center assisted many families with legal advice not directly related to strikes and boycotts. This service started in 1962 when Chçavez himself assisted families to locate an attorney. This service remained a large part of the legal department's caseload. The following is an example of such legal service. In April, three union families complained to the Service Center that they had been cheated by the Century Home Products Corporation, which operated out of Lynwood, California.

"This company sells pots and pans at extremely high prices. Door to door salesmen come to the houses of prospective customers. Usually these salesmen are Mexican-American if the family is Spanish-speaking . . . of course they do not tell what is really in the contract

The three families have come to the Service Center . . . The Service Center has written letters to the company in each case . . . We have also filed complaints with the Better Business Bureau in Bakersfield . . . Also the attorney general's office, department of commercial fraud has been informed of these cases."[42]

In May, Perelli-Minetti filed a six million dollar libel suit against UFWOC.

"UFWOC's lawyers say that should old P-M pursue this folly in the court-room, it will be thrown out for lack of evidence leaving him several thousands in court costs the loser—and we do hope at least a touch wiser."[43]

In June, UFWOC Vice-president Larry Itlong sued the John Birch Society.

"The lawsuit was filed in San Francisco last week by Larry. The Birch Society, enemies of the people, are publishers of the *Opinion* magazine in the eastern United States . . . Larry, assistant director of the United Farm Workers, said, 'I am not now, nor ever have been a communist and *American Opinion* (the Birch book) labeled me that out of ill will and hatred.' "[44]

In Mission, Texas, the Texas Rangers made over 60 arrests.[45] On May 26, a group of strikers went to Mission where the arrests occurred. Meanwhile, in Rio Grande City, Texas, the labor strike in Starr County was costing La Casita Farms over $1,000 each day.

"First they tried to stop the strike by arresting all of the huelguistas in one day. They arrested 22 people near Trophy Farms and 12 more near La Casita . . . then the workers seized upon an existing fraud law and obtained a court order from Judge Laughlin (the Judge has been formally accused of dishonesty). The Judge in effect declared the strike illegal and prevented the strikers from picketing in the camps or near the packing sheds."[46]

In July, the Visalia rent strike initiated in 1965 by NFWA members was continuing. The Linnell-Woodville rent strike was in its 106th week. The rent strikers had succeeded in blocking a one and one-third million dollar loan to the Tulare County Housing Authority by the Federal Government. The argument given to the Federal Government by the strikers and their attorneys was that it was illegal for the government to give money to a county that was trying to throw out the people who they were supposed to be helping with the money. The strikers had demanded an extension of time before evictions could begin. The extension was granted.

In Yuba City, California, DiGiorgio Corporation officials attempted to scare off union organizers when an assistant manager threatened and swung a hoe at UFWOC organizers. "The district attorney refused to bring charges against the manager."[47]

In July, the union reported that in Starr County, Texas, the police had never before arrested a boss or foreman on a complaint signed by a worker. A foreman had been charged with assault and battery against Mrs. Celia López. She went to the courthouse and filed a complaint.

The foreman was arrested and held in jail for an hour, and had to pay a bond of $400.

In August, *El Malcriado* responded to a significant legal ruling against UFWOC:

"On August 7, the kind of 'injustice' that prevails in Mississippi and Texas was dealt by a Bakersfield Judge to the United Farm Workers Organizing Committee. The union, which has been picketing the Giumarra Vineyards Corporation for four days, received an injunction from Judge J. Kelley Steele, cutting the effectiveness of the unions pickets.

"It limits the number of pickets to three per entrance, and further states that these three pickets must never come closer than fifty feet from each other. The strikers are also forbidden to wave down cars that bring the scabs to the fields, or to follow the scabs to the labor camps after work in order to talk to them about the strike.

"The ten-day restraining order is harsher even than similar injunctions which growers in Texas have secured against UFWOC's strikers. In Rio Grande Valley, the union is allowed two persons every fifty feet, and the total number of pickets is not limited.

"Giumarra repeatedly denies the existence of any strike, although nearly 300 picketers, most of them Giumarra's workers, have seriously cut Giumarra's work force . . . Giumarra is suing UFWOC for $150,000 in damages."[48]

In October, UFWOC was assisted by the California Labor Federation, AFL-CIO. The Federation filed a suit to bar the use of convict labor in the fields on October 5th. Governor Reagan's authority to use convict labor in California's fields was challenged as unconstitutional. The suit was taken under submission by San Francisco's Superior Court Judge Robert L. Drewes. He said he would request further argument on the case before granting or denying the temporary restraining order. The Federation's general counsel, Charles P. Scully, pointed out the fact that the Governor authorized the use of 200 state convicts to harvest figs in Merced County, September 28, and that the convicts actually began work October 1, a day before the correctional center was established at Denel Vocational Institute to handle them. On November 17, the Federation announced it had won the suit to bar the use of State convicts on farms. A preliminary injunction was granted.[49]

1968

Violations charged in anti-picketing injunction
Case of illegal use of green-card workers
Chávez taken to court
Court decision giving fired worker right to sue employer
The trial of 12 Texans

UFWOC organizer awarded $2,500
California grape growers sue New York Unions for $25,000,000
UFWOC sues Kern County growers for $50,000,000
Damages claimed for boycott pickets
UFWOC sues for failure to provide sanitary conditions
UFWOC denied pesticide records
Farm worker wins right to wear Union button
UFWOC challenges jury selection system
UFWOC sues city of Delano for $37,000
UFWOC sues several grape growers for $650,000
UFWOC members guilty of interrupting Tunney speech
Show cause issued regarding pesticide records
UFWOC sues growers for $50,000,000
UFWOC sues growers for $125,000
Grower suit for $75,000,000 against UFWOC
Minimum wages for women and children granted by court
Restraining order restricts picketing in San Francisco
UFWOC sues AWFWA
UFWOC sues Agricultural Commissioner

By the end of 1967, UFWOC's Legal Department was established as a result of grant monies provided for legal services. Attorney Cohen was appointed General Counselor. On February 15th, 1968, UFWOC picket captain Camacho, charged with contempt of a Giumarra anti-strike injunction in effect since August, entered a plea of not guilty in Kern County Superior Court. In addition to alleged violations of the injunction, two of the twelve counts clearly lay the groundwork for further charges of either arson, conspiracy to commit arson, or both. The case was scheduled for a "show-cause" hearing before Judge Steels on February 26. Under the "show-cause" procedure, the entire burden of proof fell on the Union, which meant in effect, that "officers and members of the Union were considered guilty until proven innocent."[50]

Almost at the same time, eleven "green carders" had been arrested at Cipriano Padillo's labor camp. When the Border Patrol gave them orders to leave, they remained because a company agent told them that the Border Patrolmen were strikers dressed up as officers. Arrests were made on the second visit. Giumarra bailed out the men, and a hearing was scheduled for March 18:

"A number of growers are working hand in glove with Giumarra to challenge the immigration law which forbids green carders to act as strike breakers. They have hired a Los Angeles attorney named Bonaparte to do the job for them. The March 18 decision can be crucial in determining whether or not a free flow of strike breakers will be permitted to cross the international border."[51]

Then, on February 27, César Chávez was taken to court, weakened by the thirteen days of his religious fast. The charge: 12 alleged violations of an anti-strike injunction issued in August 1967 by Kern County Superior Court Judge J. Kelly Stub. On the second day, the judge announced that he would not subject Chávez to the ordeal of a lengthy trial at that time. The hearing was reset for April 22 in Superior Court at Bakersfield.[52]

On April 9, Judge Ferguson of the Kern County Superior Court decided that UFWOC had a right to sue Giumarra for illegal recruitment. According to the California Labor Code, no employer in a labor dispute could recruit workers without informing them that a strike was going on. UFWOC brought suit on behalf of Mariano Esquira, asking for damages based on illegal recruitment.[53]

At the same time, the Superior Court in Bakersfield temporarily postponed the trial of Epifanio Camacho, UFWOC picket captain, and the 300 union members charged with breaking Giumarra's court injunction. Charges against Chávez were dropped entirely. The injunction said pickets must stand fifty feet apart, at each entrance, and it prohibited leafleting and visiting of scabs in their home.[54]

On April 15, UFWOC attorney Cohen appeared before the judge in a motion to release the Giumarra evidence for inspection in the contempt case against the Union, César Chávez, Epifanio Camacho, and 300 "John Does." Cohen argued that when there were criminal charges the defense attorney had a right to inspect the evidence. Judge Borten agreed, but limited the order.[55]

Meanwhile, *El Malcriado* lashed out against a Kern County ruling that had been made in Lamont, California.

"The law in Kern County ruled today that it's okay to pull a pistol on a striker, just so long as you back up the pistol threat with a sawed-off shotgun. Judge Head ruled on a case which originated last August when Miss Jessica Goven, UFWOC secretary, tried to serve a subpoena at a Giumarra labor camp."[56]

On April 18, 1968, in Bakersfield, it was decided that a worker had a right to sue his employer if he was fired for union activity.[57] Furthermore, Judge Steel dismissed contempt of court action against Chávez. The action, initiated by the Giumarra Vineyards Corporation, had charged Chávez and UFWOC with violations of a preliminary injunction. The charges were dismissed as a result of a request by Giumarra.[58]

In Texas, June 11, the trial of 12 Texans accused of conspiracy to deny UFWOC members of their constitutional rights began in Brownsville. The twelve defendants, six Texas rangers and six Starr County officials, were in court to answer charges filed by UFWOC in 1967, after the rangers and growers had "snuffed" out a strike of melon pickers. The suit also challenged the constitutionality of six Texas statutes which had virtually annihilated all strike efforts in Texas. The previous year, trains carrying "scab" melons had been guarded by machine-guns mounted on railroad cars.[59]

Then, a court decision favoring UFWOC was made in Bakersfield. Damages of $2,500 were awarded UFWOC organizer Mark Silverman by a Bakersfield judge, after a trial which proved Silverman had been attacked and beaten by Giumarra contractor Valeriano Juarez on May 16.[60]

Significantly, by July, California growers claimed that the boycott of California table grapes had cost them $25 million in the previous two months. In a suit filed in New York, over 100 grape growers claimed losses or threats of losses costing them hundreds of thousands of dollars apiece. They demanded that unions in New York, which had supported the boycott, pay damages of $25 million to make up for the losses. *El Malcriado* stated:

"The NLRA also forbids secondary boycotts (but not consumer boycotts). Growers now claim that while the law does not protect the farm workers, it should protect the employers against the boycott. This is the basis of the $25 million suit."[61]

On July 10, in Fresno, California, an extension of time for further consideration of arguments was granted by presiding Judge Conley of the District Court of Appeals in the case of Giumarra Corporation's suit against UFWOC for alleged violations of an anti-strike injunction.

"In the appeal court Cohen argued that the union had the right to a jury trial, since the case could involve heavy fines or imprisonment. Giumarra attorneys, John Giumarra, Jr., and William A. Quinlan, maintained that there was no right to a jury trial. Cohen said the union's lawyer and the opposition would present further arguments in writing for the consideration of the three-judge court. The trial of the union on contempt charges will not come about until the constitutional question of the jury is decided, he said."[62]

In August, fifty million dollars in compensatory and punitive damages were demanded of three Kern County growers in a suit filed by UFWOC. The UFWOC suit alleged that Bruno Dispoto Company, Sabovick Brothers and John J. Kovacevich had sold scab grapes in boxes bearing a Union label. The suit was filed in an attempt to halt the false labelling, as well as to secure damages for the effect on the Union of the alleged fraud.[63]

Meanwhile, on August 15, UFWOC made the following claims: The largest claim had been filed on behalf of Bill Richardson, a young Seminarian who was brutally beaten in a Coachella Valley vineyard July 2. Richardson demanded $410,000 in Actual and punitive damages from Ralph S. Jacobs and David Freedman and Co., a major Coachello grower. UFWOC lawyers were also representing Peter Williamson, a law student volunteer, who had alleged that on July 18 Jose Mendoza pointed a rifle at his head in front of the Union headquarters. Damages sought in this case totaled $30,000. Fr. Mark Day was seeking $28,000 in damages for an alleged assault and battery on him at the Mosesian

Company. And, Dale Van Pelt, a member of the Migrant Ministry, had filed a $20,000 suit charging he was struck by Milton Freedman while marching on a picket line in the Coachella Valley.[64]

In addition, UFWOC attorneys filed suit on behalf of four California grape pickers charging their employers with failure to provide private, sanitary toilets and hand washing facilities in the fields. The four defendants were William Steele and Son, Virginia Guidera, Giumarra Vineyards, and David Freedman and Company.[65]

On August 22, 1968, Bakersfield Judge J. Kelley Stub issued a temporary restraining order prohibiting state agriculture officials from showing public records to Union investigators. The order specifically prohibited Kern County Agriculture Commissioner Sheldon Morley from showing Union officials pest control reports, permits, and applicator's reports dealing with chemical sprays, poisons, and other injurious materials used on crops. Cohen and UFWOC attorney David Averbuck filed a writ of mandate to overturn the restraining order and force the Agriculture Commissioner to show these records to the public.

"The request for the injunction was presented by Atwood Aviation Company and several other firms, and appears to have been rather hurriedly prepared. Atwood Aviation does chemical spraying for many local growers. The petition for the Morley conferred with Atwood's and growers' lawyers before the petition was filed. Within two hours, a petition for an injunction was drawn up and presented to Judge Steele, who quickly signed it."[66]

Also, in August, in Wauntoma, Wisconsin, a family of Mexican American farm workers went to court and established the right to wear their Union buttons without fear of being fired. In addition, they won $104 in back pay from grower Jon Wilcox, who had fired them and evicted them from his camp for wearing buttons that said "Viva la Causa."[67] Elsewhere, McFarland, California, Judicial District Court Judge John McNally ruled that the jury selection system used in the area was not discriminatory. The ruling was issued in response to a challenge by UFWOC attorneys maintaining that the naming of Jurors from voter registration lists was discriminatory because it did not provide for equal representation of the whole population.[68]

Meanwhile, it was announced in Bakersfield, that Manuel Rivera would be tried on November 15 on charges filed by anti-unionist Ignacio Rubio on similar charges filed by Union member Rivera.

"All charges arose after an incident on August 13 in which the Rubios and three carloads of their family and friends forced Rivera off the road, dragged him from his car and beat him unconscious. Gilbert Rubio also faces trial on October 18 on charges that he appeared at a UFWOC picket line brandishing a gun in a threatening and provocative manner."[69]

In August, after months of trying to get the city of Delano and the Delano police to treat the Union differently, the United Farm Workers Organizing Committee filed charges against the city, demanding over $37,000 in damages for illegal actions against Union members by Delano police. Elsewhere, the Fifth District Court of Appeal in Fresno denied the right of the United Farm Workers Organizing Committee and picket Epifanio Camacho Baez to a jury in their trial on contempt charges. The charges stemmed from a Giumarra Vineyards complaint against the Union and Camacho filed in February. The complaint, which originally included César Chávez as a defendant, alleged 12 violations of an anti-strike injunction issued in August of 1967 by Bakersfield Superior Court Judge J. Kelley Steele. Union attorneys appealed the case to the State Supreme Court on the basis that a jury trial was merited in cases with possible heavy penalties, either in fines or prison.[70]

On September 5, four UFWOC supporters were sentenced to 120 days in jail as a result of a decision announced by Tom Cross, judge of the Coachella Justice Court. Cross handed down the 120 day sentences after a jury found James S. Caswell of Indio; Raul Loya, Indio High School teacher and president of the Mexican American Political Association of Indio; Albert Figueroa of Blythe, a MAPA leader; and Thomas Kay, a UFWOC organizer, guilty of disturbing a public assembly during a Tunney rally.

"During the course of Tunney's speech, Figueroa raised a UFWOC sign so that Tunney would know we were still there. The crowds began to applaud spontaneously when the sign was raised, Figueroa said . . . Caswell said the conviction was based on section 403 of California Penal Code, which was passed in 1872."[71]

On September 11, in Bakersfield, damages of $650,000 were asked in a suit filed by the United Farm Workers Organizing Committee against several grape growers and the Agricultural Workers Freedom to Work Association (AWFWA). The suit charged violations of the Labor Code and what amounted to conspiracy to deny farm workers the right to organize. Named in the suit were growers Jack Pandol, Giumarra Vineyards, the AWFWA, and two of its heads, Gilbert Rubio and José Mendoza.

". . . their suit was based in part on section 1122 of the California Labor Code, which provides: 'Any person who organizes an employee group which is financed in whole or in part, interfered with or dominated or controlled by the employer or employer association shall be liable to suit by any person who is injured thereby. Said injured party shall recover the damages sustained by him and the costs of the suit.' "[72]

On September 16, in Hollister, California, UFWOC demanded that San Benito District Attorney Bernard McCullough apologize and dismiss trespassing charges against two Union members in a case that arose during a picket line in Hollister, August 30. Two members of the Union, Francisco Urike and Gilbert Tyrinia, both 17, were arrested for trespassing. UFWOC's attorney cited the famous Supreme Court decision of *Amalgamated Food Employees Union Local #590 vs. Logan Valley Plaza, Inc.*, handed down on May 20, 1968, as establishing the right of people to picket stores either on the sidewalk or, if there is a shopping center, on a large parking lot directly in front of the store entrance. However, McCullough refused to recognize this decision and went ahead with trespass charges, which were taken to Juvenile Court.[73]

At the same time, the Appellate Court in Fresno demanded that the State Department of Agriculture and Judge J. Kelley Steele appear before it on October 16 and "show cause" why they should not allow UFWOC representatives to study public records dealing with poisons and dangerous chemicals used on grapes.[74]

On September 23, in Delano, UFWOC charges against growers Bruno Dispoto, Sabovitch and Sons, John Kovacovitch and others for falsely labelling their grapes were heard in San Francisco. The $50 million suit alleged that the defendants falsely marked their grapes with DiGiorgio label in an effort to mislead consumers.[75] At the same time the Union filed a complaint in the U.S. District Court against Giumarra Vineyards Corporation, Giumarra Brothers Fruit Co., Pandol Sons, Barr Packing Company and Vincent Zaninovich and Sons for what appeared to be a clear violation of the Sherman Anti-Trust Act, sections 1-7, and the Clayton Anti-Trust Act, section 12. The complaint charged the growers with "illegal and unlawful combination in their efforts to break the Union boycott activities." The Union suit asked for $125,000 (which the court could triple to $375,000).[76]

Union lawyers filed two other suits on September 23, in San Francisco Superior Court, for violence allegedly committed against Mr. and Mrs. Lupe Murguia and Fred Ross, Jr. while the three were picketing the Mayfair store at the corner of Geary and Webster in San Francisco.[77]

On September 26, in Milwaukee, Jesus Solas, leader of the grape boycott in Wisconsin, was arrested as he and three others picketed inside a Kohl's Food Store. Trial was set for October 10 on charges of disorderly conduct.[78]

On September 30, San Francisco Federal Court Judge Lloyd Burke dismissed out of hand a request by grower groups for an injunction to halt the UFWOC boycott of California table grapes. Union General Council Cohen, who argued the case in San Francisco, said the Ballantine Produce Company, the Barr Packing Company, California Fruit Exchange, the Mendleson-Zeller Company, the Rozial Valley Fruit

Growers had asked the court to issue an order stopping boycott activities, but that Judge Burke ruled in a five-minute hearing that the court had no power to enjoin labor activities.

"The growers and shippers, in the same action, also sued UFWOC for $75 million under the Sherman Anti-Trust Act, and had requested the injunction as a temporary stop-gap until the case came to trial. Judge Burke overruled the request of the growers on the basis of provisions of the Norris-La Guardia Act."[79]

Then, in September, the State Court of Appeals in Sacramento ruled that over 100,000 women and minors should get the same minimum wage as other workers; $1.65 an hour for women, $1.35 for minors. The court ruled that workers should receive the minimum wage retroactive to February 1, 1968, when it was legally put into effect.[80]

On October 10, in San Francisco, a $75 million suit brought against the Union was requested to be dropped by counsel for California grape growers and shippers. UFWOC attorney Averbuck responded:

"We're not so sure we're going to let them drop the suit though, because there's a possibility we can sue them within the framework of the same case, Averbuck explained."[81]

On October 18, at a hearing in San Francisco, growers and shippers obtained a temporary restraining order restricting picketing to within 50 yards of the dock area. However, UFWOC's Cohen explained the purpose of the picketing and appealed the injunction. Judge Eyman of Superior Court of San Francisco limited the force of the injunction, allowing two pickets to be placed 15 feet on either side of each entrance to the docks. In Los Angeles, an injunction prohibiting Union picketing was issued at the request of 17 different chain stores on October 23. The following day the injunction was appealed and the judge ruled that four pickets could be placed at store entrances, four at store driveways, and that the bullhorn could be used 25 feet from the store.[82]

On October 28, in San Luis Obispo, California, José Mendoza, officer of the sporadic Agricultural Workers Freedom to Work Association, showed up for a debate at the San Luis Obispo Campus of California State Polytechnic College (Cal Poly) and was promptly served with a UFWOC complaint which asked $650,000 damages for his "union-busting" activities.[83]

Also in October, Epifranio Camacho-Baez argued in Superior Court of Kern County, that jury selection in Kern County was unfair. Camacho, charged with malicious mischief growing out of a February 5th complaint, felt he would not be judged by a jury "of his peers" as guaranteed by the Constitution.

Furthermore, in October, the UFWOC was suing Agricultural Commissioner Morley for not allowing Cohen, on June 20, access to public records, and the Kern County Superior Court for issuing an injunction the following day prohibiting Cohen's examination of the pesticide records.

In Chicago, William G. Clark, Attorney General of the State of Illinois, filed against the Chicago distributor of Giumarra grapes for selling falsely labelled grapes. Clark charged in the complaint, "to avoid the impact of the boycott, Giumarra entered into an agreement with other grape growers to use their brand names and labels." Selling these mislabelled grapes was in violation of the state consumer fraud act.[84]

On November 4, in San Francisco, the attempt by grape growers and shippers to halt the UFWOC consumer boycott of California table grapes with a $75 million suit against the Union was dropped by the plaintiffs. Attorneys for the Ballantine Produce Company, the California Fruit Exchange, the Mendelson-Zeller Company, and the Royal Valley Fruit Growers dropped the suit, which was filed originally on September 30. UFWOC assistant general counsel, David Averbuck, said the Union filed a countersuit against the growers and shippers, charging them with a conspiracy and pricefixing in violation of the Sherman Anti-Trust Law. The UFWOC suit said the United Farm Workers had sustained $125,000 in damages to the boycott as the result of alleged illegal practices on the part of the growers.[85]

On December 13, in Delano, it was announced that hearings on a request by crop dusting firms in the Kern County area to deny access to public records on the use of pesticides to UFWOC attorneys were to be held in Bakersfield on January 29, 1969.

Later, on December 31, in Delano, it was announced that UFWOC picket captain Epifanio Camacho would be tried on charges of malicious mischief in Delano-McFarland Justice Court on January 17, with Judge McNally presiding. *El Malcriado* stated:

"If Camacho goes to trial without equal protection of the laws, a full and detailed report will be sent to the U.S. Justice Department and to the Commission on Civil Rights."[86]

Also in December, in Salem, Oregon, Marion County District Court Judge Thomas W. Hansen declared a mistrial in the case of Nick Jones, UFWOC organizer in Oregon, when Jones appeared in court December 26 to face a charge of vagrancy and disorderly conduct. The jury was unable to reach a verdict after Jones' trial.[87]

1969

Hospitals refuse to admit UFWOC Medi-Cal patients
UFWOC continues demand for access to pesticide records
UFWOC sues Coachella growers

General Electric ordered to allow gate collections
UFWOC charges conspiracy
Growers sue UFWOC for $75,000,000
Jobless file for unemployment benefits
UFWOC members fired, file suit
Growers ordered to pay back wages to women and children
UFWOC sues labor contractor
UFWOC sues another labor contractor
UFWOC member sues Bank of America
UFWOC sues AWFWA for $10,000,000

On January 7, 1969, in Visalia, California, tax supported hospitals, which formerly refused to admit Medi-Cal patients would no longer be allowed to do so, as the result of a decision of Tulare County Superior Court Judge Leonard Ginsbert.

"Farm worker and UFWOC member Eluterio P. Loredo, 59, of Poplar, had filed suit against the Sierra View Hospital District after he was refused in Porterville because the cost of his case was to be paid by the Medi-Cal program. Judge Ginsberg's ruling declared that tax-supported hospitals may not discriminate against any segment of the public in their admission policies."[88]

In February, hearings regarding pesticide records were reported. Crop dusting companies, represented by attorney Stephen Wall, were technically the plaintiffs, while Morley, represented by County Attorney Jordan, were the defendants. Cohen, represented by Averbuck, was the third party in the suit. If Judge Brown ruled that the records should be kept secret until a final decision was reached, he would cancel the temporary restraining order and replace it with a preliminary injunction, which, in effect, was just about the same thing. In that case, a new hearing would be held to determine whether a final injunction, keeping the records permanently secret should be issued, or if a writ of mandate should be served on the Agricultural Commissioner, forcing him to reveal the records.[89]

On March 27, in Bakersfield, Judge George A. Brown ruled that UFWOC Attorney Jerome Cohen and the other representatives of the Union should be denied access to all public records on pesticide and herbicide poison applications filed with the County Agricultural Commissions.

"The Judge further stated, 'The importance of the agricultural chemical industry to this valley and this state is enormous, not only in terms of the employment and income which it generates, but in terms of the astronomical increase in productivity and improvement in quality of food and fiber that has accompanied widespread use of agricultural chemicals.' "[90]

On April 1, in Coachella, members of the Desert Grape Growers

League, and President Mike Bozick were named defendants in a $1 million libel suit filed by United Farm Workers Organizing Committee:

"Chávez said today Bozick 'knowingly made unfounded statements March 26 when he told the press that the union and I were responsible for alleged threats on the lives of growers Keene Larsen and crew boss Josephone Garcia.' "[91]

In June, the Ninth U.S. Circuit Court of Appeals in San Francisco handed down a decision that the General Electric Company could not prohibit trade unionists from taking up collections for striking grape workers at their plant gates. The court's decision granted a request by the National Labor Relations Board for enforcement of an NLRB order at the G.E. plant in San Jose. Twice in 1966, the plant's management refused to permit Local 1507 of the Electrical Workers Union to take up voluntary collections at the plant for the AFL-CIO United Farm Workers Organizing Committee.[92]

In July, UFWOC filed a suit claiming a conspiracy by a group of growers and labor contractors to create a dummy "union," the Agricultural Workers Freedom to Work Association. The Union claimed that because of the extensive travel and publicity undertaken by Mendoza and AWFWA, the sponsors of AWFWA should pay $50,000 in actual damages, plus costs of the case and future damages to be determined.[93]

Significantly, on July 3, in Fresno, after claiming for four years that there was no strike, and after claiming for two years that the boycott of table grapes was completely ineffective, California table grape growers filed suit in Federal Court claiming that the boycott had caused losses of $25,000,000 to grape growers. The suit demanded treble damages from the United Farm Workers Organizing Committee, a total of $75,000,000. The growers said they might also demand injunctions which would in effect outlaw all union activities, and especially outlaw the consumer boycott of grapes.[94]

July 4, 1969, in Salinas, a jobless worker was judged within his rights when he refused to accept farm labor work, on the grounds that most of such jobs were in violation of state health and sanitation laws, according to Superior Court Judge Irving Perluss. The court ruled that Mauricio Muñoz, 31, of Salinas, was entitled to unemployment insurance benefits even though he refused to accept a farm job offered him through the California Department of Employment.[95]

On July 29, nine Salinas Valley carrot harvesters, who had been fired for joining the United Farm Workers Organizing Committee, won an historic decision when the First District Court of Appeals ruled that the firings were illegal and that all farm workers were protected from such firings by the California Labor Code.

"The workers, Fred Wetherton, John Watson, Jose Perez, Manuel Ortiz, Domingo

Longoria, Anthony Cervantes, Antonio Castennada and Ignacio Burgos, charged
that the Growers Farm Labor Association of Salinas had conspired to prevent farm
workers in the Salinas Valley from joining the Union, discovering that the nine
workers had joined the Union, ordered them fired. The firings took place in August
of 1967."[96]

Meanwhile, in July, the California Grape and Tree Fruit League was
under a San Francisco Court Order to pay back wages and overtime—
including interest—to thousands of women and minors in California's
after harvest industries, which had been due them for nearly six years.

"The court's decision, a victory for the California Labor Federation, AFL-CIO,
which led the fight to win the boost in pay floor for the workers and to extend
overtime protections to them in 1963 and participated in the subsequent long,
drawn-out court fight as a friend of the court, was handed down last Friday, July
18, by Superior Court Judge Joseph Karesh . . . Many such workers are now entitled to retroactive pay of 25 cents an hour from August 30, 1963 to August 30,
1964, and 30 cents an hour from August 30, 1964 to February 1, 1966, when the
federal minimum wage was increased to $1.40.[97]

On August 4, in Fresno, UFWOC moved to dismiss a $75 million
law suit by eighty-one California Grape Growers against the Union. The
suit, which claimed triple damages because the growers had lost $25
million as a result of the strike and the grape boycott launched by the
Union, appeared so vague and with no legal basis to the UFWOC attorneys that they moved for dismissal. In case the courts did not dismiss the lawsuit, the Union was preparing to seek a court order demanding that the suing growers answer 36 pages of questions dealing
with their finances and profit margins.[98]

In September, with the help of the UFWOC and its legal staff, Mr.
and Mrs. Pardos were suing Rosario Pantoja, a labor contractor, and his
foremen Roberto Pantoja and Mike Klain, and grower L. J. Williams
and the Williams Ranch. The suit was for $20,000 in exemplary and
punitive damages, for compensation, and for the time and work that
they had lost because of the firing and blacklisting.[99]

On October 7, in Avenal, California, criminal charges were filed
against Martin Murillo, a Tulare County farm labor contractor for alleged violations of the labor law and industrial welfare codes. The alleged violations of Murillo ranged from failure to provide portable
drinking water, toilet and handwashing facilities for women and minors
working in the fields, to failure to pay wages when due and provide
farm workers with itemized wage statements showing income tax,
Social Security, and State Disability Insurance deductions from wages.
The alleged violations all occurred on Westlake Farms in Stratford between June 13 and June 26, 1969.[100]

Meanwhile, in an out-of-court settlement of a civil suit filed by

UFWOC, the Lucas Company agreed to return a microphone and to pay the union $100 in damages.[101]

By November 10, in Delano, Mrs. Dolores Lorta, UFWOC member from Earlimart, had sued the Bank of America and the "Agribusiness Investment Company," a Bank of America dummy corporation, for $30,000 damages for injuries suffered when she was sprayed with agricultural chemicals while working on land that they owned. On October 16, UFWOC and Mr. Lorta filed a suit to force AIC to rehire him. The suit against agribusiness and Bank of America also named John Saninovich and S. A. Camp Ginning Company as defendants. Mr. Lorta's suit demanded his reinstatement, payment of the back wages he lost, and $50,000 punitive damages for his having been fired in direct violation of the state law which protects a worker's rights to seek the help of a union.[102]

On December 16, Judge John Jelletich of Bakersfield announced that UFWOC's $10 million suit, filed in March against the Agricultural Workers Freedom to Work Association, did not have a legal basis under California Labor Law. The suit was filed after AWFWA, a group which claimed to offer agricultural workers an alternative to UFWOC, was organized in July, 1968, by a group of growers, including the Giumarra brothers and Jack Pandol. Finally, in a decision handed down on December 18, 1969, the judge denied UFWOC members Amalia Uribe's petition for a writ of mandate to force the Agricultural Commissioner of Riverside County to give her access to the Commissioner's records on commercial pesticide applications. Arguing that the people of the state have a constitutional right to seek the records, the Attorney General asked for a court injunction requiring the Commissioner to open the files to the public for inspection. The Judge denied both Miss Uribe's petition and the injunction request by the State Attorney General.[103]

1970

> UFWOC sues CCFA and 90 growers for $115,000,000
> UFWOC sues California Department of Agriculture to outlaw DDT
> UFWOC case for toilets and sanitary facilities
> NLRB unfair labor practice complaint against UFWOC
> UFWOC sues California Farm Labor Service
> Injunction issued prohibiting picketing
> UFWOC sues Teamsters and grower-shippers
> UFWOC sues Western Conference of Teamsters for $51,000,000
> Temporary restraining order against pickets
> Grape pickers in Visalia file suit
> Grower-Shipper Vegetable Association sues UFWOC
> Temporary restraining order to prohibit picketing

Striking workers protected from summary evictions
Cel-A-Pak sues UFWOC, AFL-CIO and Western Conference of Team-
sters
UFWOC sues Salinas Valley growers
UFWOC strike ruled a jurisdictional dispute
NLRB refuses complaint against UFWOC
UFWOC files $5,000,000 pesticide suit
Chávez ordered to jail
Chávez released due to Supreme Court action
Picketing limited

On January 14, 1970, the United Farm Workers Organizing Committee took the offensive against the General California Farmers Association by filing a counterclaim against it and 90 other growers for
$115 million damages, alleging anti-trust violations on the part of the
growers. The same growers were suing UFWOC for $25 million in
losses, which growers claimed to have suffered because of the boycott
of table grapes. The growers had asked Judge M. D. Crocker of the
Federal District Court in Fresno to award its members treble damages
of $75 million, and to enjoin UFWOC's boycott of table grapes.

Then, on January 19, 1970, UFWOC asked the Federal District
Court in Los Angeles to outlaw the use of DDT and 10 pesticides said
to be even more dangerous than DDT. The amended complaint was
filed on behalf of Coachella UFWOC member Vincente Ponce, representing the class of all consumers and farm workers, against Jerry
Fielder, Director of the California Department of Agriculture.[104]

On January 8, in Bakersfield, the United Farm Workers Organizing
Committee obtained a permanent injunction against Bianco Fruit Company dealing with failure to provide toilets and other sanitary facilities
for their farm workers.[105]

In March, an attorney for the National Labor Relations Board's San
Francisco Office announced that unless a voluntary settlement could be
obtained, the Board would issue unfair labor practice complaints
against UFWOC and a number of Bay Area unions for their activities in
promoting UFWOC's boycott against California table grapes.[106]

In May, UFWOC filed suit against the California Farm Labor Service
in U.S. District court in San Diego. The suit sought to prevent farm
labor offices from sending union members to strikebound fields.[107]

In June, Jerry Cohen was sent to advise Manuel Chávez about an
injunction issued which prohibited picketing, gathering, sitting, standing, marching, and even the use of black and red flags around Abatti's
fields. Cohen had talked to the chief judge of the District Court of
Appeals in San Diego. The judge agreed to have a hearing on the injunction.[108]

On July 28, César Chávez contended that the announced agreement
between grower-shippers and Teamsters was illegal and that a suit to

prevent its consummation would be filed.[109] On July 29, two members of the Union filed suit to prevent consummation of the July 27 collective bargaining agreement between the Teamsters and Salinas-Watsonville district grower-shippers. It was a class action in behalf of all UFWOC members, contending that the Teamsters did not, could not, and would not represent them.[110] July 30, UFWOC attorneys filed a $51 million suit in Santa Maria Superior Court against the Western Conference of Teamsters. The suit, paralleling one filed in Monterey County Superior Court, sought an injunction barring Teamsters from allegedly allowing or using employers to dominate or use employees for the sake of organizing union activities.[111]

On August 10, strikers from UFWOC reappeared in front of Freshpict Food ranches in the Salinas Valley, in possible violation of a temporary injunction. The temporary restraining order had been signed by Monterey County Superior Court Judge Stanley Lawson in response to a complaint by Freshpict. On August 11, Monterey County Sheriff's deputies began enforcement of a no-picketing injunction issued by Superior Court Judge Stanley Lawson. The injunction, or temporary restraining order, barred members of UFWOC from picketing ranches of Freshpict Food, Inc. On August 12, it took 15 minutes, plus some added delay caused by Chávez himself, for the president of the striking union to accomplish the purpose of his visit—to enable Freshpict to serve him a temporary restraining order prohibiting UFWOC from picketing UFWOC Freshpict. Chávez made it clear he regarded the order as unconstitutional and had no intention of abiding by it.

On August 13, in Visalia, California, grape workers disenchanted with the organizing techniques of the Chávez union filed suit in Tulare County Superior Court to prevent unionization without representation elections. The suit asked the court to prevent the Union from forcing workers to join without an election and sought to have dues collected held in escrow until the matter was settled by the court.[112]

Meanwhile, on August 15, UFWOC said that suits filed earlier that week by both Freshpict and Pic 'N Pac were to be dropped under mutual agreement.[113]

On August 24, attorney Andrew Church, representing the Grower-Shipper Vegetable Association, said a complaint based on California's jurisdictional disputes act would be filed in Monterey County Superior Court.[114]

On August 25, a temporary restraining order was issued by the Monterey County Superior Court to 22 of the struck firms. The restraining order prohibited picketing as a violation of the state's jurisdictional strike act. Separate but similar restraining orders were issued the day before and that day to the Garin Company, Eckel Produce, Mann Packing Company, and Pic 'N Pac.[115]

By August 26, the arrest and citation total in the three-day-old

Salinas Valley farm workers strike stood at 28 as César Chávez issued a plea for non-violence and criticized the Teamsters for the alleged beating of his attorney. Twenty-seven of those arrested or cited were pickets for Chávez' Union.[116]

On August 27, striking farm workers at the Albert Hansen Labor Camp were granted a temporary restraining order protecting them among other things from summary eviction. The order was signed by Monterey County Superior Court Judged Stanley Lawson, who also signed some dozen orders that week enjoining picketing in the farm workers strike.[117]

On August 31, in San Francisco, Cel-A-Pack, Inc., Salinas Valley cauliflower producer, filed a $4,600,000 damage suit against UFWOC, the AFL-CIO, the Western Conference of Teamsters and César Chávez. Cel-A-Pak's complaint in Federal District Court said picketing by UFWOC was costing it $750,000 a day and violated the August 12 peace settlement between the Teamsters and UFWOC.[118]

On September 2, Monterey County Sheriff's deputies arrested six women and nineteen men on charges of contempt of court. They were picketing lettuce fields owned by the Bud Antle Co., Inc., and were arrested for failure to comply with a court order injunction obtained by Bud Antle.[119] And, city officials and police chief Herb Roberson assured some 60 concerned citizens and growers the city would investigate their complaints of "distinct difference in the application of law enforcement" regarding the strike related injunction. The group had asked for the meeting to relate incidences of police assistance to the process server attempting to serve injunctions against picketing at Inter Harvest, Inc., to a number of Salinas citizens demonstrating their disapproval of the company's contract with César Chávez' United Farm Workers Union.[120]

On September 3, César Chávez announced the initiation of a massive legal attack on "lawless" Salinas Valley growers as produce shipments from the strike bound valley arose to their highest level in 11 days. UFWOC attorney Jerry Cohen disclosed the filing of a lawsuit in Federal District Court in San Francisco accusing Salinas Valley growers of conspiracy to regulate lettuce production to keep the price of lettuce artificially high. The class action for lost wages was a response to "intentional underproduction." Cohen said UFWOC would be filing lawsuits against Salinas Valley growers and the Grower-Shipper Vegetable Association on behalf of consumers who were allegedly paying inflated prices for produce. Also on the court calendar that day was Bud Antle, Inc. versus United Farm Workers' Organizing Committee with Monterey County Superior Court Judge Anthony Brazil presiding. The motions and arguments went back and forth, most of them on whether or not to grant a continuance. Furthermore, within the next few days a number of growers would be moving to evict their striker tenants, according to attorneys Joseph Stave and Andrew Church, both lawyers with grower clients. That meant the Salinas Municipal Court, which took those cases, would be hearing a lot of eviction suits in the weeks ahead.[121]

On September 3, Judge Brazil pointed out that before him were only the affidavits and nothing else. "I cannot take additional notice of who César Chávez is." And, because that question remains unanswered in the affidavits, an attempt by Bud Antle, Inc. to bring contempt charges against Chávez and UFWOC was sent back to the legal drawing boards.[122]

On September 4, three persons who were arrested outside the UFWOC headquarters at 14 Wood Street later were released pending a review of the case. Statements by police were put on a tape, but the tape failed to record the report. The officials were called back to record their reports and until the case had been reviewed and a decision reached, the three men were free of any charges.[123]

On September 5, in Soledad, California, a jury trial was scheduled for October 22 in the case of 18 UFWOC pickets arrested September 2 by Sheriff's deputies. The defendants pleaded not guilty to the charge of failing to obey a court order. They were released on their own recognizance after their attorneys assured the court they would appear in court on October 22.[124]

On September 8, 1970, Superior Court Judge Brazil stated that if a strike by UFWOC against Pic 'N Pac was in fact a jurisdictional dispute, then he will issue a ban against even peaceful picketing. Judge Brazil's action of continuing the hearing on Pic 'N Pac versus César Chávez and UFWOC left a temporary restraining order against picketing in force.[125]

On September 10, El Malcriado reported that more than 200 grape workers were outraged at the manner in which they had been treated under the contracts signed between UFWOC and grape growers. They filed a suit on August 13 against the Union and growers in the Tulare County Superior Court.[126] Meanwhile, in Redwood City, at the San Mateo County Superior Court, Judge Melvin Dohn refused to issue the temporary restraining order sought by UFWOC against the Teamster Union and several Salinas Valley growers. UFWOC sought the order against the Teamsters to prevent violence, threats, and the use of obscene language in which the defendants were allegedly engaging in connection with the current Salinas Valley farm labor strike. At the same time, three cases involving the Salinas Valley farm strike were scheduled in Monterey County Superior Court but two had been quietly continued or dropped before noon. Freshpict vs. UFWOC continued to September 17. The Allow Lettuce vs. UFWOC was dropped for lack of service. And, twenty-eight UFWOC pickets were arrested by Monterey County Sheriff's deputies for contempt of court. The pickets were accused of violating a temporary restraining order prohibiting picketing at the operation of Salinas Valley produce firms being struck by UFWOC.[127]

On September 11, the California Supreme Court ordered a hearing on a temporary restraining order banning UFWOC picketing which had been granted twenty-two Salinas Valley growers by Monterey County Superior Court. At issue in the complaints for injunctive relief was whether UFWOC picketing should be prohibited as being in violation of the state's jurisdictional strike act.[128]

On September 16, Monterey County Superior Court Judge Anthony Brazil ruled that a strike by UFWOC against thirty Salinas Valley growers was a jurisdictional dispute. The ruling had the effect of banning mass picketing and virtually prohibiting any picketing by UFWOC against the thirty growers involved.[129] (Over two years later this ruling was reversed by the State Supreme Court in December 1972.)

On October 20, a hearing seeking dismissal of charges against some 120 UFWOC pickets was continued before Monterey County Superior Court Judge Anthony Brazil. All were charged with violating Superior Court restraining orders against picketing. UFWOC attorney William Carder filed writs of habeas corpus on behalf of eighty-six of the defendants whose trials were under jurisdiction of the Soledad, Castroville and Salinas Courts. Charges were dismissed. Judge Brazil stated that the restraining orders were improperly issued.[130]

On October 22, D'Arrigo Brothers was granted a preliminary injunction limiting picketing of its Salinas Valley ranches by the UFWOC. The farmworkers said the order had no practical impact due to the September 16 ruling by Judge Brazil.[131]

On November 6, the National Labor Relations Board's San Francisco district office refused to file a complaint charging UFWOC with unfair labor practices.[132]

On November 10, in Bakersfield, Kern County Superior Court Judge George A. Brown Monday issued a temporary restraining order against UFWOC limiting the number of pickets at a Delano area lettuce farm. The suit was filed by Central Farms of Delano, which sought the restraining order plus $11 million in punitive damages and $25,000 a day in actual damages.[133]

On November 12, a seasonal farm laborer for Bruce Church, Inc. filed a $5 million pesticide suit against the firm in Monterey County Superior Court. It was the third class action suit regarding use of agricultural pesticides to be brought against a Salinas Valley grower through attorneys for the UFWOC.[134]

On November 17, the trial of Gonzales farmer John H. Panziera, who was accused of going on a rampage with a caterpillar D-4 bulldozer on August 2 during the United Farm Workers' Organizing Committee strike entered its second day.[135]

On November 19, a jury trial for Father David Duran, clergyman charged with five counts of violating the Salinas City code, was set for January 7 in municipal court. He was charged with disturbing a neighborhood with a loud noise and one count of using the premises at 14 S. Wood Street for public use without a use permit.[136] And, Gonzales farmer John H. Panziers was acquitted of a charge of felonious assault by a Monterey County Superior Court jury. In addition, a UFWOC farm worker filed suit for assault and battery complaints for damages totalling $660,000 in Monterey County Superior Court. Organizer Venustiano Olguin was suing grower Albert C. Hanse, James Plemmons and Bobby Schuster for injuries allegedly sustained on the Hansen ranch August 25 on the day after the UFWOC strike began.[137]

On November 24, it was reported that César Chávez had to show cause the following week why he should not be held in contempt of court for violating an injunction prohibiting primary boycotting of Bud Antle, Inc. lettuce. UFWOC was to appear in Monterey County Superior Court on December 4. UFWOC's Chief Counsel claimed UFWOC had a constitutional right to boycott.[138] On November 27, a request for delaying the December 4 contempt hearing of César Chávez was denied by visiting Superior Court Judge Harold Holden.[139] On December 1, Chávez was demanding a jury trial for his contempt hearing Friday in Monterey County Superior Court. On December 4, 1970, Judge Gordon Campbell ordered that César Chávez be imprisoned in the Monterey County jail "until he and the union notify all UFWOC personnel to halt their boycott against Bud Antle Inc."[140]

On December 9, seven Hollister area farm workers filed a complaint for $3,170,000 against UFWOC in Monterey Superior Court. The plaintiffs, all employees of Castle Farms of Hollister, alleged that they were severely beaten by UFWOC pickets at a Fallon Road field on September 7.[141]

On December 12, the First District Court of Appeals denied without comment a petition which, if granted, would have freed UFWOC Director Chávez from Monterey County jail.[142] On December 23, César Chávez walked down the front steps of the Monterey jail to freedom after 20 days in a cell. He was released on an order by the California Supreme Court dissolving the portions of the preliminary injunction issued by Superior Court Judge Gordon Campbell, which had been the basis for his jailing for contempt on December 4.[143]

On December 29, Superior Court Judge Alfred McCourtney Monday granted a preliminary injunction to three supermarket chains limiting picketing by UFWOC at food stores.[144] And, on December 30, 1970, the California Attorney General's office found César Chávez' charge of a "complete breakdown" of local law enforcement during the August 24 - September 16 farm strike in Salinas Valley with no base or substance.[145]

1971

UFWOC files complaint against Secretary of Defense and Bud Antle
Two UFWOC members found guilty of assault
Arizona and Salinas growers sue UFWOC for $10,200,000
UFWOC chaplain found innocent on two counts, guilty on one
UFWOC sues Secretary of Defense Laird and Commander of Ft.
Hamilton
UFWOC's pesticide suit is dismissed
Court rules growers need not answer UFWOC's 555 questions
California Supreme Court takes Chávez case under submission
UFWOC battles against Monterey County injunction
UFWOC seeks preliminary injunction against Defense Secretary
Laird
UFWOC fined $750, $600 suspended
NLRB, Washington, D.C., denies appeal
San Francisco Federal Judge dismisses $240,000,000 suit
Egger-Ghio asks $350,000 damages
UFWOC sues Egger-Ghio
UFWOC sues individual and Assistant Secretary of Labor
Salinas City action against UFWOC upheld, UFWOC appeals
UFWOC files complaint charging discrimination
UFWOC and Father Duran's appeal denied
Restraining order against mass picketing signed
Discrimination case dismissed
Hearings for preliminary injunction dropped
No trial for farmworkers charged with trespassing
Hearing set on whether to enjoin mass picketing
Suits against three growers dismissed

On January 5, 1971 it was reported that the California Supreme
Court would hold a hearing to determine whether César Chávez and the
United Farm Workers Organizing Committee should be enjoined from
boycotting lettuce from Bud Antle, Inc. On February 4, the Supreme
Court took jurisdiction over the Antle-UFWOC case. Retired Judge
Gordon Campbell had issued a preliminary injunction prohibiting
UFWOC's boycott of Antle lettuce October 8. On December 4, Campbell sentenced Chávez to jail for contempt for failing to comply with
the injunction. Bud Antle contended that UFWOC's boycott was an
illegal extension of the jurisdiction dispute found to exist between
UFWOC and the Teamsters. Antle had a contract covering its field
workers with Teamsters local 890 since 1961. UFWOC claimed state
courts had no jurisdiction over secondary boycott activities. It also
disputed the trial court's ruling that its Salinas Valley strike was a
jurisdictional dispute with the Teamsters.[146]
On January 6, 1971, in Los Angeles, the United Farm Workers

Organizing Committee filed a complaint in Federal District Court seeking to stop the Armed Forces from buying greater amounts of lettuce from Bud Antle, Inc. Antle and Secretary of Defense Melvin Laird were named as defendants in the suit.[147]

Meanwhile, in Hollister, California, two members of the United Farm Workers Organizing Committee found guilty of assault charges by a jury December 1, were sentenced in San Benito County Superior Court. The assault had occurred in a field on Fallon Road on September 7, while UFWOC's strike was on.[148] Still pending against the three men and nine other defendants was a $3,170,000 civil suit filed by Castle Farm employees against UFWOC.

On January 11, twelve Arizona grape growers, including two based in Salinas, filed a $10.2 million damage suit against the United Farm Workers Organizing Committee for allegedly violating anti-trust laws. Among the plaintiffs in the complaint filed in Federal District Court in Phoenix were Admiral Packing Company and Bruce Church, Inc., both headquartered in Salinas. The complaint charged UFWOC with violating the Sherman and Arizona Anti-Trust Acts and the Arizona anti-boycott law. They sought an injunction to prevent further boycotts.[149]

On January 14, 1971, Father Duran was charged by the City of Salinas with violating its zoning ordinance in connection with assemblies held during 1970's farm strike at the United Farm Workers Organizing Committee headquarters at 14 S. Wood Street. The Salinas Municipal Court jury found Father Duran innocent of two counts and guilty of a third, but the Union was found guilty on three counts of violating the Salinas city ordinance. Both were co-charged with three counts of violating the city's zoning ordinance by holding public assemblies at UFWOC's headquarters at 14 S. Wood Street without first obtaining the required conditional use permit.[150]

On January 16, the suit, which named Defense Secretary Melvin R. Laird and the commander of the Ft. Hamilton Brooklyn Army base, charged the Defense Department with buying lettuce from the Bud Antle Company in order to help the company break the Union boycott. Chávez announced the filing of the suit in U.S. District Court; it would be the first in a series of legal actions against the Army for purchasing.[151]

Meanwhile, a dramatic increase of almost 60% in the number of illegal aliens arrested in the Salinas area was recorded in 1970, an official of the U.S. Immigration and Naturalization Service disclosed on January 20, 1971. He said the number of aliens arrested in 1970 was 2,745 as compared with 1,727 for 1969.[152]

On January 26, a pesticide suit brought by the United Farm Workers Organizing Committee against Bruce Church, Inc. was dismissed by court order.[153]

On January 30, visiting San Luis Obispo Court judge ruled in Salinas that Oshita and twenty-one other Salinas Valley growers need not answer 555 questions put to them by the United Farm Workers Organizing Committee.[154]

On February 1, it was announced that on February 4, in San Francisco, the Supreme Court would hold a hearing which could return Chávez to jail or could leave him free to continue a boycott against lettuce shipped by Bud Antle, Inc. On February 4, the California Supreme Court took under submission a decision which could return Chávez to the Monterey County jail. UFWOC attorneys petitioned the Supreme Court, asking that Monterey County be restrained from enforcing the injunction, primarily on the basis that a secondary boycott was outside the state's jurisdiction.[155]

On February 22, an attorney for the union said the action there was dismissed without prejudice so that the UFWOC could go ahead with plans to seek a preliminary injunction against Secretary of Defense Laird in a New York federal district court.[156] March 8, UFWOC was fined $750, but with $600 suspended, for holding rallies at its union headquarters in September.[157]

On March 26, the National Labor Relations Board in Washington, D.C. denied an appeal from a decision by its San Francisco district office which refused to file a complaint charging the United Farm Workers Organizing Committee with unfair labor practices. The Salinas Valley produce firms—Bud Antle, Inc., Bruce Church, Inc., and Hansen Farms—filed the unfair labor practice charge with the NLRB in San Francisco in October.[158]

On April 14, a San Francisco federal judge ruled that farm workers could not sue growers for conspiracy to raise prices in iceberg lettuce and dismissed a $240 million anti-trust suit.[159]

On April 15, it was announced in San Francisco that UFWOC could boycott lettuce growers as long as the activity remained peaceful and truthful, as the California Supreme Court had ruled.[160]

On April 19, it was announced that a hearing on an injunction to prohibit mass picketing of the Egger-Ghio fields of south San Diego County would be held before Judge Franklin Orfield. The Egger-Ghio Company was also asking $350,000 in damages. The controversy began March 26 when twelve workers were fired for wearing UFWOC buttons. Sixty-six workers then walked off the job and the remaining twenty-five workers left by March 29. New workers were hired by the company, however, resulting in the UFWOC filing the Superior Court action on April 1 demanding reinstatement of the original twelve, protection against firing, and $10,000 damages for each worker.[161]

On June 14, U.S. District Court Judge Robert F. Peckham issued an order temporarily restraining Monterey County from enforcing its new noise ordinance. The ordinance prohibits "loud and raucus" noise on any public road, sidewalk or thoroughfare in unincorporated county areas. It specifically prohibits the use of voice amplifying equipment.[162]

On July 12, in San Diego, UFWOC filed a $6 million federal court suit against California Republican Bob Wilson and a high labor department official. The suit charged that the Congressman and Assistant Secretary of Labor Paul Sasser met with Egger-Ghio Company and conspired to have a strike at the firm declared invalid.[163]

On July 15, the Salinas City action against the United Farm Workers Organizing Committee for holding unauthorized rallies was upheld by a Monterey County Superior Court panel. However, UFWOC attorney William Carder said he would take the issue before the District Court of Appeals.[164]

On July 26, in Santa Cruz, California, UFWOC filed a complaint charging Santa Cruz and Monterey County strawberry growers, charging discrimination against its members. It alleged that the growers conspired to deprive farm workers of their right under the state labor code to name a collective bargaining agent. It also alleged that berry growers had refused to hire UFWOC workers.[165]

On August 12, it was reported that the verdict against the United Farm Workers Organizing Committee and Father David Duran was being appealed for the third and possibly last time. William Carder, UFWOC attorney, confirmed that a second appeal from the Salinas Municipal Court verdict was denied earlier that month by the District Court of Appeals. He was preparing an appeal to California State Supreme Court.[166]

On September 14, UFWOC was barred from all but limited picketing in its six-day-old Salinas Valley strike against Basic Vegetable Products, Inc. The restraining order against further mass picketing was signed by Superior Court Judge Stanley Lawson. Hearings on whether to issue a preliminary injunction were set for September 24.[167]

On September 23, in Santa Cruz, the class action suit charging strawberry growers in Santa Cruz and Monterey counties with discrimination against United Farm Workers Organizing Committee members and supporters was dismissed in the Santa Cruz County Superior Court.[168]

On September 24, hearings on whether to grant preliminary injunctions against mass picketing by the United Farm Workers Organizing Committee were dropped from Monterey County Superior Court calendar.[169]

On September 29, it was announced that there would be no trial for eight farm workers charged with trespassing August 25 at the Harden Farms labor camp at 225 Natividad Road. A legal challenge of the charge by the UFWOC Attorney was sustained by Salinas Municipal Court Judge William Stewart.[170]

On October 8, an inconclusive hearing on whether to enjoin mass picketing by UFWOC against two Salinas Valley growers was held before Superior Court Judge Stanley Lawson.[171]

Finally on October 19, 1971, three farm workers who claimed they were discharged because of their membership in the United Farm Workers Organizing Committee were told to process their grievances through the Teamsters Union. The ruling accompanied an order by Superior Court Judge Stanley Lawson dismissing a suit by the three UFWOC members against California Coastal Farms, Hansen Farms, and Merrill Farms.[172]

1972

Six farm workers sue Tomato shippers
Firms of lettuce industry charged with unfair practices
La Posada families challenge state civil procedure
NLRB seeks injunction to stop boycott activities of UFW
NLRB sues UFW, charging unfair labor practices
District Appeals Court reviews injunctions prohibiting picketing
Pic 'N Pac wins right to evict families
District Appeals Court rules jurisdictional dispute, case appealed to Supreme Court
Chavez agrees to suspend boycott of nine wineries
Anti-picketing injunctions appealed to Supreme Court
Suit to enjoin enforcement of Arizona Agricultural Relations Act
State Secretary of State asked to investigate Proposition 22 signatures
UFW and AFL-CIO file petition concerning Proposition 22
Secretary of State files suit to remove Proposition 22 from ballot
UFW pickets Tulare County Sheriff's office
Farmworkers file petition to end short handle hoe
Seventy pickets arrested
Two hundred and ten union members arrested
Chávez says unionists will make citizen arrests
UFW charges laxity in law enforcement
State Supreme court rules UFW pickets against Teamster contracts legal

On January 4, 1972, six farm workers' families filed a suit against Brown and Hill Tomato Shippers seeking to block their eviction from its Little Waco Camp south of San Lucas. The suit, filed by attorney William Carder of the UFW, sought to restrain Brown and Hill from cutting off water and power at Little Waco or otherwise making it unfit for occupancy while the families remain.[173]

On January 11, twenty-four firms in the California-Arizona lettuce industry charged United Brands, Inc. with unfair practices designed to lessen competition. United Brand owns United Fruit Company, parent company of Inter-Harvest, Inc., which was put together out of several formerly independent produce firms in the Salinas Valley. The complaint alleged that the acquisition of United Fruit by AMK Corporation, later named United Brands, violated the Clayton Anti-Trust Act.

On January 26, Pic 'N Pac Food, Inc. took its first step toward eviction of the seventy-seven persons still occupying its La Posada trailer camp in Salinas. The action, *Pic 'N Pac vs. Albert Lucio and seventy-six other defendants,* was filed in Salinas Municipal Court.[174]

On January 31, farm worker families at La Posada, faced with eviction from their Salinas trailer camp, took legal countermoves to assure their residence until at least February 18. Carder's challenge was to state civil procedure which presently allowed a tenant three days to respond to an eviction action, as compared with the 10 days allowed in most other civil proceedings.[175]

On February 2, in Sacramento, a controversial new state law that set fines on employers for knowingly hiring illegal aliens drew praise from some Mexican-American leaders who called it progressive, but criticism from others who branded it racist.[176]

On March 8, in Los Angeles, the National Labor Relations Board sought a federal court injunction to halt the secondary boycott activities of UFW. Less Hubbard, president of the Free Marketing Council, said the injunction would be sought by means of a petition which was to be based on a complaint filed last December by FMC attorneys. To support their claim, FMC attorneys submitted a series of arguments and facts asserting that César Chávez' Union had, by its actions, come within the scope of the NLRB. One of these contentions was that UFW represents workers other than agricultural workers, which would place it within NLRB jurisdiction.[177]

On March 9, in Fresno, the National Labor Relations Board filed suit in federal court seeking an injunction against boycotts by the César-Chávez-led farm workers union, alleging boycotts were unfair labor practices. U.S. District Court Judge M. D. Crocker signed an order setting a hearing for UFW to show cause April 6. No restraining order was presented in the suit filed by Wilford Johansen, regional NLRB director.[178]

On March 10, at Keene, Chávez blamed the Republican party for a move by federal labor officials to blunt the strongest weapon of the farm workers union—boycotts against stores and restaurants that handle non-union wines. The move by the NLRB would have far ranging implications for farm labor. It was the first legal attempt to determine how the NLRB Act applies to the farm workers union.[179]

Meanwhile, on March 14, a key legal issue of the Salinas Valley's

1970 farm strike would be revived in an argument before the District Court of Appeals in San Francisco. Under review by the appellate court would be twenty-seven injunctions issued by Monterey County Superior Court Judge Anthony Brazil prohibiting all or most UFW picketing against growers involved. Basic to this case was Judge Brazil's decision that growers held valid union contracts for their farm workers with the Teamsters Union. This made the strike a jurisdictional dispute.[180]

On March 15, Chávez said that the NLRB suit was a result of wine boycott complaints filed by the Western Growers Association, formed by lettuce growers as an outgrowth of the Salinas Valley strike and boycott effort.[181] At the same time, Pic 'N Pac Foods, Inc. won the right to resume legal action aimed at evicting seventy-seven farm worker occupants of its La Posada Trailer Camp in Salinas. Attorney Carder, representing the farm workers, had challenged the Pic 'N Pac action as invalid because, among other things, the company had failed to file the articles of incorporation which gave them legal standing to sue in Monterey County. The ruling also upheld Pic 'N Pac's right to seek eviction against all seventy-seven tenants in a single action rather than separately as argued by Carder.[182]

On March 16, charges were made that UFW had tried to make the NLRB move a partisan political issue by retaliating with picketing of the Republican Party.[183] Furthermore, Pic 'N Pac's eviction action against seventy-seven farm worker occupants of its La Posada Trailer Camp was scheduled for Salinas Municipal Court jury trial April 11. Departures of the families was initially delayed to explore possibilities of alternate housing of the farm workers with federal aid. Further delays were the result of motions filed by the UFW attorney on behalf of the farm worker defendants, with the last of those denied by Judge Agliano March 10.[184]

On March 25, reports from Los Angeles indicated that hundreds of illegal aliens had surrendered to federal authorities as a result of a new California law which had already been declared unconstitutional. The Illegal Alien Act prohibited employers from knowingly hiring such persons.

On March 28, injunctions barring United Farm Workers from picketing against Salinas Valley growers with Teamster contracts was upheld by the District Court of Appeals. The ruling on twenty-seven injunctions issued by the Monterey County Superior Court at the peak of the Salinas Valley's 1970 farm strike came from a three judge panel headed by Justice Wakefield Taylor. The court ruled that the strike was in fact a battle between the Teamster and César Chávez' farm union over the right to represent farm workers, and Valley growers were legally entitled to protection from being caught in that dispute. Attorney Carder, who took the United Farm Workers Union appeal from Monterey

County Superior Court Judge Anthony Brazil's ruling, had said in the past that an adverse ruling would probably be appealed to the California Supreme Court.[185]

On March 29, in Washington, D.C., James G. O'Hara (D-Michigan), chairman of the House subcommittee on Agricultural Labor, accused the administration of engaging in a deliberate multiagency effort to harass farm workers whenever they try to improve their conditions through their own efforts. He felt the NLRB was acting under orders from the President to break the United Farm Workers Union "and to keep farm workers on the bottom of the economic ladder."[186]

On April 4, in Fresno, César Chávez agreed to suspend a boycott of products from nine northern California wineries.

"The Union's legal counsel, William Carder, signed a stipulated court order approved Monday by Federal Judge M. D. Crocker to postpone indefinitely a hearing on a suit filed by the National Labor Relations Board . . . The court order states UFW will refrain from boycotting the products of Beringer, Hamms, Kornell Champagne Cellars; F. Korbel & Bros., Inc.; Charles Krug Winery; Louis M. Martini; Robert Mondavi Winery; Samuele Sebastiani; Weibel Champagne Vineyards and Wente Brothers. The order also declares UFW will halt picketing aimed at enforcing the boycott at more than 60 named establishments across the country. But if the NLRB has reasonable cause to believe there is a breach of the order or that negotiations will be fruitless the order entitles it to move for a rescheduling of the hearing within three days after notifying union attorneys."[187]

On April 7, the suspension of a UFW boycott of nine California wineries was hailed by the Free Marketing Council as marking an end to UFW's secondary boycott campaign. But a UFW spokesman said that the wine boycott had only been suspended while negotiations were in progress, and in any event, they would not halt UFW's continuing boycott against Salinas Valley lettuce.

". . . We'll never accept giving up the secondary boycott, he said . . . a very strong possibility that UFW would be picketing Valley growers this summer. Injunctions barring such picketing as a violation of the state's jurisdictional strike act were upheld by the appellate court last week, but are being appealed."[188]

On April 11, in McFarland, California, members of UFW struck the Hollis Roberts Farms at McFarland, Poplar and Lamont.

"Union spokesman said the dispute centered over failure of Roberts to pay into the Union economic fund and the dismissal of the president of the union ranch committee. Roberts, who farms more than 100,000 acres in the southern San Joaquin Valley, said he had been advised by his legal counsel payments of two cents per box into the union fund would be a violation of the Taft-Hartley Act."[189]

On May 3, the UFW resumed its international boycott of lettuce:

"At the same time, union spokesman said an agreement has been reached with the

National Labor Relations Board that permits it to engage in unrestricted secondary boycotts . . . Marshall Ganz, a UFWOC organizer in Keene, said the way was cleared for unrestricted secondary boycotts by the union after it had not and did not intend to represent other than agricultural workers."[190]

On May 4, the Free Marketing Council maintained that an agreement between the United Farm Workers Union and the NLRB prohibits secondary boycotts of wineries.

"The UFW is a labor organization as defined by the NLRB, Free Marketing Council said, and it always has been in our opinion. Therefore, it is subject to the control of the National Labor Relations Board, which means that it cannot participate in secondary boycotts . . . Marshal Ganz, a UFW organizer in Keene, said . . . The FMC's position that the boycott of the wineries has been prohibited is untrue . . . the agreement does not restrict boycott activities."[191]

On May 8, the constitutionality of Salinas Valley anti-picketing injunctions against the UFW was appealed to the California Supreme Court.

"The injunctions, issued at the peak of UFW's 1970 farm strike, were upheld March 28 by the District Court of Appeals. A request for rehearing has since been denied by the appellate court; UFW attorney William Carder said his appeal to the State Supreme Court was filed Friday. Carder said a decision from the State Supreme Court whether it will hear the appeal should come within 30 days."[192]

On May 11, in Greenfield, near Salinas, California, a controversial anti-loitering ordinance brought about a subsequent boycott of merchants. The town had a population of 2,950; and 65! were Mexican-Americans. About three-fourths were members of César Chávez' UFW. A community group led by Mexican-Americans opposed the ordinance.[193] On May 17, an agreement suspended Greenfield's controversial anti-loitering ordinance and a Mexican-American boycott called in response to it. The truce came after a conference was held with about 100 members of the Mexican-American community following a city council meeting.

On June 28, in San Francisco, César Chávez asked the California Supreme Court to take over a three-day dispute involving his union, the Teamsters and vegetable growers. The *Salinas Californian* stated:

"Chávez and his farm workers union asked the high court for a hearing in their dispute with Furukawa Farms, Inc. and other vegetable growers in Santa Barbara and San Luis Obispo counties. Santa Barbara Superior Judge Marion A. Smith ruled in favor of Chávez September 25, 1970, and refused to issue an injunction requested by the growers . . . On May 23, 1972, the State Court of Appeal reversed the decision and directed the Superior Court to issue the preliminary injunction sought by the growers. The request for a Supreme Court decision was not only clearly erroneous but involves substantial and far-reaching questions of labor law and constitutional law . . ."[194]

On June 30, in Keene, California, César Chávez denounced the California farm labor initiative "as a fraud which would destroy the farm workers union in California" and that the entire state labor movement would fight it.

"Jerry Cohen, general counsel for the UFW, called the initiative unconstitutional and said it makes the action of saying 'boycott lettuce' a crime subject to a year in jail and a $5,000 fine . . . was unconstitutional because it makes it a crime to strike . . . to boycott, and it purports to set up an election procedure when it in fact deprives workers of the right to vote."[195]

On August 14, in Phoenix, Arizona, a suit requesting that state officials be enjoined from enforcing the new Arizona Agricultural Relations Act was filed in Federal Court Monday by the United Farm Workers Union.

"The union said the act was unconstitutional in that it denies equal protection under the law, places an unlawful burden on interstate commerce and violates the supremacy clause of the U.S. Constitution. The action asked that a three-judge panel be convened to hear the case and to enjoin the state from any attempts to enforce the act."[196]

On August 28, the *Salinas Californian* reported that:

"The District Court of Appeals has upheld Monterey County Superior Court injunctions against mass picketing in the Salinas Valley, but the California Supreme Court is now weighing the issue in appeal. Until a decision is reached, mass picketing—the essential element in the 1970 produce strike—is illegal, on grounds there is a jurisdictional dispute between the UFW and the Teamsters Union."[197]

On August 29, the president of the Monterey County Farm Bureau said he knew of no instances of fraud in the county in the gathering of signatures on a petition to qualify a farm labor initiative Proposition 22 for the November 7 ballot. Secretary of State Edmund G. Brown, Jr. asked two district attorneys to investigate charges that fraud was involved in the collection of signatures. Brown said he and Alan Cranston had received complaints that persons who circulated the petitions misrepresented the initiative to voters whose signatures were solicited.[198]

On September 8, in San Francisco, two labor leaders asked the California Supreme Court to remove the title and summary for Proposition 22, the farm labor initiative, from the November ballot.

"John Henning, executive director of the State AFL-CIO, and César Chávez, president of the UFWU, filed the petition Thursday, claiming that the title and summary were misleading. Chávez and Henning said Attorney General Evelle J. Younger should be required to write a summary understood by the public and Legislative Counsel George H. Murphy should be required to rewrite his analysis for the voter handbook."[199]

On September 9, a UFW strike kept the harvesting operations of

Inter-Harvest, Salinas Valley's biggest lettuce and celery grower-shipper, almost completely shutdown for the ninth day. There would be a general Salinas Valley strike unless growers ceased their alleged efforts to get their workers to break the Inter-Harvest strike.

"If this continues, we will call a general strike, injunctions or no injunctions, Mrs. Huerta said. Injunctions against mass picketing in the Salinas Valley growing out of the 1970 general produce strike led by César Chávez are on appeal with the California Supreme Court. The injunctions mean a general strike would clearly entail the possibility of mass arrests."[200]

On September 11, in Los Angeles, Secretary of State Edmund G. Brown and District Attorney Joseph Busch were taking steps against Proposition 22, the farm labor initiative, because of evidence of large scale fraud. Brown was considering court action to remove the proposition from the November ballot.[201] On September 12, Brown expanded into eight additional counties the investigation of possible fraud in the circulating of petitions for Proposition 22. He claimed that "this was the gravest case of election fraud to come to light in recent years."[202] September 13, Los Angeles County District Attorney Joseph Busch said his office had uncovered apparent "widespread fraud" in the circulation of petitions for Proposition 22.[203]

Also, on September 13, in Fresno, supporters of the farm labor initiative (Proposition 22) criticized Secretary of State Edmund G. Brown, Jr.'s investigation of alleged fraud in obtaining signatures for the petition. Brown said he would expand the probe statewide and possibly go to court to try and force the measure off the November ballot.[204] On September 14, supporters of farm labor's Proposition 22 said Secretary of State Edmund Brown, Jr. would be unsuccessful in his efforts to have the controversial measure removed from the November 7 ballot. Brown filed a lawsuit in Sacramento County Superior Court seeking to have the proposition removed from the ballot on grounds that fraud had been committed in collecting signatures on petitions to qualify the measure.[205]

On September 14, in Visalia, California, members of the UFW picketed the Tulare County Sheriff's office.

"Several union members have been arrested by Sheriff's deputies the last few days for clashes with non-union members and alleged violation of a court order limiting picketing activities at the struck ranch."[206]

On September 30, in Sacramento, a professional petition circulator acknowledged using a technique described by Secretary of State Brown as "fraudulent" in qualifying two controversial initiatives for the November ballot.[207] And, five Salinas Valley farm workers filed a petition with the Division of Industrial Safety, seeking a statewide end to agricultural use of the short handle hoe. The petition filed in San Francisco claimed the 12-inch handled hoe was an almost literally back-breaking tool that should be prohibited as unsafe for farm workers now compelled by employers to use it. Members of the state's Industrial Safety Board were expected to consider the request when they met December 5.[208]

On September 21, in Salinas, Chávez said there would be a general strike. But the timing of the strike would depend upon the outcome of an appeal before the California Supreme Court on an injunction against mass picketing issued by the Monterey County Superior Court. Chávez also said that:

"If the law (Proposition 22) passes, we will continue having boycotts, and strikes, come what may, and if they don't like it, let them put us in jail, because we're not afraid. Meanwhile, we'll continue to organize because we're under the laws of humanity."[209]

On October 2, in Poplar, California, sixty-four striking pickets were arrested at White River grape vineyards, and another six were arrested at White River property near Delano.

"They were charged with violating terms of a temporary restraining order limiting the number of pickets at entrances and along the sides of the nine White River ranches."[210]

On October 3, in Sacramento, César Chávez denied reports that his followers hurled a molotov cocktail at the home of a labor contractor in the dispute with the struck White River grape vineyards. Chávez countercharged that illegal aliens were being used as strike breakers at the vineyards and chided the U.S. Immigration Service for refusing to go into the fields to arrest illegal workers.

"Chávez also said the farm workers will continue to violate the temporary restraining order limiting the number of pickets at entrances of the nine White River ranches near Delano. He said the order and company moves were intended to sabotage the farm union movement."[211]

On October 4, it was reported that contract renewal negotiations between the UFW and White River had fallen through August 28, and therefore, the union went on strike. There were, subsequently, more than 210 union members arrested for violating a court injunction limiting picketing activities.[212]

On October 5, in Keene, California (Union headquarters), César Chávez said union members would make citizens' arrests of suspected illegal Mexican immigrants whose alleged importation to break a strike was supported by the Nixon administration.

"This is another example of President Nixon's one-sided administration of justice and his openly anti-labor position."[213]

On October 9, in Poplar, California, the United Farm Workers charged that the Tulare County Sheriff's Department stood by during repeated attacks by a mob on the union hiring hall during the weekend. One of the attackers, it was charged, was cut on the hand by broken glass and treated at the same hospital but was not arrested.[214] October 10, in Visalia, a UFW official charged a grower with using Ku Klux Klan tactics in the continuing labor dispute at the White River Farms. The Chávez led union would ask the Justice Department to investigate violence during the weekend at the Union's Poplar office.[215]

On November 7, Proposition 22 was defeated by the voters. However, the jurisdictional dispute between the teamsters and UFW continued. Then, on December 29, 1972, the State Supreme Court handed down a decision that UFW pickets were legal.

"The California Supreme Court ruled Friday that César Chávez' farm union legally can continue picketing and other labor activities against 45 California growers and shippers who have filed workers under Teamsters Union contract . . . In its 6-1 decision, the high court found that the agricultural employers had entered an exclusive five-year 'union shop' agreement for their field workers without trying to determine whether the workers supported the Teamsters . . . From a practical point of view, an employer's grant of exclusive bargaining status to a nonrepresentative union must be considered the ultimate form of favoritism, completely substituting the employer's choice of unions for his employee's desires."[216]

Under the State Jurisdictional Strike Act, the Court concluded the growers' action favoring the Teamsters was an improper interference with the Teamsters in this situation. Where such was the case, California Labor Law prevented restraining orders against the competing union, in this situation the United Farm Workers. The decision, covering nine consolidated cases, affected twenty-five Salinas growers and shippers and ten Santa Maria growers. The UFW appealed to the Supreme Court after the Monterey County Superior Court issued a preliminary restraining order against UFW and the Santa Barbara Superior Court denied a similar injunction request.[217]

PART II: The Legislative Struggle

INTRODUCTION

It has been asserted in the foregoing study dealing with the legal struggle of the farmworkers' union that a problem existed insofar as studies of farmworkers organizing activities have been largely dealt with in a unidimensional manner, i.e., overemphasis upon one facet such as strikes. The net effect of such treatment has been to present a picture of farmworkers as somewhat isolated from the rest of society, being neither influenced by the world around them nor they, themselves, having any influence upon that same world.

However, extensive scrutiny of the organizing efforts of the National Farm Workers, AFL-CIO reveals a considerably different view, much as that outlined in the review on the legal struggle. The interfacing of the farmworkers struggle with on-going legislating efforts, at the local, state, and federal levels, as will be seen, has created an historical situation in which it can be said that future studies of farmworkers organizing *must* take into account the parallel legislative efforts that accompany any union activity. For to fail to do so is again to commit the error of omission of importantly relevant information.

Just as the legal struggle dates back in time, so does the struggle in the Congress and the state legislatures. For centuries landlords have made use of their political representation in order to sustain or to expand their control over slaves, indigents, sharecroppers, migrants, and other farmworkers in general. This legislative struggle and counter-struggle continues, as attested to by the following example of some forty years ago.

The National Labor Relations Act states that an employer must sit down with, bargain with, and discuss grievances with elected representatives of his workers so that they can share in the decisions which crucially affect their lives.

When the original bill was written in 1935 it included farmworkers . . .

"But the bill was reported out of Committee two months later with farm workers specifically excluded. Adequate justification was never given. The Senate report stated 'administrative reasons,' and the House was equally vague. Representative Marcantonio fought against the exclusion in his minority report of the House Committee on Labor: 'I . . . respectfully submit that there is not a single solitary reason why agricultural workers should not be included under the provisions of this bill.'

But the bill's sponsor in the House, Representative Connery, chairman of the Labor Committee, opposed the inclusion of farm workers at that time: '. . . the committee discussed this matter carefully in executive session and decided not to include agricultural workers. We hope that the agricultural workers will be taken care of . . . I am in favor of giving agricultural workers ever protection, but just now I believe in biting off one mouthful at a time. If we can get this bill through and get it working properly, there will be opportunity later, and I hope soon, to take care of the agricultural workers.'[218]

The 92nd Congress, thirty-eight years after the NLRA was passed in 1935, considered legislation to include farmworkers under the provisions of the NLRA. But so had every Congressional session since 1935! However, farmworkers organized by the National Farm Workers now refused to support any measure that would put them under the provisions of the NLRA. This was a radical departure from the public policy position farmworkers have taken prior to 1969.

Coverage under the NLRA has not been the only major focus of the farmworkers legislative struggle. The passage of the Social Security measure of 1935 also excluded farmworkers. Thus, many of the social security benefits taken for granted by millions of industrial workers have yet to be legislated for farmworkers. Social welfare benefits, such as unemployment, retirement, disability, etc. are not within the reach of farmworkers. For this reason, social service centers throughout the nation have been organized by the National Farm Workers in order to help farmworkers obtain benefits normally available to other workers for many years now.

In this light, the California Rural Legal Assistance has distributed a report entitled "Laws Affecting Farm Workers and Their Families." This document cites laws under the California Labor Code, California Health and Safety Code, California Administrative Code, Code of Federal Regulations, United States Code Annotated, and Division of Industrial Welfare. The report provides a discussion of wages, unions and strikes, working conditions, transportation, minors, and labor camps. The report can be summarized as follows:

The discussion of wages is in six sections: I. *In general* wages are: (A) Determined by agreement. (B) Labor contractor must post wage rate at job and on vehicle. (C) No kickbacks. (D) Equal pay for women and men. (E) show-up pay—showing up and finding no work: 1. women and minors—paid for 4 hours; 2. farm labor contractor—paid for time to and from job; 3. moving to get job. II. *Minimum wages:* (A) Who gets? Women and minors 16 or 17. (B) Who pays? Only employers hiring 5 or more women or minors. (C) Minimum wage rates: 1. Hourly wage: $1.65 for women, $1.35 for minors; 2. Piece rate: a) Production records must be given; b) workers on piece rate must earn the minimum hourly rate. 3. Remedies; 4. Workers should keep records. III. *Deductions from wages:* (A) Itemized statement of deductions required. (B) What deductions are proper: Disability insurance, 1% of gross wages; social security, 5.2% of gross wages; federal income tax. (C) What deductions are not proper: 1. In general: a) cost of medical exam; b) "kickbacks." 2. Work for women or minors, nor deductions for: a) accidental breaking of equipment; b) "Rent" for uniforms or equipment; c) rest periods. IV. *Dispute as to amount owed:*

Employer must pay amount he admits is due; he cannot require worker to sign "paid in full" statement. V. *Form of payment:* Cash checks immediately; wages must be paid in cash or in check—not in "scrip." VI. When and where the worker is to be paid: (A) Regular payday. 1. Employer must post sign saying when payday is. 2. Must be at least twice a month. (B) If worker quits, is fired or is on strike: 1. Fired is paid immediately. 2. quits is paid within 72 hours in county where he worked. 3. strike is paid on next regular payday.

The discussion of unions and strikes is in two sections: I. *Right to join a labor union.* A worker has a right to join (or not to join) any labor union. He cannot be fired for joining or taking part in union activities, even if he promises the employer he wouldn't. If he thinks he has been, he should contact a lawyer immediately. II. *Strike Breakers:* (A) There is no law which prevents a strike breaker from crossing a picket line or taking a job with the employer. However, California Law requires that he know that there is a strike in existence. (B) During a strike, the employer cannot seek new workers (either by newspaper ads, by posters or by word of mouth) without telling them that there is a strike at his place. This rule applies to the grower, a farm labor contractor and employment agencies. Note: the above acts are misdemeanors and in addition, the person who commits them is liable for suits for double damages by those whom he has deceived.

The discussion of working conditions is in five sections: I. *Drinking water.* Employer must provide: covered container; no pouring or dipping; no common drinking cups. II. *Toilet and handwashing.* (A) Required if either: 1. Crew of 5 working on crops which are to be eaten, or women or minors on the job. (B) Requirements: 1. Within 5 minute walk. 2. Toilets: Privacy, toilet paper, no flies, clean. 3. Handwashing: Water and soap. III. *Meals and rest periods.* Only for women and minors: (A) Lunch break, 30 minutes if 6 hours of work. (B) Rest period, 10 minutes every 4 hours, must be counted as time worked. IV. *Working hours:* 8 hours a day, 6 days a week for minors and women, and women can work longer during harvest. V. *Safety.* (A) Injury in the field: 1. First-aid kits. 2. Work in isolated areas. (B) Preventing injury: 1. Translator. 2. Moving machinery, guard rails on tractors, signaling device on towed machines, guarding spinning blades. 3. Night work: Lights on trucks. 4. Spreading poison. 5. Dangerous jobs, minors.

The discussion of transportation of workers is in four sections: I. *In general.* Rules important; watch distinctions as to kind of truck or bus involved. II. *Passenger accommodations:* (A) All open trucks, cab must be filled, railing, tailgate closed, no standing. (B) Open trucks used regularly to transport workers: Seats, railings, steps. (C) If 7 or more passengers: Windows required; standing, overcrowding; maximum number of passengers, minimum size of seats. III. *Safety:* (A) Equipment; must be in good repair. (B) Railroad crossings. (C) Speed. (D) Tools and inflammables: Covered and tied down. (E) Broken glass. (F) Safety equipment: Flares, fire extinguisher, signaling device. (G) Exists—two at least. (H) Exhaust. (I) Fresh air. IV. *General provisions:* (A) Special driver's license. (B) No minors driving. (C) Required signs: Name and license number of labor contractor; note on "day hauler"; wage rates; maximum number of passengers. (D) Permints-day haulers.

The discussion of minors is in three sections: I. *In general.* Convincing people why the law should be enforced. II. *School.* Minors under 18 who have not graduated from high school. (A) Full-time school: 8 to age of 16. (B) Continuation school: Non high school grads 16-17. 1. If employed, 4 hours a week. 2. If unemployed, 3 hours a day. III. *Work*. (A) Permits required for all non high school graduates under 18. Employer must post warning sign. (B) Working hours for minors under 16: 8 hours a day, 48 hours a week, counting school time; not before 5 a.m. or after 10 p.m. (C) Employer must post hours. (D) Wages are at least $1.35 for minors 16 and 17. (E) Rest periods are 10 minutes for every 4 hours. (F) Lunch break is 30 minutes if work 6 hours. (G) Dangerous jobs.

The discussion of labor camps is in six sections: I. *In general:* Five or more workers must live there. II. *Buildings:* (A) Clean, keep out wind, rain and dampness; no bugs. (B) Location, 75 feet from barns. (C) Tents, no dirt floors. (D) Construction. III. *Camp Grounds.* (A) Clean, no piles of rubbish. (B) Fire hazards and dangerous objects. (C) No standing water. (D) Garbage, covered containers, emptied daily. (E) Livestock can't run free. IV. *Rooms:* In general, fire exists, ceilings, windows, fresh air, heat, overcrowding beds, toilets, showers, handwashing, kitchen, mess halls. V. *Water.* (A) In general: 35 gallons a day for each person, must be pure; hot and cold required. (B) Drinking water: Must be provided, no dipping on ground, stored in covered containers. VI. *Camps must be registered and inspected.*[219]

Given the social as well as the economic importance of the fore-going, today it can still be said that the legislative struggle by farm-workers has neither been described, documented, nor analyzed by social science studies. Yet, similar to the legal struggle, in order to achieve a full understanding of the major forces that farm workers have had to cope with in their efforts to organize, the social, economic, and theoretical importance of legislative actions and counter-actions cannot continue to be ignored.

The following survey concerning the legislative struggles by the farmworkers organization, UFW, from 1965 to 1972 constitutes an initial step toward filling this vacuum in our knowledge relative to farm labor and legislative actions. Clearly, this legislative struggle is inter-woven with other aspects of farm worker activities, as has already been noted with mention of the farmworkers service centers, and the legal struggle.

The dates in what follows are arranged in chronological order by year. This is a relatively arbitrary arrangement due to the need to present clearly such an enormous amount of data in a comprehensible form to readers who may not be acquainted with this aspect of the farm labor movement in the United States. This account begins in 1965 with a discussion of legislation from the view of AFL-CIO (state and national), NFW, and agribusiness. Publications of each of the three organized groups, as well as many other documents, have been utilized.

In general, the final outcome of every legislative bill in this historical summary is not available except insofar as access to the resources has been possible. Nevertheless, the outcome of a number of bills is noted in sufficient numbers as to provide data for the central thrust of this study.

Finally, the following account reveals one very significant factor. That is, that all through the years of the struggle in the fields, at the same time there has taken place a parallel struggle in the legislative bodies of the nation. From this it follows, naturally, that in order to understand the activities among the workers, it is also imperative to understand something about the simultaneous activities taking place in the legislative arena. The two are interlocked. They influence each other. And, it can be said, the issues which they collectively face are bigger than both of them, for they concern the future and the human beings who will be a part of it.

1965

Minimum Wages
Braceros
Unemployment Insurance
U.S. Senate Agricultural Committee Hearings
Working And Living Conditions
Small Farmer Price Support
Land Taxation
Section 14(b) Of The Taft-Hartley Act

In January, 1965, California's agribusiness was concerned about new minimum wage requirements and restrictions on the use of alien workers:

"On April 1, 1965, California's minimum wage rises to $1.40. Certification for foreign workers will be withheld if a grower employs an alien who has entered the U.S. illegally, when he knows or has reasonable grounds to believe or suspect or by reasonable inquiry could have ascertained, that the worker is not lawfully within the United States ... To obtain foreign workers, the grower must make 'reasonable efforts' to recruit domestic workers, and must offer domestics, in addition to the minimum wages, all the terms and conditions of employment that are offered to Mexican workers (under the bracero program) including a written contract embodying these conditions ... As with the bracero program, any grower involved in a strike or labor dispute would be denied foreign workers. And when domestic workers become available for jobs which foreign workers hold, the domestics are to be given preference."[220]

Furthermore, growers were opposed to the push by the California Labor Federation, AFL-CIO, to have unemployment insurance benefits for farm workers:

"Something tells us that unemployment insurance is going to be rammed down the throat of agriculture by our legislature . . . if a new group or industry is voted under the program, the employers of that group inherit a new tax of 3.2% of their payroll . . . In Sacramento, the unions are pressing to bring two new groups into the unemployment insurance society—farm workers and state employees . . . Some experts have estimated that a deficit of $50 million a year over the amount paid by the agricultural employers would be incurred . . . But we understand there is a bill being introduced that suggests the Federal Government pay up to 80% of the deficits in the agricultural account if UI is established in this state . . . the farmers of California pay somewhere around $500 million a year in farm labor wages. The tax of 3.2%, while it applies to only the first $3,800 wages, would perhaps cover most of that $500 million. In which case the tax alone means that farmers have to add $16 million to the top of their expense sheet . . . So we add one more spike to California agriculture's competitive disadvantage."[221]

In February, 1965, the struggle between growers and U.S. Secretary of Labor's office over the use of domestic labor was best depicted by the following telegram sent to the President by Bud Antle, Antle, Inc.— Grower-Shipper of California and Arizona.

"The suggestion made today by Undersecretary of Labor, John W. Henning, that we recruit from A. Green and the Agricultural Workers Organizing Committee, AFL-CIO domestic farm workers to replace our former Mexican National workers is repugnant to us and pushes beyond our ability to accept doctrinaire instructions."[222]

By late February, California's Governor Brown, under pressure from growers, requested that Secretary of Labor Wirtz allow foreign labor to come in the State because of a so-called shortage in domestic recruitment.

"At the end of February Pat (Governor Brown) suddenly rattled his cage and sent Tieburg to Wirtz with the startling message that perhaps we were not going to be able to recruit enough domestics and would Wirtz please set up the machinery to bring in Mexicans. Wirtz said 'no.' "[223]

State welfare policies were being attacked by growers who claimed that a lack of incentive on the part of unemployed farm workers to accept jobs rather than continue on welfare was a significant factor in what they called disappointing results to recruit domestics. They criticized the State Department of Social Welfare:

"It's administratively impossible to make welfare recipients available for farm work outside the immediate area and still comply with existing requirements of the law and the latest interpretations of the department."[224]

The position of the AFL-CIO State Federation was to oppose any foreign farm worker importation program. The Federation sent a letter to all Congressmen urging they support the Secretary of Labor and oppose any efforts to renew the importation of foreign workers.

State Department of Employment Director Albert Tieburg, in an interview with the *California Farmer*, told the journal:

"We are dealing with a federal law that allows the importation of foreign workers to perform work that does not interfere with domestic workers . . . the authority for making this law operate is the Attorney General. He, in turn, has delegated his authority to the Secretary of Labor. And the Secretary of Labor must certify as to the availability of domestic workers . . . I have been made responsible for determining the availability or lack of domestics. Second, if growers seek foreign labor, my office has been charged with the standards outlined by Wirtz's office."[225]

He also proposed that growers ask Wirtz to forget the guaranteed hourly minimum which could load up a grove with "loafers." Tieburg said that piece rate was a dirty word to the Secretary of Labor. He associated it with sweat shop, speed-up and slave working conditions.

The U.S. Senate held hearings before the Senate Agricultural Committee concerning the importation of foreign workers. The two Senators from California defended the growers' position. The hearings had been held January 15, 1965, on "Importation of Foreign Agricultural Worker."[226]

In April, reports were provided on the hearings conducted by the State Industrial Welfare Commission for an increase of minimum hourly wages for women from $1.00 to $1.30. Growers' representatives stated that such an increase would put this labor supply out of the economic reaches of employers. Farm workers testified that $1.30 was absurdly low.

During the early part of April the American Farm Bureau Federation's Board of Directors urged the President to use Public Law 414 to certify admission of Mexican workers. Assistant Secretary of Agriculture George Mehren visited California and "conceded" that there was a labor shortage.[227]

On April 17, a *California Farmer* editorial blamed the death of the Bracero program on the growers. "Agriculture has blown the big one. The Bracero program is dead, and our industry had no one to blame but itself."[228] This major criticism of agriculture was said to be due to the fact that:

"Agriculture put one of the most shocking displays of public relations or no public relations ever seen . . . the growers excluded the press at their Salinas Conference with Wirtz, which was a stupid move. The well-organized opposition forces invited the press in when they met with Wirtz . . . A special back of the hand to those few labor contractors who ran filthy camps, provide lousy food . . . We hope they get regulated right up to their eyeballs by county, state, and federal jackets . . . Wirtz was rabid on the subject of housing."[229]

In May, 1965, President Johnson proposed a farm bill which would provide small farmers more price support protections than large operators. The proposal was confined to wool and rice for the 1966 and 1967 crops.[230]

Meanwhile, the California Labor Federation urged that unemployment benefits be provided to farm workers:

"Every argument justifying adoption of an unemployment insurance program for workers in general applies with equal force to the inclusion of agricultural workers, a spokesman for California Labor Federation, AFL-CIO, declared this week in testifying in behalf of AB 1280, the Federation's omnibus measure to effect long overdue improvements in the unemployment insurance program."[231]

Growers continued to complain about their inability to obtain foreign labor and continued to blame welfare policies:

"The money this state spends for welfare has some correlation with our inability to hire sufficient domestic workers to replace the bracero . . . the California Taxpayers Association calls attention to several bills . . . SB 787 and SB 791 would require that an unemployed parent apply for work with the State Employment Service before making application for aid to dependent children. SB 788 would make ineligible for aid a family whose breadwinner is unemployed because he is on strike."[232]

Two other bills were proposed that were opposed by agribusiness. The first, HR 5408, which would provide unemployment insurance benefits for farm workers, would set a 2.7% tax, assuming $60 million in payment would be made to agricultural workers. Farmers would provide $24 million; the Federal Government $34.5 million; and the state general fund $1.5 million. The other bill, AB 1648, a California strikebreaker bill, was opposed because a farmer who hired a person who had worked in the last five years under strike conditions would be considered a professional strikebreaker and the employer would be subject to criminal charges.

On May 15, the Williamson Act, AB 2117, was supported by agriculture because it provided a tax shelter for growers:

"Counties (and cities) are authorized to create agricultural preserves, containing not less than 100 acres, where land use would be restricted to agricultural and compatible uses. Such preserves could include both prime and non-prime land. Prime land is restricted to Class I or Class II soils on the Soil Conservation Service Maps, or land producing $200 an acre gross annual income from crops.

"Counties and cities are authorized to enter into 10 year contracts with prime landowners within a preserve. Such contracts are automatically renewed annually unless notice of non-renewal is given by either party.

"In return for entering a contract, the landowner would receive either a freeze on an assessed value of his land, or offsetting payments in case the assessed value was increased. For any increase in assessed value after a contract is entered into, the local governing body will pay the landowner under contract 5 cents for each $1 of increase.

"The bill would also establish restrictive cancellation provisions."[233]

In the latter part of May, President Johnson submitted to Congress his labor message calling for the repeal of Section 14 (b) of the Taft-Hartley Act, considered a union-busting section or "right-to-work" clause. Secretary of Labor Wirtz told Congress it was not the right to work, but the right to decide the conditions of work they supported.

"This issue of whether the private parties to collective bargaining are, or are not, to be free to decide the union security issue as they see fit should be settled once and for all. It has cluttered up the political process in almost every state in the union and it will continue to do so as long as the federal law invites such controversy, the Labor Secretary declared."[234]

In June, the Labor Federation issued a statement pointing out how German farm public policy for farm workers compared with U.S. policy.

"Farm workers in West Germany receive two and one-half weeks vacation with pay, comprehensive medical and hospital care, and earn about 80% of the average industrial worker's wages, George Leber, a member of the West German Parliament and leader of his nation's building and construction tradesmen, disclosed in an interview in San Francisco last week. In contrast, California's domestic farm workers have no general hospital or medical coverage, get no paid vacations, and earn less than 46% of the state's average industrial worker's weekly wage."[235]

In July, Secretary of Labor Wirtz urged support for a 5-bill proposal to improve the rights of U.S. farm workers before the Subcommittee on Migratory Labor of the Senate Committee on Labor and Public Welfare. These proposals were as follows:

1. S. 1864, to extend the minimum wage (but not overtime) provisions of the Fair Labor Standards Act to farm workers employed by employers who use more than 300 man-days of hired labor in a calendar quarter.

2. S. 1865, to prohibit the employer in agriculture of children under 14 years of age except by their parents.

3. S. 1866, to bring agricultural workers under the Taft-Hartley Act.

4. S. 1867, to provide for more effective recruitment of seasonal farm labor.

5. S. 1868, to establish a National Advisory Council on Migratory Labor.[236]

Meanwhile, the first major hurdle to repeal section 14(b) was successfully overcome.

"After 18 years and more than 40 bitter, divisive and costly battles, the U.S. House of Representatives voted 221 to 203 Wednesday to cut out the cankerous cause of it all by repealing Section 14(b) of the Taft-Hartley Act. The action to eliminate the 44 word section that enabled states to impose compulsory open shop terms on workers and employers alike by banning union shop agreements culminates years of political and legislative effort by the AFL-CIO, as well as concerned civic and religious groups."[237]

In September, a bill to require farm operators to provide unemployment insurance for farm workers would have very little impact on retail food prices, a spokesman for the U.S. Department of Agriculture told the House Ways and Means Committee. Halhan Koffsky, U.S.D.A. Director of Agricultural Economics, pointed out that:

"The increase in labor cost would amount to only two tenths of one percent of total farm production expenses. Provisions of the bill stipulate that it would apply only to farmers who use 300 or more man-days of hired labor per quarter year. Labor Department estimates indicate that only about two percent of U.S. farms are in this category and employ a total of 700,000 workers."[238]

Furthermore, in September, a so-called "back door" attempt to revive the bracero program was made. Transference of authority to determine the need for foreign workers from the U.S. Labor Department to the Department of Agriculture was rejected by only one vote, that of Vice President Humphrey, in a key Senate vote:

"The closeness of the vote, a surprise to administration forces, indicated that corporate grower interests are still exerting all the pressures they can muster to try to reopen their access to a cheap, captive, foreign labor supply at the expense of the poorest paid and most ill-treated segment of the nation's labor force—the domestic farm worker."[239]

In October, a coalition of Southern Democrats and Conservative Republicans succeeded in denying the U.S. Senate an opportunity to vote democratically on the repeal of Section 14(b) of the Taft-Hartley Act. It was a filibuster to stop the repeal.[240] In November, President Johnson pledged to "come back" to the next session of Congress and remove the anti-union shop Section 14(b). He also promised to give priority to amendment and modernization of the Fair Labor Standards Act and the unemployment insurance system.[241] At the same time, in response to the Delano grape strike started in September by AWOC and NFWA, the *California Farmer* issued the following warning:

"Farm labor will have to be managed—not just turned on and off—if many of California's crops are to survive the current period of social upheaval. Improved farm labor relations is just one of the many changes . . . you're not going to get domestic laborers to do the same type of work at the speed of the braceros."[242]

In December, those reflecting on the year's controversial labor struggle commented that the bracero program had been replaced by the "green card worker" system, and that there were now many more illegal aliens:

"The wetback problem has increased just as growers predicted it would after the expiration of P.L. 78 on December 31, 1964. The U.S. Bureau of Immigration has requested an additional $3 million for patrolling the U.S. Mexican border to keep out wetbacks. Armed Forces personnel are being used, also. The Justice Department early in November asked for an additional $280,000 appropriation . . . As of January 1, 1965, there were 631,000 Mexican 'green cards' in the U.S. Less than 20% of the overall 'green card' total were from Mexico. The Russian Soviets totaled 54,000; Canadians, 365,000; United Kingdom, 257,000; West Germans, 242,000; Polish, 127,000 and Cubans, 121,000. One million came from other countries. These figures are from U.S. Bureau of Immigration Figures."[243]

Finally, agribusiness criticized Secretary of Labor Wirtz and held more hope for Congress, while Wirtz would continue to pursue labor legislation benefiting farm workers.

1966

>Minimum Wages
>Foreign Labor
>Section 14(b) Taft-Hartley Act
>Unemployment Insurance
>U.S. Senate Subcommittee On Migrant Labor Hearings
>State Senate Fact Finding Committee On Agriculture
>National Labor Relations Act
>Fringe Benefits
>Delano Labor Hearings
>State Survey Of Farm Labor
>Hawaiian Farm Labor
>National Agricultural Work Plan

In January, 1966, agribusiness proposed that a national wage board be formed with representatives from agribusiness, organized labor, government, and the public at large, which should set uniform farm wages for the entire United States. The *California Farmer* stated:

"It further suggests that wages should be set in detail for different types of farm work. These are hourly wages. Piece rates should be set so that 51% of the workers on the farm could earn the equivalent of the hourly wage. The wage rates would be set with the condition that organized labor would not be allowed to employ the strike or the secondary boycott."[244]

During a National Farm Labor Conference, held in San Antonio, Texas, attended by state employment services, Undersecretary of Labor

John Henning and Robert Goodwin, Administrator of the Bureau of Employment Security, issued a policy statement that state lines were being abolished by the U.S. Department of Labor. The *California Farmer* complained.

"The implication is that the federal government is going to take a much bigger hand in this business of recruiting labor. We can expect from these pronouncements that the State Farm Placement Service will be getting lots of 'help' from the 'feds' whether we want it or not."[245]

In February, the labor unions began a renewed effort to repeal Section 14(b) of the Taft-Hartley Act. The *California Farmer* warned growers that unless they wrote to their Congressman and Senator there would be compulsory unionism. At the same time state AFL-CIO leader Thomas Pitts announced the appointment of a Labor Task Force Committee to study the needs and develop a program to aid California's farm workers on strike in Delano.

In March, a U.S. Senate Subcommittee on Migratory Farm Labor announced that it would hold hearings to gather information on Farm Labor legislation pending in Congress and to determine if additional legislation was needed. The hearings were to include on-site investigations of conditions in Sacramento on March 14, Visalia on March 15, and Delano on March 16. Harrison Williams (D-New Jersey) was chairman of the subcommittee. After the hearings the *California Farmer* issued the following statement:

"We have just witnessed the Williams hearings on the California labor situation. Senator Williams from New Jersey and Senator Robert Kennedy tried to load the three hearings with the friends of labor and pretty well succeeded. In fact, the whole affair might have been a tremendous disaster if it had not been for the presence of Senator George Murphy."[246]

A major discussion of a farm labor bill proposed by Senator Harrison to include farm workers under the National Labor Relations Act of 1935 was held during these hearings. Senator Kennedy and Chairman Harrison stated that their objective was to insure farm workers the right to decide for themselves whether they wanted to be represented by a union in collective bargaining. Jack Miller, vice president of Agricultural Producers Labor Committee called it compulsory unionization and opposed the bill. Miller charged the proposed legislation would give unions a monopoly over agricultural labor, and through this, control over the food supply of the nation. "This, in our opinion is against public policy," he asserted. However, there was strong union support for extension of the NLRA to agriculture.[247]

Also in March, the California Labor Federation, AFL-CIO, urged support of House Bill HR 8282, which would extend unemployment coverage; and House Bill HR 10518, which would provide minimum wage law coverage for farm workers. The growers perspective on these bills was that farm workers were covered by all but unemployment insurance, with only Hawaii and the District of Columbia having unemployment insurance for farm workers. In essence, they felt that the legislative struggle would drag on and that there was no chance for a union victory prior to the 1967 general legislative session. They did admit they could lose to the "new breed" of city-oriented legislators in the future.

Furthermore, in March, the *Farm Journal* was critical of the California Labor Panel reports which called Secretary of Labor Wirtz' termination of foreign labor a success.

"Two labor panels have reviewed the results of Wirtz's policy and have termed it a 'substantial success.' The pronouncement by the California Labor Panel was immediately paraded publicly by USDL and labor union publications as unassailable proof for their position despite angry protests by growers. The panel picked by Wirtz included no farmers."[248]

In May, Senator Fred S. Farr (D-Carmel, Ca.) introduced two bills to provide emergency educational services to school districts receiving large numbers of children from farm worker families. Introduced at the request of Governor Brown, the two bills would provide up to $1,000,000 for temporary classrooms and $500,000 for teachers and supplies.

At the same time, the California Labor Federation opposed the state's policy of using state prison labor as a "substitute bracero program." The state had announced that some 500 minimum security prisoners would be put to work on a volunteer basis in asparagus fields in the San Joaquin Delta.[249]

In June, California's Republican nominee for Governor, Ronald Reagan, urged the renewal of the bracero program. And U.S. Senator Gaylord Nelson (D-Wisc.) along with U.S. Representative Joseph Karth (D-Minn.) proposed laws to forbid interstate sale and shipment of DDT. This was opposed by the *Farm Journal*.[250]

In July, a hearing was held by the state Senate Fact-finding Committee on Agriculture in Delano. Also in July, the state Labor Federation, AFL-CIO, repudiated agribusiness claims that collective bargaining would not work in agriculture.

In August, the California Citrus Association offered fringe benefits to farm workers in an attempt to prevent any program imposed by government or unions.

"Coastal Growers of Oxnard supplied its workers with major medical and hospitalization benefits up to $10,000; the workers found that they were only required to pay $100 of large medical bills. Coastal Growers may well be setting the yardstick for other growers to follow in their fringe benefit program for field workers, along with a pay schedule which puts average earnings of harvest labor at more than $2 per hour. In an interview with *California Farmer*, Harry McKee, president of the Coastal Growers, said, 'We would rather write our own program than have someone else do it for us, and it's about time we growers got off the defensive and carried the ball ourselves for a change.' "[251]

Meanwhile, the Labor Federation, AFL-CIO, at its convention in San Diego, California, declared that the fight to organize farm workers was the major battleground in California's war on poverty. It pledged a "redoubled" effort to help farm workers organize into unions and intensify legislative efforts to bring them under the coverage of the National Labor Relations Act, the Fair Labor Standards Act, and the Unemployment Insurance Program.[252]

In September, 1966, California state Assemblyman John C. Williamson (D-Bakersfield), Chairman of the Assembly Committee on Agriculture, announced that the U.S. Bureau of Employment Security granted $146,080 to the State Department of Employment to do a survey of the California Farm Labor Force:

"Williamson stated the survey was part of a comprehensive farm labor research program that his committee has been working on since last year with the assistance of an advisory committee composed of three farm employer and three farm employee representatives. Members of the advisory committee are: J. J. Miller, executive vice president, Agricultural Producers Labor Committee; Richard W. Owens, Secretary-Treasurer, California Farm Bureau Federation; William Hunt Conrad, Kern County Land Company; Michael Peevey, Research Director, California Labor Federation, AFL-CIO; Thomas L. Harris, Social Insurance analyst, California Teamsters Legislative Council; and Bard McAllister, Farm Labor Secretary, American Friends Service Committee."[253]

Then, in October, at the request of growers, a representative for the Western Growers Association, Ross Gast, visited Hawaii to investigate statements made by Harry Bridges, President of the International Longshoremen's and Warehousemen's Union. Bridges appeared before Senator Williams' subcommittee hearings on migratory labor and stated that the only way to make California farmer "cave in" and accept unionization was to "close down the agricultural industry of California." Gast summarized his study as follows:

"Hawaiian agricultural employers are all highly industrialized operations controlling not only the processing of their products, but many of their sources of supply, and are not dependent on farming products for survival. Thus, they are far different than the average California farm labor employer, who hires mostly seasonal labor, and has his survival riding on the profits from any one year's operations. California does have the DiGiorgio and other corporate farms, much like the Hawaiian agricultural operations, but such outfits represent only slightly above one percent of the California farm employment."[254]

In November, the *California Farmer* reported that a National Agricultural Research Plan was submitted to the U.S. Senate which was designed to meet the expanding needs of the nation. The Plan was submitted to the Subcommittee on Agriculture and Related Agencies of the Senate Appropriations Committee by Secretary of Agriculture Orville L. Freeman and David D. Henry, Chairman of the Association of State Universities and Land Grant Colleges.[255]

Also, in November, jobless or unemployment insurance was again urged by the AFL-CIO Labor Federation for California's farm workers.

"California's huge $3.8 billion farm industry can well afford the relatively slight cost of extending unemployment insurance to farm workers—the lowest paid workers in the state—and such a move would benefit not only some 275,000 farm workers and the state's economy, but by reducing welfare costs, the state's general taxpayers as well, state AFL-CIO declared this week."[256]

Finally, in December, the California AFL-CIO Federation, at a hearing in San Francisco, urged that the U.S. Labor Department bar all foreign farm workers from California, failing this, they proposed to require California growers to offer domestic workers at least $2.25 an hour and $90 a week before allowing them to import aliens.[257]

1967

Collective Bargaining
Increased Wage Rate
Unemployment Insurance
U.S. Reclamation Law
Green Card Workers
New Bureau Of Employment Agencies
Weakened Protection For Working Women
Use of Braceros
Newly Accepted 40 Hour Week
Illegal Use Of Convict Labor
Landrum-Griffin Act

In January, 1967, the AFL-CIO Labor Federation criticized the growers push to increase their own bargaining rights:

"The best, most recent reflection of this unreasonable transformation is provided by the latest edition of one of the State's Agribusiness-oriented publications, the *California Farmer*, which levels its editorial barrage against big processor lobbyists who are opposing congressional legislation that would protect the growers' right to join associations that would bargain collectively with the processors to improve the prices the growers get for their products."[258]

William Kirches, National Director of Organization for AFL-CIO, told members of a U.S. Advisory Commission on Food and Fiber in San Francisco that farm workers in California and throughout the nation must be accorded full collective bargaining rights and the benefits of other protective social welfare legislation.[259]

In March, State AFL-CIO leader Thomas Pitts took sharp issue with the new $1.60 wage rate which California agribusiness interests had to offer domestic workers before being permitted to import braceros. "It's not enough," Pitts said of the rate announced by the U.S. Labor Department.[260]

Also in March, California Assemblyman John Burton (D-San Francisco) introduced an unemployment insurance bill for farm workers:

"The bill, AB937, initiated by the California Labor Federation, would extend jobless insurance benefits to farm workers, workers in domestic service and to public employees and employees of certain non-profit organizations."[261]

The following month, in April, the farm workers press, through *El Malcriado,* issued one of its earliest statements regarding legislation. It informed the workers that a bill to extend National Labor Relations Act coverage to farm workers had finally passed the House, Education, and Labor Committee which was chaired by Congressman Phil Burton (D-California). The bill, HR4769, was sent to the floor of Congress where it could "easily be trampled."[262]

Also, in April, California's Labor Federation urged the Assembly Finance and Insurance Committee's Subcommittee on Unemployment Insurance to act favorably on AB937-Burton-initiated bill to extend jobless pay benefits to farm workers.

In May, National AFL-CIO and the Johnson Administration joined in supporting legislation to give farm workers the right to organize and bargain with their employers.

"Farm workers, excluded from the National Labor Relations Act, face 'firings, blacklists, yellow-dog contracts, even arrest on trumped-up charges' when they try to organize, AFL-CIO President George Meany told a House Labor Subcommittee Monday. Meany stressed that the bitter farm worker strikes of the past years have been primarily 'for the fundamental right to bargain collectively.' "[263]

In June, California's AFL-CIO criticized the U.S. Reclamation Law. The basic principle of the law was that the benefits of projects paid by public funds should benefit the public at large as much as possible, and not be funneled automatically into the hands of large land owners and land speculators. Moreover, contrary to claims of the large landowners, the 160-acre limit applied to ownership, not to operations. The present reclamation law, in other words, did not restrict the operational capability of vast corporate agricultural holdings in any way. It just said that they had to pay a reasonable rate for the water they used on their excess acreage instead of getting it for practically nothing. The public paid higher state and federal taxes, while cash benefits of the publically financed project flowed into the hands of the rich, according to the *California AFL-CIO News.*[264]

Meanwhile, César Chávez led a demonstration in Washington and spoke to the nation's leaders about why the National Labor Relations Act should be extended to protect farm workers.

In August, the California Labor Federation requested federal action to ban the use of "green card" workers from Mexico as strikebreakers in a farm labor dispute at the properties of Giumarra Vineyard Corporation in Kern County.[265]

In September, California's Governor Reagan signed AB1030-Moretti, which weakened the protection afforded women workers by the State's historic 8-hour law. Women in most industries covered by the Federal Fair Labor Standards Act would be encouraged to work up to 10 hours a day and 58 hours a week.

Furthermore, the State AFL-CIO Federation demanded that Secretary of Labor Wirtz bar the use of braceros. Importation of 8,100 foreign farm workers to harvest tomatoes in California, labor contended, would shortchange domestic workers of higher wages and boost the welfare load on California's general taxpayers. The U.S. Labor Department agreed to a unique pact to increase its investigation of charges of grower violations of rules previously set up to assure that no foreign farm workers would be imported into California so long as domestic workers were available.[266]

By the end of September it was announced that the Industrial Welfare Commission increased the pay floor and adopted a 40-hour week for farm workers:

" 'The Industrial Welfare Commission's final decision to boost the State's minimum wage from $1.30 to $1.65 an hour, wipe out the inequity of a lower minimum for farm workers, and cut the maximum straight-time work week from 48 to 40 hours is without a doubt the most meaningful step taken in recent years to improve the lot of millions of low-income workers in California but it still leaves much to be desired,' State AFL-CIO leader Thomas L. Pitts said this week."[267]

In October, the AFL-CIO Federation filed suit to bar the use of convict labor and challenged Governor Reagan's authority to use convict labor in California's fields as unconstitutional in a court action initiated in San Francisco. Citing Article 10, Section 1 of the State Constitution, which according to State AFL-CIO leader Thomas L. Pitts, specifically prohibits such exploitation of convict labor as had been authorized by Governor Reagan, the Federation asked for an *ex parte* temporary restraining order, but scheduled a "show cause" hearing on the issue for Monday, October 16.[268]

In November, the AFL-CIO Federation testified before the Assembly Constitutional Amendments Committee. Thomas Pitts declared:

"We strenuously object to any change in the Constitution which would allow the use of prisoners to undercut or circumvent a free labor market by contracting our prisoners to any private employer. In opposing proposals to strike Paragraph 3 of Article X of the State Constitution the Federation said that the obvious danger of such a move is that it might well open the floodgate to just such unscrupulous action. Paragraph 3 of Article X states: The labor of convicts shall not be let out by contract to any person, co-partnership, company or corporation, and the Legislature shall, by law, provide the working of convicts for the benefit of the State."[269]

The AFL-CIO Federation won its suit to bar the use of State convicts on farms. Authorization of a preliminary injunction barring use of convict labor to harvest California crops was viewed as a victory for the California Labor Federation as well as for the State's grossly underpaid farm workers. The order, issued by San Francisco Superior Court Judge Robert Drewes, resulted from a suit filed October 5.

"The suit charged Governor Ronald Reagan with violating the State Constitution when the Governor authorized the use of some 300 State prison convicts to harvest figs and grapes in Merced and San Bernardino Counties. In announcing his decision, Judge Drewes agreed with the California Federation's contention that Governor Reagan's authorization of the use of convicts to harvest private crops does not follow the rules of the work-furlough program. It does not resemble a rehabilitation program in any important respect, Judge Drewes said."[270]

Shortly after this legal decision, the California Constitution Revision Commission, voted unanimously against changing paragraph 3 of Article 10 of the State Constitution.

Finally, in December, a study was released indicating that the Landrum-Griffin Act was a "bad law" compounded by "administrative abuses." A committee of 21 experienced lawyers published "A Report After Eight Years of Landrum-Griffin Act," for the AFL-CIO Maritime Trades Department and its president Paul Hall of the Seafarers.

1968

New Farm Worker Lobby Called The National Campaign For Agricultural Democracy
Proposed Coverage Under NLRA For Workers (HR 5769 And S. 8)
California Land Conservation Act Under Legal Attack
Unemployment Insurance Bills AB 273 and AB 182
Hearings On Foreign Workers And Green-Carders
Senator Kennedy's Bill To Prohibit Green-Carder Commuter Traffic (S. 2790)
Federal Reclamation Law Subsidies Under Attack
Minimum Wage Of $1.35 For Minors Working In Agriculture

In January, 1968, there appeared a new registered lobby in Washington. It was called the National Campaign for Agricultural Democracy. The lobby's aim was to give the National Labor Relations Board authority to require farmer-employers to recognize a union as a bargaining agent for their employees. Two bills were introduced: HR 5769 and S. 8, which would put agriculture under the NLRB. The original participants in the lobby were the AFL-CIO, the National Council of Churches, the Bishops Committee for the Spanish-Speaking, the National Catholic Rural Life Conference, the Methodist Church, the United Church of Christ, the National Advisory Committee on Farm Labor, Walter Reuther's Industrial Union Department, the Amalgamated Meat Cutters and Butcher Workmen, and several state migrant ministries. Heading the lobbying activity was Reverend Eugene Boutillier, who was formerly National Boycott Coordinator of Grape Products for César Chávez and the United Farm Workers' Organizing Committee.[271]

At the same time the California Land Conservation Act, supported by growers because it offered a tax break for agricultural land use, was under legal attack. The *California Farmer* urged agriculture to state its case before the John Knox Committee that was defining open space and acceptable land use restrictions as presented under Proposition 3 in the November 1966 elections. Legal counsel stated that:

"It is this attorney's opinion: Article XIII, Section VI of the California Constitution specifically forbids contracts which shall surrender or suspend the power of taxation to which the State is a party, and the Tax Scheme of the State of California and particularly the Williamson Act, which is specifically in violation of Article XIII, Section VI of the State Constitution in this regard . . ."[272]

In February, a series of legislative bills were introduced by California Assemblyman John L. Burton (D-San Francisco) that would affirm the collective bargaining rights of farm workers and public employees and improve the protections and benefits under the unemployment insurance program. AB 273 would extend unemployment benefits to farm workers, domestic servants, public employees and election campaign employees. AB 282 would declare, as a matter of state policy, that workers may select a collective bargaining agent by a majority of those voting in a work unit and would authorize state certification of that agent as sole bargaining agent for the workers for up to two years. AB 283 would authorize state and other public bodies to make contracts and agreements with collective bargaining agents and labor groups.[273]

In addition, the AFL-CIO Federation urged a complete ban on the importation of foreign farm workers. This took place at a hearing in San Francisco held by the Labor Department to gather testimony on updating the $1.60 hourly adverse effect wage rate growers had to offer domestic workers before being allowed to seek foreign workers.

"In calling on the Labor Department to take 'the final step' in 1968 to eliminate foreign farm workers from California's fields, a statement submitted to John Mealy, Labor Department hearing examiner, in behalf of state AFL-CIO leader Thomas L. Pitts, said that the 100,000 increase in domestic farm worker employment, coupled with the rise in their earnings from $616 million in 1964 to an estimated $815 million in 1967, along with the steady increase in gross farm income, has made it overwhelmingly clear that domestic farm workers, growers and small merchants in rural communities have benefited from the end of massive foreign farm worker importation."[274]

The Labor Federation also urged a U.S. Commission in San Diego, California, to end the perpetuation of the so-called green-card system that permitted Mexican citizens to commute to jobs in the U.S. while keeping their residence in Mexico.

"In testimony submitted to the U.S. Select Commission on Immigration on behalf of Thomas L. Pitts, Secretary-Treasurer of the California Labor Federation, the state AFL-CIO cited figures from the State Department of Employment and the U.S. Department of Labor to prove that working conditions as well as wages are adversely affected by the green-card system that brings more than 16,000 aliens into San Diego and Imperial Counties each day."[275]

An editorial by the *California Farmer,* February 17, questioned proposals for government reorganization in Sacramento. It was noted that when Governor Reagan first took office he placed all but agriculture under three cabinet secretaries, and agriculture stood alone. A task force of businessmen recommended that the 37 divisions of state government be more evenly divided under four secretaries.

Then, in February, the AFL-CIO Federation supported the charges that many growers and farm labor contractors continue to disregard the few state laws designed to protect California farm workers and consumers. A survey was completed by the Marysville office of the California Rural Legal Assistance. The survey, conducted in December 1967, and January 1968, was undertaken by the CRLA in behalf of a worker who was denied unemployment insurance benefits for refusing to accept farm work.

"The worker, Magdaleno Botello, refused farm labor on the grounds that it was not covered by unemployment insurance, the Fair Labor Standards Act or the National Labor Relations Act, and the farm employers do not obey state laws requiring them to provide clean and sanitary drinking water, toilets, and hand washing facilities for their workers."[276]

In March, there was a proposal by U.S. Senator Edward M. Kennedy which, if passed, would close the border to green card holders who commute from Mexico to work in the U.S.

"While the proposal, S. 2790, would apply to Canada as well as Mexico, the Senator himself made it obvious that his measure was aimed at the Mexican border. While the Senator accompanied his proposal with a mass of charges and statistics, none of the data was concerned with immigrants from Canada. A hearing on the proposal was held recently in San Diego by the Select Commission on Western Hemisphere Immigration, composed of 15 members. The Commission is made up of five Senators, five Congressmen, and five presidential appointees. Senate Bill 2790 would amend Section 212 of the Immigration and Nationality Act, and would virtually give the Secretary of Labor the authority to open and close the border to immigrant workers who choose to maintain a residence in Mexico."[277]

During the same month, the *California Farmer* informed farmers that when they fired one of their workers they did not have to give advance notice, but the employer had to provide a paycheck at the time of discharge. If he did not, then the grower was guilty of violating the California Labor Code, according to a Deputy Labor Commissioner.[278]

Also in March, the U.S. House Committee approved Federal legislation that would assure farm workers collective bargaining rights. The measure, estimated to apply to some 500,000 farm workers, would bring workers on larger farms under the National Labor Relations Act. AFL-CIO President George Meany testified in support of it at both House and Senate hearings. As approved on a 16 to 12 vote by the committee, the measure, sponsored by Republican James G. O'Hara (D-Michigan), would extend NLRA coverage to workers on farms that employ more than 12 workers at any time during the year and have a total payroll of more than $100,000 a year.[279]

In April, the farm workers press, *El Malcriado,* indicated that when the workers won a contract with DiGiorgio, the Union demanded that DiGiorgio pay his workers unemployment insurance. If a worker earned $880 during a three month period, he would be eligible for unemployment insurance benefits.

A task force appointed by Governor Reagan to study the 160-acre limitation provisions of the Federal Reclamation Law reported that it applied only in the case of the subsidy to farmers who wanted to buy an irrigation water supply from a federal reclamation project.[280]

On April 3, 1968, a farm worker from Tulare County confronted the state assembly subcommittee on unemployment insurance. The subcommittee was considering Assembly Bill 182, introduced by Yvonne Braithwaite, Black assemblywoman from Los Angeles. The bill would extend unemployment coverage for farm workers, reported the United Farm Workers Union. The union also supported HR 16014, which would include farm workers under the NLRA. The bill would cover 1% of the nation's farms while covering 50% of the nation's farm workers.

". . . the growers are now taking a second look at NLRA in order to protect themselves from the long, drawn out battles which they know we are ready to fight for union recognition, and to protect themselves from the boycott which hits them in the money belt."[281]

In May, 1968, the State Supreme Court agreed to hear a petition brought by State Attorney General Thomas Lynch to prevent litigation initiated by growers denying some 100,000 women and minors working in agriculture the benefits of an increase in the minimum hourly wage and a shorter workday, ordered for them by the State Industrial Welfare Commission.

"In a petition filed with Chief Justice Roger J. Traynor on April 22, Lynch pointed out that if orders issued by Superior Courts in Los Angeles and San Francisco Counties that presently prevent enforcement of the IWC order in those jurisdictions are allowed to stand, the rights of many farm workers may be lost irrevocably."[282]

On May 15, the United Farm Workers issued a statement criticizing the American Farm Bureau's attack on legislative proposals that would provide NLRB coverage for farm workers.[283]

In July, the *California Farmer* reported that the word boycott was sending a chill up the spine of agriculture. Growers were faced with a secondary boycott which was a violation of the National Labor Relations Act Section 8(b) (4) (ii) (B). This section was generally referred to as 864. A second section dealing with the present grower situation was 8e. Each was examined in the article.[284]

Meanwhile, the United Farm Workers' Organizing Committee announced that a strike breaking bill sponsored by long time UFWOC foe, California Senator Hugh Burns, died in committee July 2. Members of the Senate Labor Committee decided against bringing the hot cargo and secondary boycott bill to the floor of the Senate. By a three to one vote, the committee refused to go ahead with the bill, which would have prohibited informational picketing throughout the State.[285] And, UFWOC announced support from U.S. Senate nominee Alan Cranston for HR 16014 to give farm workers collective bargaining protection under the National Labor Relations Act.

In August, a trial was held in U.S. District Court in Los Angeles on the legality of an Immigration Service Regulation which prohibited green-card holders from crossing a U.S. Border to work for firms involved in labor disputes. The U.S. Immigration Service was attempting to deport 10 green card holders who had been working at Giumarra Vineyards. The regulation under which Immigration was seeking the deportations had been used before the Giumarra case.

In September, the validity of three state minimum wage orders boosting hourly wages for 100,000 women and children working on California farms had been unanimously upheld by the State Court of Appeals. The ruling would hike the minimum hourly wage for women by 35 cents from $1.30 to $1.65, and that of minors by 25 cents from $1.10 to $1.35. Agribusiness appealed this decision in October, 1968. The AFL-CIO Labor Federation said the following about the decision:

"Payment of the new minimums had been thwarted by three Superior Court suits filed by agribusiness interests headed by the California Farm Bureau Federation and including the California Grape and Tree Fruit League. The 42-page Appellate Court decision written by Judge Leonard M. Friedman and concurred with by Judges Fred R. Pierce and Edwin J. Regan, ruled that the IWC had full legal authority to act, ordered the three suits dissolved, and directed the IWC to enforce the new minimum wage floors in farm labor immediately."[286]

In November, the United Farm Workers' Organizing Committee, in San Francisco, presented a 20,000 signature petition in support of the extension of the National Labor Relations Act coverage to farm workers to California Congressman Phil Burton. The petition was presented by UFWOC representatives Mr. & Mrs. Lupe Murgia, Pete Velasco and Anne Draper, Citizens for Farm Labor.[287]

On November 2, the *California Farmer* published an article entitled "Hidden Dangers in the NLRB." Stewart Rothman, former General Counsel of the National Labor Relations Board, which administers the NLRA, said the NLRB could limit the growers right to sell or dispose of their property or prevent them from going out of business, move their operation or any part of it to a new location, hire a contractor to do work that they formerly did themselves, and that it had done these things many times to industrial employers.[288]

Meanwhile, the Third District Appellate Court in Sacramento issued a writ calling for the dismissal of suits filed by agribusiness interests that had succeeded in blocking a boost (scheduled to go into effect February 1, 1968) in the minimum wage to $1.65 for women and $1.35 for minors. It was then retroactive to that date.[289]

In December, AFL-CIO Secretary-Treasurer of the California Labor Federation denounced the Governor's opposition to National Labor Relations Act coverage for farm workers. And, in San Francisco, on December 4, O. W. Filleriup, head of the Council of California Growers, advocated prompt action in state and federal legislation to settle farm labor disputes. He proposed a special board or commission which would take into account the "unique factors of agriculture such as the perishable nature of the product."[290] On December 3, 1968, Governor Reagan issued a statement that the executive branch of government had heard proposals for additional farm labor legislation. He said the application of principles in the NLRA to farming was unwise.[291]

1969

Employment Insurance
Pesticides
Taft-Hartley Provisions Of NLRA

Aliens
Anti-Secondary Boycotts
Right-To-Work
Agricultural Conciliation Service
Nixon Farm Worker Plan
Immigration And Nationalist Act
NLRA Coverage For Farm Workers
Labor Contractors
Green-Card Workers
Farm Subsidies
Sanitary Facilities
Sen. Murphy's Consumer Agricultural Food Protection Act Of 1969
Fair Employment Practice Act
Assembly Agriculture Committee Study

In January, 1969, Governor Reagan in his State of the State Address to the joint session of the legislature said he intended to "seek and support legislation in the area of farm labor-management relations."

"Such legislation, he said, will establish, ground rules to supervise free elections to determine first if the workers want to be represented by a labor union or association and if they do, choose which one without fear, intimidation or reprisal."[292]

However, he did indicate opposition to full free collective bargaining rights for farm workers when he said that:

"This legislation should spell out the role that arbitration should play and it should clearly establish a prohibition of strikes and other work stoppages in harvest and critical times."[293]

Reagan's proposals appeared to have been prompted by apprehensions over the possibility of more adequate legislation being enacted on the federal level. UFWOC had been fighting for free elections for farm workers for years, but the states agribusiness steadfastly opposed them. Nevertheless, in more than a dozen representative elections, UFWOC won overwhelmingly.

During January, SB2613 was proposed to keep tax-loss capital out of agriculture, or how to prevent non-farmers from climbing into agriculture for "tax loss" purposes.[294]

In February, the *California Farmer* issued a statement that unemployment insurance for farm workers appeared to be inevitable. The Chamber of Commerce's agricultural committee at its meeting in Los Angeles stated that it did not object to unemployment insurance being extended, but did question how farmers would pay for the bill, without at the same time being able to establish a price for their products.[295]

California's Labor Federation, AFL-CIO supported Assembly Bill, AB299, which would extend unemployment insurance coverage to agricultural, domestic, non-profit and public employees in February.

The *California Farmer,* in March, 1969 stated that agribusiness was trying to accomplish several important steps in the matter of farm labor relations. One step was the inclusion of farm labor under unemployment insurance. If they had unemployment insurance on either a state or federal basis, it would "certainly blunt the unionization drive."[296]

In March, legislators were attacking UFWOC's anti-pesticide campaign. Two legislators attacked those who would banish all agricultural pesticides because of alleged danger in the use of the products. California Assemblyman Kent Stacey and U.S. Senator James B. Pearson of Kansas had spoken in favor of pesticide use.

Significantly, President Nixon in March 1969, requested that a study be undertaken of the possibility of extending the Taft-Hartley provisions of the NLRA to cover farm workers. The Taft-Hartley Act restricted the rights of unions and outlawed boycotts. It also allowed the President to order striking workers to go back to work if he felt a strike was a national emergency.[297]

On March 14, the California Labor Federation opposed Assembly Bill 807, which purported to bring agricultural workers under the state unemployment insurance program.

"The flaws and faults in AB807 are so many that its enactment would do far more danger than good to the unemployment insurance program in California."[298]

The Federation was sponsoring AB299 by Assemblyman Leo Ralph. AB807 would increase the qualifying annual wage for all workers by more than a third, from $720 to $1,000. That feature would mean exclusion of over 400,000, who would be presently covered. It would still leave a major portion of farm workers out from under the protection sought, and would tax farm owners and manipulate the fund to the detriment of the workers involved, while major employers would benefit many millions of dollars.

Meanwhile, Allan Grant, Chairman of the California State Board of Agriculture said he had been told that if agricultural legislation covering farm workers was approved but still opposed by UFWOC, the Union would not abide by the law. The Board urged Congressmen from both parties to seek legislation which would bring a solution to the existing boycott as soon as possible. The economic boycott was having its effect.

"John Giumarra, Jr., in his remarks before the California Tomato Growers Association, noted that union activities are making it more difficult to borrow money to raise crops. Lending institutions fear strikes, walk-outs or slow downs at harvest or other critical periods during the year could result in partial or total crop loss, resulting in the inability of the farmer to repay the loan."[299]

On March 21, the California Labor Federation, AFL-CIO indicated its opposition to Assembly bills AB210 and AB807. Both bills dealt with unemployment insurance for farm workers, but actually decreased benefits for all other workers.[300] Furthermore, the annual report of the Senate Subcommittee on Migratory Labor proposed inclusion of agricultural workers under the NLRA.[301]

In April, Congressman John Tunney proposed curbs to prohibit aliens from employment. This position was sent in letters to the Chairman of the Senate and House Judiciary Committees. Tunney criticized the deficiencies in immigration laws and regulations and laxity in enforcement. Also, he proposed that employers be regulated under a provision that would make it a crime to knowingly harbor or conceal illegal immigrants or to encourage illegal entry. Employers were exempted from such a provision. The second reform would require a periodic review of the status of immigrants who had legally entered the country for business or pleasure in order to insure that the immigrant had not taken a job.

The AFL-CIO Labor Federation, in April, was opposing anti-labor legislation: Senate Bill, SB544 would outlaw the secondary boycott, and Assembly Bill, AB522 would delay payment to seasonal agricultural workers.

On April 16, 1969, Dolores Huerta appeared before the Senate Subcommittee on Migratory Labor and read César Chávez' prepared statement on collective bargaining legislation.

"We too need our decent period of time to develop and grow strong under the life-giving sum of a favorable public policy which affirmatively favors the growth of farm unionism.

"Of utmost importance is an exemption for a time from the Taft-Hartley and Landrum-Griffin restrictions on traditional union activity. The bans on recognition and organizational picketing and on the so-called secondary boycott would be particularly harmful, and the mandatory injunction in both cases makes them truly disastrous.

"The relief we seek from Congress today, however, is neither very new nor very revolutionary. It has proved beneficial to the nation in the past when unions were weak and industry strong. We need and favor NLRA amendments along the lines of the original Wagner Act, but we oppose for this period in history the restrictions of Taft-Hartley and Landrum-Griffin."[302]

In May, the Labor Federation opposed Governor Reagan's proposed changes in child labor laws, which would serve as union-busting efforts; and Senator Harmer's bill, SB544, which would ban secondary boycotts. The Federation did, however, initiate a measure to extend the Fair Employment Practices Act to farm workers.[303]

Also in May, the AFL-CIO Labor Federation opposed California Senate Bill 1119, which proposed to establish the "right-to-work" principle in the field of farm labor relations, as well as Assembly Bill

AB1333, which would create an Agricultural Conciliation Service to provide "services" to employers and labor organizations, prescribing powers, duties, and functions. The service would be under the direction and control of a chief conciliator, who would be appointed by the State Director of Agriculture upon nomination by the State Board of Agriculture. The bill was sent to the Agricultural Committee on May 19.

On May 20, 1969, U.S. Senator Murphy introduced the strongest anti-farm labor bill proposed, S2203, cited as the "Consumer Agricultural Food Protection Act of 1969." The following were the key provisions of the act:

"Sec. 101. It shall be unlawful . . . (1) to induce or encourage any individual employed by any person engaged in commerce or in any industry affecting commerce to engage in a strike or refusal to use, process, transport, display for sale, sell, or otherwise handle or work on any agricultural commodity after such commodity leaves the farm or cities where grown or produced, or to picket or threaten to picket any other person . . .

Sec. 201. (a) There is hereby established a board which shall be known as the Farm Labor Relations Board . . . which shall consist of three members. (b) There shall be in the Department of Agriculture an Assistant Secretary for Farm Labor Relations who shall be a member of the Board and shall serve as its chairman. The Assistant Secretary for Farm Labor Relations and two additional members of the Board shall be appointed by the President . . . (c) There shall be a General Counsel of the Board who shall be appointed by the President . . ."[304]

Furthermore, secret ballot elections and unfair labor practices would be determined by the Board.

On May 23, the Labor Federation indicated that AB837 was given a "do pass" recommendation by the Assembly Ways and Means Committee. It forestalled the expulsion of certain agricultural workers and employees from the scope of the California Fair Employment Practice Act. The Assembly Agriculture Committee took under submission for further study AB1333, opposed by labor, which would set up an agricultural conciliation service.

At the same time, George Meany criticized President Nixon's Farm Worker Plan. Meany claimed that the proposal amounted to a number of special rules and procedures to make it more difficult for farm workers to form unions and to secure recognition than other workers.

"The rules proposed by the administration would be administered by a special Farm Labor Relations Board 'stacked' in favor of big agricultural employers . . . would restrict the workers right to strike during harvest seasons or any 30-day period selected by the grower and impose binding arbitration on a union after a harvest was in a period when strike action would be useless."[305]

George Meany, National AFL-CIO, advocated inclusion of farm workers under the National Labor Relations Act. Chávez meanwhile opposed the Nixon proposals advanced by U.S. Secretary of Labor George P. Shultz which recommended creation of the separate three-member Farm Labor Relations Board. Chávez said:

"This is more evidence that Nixon has entered into an unholy alliance with Governor Reagan and U.S. Senator Murphy to insure that there will be no meaningful legislation for farm workers this year."[306]

On May 30, SB544 to ban the secondary boycott was defeated in the Senate Labor and Social Welfare Committee. The Senate Agricultural Committee set a hearing on SB1119, for June 5, which would put a right-to-work provision into law with respect to agricultural employees.[307]

In June, the *Farm Journal* issued an article on "The Fight to Ban DDT." It pointed out that "pressure groups" claimed DDT was obsolete and harmed wildlife:

"The insecticide, regarded as a 'wonder' chemical when it won the discoverer a Nobel Prize in Medicine 24 years ago, came under critical attack from conservationists' and sportsmen's groups in the legislatures of California and Illinois and others states in 1969. Registration for all uses was cancelled in Michigan in 1969."[308]

On June 7, the *California Farmer* reported that the State Agriculture Board unanimously adopted a resolution expressing its opposition to Senate Bill 1694 and House resolution 9505 in the 91st Congress, both of which would amend the Immigration and Nationality Act to limit the availability of immigrants from Mexico and Canada for employment in agriculture and other industries.

"Board President Allen Grant said that there was a growing realization throughout the country that agriculture needs a separate labor law, which will protect the nation's food supply from strikes at harvest time and prohibit secondary boycotts of farm produce."[309]

U.S. Senator Alan Cranston, in an address at the Mid-Continent Migrant Health Conference in New Mexico, expressed his view of farm labor relations:

"Farm workers should be included in the National Labor Relations Act. I've joined with other Senators in sponsoring legislation to this end. Compulsory workmen's compensation and unemployment insurance should be extended to farm workers in every state in the nation. We must end the discriminatory residence requirements which deny to migrants federally supported public assistance programs and other benefits."[310]

At the same time, Senator Edward Kennedy attacked farm subsidies, and Senator John Tunney introduced legislation to place farm workers under the National Labor Relations Act, but at the same time he refused to support the grape boycott.

In June, California Child Labor Bills AB1978 and AB2104 were taken under submission by the Assembly Labor Relations Committee. Both would have relaxed vital protections for minors in California. Assembly Bill AB1993 was scheduled for hearings before the Senate Agriculture Committee. It would increase the surety bond required of farm labor contractors from $1,500 to $5,000 and otherwise strengthen the law controlling such contractors. AB1993, which passed the Assembly, was supported by labor.[311]

There were bills in the U.S. Congress which would restrict the use of green card workers in agriculture. Testifying in opposition before a Subcommittee of the California State Senate Committee on judiciary, R. Daniels of the Agricultural Producers Labor Committee said:

"Proponents of this bill allege depressed wages, high unemployment and are responsible for low annual earnings. Agriculture knows that the immigrant aliens from Mexico are extremely valuable to the economy of California and to agriculture in particular . . . It is hoped that no legislation will pass which will unduly restrict the opportunity of our neighbors to the south work with us."[312]

Also in June, the U.S. Department of Labor had returned authority to determine where a labor dispute existed to the State Department of Employment.

In July, the *Farm Journal* published an article entitled "Should We Limit Government Payments Per Farm?" Congressman Paul Findly (Ill.), former member of the House Agriculture Committee proposed that there should be a limit:

"Those of us in Congress who are close to agriculture know that legislation is absolutely essential to help farmers adjust to changing technology in the years immediately ahead. Others don't feel this way. They are increasingly inclined to view all farm legislation as hopeless and wasteful. They are weary of hearing the same empty platitudes year after year to justify extending present programs. They especially resent the large payments to individual farmers and the lack of initiative for reform by Congressional Committees.

Last year, 5,885 farmers each received government payments of more than $25,000; meanwhile 1,084,000 farmers were paid less than $500 each."[313]

Congressman Poage (Texas), Chairman of the House Agriculture Committee proposed that there should be no limit:

"The case in favor of limiting the size of government farm payments to an individual farmer rests very largely on the lack of understanding of our farm income support program. Basically, we support farm income in order the farmers may produce abundantly, and thus supply consumers with inexpensive food. Unless farmers can get enough income from some source to meet today's production costs, it is obvious they cannot use modern equipment, fertilizer, insecticides, etc. All these techniques are expensive, and they must be paid for at the 1969 wages and profits enjoyed by laborers and businessmen."[314]

By July, Senate Bill 1119, the right-to-work provision, was taken under submission (killed) by the Senate Labor and Social Welfare Committee. Assembly Bill 1333, by Assemblyman Victor Veysey (R-Brawley), which would impose right-to-work provisions on farm workers was still pending.

George Meany, National AFL-CIO, testified before the U.S. Senate Subcommittee in opposition to the Nixon proposals for farm labor. The California Finance and Insurance Committee blocked passage of a proposal to provide unemployment insurance for farm workers, AB299, by Leon Ralph (D-Los Angeles) and sponsored by the Labor Federation.[315] In addition, Assembly Bill 1333, an anti-labor bill adversely affecting the rights of farm workers in collective bargaining was taken under submission (killed) by the Assembly Agriculture Committee. This bill would have set up an agricultural conciliator to be appointed by the Governor.

In August, the California Table Grape Commission proposed that State and federal agencies take appropriate action to halt "deliberate untruths and misleading information," about pesticide effects on table grapes made by the United Farm Workers Organizing Committee, AFL-CIO.

August 8, the Labor Federation reported that the Assembly passed SB721 by Senator Bielenson (D-Los Angeles, Ca.), which gave added strength to laws providing sanitary facilities for agricultural workers in the field. Another bill, AB1993, by the late Assemblyman Alan Pattie of Salinas, increasing the surety bond for labor contractors to $5,000 for more adequate protection of wage earners, was passed by the California Senate and sent to the Governor.

A statement pledging support to the farm workers struggle for union recognition was provided by the Executive Council of the California Labor Federation, AFL-CIO, at its mid-summer meeting, pointed out its opposition to Senator Murphy's Consumer Agricultural Food Protection Act of 1969, S2203.

"This vicious bill would ban boycotts, organizational picketing, and prohibit strikes. Significantly, Secretary of Agriculture Clifford M. Hardin supports this bill. This bill and other anti-labor legislation law suits to harass and distract, and the hiring of public relations firms testify to the success of the grape boycott."[316]

On August 15, the Labor Federation reported that AB837, by Assemblyman John Miller (D-Oakland, Ca.), was sent to the Governor's office. It would extend coverage under the Fair Employment Practice Act to agricultural workers. Presented to the Senate by Senator Lewis Sherman (R-Oakland), AB837 was passed 22 to 8. Also, labor was alerted to HR484 by Assemblyman William Ketchum (R-Bakersfield). Introduced late in August HR484 asks for an interim study of the subject of farm labor, including but not limited to labor management relations and the conditions of employment. If the resolution was implemented, a report of findings and recommendations would be made to the legislature not later than the fifth legislative day of the 1970 session. On the Senate side, California Senator John Schmitz (R-Rustin) introduced SR378, relative to child labor laws. The resolution called for an interim study of the subject. He had introduced "right-to-work" legislation, and labor was going to scrutinize any study he proposed.[317]

In August, a study of farm worker wage rates was released by the U.S. Department of Labor:

"It found that the national average farm wage for 1968 was $1.43 an hour . . . In contrast, the minimum hourly wage for farm workers protected by union contracts negotiated by the United Farm Workers Organizing Committee in California is $2.00 . . . Under amendments to the Fair Labor Standards Act won by organized labor in 1966 some 400,000 farm workers, about one-third of the annual average number hired farm workers in the nation; were brought under FLSA coverage. The federal pay floor for convered farm workers rose to $1.30 on February 1, 1969."[318]

On August 29, the State Labor Federation issued a statement reviewing Senator Murphy's record on labor. In particular, the Federation stated that:

"Murphy has generally reflected the interests of the State's corporate farms and banking interests. On September 13, 1965, for example, he voted against a motion to delete a proposal made by the conservative Senate Agriculture Committee to transfer authority over the importation of foreign farm workers from the Secretary of Labor to the Secretary of Agriculture. In short, Murphy favored the transfer . . . it boiled down to a backdoor attempt to revive the discredited bracero program . . ."[319]

In September, the pesticide issue was predominant. Senator Murphy charged UFWOC with providing false evidence to the Subcommittee on Migratory Labor. UFWOC filed suit to obtain pesticide records. And the *California Farmer* criticized the CRLA for joining the pesticide issue and said that "CRLA attempts to do for farm workers some of the things that the Farm Bureau has attempted to do for farmers."[320]

In October, the Labor Federation discussed a six-year legislative study of farm laborers that was released by Assembly Agriculture Committee chaired by William Ketchum of Paso Robles.

". . . workers (in agriculture) who got jobs through a union had a medium earning of almost four times those of the total sample . . . the study, begun in 1964 by the Agriculture's Committee's Advisory Committee on Farm Labor Research, included a survey of the earnings, family status and living conditions of 3,488 workers."[321]

On December 13, the *California Farmer* issued an article entitled "Is There Hope of Federal Farm Labor Law Soon?"

"The only permanent solution to the issue of attempted farm worker unionization is federal legislation—either Senator George Murphy's 'Consumers Agricultural Food Protection Act' or a suitable compromise version thereof, Giumarra said."[322]

Finally, another article was printed entitled "Grapes in Serious Trouble Unless Legislation Passes." Jack T. Baillie, president of Perishable Agricultural Commodities Corporation proposed legislation. There was a strong indication that "food chain stores feeling boycott pressure," and making the boycott illegal was the answer to grape growers economic troubles.

1970

Pesticide Study
Consumer Agricultural Food Protection Act
Congressional Record on Farm Subsidies
Governor Reagan's Plan for Farm Labor
State Conciliation Service
Economic Poison Safety Act of 1970
Farm Act of 1973

In January, 1970, the *Farm Journal* issued an article entitled "Governments Plan to Phase Out Persistent Chemicals." It stated that on November 20, 1969, the White House announced the ending of most uses of DDT. Beginning March 1970, action regarding other persistent pesticides would be taken using the same criteria and procedures being applied to DDT. USDA Secretary Clifford Hardin defined persistent pesticides as those which would persist in the environment beyond the current growing season for a crop, or one year for non-crop uses. The Environmental Quality Council reviewed the recommendations of the Mrak Commission, a blue ribbon panel appointed by Robert Finch, Secretary of HEW, to study the effect of pesticides. The Council also established a new Committee on Pesticides use which would set up a working group to provide day-to-day coordination in developing a program and policy for future pesticide use. The phase-out action would be taken in two steps, according to Ned. D. Bayley, Director of Science and Education for the USDA.

"The first step may be a notice to cancel some of the present uses of the persistent pesticides which are not essential or for which suitable substitutes are already available. This notice goes to manufacturers, formulators, distributors and registrants of economic poisons.

The second step is publication in the Federal Register of intent to cancel all other uses with a request for comment within 90 days. Exceptions would be made where the chemical is essential to farm or forest production and to human health, and where no safe and effective alternatives are available."[323]

At the same time, the *California Farmer* supported Coachella Valley grower Michael Bozick, who said Senator Murphy's bill was important because the solution had to be national. He felt a state law should be enacted setting up certain guidelines for collective bargaining for farm workers, "but what effect will it have upon the national boycott?" At the same time Virgil Rasmussen, a Sanger farmer, said "we need laws which will set the ground rules for collective bargaining."[324] He too called for federal legislation:

"The change in federal farm labor policies in the past decade are probably the most important changes in agricultural production. Farm labor policies and programs were in the direction of providing a labor supply for fruit and vegetable industry. In the past five years emphasis has shifted toward the concern for welfare of the farm workers."[325]

Also in January, the State Federation of Labor, AFL-CIO, protested a declaration by the State Board of Agriculture that it planned to take part in a campaign opposing consumer boycotts of California grapes initiated by the United Farm Workers Organizing Committee, AFL-CIO.

"Thomas L. Pitts, secretary-treasurer of the California Labor Federation, AFL-CIO, today made public a letter sent to Governor Reagan earlier in which he termed the State Board's action 'a willful violation of public trust' and called on the Board to 'immediately cancel its partisan promotional activities against the grape boycott.' "[326]

Then, in February, the State Department of Public Health released a study on "walking death," or the incidence of pesticide poisoning among California farm workers, as far higher than previous official state reports.

"The study, which reinforces the campaign initiated more than two years ago by the AFL-CIO United Farm Workers' Organizing Committee for effective safeguards from pesticide poisoning for farm workers found that there may be more than 150 cases of such poisoning for every 1,000 farm workers instead of only 1 per 1,000.

The higher rate would mean that instead of only about 250 poisonings a year it's more likely that there are actually some 37,500 cases among the state's 250,000 farm workers.

The study involved a door-to-door survey of 1,120 farm families. It was conducted by the Health Department of Tulare County between January, 1968, and September, 1969."[327]

In March, several days of hearings produced support for Senator Murphy's S. 2203, opposed by UFWOC. The Murphy Bill would establish a Farm Labor Relations Board in the U.S. Department of Agriculture and be independent of the National Labor Relations Board.

In April, 1970, Oregon State's farm labor camp regulations called for better living and health conditions.

Meanwhile, in Washington, D.C., the Congressional Record included figures inserted by Republican Paul Findley (Illinois) indicating that federal subsidies totaling $7,613 million were passed out to 1,397 California farms in 1969 and that 85% of the money went to recipients who got $25,000 or more. Some 783 California growers shared in $64.5 million in federal production control payments that went to growers who received $25,000 and up. 614 California growers received payments ranging between $15,000 and $25,000 which totalled $11.8 million. Republican Findley introduced a bill to limit individual payments to $20,000 a year for the next two years. The House approved such a limit the previous year, but it was killed in the Senate. Findley indicated he would press for adoption of similar limits on farm supports for 1970.

"In fact, six California companies received more than $1 million apiece in farm subsidies last year, with two of these receiving more than $3 million. Disclosure of these figures point up the need for the AFL-CIO backed legislation to limit subsidy payments to $20,000 a year, a proposal that California's Senior Senator George Murphy voted against last year. Ironically, a number of firms receiving these huge federal handouts are also vigorously opposed to any realistic moves to give farm workers full and effective collective bargaining rights. The two California firms receiving more than $3 million each were: the J. G. Boswell Co. of Corcoran, $4,370,657, and Griffin Inc. of Huron, $3,412,869. The other four California firms receiving over $1 million are: South Lake Farms, Fresno, $1,807,690; Sylyer Land Company, Corcoran, $1,637,961; Mt. Whitney Farms, Five Points, $1,152,294; and the Kern County Land Co. of Bakersfield, $1,080,533. Another five California corporate farms that were among the 14 that received more than $500,000 were: S. A. Camp Farms, Shaffer, $928,917; Vista Del Llano Farms, Firebaugh, $778,586; Sista Del Llano Farms, Firebaugh, $673,410; Boston Ranch Co., Lemoore, $643,006; and Telles Ranch, Inc., Firebaugh, $503,285."[328]

In May, the California Labor Federation, AFL-CIO, announced that Paul S. Taylor, former Chairman of the Department of Economics at the University of California at Berkeley, had been appointed Economist and Research Director. Dr. Taylor is a recognized authority on U.S. reclamation law and has served as a consultant to the United Nations, the Social Security Administration and the U.S. Department of Interior.

Furthermore, and significantly, it was reported in May that the National Labor Relations Board's general counsel authorized a complaint against the AFL-CIO and UFWOC and 10 other labor organizations asserting that when UFWOC worked in concert with others it was subject to action by the NLRB.[329]

By July, the Salinas Californian reported that U.S. Senator Murphy's Consumer Agricultural Food Protection Act was buried in a Senate subcommittee. Agribusiness assumed Chávez was employing the "domino" strategy—"picking off" growers one at a time.[330]

During the same month, the California Labor Federation, AFL-CIO, opposed Governor Reagan's Plan for farm labor elections. In 1969, the Governor strongly opposed a bill authored by Senator Nicholas Petris (D-Oakland) that would have created collective bargaining for farm workers. He was supporting federal legislation being proposed by Senator Murphy's Consumer Agricultural Food Protection Act that would outlaw strikes at harvest time. On July 10, Reagan issued a statement criticizing farm union leaders for not grasping the opportunity on June 29 to make State Conciliation Service available to supervise farm workers elections. He said:

"It is hard to believe that any individual having the responsibility for union leadership should be unwilling to grasp this opportunity for bringing about the solution to the chaotic situation that now exists."[331]

Reagan's statement was issued the day after UFWOC rejected the offer saying it had no confidence in the State Conciliation Service or its Director Ralph Duncan, who they described as a "growers' lackey." On July 6, fifty-two major grape growers in Kern and Tulare Counties had asked Duncan for elections. On July 10 Reagan acknowledged the growers' request.

"I am reliably informed that a substantial number of growers in the San Joaquin Valley have petitioned the State Conciliation Service to conduct such an election— by secret ballot—for their workers regarding their possible unionization."[332]

The Labor Federation disputed the Governor's information. The Federation claimed that Luis Gilbert, presiding counsel of the Los Angeles office of the State Conciliation Service, said that he had been approached by a management consulting firm representing "a large number of growers." They had asked that a meeting be set up between the growers' representatives and the UFWOC. The rules proposed by Reagan under which elections would be held gave the Conciliation Service sole authority to determine the time and place of the election, the length of prior employment required to be eligible to vote, the wording on the ballot, and the language or languages to be used. In short, the farm workers union felt it would face a "stacked deck."[333]

In August, the AFL-CIO News attacked the Farm Bureau for its major role in killing a pesticide bill, or the "Economic Poison Safety Act of 1970":

"The bad legislation in the view of the corporate grower-dominated Farm Bureau was SB 1347, introduced by Senator Nicholas Petris (D-Oakland), which would have enacted the 'Economic Poison Safety Act of 1970.' This legislation would have provided the conditions that must be met for the safety of workers and the public in the use of economic poisons."[334]

On September 2, the *Salinas Californian* published an article entitled "Farm Bill Condemned by Labor." The California Labor Federation's Convention had recently issued a statement that Murphy's bill was "an attempt to perpetuate discriminatory treatment of agricultural workers in labor, social or immigration legislation."[335]

On October 3, 1970, the *California Farmer* admitted that the anti-farm labor movement was lost to UFWOC.

"There is legislation that could have saved us, but there wasn't enough political guts in Washington to buck the unions in an election year. Governor R. Reagan tried on the State level, for a conciliation bill but was politically smothered. Senator George Murphy tried, on the national level, but Congress, trembling in fear of organized labor, caused the bill to be buried."[336]

In November, the *Farm Journal* discussed the new farm law that set up a farm program for the following three years, 1971-1973. It replaced the 1965 farm act that expired in 1961, but which was extended one additional year. Significantly, the bill set $55,000 limit on government payments per crop per person for feed, grain, wheat and cotton.[337]

Finally, in December, the *California Farmer* emphasized that legislation was the answer, that states were to introduce federal legislation, and that "one thing this would do is give agriculture use of the courts."[338]

In summary, Senator Murphy's Consumer Agricultural Food Protection Act symbolized the year's legislative struggle. A concerted effort to limit farm subsidies began to emerge as another legislative issue, along with a continued drive for unemployment and better wages. Pesticides were a major legislative target. The State Legislature stepped up its attack on farm workers organizing, particularly the boycott.

1971

Secret Ballot Election Proposals
Amendments To The NLRB
Consumer Agricultural Food Protection Act Of 1971
Farm Workers Bill Of Rights
Farm Workers Collective Bargaining Act
Bans On Secondary Boycotts
Ban On Strikes
Unemployment Insurance Benefits
California Agricultural Labor Relations Act Of 1971
Housing
Illegal Aliens: Dixon Arnett Bill

Oregon Farm Labor Law Veto
Farm Subsidies
National Farm Labor Relations Act
Workmen's Compensation
National Agricultural Bargaining Board
Farm Labor Secret Ballot Initiative

On January 5, 1971, California State Senator Harmer introduced SB 40 which was sent to the Senate Committee on Industrial Relations. It was adamantly opposed by UFWOC and the State Federation, AFL-CIO, because it called for elections supervised by the Governor's office through the Department of Industrial Relations. More specifically SB 40:

"Declares state policy to be that agricultural labor workers, as defined, in a given unit shall have the opportunity to select a collective bargaining agent by majority vote of those voting.

"Authorizes any agricultural labor organization claiming to represent a majority of agricultural labor workers in a unit of workers of an employer to file a petition with the Department of Industrial Relations.

"Requires the department, upon petition of an agricultural labor organization, to investigate and conduct such hearings and elections as are necessary to determine the appropriateness of a unit of agricultural labor workers and whether or not a majority of the workers therein desire to be represented by a petitioning labor organization.

"Provides that after conducting such investigation and election the department shall certify the appropriate agricultural labor organization receiving a majority of the votes cast as the exclusive representative of the workers in the designated unit for a period of one year or until the expiration date of a collective bargaining agreement not to exceed two years.

"Defines terms used.

"Authorizes the department to take all proceedings necessary to enforce the provisions of act, including action in a superior court, and permits any person aggrieved by a final decision or order of the department to obtain judicial review by writ of mandate."[339]

One day later, on January 6, Assembly Bill 53 was introduced by Assemblymen Burton, Brown, Garcia, proposing collective bargaining legislation. The Bill:

"Provides for certification by State Conciliation Service, pursuant to prescribed procedures, of collective bargaining representatives of appropriate units of agricultural workers where a majority of the workers voting on the question indicate a desire to be represented by such a representative. Provides that an agricultural employer should bargain with a representative so certified and, if any understanding is reached, that understanding should be embodied, upon request, in a signed agreement.

Declares public policy of Section 923 of Labor Code included in, and shall govern construction of, such provision."[340]

On January 11, California Assemblyman Wood (R-Greenfield) proposed anti-farm labor bill AB 83 which called for secret ballot elections. AB 83

"Makes provision for secret ballot elections, conducted and supervised by the Division of Conciliation of the Department of Industrial Relations, to determine whether employees shall or shall not be represented by a labor organization. Provides for certification by such department of labor organization winning election as exclusive bargaining representative of employees.

"Makes it unlawful for any labor organization, as defined, or its agents, to commit specified acts, including certain secondary boycotts, jurisdictional disputes, and hot cargo agreements with respect to producer or processor of agricultural products or agricultural marketing organization.

"Makes it unlawful for any person not an employee or former employee to picket, or cause to be picketed in order to change wages, hours, or working conditions, any farm, ranch, or orchard where perishable agricultural commodities are produced.

"Provides injunctive relief and damages for persons injured or threatened with injury from such unlawful acts.

"Specifies act shall not be applicable to any matter subject to National Labor Relations Act."[341]

On January 12, a survey by California Representative Talcott (R-Salinas), revealed that 63.3% of those in his district favored extension of NLRA coverage to farm workers. He opposed such coverage by the NLRB.

Meanwhile, the California Labor Federation called on the National AFL-CIO to push for legislation to bar the use of "wetbacks," or so-called green card commuters, as strikebreakers and cut-rate workers in Southern California and along the southwest border. Fifteen months before, delegates to the National AFL-CIO Convention in San Francisco had adopted a policy resolution that urged Congress to enact a law with strong enforcement against the use of Mexican commuters which undermine wages, labor standards, narrow employment opportunities for American workers, and provide a constant threat of strikebreaking.[342]

On January 22, U.S. Representative Leggett of California introduced HR 1410 to the House Committee on Education and Labor. This bill proposed NLRB coverage for farm workers,

"To amend the National Labor Relations Act, as amended, to amend the definition of 'employee' to include certain agriculture employees, and to permit certain provisions in agreements between agricultural employers and employees . . . Brings agricultural laborers under coverage of LMRA by striking the present exclusion of these employees in section 2(3) of NLRA. Adds a new section to NLRA, section 8(g), providing that it shall be an unfair labor practice to make a prehire agreement in agriculture requiring union membership within 7 days of hiring and that priority in hiring may. be given to those with seniority with the employer, in the industry or in the particular geographical area. This provision is similar to section 8(b) of the NLRA covering the building and construction industry."[343]

Identical bills were introduced by three other legislators: HR 2546, Mr. Roybal, January 29, 1971; HR 3571, Mrs. Mink, February 4, 1971; and HR 4438, Mr. Ryan, February 17, 1971.

U.S. Representative Talcott introduced HR 1689, the Consumer Agricultural Food Protection Act of 1971, on January 22 of the same year. This agribusiness supported bill proposed that an employee work 100 days the previous year to be covered; that secondary boycotts were illegal, and that a Farm Labor Relations Board and Federal Mediation and Conciliation Service would be provided.

"HR 1689 makes it unlawful to engage in any secondary boycott of agricultural products, to conduct a primary boycott or to induce an ultimate consumer to refrain from purchasing, consuming or using an agricultural commodity . . . creates a Farm Labor Relations Board, consisting of an Assistant Secretary of Agriculture, who shall chair the Board, and two other members, appointed by the President, subject to confirmation for staggered 10-year terms . . . Federal Mediation and Conciliation Service provisions . . . prohibits all strikes and lockouts, providing instead for a five-member board of arbitration, which may settle disputes on a final offer selection basis."[344]

On January 26, four U.S. Senate bills regarding agricultural workers were introduced. Senate Bill 660 was introduced by Senator Nelson and Senator Humphrey. It proposed the establishment of the "National Pesticide Control and Protection Act." Simultaneously, Senate Bill 727 was introduced by Senator Mondale and Senators Church, Cranston, Harris, Hart, Humphrey, McGee, McGovern, Mansfield, and Young proposing the establishment of the "National Agricultural Marketing Act." In addition, Senate Bill 726 was introduced by Senator Mondale and Senators Church, Burdick, Cranston, Harris, McGee, Humphrey, McGovern, Mansfield, and Young proposing the establishment of the "National Agricultural Bargaining Act" which would create a National Agricultural Relations Board. Then, Senate Bill 745 was introduced by Senator Packwood proposing the establishment of the "Federal Environmental Pesticide Control Act of 1971."

On February 4, Representative Gonzales of Texas introduced HR 3625 to the House Committee on Education and Labor. It proposed to include farm workers under the NLRA, but with some restrictions. HR 3625

"Brings agricultural laborers under coverage of the NLRA by striking the present exclusion of these employees in Section 2(3) of the National Labor Relations Act, except that the exclusion would continue for agricultural laborers 'employed by an employer who at no time during the preceding calendar year employed more than 12 employees or who during the preceding calendar year had labor costs of less than $10,000 . . . provides for a 'prehire' arrangement in agriculture, like that now prevailing in construction."[345]

Then, on February 25, Representative O'Hara introduced HR 5010 to the House Committee on Education and Labor. It was known as the "Farm Workers' Bill of Rights." The bill had six titles, each related to a separate aspect of farm worker legislation. Title I covered collective bargaining; Title II workmen's compensation; Title III manpower services; Title IV wage and hour standards; Title V unemployment compensation; and Title VI an advisory council on farm labor. Identical bills were introduced by Republican Thompson of New Jersey, March 1, 1971: HR 5281, and an earlier version by Republican Helstoski: HR 12486, January 19, 1972. Title I of the O'Hara bill was called the "Farm Workers Collective Bargaining Act." Its provision stated that it

"Brings agricultural laborers under coverage of NLRA by striking the present exclusion of these employees in Section 2(3) of NLRA.

"Exempts agricultural labor unions from the following prohibitions and limitations listed as unfair labor practices in the NLRA: (1) The secondary boycott; (2) picketing to obtain recognition from an employer or to organize workers; and (3) the 'hot cargo' agreement . . . Exempts agricultural employment from section 14(b) of NLRA. The effect of this exemption is to permit the union shop for agricultural workers in commerce in all states including those which prohibit the requirement of union membership as a condition of employment."[346]

Meanwhile, the United Farm Workers' Organizing Committee was concerned with the possibility that Oregon would be the first state to prohibit the secondary boycott and strikes. The Oregon legislature passed such a bill and UFWOC and AFL-CIO called for Governor McCall of Oregon to veto the measure. This was the first time in American history that such a bill had passed through a state legislature.

On February 6, California Assemblyman Wood's Bill 83, co-authored by Senator Grunsky, called for secret elections and a ban on secondary boycott or hot cargo. It would prevent threats or coercion to enforce a secondary boycott or hot cargo agreement, and prevent picketing by other than an employee.

On February 12, the *Salinas Californian* reported that Allen Grant, speaking at the Farm Bureau Federation Convention, had said that pressure for unionization was widespread. However, Grant felt that if national legislation sought by farmers was passed, no large part of agriculture would need to be unionized and that farmers should concern themselves with labor, international trade, agricultural marketing, credit and environmental problems. Grant urged growers to become involved in ecological problems.[347]

Significantly, on February 16, California growers changed their by-laws to permit them to pursue legislation to protect them. J. Hayes, President of the Salinas Valley Independent Growers Association, reported that efforts to achieve federal legislation were promising and state legislative proposals were progressing. By-laws changes permitted wider membership participation.[348] This was a significant change in tactics.

On February 24, California Assemblymen Ketchum, Wood, Maddy, Mobley, Duffy, Seeley, Stacey, Ray E. Johnson, MacGillivray, Monagan, Murphy introduced AB 639, or the "Agricultural Labor Relations Act of 1971." It would create the Agricultural Labor Relations Board appointed by the Governor, subject to confirmation by the Senate; and this bill was supported by agribusiness while it was opposed by UFWOC as an anti-farm labor organizing measure. The measure was sent to the Assembly Committee on Labor Relations and amended in the Assembly August 9, 1971.[349]

In February, also, Senator Petris introduced SB 165, a collective bargaining bill. SB 165

"Makes recognition of a labor organization as a collective representative for farm workers duty of agricultural employer upon demand of a labor organization unless employer has good faith doubt that the demand is supported by a majority of farm workers in a unit appropriate for collective bargaining, and specifies details of representation of farm workers by labor organizations . . .

"Provides that the Director of Industrial Relations upon being petitioned by a labor organization may issue, under certain conditions and after investigation and a hearing, an order sought by petitioner in order to effectuate policies of chapter.

"Specifies procedure for and requirements of representation elections and duties of the director in connection with such elections.

"Specifies grievance procedure for agricultural employers.

"Declares public policy of state to be voluntary settlement of labor disputes.

"Provides that it is the duty of an agricultural employer to bargain in good faith concerning wages, hours and other terms and conditions of employment with a lawfully recognized or certified labor organization. Provides for corresponding duty to bargain in good faith on part of such labor organization.

"Specifies duties and powers of director and directs him to adopt regulations to effectuate intent of chapter.

"Provides that in case of conflict between this chapter and provisions relating to state labor policy set out in Section 923, Lab. C., this chapter shall prevail.

"Provides that chapter shall not apply to any representation matter over which the National Labor Relations Board would assert jurisdiction."[350]

On March 1, 1971, Senator Petris introduced SB 432, a pesticide bill promoting health and safety. SB 432

"Sets forth specific safety requirements for handling of defined economic poisons, including requiring specified handwashing facilities. Requires posting of notices on fields that have been or will be treated with economic poisons designated by the State Department of Public Health as constituting a serious menace to employees' lives, health or safety. Provides for inspections by county health officer and accompanying fees. Specifies county health officer may direct the person who authorized the application of economic poisons to eliminate any menace or order specified areas which constitute menace to employees' lives, health, or safety closed, such order to be appealable to the department.

"Specifies primary responsibility for enforcement of act is with county health officers, with the assistance of the State Department of Public Health."[351]

On March 12, a series of pesticide bills were introduced in the California Assembly:

"Organic phosphates, widely used as agricultural pesticides, are extremely toxic poisons. Like nerve gas these substances destroy cholinesterase, a chemical in our bodies that controls nerve impulses. Consequently, overexposure to an organic phosphate can cause muscular convulsions, coma, and death.

"Assemblyman William Ketchum (R-Paso Robles) has introduced AB 349, which would make it a misdemeanor for an employer to employ a person in the application of organic phosphate pesticides, unless the employee can furnish a certificate indicating recent and satisfactory cholinesterase level tests. Local public health departments would be required to administer tests to all who request them.

"AB 349 would also prohibit the employment of anyone applying organic phosphates whose cholinesterase level is below the normal average as established by the State Department of Public Health.

"Another bill that might affect farm workers is AB 198 (Jack R. Fenton, D-Montebello). It would regulate the frequency of Division of Industrial Safety inspection in accordance with the level of hazard of a profession. Since farm work is among the most dangerous occupations the working conditions of farm workers would be subject to more frequent scrutiny."[352]

A week earlier, on March 5, the California Church Council's Legislative News Alert summarized the farm labor bills introduced in both houses:

"Many bills dealing with the Agribusiness vs. farm labor struggle are being introduced this session. Assemblyman Robert G. Wood (R-Salinas) has introduced AB 83, which would forbid a grower from recognizing a union as representative of his employees unless it has won a secret election and has been certified as the employees' collective bargaining agent by the State Conciliation Service.

"AB 83 would also prohibit boycotts, jurisdictional disputes, and hot cargo agreements in agriculture. A hot cargo agreement is defined as an agreement between a union and an employer with whom the union has a dispute. A similar bill, SB 40, by John L. Harmer (R-Glendale), has been introduced in the other house.

"Bills more favorable to the farm workers' cause have also been introduced. Assemblyman John Burton (D-S.F.) has reintroduced a bill, AB 53, that would permit a grower to recognize union without an election, if he were satisfied that the union represented a majority of his workers. If the employer questioned the right of a union to represent his workers, the State Conciliation Service would make the determination either by card check or by secret ballot. The employer would be required to bargain in good faith with a union certified by the Conciliation Service and to put any agreement reached into writing. A similar measure, SB 165, has been introduced in the Senate by Nicholas Petris (D-Oakland).

"Children of farm workers who come from homes where English is not spoken would benefit by the establishment of special school programs provided for under AB 115 and AB 116, introduced by Wadie P. Deddeh (D-Chula Vista).[353]

On March 8, Assemblyman Burton introduced AB 844 which provided a method for the selection of collective bargaining agent with the assistance of the Department of Industrial Relations.[354]

On March 12, the California AFL-CIO reported that a legal battle they had launched over 3 years before to bar the use of convicts in agriculture had been won. The California Supreme Court denied a petition filed by State Attorney General Younger for a hearing on the case. The AFL-CIO won a temporary injunction in November 1967 after Governor Reagan authorized the use of 300 state prison convicts to harvest figs and grapes in Merced and San Bernardino.[355]

The legislative moves continued. On March 15, Assemblymen Cory, Wood, and La Coste introduced AB 964 or the "Agricultural Labor Relations Act of 1971." It was supported by agribusiness because of its almost identical provisions as AB 639, the Ketchum bill. The *Salinas Californian* called the measure an intention to protect farm workers rights to organize and protect growers and consumers against a disrupted supply of produce on farms and in the marketplace.[356] The Free Marketing Council urged support of AB 964 because it called for secret ballot elections supervised by the Governor's office, made the secondary boycott illegal, and gave growers management rights protection.

In Washington, meanwhile, on March 23, U.S. Senator Kennedy had introduced S. 1373 to revise the Immigration and Nationality Act. Co-authors included Senators Fong, Anderson, Bayh, Case, Gravel, Hart, Hughes, Humphrey, Inouye, Lavits, Magnuson, Pastore, Pell, Percy, Randolph, and Stevens. The act was called the "Immigration and Nationality Act Amendments of 1971." Section 7 of the Act refers to the influx of alien workers from Mexico and Canada.

"Section 7 of the bill refines the so-called 'alien commuter system' administered by the Immigration and Naturalization Service . . . The amendment simply says that each commuter alien must be regularly certified every 6 months by the Department of Labor, that his presence in the United States to seek or continue employment does not adversely affect the wages and working conditions of American workers similarly employed. The amendment provides for the revocation of a commuter alien's labor clearance, if he violated administrative regulations, such as a ban on strikebreaking—and this regulation needs strengthening—prescribed by the Department of Labor and the Immigration and Naturalization Service to carry out the purpose of this amendment. Section 14 of the bill, among other things, imposes criminal sanctions on employers who knowingly employ illegal entrants or those in an immigration status in which employment is not authorized."[357]

Back in California, on March 30, 1971, Assemblymen Fenton, Moretti, La Coste, Brathwaite, Brown, Burton, Chacon, Cory, Deddeh, Garcia, Leroy F. Greene, Harvey, Johnson, Knox, MacDonald, McAlister, McCathy, Meade, Pierson, Porter, Robert Townsend, Warren, and Waxman introduced AB 1355, or, unemployment insurance benefits for farm workers. AB 1355

"Deletes provisions that exclude agricultural workers from the provisions of the Unemployment Insurance Code and makes unemployment insurance law applicable to agricultural labor. Provides for additional tax on certain employers on wages paid to their agricultural employees."[358]

AB 1355 was amended in the Senate on June 7, July 8, and July 19, 1971. The bill was initially referred to the Assembly Committee on Government Administration. A similar bill was introduced on April 1, by Assemblyman Waxman and sponsored by the State AFL-CIO. It proposed to provide unemployment insurance benefits for approximately 215,000 farm workers. The *Salinas Californian* printed an article about the Waxman bill which stated, "in 32 years of effort the labor lobby has never been able to enact legislation that would include farm workers as recipients of government largesse in the form of unemployment insurance."[359]

On April 8, the *Salinas Californian* published an article entitled "Outlook Favorable for Bill for Expanding Farm Credit." It indicated that a bill introduced in the House by Republican J. MacMillan and in the Senate by Chairman Talmadge of the Senate Agricultural Committee would broaden Farm Credit Systems lending authority, allow it to move into several new rural credit fields, authorize Federal Land Banks to make mortgage loans for non-farm homes, etc. Critics of the bill charged it threatened to reduce the pool of loanable funds in rural America.[360]

On April 12, the *Nation,* in an article entitled "Why Chávez Spurns the Labor Act," reported that a coalition of California farm groups with the support of the Nixon and Reagan Administrations wanted to bring agriculture under the National Labor Relations Act. The federal proposals would be similar to those put forth by Secretary of Labor George Shultz in 1970. Assistant Secretary of Labor W. L. Usery and Under Secretary Silverman provided these outlines. The administration package would exempt small farmers (Shultz mentioned the hiring of 500 man-days of labor in a peak quarter as the line between large and small); it would establish union recognition procedures, and it would define unfair labor practices to include secondary boycotts.[361]

While growers said they would give up the "no strike at harvest" clauses, Labor Department officials talked of "protecting" perishable crops from strikes, while somehow guaranteeing the workers the right to strike. Shultz proposed that unions give ten days notice of intent to strike. The grower then could seek a thirty day cooling off and fact-finding period that would result in arbitration binding on the grower. However, if the union disliked the arbitrator's findings, it would be free to strike.

Meanwhile, in Sacramento, an ad hoc committee representing seven major farm organizations was drafting a state farm labor relations bill. Committee chairman Robert Brown, director of the California Tax-payers Association, hoped the bill would pass that spring. It was part of a "game plan" calling for similar legislative efforts in *twenty-five states.* Farm leaders believed that such state actions would put additional pressures on Congress to pass a "favorable" farm labor relations amendment to the NLRA. The State Agriculture Department had chairman Brown present the committee proposals to the State Board of Agriculture, whose chairman, Allan Grant, was a Reagan appointee and also a member of Brown's committee. In addition, Grant was president of the California Farm Bureau Federation and a member of the Board of Directors of the American Farm Bureau. He visited all the farm states helping to coordinate the labor legislation. Grant's work was also co-ordinated through the National Council of Agriculture Employers, based in Washington. During the WCAE's convention in Atlanta, that year, farmers from thirty-seven states heard a top U.S. Department Labor Official say that one of the President's "major legislative goals" was farm legislation similar to the NLRA—but one that recognized the unique nature of farming.

The membership of Robert Brown's committee included representatives from the farm bureau, the Western Growers Association, the Free Marketing Council, the California Grape and Tree Fruit League, the Agricultural Council of California and two large grower-operated labor procurement organizations.

At another level, on April 16, California Assemblyman Wilson introduced AB 3049, which would require the Commission of Housing and Community Development to adopt, and the Department of Housing

and Community Development to enforce, regulations relating to specified aspects of housing, pursuant to Farm Labor Center Law. It provided that all buildings in labor camps would comply with regulations
adopted pursuant to Employee Housing Act, etc.[362]

On May 4, hearings were held by the Senate Finance and Insurance
Committee regarding AB 1257 by Assemblyman Waxman (D-Los Angeles) on unemployment insurance benefits for farm workers. AB 1340
by David Pierson (D-Inglewood) would also cover farm workers the
same as other presently covered workers.

After all these years, foreign workers continued to be a major issue.
In May, Assemblyman Dixon Arnett's bill, AB 528, which would prohibit employers from knowingly hiring aliens who were not entitled to
legal residence in the United States, was reported defeated. However,
the bill was amended and passed by the Assembly on July 29, 1971, by
a vote of 55 to 8.

On May 7, the Labor Federation reported that the California Senate
Finance and Insurance Committee had taken under submission (killed)
AB 1257 (Waxman). UFWOC vice-president Andy Imutan and John
Henning, executive secretary of California AFL-CIO, had testified in
support of the bill.[363] Meanwhile, AB 964 (Cory, Wood), AB 639
(Ketchum), and AB 83 (Wood), three bills opposed by the AFL-CIO, as
well as churches and UFWOC, were set to be heard in June before the
Assembly Labor Relations Committee.

On May 21, the California Church Council reported on the rescheduling of farm labor bills.

"A number of farm labor bills originally scheduled for a hearing May 5th have been
re-scheduled before the Labor Relations Committee of the Assembly. The bills,
including AB 964 by Kenneth Cory (D-Anaheim), AB 844 by John Burton
(D-S.F.), and AB 566 by Willie Brown (D-S.F.), have been scheduled for a hearing
at 9:30 a.m. in Room 2170 of the Capitol on Wednesday, May 26th. The bills are
described in ALERT #13, April 30th."[364]

May was a busy month. Senator Alan Cranston (D-Calif.) joined in
by calling for a tenfold increase in funds for farm labor housing programs operated by the Farmers Home Administration. He pointed out
that the Nixon Administration's proposed budget for fiscal year 1972
requested only $2.5 million for the program. The previous year amend-
ments co-sponsored by Cranston were enacted in the Housing and Urban Development Act of 1970. They had raised the maximum grant
limitation to 90% of the cost of construction and expanded eligibility
to include non-profit organizations of farm workers, and broadly based
organizations incorporated in a state, for the purpose of providing housing and related facilities for domestic farm workers.[365]

By June 1, collective bargaining for farm workers was an issue that had "smoldered" in the California Assembly and Senate committees during May, and now threatened to get even more heated. All bills to establish collective bargaining procedures for agriculture still awaited their first hearing in the Assembly Labor Relations and Senate Industrial Relations: AB 83 (Wood), AB 639 (Ketchum), a similar bill, SB 40 (Harmer), and AB 964 (Cory). AB 639, AB 964 and SB 40 all placed final enforcement powers in the courts.

On June 4, legislation supported by the State AFL-CIO to prohibit employers from knowingly employing an alien who was not entitled to lawful residence in the United States was reported out of the Assembly Labor Relations Committee with a "Do Pass" recommendation. The bill, AB 528, introduced by Dixon Arnett (R-Redwood City) was designed to discourage trafficking in illegal aliens by unscrupulous employers.[366]

Four days later, the *Salinas Californian* issued an article entitled "Cory Wood Bill Passage Hopeful." Cory indicated his optimism of AB 964 passage due to increased support from those who had opposed the bill because it did not prohibit strikes at harvest. California farmers had been reluctant to push for state legislation, claiming that laws pertaining only to agriculture in California would further restrict industry on a highly competitive market. Cory felt that a solution to farm labor would have to come from California, although he preferred legislation that would apply nationwide.[367]

In June, AB 83 (Wood), AB 639 (Ketchum), and AB 964 (Cory), antilabor bills, were joined by AB 704 (Wood). This latter bill would affect the employment of minors in farm labor.[368]

On June 22, UFWOC's vice president and legislative analyst, Dolores Huerta, criticized AB 964 by Cory. She said that the union could win elections, but they would not be significant if UFWOC could not get the kind of contracts it wanted. She complained that legislators guaranteed improved working conditions for farm workers and higher minimum wage laws, but that they were not being enforced. UFWOC attorney Carder accused Assemblyman Cory of having his measure drafted by a sophisticated management attorney.[369]

Meanwhile, passage was predicted for Assemblyman J. Fenton's measure extending unemployment insurance benefits. Supported by UFWOC and the Teamsters Union, it was opposed by the California Farm Bureau Federation.

On June 24, despite solid opposition by UFWOC and the state AFL-CIO, the Assembly Labor Relations Committee approved AB 964, the Cory-Wood bill which would cripple consumer boycott activities. UFWOC Vice President, Dolores Huerta, and John Henning from the State AFL-CIO, church groups and others, had testified against the measure.

"The bill, AB 964 was approved on a split party, voice vote of the nine-member committee which includes five Democrats and four Republicans. Voting for the bill were four Republicans—Ketchum, MacGillivray, Wakefield, and Biddle, and one Democrat, Alex Garcia. Voting against the bill . . . Chairman Assemblyman Roberti, Chacon, Gonsalves, and McAlister, all Democrats. The measure, which remains anti-worker despite recent amendments, was introduced by Assemblyman Kenneth Cory. It has been referred to 21 member Assembly Ways and Means Committee."[370]

On June 23, AB 1355 (Fenton), State AFL-CIO supported legislation to extend unemployment insurance to farm workers, was passed out of the Assembly Ways and Means Committee. Also, AB 2224, introduced by Assemblyman John J. Miller (D-Oakland) and sponsored by the State AFL-CIO was taken under submission by the Assembly Water Committee. This bill would curb the unjust enrichment of large landowners and speculators from publically financial state water projects. Paul Taylor, economic consultant for the AFL-CIO Federation and recognized authority on U.S. Reclamation Law, testified in support of the bill.

By July 1, 1971, the "Friends Committee on Legislation Newsletter," analyzed the situation this way:

"A split in Democratic ranks over collective bargaining for farm labor in late June created a life-or-death crisis for César Chávez' Farm Workers' Organizing Committee, which in the past has counted heavily on Democrats to protect it from grower-oriented legislative proposals.

The crisis arose when Assemblyman Kenneth Cory, (D., Garden Grove) persisted in pushing his AB 964 despite the strong opposition of the UFWOC, AFL-CIO and many of his fellow Democrats. The bill was viewed by Chávez and his co-workers as designed to kill their efforts to organize farm labor . . .

Cory's persistence paid off when the Assembly Labor Relations Committee, after a number of delays, on June 24, gave a "do pass" recommendation to his bill. Democrat Alex P. Garcia (D., L.A.) joined the four Republicans on the committee for a 5-4 Cory victory . . .

During the days that a major battle was brewing over AB 964, a bill to provide unemployment insurance coverage for farm workers won a "do pass" recommendation from the Assembly Committee on Finance and Insurance. Almost unnoticed AB 1355 (Fenton, D., Montebello) passed the Assembly Ways and Means Committee and on June 30 was given a 44-24 approval on the Assembly floor.

Since the course of events in the AB 964 controversy is not explicable in terms of the usual ideological and party divisions, theories to explain them in other terms coursed the corridors of the Capitol. Some theories cast dark aspersions upon the motivations of chief participants in the fray. Two of the less scandalous were:

Theory 1: the Democrats are seeking the best of all possible worlds, in which they can pose as the champions of farm workers, giving them what years of earlier efforts could not achieve, namely unemployment insurance coverage, and in which they can also pose as those who finally have brought peace to the orchards, vineyards and fields. (The peace of the graveyard, farm worker leaders reply bitterly.)

Theory 2: Democrats want to redraw the boundaries of legislative districts with the least possible disturbance to incumbent Democrats. Militant Chicanos have been demanding boundaries that would give Spanish-speaking citizens a more just share of representation in the legislature. To do this would threaten the Democratic status quo. The Democratic leadership is using AB 964 as a threat, telling the farm workers and their allies in effect, "You lay off your demands for more Mexican-American legislative seats and we will kill AB 964."[371]

On July 2, AB 1355 (Fenton) won bipartisan support of the Assembly by a margin of 44-24. Rising to speak for the measure were Assemblymen Fenton, Wood (who is a farmer himself), Chacon and Frank Murphy, Jr. Opposition to the bill was voiced by Assemblyman Ketchum, also a farmer. It then was sent to the seven-member Senate Committee on Industrial Relations, chaired by Senator Alan Short (D-Stockton).

Meantime, Assemblyman David Roberti (D-Los Angeles) issued a warning that if AB 964 passed, it would mean the death of the farm workers' movement in California. In exchange, the workers would receive a pro-management version of the Taft-Hartley Bill loaded in favor of the agribusiness employees. Roberti said that AB 964 is:

"a very extensive piece of legislation that would affect all aspects of the employer-employee relationship in agriculture and noted that its jurisdiction would even extend to out-of-state consumer boycotts."[372]

On July 3, the *Salinas Californian* reported that the Oregon farm labor bill had been vetoed by Governor McCall. César Chávez had demonstrated at the State Capital in Oregon after the bill was passed and threatened civil disobedience and a nationwide boycott of Oregon products. Chávez charged the bill would take away the right to organize, and the right to strike. In particular, Chávez opposed the provision that farm labor "unions" would have to register with an agricultural labor relations board, the procedures for organizing unions and qualifying to represent the workers. Strikes therefore could be blocked during harvest while the dispute was submitted to arbitration.[373]

By July 6, the Cory-Wood agricultural bill AB 964 was sent to a select study committee during the Assembly's August adjournment. The democratically controlled Ways and Means Committee seemed to make passage of the bill impossible, therefore it was sent to committee for study. Assemblyman Wood was hopeful problems could be ironed out for later acceptance by the majority.

However, on July 9, the California Church Council reported on the successful defeat of AB 964.

"A massive demonstration on the steps of the State Capitol by César Chávez's United Farm Workers Organizing Committee on July 7th against AB 964 (Ken Cory, D-Garden Grove) has helped to kill that bill. His measure, establishing collective bargaining procedures and outlawing mass picketing and secondary boycotts, would have virtually killed UFWOC. Such restrictions would have prohibited UFWOC from achieving a position strong enough to bargain effectively with the growers. Opposition from the Assembly Democratic leadership and a large expression of public support for UFWOC helped defeat the bill. In accordance with the Statement of Legislative Principles, the Church Council helped oppose AB 964 and was publicly thanked by César Chávez at the rally."[374]

Shortly thereafter, on July 8, the *Salinas Californian* reported that the Cory-Wood bill was killed by pressure from UFWOC and the State AFL-CIO.[375] The report went on to say that

"Vigorous action by organized labor at all levels was credited this week with the defeat of AB 964, a proposed state Agricultural Labor Relations Act introduced by Assemblyman Kenneth Cory (D-Anaheim) and opposed by the State AFL-CIO on grounds that it was a strongly anti-worker bill.

National leaders opposing the Cory anti-labor farm workers' bill included: George Meany, President of AFL-CIO, Larry O'Brien, Chairman of Democratic National Committee, and U.S. Senators Ted Kennedy, Hubert H. Humphrey, Henry Jackson, John V. Tunney, and Alan Cranston."[376]

Meanwhile, Nixon Administration officials proposed that the Senate reject a $20,000 farm subsidy ceiling that had been approved in the House. The farm bloc leaders were utilizing a strategy used in similar situations in past years by killing the limitation in a Senate-House conference committee. Agribusiness was claiming the House action was costly to farmers, and would lead to surplus production of grain crops without achieving real savings in government costs.

Green card workers continued to attract attention. On July 17, the *California Farmer* announced that green card workers were allowed to continue working in the U.S. The assurance came when the U.S. Supreme Court refused to examine a lawsuit brought by two southern California farm workers.[377] At the same time, Assemblyman Ray Seely introduced a measure which would make farm labor unions make public the dues of their members.

On July 27, Assemblyman Cory launched a campaign to correct misconceptions about AB 964 and to move legislation in 1971. Chávez had called on powerful political friends. According to the *Salinas Californian,* Cory felt the pressure and asked for the bill's submission. He was convinced the bill would pass if it could overcome the UFWOC "propaganda" drive. Interestingly, the Teamsters Union supported the Cory bill, while Chávez made it clear that UFWOC wanted nothing to do with it.[378] Governor Reagan supported AB 964 at a gathering of 300 farmers.[379]

On July 29, 1971, the Dixon-Arnett illegal alien bill, AB 528, passed the California Assembly by a vote of 55 to 8.[380]

On July 30, the California Church Council reported that AB 1355 (Fenton) progressed because,

"Assignment of the bill to the Industrial Relations Committee instead of to the more conservative Committee on Insurance and Financial Institutions was in itself an indication that the Senate leadership wanted the bill to pass. A majority of the members of the Industrial Relations Committee were expected to favor the measure. However, employer groups are strongly opposing AB 1355. Those favoring equal treatment for farm workers should urge early and favorable action upon Senator Alan Short (D-Stockton), the committee chairman."[381]

In August, U.S. Congressman O'Hara's office introduced the Agricultural Child Labor Act, H.R. 10499. The provisions listed by the Committee on Education and Labor in a summary statement included the following:

"1. Under present law, children of any age may be employed in agriculture, except during school hours for the school district in which they live while so employed. Under H.R. 10499, children between 14 and 16 can be employed in agriculture only if the Secretary of Labor finds that such employment will not interfere with their education and children under 14 cannot be employed at all.

2. Under present law, the employment of children below the age of 16 can be prohibited by the Secretary of Labor in occupations which he finds particularly hazardous for such children. H.R. 10499 would prohibit the employment of children between the age of 14 and 16 unless the Secretary of Labor finds such employment will not interfere with their safety, health, or well-being.

3. Under present law, none of the above restrictions apply to children employed on a farm belonging to their parent or guardian. H.R. 10499 continues this provision of law.

4. Under present law, children under 16, working as hand harvesters, paid by piece rate in an operation customarily so paid for, are not covered by the minimum wage provisions of the Fair Labor Standards Act. H.R. 10499 would repeal this exemption.

5. H.R. 10499 provides that the enforcement authority of the Secretary of Labor under the Fair Labor Standards Act shall also apply to this new act. Willful violations are punishable by fine of no more than $10,000, or (for repeated offenses only) imprisonment of not more than 6 months."[382]

On August 6, 1971, Republican O'Hara announced hearings to be held on his bill.

On August 4, Lt. Governor Reineke supported the struggle to revive AB 964. He joined the Teamsters Union, the California Farm Bureau Federation, and the Free Marketing Association in support of the bill.[383] In an article entitled, "GOP trying to revive Farm Labor Relations Bill," the Salinas Californian reported formal confirmation by

Assembly Speaker Moretti that the Cory-Wood bill was dead. Assembly-man Ketchum announced he would revive his pending bill.[384]

Meanwhile, on August 5, Congressmen Sisk and McFall introduced H.R. 10445 and submitted it to the House Committee on Education and Labor. It proposed:

"To amend the National Labor Relations Act, as amended, to amend the definition of 'employee' to include certain agricultural employees . . . Brings agricultural labors under coverage of LMRA, by striking the present exclusion of these employees, Section 2(3) of NLRA."[385]

And, Congressman Veysey introduced H.R. 10459, cited as the "National Farm Labor Relations Act." It would establish a Farm Labor Relations Board to prescribe and protect the collective bargaining rights of agricultural employees and agricultural employers, so as to avoid disruptive labor disputes in agriculture. It too was submitted to the House Committee on Education and Labor.[386]

At this point the *Salinas Californian* editorialized:

"One area in which effective labor law is lacking is agriculture. Farm leaders used to squeal like stuck pigs at the thought of extending the NLRA to agriculture, and it was their influence that kept the labor laws out of the farm picture . . . The absence of labor law in agriculture means that workers and employers alike are denied certain privileges which are granted by law in industry, and . . . denied certain obligations . . . The laborer is being denied the right to specific language in state law settling . . . his right to form or join a labor organization and bargain for a contract . . . the laborer is being denied the right to secret ballot . . . and business-men . . . are being denied legal protection against the secondary boycott . . . the bill, co-authored by Assemblyman Bob Wood, R. Greenfield, was killed . . . The executioners were César Chávez, the UFWOC leader; the National AFL-CIO with whom Mr. Chávez is affiliated, and the top leadership of the National Democratic party . . .

Now Mr. Wood, Assemblyman Frank Murphy, Jr., (R., Santa Cruz) and eight other assemblymen have revived their proposal in bare-bones fashion. They propose only three basics—the guarantee of labor's right to organize, the protection of the secret ballot, and the prohibition of the secondary boycott."[387]

Back in California, in September, an analysis of the effort to pass collective bargaining legislation that UFWOC vigorously opposed was made by the Friends Committee.

"The new attack came from an unexpected quarter, the Senate Industrial Relations Committee. This committee, on July 12, with a majority of Democrats considered friendly to labor, had sent SB 40 to the Senate Rules Committee for assignment to interim study. Ordinarily the bill would have been dead. However, late in the month Senator Harmer obtained consent from the Industrial Relations Committee for reconsideration of his measure and was able to have the bill amended on the Senate floor and returned from Rules to Industrial Relations.

Harmer had written his amendment well. It consisted of the text of a bill for farm labor elections and union recognition which the AFL-CIO had sponsored in 1969 and which Senator Alan Short (D., Stockton) had authored. The new SB 40 was clearly a bill which the AFL-CIO would have a hard time opposing and which presumably would have the support of Short, Chairman of the Industrial Relations Committee.

Despite the original AFL-CIO draftsmanship, the bill contained serious flaws. It would give great powers to the Department of Industrial Relations. The Department would schedule elections and hearings and would establish its own procedures and regulations. It would determine who could vote in an election. All of these powers could be used to favor either the growers or the unions—and the Director of the Department is a political appointee.

SB 40 also left it unclear whether, once a union had been certified as collective bargaining agent for a farm unit, the employer would be required to bargain in good faith. Nor did the bill spell out what would be unfair labor practices by either the employer or the union. Winning an election does not give the union a contract. A requirement that the employer bargain in good faith and the clear delineation of unfair labor practices are essential elements of a good collective bargaining act."[388]

On September 15, a hearing for another reserved farm labor bill, AB 639, sponsored by California Assemblyman Ketchum (R-Paso Robles), was held. The *Salinas Californian* supported this bill also.

"The bill was introduced after a bill sponsored by Assemblyman Bob Wood, R. Greenfield, and Kenneth Cory (D-Garden Grove), was killed. It is basic and constructive legislation written to protect both the California farmer and farm workers, Ketchum said of his new bill."[389]

In this situation, more than 200 supporters of a farm labor bill to outlaw secondary boycotting and require secret ballot elections were called to testify on the Ketchum measure. Despite the demonstration supporting the Ketchum measure, it was killed in committee.

UFWOC and labor had objections to the Ketchum bill AB 639: the bill's definition of an eligible farm worker (requiring the worker to have been employed for at least 100 days) disqualified any striker who had subsequently obtained regular and "substantially equivalent" employment. Under federal law, a striking worker was eligible to vote regardless of what employment he became engaged in.[390]

On September 16, two bills supported by the State AFL-CIO, which would extend unemployment insurance to farm workers and strengthen workmen's compensation benefits, were passed out of the Senate Industrial Relations Committee and referred to the Senate Finance Committee. They were Fenton bills AB 486 and AB 1355. AB 486 would increase the maximum weekly temporary disability benefits from $87.50 to $105. It would also increase maximum weekly permanent disability benefits from $52.50 to $70 and increase death benefits under workmen's compensation program from $20,000 to $25,000. AB 1355 would extend unemployment insurance to farm workers.[391]

Two days later, the *California Farmer* supported a bill introduced by B. Sisk (D-Calif.) and co-sponsored by 83 members of the House of Representatives and 16 Senators.

"The bill is [an] attempt to develop an appropriate climate for agricultural bargaining. It could create a National Agricultural Bargaining Board, to provide standards of qualification of associations of producers, to define the mutual obligations of handlers and associations of producers to negotiate regarding agricultural products, and for other purposes."[392]

Also, the Colorado legislature was considering legislation similar to the Cory bill which would provide for secret ballot elections and make the secondary boycott by farm workers illegal.[393]

On September 20, California Senator Harmer's SB 40 cleared the Senate Finance Committee, but it had to work its way through a crowded Senate calendar and from there to the Assembly. It was predicted that Harmer's bill would pass the Senate, but would meet the same fate as the Cory and Ketchum bills in the Assembly.

On September 23, Robert E. McMilben testified for UFWOC at Congressional Hearings in Washington on the Agricultural Child Labor Act (H.R. 10499). UFWOC supported the bill. U.S. Congressman O'Hara (D-Michigan), who was a long time friend of UFWOC, was planning hearings on the bill in Ohio in November at UFWOC's initiative.[394]

At the same time, the Senate Subcommittee on Migratory Labor announced a series of hearings and investigations on the problems of farm workers. The first was held July 22, according to the Congressional Record.[395]

In October the farm worker press, *El Malcriado,* issued an emergency issue urging UFWOC members to support AB 1355, the unemployment insurance bill.

"In 1966 United Farm Worker Organizing Committee Officer Antonio Orendain said, 'I predict that there will be a man on the moon before we receive Unemployment Insurance . . .' Also in the early 60's our Director César Chávez said, 'We are not going to get Unemployment Insurance until we have a union. We have a union. Now we are going to get our Unemployment Insurance.' "[396]

On October 1, Senator Harmer's SB 40 passed the Senate. It was supported by Governor Reagan, but again its future appeared dim in the Assembly.

"During committee hearings on the bill, the UFWOC opposed it on the grounds that it would cost the state too much and that the Department of Industrial Relations was not equipped to handle such problems. Harmer's proposal faces opposition in the Assembly from Assembly Speaker Bob Moretti."[397]

Then, on October 27, SB 40 was killed in the Assembly Labor Relations Committee on a 5-3 vote. SB 432 by Petris moved to the Assembly Ways and Means Committee. SB 432 had wide support from labor and church groups.

On November 5 UFWOC held a rally at their Salinas hiring hall in support of AB 1355. It had been approved by the Finance Committee chaired by Senator Collier (D-Eureka), and was sent to the Senate floor for passage.

"The bill, supported by Senator Donald Grunsky, R-Watsonville, appeared to have good prospect for passage, with backing from both farm workers and grower spokesmen. . . . It would provide about $66 million annually in unemployment benefits for farm workers, until now excluded from unemployment coverage . . . be financed by $34.5 million in contributions from farm employers and another $21.5 million from non-farm employers who provided major opposition . . ."[398]

On November 8, the most significant piece of legislation affecting farm workers was signed by Governor Reagan. It prohibited the hiring of illegal aliens in California. The State Department of Industrial Relations data had indicated that there were 250,000 illegal aliens in California in 1969, 100,000 working and earning over $100 million in wages. The AFL-CIO had earlier adopted a policy calling for legislation which would attack the availability of illegal wetbacks. UFWOC certainly viewed this as a victory. AB 528 (Dixon-Arnett Bill) states:

"Section 1. Section 2805 is added to the Labor Code to read: 2805 (a) No employer shall knowingly employ an alien who is not entitled to lawful residence in the United States if such employment would have an adverse effect on lawful residence workers. (b) A person found guilty of a violation of subdivision (a) is punishable by a fine of not less than two hundred dollars nor more than five hundred dollars for each offense. (c) The foregoing provisions shall not be a bar to civil action against the employer based upon violation of subdivision (a)."[399]

On the same day, November 8, the Senate Finance Committee passed AB 1355 (Fenton), extending unemployment to 245,000 California farm workers. The bill was sent to the Senate Floor. AB 1355 won passage on June 30 in a 44 to 24 vote.[400] Legislation to protect farm workers and consumers by establishing specific safety requirements for handling pesticides won approval of the Assembly Ways and Means Committee, and was sent to the Assembly Floor.

"The Senate-passed measure SB 432, introduced by Nicolas C. Petris (D-Oakland), has the support of the California Labor Federation, AFL-CIO, County Health Officers Association, the United Farm Workers Organizing Committee, the Teamsters, and California Rural Legal Assistance . . . An assembly floor fight is expected in the measure since agribusiness interests are reportedly attempting to shift the authority from establishing regulations from the Department of Public Health to State Department of Agriculture, an agency that has been charged . . . with paying more

LEGISLATIVE SUMMARY

First Session — 92nd Congress

AGRICULTURE

Bill	Nature of Bill	Congressional Action
H.R. 318 (O'Hara)	Extends unemployment insurance coverage to employers of agricultural workers on the same basis as other workers.	*House:* Pending in Ways & Means Committee. (Hearings not scheduled.)
H.R. 5010 Farmworkers' Bill of Rights (O'Hara)	Assures equal access for farm workers to programs and procedures instituted for protection of American working men and women.	*House:* Subcommittee on Agricultural Labor of the Education and Labor Committee held background hearing 6/30/71. Report requested from Department of Labor 7/1/71.
H.R. 5945 (Corman)	Extends unemployment insurance coverage to employers employing four or more agricultural workers for each of 20 or more weeks.	*House:* Pending in Ways and Means Committee. (Hearings not scheduled.)
H.R. 11007 Farmworkers' Compensation Act (O'Hara)	Provides compensation for injury, illness, disability, or death of employees in agriculture, and for other purposes.	*House:* Subcommittee on Agricultural Labor concluded hearings.
H.R. 10499 Agricultural Child Labor Act of 1971 (O'Hara)	Bans oppressive child labor in agriculture, and for other purposes.	*House:* Subcommittee on Agricultural Labor approved for full committee. (Steve Bossi testified.)
H.R. 10867 Rural Development Act of 1971 (Page)	Provides for improving the economy and living conditions in rural America.	*House:* Agriculture Committee concluded hearings 10/14/71; executive sessions held 10/26,27; adjourned subject to call.

S. 1612
Rural Community Development Revenue Sharing Act of 1971
(Miller)

Revenue Sharing Plan for rural community development.

Senate: Subcommittee on Rural Development held hearings; Full committee in executive sessions 11/3,9,15. Session resumes 1/25/72.

S. 742
Rural Community Development Bank Act of 1971
(Pearson)

Creates a rural community development bank to assist in rural community development by making financial, technical, and other assistance available for the establishment or expansion of commercial, industrial, and related private and public facilities and services, and for other purposes.

Senate: Pending in committee on Banking, Housing, and Urban Affairs.

H. 7597
National Agricultural Marketing and Bargaining Acts
(Sisk)

Creates a National Agricultural Bargaining Board and expands coverage of Agricultural Bargaining Act.

House: Subcommittee on Domestic Marketing & Consumer Relations held hearings. Executive session 11/30/71. (Agriculture Department report unfavorable.)

H.R. 8886-7
National Agricultural Marketing and Bargaining Acts
(Bergland)

Creates a National Agricultural Bargaining Board and expands coverage of Agricultural Bargaining Act.

House: Subcommittee on Domestic Marketing & Consumer Relations held hearings. Executive session held 11/30/71. (Agriculture Department report unfavorable.)

S. 726-727
National Agricultural Marketing and Bargaining Acts
(Mondale)

Creates a National Agricultural Bargaining Board and expands coverage of Agricultural Bargaining Act.

Senate: Hearings concluded 11/23/71; Msgr. Webber testified.

heed to the economic consideration to the State's corporate farm interest than with the Safety of workers and consumers."[401]

The November 20 issue of the *California Farmer* supported the use of the initiative to achieve labor legislation which by-passed the legislature and the Governor. It did, however, criticize the new farm labor law initiative sponsored by the Citizens' Committees.

"It reads well, but a good labor lawyer will tell you that the initiative is so poorly written that it would be a huge mistake to vote for it. The important thing in such legislation is 'definitions.' "[402]

On November 23 the legislature passed and sent to Governor Reagan unemployment insurance benefits for farm workers, AB 1355, sponsored by Assemblyman Fenton. Under the bill an unemployed farm worker could receive a maximum of $65 per week for up to 26 weeks, the same as a jobless worker in industry.[403]

Soon after, the November 29 issue of the *Salinas Californian* reported on the farm labor initiative, claiming,

"The Farm Workers Secret Ballot Initiative is a concerted effort of nearly 6,300 farm workers, laboring in the farming valleys across California, to procure protective farm legislation . . . establishes the right of farm workers to form and join labor organization and bargain collectively through representatives. It also gives them the right to refrain from such activities . . . puts California agriculture under the Department of Industrial Relations which will conduct secret ballot elections . . . prohibits the use of secondary boycotting by agricultural labor organizations."[404]

In December the center of attention changed and vigorous opposition to the confirmation of Mrs. Ramona Acosta Banuelos as Treasurer of the United States was voiced by AFL-CIO and the United Farm Workers Organizing Committee.

"Referring to the fact that Mrs. Banuelos' $6 million a year Mexican food factory in Gardena has been raided six times in the past four years for employing illegal aliens . . . UFWOC Director César Chávez sent a statement to a Senate Committee . . . It is unthinkable that practices which exploit the poor and actually reflect the opposition of this nation's best principles should be given the presidential and congressional blessing by the appointment of Señora Banuelos. Chávez said that this kind of appointment 'frustrates the organizing efforts of legitimate unions throughout the country.' Our experience is use of illegal entrants as strikebreakers in the organizing efforts of farm workers."[405]

Elsewhere, the American Friends criticized the secret ballot initiative.

"The initiative is sponsored by a Farm Workers' Secret Ballot Election Committee headed by Dolores S. Mendoza, a farm worker, and by the Rev. Michael L. Cross, a priest. Both were active in the 1971 session in support of collective bargaining bills opposed by the César Chávez group, the United Farm Workers' Organizing Committee, AFL-CIO. As far as can be determined, no major grower groups are supporting the initiative.

"The initiative statute follows the language of the National Labor Relations Act (NLRA) with few deviations but with significant omissions. The proposed law, unlike the NLRA, does not establish an administrative agency to administer and police its provisions. Instead, the Department of Industrial Relations is given broad powers to conduct elections and certify results.

"The initiative would change the state's labor law. To qualify the measure for the June, 1972 primary ballot, only 325,000 signatures are required. An initiative statute cannot be vetoed by the Governor nor can it be repealed or amended except by another vote of the people."[406]

On December 11, 1971, the *California Farmer* criticized the farm labor initiative again as "superficial and an unsophisticated effort," to deal with a very complicated and involved area of labor relations.[407]

Significantly, Governor Reagan vetoed unemployment insurance benefits for farm workers on December 22, 1971. He said:

"I cannot approve legislation that would further increase the competitive disadvantages faced by California agricultural community . . . the Nixon administration currently is drafting a national unemployment insurance program for farm workers and I intend to support this proposal when it is presented to the Congress."[408]

Obviously, the governor was strongly criticized by Fenton for his veto of AB 1355. The State Labor Federation immediately announced it would reintroduce the bill in 1972.

Finally, on December 27, critics of big government farm subsidies announced they had lost their drive to lower the ceiling of payment to individual farms in 1972. Under an existing law, which expired at the end of 1973, the payment limit was $55,000 per farmer on each of three crops—wheat, feed grains, and cotton. Representatives of Findley's rider would have put a $20,000 per farmer limit.[409]

1972

California Labor Relations Act of 1972
U.S. Senate Subcommittee On Migratory Labor Hearings
Unemployment Insurance Benefits
Illegal Aliens: Brophy and Arnett Measures
National Labor Relations Board
National Agricultural Labor Relations Act of 1972
Pesticide Bill
Family Farmer Bill
Fair Labor Standards Act: Minimum Wage
Hawaii Employment Relations Act

Idaho Agricultural Labor Act, 1972 (Passed)
Kansas Agricultural Employment Relations Act, 1972 (Passed)
Arizona Agricultural Employment Relations Act, 1972 (Passed)
California Agricultural Labor Relations Initiative—Proposition 22

Among the first bills to be introduced in the 1972 California legislature were measures dealing with collective bargaining in agriculture, authored by the same legislators who pushed anti-union bills in 1971.

On January 3, Senator Harmer introduced SB 16, the Agriculture Labor Relations Act. On January 4, Assemblyman Wood introduced AB 9, the Agricultural Labor Relations Act of 1972, creating an Agricultural Labor Relations Board.

"Wood said the bill differed from last year's defeated farm labor bill . . . only in the removal of clause prohibiting the secondary boycott . . . Wood's proposal was drafted to conform with the National Labor Relations Act . . . Wood said he does not believe his measure will conflict with an initiative effort by the Citizen's Committee for Agriculture to place a secret ballot election proposal before voters. The initiative has a right to work clause; mine does not . . ."[410]

In January, the U.S. Senate Subcommittee on Migratory Labor of the Senate Committee on Labor and Public Welfare, started three days of hearings in San Francisco and Fresno to investigate "corporate feudalism," and the quality of rural life in California. The State Federation, AFL-CIO called for immediate congressional action to extend the NLRA to farm workers. The focus of the hearings was not legislation, but land holding.

"In California, for example, 3.7 million acres of farm land are now owned by 45 corporate farms; one corporation, Tenneco, controls more than a million acres in California. Nearly half the agricultural land in the state is owned by a small fraction of the population.

"In 1960, only one percent of Florida's citrus lands were held by large farming-canning corporations. Now fully 20 percent of those lands are in such ownership."

"In 1969, the largest 40,000 farms in America, less than two percent of the total number accounted for more than one-third of all farm sales—U.S. Senator Adlai E. Stevenson, III."[411]

The lack of enforcement of the U.S. reclamation law was pointed out as a major contributor to increase corporate power over land. Paul Taylor, State AFL-CIO expert on U.S. reclamation law cited a unanimous U.S. Supreme Court decision in 1958 that revised a California Supreme Court opinion holding acreage limitation unconstitutional. He noted that in 1959-60 Congress refused to exempt a California water project jointly using federal reservoirs, pumps and canals, from acreage limitation. Taylor emphasized that the administrative branch shortly nullified the congressional debate and action by giving the exemption anyway.[412]

Then, on January 25, Assemblyman Fenton reintroduced unemployment insurance benefits for farm workers, AB 205, which was referred to Committee on Finance and Insurance. On January 27, Assemblyman Wood introduced a pesticide bill: AB 246, the pesticide bill,

"Declares legislative intent regarding the safe use of pesticides and safe working conditions for farm workers, pest control application, and other persons handling, storing, or applying pesticides, or working in and about pesticide-treated areas. Requires the Director of Agriculture to adopt regulations to carry out such provisions. Requires the State Department of Public Health to participate in the development of such regulations and requires that regulations which relate to health effects be based upon the recommendations of the State Department of Public Health. Requires designated information relating to such recommendations to be made available upon request to any person.

"Requires the director and each county agricultural commissioner under the direction and supervision of the director, to enforce such provisions and any regulations adopted pursuant thereto. Authorizes the local health officer to assist the director and commissioner. Requires local health officer to investigate any conditions where a health hazard from pesticide use exists, and to take action in cooperation with the commissioner, to abate any such condition. Authorizes the local health officer to call upon the State Department of Public Health for assistance, pursuant to specified provisions."[413]

On January 29, Catholic priest, Father Michael Cross, Salinas County Chairman of the Farm Workers Initiative Committee, announced that more than 100,000 signatures had been collected. Petitions for the initiative were filed on January 24, in every county of the State. The statewide initiative, which had to be signed by 325,000 valid signatures would give control over secret ballot elections to the Governor and make the secondary boycott illegal.[414]

The National Farm Worker Ministry Director, Rev. Wayne C. Hartmire, Jr. issued a statement entitled, "Understanding the Farm Worker's Position on Legislation," in January, 1972.

"What is the UFWOC position on legislation? On April 16, 1969 Dolores Huerta appeared before the Senate Subcommittee on Migratory labor and read César Chávez' prepared statement on collective bargaining legislation. UFWOC's position favors extension of the National Labor Relations Act (NLRA) to farm workers but without the crippling Taft-Hartley and Landrum Griffin amendments (see attached historical sheet). UFWOC favors the same kind of protections that industrial workers had when they were first protected by the Wagner Act in 1935. Friends of the farm workers argue that it is impossible to get the original Wagner Act for farm workers. They point out that growers and chain stores are organized in every state. The farm workers are organized in only a few places. Only 10% of America's farm workers are covered by union contracts. It seems inevitable that a strong UFWOC

collective bargaining bill introduced in Washington, D.C. would be amended and watered down and farm workers would be stuck with legislation that provides for elections but robs them of the power to gain good contracts. So the farm workers have chosen to keep struggling without legislation. They prefer to make gains slowly and surely and to build a democratic union that may some day have the strength to gain good Federal collective bargaining legislation. In the meantime they are forced to oppose all the repressive legislation that will keep appearing in state after state."[415]

Furthermore, Rev. Hartmire warned that agribusiness interests, the Farm Bureau and the John Birch Society, had decided to attack the farm workers union. For example, the Farm Bureau was arguing that the May UFWOC elections were not valid elections and legislation was needed to protect the workers. Rev. Hartmire's answer to that was:

"From 1965 to 1971, there have been well over 50 valid elections in California, Arizona and Washington agriculture. In every case but one the election has been won by United Farm Workers. The one exception is being appealed because the labor contractor illegally intimidated his Filipino workers ('If Chávez wins you will all be fired and replaced by Mexicans') . . .

The Farm Bureau has tried to argue that these many elections were not valid elections. But the evidence proves that they were:
(a) The elections were supervised by a neutral arbitrator chosen by all parties to the elections, e.g., American Arbitration Association, Federal Mediation & Conciliation Service, Protestant Clergy like the Rev. Lloyd Saatjian of the Methodist Church of Palm Springs and the Roman Catholic Bishops Committee.
(b) The rules and procedures for every election were agreed to in advance by all parties to the elections.
(c) The different kinds of elections used (card check, secret ballot and ratification) are all approved by the NLRA as valid expressions of the will of the workers (under many circumstances strikes are also recognized by the NLRA as valid expressions of the will of the workers.)."[416]

In a book entitled *Dollar Harvest: the Story of the Farm Bureau*, 1971, César Chávez states in the Foreward that:

"The Farm Bureau has been one of the most steadfast and consistent opponents of our efforts to unionize the country's farm workers. Arm in arm with other reactionary forces, it has resisted the attempt of farm workers to join together to bargain effectively and lift themselves from the bottom of the economic ladder. It has attempted to defame and discredit our Union and break our strikes. It has led the battle in Washington to cripple unionization with restrictive legislation. It has fought every attempt to improve the conditions of farm workers by opposing legislation to give us such minimum protections as Social Security unemployment and minimum wage hour legislation."[417]

On February 2, one of several hearings was held by the Assembly Labor Relations Committee on the illegal alien bill by Dixon Arnett which would take effect March 4. The measure which was quietly passed and signed had become controversial, even among Chicano groups. The bill was supported by CRLA general counsel Sheldon Greene, and the U.S. Catholic Conference, Division for the Spanish Speaking, West Coast Office urged the bill be strengthened. It was opposed by a Mexican American organization in east Los Angeles, CASA. On Febraury 3, Assemblyman Brophy introduced a repeal bill to the Arnett Bill 2805. AB 315 by Brophy did not pass.[418]

On February 4, the California Labor Federation's Research Director was reported urging that the Dixon Arnett bill, AB 528, should be strengthened. Specifically, he suggested that the $200 to $500 fines were too low and should be increased.[419]

Section 2805 of the Labor Code, the Arnett law on illegal aliens signed into law November 8, 1971, was declared unconstitutional in February, 1972 by Los Angeles Superior Court Judge Charles Church. The ruling was based on the grounds that the law was too vague in defining illegal aliens. An appeal was being prepared by the California Division of Labor Law Enforcement before the State Supreme Court. The sponsor prepared an amended version to be introduced during the year.

Significantly, on March 9, the federal government asked a U.S. District Court in Fresno to stop the United Farm Workers from picketing stores and restaurants selling nonunion wines. The National Labor Relations Board contended the picketing was an illegal secondary boycott. This was precedent-setting because farm workers always had been outside the jurisdiction of the NLRA.

"César Chávez' farm labor union has charged the White House advisors and members of the Republican National Committee 'master minded' government action against a union boycott of firms which sell nonunion California wines . . . In every state and every city where Republicans are seeking re-election, we're going to bring our life and death struggle to them . . . they're trying to take the boycott away from the movement, and they're going to pay the price for it . . . Sources inside the GOP are telling us the decision was made by the White House advisors and persons associated with the Republican National Committee."[420]

A hearing in Fresno was scheduled for April 6, 1972. By that date one million letters of protest had been sent to Senator Robert Dole, Chairman of the Republican National Committee by farm workers and their supporters. The hearing was never held because of a joint agreement between UFWOC and NLRB counsel. Boycott activities resumed in May. The State AFL-CIO executive officer John Henning said:

"In the light of the Nixon Administration's anti-labor track record—its drive to wipe out free collective bargaining in transportation industry and its so-called wage-price controls that have frozen wages while letting prices and profits run—it's not surprising that the farm workers' union should regard this latest attempt to label its efforts to bring economic security to some of the most exploited workers in our nation as 'purely political.' "[421]

Significantly, the first state collective bargaining measure for farm workers was signed into law in the state of Idaho, March 22, 1972. Senate Bill 1604 was anti-farm worker legislation prohibiting the secondary boycott, establishing an Idaho Agricultural Board which supervises elections, etc. This measure was cited as the "Idaho Agricultural Labor Act." It states:

"SECTION 3. (1) There is hereby created a board to be known as the Idaho agricultural labor board . . . composed of five (5) members, appointed by the governor and subject to confirmation by the senate. Two (2) of the members shall be appointed from a list of names submitted by labor organizations. Two (2) shall be appointed from a list of names submitted by agricultural produce groups. One (1) member shall be representative of the public and shall be selected from a mutually agreed upon list of not less than three (3) persons submitted to the governor by the four (4) other members of the board. The public representative of the board will act as its chairman . . ."[422]

Meanwhile, Representatives Leggett, Quie, Ullman, and Teague of California introduced HR 13981, the Agricultural Relations Act of 1972, to the U.S. House Committee on Education and Labor. This anti-union measure would establish a separate Agricultural Labor Relations Board appointed by the President for 5 year terms.

By March 27, AB 246 (Wood), alleged to provide protection to farm workers who work in fields and orchards with pesticides, had moved its way to the Assembly Ways and Means Committee. Key faults of the bill were listed as:

"(1) The Director of Agriculture would be given the responsibility of issuing and enforcing regulations relating to pesticides and worker safety. The State Department of Public Health would 'participate'—the term is not defined—in the development of regulations. 'The final decision on matters of public health under the bill would be jointly to Public Health and Agriculture. This would mean that the Department of Agriculture would have a veto power over public health questions relating to pesticides.

"(2) Local enforcement would be left to the county Agriculture Commissioner, not the local health officer. The latter could assist the county Agriculture Commissioner and would have the responsibility of investigating any condition where a health hazard from pesticide use exists. At best, this would be the authority to investigate whether the barn door should be closed after the horse has been stolen."[423]

Then, on March 29, Senator Edward Kennedy issued a statement opposing the action of the NLRB to impose the provisions of the NLRA:

". . . the action represents the federal government's intercession on the part of corporate agriculture . . . it becomes flagrantly unjust to use the punitive provision of that act against the union representing farm workers . . . there has been vigorous opposition to consideration of farm workers under the NRLA on the part of Congress. This has been manifest in the law itself as well as the rider which has been attached to appropriation bills every year since 1946."[424]

Senator Kennedy and Sen. Williams thus, requested an opinion of the propriety of expenditures of funds by the NLRB of the Comptroller General. The letter states:

"Our concern is that the Board's use of funds for investigative purposes and its activities with regard to the United Farm Workers violates the provision attached to appropriation measures since 1947 providing that 'no part of the appropriation shall be available . . . or used in connection with investigation, hearings, directives, or orders concerning bargaining units composed of agricultural laborers.' "[425]

On April 19, a new plan for anti-pollution subsidies to farmers had gone before the Senate. If the measure was approved it would authorize federal subsidies to reduce air pollution in rural areas.[426]

By April 28, Wood's pesticide bill passed the Assembly, and a bill by Assemblyman Burton was introduced to protect family type farmers.

"Assemblyman John Burton (D.-San Francisco) has introduced a constitutional amendment to give the legislature the power to impose graduated real property taxes on persons or businesses owning huge parcels of California land. AB 97 would arrest the tendency of large industries, corporations and conglomerates to acquire large land parcels. This major effort at land reform would also help preserve the family farm and could encourage migration from overcrowded urban areas to rural areas.

"The tax rates would be low on the first steps of the proposed scale to protect small growers, but would increase when the total acreage reaches the range of the 'super farms.' Burton claims 'The big landowners in this state, especially the corporate farms, have so many governmental advantages over the small farmer and the average taxpayer that the situation is nearly criminal.' "[427]

Then, from their national headquarters in Chicago, the American Farm Bureau president William Kuhfuss said a nationwide campaign to attack and discredit the AFBF was threatened by César Chávez. On April 26, the United Farm Workers informed UFBF that unless it withdrew its efforts to get anti-farm labor legislation enacted, the Union's national boycott apparatus would be put into an informational campaign against the farm bureau in 40 cities. Kuhfuss responded by stating that AFBF was going to continue lobbying in Congress and in several states for legislation to guarantee secret ballot elections, and to ban the secondary boycott in agriculture.[428]

This was followed by the governor of Arizona who signed into law anti-farm labor legislation on May 11, 1972. This followed legislation passed in Idaho and Kansas in 1972. The Arizona bill, House Bill 2134 reads:

"There is established an Agricultural Employment Relations Board which consists of seven members . . . The members of the Board shall be appointed by the governor, two of the members shall be appointed as representatives of agriculture employers, two of the members appointed shall be representatives of organized agricultural labor and the three additional members, one of who shall be the chairman of the board, shall be appointed representatives of the general public . . ."[429]

Obviously, the farm workers union, UFW, denounced this bill and warned that passage would mean greater unionization efforts in Arizona. "The new law signed by Governor Jack Williams Thursday gave the Farm Workers Union the one issue it needs to further unionize in Arizona, Chávez told 400 cheering supporters at the State Capitol Friday."[430] On May 11, Chávez started a fast to protest the enactment of the labor law. The following is taken from a letter from Chávez to Farm Workers and to supporters of the farm workers cause.

"In Arizona—a major lettuce producing state—the growers and the politicians have just passed a law that destroys the right of farm workers to have a union. Farm workers under this law cannot engage in consumer boycotts. Supporters of our union could be arrested for telling their friends not to buy lettuce. Farm workers are put in the humiliating position of having to go to a special Agricultural Labor Relations Board (appointed by Republican Governor Jack Williams) for a government conducted election to determine their right to strike. The law provides for union representation elections but establishes so many steps and procedures that seasonal and migrant workers would never have a chance to vote. Growers can not only frustrate an election for 2-3 months, they can actually avoid elections by a minor change in hiring practices. Even if workers should vote for the union, an employer can seek a decertification election after only a 3 month waiting period. The bill is discriminatory. It is aimed only at farm workers who are mostly black, brown, and Indian. No other labor force is asked to live with these repressive measures. This is what the Farm Bureau means when they advocate 'free elections' and 'responsible legislation' . . .

My major concern is not this particular Arizona law. The fast is not out of anger against the growers. My concern is the spirit of fear that lies behind such laws in the hearts of growers and legislators across the country. Somehow these powerful men and women must be helped to realize that there is nothing to fear from treating their workers as fellow human beings. We do not seek to destroy the growers. We only wish an opportunity to organize our union and to work nonviolently to bring a new day of hope and justice to the farm workers of our country."[431]

Twenty-four days later Chávez ended his fast honoring the workers who went on strike in Arizona, thanking those who had joined the lettuce boycott, honoring those who had given their lives to their movement during the year (Nan Freeman and Sal Santos), and acknowledging that people who choose to work in the non-violent struggle would know hardship and sacrifice. The struggle continued in Arizona. UFW set forth to have the governor removed, and a suit was filed to challenge the law.

On June 15, Richard Thornton, new executive vice president of the Grower-Shipper Vegetable Exchange in Salinas issued a statement that federal legislation was inevitable. He had worked to have the House of Representatives support an Agricultural Labor Relations Act measure. The bill was sponsored by Congressman Leggett (D-Calif.), Quie (R-Minn.), Teague (R-Calif.), and Ullman (D-Ore.). Meanwhile, the *Salinas Californian* editorial on June 19, 1972, stated,

"Unquestionably, the Arizona law represents a social justice for Arizona's farmers whose hard work should not be destroyed by an edict from a tyrannical union boss . . . If the outlook is dismal at the federal level, the example of Arizona is evidence of what grassroots struggles against monopoly unionism can be achieved . . ."[432]

Meanwhile, on June 13, Assemblyman Wood withdrew AB 9, because he could not gather sufficient support. AB 1214 by Assemblyman Powers (D-Sacramento) was pending. Nationally, the Democratic Platform Committee endorsed the UFW led by Chávez and called for support of the boycott on non-union iceberg lettuce. Meanwhile, another major struggle had developed when the anti-farm labor initiative qualified for the November ballot in California.

On June 30, from the national headquarters of UFW, César Chávez denounced the California farm labor initiative that had qualified for the November ballot as a fraud which would destroy the farm workers union in California, and said the entire state labor movement would fight it. He called the initiative repressive and anti-union legislation which was pushed by both the farm bureau and the John Birch Society.[433]

In neighboring Arizona, on July 15, Governor Williams defended the new labor law stating it did not prevent labor unions from organizing, did not outlaw the strike, offered no impediment to wage increases, did not prevent any steps to improve safety and working conditions, and did not prevent people from criticizing the quality of any agricultural product.

Shortly before, on July 1, the third major legislative anti-farm labor state bill was signed into law in Kansas. Kansas Senate Bill 291 establishes an agricultural labor relations board, prohibits organizational pickets at an agricultural residence, prohibits strikes during periods of marketing or during a critical period of production or harvesting of crops or during mediation, and prohibits engaging in a secondary boycott.

"Sec. 3 (a) There is hereby created the Agricultural Labor Relations Board, which shall consist of three (3) members two (2) of whom shall be appointed by the governors, with the advice and consent of the Senate, for terms of (4) years each. One member shall be representative of agricultural employees, one member shall be representative of agricultural employers, and one member representative of the public. The appointment of the agricultural employee representative member of said board shall be made by the governor from a list of (3) nominations submitted to him by the Kansas State Board of Agriculture . . . shall be made by the members appointed by the governor . . . if the two (2) do not agree and make the appointment of the third member within thirty (30) days, then the governor shall appoint such representative of the public."[434]

On August 15, Governor Reagan vetoed unemployment insurance benefits for farm workers for the second consecutive year.

On August 30, Chávez once again appealed to the churches to help win the struggle against Proposition 22. In a letter to churchmen he said:

"It hurts farm workers when they find out that such an unfair law is going to be on the ballot. I have told them that many Californians were tricked into signing the initiative. Thousands of our friends who signed the petition in May and June were told that this Agricultural Initiative would help farm workers. Others were told that the farm workers union was in favor of the initiative. Still others were told that 'lower food prices.' Perhaps some of you were approached in that way and even signed the petition.

Proposition 22 is dishonest. The growers paid over $240,000 to gather the signatures. They say it will help farm workers but they did not consult farm workers. Now they have said publicly (The Packer, 8/26/72) that they will restrict their campaign on behalf of Proposition 22 to the last few weeks so that UFW members will not be able to refute their propaganda. They also report that upwards of $600,000 will be spent on their media campaign."[435]

On September 4, the Catholic Bishops of California joined labor and many other groups in denouncing Proposition 22. They said "it . . . deviates so widely from a just and equitable approach to settling agricultural labor problems," that they could not support the initiative.[436]

By September 30, California Secretary of State Brown had asked the State Superior Court to take Proposition 22 off the November ballot because of what he called the "worst case of election fraud" ever uncovered in the state.

Proposition 22 was opposed for the following reasons, according to Gerry Cohen, United Farm Workers General Counsel:

"I. THE BOYCOTT (See section 1143)

    A.   It makes secondary boycotting illegal and punishable by one year in jail and a $5,000 fine. PRIMARY ACTIVITY IS MADE A *CRIME*.

    B.   It makes it illegal to use 'publicity directed against any trademark, trade name or generic name which includes agricultural products of another producer or user of such trademark, trade name or generic name.'

Since lettuce is a generic name saying 'BOYCOTT LETTUCE' becomes a crime punishable by one year in jail and a $5,000 fine.

IT BECOMES A *CRIME* TO PICKET A RETAIL ESTABLISHMENT. (Even primary picketing is outlawed.)

These boycott restrictions are *unconstitutional.*

II. THE RIGHT TO STRIKE (See sections 1143 & 1156)

Strikes can be halted by 60 day temporary restraining orders granted without notice. This of course effectively abolishes the right to strike. It too is *unconstitutional.* Even without this provision the structure of the act is set up to prohibit a strike without complying with the terms. Such compliance will always take longer than the harvest.

III. BARGAINING

The initiative ends bargaining about 'management rights.' These management rights include:

1. The right to discontinue the entire farming operation or part thereof. (This means it would be illegal to bargain for a successor clause.)

2. The right to contract out any part of the work. (This means it is illegal to bargain for a subcontracting clause.)

3. The right to determine the methods, equipment and facilities to be used. (God only knows what this means but since pesticide application is clearly a method used in the production of agricultural crops it is clear that if we insist on pesticide protection we are violating the law.)"[437]

The initiative was defeated in the November ballot, and marked the end of an unprecedented attack on farm labor organizing by legislative means. Historically, legal suits, deportation of union leaders, war efforts, and the use of illegal aliens to break strikes had been agribusiness' most effective weapon. Chávez, a historian as well as labor leader, defended the union's efforts knowing full well that these opposing efforts would be applied. When it became obvious that the secondary boycott was the unions most effective weapon, protected by legal sanction, agribusiness along with the American Farm Bureau introduced legislation at the statewide and national levels to make the boycott illegal. It succeeded in three states, Idaho, Kansas, and Arizona. Meanwhile, the union renewed its largest boycott effort against Salinas, and Santa Maria lettuce growers in an attempt to win over contracts that had been made between the growers and teamsters union in "sweetheart" agreements.

At the national level the farmworkers legislative struggle was at a standstill. The following is an example of what happened during the 92nd Congress to progressive farm labor legislation that was proposed. On July 20, 1972, the Senate voted 47-46 to defeat the Republican substitute offered to the Fair Labor Standards Act. By the one-vote margin, coverage of farmworkers was greatly expanded with all of the 1966 exemptions and exclusions deleted leaving only the 500 man-day test remaining for farmworkers coverage. The new minimum wage for all workers would have been $2.20 per hour. There were restrictions on the employment of children. An illegal alien amendment providing criminal penalties for the knowing employment of illegals was also included. There was extended argument on the floor regarding the section on illegal aliens therefore insuring that it would be dropped in any Senate-House conference.

The House of Representatives decided in August, by an eight vote margin, against sending its minimum wage bill to conference. The House had rejected the bill reported out by its own Committee on Education and Labor. It had accepted the Nixon Administration substitute bill introduced by Rep. John Erlencorn (R-Ill.) who was then able to block the Committee's attempt to go to conference with the Senate version because he had heard that the House members on the conference committee would immediately agree to the Senate bill. After considerable negotiations and lobbying, the Chairman Carl Perkins (D-Ky.) again failed to get the bill to conference on October 3, and therefore the amendments to the Fair Labor Standards Act were killed in the 92nd Congress. Thus, labor and its Congressional allies had failed to get a minimum wage bill out of Congress that would have included farmworkers.

The following chart was released in May 1972 as part of the "Summaries of Legislative Proposals Relating to Labor-Management Relations in Agriculture," as introduced in the 92nd Congress through April 1972. It was prepared for use of the Subcommittee on Agricultural Labor of the Committee on Education and Labor House of Representatives.[438]

MAJOR PROVISIONS OF PENDING AGRICULTURAL LABOR-MANAGEMENT RELATIONS BILLS

Provisions	H.R. 1410 2546, 3571, 4438.	H.R. 1689	H.R. 3625	H.R. 5010 5281, 12486	H.R. 10445	H.R. 10459	H.R. 13981
Covers all farmworkers	X			X	X		
Covers employers of larger farms only:							
(a) Farms using 500 man-days of agricultural labor in a calendar quarter		X[1]				X	X
(b) Farms using over 12 employees, or having labor costs over $10,000 per annum			X				
Excludes supervisors	X	X	X	X	X	X	X
Brings farmworkers under LMRA	X		X		X		
Brings farmworkers under NLRA, excluding many Taft-Hartley and Landrum-Griffin amendments				X			
Permits union shop agreements in which farmworkers may be required to join the union within 7 days of employment	X		X	X			X
Permits union shop: (a) In any State				X			
(b) Only where State law does not forbid	X	X	X		X	X	X
Permits hiring hall arrangements						X	
Administered by NLRB	X		X	X	X		
Establishes new Board		X				X	X
Permits secondary boycotts or hot cargo agreements				X			
Prohibits use of green carders as strike breakers				X			
Prohibits knowing employment of illegal aliens							X
Prohibits strikes or lockouts		X					
Provision for delaying strike or lockout:							
For 30 days						X	
For 40 days							X
For 80 days, in case of national emergency strike, as determined by President and the courts	X		X	X	X		
Secret ballot elections: 1. for selection of bargaining representatives by workers: (a) Mandatory		X					
(b) required "if the Board finds a question of representation exists"	X		X	X	X	X	X[3]
2. For election of union officers	X[4]	X[5]	X[4]	X[4]	X[4]		

1 "Agricultural employee" is defined as one who has worked for the same employer 14 days out of the previous month, and for at least 100 days for him or another agricultural employer, in the previous calendar year.
2 The Chairman of the Board is an Assistant Secretary of Agriculture, and USDA regional offices perform the functions of NLRB regional offices.
3 H.R. 13981 permits the Board to certify a union as the bargaining representative even where that union has lost the election where aggravated unfair labor practices by the employer have resulted in the defeat of the union in the election.
4 The bills which extend NLRA to agriculture have the effect of requiring secret ballot elections of officers (or of delegates to conventions electing officers) since provisions of the Labor-Management Reporting and Disclosure Act of 1959 apply, by reference, to any labor organization certified as a bargaining representative under NLRA.
5 H.R. 1689 specifically directs the Board to conduct such elections.

CONCLUSION

The Legal Struggle

The farm workers' legal struggle between 1965 and 1972 involved the following: labor contractors, rent strike, illegal aliens, assaults, anti-picketing injunctions, transgression, libel suits, convict labor, green-carders, illegal aliens, anti-boycotting cases, sanitary conditions, pesticide records, jury selection system, minimum wages, conspiracy, unemployment benefits, farm labor service, Teamsters, evictions, jurisdictional dispute charges, pesticides and ecology, Defense Department, Labor Department, discrimination, restraining orders, unfair labor practices, National Labor Relations Board suits, anti-secondary boycotting, legislation in Arizona, Proposition 22 in California, the short handle hoe, as well as other suits.

For the most part, the legal suits emanated from the farm workers Union. Major legal struggles almost always involved the anti-picketing injunctions granted to growers whenever the Union went on strike. Arrests followed along with assaults, evictions, charges of transgression, etc. Counter suits by the Union involved the illegal use of alien workers and green-card workers used to break the strikes. Then followed anti-boycotting suits by growers and Union counter suits to protect the boycott. The legal suits against state legislative proposals did not follow until the boycott had repeatedly proven a success between 1965-1970. Then, anti-picketing injunctions in Salinas, California, granted in Monterey County, were kept in effect for two years until they were overturned by the state Supreme Court. However, during this time, growers launched a major drive to introduce legislation that would prohibit secondary boycotts by the United Farm Workers, AFL-CIO.

From the foregoing account of the legal struggle, it is readily apparent that the legal struggle for the farmworkers' Union has not been static. In fact, it appears that the United Farm Workers, AFL-CIO, exhibited a knowledge of previous legal struggles and consequently set forth its own legal strategy. The Union's communications media focused considerable effort toward the understanding of such past legal history. Thus, with a historical perspective upon which to base contemporary activities, the Union instituted its own legal department within its complex and developing organizational structure. This development of its own legal institution ultimately controlled by farmworkers, has provided the Union and its membership with both a protective legal arm and a forum for a progressive legal thrust. Briefly, the legal department is protective in that it works to preserve the integrity of the organization. Simultaneously, it is progressive in that it seeks to break new legal ground with respect to farmworkers and the law.

The legal thrust has been protective to the membership and the organization as a whole. The membership is now provided with a voice in an arena that heretofore had been neglected. It provides a vigilant instrument over activities dealing with workers' rights previously legislated or contracted for. It also promotes interdependence between the individual and their organization insofar as the result of cases more often than not affects many others. The organization is protected, allowing it to preserve integrity of the postulates under which the organization has been formed and sustained. It also reflects group decisions regarding the allocation of resources for the legal defense.

The progressive thrust of this legal struggle has been such that the César Chávez led United Farm Workers has been able to develop institutions long sought by farm workers all over the world. This legal struggle has, in part, contributed to the progress and growth of the membership of the Union. The membership has improved its socio-economic conditions, and, in addition, is provided with a wide range of legal services heretofore not readily available to farm workers. The organization has been progressive in seeking changes in the National Labor Relations Act, unemployment insurance, pesticide control, progressive contracts, and its own cooperative institutions.

The organization in particular has been progressive in providing legal support for the central facets of the Union's cooperative structure within which there are eleven legal entities: clinics, medical plan, coop garage, credit union, retirement village, service centers, death benefit plan, hiring halls, ranch committees, farm workers press, organizing department, contracts, negotiation and arbitration, research department, accounting department, strike fund, economic development fund, legal defense fund, legal department, strike store and kitchen, boycott offices, huelga school, child care nursery, non-violent training center at La Paz, overall administration, and most important, services to the families of the membership.

While the major focus of the foregoing in Part I has related primarily to the struggle of the organization, the ramifications of the overall legal activities extend beyond the organization itself. Of these extensions, probably the most closely related lies in the field of legislation and the activities that surround the creation of new legislation and the abolishment of old. To fully understand the legal activities described here, one must equally understand the legislative struggle of the farm workers.

The Legislative Struggle

In the arena of the farmworkers' legislative struggle, the following has been discussed: minimum wages, braceros, unemployment insurance, right-to-work laws, illegal aliens, green-carders, National Labor

Relations coverage, convict labor, pesticides and ecology, anti-secondary boycotts, labor contractors, elections, workmen's compensation, housing, as well as other areas. The different social forces that have dealt with farm labor legislation have consistently been at odds, with the interest of agribusiness continually dominating.

To date, there have been only a few breakthroughs for farm workers in the legislative arena. For example, the bracero program ended. However, it was replaced by the use of illegal aliens and green-card workers used to break strikes and lower wages. Similarly, unemployment insurance moved one step further. Legislation was passed in California when, for two consecutive years, the legislature passed unemployment benefits. However, these were vetoed each time by the Governor. Pesticide legislation met powerful opposition in the legislature, thus preventing it from being passed. Convict labor was prohibited in the fields after a legal struggle, but continued to be used elsewhere throughout the nation. Anti-secondary boycott legislation was passed in Idaho, Kansas, and Arizona, while similar legislative proposals were killed in thirty-six states in 1972. Passage in these three states represented a breakthrough for agribusiness forces such as the Farm Bureau, which had been leading such a thrust since 1970. In addition, agribusiness reversed its public policy regarding coverage for farm workers under the National Labor Relations Act provisions. By supporting such coverage for farm workers, agribusiness then could hope to be effectively protected from the secondary consumer boycotts conducted by the United Farm Workers, AFL-CIO against their products.

Because of the past record in legislation, 1965-1972, it appears that farmworkers' protective legislation prospects for the future continue to be bleak indeed. It seems clear that for the immediate future, farmworkers cannot count on protective legislation either at the state or national level. Therefore, what is indicated from the foregoing in Part II is that restrictive legislation such as that passed in Idaho, Kansas, and Arizona, will continue to be proposed at the state levels as well as nationally. As a result, the Union has had to develop a protective strategy in order to sustain its organizational integrity. Toward this end, a legislative department has been formed within the Union's overall structure. Now, despite the lack of progress in the legislative arena, the Union will be enabled to continue its efforts to reach the goal of protective legislation for farmworkers. Perhaps a resolution will be found in representation at the highest levels of government, such as that presently enjoyed by the Teamsters in the Nixon Administration.

Thus, it can be concluded that in the legal arena some advances can be pinpointed as related to the organizing of farmworkers, such as those cases which enabled the Union to bring its efforts to bear on growers (strikes, picketing, boycott, etc.), particularly the State Supreme Court decision of December 29, 1972. While in the past such legal cases have spelled the demise of other union activities, the same cannot be said for the United Farm Workers. Thus far, the UFW has engaged the issues in the legal sphere and emerged with some successes without dissolution of the Union.

The same, however, cannot be said for the legislative struggle. Here it appears that there has been little, if any, progress principally due to the fact that the tools of bargaining (boycott, etc.) are under increasing attack in legislatures. Thus, the end of the bracero program, while initially viewed as a step forward in reality has resulted in little or no change. This has been principally due to the continued use of illegal aliens and green-card workers who have, to a high degree, tended to replace braceros in the fields. Thus, ten years after the end of the bracero program, the original problem of foreign labor continues. In the absence of effective legislation, therefore, the United Farm Workers has had to institute organizing efforts along the border regions in order to limit, if not eliminate, the continuing importation of labor.

Meanwhile, the present prospects indicate that, legally and legislatively speaking, the present situation from the viewpoint of farmworkers organizing will become worse rather than better. The indications have been that as the Union grows, so does the legal and legislative opposition. This being the case, over time, each legal and legislative counter move becomes increasingly important in terms of the survival of the Union. Thus, restrictive legal and legislative action increasingly affects the survival of the Union.

The final outcome, of course, still concerns one of the initial reasons for originally attempting to organize farmworkers. That is: will or will not the farmworkers and their organization have a voice in the courts and legislatures of the land, a voice that ultimately results in specific actions. As the struggle continues, more and more farmworkers are presently turning toward individual and group efforts to influence future legislation, as well as actions in the courts. It is in this context that the organizing, the bargaining, the legal, and the legislative aspects of farmworker organizing have become so interwoven that what happens in one arena inevitably affects all the others.

That is why, in the introductions to this study, this interdependence was indicated. And that is why full knowledge of all these aspects of farm labor is so essential. It is no longer, if indeed it ever was, sufficient to merely describe a few workers in poverty, or to focus merely upon the more dramatic aspects of Huelga, as has been done in past books concerning this Union. Today, the central issue is not merely better wages, but rather: will or will not the farmworkers have a legal and legislative voice in their future destinies that will protect their rights to self-determination. It is toward this end that the United Farm Workers has focused much of its present efforts.

While much of the present study has been referred to as the struggle of the farmworkers, there are those who say, with some justification, that the real struggle is yet to come.

EPILOGUE

It was stated before that as the Union grows, so does the nature of the forces opposing it. Since the end of this study, this seems to have been born out by recent developments. It was also stated that with such growth in the opposition, each subsequent move has tended to influence the entire Union and its survival. This also has been borne out by recent developments.

In accordance with its past history, the Union has responded, and only the future will tell what the final outcome of the present situation will be. For the present, the field, the legal, and the legislative efforts are all equally important in determining the final results.

In the past, due to legal maneuverings, and the slow-paced deliberations in legislative halls, final resolutions have been slow in coming, as in the case of the Salinas anti-picketing injunctions which were in court for two years. Based on this past experience, it would seem safe to predict that the recent developments in California agriculture, i.e., the situation with the Teamsters and the growers, signal the beginning of an extended effort to regain formal representation. This effort promises to last a considerable period of time.

At stake, of course, are not only the legal and legislative rights of farm workers, but also the important services to the workers that have been developed and provided by the U.F.W. and which were mentioned in the introduction to this study. In short, what is also at stake in the present struggle is whether or not the U.F.W. can continue to provide the farm workers with medical benefits, clinics, death benefits, hiring halls, pesticide and ecological protection, a retirement village, service centers, a credit union, an economic development fund, a school for children, day care nursery services, a farmworkers press, ranch committees for field representation, a co-operative garage, a research department for economic and social problems, a legal defense fund for individuals as well as the organization, all controlled by the workers, and thus providing the farm workers with a significant voice in the determination of their own destinies.

NOTES

The Legal Struggle

1. National Advisory Committee on Farm Labor, "First Organizing Attempts in California," *Farm Labor Organizing 1905-1967: A Brief History* (New York, N.Y.), July, 1967, p. 14.

2. Governor C. C. Young's Mexican Fact-Finding Committee, "The Strike of Mexican Cantaloupe Pickers," *Mexicans in California* (San Francisco: State Building, California), October, 1930, p. 143.

3. National Advisory Committee on Farm Labor, "The Southern Tenant Farmers Union," op. cit., p. 23.

4. London, Joan and Henry Anderson. *So Shall Ye Reap.* New York: Thomas Y. Crowell Company, 1970.

5. National Advisory Committee on Farm Labor, "The AFL, the CIO and Farm Workers After World War II," op. cit., pp. 38-39.

6. Galarza, Ernesto, *Spiders In The House And Workers In The Field,* University of Notre Dame Press, 1970, pp. 3-4.

7. National Advisory Committee on Farm Labor, op. cit., p. 40.

8. Galarza, pp. 4-5.

9. National Advisory Committee on Farm Labor, op. cit., p. 42.

10. Galarza, pp. xi-xii.

11. "El Caso Contra 'HRONIS,' " *El Malcriado,* No. 11, p. 2.

12. "Se Prende La Metcha," *El Malcriado,* No. 11, p. 7.

13. "Cienes Rehusan Pagar La Renta De Los Jacales De Linnell y Woodville," *El Malcriado,* No. 12, p. 5.

14. "Relampago," *El Malcriado,* No. 12, p. 5.

15. "Contratista De Curceran Hiere Un Socio," *El Malcriado,* No. 14, p. 3.

16. "El Herido Demands $15,000, Del Contratista De Kings," *El Malcriado,* No. 15, p. 7.

17. "Los Rancheros Se Creen Mas Que La Ley," *El Malcriado,* No. 15, p. 12.

18. "Se Investigan Los Campos Por Autoridades Del Condado y El Estado," *El Malcriado,* August, 1965, p. 5.

19. "Huelga De Renta Presion Forzo Al Comision Tratar Con Los Renteros," *El Malcriado,* September, 1965, p. 8.

20. "Puso Quejas Al Federal Contra Exeter Dehydrater," *El Malcriado,* No. 19, p. 4.

21. "Policia Golpeo A Socios," *El Malcriado,* No. 19, p. 4.

22. "Justice In The Valley," *El Malcriado,* No. 19, p. 7.

23. "Mrs. Huerta Jailed," *El Malcriado,* No. 22, p. 8.

24. "Trabajadores y Ministros Tomaran Su Dia En La Corte," *El Malcriado,* No. 23, p. 3.

25. "La Gente Triunfa," *El Malcriado,* No. 23, p. 7.

26. "New Investigations Of Tulare Housing Scandals," *El Malcriado,* No. 25, p. 7.

27. "An Open Letter From César Chávez," *El Malcriado,* No. 25, p. 8.

28. "DiGiorgio Loses $300,000," *El Malcriado*, No. 29, February 12, 1966, p. 3.

29. "The Hot Line," *El Malcriado*, February, 1966, p. 14.

30. "Campesinos Hacen Demanda A DiGiorgio Para $640,000," *El Malcriado*, May, 1966, p. 4.

31. "The Hot Line," *El Malcriado*, May, 1966, p. 22.

32. "DiGiorgio Demands New Law To Break Strike," *El Malcriado*, June, 1966, p. 6.

33. "Conspiracion Entre Ranchero-y-Policia," *El Malcriado*, No. 39, June 30, 1966, p. 14.

34. "Chávez on Trial," *El Malcriado*, August, 1966, p. 5.

35. "A Broken Head And Eight Months In Jail," *El Malcriado*, October, 1966, p. 11.

36. "The Largest Lettuce Grower In The World Sues El Malcriado, For One Million Dollars," *El Malcriado*, November, 1966, p. 11.

37. "Lettuce Grower Fails Again," *El Malcriado*, January 18, 1967, p. 11.

38. "Even Playing To God Is A Crime," *El Malcriado*, January 13, 1967, p. 23.

39. "FBI Investigates Texas Arrests," *El Malcriado*, March 1, 1967, p. 13.

40. "Victory And Violence In S.F.," *El Malcriado*, March 15, 1967, p. 16.

41. "Violence," *El Malcriado*, April 12, 1967, p. 20.

42. "Union Families Say They Were Taken By Company," *El Malcriado*, April 13, 1967, p. 30.

43. "Perelli & Minetti vs. El Malcriado," *El Malcriado*, May 24, 1967, p. 6.

44. "Lary Itliong Sues Birch Society," *El Malcriado*, June 10, 1967, p. 6.

45. "Ranger Violence," *El Malcriado*, June, 1967, p. 11.

46. "How It Happened," *El Malcriado*, June, 1967, p. 11.

47. "Victory For Rent Strikers," *El Malcriado*, July 5, 1967, p. 1.

48. "Texas Justice In California," *El Malcriado*, August 16, 1967.

49. "Fed Wins Suit To Ban Use Of State Convicts On Farms," *California AFL-CIO News*, IV, 46 (November, 1967), 1.

50. "Frame Up," *El Malcriado*, February 21, 1968, pp. 1-3.

51. "Greencard Scabs And The Law," *El Malcriado*, March 15, 1968, p. 7.

52. "Trial Set To April 22," *El Malcriado*, March 15, 1968, p. 4.

53. "Court Concedes," *El Malcriado*, May 1, 1968, p. 2.

54. "Strike Tempo Quickens," *El Malcriado*, May 1, 1968, p. 6.

55. "April Fool's Day In Court," *El Malcriado*, April 15, 1968, pp. 7-8.

56. "Court Okays Gun Threat," *El Malcriado*, April 15, 1968, p. 15.

57. "Tantrum Fails In Court," *El Malcriado*, May 1, 1968, p. 8.

58. "Strike Tempo Quickens," *El Malcriado*, May 1, 1968, p. 6.

59. "The Trial Of The Texas Rangers," *El Malcriado*, July 1, 1968, p. 5.

60. "Contractor Must Pay $2,500 For Hitting Striker," *El Malcriado*, July 1, 1968, p. 4.

61. "Growers Claim $25 Million Boycott Loss," *El Malcriado*, July 15, 1968, p. 4.

62. "Union Asks For Jury Trial," *El Malcriado*, August 1, 1968, p. 6.

63. "Union Files $50,000,000 Suit," *El Malcriado*, August 15, 1968, p. 5.

64. "Enough Is Enough," *El Malcriado*, August 15, 1968, p. 7.

65. "Woodville Tenant Support Boycott," *El Malcriado*, August 15, 1968, p. 9.

66. "Growers Hide Facts On Poisons," *El Malcriado*, September 1, 1968, p. 6.

67. "Wisconsin Court Victory," *El Malcriado*, September 1, 1968, p. 7.

68. "Judge Denies Jury Challenge," *El Malcriado*, September 1, 1968, p. 12.

69. "Trials Set For Rubio Rivera," *El Malcriado*, September 1, 1968, p. 12.

70. "Union Files $37,000 On Demand Against Cops," *El Malcriado*, September 1, 1968, p. 14.

71. "Clapping Illegal In Coachella," *El Malcriado*, September 15, 1968, p. 13.

72. "Growers Conspire With Phony Union," *El Malcriado*, September 15, 1968, p. 6.

73. "Hollister D.A. vs. U.S. Supreme Court," *El Malcriado*, September 15, 1968, p. 5.

74. "Court Questions Poison Injuction," *El Malcriado*, September 15, 1968, p. 6.

75. "Hearing On Label Suit Set For 23," *El Malcriado*, September 15, 1968, p. 13.

76. "Anti-Trust Action Against Grape Growers," *El Malcriado*, October 1, 1968, p. 5.

77. "Workers File Charges, Against Mayfair Markets," *El Malcriado*, October 1, 1968, p. 7.

78. "HHH Upholds Grape Boycott," *El Malcriado*, October 15, 1968, p. 4.

79. "Judge Denies Grower Charges," *El Malcriado*, October 1, 1968, p. 5.

80. "State Officials Ignore Wage Law," *El Malcriado*, October 1, 1968, p. 11.

81. "Growers Try To Drop $75 Million Claim," *El Malcriado*, October 15, 1968, p. 4.

82. "Injunctions Fail To Slow Boycott," *El Malcriado*, November 1, 1968, p. 8.

83. "SCAB Clique Faces $650,000 Suit," *El Malcriado*, November 1, 1968, p. 4.

84. "Giumarra Charged Consumer Fraud," *El Malcriado*, November 1, 1968, p. 12.

85. "S.F. Judge Dismisses Grower Suit," *El Malcriado*, November 15, 1968, p. 11.

86. "Camacho Challenges Court," *El Malcriado*, January 1, 1968, p. 7.

87. "Cops Arrest Picket Line," *El Malcriado*, December 13, 1968, p. 6.

88. "Hospital Segregation Challenged," *El Malcriado*, January 15, 1969, p. 8.

89. "What Are They Hiding?" *El Malcriado*, February 7, 1969, p. 4.

90. "Judge Denies UFWOC Access To Poison Info," *El Malcriado*, April 1, 1969, p. 2.

91. "UFWOC Sues Over Coachella Grower's Phony Charges," *El Malcriado*, April 1, 1969, p. 3.

92. "Collections At Gate For Farm Workers Upheld," *California AFL-CIO News*, 11, 23 (June 2, 1969), 2.

93. "Growers Running From The Law," *El Malcriado*, July 1, 1969, p. 10.

94. "Court Upholds Farm Workers Right To Join Union," *El Malcriado*, July 15, 1969, p. 5.

95. "Judge Rules Ag Labor Not Suitable Employment," *El Malcriado*, July 15, 1969, p. 11.

96. "Court Upholds Farm Workers Right To Join Union," *El Malcriado*, August 1, 1969, p. 14.

97. "Back Pay And Overtime For Farm Workers Upheld," *El Malcriado*, July 25, 1969, p. 1, 4.

98. "UFWOC Moves To Dismiss Growers," *El Malcriado*, August 1, 1969, p. 5.

99. "UFWOC Defends Orange Cove Workers, Sues Labor Contractors," *El Malcriado*, August 15-September 15, 1969, p. 10.

100. "Contractor Charged With Law Violations," *El Malcriado*, October 15, 1969, p. 6.

101. "Thieving Grape Grower Admits Guilt," *El Malcriado*, November 1, 1969, p. 6.

102. "B of A Charged With Poisoning, Firing Farm Workers," *El Malcriado*, November 1, 1969, p. 6.

103. "Rotten Decision—Judge Protects Pesticide Service," *El Malcriado*, January 15, 1970, p. 18.

104. "UFWOC Sues Growers," *El Malcriado*, February 1, 1970, p. 2.

105. "Workers Win Court Injunction To Enforce Sanitation Law," *El Malcriado*, March 1, 1970, p. 12.

106. "NRLB Action Threatened," *El Malcriado*, April 15, 1970, p. 5.

107. "Chávez Files Suit Against State Farm Labor Service," *El Malcriado*, May 16, 1970, p. 31.

108. "UFWOC To Represent Melon Workers," *El Malcriado*, June 15, 1970, p. 1.

109. "30 Growers Sign Teamster Contract," *Salinas Californian*, July 28, 1970, p. 1.

110. "Agricultural Workers Union Sues To Block Teamster Pact," *Salinas Californian*, July 29, 1970, p. 1.

111. "Chávez Backers Start March To Salinas Rally," *Salinas Californian*, July 31, 1970, p. 1.

112. "Chávez Pact For Grapes Protested," *Salinas Californian*, August 13, 1970, p. 1.

113. "Farm Union Reports Freshpick Talks Due," *Salinas Californian*, August 15, 1970, p. 1.

114. "Bishop Hopeful Of Talks," *Salinas Californian*, August 24, 1970, p. 1.

115. "Court Bans Pickets As Tension Grows," *Salinas Californian*, August 25, 1970, p. 1.

116. "Strike Arrests Total 28; Chávez Urges Non-Violence," *Salinas Californian*, August 26, 1970, p. 1.

117. "Court Order Bans Eviction Of Striker," *Salinas Californian*, August 28, 1970, p. 13.

118. "Col-A-Pak Files Against Unions," *Salinas Californian*, August 31, 1970, p. 1.

119. "25 Pickets Are Arrested For Failing To Disperse," *Salinas Californian*, September 2, 1970, p. 1.

120. "Salinas Officials Assure Citizens Of Probe On Injunction Serving," *Salinas Californian*, September 2, 1970, p. 1.

121. "Courts Face Floods Of Eviction Suits," *Salinas Californian*, September 3, 1970, p. 1.

122. "Contempt Action Fails Against Chávez By Technicality," *Salinas Californian*, September 4, 1970, p. 9.

123. "3 Freed Following Arrests," *Salinas Californian*, September 4, 1970, p. 1.

124. "Jury Trial Set For 18 Pickets," *Salinas Californian*, September 5, 1970, p. 1.

125. "Judge Brazil Ponders Picket Ban On Jurisdictional Strike," *Salinas Californian*, September 9, 1970, p. 1.

126. "Farm Workers File Suit Against UFWOC, Growers," *Salinas Californian*, September 10, 1970, p. 4.

127. "Deputies Step Up Arrests Of UFWOC Valley Pickets," *Salinas Californian*, September 10, 1970, p. 1.

128. "Artichoke Grower Recognizes Union," *Salinas Californian*, September 12, 1970, p. 1.

129. "Judge Rules Farm Strike Union Fight," *Salinas Californian*, September 16, 1970, p. 1.

130. "Judge Drops Charges Against Farm Pickets," *Salinas Californian*, October 20, 1970, p. 1.

131. "D'Arrigo Granted Picket Injunction," *Salinas Californian*, October 22, 1970, p. 1.

132. "National Labor Board To Issue Complaint Against UFWOC," *Salinas Californian*, November 6, 1970, p. 2.

133. "National Labor Board Refuses To Issue Complaint Against UFWOC," *Salinas Californian*, November 6, 1970, p. 2.

134. "Farm Laborer Files Lawsuit Against Use Of Pesticides," *Salinas Californian*, November 12, 1970, p. 26.

135. "Bulldozer Incident Related By Worker," *Salinas Californian*, November 17, 1970, p. 1.

136. "Father Duran's Trial Scheduled On Jan. 7 For UFWOC Rallies," *Salinas Californian*, November 19, 1970, p. 11.

137. "Farm Labor Organizer Seeks Damages In Suit," *Salinas Californian*, November 20, 1970, p. 17.

138. "Chávez Must Defend Antle Produce Boycott," *Salinas Californian*, November 21, 1970, p. 1.

139. "Judge Denies Chávez Move," *Salinas Californian*, November 27, 1970, p. 1.

140. "Jury Trial Requested By Chávez In Court," *Salinas Californian*, December 1, 1970, p. 1.

141. "UFWOC Pickets Sued By Hollister Workers," *Salinas Californian*, December 9, 1970, p. 1.

142. "Farm Workers Union Suffers Twin Setbacks," *Salinas Californian*, December 12, 1970, p. 1.

143. "State Court Lets Chávez Out Of Jail," *Salinas Californian*, December 24, 1970, p. 1.

144. "UFWOC Pickets Curbed By Los Angeles Judge," *Salinas Californian*, December 22, 1970, p. 1.

145. "Attorney General's Office Refutes Chávez's Charge Of Law Breakdown," *Salinas Californian*, December 30, 1970, p. 1.

146. "State Court To Hear Chávez Case Feb. 4," *Salinas Californian*, January 5, 1971, p. 1.

147. "UFWOC Sues Antle, Laird," *Salinas Californian*, January 6, 1971, p. 27.

148. "2 UFWOC Members Sentenced," *Salinas Californian*, January 6, 1971, p. 15.

149. "Arizona Growers Sue Union," *Salinas Californian*, January 12, 1971, p. 11.

150. "Jury Finds UFWOC, Priest Guilty," *Salinas Californian*, January 12, 1971, p. 1.

151. "UFWOC Files New York Suit On Purchases," *Salinas Californian*, January 16, 1971, p. 2.

152. "Alien Arrests Rise Sharply In Salinas Area," *Salinas Californian*, January 20, 1971, p. 1.

153. "Court Dismisses Pesticide Lawsuit By UFWOC," *Salinas Californian*, January 26, 1971, p. 22.

154. "Judge Rules Oshita, Others Won't Answer UFWOC," *Salinas Californian*, January 30, 1971, p. 7.

155. "Court Hears Argument In Chávez Boycott Ban," *Salinas Californian*, February 4, 1971, p. 1.

156. "UFWOC Drops Pentagon Suit," *Salinas Californian*, February 23, 1971, p. 2.

157. "UFWOC Fined Net $150 For Rallies In September," *Salinas Californian*, March 8, 1971, p. 1.

158. "Chávez Announces Pact With Teamsters Union," *Salinas Californian*, March 26, 1971, p. 6.

159. "Judge Quashes UFWOC Suit," *Salinas Californian*, April 14, 1971, p. 1.

160. "California Court Rules Chávez Boycott Legal," *Salinas Californian*, April 15, 1971, p. 1.

161. "UFWOC Taken To Court In San Diego County Case," *Salinas Californian*, April 19, 1971, p. 1.

162. "Noise Ban Is Snagged By UFWOC," *Salinas Californian*, June 14, 1971, p. 2.

163. "UFWOC Sues A Congressman," *Salinas Californian*, July 13, 1971, p. 12.

164. "UFWOC Loses Decision On Appeal," *Salinas Californian*, July 15, 1971, p. 4.

165. "UFWOC Charges Growers Biased," *Salinas Californian*, July 26, 1971, p. 13.

166. "UFWOC Plans Appeal From Salinas Rally Verdict," *Salinas Californian*, August 12, 1971, p. 4.

167. "UFWOC Picketing Limited," *Salinas Californian*, September 15, 1971, p. 1.

168. "UFWOC Suit Dismissed By Judge In Santa Cruz," *Salinas Californian*, September 23, 1971, p. 24.

169. "Picket Hearings Charged Probably Due On Oct. 1," *Salinas Californian*, September 24, 1971, p. 2.

170. "Trespass Charges Dropped Against Eight UFWOC Members," *Salinas Californian,* September 29, 1971, p. 21.

171. "UFWOC Picketing Hearing Undecided," *Salinas Californian,* October 9, 1971, p. 2.

172. "Discharged Farm Workers' Suit Dismissed By Judge," *Salinas Californian,* October 19, 1971, p. 13.

173. "UFWOC Sues To Prevent San Lucas Camp Closure," *Salinas Californian,* January 5, 1972, p. 2.

174. "Pic 'N Pac Moves For Evictions," *Salinas Californian,* January 27, 1972, p. 3.

175. "La Posada Families Win Another Eviction Delay," *Salinas Californian,* February 1, 1972, p. 3.

176. "Alien Law Disputed," *Salinas Californian,* February 2, 1972, p. 23.

177. "Injunction Sought To Bar Farm Secondary Boycott," *Salinas Californian,* March 8, 1972, p. 1.

178. "Suit Aims At Chávez Boycotts," *Salinas Californian,* March 9, 1972, p. 1.

179. "Chávez Blames Republicans For Move To Halt Boycott," *Salinas Californian,* March 10, 1972, p. 1.

180. "$248,000 Grant To Finance Co-op," *Salinas Californian,* March 13, 1972, p. 1.

181. "United Farm Workers Plan Lettuce Boycott," *Salinas Californian,* March 15, 1972, p. 1.

182. "Pic 'N Pac Now Can Resume Eviction Action," *Salinas Californian,* March 15, 1972, p. 5.

183. "Chávez Will Launch Lettuce Strike," *Salinas Californian,* March 16, 1972, p. 1.

184. "Pic 'N Pac's Eviction Case To Await Naming A Judge," *Salinas Californian,* March 29, 1972, p. 1.

185. "Picket Injunction Hit," *Salinas Californian,* March 29, 1972, p. 1.

186. "Harassment Of Chávez's Union Charged," *Salinas Californian,* March 29, 1972, p. 24.

187. "UFW Suspends Wine Boycott," *Salinas Californian,* April 4, 1972, p. 1.

188. "UFW Says Lettuce Boycott Still On," *Salinas Californian,* April 7, 1972, p. 2.

189. "UFW Strikes Roberts Farm," *Salinas Californian,* April 12, 1972, p. 2.

190. "Farm Bureau Chief Reveals Chávez Threat," *Salinas Californian,* May 3, 1972, p. 4.

191. "Winery Boycott Must Stop, Free Market Council Claims," *Salinas Californian,* May 4, 1972, p. 2.

192. "UFW Appeals Injunctions To High Court," *Salinas Californian,* May 8, 1972, p. 3.

193. "Greenfield Casualty In Ideological War," *Salinas Californian,* May 11, 1972, p. 1.

194. "Chávez Asks High Court To Resolve Dispute," *Salinas Californian,* June 29, 1972, p. 18.

195. "Chávez Raps Farm Initiative," *Salinas Californian,* June 31, 1972, p. 1.

196. "UFW Files Suit To Kill Arizona Farm Labor Law," *Salinas Californian,* August 15, 1972, p. 15.

197. "UFW Inter-Harvest Meet On New Pact," *Salinas Californian*, August 28, 1972, p. 3.

198. "County Farm Bureau Chief Discounts Petition Fraud," *Salinas Californian*, August 28, 1972, p. 13.

199. "Chávez, Henning Petition To Remove Prop. 22 Summary," *Salinas Californian*, September 8, 1972, p. 19.

200. "Inter-Harvest Strike Talks Resume Monday," *Salinas Californian*, September 12, 1972, p. 1.

201. "Brown Moves Against Proposition 22," *Salinas Californian*, September 11, 1972, p. 5.

202. "Prop. 22 Investigation Expanded to 8 Counties," *Salinas Californian*, September 12, 1972, p. 12.

203. "Voters May Decide Festering Farm Labor Problems," *Salinas Californian*, September 13, 1972, p. 29.

204. "Prop. 22 Backers Say Brown's Move 'Bunch of Baloney,' " *Salinas Californian*, September 14, 1972, p. 3.

205. "Prop. 22 Backers Scoff At Suit," *Salinas Californian*, September 15, 1972, p. 1.

206. "UFW Pickets Sheriff's Tulare County Office," *Salinas Californian*, September 15, 1972, p. 5.

207. "Prop. 22 Charges Disputes Brown's Prop. 22 Charges," *Salinas Californian*, September 20, 1972, p. 4.

208. "Farm Workers Ask Bar On Short Handle Hoe," *Salinas Californian*, September 20, 1972, p. 13.

209. "Chávez Urges Workers' Political Involvement," *Salinas Californian*, September 21, 1972, p. 1.

210. "64 UFW Pickets Arrested At White River Vineyards," *Salinas Californian*, October 3, 1972, p. 12.

211. "Otsuki Bros. File Suit Over Pic 'N Pac Deal," *Salinas Californian*, October 3, 1972, p. 13.

212. "Chávez Locked In Bitter Dispute Where It All Started," *Salinas Californian*, October 4, 1972, p. 22.

213. "Chávez Says UFW May Make Own Arrests," *Salinas Californian*, October 5, 1972, p. 32.

214. "UFW Says Tulare Sheriff Watched Union Hall Attacks," *Salinas Californian*, October 9, 1972, p. 3.

215. "UFW Loses Battle In Court Charges 'Klan' Tactics Used," *Salinas Californian*, October 11, 1972, p. 25.

216. "Farm Workers Pickets Legal; Chávez Threatens A Strike," *San Jose Mercury*, December 30, 1972, p. 33.

217. *Ibid.*

The Legislative Struggle

218. National Advisory Committee on Farm Labor, "Farm Workers and the National Labor Relations Act," *Farm Labor Organizing 1905-1967: A Brief History*, (New York, N.Y.) July, 1967, p. 10.

219. California Rural Legal Assistance, "Laws Affecting Farm Workers and Their Families," (report), 1972.

220. "You Can Get Braceros If," *California Farmer*, January 16, 1965, p. 5.

221. Pickett, Jack, "Editorially Speaking: Unemployment Insurance Coming To Agriculture," *California Farmer*, January 16, 1965, p. 4.

222. "Antle Spells Out Labor Problem For LBJ," *California Farmer*, February 6, 1965, p. 46.

223. Pickett, Jack, "Editorially Speaking: Pat Discovers Labor Shortage," *California Farmer*, March 20, 1965, p. 4.

224. Pickett, Jack, "Editorially Speaking: Our Labor Headache," *California Farmer*, February 20, 1965, p. 4.

225. "Tieburg's Views On The Farm Labor Situation," *California Farmer*, March 6, 1965, p. 7.

226. "Senate Ag Committee's Farm Labor Hearing Is Lively," *California Farmer*, March 6, 1965, p. 25.

227. "AFBF Asks President For Farm Labor," *California Farmer*, April 3, 1965, p. 37.

228. Razee, Don, "Agriculture Kicks Itself Around On Wirtz Tour," *California Farmer*, April 17, 1965, p. 5.

229. Pickett, Jack, "Editorially Speaking: The Wirtz Visit Was A Fiasco," *California Farmer*, April 17, 1965, p. 4.

230. "LBJ Farm Bill Favors Small Operators," *California Farmer*, May 1, 1965, p. 39.

231. "Extend Jobless Pay Program To Farm Workers And Update Benefits, Feds Urges," *California AFL-CIO Weekly News Letter*, VII, 19, (May, 1965), 1.

232. Pickett, Jack, "Editorially Speaking: Welfare U.S. Farm Labor," *California Farmer*, May 15, 1965, p. 8.

233. Pickett, Jack, "Editorially Speaking: What's Doing On The Legislative Front?" *California Farmer*, May 15, 1965, p. 8.

234. "Fight To End 14(b) Opens As LBJ Urged Its Repeal," *California AFL-CIO Weekly News Letter*, VII, 21, (May, 1965), 1.

235. "German Farm Workers Fare Better Than U.S.," *California AFL-CIO Weekly News Letter*, VII, 24 (June, 1965), 2.

236. "Wirtz Urges Support for 5-Bill Package To Improve Rights of U.S. Farm Workers," *California AFL-CIO Weekly News Letter*, VII, 29, (July, 1965), 1.

237. "Repeal Of Sec. 14 (b) Wins House Approval By Vote Of 221 To 203," *California AFL-CIO Weekly News Letter*, VII, 31, (July, 1965), 1.

238. "Expert Backs Jobless Pay For Farm Workers," *California AFL-CIO Weekly News Letter*, VII, 36, (September, 1965), 3.

239. " 'Backdoor' Effort to Revive Bracero Program Repulsed by Just One Vote," *California AFL-CIO Weekly News Letter*, VII, 38, (September, 1965), 1.

240. "Dixiecrat-GOP Filibuster Balks Move To Repeal Section 14(b)," *California Weekly News Letter*, VII, 42, (October, 1965), 1.

241. "LBJ Pledge On 14(b)," *California Weekly News Letter*, VII, 48, (November, 1965), 1.

242. Upton, Don, "A New Era Ahead In Farm Labor Relations," *California Farmer*, November 6, 1965, p. 7.

243. "Oregon Looks At Labor Problems," *California Farmer*, December 18, 1965, p. 15.

244. Pickett, Jack, "Editorially Speaking, National Farm Wage Rates," *California Farmer*, January 15, 1966, p. 4.

245. Pickett, Jack, "Editorially Speaking, The Feds Are Moving In," *California Farmer*, February 5, 1966, p. 4.

246. Pickett, Jack, "Editorially Speaking, Labor Pains," *California Farmer*, April 2, 1966, p. 6.

247. Upton, Don, "NRLA Coverage Denounces In Senate Hearings," *Farm Journal*, April, 1966, p. 6.

248. Logsdon, Gene, "The Fight For Farm Labor," *Farm Journal*, March, 1966, p. 89.

249. "Pitts Acts To Halt Mass Use Of Prison Labor On Farms," *California AFL-CIO News*, VIII, 21 (May, 1966), 1.

250. "Farm Business," *Farm Journal*, June, 1966, p. 15.

251. Pryor, Alton, "Citrus Association Offers Fringe Benefits In A Big Way," *California Farmer*, August 6, 1966, p. 7.

252. "Brown Spells Out Program To Improve Labor Laws," *California AFL-CIO News*, VIII, 32 (August, 1966), 1.

253. "Federal Grant Underwrites State Survey Of Farm Labor," *California Farmer*, September 3, 1966, p. 18.

254. "A Californian Looks At Hawaiian Farm Labor Income," *California Farmer*, October 15, 1966, p. 5.

255. State Agriculture Department Releases Foreign Trade Study," *California Farmer*, November 5, 1966, p. 12.

256. "Jobless Pay Urged For State's Farm Workers," *California AFL-CIO*, VII, 47 (November, 1966), 1.

257. "Bar Foreign Workers, Fed Urges At Hearing In S.F.," *California AFL-CIO News*, VIII, 50 (December, 1966), 1.

258. "Growers Push Bill To Bolster Their Own Bargain Rights," *California AFL-CIO News*, IX, 2, (January, 1967), 1.

259. "Bargaining Right For Farm Workers Urged At Hearing," *California AFL-CIO News*, IX, 2 (January, 1967), 1.

260. "Pitts Raps Labor Dept's New Farm Rate As Not Enough," *California AFL-CIO News*, IX, 10, (March, 1967), 1.

261. "Fed Seeks U. I. Benefits For Farm Workers," *California AFL-CIO News*, IX, 13, (March, 1967), 1.

262. "In Congress: The Quiet Struggle," *El Malcriado*, 59, (April 26, 1967), 30.

263. "Meany Seeks NRLA Rights For Farm Workers," *California AFL-CIO News*, IX, 18, (May, 1967), 1.

264. "What's The 160 Acre Limit Fight All About?" *California AFL-CIO News*, IX, 24, (June, 1967), 3.

265. "Wirtz Asked To Bar 'Green Card' Strike Breakers," *California AFL-CIO News*, IX, 34, (August, 1967), 1.

266. "Pitts Asks Wirtz To Bar Braceros," *California AFL-CIO News*, IX, 37, (September, 1967).1.

267. "IWC Ups Pay Floor To $1.65: Farm Workers Win Pay Parity as Board Adopts 40-Hr. Week," *California AFL-CIO News*, IX, 39 (September, 1967), 1.

268. "Feds File Suit To Bar Use of Convict Labor," *California AFL-CIO News,* IX, 40 (October, 1967), 1.

269. "Keep Ban On Con Labor, Fed Urged," *California AFL-CIO News,* IX, 45, (November, 1967), 1.

270. "Feds Win Suit To Bar Use Of State Convicts On Farms, *California AFL-CIO News,* IX, 46, (November, 1967), 1.

271. Pickett, Jack, "Editorially Speaking, Picket Line Acrss The Pearly Gates," *California Farmer,* January 6, 1968, p. 4.

272. "Attorney Contends That Williamson Act Is Illegal," *California Farmer,* January 6, 1968, p. 18.

273. "Bills To Boost U.I. Pay, Bargaining Rights Introduced," *California AFL-CIO News,* X, 6 (February, 1968), 1.

274. "Ban Alien Farm Hands, Fed Urges," *California AFL-CIO News,* X, 6 (February, 1968), p. 1.

275. "End Green Card Invasion, Labor Urges U.S. Board," *California AFL-CIO News,* X, 6 (February, 1968), 1.

276. "Do Growers Flout The Law?" *California AFL-CIO News,* X, 8 (February, 1968), 1.

277. Pryor, Alton, "Green Card Workers May Go The Way Of The Bracero," *California Farmer,* March 2, 1968, p. 11.

278. "Labor Law Provisions That Farmers Should Know About," *California Farmer,* March 2, 1968, p. 3.

279. "Farm Bargaining Rights Bill Ok'd By House Unit," *California AFL-CIO News,* X, 12 (March, 1968), 3.

280. Pryor, Alton, "Task Force Presents A Good Case Against 160-Acre Limitation," *California Farmer,* April 6, 1968, p. 7.

281. "Farm Workers Speak Out," *El Malcriado,* II, 5, (May, 1968), 7.

282. "High Court To Act In Cases Balking IWC Farm Wage Boosts," *California AFL-CIO News,* X, 18 (May, 1968), 1.

283. "Agri-Power Blasts NLRB," *El Malcriado,* II, 6, (May, 1968), 12.

284. Razee, Don, "Boycott Jeopordizes Entire Grape Crop," *California Farmer,* July 6, 1968, p. 7.

285. "Burns' Bad Bill," *El Malcriado,* II, 10, (July, 1968), 13.

286. "Court Upholds New State Farm Pay Floor," *California AFL-CIO News,* X, 37 (September, 1968), 1.

287. "Petition Demands Labor Law Coverage For Farm Workers," *El Malcriado,* 11, 12 (November 1, 1968), 15.

288. Norris, Murry, "Hidden Dangers In The NLRB," *California Farmer,* November 2, 1968, p. 6.

289. "Women Farm Workers Rate Back Pay For 1968," *California AFL-CIO News,* X, 46 (November, 1968), p. 1.

290. "Grower Proposes Anti-Strike Bill," *El Malcriado,* 11, 20 (December 15, 1968), 12.

291. "Reagan's Stand Against Farm Worker Rights Draws Fire," *California AFL-CIO News,* X, 49 (December, 1968), 1.

292. "Reagan To Seek Farm Labor Law," *California AFL-CIO News,* XI, 2, (January, 1969), 1.

293. Ibid.

294. Pickett, Jack, "Editorially Speaking: A Bill To Keep Tax-Loss Capital Out Of Agriculture," *California Farmer,* January 15, 1969, p. 4.

295. Pryor, Alton, "Unemployment Insurance For Farm Workers Appears To Be Inevitable," *California Farmer,* February 1, 1969, p. 2.

296. Pickett, Jack, "Editorially Speaking: Wrong If You Do, Wrong If You Don't," *California Farmer,* March 1, 1969, p. 10.

297. "Nixon Eyes Farm Labor," *El Malcriado,* III, 1, (March, 1969), 8.

298. "Pitts Assails AB 807," *California AFL-CIO News,* XI, 11, (March, 1969), p. 1.

299. "Table Grape Boycott Viewed From The Inside," *California Farmer,* March 1, 1969, p. 41.

300. "State AFL-CIO Warns Of Two Bad Jobless Paybills," *California AFL-CIO News,* XI, 12, (March, 1969), 2.

301. "AB 119 Put Over To April 2," *California AFL-CIO News,* XI, 13, (March, 1969), 1.

302. Statement by César E. Chávez before the Sub-Committee on Labor, April 16, 1969.

303. "State Fed Compiles A Long List Of Bad Bills," *California AFL-CIO News,* XI, 18 (May, 1969), 4.

304. "Labor At The Legislature," *California AFL-CIO News,* XI, 19 (May, 1969), 1.

305. "Meany Raps Nixon Farm Worker Plan," *California AFL-CIO News,* XI, 21 (May, 1969), 4.

306. Ibid.

307. "Hearings Set On RTW Threat to Farm Workers," *California AFL-CIO News,* XI, 22, (May, 1969), 1.

308. "The Fight To Ban DDT," *Farm Journal,* June 1969, p. 15.

309. "State Agriculture Board Takes Stand On Labor," *California Farmer,* June 7, 1969, p. 12A.

310. Pickett, Jack, "Editorially Speaking, Senator Cranston's Views On Farm Labor," *California Farmer,* June 7, 1969, p. 6.

311. "Labor At The Legislature," *California AFL-CIO News,* XI, 25 (June, 1969), 4.

312. Pryor, Alton, "Farm Union Must Dance To A Different Tune," *California Farmer,* June 21, 1969, p. 9.

313. Finley, Paul, "Should We Limit Government Payments For Farm," *Farm Journal,* July, 1969, p. 15.

314. Gong, W. R. Paage (Tex), "Should We Limit Government Payments For Farm," *Farm Journal,* July, 1969, p. 1.

315. "Meany Debunks Grower Claims At Senate Hearing," *California AFL-CIO News,* XI, 29 (July, 1969), 1.

316. "Labor At The Legislature," *California AFL-CIO News,* XI, 34 (August, 1969), 1.

317. "Murphy's Bill Hit," *California AFL-CIO News,* XI, 34 (August, 1969), 4.

318. "Two Federation Bills To Governor's Desk," *California AFL-CIO News,* XI, 33 (August, 1969), p. 1.

319. "What's A Senator Done For—Or To—You Since 1964?" *California AFL-CIO News,* XI, 35 (August, 1969), p. 2.

320. "Pesticide Scare Attempt By Union Gets Court Hearing," *California Farmer*, September 20, 1969, p. 24.

321. "State Farm Study Points Up Value Of Unions," *California AFL-CIO News*, XI, 40 (October, 1969), 1.

322. "Is There Hope Of Federal Farm Labor Law Soon?" *California Farmer*, December 13, 1969, p. 7.

323. "Government's Plan To Phase Out 'Persistent' Chemicals," *Farm Journal*, January, 1970, pp. 20, 21.

324. "Neither Growers Nor Unions Want State Labor Legislation," *California Farmer*, January 3, 1970, p. 18.

325. Ibid.

326. "Fed Raps Farm Bd's Action On Grape Boycott," *California AFL-CIO News*, XII, 2, (January, 1970), 1.

327. "Far More Farm Workers Poisoned, State Study Finds," *California AFL-CIO News*, XII, 6, (February, 1970), 3.

328. "Big Calif. Farms Get Lion's Share of Federal Handout," *California AFL-CIO News*, XII, 17, (April, 1970), 1, 4. See also, U.S. *Congressional Record*, 91st Cong., 2d Sess., (1970), CXVI, No. 9, 11307.

329. "NLRB Moves Against Chávez," *California Farmer*, May 2, 1970, p. 10.

330. "Senator Murphy's Farm Labor Bill Clears Hurdle," *Salinas Californian*, July 18, 1972, pp. 1, 2.

331. "A Closer Look At Gov. Reagan's Plan For Farm Labor Elections," *California AFL-CIO News*, XIII, 30, (July, 1970), 4.

332. Ibid.

333. Ibid.

334. "Farm Bureau's Proud Of Killing Pesticide Bill," *California AFL-CIO News*, XIII, 35, (August, 1970), 1.

335. "Farm Bill Condemned By Labor," *Salinas Californian*, September 3, 1970, p. 2.

336. Pickett, "Editorially Speaking: Who Lost the Most?" *California Farmer*, October 3, 1970, p. 6.

337. Gifford, Claude W., "What's In That New Farm Law," *Farm Journal*, November, 1970, p. 17.

338. "Growers Told, 'Legislation Is Answer,'" *California Farmer*, December 12, 1970, p. 22.

339. SB40, Harmer, (Section 1137), January 5, 1971, pp. 1-2.

340. AB53, Burton, Brown, and Garcia (Section 1161), January 6, 1971, p. 1.

341. AB83, Wood (Section 1130), January 11, 1971, p. 1.

342. "Fed Asks Action To Prohibit 'Wetback' Strikebreakers," *California AFL-CIO News*, XLV, 3 (January, 1971), 1.

343. U.S. House, Committee on Education and Labor House of Representatives, Subcommittee on Agricultural Labor, *Summaries of Legislative Proposals Relating To Labor Management Relations In Agriculture*, 92nd Congress, 2d Sess., April, 1972, (Washington: Government Printing Office, 1972), p. 5.

344. Ibid., p. 6-7.

345. Ibid., p. 8.

346. Ibid., p. 9.

347. "Farmers Seeking New Legislation," *Salinas Californian,* February 12, 1971, p. 17.

348. "Growers Change By-Laws; Discuss Farm Labor Legislation," *Salinas Californian,* February 16, 1971, p. 13.

349. AB639, Ketchum and others, (Section 1140), February 24, 1971.

350. Burke, William R. "Health and Welfare Bills," *Legislative Bulletin,* No. 2 (February 26, 1971), 1.

351. SB432, Petris, (Section 24375), March 1, 1971, p. 1.

352. California Church Council, "Agribusiness Farm Labor Struggle," *Legislative News Alert,* No. 6 (March 12, 1971), 2.

353. California Church Council, "Agribusiness Farm Labor Struggle," *Legislative News Alert,* No. 5 (March 5, 1971), 2.

354. AB844, Burton (Section 1137), March 8, 1971.

355. "State AFL-CIO Wins Final Victory In Con Labor Suit," *California AFL-CIO News,* XIV, 11 (March 1971), 1.

356. "State Farm Labor Measure Proposed," *Salinas Californian,* March 16, 1971, p. 1.

357. U.S., *Congressional Record,* 92d Cong., 1st Session (1971), CXVII, No. 42.

358. AB1355, Fenton, March 30, 1971, p. 1.

359. "Farm Labor Bill Support Urged," *Salinas Californian,* March 29, 1971, p. 1.

360. "Out Look Favorable For Expanding Farm Credit," *Salinas Californian,* April 8, 1971, p. 5.

361. "Why Chávez Spurns The Labor Act," *The Nation,* April 12, 1971, p. 454-455.

362. AB3049, Wilson, April 16, 1971.

363. "Bills To Extend U. I. Coverage Taken Under Submission," *California AFL-CIO News,* XIV, 19 (May, 1971), p. 2.

364. California Church Council, *Legislative News Alert,* April 30, 1971, p. 1.

365. "Cranston Urges 10 Fold Increase In Funds For Farm Labor," *California AFL-CIO News,* XIV, 22 (June, 1971), p. 2.

366. "Bill To Curb Use Of Illegal Aliens Ok'd," *California AFL-CIO News,* XIV, 23 (June, 1971), p. 2.

367. "Cory-Wood Bill Passage Hopeful," *Salinas Californian,* June 10, 1971, p. 4.

368. "What's Up . . . In Sacramento," *California AFL-CIO News,* XLV, 23 (June, 1971), p. 3.

369. "UFWOC Opposes Farm Labor Bill," *Salinas Californian,* June 22, 1971, p. 4.

370. "Cory-Wood Bill Clears Hurdle," *Salinas Californian,* June 24, 1971, p. 15.

371. *Friends Committee On Legislation Newsletter,* XX; 7 (July, 1971), p. 3.

372. "State Labor Council Urges Solons To Act In Job Crisis," *California AFL-CIO News,* XIV, 27 (July, 1971), p. 1.

373. "Oregon Farm Labor Bill Vetoed; Threats Criticized," *Salinas Californian,* July 3, 1971, p. 15.

374. California Church Council, "Farm Labor Bill Killed," *Legislative News Alert,* No. 23 (July 9, 1971), p. 1.

375. "No Farm Labor Bill Is Inexcusable; UFWOC Workers Skip Valley Harvesting," *Salinas Californian,* July 8, 1971, p. 6.

376. "3000 Hail Defeat of Farm Labor Bill: Strong Protest by Unions Torpedo Anti-UFWOC Measure," *California AFL-CIO News,* XIV, 28 (July, 1971), p. 1.

377. "Green Card Commuters To Continue Work," *California Farmer,* July 17, 1971, p. 48.

378. "Chávez Fears Farm Labor Bill," *Salinas Californian,* July 27, 1971, p. 4.

379. "Reagan Backs Farm Labor Secret Ballot," *Salinas Californian,* July 29, 1971, p. 1.

380. "Illegal Alien's Curb Gets Assembly OK," *California AFL-CIO News,* XIV, 31, (July, 1971), p. 1.

381. California Church Council, "U.I. for Farm Workers," *Legislative News Alert,* No. 26 (July 30, 1971), p. 2.

382. H.R. 10499, 92d Cong., 1st Sess., August 6, 1971.

383. "Farm Labor Vote Back By Reinecke," *Salinas Californian,* August 4, 1971, p. 3.

384. Ibid., p. 21.

385. U.S., House, Committee on Education and Labor House of Representatives Subcommittee on Agricultural Labor, *Summaries of Legislative Proposals Relating to Labor Management Relations In Agriculture,* 92d Congress, 2d Sess., April, 1971 (Washington: Government Printing Office, 1972), p. 90.

386. Ibid., p. 91.

387. "The Orderly Way In Labor Relations," *Salinas Californian,* August 26, 1971, p. 2.

388. *Friends Committee on Legislation Newsletter,* XX: 7 (August-September, 1971).

389. *Salinas Californian,* loc. cit.

390. "Anti-Worker Farm Labor Bill Defeated In Assembly," *California AFL-CIO News,* XIV, 38 (September, 1971), p. 1.

391. "Farm U.I. Pay and Workman's Comp. Bills Move Ahead," *California AFL-CIO News,* XIV, 39 (September, 1971), p. 1.

392. "Bill Would Help Farm Bargaining Groups," *California Farmer,* September 18, 1971, p. 20.

393. "Colorado To Enact Farm Bill," *Salinas Californian,* September 18, 1971, p. 2.

394. Based on correspondence between United Farm Workers, AFL-CIO, San Jose Office and Union supporters, (October 25, 1971).

395. U.S., *Congressional Record,* 92d Cong., 1st Sess., (1971) CXVII, No. 139.

396. "Twenty Years Of Struggle," *El Malcriado,* Emergency Issue (October, 1971), p. 2.

397. "Harmer Farm Labor Bill Passes Senate," *Salinas Californian,* October 5, 1971, p. 1.

398. "Farm Jobless Bill Approved," *Salinas Californian,* November 8, 1971, p. 1.

399. AB 528, Dixon-Arnett (Section 2805), November 8, 1971, p. 1.

400. "U.I. Pay for Farm Workers Up for Full Senate Vote," *California AFL-CIO News,* XIV, 46 (November, 1971), p. 4.

401. "Farm U.I. Pay Bill Wins Senate Approval 22-11," *California AFL-CIO News*, XIV, 47 (November, 1971), p. 1.

402. Pickett, Jack, "Editorially Speaking: Forced to Turn to the Initiative Route," *California Farmer*, November 20, 1971, p. 6.

403. "Farm Jobless Insurance Bill Provides S65 Weekly Checks," *Salinas Californian*, November 23, 1971, p. 17.

404. "Future of State's Farm Workers Rests With Voters," *Salinas Californian*, November 29, 1971, p. 4.

405. "AFL-CIO, Chávez Oppose Banuelos Appointment; Cranston Backs Her," *California AFL-CIO News*, XIV, 49 (December, 1971), p. 1.

406. *Friends Committee on Legislation Newsletter*, XX: 11 (December, 1971), p. 2.

407. "The Farm Labor Initiative," *California Farmer*, December 11, 1971, p. 7.

408. "Farm Worker Jobless Insurance Bill Vetoed," *Salinas Californian*, December 11, 1971, p. 7.

409. "Big Farm Subsidy Foe Sees Crackdown in '73," *Salinas Californian*, December 27, 1971, p. 29.

410. "Wood Puts In Farm Bill," *Salinas Californian*, January 3, 1972, p. 1.

411. "Farm Union Key To Better Living Standards, Fed Says," *California AFL-CIO News*, XV, 2 (January, 1972), p. 1.

412. Ibid., 2.

413. AB 246, Wood and others (Section 12980), January 27, 1972, 1-2.

414. "Signatures Still Sought for Farm Initiative," *Salinas Californian*, January 29, 1972, p. 2.

415. Hartmire, Jr., Wayne C., "Understanding The Farm Workers' Position On Legislation," *National Farm Worker Ministry*, (January, 1972).

416. Hartmire, Jr., Wayne C., "Elections And Legislation In Agriculture," *National Farm Worker Ministry*, (January, 1972).

417. Berger, Samuel F., *Dollar Harvest: The Story Of The Farm Bureau*, (Massachusetts: Heath-Lexington, and Company, 1971), VIII.

418. AB 315, Brophy, (Section 2803), February 3, 1972.

419. "Strikebreaker Ban Needed, Fed Tells Panel," *California AFL-CIO News*, XV, 5 (February, 1972).

420. *San Jose Mercury*, March 11, 1972, p. 2.

421. "NLRB Ploy To Curb Farm Union Rapped As Unjust," *California AFL-CIO News*, XV, 11 (March, 1972).

422. "Collective Bargaining By Agricultural Employees: Idaho Agricultural Labor Act," *Labor Law Reports* (April 7, 1972).

423. *Friends Committee On Legislation Newsletter*, XXI, 3 (March 27, 1972).

424. Statement by Senator Edward M. Kennedy, March 29, 1972.

425. Ibid., 2.

426. "Senate Considering Farm Antipollution Subsidies," *Salinas Californian*, April 19, 1972, p. 18.

427. California Church Council, "Protect Family Type Farmer," *Legislative News Alert*, 12 (April 28, 1972), p. 2.

428. "Plan To Discredit Farm Bureau Told," *Salinas Californian*, May 2, 1972, p. 13.

429. HB 2134, 30th Legislature, 2d Session, Chapter 137.

430. "Chávez Opposes New Bill," *Salinas Californian,* May 13, 1972, p. 2.

431. Based on personal correspondence between César Chávez, Director, United Farm Workers, AFL-CIO and Union Supporters (May 15, 1972).

432. "Arizona Sets Example," *Salinas Californian,* June 19, 1972, p. 4.

433. "Chávez Raps Farm Initiative," *Salinas Californian,* June 30, 1972, p. 1.

434. "Collective Bargaining By Agricultural Employees: The Kansas Agricultural Employment Relations Act," *Labor Law Reports* (November 3, 1972).

435. Based on correspondence from César Chávez, Director, United Farm Workers, AFL-CIO to Churches (August 30, 1972).

436. "State's Bishops Oppose Proposition 22," *California Citizens' No On Proposition 22 Committee* (1972), p. 3.

437. Based on statement by Jerry Cohen, General Legal Counsel for United Farm Workers, AFL-CIO on Proposition 22.

438. U.S., House, Committee on Education and Labor House of Representatives, Subcommittee on Agricultural Labor, *Summaries of Legislative Proposals Relating To Labor Management Relations In Agriculture,* 92d Congress, 2d Sess., April, 1972, (Washington: Government Printing Office, 1972), p. 13.

PART IV

LA EDUCACION

INTRODUCTION

Just as the articles in PART III represent original and outstanding articulations by Chicano writers toward our better understanding of Chicano history, so too do the following articles enable us to better understand the web of relationships which currently exist between the Chicano community and the world of socialization which is called education.

The selections on education begin with the most comprehensive study ever written that deals with schools, Mexican-Americans, segregation and desegregation, "Mexican-Americans and the Desegregation of Schools in the Southwest" by Guadalupe Salinas. Here, once again, the Chicano population is seen as active and participating in issues of importance to them. Just as community organizing goes back for decades, just as union activities similarly date back equally long, just as Chicano influence upon contemporary music patterns also extends back in time, as so many other facets of Chicano activities, so, too, does the Chicano struggle for adequate and significant education trace back in history. Mr. Salinas, now with M.A.L.D.E.F. in San Antonio, Texas, has very competently provided us with this very comprehensive panorama.

Mr. Manuel Ramirez then pinpoints equally important issues that, basically, keep open the questions that surround the relationships between education and acculturation. The contents of this article provide enough leads for future research to keep someone busy for some time to come. Needless to say, the last word on this subject has not been heard.

Hardly a Chicano exists who has not at one time or another pondered about those procedures and processes which result in the placing of Chicano children in public school classes for the mentally and educationally retarded. Mr. Frank Ortega not only pondered the question, he delved into the intricacies of the processes by which this is done. His findings constitute what many had previously suspected, but not documented. That is, the assignment of Mexican-American children to such classes exceeds what can be expected under a fair, impartial, and normal process. Recently, protests about these practices have taken place from California to the state of Michigan, virtually wherever Chicanos live.

Those who choose to pursue this matter further, either in research or in educational policy, by all means should digest the contents of the next article, "Problems Related to Present Testing Instruments" by

Steve Moreno. Herein, Mr. Moreno questions the validity (and reliability) of testing instruments as applied to Chicano children.

This selection of articles on education is closed, or should I say highlighted, by the remarkable study of language, linguistics, and education by Rosaura Sánchez. This work, clearly, is of fundamental importance to the issues raised by Salinas, Ramirez, Ortega, and Moreno. In short, the questions involving segregation, ethnic identifiability, acculturation, testing, bilingualism, and biculturalism are all dealt with by these authors. In addition, it goes without saying that these questions have been and continue to be of central concern to Chicano communities across the nation.

At this juncture, one can only add that there is an extremely strong temptation to commend the following authors for their serious and competent efforts which have opened so many new doors, and, equally important, have kept so many old doors open as well.

The following article by Mr. Guadalupe Salinas originally appeared in the HOUSTON LAW REVIEW, Volume 8, 1971, pp. 929-951. (Copyright: HOUSTON LAW REVIEW). It is reprinted here with permission from the Editor of the REVIEW and the author. Although it is not the usual policy of EL GRITO to reprint articles published elsewhere, an exception is made in this case because of the significance of the subject matter, and in order to bring it to the attention of the nation's largest Chicano reading audience of Chicano literature.

In the SUPPLEMENT, which immediately follows the original article, the author discusses more recent developments that concern segregation-desegregation and Mexican-Americans. The SUPPLEMENT was written by Mr. Salinas especially for EL GRITO. —The Editors

— MEXICAN-AMERICANS AND THE DESEGREGATION — OF SCHOOLS IN THE SOUTHWEST

Guadalupe Salinas

I. INTRODUCTION

On June 4, 1970, Federal District Judge Woodrow Seals, in *Cisneros v. Corpus Christi Independent School District*,[1] held that Mexican-Americans are an "identifiable ethnic minority group" for the purpose of public school desegregation.[2] Because Mexican-Americans are an identifiable group and have been subjected to discrimination in the Corpus Christi, Texas area, Judge Seals stated that Mexican-Americans are entitled to the same protection afforded Negroes under the landmark decision of *Brown v. Board of Education*.[3] The court found that the school district segregated Mexican-Americans, as well as Negroes, to such an extent that a dual school system resulted.[4] The parties were then asked to submit a desegregation plan which considered the three major ethnic groups: Negro, Mexican-American, and Anglo, that is, other whites besides Mexican-Americans.[5]

Cisneros is unique in that it is the first case in which a court officially recognized Mexican-Americans as an *identifiable ethnic minority group* for the purposes of public school desegregation. Before proceeding with a discussion of the significance of being an *identifiable ethnic minority group*, a definition of the phrase may be conducive to a better understanding of the court's holding. Mexican-Americans are considered by some to be a non-white racial group. However, the predominant view is that Mexican-Americans are white, even though many are *mestizos* (a hybrid of white and Indian). Nevertheless, like other white nationality groups who have been victims of discrimination, for example, the Jewish and Italian-Americans, Mexican-Americans have inherent characteristics which make them easily identifiable and susceptible to discrimination. Among these characteristics are brown skin color, a Spanish surname, and the Spanish language. The fact that this group is of Mexican descent and has certain inherent characteristics makes it an *identifiable ethnic group.*

Judge Seals characterized Mexican-Americans as an ethnic *minority* group. Mexican-Americans definitely are a numerical minority in the United States, representing about 2.5 percent of the population.[6] In Texas, this ethnic group comprises 14.5 percent of the population.[7] In Corpus Christi, where *Cisneros* arose, Mexican-Americans comprise 35.7 percent of the population.[8] However, Judge Seals does not rely on mere numbers to determine whether an ethnic group is a minority group. His principal test is whether the group is discriminated against in the schools through segregation, a discrimination facilitated by the group's economic and political impotence.[9] Thus, Mexican-Americans are an *identifiable ethnic minority group,* even in areas where they are the majority since many are economically and politically disadvantaged.

The court's holding, that Mexican-Americans are entitled to the protection given Negroes by *Brown,* is significant because it introduces a new group into the desegregation process. Federal courts should consider Mexican-American students in determining whether a unitary school system is in operation. More importantly, the court's recognition of Mexican-Americans should serve as a restraint on school districts which utilize the Mexican-American's classification of white by integrating them with Negroes to satisfy court desegregation orders. Further discussion about the mixing of Negroes and Mexican-Americans in minority schools is presented in parts IV and VI-B.

This comment seeks to analyze whether Mexican-Americans should be considered an identifiable ethnic minority group for purposes of public school desegregation. After providing a brief history of the American of Mexican descent, the writer will discuss various civil rights problems encountered by Mexican-Americans and, more importantly the evolution of the desegregation doctrine as it pertains to Mexican-Americans.

II. HISTORICAL BACKGROUND
OF THE MEXICAN-AMERICAN

Mexican-Americans are the second largest minority group in the United States.[10] In the Southwest (an area including Arizona, California, Colorado, New Mexico, and Texas), where 87 percent of this minority group resides, Mexican-Americans are the largest minority group.[11]

In the 1500's the Spanish began to settle this area, many years before the English established the first settlement at Jamestown in 1607. This early Spanish influence is evidenced in the number of States, cities, and rivers with Spanish names.[12] These Southwestern States came under Mexican rule after Mexico won her independence from Spain in 1821.

However, the vast Mexican nation encountered internal problems when Texas seceded in 1836 and again when the United States Congress voted in 1845 to allow Texas to enter the Union. Mexico had warned that admission into the Union would be equivalent to an act of war. In spite of Mexico's relative military weakness compared to the United States, the two countries engaged in armed conflict. The result was the defeat of Mexico and the signing of the Treaty of Guadalupe Hidalgo on February 2, 1848.[13] By the terms of the treaty, Mexico acknowledged the annexation of Texas and ceded the rest of the Southwest to the United States. In addition, the treaty guaranteed civil and property rights to those who became American citizens.[14]

Approximately 75,000 Mexicans decided to remain and receive American citizenship.[15] These Mexican-Americans were later supplemented by vast emigrations from Mexico. The first influx, precipitated by the social revolution in Mexico, began in 1910. A second wave of immigrants resulted in the increase of the Mexican-American population by nearly one million from 1910 to 1930. During and after World War II, attracted by the agricultural labor market, a third group of Mexicans came to the United States.[16] In addition, about 3500 Mexicans immigrate to this country each month, thus continuing the steady growth of the Mexican-American population.[17]

With the increase of the Mexican-American population, there was an increase in the prejudice of the predominant Anglo society. For example, Mexican-Americans, as well as Mexican nationals, were deported during the Great Depression to reduce the welfare rolls.[18] This prejudice resulted in the "largest mass trial for murder ever in the United States."[19] Such prejudice also led to the so-called "zoot suit" riots of 1943 in Los Angeles. The riots began when city police refused to intervene while over a hundred sailors roamed the streets for nearly a week beating and stripping Mexican-American youths in retaliation for the beating some sailors had received earlier from a gang of "zoot suiters."[20]

As a result of these and similar discriminatory practices, Mexican-American interest groups began to organize in order to defend La Raza (the race), as Mexican-Americans call themselves. In 1927 the League of United Latin American Citizens (LULAC) was formed in Texas. Shortly thereafter LULAC helped fund the first challenge against the segregation of Mexican-American school children.[21] In 1948, a Mexican-American war veteran, Dr. Hector P. Garcia, founded the American GI Forum for the purpose of protecting Mexican-American veterans from discriminatory practices which they "were being subjected to in the areas of education, employment, medical attention and housing . . . ."[22] The American GI Forum, which now has many chapters throughout the United States, has also helped support civil rights litigation.

In spite of the successes which LULAC and the GI Forum have accomplished, many Mexican-American youths have not been satisfied. Unlike their elders, Mexican-American youth activists, or *Chicanos* (the term is a derivation of *mejicano,* which is the Spanish term for Mexican), as they like to be called, refuse to be satisfied with justice on the installment plan, that is, gradual social progress. Instead, this new breed demands justice and equality for *La Raza* now.

In order to promote the advancement of Mexican-Americans, *Chicanos* throughout the Southwest have organized in recent years, mainly on college campuses.[23] For example, the Mexican-American Youth Organization (MAYO), which was founded in 1967 by San Antonio college students,[24] is currently organized at the two largest universities in Texas, The University of Texas and the University of Houston. In addition, MAYO chapters are active in the *barrios* (neighborhoods where the Mexican-American population is predominant).

The Mexican-American Legal Defense and Educational Fund (MALDEF), a *Chicano* (the term is not limited in its application to the youth activists) civil rights organization which was created in 1968,[25] is even more effective than these political groups. The previous lack of a legal defense organization perhaps best explains why Mexican-Americans have not been too active in civil rights litigation. In fact, the Supreme Court of the United States has decided a *Chicano* civil rights issue on only one occasion.[26] However, legal activities of MALDEF prompted a newspaper to note that "[m]ore legal attention has been focused on the problems of Texas' nearly two million Mexican-Americans during the past 11 months than during the entire history of *La Raza* in Texas."[27] This statement is applicable as well to the rest of the Southwest.[28]

III. THE MEXICAN-AMERICAN—AN IDENTIFIABLE ETHNIC MINORITY GROUP

A. *The Mexican-American*

Mexican-Americans, as a group, have been widely discriminated against. As a result, many Mexican-Americans have easily been able to identify with *La Raza.* On the other hand, there are many Mexican-Americans who have never personally experienced an act of discrimination and thus, find it difficult to empathize with the civil rights movement. Many of these adamantly assert that they are Americans and fail to identify with Mexican-Americans. In many cases, a light-skinned complexion has helped make life more "American" for them.[29] In addition, there are some who feel a stigma or a handicap if the term "Mexican" is used to describe them and who prefer a euphemistic label like Latin American or Spanish-speaking American. Finally, there is a group who, because of their ancestry of early Spanish colonists, call themselves Spanish-Americans and Hispanos. Nevertheless, in spite of what Spanish-surnamed Americans of the Southwest prefer to be called, the name Mexican-American is perhaps the best designation which can be applied objectively. Regardless of what they call themselves, one fact is clear—either they or their ancestors, including the Spanish colonists, came "north from Mexico."[30]

B. *Discrimination in Areas Besides Education*

1. *Employment*

Mexican-Americans, like Negroes, have encountered discriminatory practices by employers in hiring and promotion. What is worse, is that much of this discrimination is subtle. Employers often use the "high school diploma" or "we'll call you" tactics since they can no longer discriminate openly with impunity. As a result, it is often difficult to maintain a civil rights action. Since the Civil Rights Act of 1964[31] was passed, at least one Mexican-American has been successful, and many more cases have been filed. The one successful claim is the agreement reached in the case of *Urquidez v. General Telephone Co.*[32] The suit, a class action, resulted from the fact that Urquidez applied for employment, passed the tests, and had more job-related experience and education than several Anglo applicants who were subsequently hired. The settlement agreement acknowledged that Urquidez had a prima facie case of discrimination, awarded him $2,000, and provided that General Telephone would take definite steps to remedy past discriminatory practices.

In spite of the unusually small number of cases in the field of employment discrimination, the statistics and evidence indicate that discriminatory practices are very prevalent. For example, considering the Southwest alone, the unemployment rate among Mexican-Americans is double the Anglo rate—a statistic which understates the severity of the situation since farm workers are not included in unemployment statistics.[33] In addition, in 1960, 79 percent of all Mexican-American workers held unskilled and semi-skilled jobs.[34]

While some of the employment problems facing Mexican-Americans are attributable to their relatively low educational attainment,[35] there are indications of discrimination to offset much of that argument. For instance, in comparing the income of Mexican-Americans and Anglos who have completed the same number of school years, the income of Mexican-Americans is only 60 to 80 percent of the Anglo income.[36] Since passage of the Civil Rights Act of 1964, employers have resorted to more subtle practices, such as promoting Anglos before Mexican-Americans, even if the former are less educated and less skilled. Many employers, when questioned about such practices, rationalize that Anglo workers will not take orders from Mexican-Americans.[37] Consequently, the Mexican-American is denied the equal protection of the laws as guaranteed him by the Constitution of the United States[38] and by the Civil Rights Act of 1964.

As previously stated, many employment discrimination cases have been instituted, mostly by MALDEF-assisted plaintiffs. Two of these cases were delayed by motions to dismiss which have been denied,[39] and the cases are set for a hearing on the merits. MALDEF lists 15 additional pending cases.[40] Among the grounds urged for relief are: (1) refusal to hire because of national origin; (2) failure to promote over less-educated and less-experienced Anglos; (3) hiring Mexican-Americans only for low-paying positions; (4) paying different wages to Mexican-Americans and Anglos; and (5) underemployment while Anglos with less seniority are allowed more work time.[41]

One pending case, *Quiroz v. James H. Matthews & Co.*,[42] challenges some of the subtle, covert practices employers commonly use to deny Mexican-Americans equal opportunity. Quiroz alleges violation of his equal employment rights under Title VII of the Civil Rights Act of 1964.[43] The plaintiff, who had 16 years' experience, was replaced by an Anglo who had less job-related experience. Furthermore, Quiroz contends that the defendant pays Mexican-American employees less than fellow Anglo employees receive for doing the same kind of work.[44]

2. Spanish and Mexican Land Grants

Mexican-Americans have also suffered unjustly in the area of Spanish and Mexican land grants, an issue encountered generally in New Mexico and Colorado. The issue is whether Mexican-American land grantees or the heirs of these grantees, who by some means were defrauded of their land by various state officials, are entitled to compensation.

This issue was raised in *Vigil v. United States*,[45] a class action filed for those descendants of Spanish-surnamed Americans who lived in areas ceded to the United States by Mexico in 1848. The plaintiffs sought $1 million actual damages and $1 million punitive damages for each individual who was part of the class. However, the court held that the vague allegations in the complaint failed to satisfy the Federal Tort Claims Act and that there was no claim against the United States under the Civil Rights Acts for deprivation of property.

Although that complaint was vague, one *Chicano* writer has been more specific.[46] He claims Mexican-Americans have lost nearly four million acres of land.[47] This loss has occurred even though Article VIII of the Treaty of Guadalupe Hidalgo provides:

> The present owners, the heirs of these, and all Mexicans who may hereafter acquire said property by contract, shall enjoy with respect to it guaranties equally ample as if the same belonged to citizens of the United States.[48]

The writer argues that the shift from the Mexican legal system, where grant lands were immune from taxation and titles were unregistered, to the Anglo legal system of land taxation and title recordation was the major factor in the land losses which Mexican-Americans suffered.[49] Many landowners were divested of title by wealthy Anglo ranchers purchasing deeds at tax sales or by recording a claim to the property before the true owner.[50] Perhaps federal courts will grant relief to these aggrieved heirs of the land grantees when and if the complaints are clarified.

3. Public Accommodations

Mexican-Americans have been excluded from public accommodations. Fortunately the practice has subsided since the 1940's when Mexican-Americans were segregated from restaurants, theaters, and swimming pools.[51] Nevertheless, prejudice and overt acts of discrimination have contributed to making Mexican-Americans an identifiable ethnic minority group.

In 1944 Texas upheld the right of a proprietor to exclude any person for any reason whatsoever, including the fact that the person was of Mexican descent.[52] However, that same year a federal court in California held that Mexican-Americans *are* entitled to public accommodations such as other citizens enjoy.[53] In spite of this ruling and the Civil Rights Act of 1964, a federal court in 1968 found it necessary to enjoin the exclusion of Mexican-Americans from public swimming pool facilities.[54]

4. Administration of Justice

Mexican-Americans also face serious discrimination in the administration of justice. This discrimination, as well as the personal prejudice of police officers, often leads to physical and psychological injury to Mexican-Americans.[55] However, Mexican-Americans, like other minority groups, have encountered difficulty in getting grand juries to return indictments against police officers who use excessive force and insulting, derogatory language.[56] In one case a Mexican-American woman won a civil damages suit against a police officer.[57] The plaintiff claimed she had suffered physical and mental damages because of being forcefully undressed by two policewomen and two policemen to see if she had any concealed narcotics. Earlier, when the officers had entered the plaintiff's residence without a search warrant, the plaintiff demanded respect for her constitutional rights, but one officer told her to "go back to Mexico."[58]

Besides the treatment received from law enforcement officials,[59] Mexican-Americans are often inadequately represented on juries. Consequently, the juries hearing cases involving Mexican-American defendants are not "impartial"[60] juries since they fail to represent the community. These inequities still occur frequently, even though the United States Supreme Court held in *Hernandez v. Texas*[61] that "[t]he exclusion of otherwise eligible [Mexican-Americans] from jury service solely because of their ancestry or national origin is discrimination prohibited by the Fourteenth Amendment."[62] The Court stated that the absence of a Mexican-American juror for 25 years in a county where this ethnic group comprised 14 percent of the population "bespeaks discrimination, whether or not it was a conscious decision on the part of any individual jury commissioner."[63]

Prior to *Hernandez*, Texas courts refused to recognize the Mexican-American as a separate class—distinct from other whites—for purposes of determining whether there was an unconstitutional exclusion from juries.[64] The Texas courts limited the application of the equal protection clause to two classes, whites and Negroes. Since Mexican-Americans were legally considered white, the equal protection clause did not apply.

Nevertheless, this weak argument was overruled by the Supreme Court in *Hernandez* when it held that Mexican-Americans are a separate class, distinct from whites. The Court noted that historically "differences in race and color have defined *easily identifiable* groups which have at times required the aid of the courts in securing equal treatment under the laws."[65] Since *Hernandez*, courts have recognized Mexican-Americans as an identifiable ethnic group, although they have not always found discrimination.[66]

Recently, the Fifth Circuit overturned the 1942 rape conviction of a Mexican-American in El Paso County, Texas, because the juries that indicted and convicted him had excluded persons of his ethnic group.[67] Only 18 of the 600 grand jurors who served from 1936 to 1947 were Mexican-Americans, even though the county population was 15 to 20 percent Mexican-American.[68] The court stated that these figures "cry out 'discrimination' with unmistakable clarity."[69]

Although the discussion of discrimination toward Mexican-Americans dealt only with the issues of employment, land grants, public accommodations, and the administration of justice, this in no way limits the areas in which Mexican-Americans encounter injustices.[70] The issues discussed were selected to justify the holding in *Cisneros*, that Mexican-Americans are an identifiable ethnic minority group entitled to the protection of the 14th amendment in the area of school desegregation in the Southwest.

C. *Non-Judicial Recognition*

The Mexican-American has been recognized as a separate, identifiable group not only by the courts but also by other governmental institutions. For instance, the Civil Rights Act of 1964, by use of the term "national origin,"[71] impliedly includes Mexican-Americans and other "national origin" minority groups such as Puerto Ricans. Furthermore, recognizing the problems facing many Mexican-American school children, Congress passed the Bilingual Education Act[72] which seeks to facilitate the learning of English and at the same time allow the Spanish-speaking child to perfect his mother language and regain self-esteem through the encouraged learning of Spanish.[73] In addition, Congress created a cabinet committee whose purpose is to assure that federal programs are reaching Mexican-Americans and all other Spanish-speaking groups.[74] Also, through the creation of the United States Civil Rights Commission in 1957, Congress and the public have become better informed as to the injustices Mexican-Americans endure.[75] Other governmental agencies have researched the living conditions of the Mexican-American.[76] Finally, the Department of Health, Education, and Welfare (HEW) has issued regulations which prohibit the denial of equal educational opportunity on the basis of English language deficiency. The regulations apply to school districts accepting federally assisted programs and having at least 5 percent Mexican-American enrollment.[77]

IV. THE CHICANO SCHOOL CASES

Since all three branches of government recognize Mexican-Americans as a minority group, the question which must be answered is whether *Chicano* students have been discriminated against by school districts to such an extent as to warrant their inclusion as a separate ethnic group in the desegregation plans for public schools in the Southwest. In other words, does the history of Mexican-American school children in the predominantly Anglo school systems of the Southwest demand recognition of this educationally disadvantaged group as being separate and distinct from whites?

The practice of maintaining separate schools throughout the Southwest was never sanctioned by any State statute, although in California, a statute allowing separate schools for "Mongolians" and "Indians" was interpreted to include Mexican-Americans in the latter group.[78] Generally, the segregation of Mexican-Americans was enforced by the customs and regulations of school districts throughout the Southwest. Nevertheless, the segregation was de jure since sufficient State action was involved.

The struggle by Mexican-Americans against separate and unequal schools has been lengthy. In 1930 a Texas appellate court held in *Independent School District v. Salvatierra*[79] that school authorities in Del Rio, or anywhere else, have no power to segregate *Chicano* children "merely or solely because they are [Mexican-Americans]."[80] However, the school district successfully argued that the children's language deficiencies warranted their separate schooling, even though the superintendent conceded that "generally the best way to learn a language is to be associated with the people who speak that language."[81] The Attorney General of Texas later supported this holding by justifying education of the linguistically deficient in separate classrooms and even in separate buildings if necessary.[82]

The first federal district court decision in this area was *Mendez v. Westminister School District*[83] in 1946. The court held that the equal protection of the laws pertaining to the public school system in California is not met by providing "separate schools [with] the same technical facilities"[84] for Mexican-American children—words which are strikingly similar to the Supreme Court's holding in *Brown* 8 years later that "[s]eparate education facilities are inherently unequal."[85] The court observed that "[a] paramount requisite in the American system of public education is social equality. It must be open to all children by unified school association regardless of lineage."[86]

On appeal, the Ninth Circuit affirmed *Mendez*, finding that the school officials had acted "under color of State law" in segregating the Mexican-American students.[87] The appellate court reasoned that since the California segregation statute did not expressly include Mexican-Americans, their segregation denied due process and the equal protection of the laws.[88]

Following the landmark ruling in *Mendez*, a federal district court in Texas, in *Delgado v. Bastrop Independent School District*,[89] held that the segregation practices of the district were "arbitrary and discriminatory and in violation of [the 14th amendment]."[90] In addition, the court's instructions to Texas school districts stipulated that separate classes for those which language deficiencies must be on the same campus with all other students,[91] thereby denying school officials the power to justify completely separate Mexican-American schools by use of the language deficiency argument.

Nevertheless, the *Delgado* requirement did not prevent the creation of evasive schemes in order to maintain segregated school facilities. For example, in Driscoll, Texas, school authorities customarily required a majority of the Mexican-American children to spend 3 years in the first grade before promotion to the second.[92] After the *Delgado* case, Driscoll abandoned the maintenance of separate schools for Anglos and Mexican-Americans. However, the school district exploited the *Salvatierra* doctrine, by drawing the line designating who must attend the language deficiency classes on a racial rather than a merit basis.[93] In *Hernandez v. Driscoll Consolidated Independent School District*[94] a Mexican-American child who could not speak Spanish was denied admission to the Anglo section until a lawyer was contacted. The court held that abusing the language deficiency of the Mexican-American children is "unreasonable race discrimination."[95] In a situation similar to *Driscoll,* Judge Seals, who later wrote the *Cisneros* opinion, enjoined the Odem Independent School District from operating and maintaining a separate school solely for Mexican-American children.[96]

After *Brown v. Board of Education*[97] the *Chicano* school cases began to assume a new dimension. Since Mexican-Americans were generally classified as whites, school districts began to integrate Negroes and Mexican-Americans while Anglos were assigned to all-Anglo schools. As a result, two educationally disadvantaged minority groups have been prevented from having maximum interaction with students of the predominant Anglo group. For example, in 1955 Negro and Mexican-Americans sued the El Centro School District in California for alleged "ethnic and racial discrimination and segregation by regulation, custom and usage."[98] In a rather narrow reading of *Brown,* the district court stated that *Brown,* which involved constitutional and statutory provisions, did not apply in situations where only customs and regulations were alleged. The court dismissed the complaint, claiming that where no specific regulation was set forth, plaintiffs must seek construction of the regulation in a State court.[99] On appeal, the Ninth Circuit reversed and remanded the case,[100] holding that when the complaint alleged segregation of public school facilities on the basis of race or color, a federal constitutional issue had been raised, requiring the district court to exercise its jurisdiction. Instead of going to trial, the case apparently was settled out of court, but the segregation of Negroes and Mexican-Americans has continued in most of the Southwest.

Whether integrating Negroes and Mexican-Americans produces a unitary school system was the issue raised in *Keyes v. School District Number One.*[101] In *Keyes,* the court questioned the permissibility of adding the number of Negroes and Hispanos (as Mexican-Americans are referred to in Colorado) to reach a single minority category in order to classify the school as a segregated school.[102] Nevertheless, the court stated that "to the extent that Hispanos . . . are isolated in concentrated numbers, a school in which this has occurred is to be regarded as a segregated school, either *de facto* or *de jure.*"[103] Failing to find de jure segregation, the court held that where the de facto segregated schools exist, they must provide equal educational opportunity, or a constitutional violation may exist.[104] As a result, the *Keyes* court revived the separate-but-equal doctrine[105] as to de facto segregated schools.

While *Keyes* did not answer whether mixing Blacks and *Chicanos* satisfies constitutional requirements, *Cisneros* did, holding that placing Negroes and Mexican-Americans in the same school did not achieve a unitary system.[106] However, *Keyes* involved de facto segregation, whereas *Cisneros* involved de jure segregation in the form of (1) locating schools in the Negro and Mexican-American neighborhoods; (2) bussing Anglo students to avoid the minority group schools; and (3) assigning Negro and Mexican-American teachers in disproportionate ratios to the segregated schools.[107]

In *Ross v. Eckels*[108] the Fifth Circuit appears to have disregarded the arguments advanced by Mexican-Americans and Negroes that mixing these minorities does not provide the equal educational opportunity of a unitary school system. In *Ross* the court implemented a pairing plan for the elementary schools of Houston, Texas. resulting in merging predominantly Negro schools with predominantly Mexican-American schools. Judge Clark, dissenting, relied on *Cisneros* in stating:

I say it is a mock justice when we "force" the numbers by pairing disadvantaged Negro students into schools with members of this equally disadvantaged ethnic group [Mexican-Americans].[109]

Ross is an important case. First, *Ross* involves the sixth largest school district in the United States, having approximately 235,000 students.[110] Second, *Ross* involves a Southwestern city which, like Corpus Christi, has a tri-racial rather than a bi-racial student population. This tri-racial situation was recognized by the Houston school board when they voted unanimously to appeal the *Ross* case to the United States Supreme Court.[111]

Another case involving segregation of Mexican-Americans, *Perez v. Sonora Independent School District,*[112] held that the Sonora, Texas schools were operating in a "unitary, nondiscriminatory, fully desegregated school system."[113] MALDEF had offered evidence to show that in 1938 the Sonora school board passed a resolution enrolling Mexican-American children in the "Mexican School."[114] *Perez* is an important case for Mexican-Americans and the desegregation of schools in the Southwest in that it is the first desegregation case in which the Justice Department has intervened on behalf of Mexican-Americans.[115]

Since *Salvatierra* in 1930 the Mexican-American desegregation struggle has progressed slowly, considering the injustices which resulted first, from almost total segregation by the regulations of the various school districts, and second, from exploitation of the classification of Mexican-Americans as white. As *Brown* held, it is unconstitutional to segregate Blacks in the public school systems. Similarly, cases from *Mendez* in 1947 to *Perez* in 1970 have held that it is a violation of the equal protection clause of the 14th Amendment to maintain by "custom or regulation" segregated schools for Mexican-Americans. Consequently, assigning Negroes and Mexican-Americans to the same schools and excluding Anglos accomplishes an end that is exactly opposite to the goal desired by the educationally disadvantaged, that goal being the social encounters and interactions between the identifiable minority groups and Anglo-Americans. As a result, the desegregation or assignment plans, which school districts in the Southwest formulate in tri-racial situations, should include the three ethnic groups on a more or less proportionate basis. The necessity for this can perhaps be demonstrated by an analogy from criminal law:

1. If it is a crime to commit A, and
2. If it is a crime to commit B, then
3. One cannot commit A and B simultaneously and be absolved of the crimes.

The same applies to school districts which continue to segregate Negroes and Mexican-Americans from predominantly Anglo schools on the theory that a unitary school system is achieved by integrating the two minority groups, merely because one is technically classified as white. Actually the public school system remains a dual one with identifiable white schools and identifiable minority schools, thus justifying intervention of courts in situations where either identifiable minority group seeks relief.

Forty-one years have passed since Mexican-Americans first sought an equal educational opportunity by attendance at racially integrated schools. In many cases this goal has not been realized, even though Mexican-Americans have been successful in almost every case since *Mendez*.[116] Consequently, an affirmative answer is required for the question whether the history of the Mexican-American school children in the predominantly Anglo school systems of the Southwest demands recognition of them as an identifiable ethnic minority group.

V. FACTORS LEADING TO THE SEGREGATION OF MEXICAN-AMERICAN CHILDREN

A. *Residential Segregation*

Residential segregation, whether resulting from economic necessity or discriminatory racial covenants, is a substantial factor in the de facto school segregation of Mexican-Americans. The residential segregation of Mexican-Americans ranges from a low of 30 percent in Sacramento, California to a high of 76 percent in Odessa, Texas.[117] The *Chicano* school cases can be compared to the amount of residential segregation in the areas where the cases arose, perhaps establishing a correlation between the residential segregation and allegations of unequal protection in the public school system:

Cases	Areas	Percentage of Mexican-American Residential Segregation[118]
Mendez (1946)	San Bernardino, California	67.9
Delgado (1948)	Austin, Texas	63.3
Gonzales (1951)	Phoenix, Arizona	57.8
Keyes (1970)	Denver, Colorado	60.0
Cisneros (1970)	Corpus Christi, Texas	72.2
Ross (1970)	Houston, Texas	65.2
Perez (1970)	San Angelo, Texas	65.7

This table reflects a positive correlation between de jure segregated schools and substantial racial segregation. This should be sufficient to shift the burden of proof to the defendant school districts in cases where de facto segregation is alleged.

Furthermore, *Dowell v. School Board*,[119] which holds that a neighborhood school policy is invalid when superimposed on residential segregation which was initiated by State enforcement of racial covenants, should be an aid to the Mexican-American's quest for an equal educational opportunity. There is support for the view that Mexican-Americans have been denied access to homes and apartments in predominantly Anglo areas.[120] These denials are aggravated by the economic reality that when one settles for a home in a residentially segregated neighborhood, the home is usually retained for some time.[121]

In 1948 *Shelley v. Kraemer*[122] held that State enforcement of private racial covenants is unconstitutional. As a result, State courts in California[123] and Texas[124] refused to enforce racial convenants which provided that "[n]o person or persons of the Mexican race or other than the Caucasian race shall use or occupy any buildings or any lot."[125] The patterns that developed prior to *Shelley* have not receded. School districts in the Southwest should not be allowed to allege that school segregation is merely de facto if there has been State action in pre-*Shelley* days. A plaintiff should not be required to prove any specific act of residential discrimination where a pattern of segregation appears. Requirements of actual proof allow unjustifiable delay in the immediate transformation to unitary school systems, an issue the Supreme Court considers to be of "paramount importance."[126]

B. *Ability Grouping*

Like residential segregation, ability grouping (grouping students according to their talents and aptitudes) often leads to segregated education. However, unlike residential segregation, a factor external to the public school system, ability grouping is practiced within the school system. In schools that are to some extent desegregated, the tests and guides which are used indirectly lead to classes in which many Negroes, Mexican-Americans, or both are grouped into segregated classrooms. The results are by no means attributable to any inherent inadequacy on the part of minority group children. Instead, ability grouping which leads to ethnic and racial segregation can be traced to the nature of the social and environmental conditions which minority group children experience. When their aptitude is measured by a standardized national test, which is geared to represent the average white middle class student, the results are inherently biased against children who are culturally different from whites.[127]

In *Hobson v. Hansen*,[128] Judge Skelly Wright held that the school district's track system, a method of ability grouping, must be abolished because "[i]n practice, if not in concept, it discriminates against the disadvantaged child, particularly the Negro."[129] Judge Wright did not condemn all forms of ability grouping. However, he did question ability grouping when it unreasonably leads to or maintains continous racial or socioeconomic segregation. In cases of such segregation, the effect is unreasonable and discriminatory because it fails to accomplish its aim—the grouping of pupils according to their capacities to learn. Because minority group children have had an educationally disadvantaged experience does not mean they must be permanently restricted to low achievement.

Hobson may contribute much to the fall of the track systems employed in the Southwest. After all, when tests are given which result in highly disproportionate numbers of Mexican-Americans in the retarded or below average category, the classification is constitutionally suspect. The Supreme Court's language in *Hernandez* applies by analogy to the discriminatory effects of ability grouping in the Southwest:
"The result [of an overrepresentation of Mexican-Americans in the below average category] bespeaks discrimination, whether or not it was a conscious decision on the part of any individual [school official]."[130]

Besides the language deficiency argument, other devices result in the segregation of Mexican-Americans, even in racially mixed schools. For example, standardized tests fail to judge accurately the Mexican-American's innate capacity to learn. The national tests may ask the *Chicano* child to match a picture with a word that is foreign to him but may be quite common to the middle class white child, who may have encountered its use within his environment. One must realize that these tests are geared to measure the average middle class white American. Consequently, *Chicano* children continue to score very low and to be placed in the lower intelligence sections, from which escape is practically impossible.[131]

An even more damaging practice is common in California. Mexican-American children, many of whom come from homes where Spanish is spoken daily, are given tests in English to determine their group level. Consequently, the language obstacle hinders the Spanish-speaking child and contributes to his lower score. As a result, many children score low enough to be classified as "Educable Mentally Retarded" (EMR). Once a child is placed in a special education class, his chance of escaping is minimal. In the San Diego, California school district, Mexican-Americans have challenged the unfair testing schemes which are employed and which result in disproportionate numbers of *Chicanos* in the EMR classes.[132]

In order to realize how examinations such as these deny equal protection to the Mexican-American student, one must perceive the discrepancy which results when the *Chicano* child is tested under varying conditions. Using the Wechsler Intelligence Scale for Children, 44 scored below 80 when tested in English. But when the test was administered to the same group in Spanish, only 20 scored below 80.[133] Consequently, when applied to children with a limited background in English, these tests are inadequate since they are unable to measure a child's capacity to learn and thus result in harmful discrimination to the Mexican-American child in the public schools of the Southwest.

VI. MEXICAN-AMERICAN DESEGREGATION—THE FUTURE

A. *The Southwest Generally*

Overall, there are many areas of the Southwest where segregated schools should be challenged as denying the equal protection of the laws. For example, Del Rio, Texas, the scene of the *Salvatierra* case in 1930, although it is a rather small town, has two school districts within the city limits: The Del Rio Independent School District, which is predominantly Anglo, and the San Felipe Independent School District, which is almost entirely Mexican-American.[134] Since the Del Rio schools are much better, the Anglo children from a nearby Air Force base are bussed at State expense to the Del Rio district schools, even though the base is located in the San Felipe district.[135] Although there are two technically separate school districts in Del Rio, they should be treated as one for purposes of school desegregation. The obvious reluctance of the Del Rio district to accept Mexican-Americans is evidenced by the fact that this school district's accreditation was questioned in 1949 for failure to integrate Mexican-American students.[136] This may support a claim of unconstitutional State action. However, assuming the Del Rio public school system is segregated on a de facto basis, the *Keyes*[137] separate-but-equal formula may play a decisive role in the desegregation of these schools. *Keyes* demands that segregated schools offer equal educational opportunity if they are to be constitutionally allowable. However, both physically and academically, the Del Rio district schools are superior. Besides being newer, Del Rio High School (mostly Anglo) offers 75 to 100 courses. On the other hand, San Felipe High School (Mexican-American) offers only 36 courses and cannot afford a vocational program.[138]

San Antonio, Texas, which is nearly 50 percent Mexican-American, employs a similar public school system. There are 13 school districts in and around the San Antonio area, of which five are predominantly Mexican-American and eight are predominantly Anglo-American.[139] Ninety percent or 82,000 of the Mexican-American students attend school in five predominantly Mexican-American districts. Because of the financial and educational inequities which result from having various independent school districts, residents of a nearly 100 percent Mexican-American school district have sued all the school districts in the San Antonio area.[140] The plaintiffs allege the Texas system of school financing, which allows each school district to collect taxes for use exclusively within that particular school system, violates the constitutional rights of children in the poorer districts to an equal educational opportunity. In a case of this type, *Hobson*, which also held that school boards cannot discriminate on the basis of poverty,[141] may be controlling, since the financing scheme does result, whether intentionally or not, in an unreasonable discrimination against the poor.

Ethnic isolation or concentration, as it exists in the Del Rio and San Antonio, Texas systems, is similar to that found throughout the Southwest, although it is least serious in California and most serious in Texas.[142] It is interesting to note that there is an inverse relationship between the educational level of Mexican-Americans in these two States.[143] In other words, where the ethnic segregation increases, the educational level decreases, and vice versa. This reaffirms the accepted view in desegregation cases that segregated educational facilities fail to offer an equal educational opportunity.[144]

B.   Ross v. Eckels—The Houston Situation

As previously mentioned Ross v. Eckels[145] is a Fifth Circuit case in which a pairing order was issued for some Houston, Texas elementary schools. The result was the pairing of 27 predominantly Black and Chicano schools, whose segregated facilities resulted mostly from the de jure segregation of pre-1954 years and from the de facto segregation which developed as a result of the high rate of residential segregation in Houston. In many areas of the city, Negro neighborhoods are adjacent to Mexican-American barrios. Consequently, much of the neighborhood school "integration" which Houston does have is black-brown integration, lacking the white student population necessary in order to make the school system responsive both politically and educationally to the needs of the minority group population of Houston.

In the Southwest more than 50 percent of the Mexican-American students at the elementary school level attend predominantly Mexican-American schools.[146] For this reason, and since the Ross pairing order involved only elementary school children, this discussion will be limited to the elementary schools in Houston.

Judge Clark, in his dissenting opinion in Ross, denounced the pairing order as "mock justice" because it paired Negroes with another educationally disadvantaged group. An analysis of the school populations may prove Judge Clark's dissent to be more consistent with the prior development in the desegregation cases involving Blacks and Chicanos.[147]

The elementary grade level students in the Houston public schools number approximately 143,400.[148] Of these, 66,612 are Anglo; 53,875 are Negro; and 23,000 are Mexican-American. The respective percentages of each group in relation to the total student population in the elementary schools are 46.5 percent Anglo, 37.5 percent Negro, and 16 percent Mexican-American. Comparing the Anglo with the combined minority groups, Black and Chicano students comprise 53.5 percent of the student population. In addition, in 23 of the 170 elementary schools, the Mexican-American student population exceeds 50 percent, thus leading to ethnic imbalance. This does not include the many other schools where the combined minority group population greatly exceeds the 53.5 percent this combined group represents. In these 23 elementary schools, Mexican-Americans account for 74.9 percent of the total enrollment (13,300 out of a total of 17,750). In comparison to the entire Mexican-American school population, the 13,300 students in these ethnically concentrated schools account for 57.8 percent of the total *Chicano* population in elementary schools. As a result, Houston is typical of the elementary school segregation norm in the Southwest: Over 50 percent ethnic isolation.

Of the 27 schools involved in the *Ross* pairing order, only one was predominantly (50 percent or more) Anglo. It appears that the desegregation order excluded any meaningful integration of the Anglo student with the other identifiable groups in Houston. Overall, there were 2,368 Anglo, 6,233 Mexican-American, and 14,942 Negro students involved in the pairing plan. Consequently, 21,175 of the total 23,543 students, or 89.9 percent, were children of educationally disadvantaged backgrounds. The purpose of the desegregation cases, which is to establish unitary school systems and thereby provide meaningful social and educational encounters between students of all racial backgrounds, is not achieved by the *Ross* pairing order.[149]

VII. CONCLUSION

Throughout the Southwest, the approximately 1.4 million Mexican-American students represent 17 percent of the total enrollment. Thus, *Chicanos* constitute the largest minority student group in this part of the United States.[150] These students have been neglected, both educationally[151] and legally. The low educational levels of Mexican-Americans imply that the school systems have failed to deal with this bilingual, bicultural group. Legally, the past failure of courts to require total disestablishment of dual school systems, such as in Del Rio, Texas after *Salvatierra*, has provided much support to the publicly-elected school boards in their attempt to maintain the segregation of Mexican-Americans.

As a result, Judge Seals' landmark ruling in *Cisneros* is cause for much optimism on the part of the Mexican-American population in the Southwest regarding the educational future of their children. In all respects, the holdings in *Brown* and its progeny apply to Mexican-Americans as well as to any other identifiable minority groups.

Cisneros is consistent with prior judicial development. Historically, Congress and the courts have granted Mexican-Americans protection from unreasonable discrimination in housing, employment, public accommodations, voting, the administration of justice, and in the field of equal educational opportunity. This protection has resulted from a recognition that Mexican-Americans are an identifiable ethnic minority group, whether because of physical characteristics, language, predominant religion, distinct culture, or Spanish surname[152] and are entitled to equal protection of the laws in the area of public school desegregation.

NOTES

1. Civil Action No. 68-C-95 (S.D. Tex., June 4, 1970) [hereinafter cited as *Cisneros*], noted, 49 TEX.L. REV. 337 (1971).
2. *Id.* at 9-10.
3. 347 U.S. 483 (1954). *See also* Swann v. Charlotte-Mecklenburg Bd. of Educ., 91 S.Ct. 1267 (1971).
4. *Cisneros* at 13-14.
5. *Id.* at 20-21.
6. *See* THE NEW YORK TIMES ENCYCLOPEDIC ALMANAC 35, 288 (2d ed. 1970).
7. *Id.* at 245, 288.
8. *Cisneros* at 10 n.34.
9. *Id.* at 8 n.28.
10. L. GREBLER, J. MOORE, & R. GUZMAN, THE MEXICAN-AMERICAN PEOPLE 14-15 (1970) [hereinafter cited as GREBLER, MOORE, & GUZMAN]. The authors cite the Mexican-American population in 1960 as 3.8 million and estimate the 1970 count to be 5.6 million.
11. *Id.* at 15.
12. *E.g.,* States: Arizona, California, Colorado, Texas; cities: San Antonio, Del Rio, San Francisco, Santa Fe, Pueblo; rivers: Rio Grande, Brazos, Guadalupe.
13. 9 Stat. 922 (1848).
14. *Id.* at 929-30, art. VIII.
15. C. McWILLIAMS, NORTH FROM MEXICO 52 (1948) [hereinafter cited as McWILLIAMS].
16. L. F. HERNANDEZ, A FORGOTTEN AMERICAN 8 (1969).
17. U.S. BUREAU OF THE CENSUS, WE THE MEXICAN AMERICANS 2 (1970).
18. McWILLIAMS 193.
19. R. DANIELS & H. H. L. KITANO, AMERICAN RACISM 74 (1970). The authors refer to People v. Zammora, 66 Cal. App. 2d 166, 152 P.2d 180 (1944), in which 17 Mexican-American youths were indicted and convicted for murder, without any tangible evidence, in the death of another youth who was killed in a gang fight. The California appellate court reversed and remanded all the convictions.
20. *Id.* at 77. The name "zoot suiters" was derived from the gaudy clothing worn by some of the *Chicano* youths.
21. *See* Independent School Dist. v. Salvatierra, 33 S.W.2d 790 (Tex. Civ. App.—San Antonio 1930), *cert. denied*, 284 U.S. 580 (1931).
22. AMERICAN GI FORUM, 21st ANNUAL CONVENTION, July 4, 1969. The incident leading to the creation of the GI Forum was the refusal in 1948 of Anglo citizens in Three Rivers, Texas to have a deceased Mexican-American veteran buried in the city's cemetery. The soldier, Felix Longoria, was buried with honors in Arlington National Cemetery. San Angelo Standard-Times, July 6, 1969, § 1, at 1, col. 1.
23. Judge Seals listed MAYO, LULAC, and the GI Forum as products of discriminatory practices. *Cisneros* 12.
24. Steiner, Chicano Power, THE NEW REPUBLIC, June 20, 1970, at 17.
25. The Texas Observer, April 11, 1969, at 6, col. 1. MALDEF is operating under an 8-year, $2.2 million Ford Foundation grant.
26. *See* Hernandez v. Texas, 347 U.S. 475 (1954). The Supreme Court found that Mexican-Americans had been discriminated against in the selection of jurors in

Jackson County, Texas. *See also* Tijerina v. Henry, 48 F.R.D. 274 (D.N.M.), *appeal dismissed*, 90 S. Ct. 1718 (1969) (Douglas, J., dissenting).

27. The Texas Observer, April 11, 1969, at 6, col. 1.

28. As of December 1969, MALDEF had filed civil rights suits against discrimination in hiring and promotion, the enforcement of the laws, voting rights, public accommodations, and education. See MALDEF Docket Report (Dec. 1969) [hereinafter cited as Docket Report].

29. One author contends that the "brown skin color" of most Mexican-Americans makes them susceptible to Anglo prejudice against darker-skinned persons. *See* Forbes, *Race and Color in Mexican-American Problems*, 16 J. HUMAN REL. 55 (1968).

30. McWILLIAMS.

31. 42 U.S.C. § 200e-2 (1964).

32. Civil Action No. 7680 (D.N.M., Sept. 24, 1969), discussed in 1 MALDEF Newsletter 1, Nov., 1969.

33. H. ROWAN, THE MEXICAN AMERICAN 38, (Paper prepared for U.S. Comm'n on Civil Rights 1968).

34. *Id.* at 39.

35. The median school years completed by Mexican-Americans is 8.1, much lower than the 12.0 years achieved by Anglo students. GREBLER, MOORE, & GUZMAN 143.

36. W. FOGEL, MEXICAN AMERICANS IN SOUTHWEST LABOR MARKETS 191 (U.C.L.A. Mexican-American Study Project: Advance Report No. 10, 1967).

37. H. ROWAN, THE MEXICAN AMERICAN 45, U.S. Comm'n on Civil Rights (1968).

38. U.S. CONST. amend. XIV provides: "No State shall . . . deny to any person within its jurisdiction the equal protection of the laws." The Justice Department has sued an Arizona copper company for job opportunity discrimination against Mexican-Americans and Indians. Arizona Daily Star, Mar. 4, 1971, § B, at 1, col. 6.

39. *See* Vigil v. American Tel. & Tel. Co., 305 F. Supp. 44 (D. Colo. 1969); Pena v. Hunt Tool Co., 296 F. Supp. 1003 (S.D. Tex. 1968). In another employment case, Moreno v. Henckel, 431 F.2d 1299 (5th Cir. 1970), the plaintiff was fired for circulating a petition of grievances concerning dissatisfaction with the rate of promotion for Mexican-American workers. The case was remanded since the district court incorrectly dismissed the case.

40. *See generally* Docket Report, Tit. 2, Job Discrimination. The Justice Department has sued an Arizona firm and some unions for job opportunity discrimination against Mexican-Americans and Indians. Arizona Daily Star, Mar. 4, 1971, § B, at 1, col. 6.

41. *Id.*

42. Civil Action No. 69H-1082 (S.D. Tex., filed Nov. 4, 1969).

43. 42 U.S.C. § 2000e-2 (1964) makes it unlawful for an employer to discriminate because of race, color, religion, sex, or national origin.

44. Docket Report, Tit. 2, at 7.

45. 293 F. Supp. 1176 (D. Colo. 1968).

46. Valdez, *Insurrection in New Mexico*, 1 EL GRITO 14 (Fall, 1967).

47. *Id.* at 19-20.

48. 9 Stat. 922, 929-30 (1848).

49. Valdez, *Insurrection in New Mexico*, 1 EL GRITO 14, 20-21 (Fall, 1967).

50. *See* McWILLIAMS 76-78, *supra* note 15.

51. For actual cases of ethnic discrimination in Texas see A. PERALES, ARE WE GOOD NEIGHBORS? 139-227 (1948) [hereinafter cited as PERALES].

52. Terrell Wells Swimming Pool v. Rodriguez, 182 S.W.2d 824 (Tex. Civ. App.–San Antonio 1944, no writ); cf. Lueras v. Town of Lafayette, 100 Colo. 124, 65 P.2d 1431 (1937).

53. Lopez v. Seccombe, 71 F. Supp. 769 (S.D. Cal. 1944).

54. Beltran v. Patterson, Civil Action No. 68-59-W (W.D. Tex. 1968), cited in Brief for MALDEF as Amicus Curiae at 3, Ross v. Eckels, 434 F.2d 1140 (5th Cir. 1970).

55. U.S. COMM'N ON CIVIL RIGHTS, MEXICAN AMERICANS AND THE ADMINISTRATION OF JUSTICE IN THE SOUTHWEST 2-6 (1970) [hereinafter cited as ADMINISTRATION OF JUSTICE].

56. Id. at 4 n.15.

57. Lucero v. Donovan, 258 F. Supp. 979 (C.D. Cal. 1966).

58. Lucero v. Donovan, 354 F.2d 16, 18 (9th Cir. 1965). Mrs. Lucero was a native-born citizen of the United States.

59. For an insight into the distrust of the Texas Rangers by South Texas Chicanos, see ADMINISTRATION OF JUSTICE 16-17.

60. See U.S. CONST. amend. VI.

61. 347 U.S. 475 (1954).

62. Id. at 479.

63. Id. at 482.

64. Hernandez v. State, 160 Tex. Crim. 72, 251 S.W.2d 531 (1952); Sanchez v. State, 156 Tex. Crim. 468, 243 S.W.2d 700 (1951); Salazar v. State, 149 Tex. Crim. 260, 193 S.W.2d 211 (1946); Sanchez v. State, 147 Tex. Crim. 436, 181 S.W.2d 87 (1944).

65. 347 U.S. 475, 478 (1954) (emphasis added).

66. See United States v. Hunt, 265 F. Supp. 178 (W.D. Tex. 1967); Gonzales v. State, 414 S.W.2d 181 (Tex. Crim. App. 1967); Montoya v. People, 345 P.2d 1062 (Colo. 1959).

67. Muniz v. Beto, 434 F.2d 697 (5th Cir. 1970).

68. Id. at 703.

69. Id. at 702.

70. E.g., Voting rights: Mexican-American Federation v. Naff, 299 F. Supp. 587 (E.D. Wash. 1969), rev'd, 39 U.S.L.W. 3296 (U.S. Jan. 12, 1971) (English literacy requirement upheld by the lower court); Castro v. State, 2 Cal. 3d 223, 466 P.2d 244, 85 Cal. Rptr. 20 (1970) (English literacy requirement held unconstitutional). Housing: Valtierra v. Housing Authority, 313 F. Supp. 1 (N.D. Cal. 1970), rev'd sub nom. James v. Valtierra, 91 S.Ct. 1331 (1971). Judicial prejudice: Judge Gerald S. Chargin Speaks, 2 EL GRITO 4 (1969). In this juvenile court proceeding, Judge Chargin denounced a Chicano youth, who was charged with incest, and the "Mexican people" for acting "like an animal" and for being "miserable, lousy, rotten people." Chargin also stated that "[m]aybe Hitler was right" about having to destroy the animals in our society.

71. 42 U.S.C. § 2000(a) (1964).

72. 20 U.S.C. § 880b (Supp. V, 1970).

73. The Mexican-American student has suffered serious emotional scars because of the "No Spanish" rule, whose violation by speaking Spanish on school grounds often has led to scolding and/or detention after school as punishment. The rule was probably derived from Tex. Laws 1933, ch. 125, § 1, at 325 (repealed 1969), which required all school business, except foreign language classes, to be conducted in English.

74. 42 U.S.C. § 4301 (Supp. V, 1970).

75. For example, the following reports have been published: U.S. COMM'N ON CIVIL RIGHTS, MEXICAN AMERICAN EDUCATION STUDY, REPORT I: ETHNIC ISOLATION OF MEXICAN AMERICANS IN THE PUBLIC SCHOOLS OF THE SOUTHWEST (1970); U.S. COMM'N ON CIVIL RIGHTS, MEXICAN AMERICANS AND THE ADMINISTRATION OF JUSTICE IN THE SOUTHWEST

(1970); H. ROWAN, THE MEXICAN AMERICAN, U.S. Comm'n on Civil Rights (1968); U.S. COMM'N ON CIVIL RIGHTS, HEARING HELD IN SAN ANTONIO, TEXAS, DECEMBER 9-14, 1968 (1968).

76. U.S. BUREAU OF THE CENSUS, WE THE MEXICAN AMERICANS (1970); F. H. SCHMIDT, SPANISH SURNAMED AMERICAN EMPLOYMENT IN THE SOUTHWEST (1970) (A Study Prepared for the Colorado Civil Rights Comm'n under the auspices of the Equal Employment Opportunity Comm'n).

77. Pottinger, Memorandum to School Districts with More Than Five Percent National Origin-Minority Group Children, May 25, 1970. Memorandum on file in Univ. of Houston Law Library. See also 35 Fed. Reg. 13442 (1970). The Department of Health, Education, and Welfare suggested to the Houston school district that Mexican-Americans be appointed to the district's biracial committee. Houston Chronicle, Dec. 18, 1970, § 1, at 1, col. 8.

78. T. I. EMERSON, 2 POLITICAL AND CIVIL RIGHTS IN THE UNITED STATES 1734 (3d ed. 1967), citing NATIONAL ASS'N OF INTERGROUP RELATIONS, Public School Segregation and Integration in the North, J. INTER-GROUP REL. 1 (1963).

79. 33 S.W.2d 790 (Tex. Civ. App.—San Antonio 1930), cert. denied, 284 U.S. 580 (1931).

80. Id. at 795.

81. Id. at 793.

82. TEX. ATT'Y GEN. OP. No. V-128 (1947), reported in J. C. HINSLEY, TEXAS SCHOOL LAW 1109 (4th ed. 1968).

83. 64 F. Supp. 544 (S.D. Cal. 1946), aff'd, 161 F.2d 774 (9th Cir. 1947).

84. Id. at 549.

85. Brown v. Board of Educ., 347 U.S. 483, 495 (1954).

86. 64 F. Supp. at 549.

87. School Dist. v. Mendez, 161 F.2d 774, 779 (9th Cir. 1947), aff'g 64 F. Supp. 544 (S.D. Cal. 1946).

88. Id. at 781.

89. Civil Action No. 388 (W.D. Tex., June 15, 1948) (unreported); accord, Gonzales v. Sheely, 96 F. Supp. 1004 (D. Ariz. 1951).

90. Id. at 1.

91. Id. at 2.

92. See Hernandez v. Driscoll Consol. Ind. School Dist., 2 RACE REL. L. REP. 329 (S.D. Tex. 1957).

93. Id. at 331.

94. 2 RACE REL. L. REP. 329 (S.D. Tex. 1957).

95. Id. at 331-32.

96. Chapa v. Odem Ind. School Dist., Civil Action No. 66-C-92 (S.D. Tex., July 28, 1967) (unreported).

97. 347 U.S. 483 (1954).

98. Romero v. Weakley, 131 F. Supp. 818, 820 (S.D. Cal.), rev'd, 226 F.2d 399 (9th Cir. 1955).

99. Id. at 831.

100. 226 F.2d 399 (9th Cir. 1955).

101. 313 F. Supp. 61 (D. Colo. 1970). (This opinion deals only with the issue of segregation in the school.)

102. Id. at 69.

103. Id. On the issue of the desegregation plan, the court expressed that apportionment of the three ethnic groups was desirable but not required. Id. at 98.

104. Id. at 82-83. For another de facto case involving Chicanos and Blacks, see United States v. Lubbock Ind. School Dist., 316 F. Supp. 1310 (N.D. Tex. 1970).

105. See Plessy v. Ferguson, 163 U.S. 537 (1896). The separate-but-equal doctrine was repudiated as to de jure school segregation by Brown v. Board of Educ., 347 U.S. 483 (1954).

106. *Cisneros* at 13.

107. *Id.* at 14-15.

108. 434 F.2d 1140 (5th Cir. 1970).

109. *Id.* at 1150 (dissenting opinion).

110. *Id.* at 1141.

111. Houston Chronicle, Sept. 15, 1970 § 1, at 1, col. 1.

112. Civil Action No. 6-224 (N.D. Tex., Nov. 5, 1970). Sonora, Texas, had a "Mexican" elementary school which was 2 percent black and an all-Anglo elementary school.

113. *Id.* at 2.

114. Plaintiff's Motion for a Preliminary Injunction at 4, Perez v. Sonora Ind. School Dist., Civil Action No. 6-224 (N.D. Tex., Nov. 5, 1970).

115. Houston Chronicle, Nov. 6, 1970, § 1, at 9, col. 7. The United States has also objected to the adoption of a desegregation plan in Austin, Texas whereby Blacks and *Chicanos* were integrated to the exclusion of Anglos, thus maintaining ethnically and racially identifiable schools. United States v. Texas Educ. Agency, Civil Action No. A-70-CA-80, (W.D. Tex., filed Aug. 7, 1970), cited in Brief for MALDEF as Amicus Curiae at 14, Ross v. Eckels, 434 F.2d 1140 (5th Cir. 1970).

116. One case where Mexican-Americans and Negroes were denied relief is United States v. Lubbock Ind. School Dist., 316 F. Supp. 1310 (N.D. Tex. 1970), where the court found the segregation to be de facto.

117. GREBLER, MOORE, & GUZMAN 274, *supra* note 10. Zero percent segregation connotes a random scattering throughout the population; 100 percent represents total segregation.

118. *Id.* at 275.

119. 244 F. Supp. 971 (W.D. Okla.), *aff'd sub nom.* Board of Educ. v. Dowell, 375 F.2d 158 (10th Cir. 1965), *cert. denied,* 387 U.S. 931 (1967).

120. PERALES 139-46, *supra* note 51.

121. Kaplan, *Segregation Litigation and the Schools—Part II: The General Northern Problem,* 58 Nw. U.L. REV. 157, 212 (1964).

122. 334 U.S. 1 (1948).

123. Matthews v. Andrade, 87 Cal. App. 2d 906, 198 P.2d 66 (1948).

124. Clifton v. Puente, 218 S.W.2d 272 (Tex. Civ. App.—San Antonio 1948, writ ref'd n.r.e.).

125. 87 Cal App. 2d 906, 198 P.2d 66 (1948). The language in *Clifton* was similar to that cited here.

126. 396 U.S. 19, 20 (1969). *See generally* Wright, *Public School Desegregation: Legal Remedies for De Facto Segregation,* 16 W. RES. L. REV. 478 (1965).

127. Hobson v. Hansen, 269 F. Supp. 401, 484-85 (D.D.C. 1967), *appeal dismissed,* 393 U.S. 801 (1968), *aff'd sub nom., Smuck v. Hobson,* 408 F.2d 175 (D.C. Cir. 1969).

128. *Id.*

129. *Id.* at 515; *accord,* Dove v. Parham, 282 F.2d 256, 261 (8th Cir. 1960).

130. Hernandez v. Texas, 347 U.S. 475, 482 (1954).

131. A suit has been filed in Texas against a district alleging segregation resulting both from design and from a rigid system of ability grouping. Zamora v. New Braunfels Ind. School Dist., Civil Action No. 68-205-SA (W.D. Tex., filed Aug. 28, 1968), *cited in* Docket Report, Tit. 3, Education, at 1.

132. Covarrubias v. San Diego Unified School Dist., Civil Action No. 70-394-T (S.D. Cal., filed Dec. 1, 1970).

133. M. WEINBERG, DESEGREGATION RESEARCH: AN APPRAISAL 265-66 (2d ed. 1970).

134. U.S. COMM'N ON CIVIL RIGHTS, HEARING HELD IN SAN ANTONIO, TEXAS, December 9-14, 1968, at 295-304 (1968).

135. *Id.* at 304.

136. *Id.* at 305.

137. 313 F. Supp. 61 (D. Colo. 1970).

138. 2 Civil Rights Digest 16, 20 (1969).

139. U.S. COMM'N ON CIVIL RIGHTS, MEXICAN AMERICAN EDUCA-TION STUDY, REPORT I: ETHNIC ISOLATION OF MEXICAN AMERICANS IN THE PUBLIC SCHOOLS OF THE SOUTHWEST 26 (1970) [hereinafter cited as ETHNIC ISOLATION].

140. Rodriguez v. San Antonio Ind. School Dist., 299 F. Supp. 476 (W.D. Tex. 1969) (issue here limited to whether a three-judge panel should hear the case).

141. 269 F. Supp. at 513.

142. ETHNIC ISOLATION 30.

143. *See* GREBLER, MOORE, & GUZMAN 144, *supra* note 10.

144. A Connecticut Department of Education study shows that children bussed to suburban classrooms from inner-city schools accelerate their reading ability as much as 18 months ahead of their uban counterparts who remain be-hind. Houston Chronicle, Nov. 8, 1970, § 1, at 2, col. 7.

145. 434 F.2d 1140 (5th Cir. 1970).

146. ETHNIC ISOLATION 35.

147. *E.g.,* Cisneros v. Corpus Christi Ind. School Dist., Civil Action No. 68-C-95 (S.D. Tex. June 4, 1970); Keyes v. School Dist. Number One, 313 F. Supp. 61 (D. Colo. 1970); Romero v. Weakley, 131 F. Supp. 818 (S.D. Cal.), *rev'd,* 226 F.2d 399 (9th Cir. 1955). These three cases involved segregation of Negroes and Mexican-Americans into minority schools.

148. Houston Chronicle, oct. 1, 1970, § 1, at 13, col. 1-2. All figures and percentages used in the analysis of the Houston elementary schools were derived from this article.

149. Ross v. Eckels, 434 F.2d 1140 (5th Cir. 1970) was appealed to the Supreme Court of the United States by the Houston Independent School District because the court pairing order integrated two minority groups. Houston Chron-icle, Sept. 15, 1970, § 1, at 1, col. 1. A motion to stay the pairing order was denied by the Supreme Court. Houston Chronicle, March 1, 1971, § 1, at 1, col. 1.

150. ETHNIC ISOLATION 89.

151. *See* T. P. CARTER, MEXICAN AMERICANS IN SCHOOL: A HISTORY OF EDUCATIONAL NEGLECT (1970).

152. Cisneros v. Corpus Christi Ind. School Dist., Civil Action No. 68-C-95, at 10-11 (S.D. Tex. June 4, 1970).

MEXICAN-AMERICANS AND THE DESEGREGATION OF SCHOOLS IN THE SOUTHWEST — A SUPPLEMENT

by Guadalupe Salinas

I. INTRODUCTION

Since the original publication of this writer's article in the Houston Law Review, there have been additional cases of interest in the Chicano civil rights field. Also, there are some cases which the writer omitted but desires to discuss in this supplement.

II. HISTORICAL BACKGROUND OF THE MEXICAN-AMERICAN

One year after the Treaty of Guadalupe Hidalgo in 1848, those Mexicans who remained in the United States became American citizens. However, this did not clear up the citizenship problem for Chicanos. In the late 1890's Ricardo Rodriguez, a legal United States resident, filed an application to become a naturalized citizen. The United States denied it because *the law restricted naturalization to whites and persons of African descent.* The contention, therefore, was that Rodriguez was neither white nor black. In fact, the opposing lawyers described him as having "chocolate brown skin."[1] As a result, Rodriguez took his claim to court where the issue presented was, "Is Rodriguez ineligible for citizenship because he is not a 'white' person and apparently belongs to the Indian or red race?"[2]

In re Rodriguez[3] held that Rodriguez was entitled to citizenship, even though the court recognized that anthropologically, Rodriguez "would probably not be classed as white."[4] Consequently, *this case verifies that historically the Chicano has been viewed as a separate group, distinct from whites, for generations.*[5]

III. THE MEXICAN-AMERICAN
AN IDENTIFIABLE ETHNIC MINORITY GROUP

A. *The Mexican American*

B. *Discrimination in Areas Besides Education*

    1. *Employment*

Of enormous importance to Chicanos, Blacks, and Indians alike is the case of *Griggs v. Duke Power Company,*[6] where the United States Supreme Court said:

> If an employment practice [e.g., aptitude test] which operates to exclude Negroes [Chicanos and Indians] cannot be shown to be related to job performance, the practice is prohibited.[7]

This case implies employers can no longer deny jobs because they fail a test, lack a high school diploma, or are unable to speak fluent English *unless* the employer can show the requirement is related to the job. For example, one does not have to pass an English vocabulary test to be qualified for a job as a telephone installer. Such a test merely serves to weed Chicanos out from many of these jobs. Therefore, Raza lawyers should study *Griggs* closely.

    2. *Spanish and Mexican Land Grants*

Of significant legal and historical value in the land grant area are the Supreme Court cases of *United States v. Rio Arriba Land and Cattle*

Company (1897),[8] *United States v. Sandoval* (1897),[9] and *United States v. Santa Fe* (1897).[10] These cases are considered the "bulwark against the property rights of the impoverished Indo-Hispano (Chicano) of the Southwest."[11]

3. Public Accommodations

In the case of *In re Rodriguez* the Chicano was described as belonging to the Indian race. Apparently this view is still current in Arizona. In June, 1971, a Chicano friend of the writer, his family, and some friends went to the Grand Canyon on their vacation. On the way they stopped for breakfast at a restaurant in Cameron, Arizona. They sat down and waited . . . and waited. Meanwhile, the other customers were being served. After thirty minutes, they asked what they had to do to obtain service. The waitress, an Indian girl, told him that it was not the policy of the management to serve Indians! After a few demands, the Chicanos were served, but the rude manner in which the food was served amounted to a denial of services. The Department of Justice is currently investigating the incident.[12]

4. Administration of Justice

In *Tate v. Short*,[13] Peter Sanchez Navarro, a Chicano lawyer then with the Houston Legal Foundation, convinced the Supreme Court that one should not be confined to jail to work off a traffic fine. This case should serve as a basis for the release of a large number of Chicanos who remain jailed merely because they are too poor to pay the fine imposed.

5. Social Welfare

In *Graham v. Richardson*[14] the Supreme Court ruled that State statutes which deny welfare benefits to resident aliens or to aliens who have not resided in the United States for a specified number of years violate the equal protection clause of the 14th Amendment. *Graham's* enforcement in Texas is currently being sought by a Mexican alien who has resided in the United States for 54 of her 60 years.[15]

6. Voting

In *Garza v. Smith*[16] a federal district court ruled that the Texas Election Code denies illiterate voters equal protection because the Code allows assistance in the voting booth only to those that are physically handicapped and by implication, denies it to the "mentally" handicapped. The court said that the illiterate "is just as surely disabled as the blind or physically incapacitated voter, and therefore equally in need of assistance, yet the statutes forbid anyone to help him."[17]

7. Migrant Workers

In October, 1971, a federal district court in Michigan ruled that migrant workers are entitled to basic civil rights just as any other person. The facts were that a Chicano named Folgueras, representing a federal program designed for migrant workers, tried to enter Hassle's property to visit some migrants. However, Hassle beat Folgueras and got two deputy sheriffs to arrest him for criminal trespass. Folgueras recovered a money judgment against the three as well as a constitutional rule that property rights are subordinate to the farm workers' civil rights.[18]

IV. THE CHICANO SCHOOL CASES

A. *California*

Although Texas leads in the quantity of recent Chicano school cases, California leads in the quality of the legal reasoning. For example, in *People v. San Diego Unified School District*[19] a State appellate court held that the school district must take reasonably feasible steps to alleviate racial imbalance in the schools because it resulted from racially motivated State action perpetuating a previously existing imbalance whatever may have been its initial cause. The suit was brought by the attorney general on behalf of Mexican-American, Black, Oriental, and American Indian students.

Another important Chicano case is *Soria v. Oxnard School District*.[20] This federal district court case held that "separate education for the Mexican American and Negro American students in the Oxnard Elementary Schools is inferior to education in racially balanced schools within the district."[21]

Perhaps the most far-reaching case since *Brown* in 1954 is *Serrano v. Priest*,[22] decided on August 30, 1971, by the California Supreme Court. *Serrano* held that the State's financing of the public school system, with its substantial dependence on local property taxes and resultant wide disparities in school revenue, violates the equal protection clause. The Court said:

> [T]his funding scheme invidiously discriminates against the poor because it makes the quality of a child's education a function of the wealth of his parents and neighbors.[23]

B. *Colorado*

Unlike the vigorous duty required by California courts to overcome racial and ethnic imbalance, the Tenth Circuit, which includes Colorado, has reversed *Keyes* and ruled that in de facto cases, the school district is not required to develop a desegregation plan unless the imbalance resulted from racially motivated conduct.[24]

C. *Texas*

1. *Houston*

In Houston *Ross v. Eckels*, which calls for the pairing of Black and Chicano children, is still the law. On May 24, 1971, Judge Ben C.

Connally threw La Raza out of court. The Mexican-American Education Council (MAEC) was seeking, through various Chicano parents, to intervene in the Houston school case.

Before the Houston school district was given serious orders to desegregate, Anglos went to white schools, Blacks went to black schools, and La Raza went to the brown schools. To some extent there has been white-brown integration. After the district received orders to desegregate the dual school system, the residentially segregated Blacks and Chicanos were paired into their neighborhood schools. As a result of being *used* as whites and not *treated* as whites, the Houston Chicanos boycotted the schools in September, 1970 and opened their own Huelga Schools. These Huelga Schools are presently operating with the assistance of volunteer teachers.

During the boycott, the school superintendent recognized Chicanos as an identifiable ethnic minority group. However, it was not binding unless Judge Connally could be convinced that Chicanos have been and are a separate ethnic group. The Judge, in his opinion on the motion to intervene, displayed his ignorance of Chicano history and of the Texas Chicano school cases in saying:

> The Houston Independent School District (*as I believe has been true generally for school purposes throughout this state*) has always treated Latin-Americans as of the *Anglo* or White race.[25]

First, Judge Connally disregards reality when he claims Chicanos have always been treated as Whites in Texas schools. Generally, the documentation this writer has presented refutes that statement. More specifically, *Salvatierra, Delgado, Hernandez, Cisneros, Perez,* and many other cases are legal proof that Chicanos have been discriminated against because of their race and/or color. Second, the Judge grossly exaggerates when he states that Latin-Americans have always been treated as of the *Anglo* race.

Judge Connally then implicitly accuses Chicanos of being racists:

> Content to be "White" for these many years, now, when the shoe begins to pinch, the would-be Intervenors wish to be treated not as Whites but as an "identifiable minority group." *In short, they wish to be "integrated" with Whites, not Blacks.*[26]

What worries this writer is that Judge Connally never cited legal authority for his conclusions. Instead, his decision appears to reveal more of an individual personal opinion. The truth of the matter is that whenever MAEC presented official demands, one of them always called for a *tri-ethnic* desegregation plan, including Anglos, Chicanos, *and* Blacks. Nevertheless, the only relief Chicanos and Blacks can hope for is from the Fifth Circuit, the court which will soon rule on *Cisneros v. Corpus Christi Independent School District.*[27]

2. Austin

In *United States v. Austin Independent School District*[28] the central issue was whether Chicanos had been segregated by acts of the school district. Austin is 64.6% Anglo, 20.4% Chicano, and 15.1% Black. Judge Roberts conceded that even the most casual examination of Chicano culture discloses Chicanos are a separate ethnic group. Nevertheless, the court added:

> But the mere existence of an ethnic group, regardless of its racial origin, and standing alone, does not establish a case for integrating it with the remainder of the school population. Rather the plaintiff (HEW) must show that there had been some form of de jure (official) segregation against the ethnic minority.[29]

Judge Roberts held the Austin district had never segregated Chicanos, but he did note the inequity of integrating Blacks and Browns only:

> [T]here will be little educational value in a plan which merely integrates one socially and economically disadvantaged group, the blacks, with another, the Mexican-Americans.[30]

3. Dallas

Tasby v. Estes,[31] the Dallas school case, is a class action filed by the Dallas Legal Services on behalf of Black and Chicano school children. The court held that Chicanos, although they constitute a clearly separate and identifiable ethnic group, failed to show official segregation by the Dallas school district. However, the court directed that any desegregation plan would take Chicanos into account. In addition, the court called for the creation of a tri-ethnic rather than a bi-racial committee and named five citizens from each of the three groups.

The plan in *Tasby* is unique in two ways. First, it encourages desegregation by providing a four-day week for students who volunteer to transfer from schools where they are the majority to schools where their race is the minority. Second, the plan substitutes physical contact among the different groups with a simultaneous two-way oral and visual communication on television.[32] The case is currently on appeal to the Fifth Circuit.

4. Bryan

When the original school suit was filed in Bryan in 1961, it was filed by Blacks. This year the United States intervened, contending that Bryan operated 14 schools, three attended exclusively by Blacks and one attended predominantly by Chicanos. The district is 26.5% Black and 13.4% Chicano. The court found that 40% of the district's Chicano children attended a school where their race is in a large majority. Consequently, the court ordered Bryan to abstain from discriminating on the basis of race, color, *or ethnic origin,* thereby implying that Chicanos had been segregated officially by the district.[33]

5. *Victoria*

Not all school desegregation requires court action. The Department of Health, Education and Welfare (HEW) can order the submission of a plan whenever it feels discriminatory conditions exist in a school district. This is what occurred in Victoria with regard to three elementary schools. The school board feels these schools are integrated, but as a MAYO member told the board, "All you have to do is to go to those schools to see that they are mostly Black and Chicano."[34] The status of the action in Victoria at the present time is unknown.

6. *Weslaco*

HEW also filed a civil rights "non-compliance" notice against the Weslaco school district. The district, whose student composition is 85.7% Chicano, has only 78 or 27.2% Chicano teachers. Another alleged violation is that four of the six elementary schools are nearly 100% Chicano.[35] To keep their federal funds, Weslaco adopted a single-grade campus, *i.e.,* each elementary school has only one grade.

7. *San Antonio*

In *Rodriguez v. San Antonio Independent School District,*[36] the Chicano plaintiffs are seeking to invalidate the property tax system of school financing as California Chicanos did in *Serrano v. Priest.* However, Judge Spears has purposely delayed hearing the suit to wait for the Texas Legislature to remedy the situation.[37] Even though the legislature failed to act, the case has yet to be heard.

Another legal issue arising in San Antonio is the location of a new school. The NAACP claims that the construction of a new school in a particular location will result in the incorporation of two "handicapped groups"—Blacks and Chicanos—with only a small percentage of white students.[38]

8. *Del Rio*

This writer urged in his previous article that the Del Rio and San Felipe school districts should be treated as one for desegregation purposes.[39] In *United States v. State of Texas*[40] Judge Justice accomplished this by consolidating these two districts. The action arose after the Texas Education Agency refused to accept Anglo transfers to Del Rio from an Air Force base located within the San Felipe district. The refusal was based on the theory that allowing Anglo school children to escape attending an ethnically imbalanced school impedes the desegregation of the districts.[41] The district is now known as the San Felipe Del Rio Consolidated Independent School District.

9. El Paso

In *Alvarado v. El Paso Independent School District*[42] the Fifth Circuit reversed a lower court's dismissal of a Chicano class action desegregation suit alleging racial and ethnic discrimination. The lower court judge said the plaintiffs had "failed to allege any specific act of discrimination which specifically affects any one of the Plaintiffs."[43] On the other hand, the Fifth Circuit held that "the complaint clearly states a cause of action," citing a few cases as authority *"and other cases too numerous to list."*[44]

Alvarado is important for the Texas school cases because it is the first time the Fifth Circuit has addressed itself *directly* to a Chicano school desegregation issue. The court did not rule on the legal questions involved, but it still recognized the identifiability of Mexican-Americans.

The Fifth Circuit first had occasion to deal with the Chicano issue in *Ross v. Eckels,* the Houston case. However, the reason the court allowed the pairing of Black and Chicano schools probably was because the issue was not ripe for decision. The court lacked the value of legal argument by an interest group like MALDEF (Mexican American Legal and Defense Education Fund). And more crucial, there were no Chicano plaintiffs (and there still are none) in *Ross.* This did not prevent Judge Clark from denouncing the Black-Brown integration as "mock justice." Any further developments in this field will be determined by the Fifth Circuit's decisions in the Corpus Christi, Austin, Dallas, El Paso, and Houston cases.

10. Uvalde

In *Morales v. Uvalde Independent School District,*[45] the district court dismissed a suit which is similar to the allegations made in *Alvarado.* The court said that any segregation in Uvalde schools was de facto, *i.e.,* based on voluntary, residential patterns. In addition, the court claimed it could not allow "any and all groups of private individuals to institute suits to revamp and revise an entire school system which has been elected under the democratic process by the people."[46] Because of the similarity to *Alvarado,* the court has decided to delay the Uvalde case until *Alvarado* is finally decided by a higher court.

11. Corpus Christi

Cisneros v. Corpus Christi Independent School District is the landmark case that set off the current rash of Chicano school cases. Briefly, Judge Seals ruled that Chicanos are entitled to the protection of *Brown* and every other school case regarding Blacks since. Also, he held that integration of Blacks and Chicanos fails to produce a unitary school system.

Cisneros is tentatively set to be heard on November 16, 1971. It was originally decided in June, 1970. In October, 1970, Judge Seals allowed the Department of Justice and HEW to intervene, even though an anti-bussing group was denied. The reason for the differing treatment is that the national policy was then one favoring integration.

On July 2, 1971, Judge Seals issued his decision to bus 15,000 students in order to desegregate Corpus Christi, basing this remedy on *Swann v. Charlotte-Mecklenburg Board of Education.*[48] This decision was appealed by the school district to the late Justice Black, who granted a stay. Justice Black said the Corpus Christi situation is "very anomalous, new and confusing."[49] Also, the Department of Justice said there was a "serious question" that there had been discrimination against Chicanos.[50]

On October 7, 1971, the Fifth Circuit voted against hearing *Cisneros* as a full court (16 judges), even though serious questions are involved.[51] Judge Bell, the only one in favor of having the entire court hear the case, stated that:

> [w]e have here a Mexican-American and Anglo segregation problem in a school district where school segregation between the two groups has never been required by law.[52]

Judge Bell fails to recognize that "law" includes not only State legislation and constitutions but also school board customs, regulations, and practices. It was school board practices that Judge Seals found had segregated Mexican-Americans from Anglo children. Nevertheless, it remains for the Fifth Circuit to rule on this question in *Cisneros.*

V. FACTORS LEADING TO THE SEGREGATION OF MEXICAN-AMERICAN CHILDREN

A. *Residential Segregation*

B. *Ability Grouping*

In *Diana v. State Board of Education*[53] the plaintiff Chicano children contended that California's administration of intelligence tests resulted in a disproportionate number of Chicanos in Educable Mentally Retarded classes. The reason for this was that the tests 1) stress verbal skills and 2) are culturally biased since they are geared to measure the average middle class white child.

As a remedy, the court order and agreement requires, among other things, that all children whose primary home language is other than English from now on must be tested in both their primary language and in English with tests which put less stress on verbal skills.

VI. MEXICAN-AMERICAN DESEGREGATION—THE FUTURE

A. *The Southwest Generally*

As previously mentioned, the Del Rio, Texas school case is apparently settled with the consolidation of the Del Rio and San Felipe school districts.

In San Antonio, no decision has been rendered in *Rodriguez*, but *Serrano*, the California property tax case, is extremely relevant.

B. *Ross v. Eckels—The Houston Situation*

For the *Ross* discussion, see IV (C) (1) above.

VII. CONCLUSION

It is hoped that this supplement will offer the reader an insight into the ramifications *Cisneros* could have on the public schools of the Southwest. In addition, the supplement hopefully serves to inform the reader of other recent cases involving the civil rights of Mexican-Americans. The overall objective, however, is to convince the American judicial system that La Raza—Mexican-Americans, Chicanos, Hispanos, Latinos—has been treated unjustly educationally and legally, therefore requiring the intervention of the judiciary in areas of interest to La Raza. Otherwise, the constitutional rule of equal protection of the laws will be nothing more than an empty, unenforcible promise for Chicanos.

NOTES

1. In re Rodriguez, 81 F. 337, 345 (W.D. Tex. 1897).

2. *Id.* at 340.

3. 81 F. 337 (W.D. Tex, 1897).

4. *Id.* at 349.

5. *See also* Sanchez, *Pachucos in the Making*, 4 COMMON GROUND 13 (1943), where Dr. George I. Sanchez of the University of Texas theorizes that discrimination has a causal relationship to the development of pachucos.

6. 401 U.S. 424, 91 S. Ct. 849 (1971).

7. 91 S. Ct. 849, 853 (1971).

8. 167 U.S. 298 (1897).

9. 167 U.S. 278 (1897).

10. 165 U.S. 675 (1897).

11. Letter from William L. Higgs to the United States Supreme Court, February 21, 1971.

12. Interview with Jesse Cruz, July, 1971.

13. 401 U.S. 395 (1971).

14. Graham v. Richardson, 403 U.S. 365, 39 U.S.L.W. 4732 (U.S. June 14, 1971).

15. Perez v. Hackney, Civil Action No. 70-H-1398 (S.D. Tex., filed July 16, 1971). *See* Comment, *State Discrimination Against Mexican Aliens*, 38 GEO. WASH. L. REV. 1091 (1970).

16. 320 F. Supp. 131 (W.D. Tex. 1970).

17. *Id.* at 137.

18. Houston Chronicle, Oct. 4, 1971, § 1, at 11, col. 1. *See also* Gomez v. Florida State Employment Service, 417 F.2d 569 (5th Cir. 1969), where a migrant worker was allowed a civil rights action for damages.

19. 96 Cal. Rptr. 658 (Cal. App. 1971).

20. 328 F. Supp. 155 (C.D. Cal. 1971).

21. *Id.* at 157.

22. 96 Cal. Rptr. 601 (1971). *See also* Rodriguez v. San Antonio Ind. School Dist., 299 F. Supp. 476 (W.D. Tex. 1969).

23. *Id.* at 604.

24. Keyes v. School Dist. No. 1, 445 F.2d 990 (10th Cir. 1971), *rev'g* 313 F. Supp. 61, 313 F. Supp. 90 (D. Colo. 1970).

25. Ross v. Eckels, Civil Action No. 10444, at 6 (S.D. Tex. May 24, 1971) (emphasis added).

26. *Id.* at 7 (emphasis added).

27. *Cisneros* is scheduled for argument on November 16, 1971.

28. Civil Action No. A-70-CA-80 (W.D. Tex. June 28, 1971).

29. Corpus Christi Caller, June 29, 1971, § A, at 2, col. 3.

30. *Id.* at col. 4. The Fifth Circuit Court of Appeals has decided to allow the NAACP and MALDEF to intervene. The groups felt the government would not adequately represent the Black and Chicano school children's needs. San Antonio Express, Aug. 25, 1971, § A, at 16, col. 1.

31. Civil Action No. 3-4211-C (N.D. Tex. Aug. 2, 1971).

32. *Id.* at 7, 17.

33. Thomas v. Bryan Ind. School Dist., Civil Action No. 13850, at 3-6 (S.D. Tex. July 23, 1971).

34. Corpus Christi Caller, June 25, 1971, § D, at 16, col. 4.

35. The McAllen Monitor, July 28, 1971, § A, at 1, col. 2.

36. 299 F. Supp. 476 (W.D. Tex. 1969).

37. San Antonio Express, Sept. 2, 1971, § A, at 1, col. 2.

38. San Antonio Express, July 18, 1971, § D, at 2, col. 2.

39. 8 HOUST. L. REV. 929, 948 (1971).

40. Civil Action No. 5281 (E.D. Tex. Aug. 26, 1971).

41. *See* United States v. State of Texas, 330 F. Supp. 235, 243 (E.D. Tex. 1971).

42. 445 F.2d 1011 (5th Cir.), *rev'g* 326 F. Supp. 674 (W.D. Tex. 1971).

43. 326 F. Supp. 674, 675 (W.D. Tex. 1971).

44. Alvarado v. El Paso Ind. School Dist., 445 F.2d 1011 (5th Cir. 1971) (emphasis added).

45. Civil Action No. _____ (W.D. Tex. June 1, 1971).

46. San Antonio Express, June 25, 1971, § A, at 1, col. 2.

47. 324 F. Supp. 599 (S.D. Tex. 1970).

48. 402 U.S. 1 (1971). *See generally* Exelrod, *Chicano Education: In Swann's Way?*, INEQUALITY IN EDUCATION 28 (1971).

49. San Antonio Express, Aug. 20, 1971, § A, at 1, col. 3. Earlier, Judge Cox, a federal district court judge, issued a stay of Judge Seals' bussing mandate. The Fifth Circuit reversed.

50. *Id.*

51. No. 71-2397 (5th Cir. Oct. 7, 1971).

52. *Id.* at 2.

53. Civil Action No. C-70-37 RFP (N.D. Cal. Feb. 3, 1970).

THE RELATIONSHIP OF ACCULTURATION TO EDUCATIONAL ACHIEVEMENT AND PSYCHOLOGICAL ADJUSTMENT IN CHICANO CHILDREN AND ADOLESCENTS: A REVIEW OF THE LITERATURE[1,2]

Manuel Ramirez III

Introduction

Studies that attempt to relate acculturation to educational achievement and/or personality adjustment in Mexican-Americans invariably concern themselves with one central issue—is identification with the ethnic group an asset or a liability for the Chicano? Information relative to this issue is very critical at present because of the recent emergence of the philosophy of cultural democracy on the American educational scene. Thus, data relative to the effects of acculturation on education and personality will undoubtedly come to determine whether cultural democracy will replace the melting pot as the guiding philosophy of education and mental health programs designed for Mexican-Americans. Should research results show that to maintain identification with the ethnic group is detrimental to the child's educational achievement and his psychological adjustment, the emergent philosophy of cultural democracy will be called into question. Conversely, if identification with the ethnic group is found to be a necessary ingredient of academic success and a positive self-image, then, the policy of cultural relevancy must come to dominate efforts in developing experimental educational and mental health programs for Chicanos.

Review of the Literature

Studies of the relationship of acculturation to education.

The most recent study in this area (Schwartz, 1969) focused on Mexican-American and Anglo-American high school students from schools in the Los Angeles area. The experimenter administered an attitudes inventory to the subjects. The results indicated that there were substantial differences in some special value orientations between Mexican-American and Anglo American pupils from similar socio-economic backgrounds. Namely, Chicanos indicated greater acceptance of wide-scope family authority, viewed their fellow man with caution and viewed their own destiny with resignation. Schwartz found that orientation to the family was the most obvious of these value differences, i.e., more Chicanos than Anglos indicated a desire for parental guidance and approval. Furthermore, scores based on reading tests showed that achieving Chicanos differed from their achieving Anglo counterparts chiefly in their orientation to authority, that is, in their reluctance to exercise control over others and in their lack of independence from parental authority. However, achieving Mexican-Americans indicated that they were more independent from parental control than non-achieving Mexican-Americans and also that they had greater concern for peer than adult disapproval. *In an attempt to explain these findings, the author concluded that by moving away from the strong influence of the family the Chicano pupil frees himself of the cultural ties which may inhibit his achievement.* That is, with independence from family authority, the pupil is said to be emotionally free to change his major reference group and acquire new values and behaviors. The author goes on to state, "One can conclude from this analysis that as opportunities are presented to Mexican-American youth for some acculturation to Anglo values, so are opportunities presented for greater educational achievement."

A recent study by Cordova (1969) has obtained findings which are somewhat different from those obtained by Schwartz. Spanish-American[3] sixth grade students from Albuquerque and from school districts in Northern New Mexico were administered a questionnaire. The results obtained show that values and beliefs in the area of politics (importance attributed to taxes, policemen, judges, etc.) and education (importance attributed to attendance, school activities, etc.) were negatively related to a general feeling of alienation and feelings that school activities were not rewarding or valuable, thus, as there is an increase in the acceptance by Spanish-American students of the values and beliefs concerning education and politics there is a decrease in their feelings of alienation. Acculturation with respect to family values was found to be related to feelings of powerlessness, i.e., the subjects felt that their behaviors could not obtain the goals and reinforcements they sought. Finally, as acculturation in the areas of family and politics increased the achievement of urban middle class students decreased. From this Cordova concluded "These findings imply that previous assumptions that acculturation is a cure-all for educational problems of Spanish-American students is not accurate."

A study by Henderson and Merritt (1968) throws some additional light on the relationship of acculturation to educational achievement. Two groups of Chicano mothers of six-year-old children attending schools in Tucson, Arizona were given an interview which attempted to assess nine environmental process variables, i.e., achievement press, language models, academic guidance, activeness of family, identification with models, range of social interaction, and perception of practical values of education. There were two groups of mothers interviewed—one group was composed of mothers of high potential children, identified as such by their scores on the Goodenough Harris Drawing Test and the Van Alstyne Picture Vocabulary, and another group was composed of mothers of children who had scored low on these same tests (i.e., low potential group). The results showed that as expected the means on all environmental process variables were higher for the high potential group, thus, indicating that children in the high potential group were exposed to a wider variety of stimulating experiences. The most interesting finding of the study, however, was that *high potential children scored better than low potential children on a test of Spanish vocabulary.* The authors concluded, "The data seemed to refute the common assumption that children from families that are the most 'Mexican' in their behavior and outlook will have difficulty in school, it appears that high potential families may participate more fully than families of low potential children in both Anglo American and Mexican-American cultures." A study somewhat related to that of Henderson and Merritt but involving graduate students rather than elementary school children produced similar results. Long and Padilla (1971) administered a questionnaire to 50 students with Spanish surnames who had succeeded in obtained graduate degrees at the University of New Mexico and compared their responses to those of unsuccessful Spanish surnamed students who had dropped out of the university. The results showed that 94 per cent of the successful but only 7.6 per cent of the unsuccessful students reported having been reared in bilingual homes. Most of the unsuccessful students had come from homes in which only English was spoken, thus, indicating a high degree of acculturation. On the basis of this finding Long and Padilla concluded, "The present finding of a very high rate of bilingualism in the sample of successful Spanish-American students suggests that these students may have been better able to interact readily with members of both their own culture and that of the dominant American culture. These individuals may simply be better adjusted members of both their cultures. The lack of bilingual background suggested in the sample of unsuccessful students may reflect the conflict of marginality often seen in members of ethnic minority groups . . ."

Studies dealing with the relationship of acculturation to personality.

Derbyshire (1968) selected Chicano adolescents living in a low income neighborhood in East Los Angeles for study. They were given a thirty-four page questionnaire which covered personal and family history as well as subjective feelings and attitudes toward persons and values significant in their lives. The questionnaire included a series of concepts (i.e., father, mother, self, Mexican) to be rated on an Osgood Semantic Differential Scale. The results indicated that Chicanos who identified with the Mexican way of life to a greater extent were more educationally minded, more sympathetic and adaptable to deviants, maintained more respect for authority, and were more adaptable to conflicting situations. From these findings the author concluded, "The data indicates that the maintenance, perpetuation, and integration of the Mexican heritage and culture is important to the maintenance of a stable sense of identity while growing up in the U.S." Ramirez (1969) also studied Chicano adolescents in California. He administered a Mexican-American values inventory to two hundred Chicano adolescents in Sacramento. The ten subjects who expressed the greatest degree of agreement with these values and the ten who expressed the least degree of agreement were administered the Bell Adjustment Inventory (Student Form). The findings obtained were as follows: 1. Subjects who rejected Chicano values reported experiencing more conflicts with parents, more health problems, and more guilt and tension than those who had agreed with the values while 2. Chicano females who expressed agreement with the values scored higher on submissiveness and hostility than any of the other subgroups, and 3. males who expressed agreement with the values seemed to be best adjusted of all the sub-groups. This would seem to indicate that Chicano adolescents who rejected Chicano values experienced more difficulty in human relations than those who identified with them. Especially important appears to be the fact that subjects who rejected Chicano values reported experiencing more conflicts with their parents. This, along with the fact that they reported feeling more guilt and tension and more health problems, seems to suggest that conflict with parents resulted in tensions which in turn was expressed in the way of psychosomatic complaints. This could certainly be in line with observations made by other researchers (Cleveland and Longakre 1967) of non-Chicanos who have experienced value conflicts with their parents.

Jessor, Graves, Hanson, and Jessor (1968) studied Spanish-Americans,[4] Anglo Americans, and Indian-Americans in a small town in southwestern Colorado. Adults were interviewed and a variety of different instruments were used to assess the adolescents including self reports, group questionnaires, interviews, sociometrics, behavior tests, teacher ratings, and school records. The results showed that differences in values between the ethnic groups were relatively minor and that what emerged as crucially important were differences in expectation for achieving what was valued. With respect to social control and deviance proneness the data pointed to the critical role played by social controls especially with respect to Indians and Spanish-Americans. Both groups were subjected to strong pressures toward deviance yet the Spanish-Americans embedded in a persisting structure of religious, family and interpersonal sanctions contributed far less to the deviance rates than the Indians for whom the control structure was fragmented and weak. This implies that acculturation would tend to increase deviancy in Chicanos since the usual trend of acculturation is to reduce social controls of religion and family.

Studies attempting to relate acculturation to both educational and personality variables.

There is one study (Ramirez, Taylor, and Petersen, 1970) which attempted to deal with both educational and personality variables. The study consisted of two experiments. The initial effort involved administering an attitudes toward education inventory to junior and senior high Mexican-American and Anglo students of the lower socio-economic class in Sacramento, California. The second part consisted of administering a projective technique, a story telling procedure, to three Chicano and three Anglo sub-groups from the original sample. The three groups within each ethnic group were selected according to their score on the attitude scale as follows: 1. those who had expressed positive attitudes toward education, 2. those who had expressed negative attitudes and 3. those whose scores were close to the mean. The results of the first part of the study showed that Chicanos expressed views toward education which were significantly less positive than those of Anglos. Items which differentiated significantly between the two ethnic groups appeared to reflect differences between the value orientations of the groups. Data obtained with the projective technique in the second phase of the study revealed that Chicanos had scored higher than Anglos on need Power, and need Rejection but had scored lower on need Achievement. Again, the differences in motivational style were explained in terms of differences between value systems of the two ethnic groups and the present structure of the educational system which in many cases is alien to the beliefs and prior learning experiences of Chicanos. Furthermore, stories obtained with the projective technique seemed to indicate that Chicano students experienced more conflicts with both their parents and their teachers because they served as the carriers of values from both school and home. Since in many instances parents and teachers were ignorant of one another's values and life styles, disagreement between them with negative consequences for the Chicano student was the end result. The authors stated "to improve the chances for academic success of the Mexican-American child changes must be made in both the educational system and in some of the attitudes perceptions and behaviors of the child . . . by altering the structure of the educational system and by helping school personnel to become aware of the unique needs, perceptions, and attitudes of Chicano students most of the characteristics engendered by the Mexican-American culture in children can become an asset rather than a liability in the classroom."

Discussion

Education Studies

The studies reviewed emphasize the complexity of the acculturation issue. Schwartz (1969) found in her study of a Los Angeles sample of

Chicanos that acculturation is positively related to academic achievement, yet Cordova (1969), and also Henderson and Merritt (1968) found the opposite to be true in New Mexico and Arizona, respectively. These findings seem to indicate that the milieu plays a crucial role here. It is altogether possible for example that the schools from which Schwartz sampled in Los Angeles did not reinforce the child for his "Chicanismo," on the other hand, schools from which Cordova and Henderson and Merritt selected their subjects in New Mexico and Arizona may follow a different policy. Here there may be more reinforcement or at least less punishment for being identified with the Mexican-American value system.

The research reviewed here also suggests that socio-economic variables may be central to this issue. Cordova's results support this latter finding. He found that for the middle class Spanish surnamed students in his sample, acculturation to family values was negatively related to performance in school. What appears to be suggested here is that the relationship of acculturation (at least with respect to family values) to academic performance is linked to socio-economic class. Is it possible, then, that for Cordova's samples acculturation was negatively related to achievement in middle class students, but positively related in those of the lower class?

The fact that the middle class Chicano family, because of its greater economic resources, may be capable of maintaining its ethnic identity makes this likely. That is, the middle class family may be more capable than the lower class family of protecting some of its values from the onslaught of schools which are out to Anglicize its members. In addition, teachers may be more supportive of cultural differences in middle class Chicano children than in lower class children. In other words, the same cultural differences which they see as prestigious and interesting in middle class children they may be viewing as cultural deprivation and disadvantage in poor children. It is obvious that future studies in this area cannot ignore these variables.

The achievement test validity issue may also be critical here. In most of the studies reviewed here, degree of achievement in school was defined in terms of performance on standardized achievement tests. Unacculturated Chicano children are most likely to have performed poorly on these tests because a traditional orientation to family values is usually correlated with lack of acculturation in areas most commonly tapped by these instruments. For example: (1) the primary langauge of unacculturated Chicano children is Spanish, thus, they are not familiar with the English vocabulary of these tests, (2) most of these children also have never been exposed to the Anglo middle class cultural information reflected in the test items and, (3) there is nothing in their past experiences which prepares them for the testing situation itself. The achievement test data is thus, confounded by the weaknesses of the instruments used for evaluating these children.

Personality studies.

Results of the personality studies are much more consistent than those in education. They reveal that acculturation in the form of reducing the Chicano's identity with his ethnic group tends to result in negative consequences for psychological adjustment. The methodology of these studies, however, is not nearly as sophisticated as those reviewed in the education section. Almost all of these studies have employed paper and pencil instruments and have involved only superficial and short term study of subjects.

Recommendations

Almost every review of the literature ends in a call for additional research and this one is no exception. There is a great need for longitudinal studies in this area. Specifically there is need for extensive studies of how milieu, and socio-economic class interact with acculturation to affect personality and education. The Chicano is now socio-economically diverse, and is found in so many different milieus that it will be necessary to do studies in rural and urban areas and in different states of the Southwest and Midwest. Who can deny that conditions for acculturation in Texas differ from those in California, or that those in East Los Angeles differ from those in Chicago? Furthermore, there is need for studies on family dynamics. *All studies reviewed showed that the family is closely tied to the effects which the Chicano child experiences in the process of becoming acculturated, yet we have little data available on Chicano family dynamics, and especially so on urban Chicano families.*

There is, therefore, a critical need for more enlightened research relevant to acculturation of Chicanos. There is an even greater need to insure that the results of this research will be incorporated into education and community mental health programs. This is especially important since many of these programs are continuing to follow the old and inappropriate model of assimilation into the mainstream American middle-class. There is, thus, a very crucial issue at stake here—the outcome of the struggle for cultural democracy in American mental health and education.

NOTES

1. The author would like to thank Dr. Alfredo Castaneda, Chairman of Mexican-American Studies at the University of California, Riverside for his help and encouragement in the preparation of this paper.

2. This paper was written for the Southwestern Cooperative Educational Laboratory as part of a project sponsored by the Bureau of Research, U.S. Office of Education. Dr. Atilano Valencia served as director of the project.

3. Cordova's terminology.

4. Jessor's terminology.

REFERENCES

Cleveland, E. J. and Longakre, W. D., Neurotic patterns in the family. In G. Handel (ed.) *The Psychosocial interior of the family.*, Chicago: Aldine, 1967, p. 159-185.

Cordova, I. R., The relationship of acculturation, · achievement, and alienation among Spanish-American sixth grade students., Prepared for the Conference on Teacher Education for Mexican-Americans: New Mexico State University: ERIC: CRESS, February, 1969.

Derbyshire, R. L., Adolescent identity crisis in urban Mexican-Americans in East Los Angeles., In E. B. Brody, *Minority group adolescents in the United States.*, Baltimore: The Williams and Wilkens Company, 1968, 73-110.

Henderson, R. W. and Merritt, C. C. Environmental backgrounds of Mexican-American children with different potentials for school success. *The Journal of Social Psychology.*, 1969, 75, 101-106.

Jessor, R., Graves, T. D., Hanson, R. C. and Jessor, S. L., *Society, personality, and deviant behavior: a study of a tri-ethnic community.* New York: Holt, Rinehart and Winston, Inc., 1968.

Long, K. K. and Padilla, A. M. Evidence for bilingual antecedents of academic success in the groups of Spanish-American college students., *Journal of Cross-Cultural Psychology*, 1971.

Ramirez, M., Identification with Mexican-American values and psychological adjustment in Mexican-American adolescents. *International Journal of Social Psychiatry*, 1969, 11 (2), 151-156.

Ramirez, M., and Taylor, C., Sex role determinants in attitudes toward education among Mexican-American adolescents, Report submitted to the Department of Health, Education and Welfare., Office of Education, Bureau of Research., November, 1967.

Ramirez, M., Taylor, C. and Petersen, B., Mexican-American cultural membership and adjustment to school., *Developmental Psychology*, 1971, 4 (2), 141-148.

Schwartz, A. J., Comparative values and achievement of Mexican-American and Anglo pupils., Center for the Study of Evaluation, UCLA Graduate School of Education., Report No. 37, February, 1969.

SPECIAL EDUCATION PLACEMENT AND MEXICAN AMERICANS
Frank Ortega

Several million Mexican American children living within a five-state area in the Southwest never will get beyond the eighth grade. Whatever their background, they are herded into classes wherein all courses are taught in English. In many cases, they are forbidden to speak Spanish in the classrooms and even on the playground. How can one determine the intellectual functioning of these children?

Thus far, in determining the intellectual functioning of Mexican American children, the principal problems appear to be:

1. The content of the intelligence tests. The Mexican American children may not have acquired the habits and tools that are tapped by I.Q. tests.

2. The inadequacy of non-verbal tests to ascertain the intelligence of Mexican American children. Non-verbal tests are as culturally biased as the verbal tests, and they cannot test what is not there. *Non-verbal performance tasks actually require verbal mediation.*

3. The use of translated tests. Even after translation, cultural factors may remain which may render the test invalid for Mexican American children.

4. The level of verbal competency of the Mexican American children taking the standardized intelligence test, especially when it is administered in Spanish. The Spanish spoken in the home may contain many dialectical variations and Anglicisms.

5. Interpretation of test scores is an important factor. Until recently, it was commonly held that I.Q. was an innate capacity fixed at birth by genetic determinants.

Some Definitions

EDUCABLE MENTALLY RETARDED (EMR): An educable mentally retarded child is one whose Intelligence Quotient ranges roughly between 50 and 70, and who, under favorable circumstances and adequate training, can become self-supporting and in many cases will require little or no supervision. Educationally such a student may attain a level between the first and fourth grade.

EDUCATIONALLY HANDICAPPED (EH): Educationally handicapped children are minors, other than physically handicapped or mentally retarded minors, who, by reason of marked learning or behavioral problems or a combination thereof, cannot receive the reasonable benefit of ordinary educational facilities.

TRAINABLE MENTALLY RETARDED (TMR): A trainable mentally retarded child can be defined as one having a mentality from four to eight years of age at full maturity and who will always require supervision in performing useful tasks.

INTELLIGENCE QUOTIENT (I.Q.): Intelligence quotient is defined as numerical representation of level of intelligence.

The Problem

In California, is there a disproportionate placement of Mexican American children in classes for the educable mentally retarded? To answer this question, the following hypotheses have been formulated:

Hypothesis I: With the total school population as a base, the placement of Spanish speaking and "other white" students in Special Education (EMR, TMR) will follow the normal curve.

Hypothesis II: With the total handicapped population as a base, the placement of Spanish speaking and "other white" students in Special Education (EMR, TMR) will follow the normal curve.

Hypothesis III: The placement of "other whites" in EMR and TMR classes does follow the normal distribution curve.

Hypothesis IV: The placement of Mexican American students in EMR and TMR classes does not follow the normal curve.

The Study

The data utilized in this study (See Tables I, II, III, IV) is contained in the California State Department of Education report entitled, "A Report to State Board of Education Regarding House Resolution No. 444 Relative to Special Education." A chi square analysis was made to determine if EMR class placement in the state of California follows the theory of normal distribution. In other words, what is being looked at is the amount of discrepancy between what is expected and what is actually observed.

We know that there are vast differences in the range of intellectual ability among' children. Most children, however, tend to cluster around a central point in the distribution of intelligence. This is called the mean or the average. Any given child may rank at any point from "inferior" to "very superior" from the standpoint of intelligence. From a quantitative point of view, it is important to consider how I.Q. is distributed through the general population. The distribution depicted by Figure A is representative of many human traits, i.e., height, weight, etc.

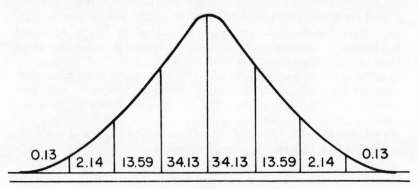

FIGURE A
PERCENT OF CASES UNDER PORTIONS OF THE NORMAL CURVE

This curve is known as the normal distribution curve, or the curve of normal probability. It is used in plotting the distribution of intelligence in the general population. Generally speaking, the statistical average in I.Q.'s falls between 95 and 104. People who are within this range are considered to be "average" or "normal" in intelligence.

Statisticians have determined that the following relationship always holds for any normal distribution or measurement: 68.26% of the population falls between one standard deviation above and one standard deviation below the mean; 95% of all cases fall between two standard deviations above and below the mean; and 99.7% of all cases fall between points three standard deviations above and below the mean.

Although the numerical value of the mean I.Q., and the size of the standard deviation vary according to the specific intelligence test used (since any given test contains some errors of measurement), it is believed that intelligence is distributed over the total population in a similar manner, regardless of the test used for its measurement. *Any statistical or proportional deviation that suggests intelligence is not equally distributed among racial, ethnic, or socio-economic groups is completely antithetical to the basic theory of distribution.*

Results of the Study

The hypothesis that, with the total school population as a base, the placement of Spanish speaking and "other white" students in Special Education (EMR, TMR) follows the normal curve is rejected. Table I demonstrates that special education placement did not follow the normal distribution curve for the "other white" EMR students, although placement can be considered normal for TMR classes.

The hypothesis that, with the total handicapped population as a base, the placement of Spanish speaking and "other white" students in Special Education (EMR, TMR) is rejected. Table II shows that within the handicapped population Mexican Americans made up 28.34% of the EMR population, yet only 15.22% of the total school population. "Other whites" were 72.40% of the total school population, yet they constituted only 44.27 of the EMR population. Table II also indicates clearly that Mexican American students are not being properly served in the EH program.

Hypothesis number III, that placement of "other whites" in EMR and TMR classes follows the normal distribution curve is rejected. Table III clearly indicates that "other whites" were placed in EMR programs in smaller numbers than would be expected according to the normal distribution curve.

Hypothesis IV, that the placement of Mexican American students in EMR and TMR classes does not follow the normal distribution curve is rejected. Table IV indicates that actual placement of Mexican American children did follow the normal distribution curve.

Summary

The data support the contention that special education placement in California does not follow expectations according to the curve of normal probability. There is a clear lack of relationship between the Mexican American composition of classes for the educable mentally retarded and regular education classes. A clear disproportion of special classes for the educable mentally retarded are composed of Mexican American children.

Including all pupils in California schools, 1.16% of all pupils have been diagnosed as educable mentally retarded. However, among the Mexican Americans 2.14% have been so diagnosed and placed in programs for the educable mentally retarded. Only .71% of "other white" pupils have been so diagnosed! This means that fewer "other whites" are placed in educable mentally retarded classes than expected according to the normal curve.

Conclusions

From the foregoing it is possible to draw several conclusions regarding the enrollment of Mexican Americans in programs for the educable mentally retarded.

First, the disproportionate representation of Spanish speaking students in programs for the educable mentally retarded is a statewide problem.

Second, it is apparent that "intelligence" in California is not stable, but dependent upon the *right* psychologists and special education per-

TABLE I

A COMPARISON OF RACIAL AND ETHNIC POPULATION PLACED IN SPECIAL EDUCATION PROGRAMS: PERCENTAGE OF THE TOTAL POPULATION USED AS A BASE

	Spanish Surnamed	Other White	
EMR	2.14	.71	2.85
TMR	.25	.19	.44
EH	.32	.57	.89
	2.71	1.47	4.18

NOTE: Chi square equals 43.0423 with 2 degrees of freedom. It is statistically significant beyond the .01 level.

TABLE II

A COMPARISON OF RACIAL AND ETHNIC POPULATION PLACED IN SPECIAL EDUCATION PROGRAMS: PERCENTAGE OF THE TOTAL HANDICAPPED POPULATION USED AS A BASE

	Spanish Surname	Other White	
EMR	28.34	44.27	72.61
TMR	18.88	66.91	85.79
EH	9.42	79.59	89.01
	56.64	190.77	247.41

NOTE: Chi square equals 18.3908 with 2 degrees of freedom. It is statistically significant beyond the .01 level.

TABLE III

PLACEMENT OF HANDICAPPED OTHER WHITES COMPARED WITH NORMAL DISTRIBUTION CURVE

	Normal Probability	Actual Placement of Other Whites	
EMR	2.14	.71	2.85
TMR	.13	.19	.32
	2.27	.90	3.17

NOTE: Chi square equals 22.6991 with 1 degree of freedom. It is statistically significant at the .01 level.

TABLE IV

PLACEMENT OF MEXICAN AMERICAN HANDICAPPED COMPARED WITH NORMAL DISTRIBUTION CURVE

	Normal Probability	Actual Placement of Mexican Americans	
EMR	2.14	2.14	4.28
TMR	.13	.25	.38
	2.27	2.39	4.66

NOTE: Chi square equals 0.0129 with 1 degree of freedom. It is not statistically significant.

sonnel. The entire concept of intelligence in California has been completely contradictory to the basic premise upon which special classes are based.

Third, the procedure used to label students as mentally retarded, as used in California, is ambiguous. The actual problem appears to be the fact that educators have been unwilling to accept language and cultural differences in children, and to modify their curricula for the specific needs of children. They have succumbed to the easier panacea of labeling Spanish speaking children as educable mentally retarded. Thus the inferior image of the Mexican American population, accompanied by a pessimistic academic expectancy becomes commonplace in educational circles. Because of the over-representation of the Mexican Americans in the EMR programs, how many children are mislabeled for life each year in California schools?

Problems Related to the Availability, Use and
Effects of Present American Testing Instruments
and Methods with Mexican Americans

Problems Related to Present Testing Instruments

Steve Moreno

The Problem

Achievement, aptitude and intelligence tests have been developed for, and standardized on, an entirely English speaking population. The norms thus developed were designed to provide descriptive information and predictive validity about the various skills, aptitudes, and abilities measured. The tests clearly reflect middle-class American culture, values, and language.

The *major* problem facing most Mexican-Americans is that they represent a different culture, possess many different values, and speak a different language than that contained in the American tests. As a result of cultural differences, the Mexican American is obviously at a disadvantage when he is exposed to most tests. The Mexican American usually scores much lower than his English speaking American contemporary. As a result of his lower score, the Mexican American has been relegated to an image of stupid, lazy, dumb, slow, educable mentally retarded, etc. Many questions have been raised recently as a result of the lower scores for Mexican-Americans. Those questions most asked by concerned Mexican-American educators are:

1. How valid are English test scores on Spanish-speaking or bilingual children?

2. How reliable are English test scores on Spanish-speaking or bilingual children?

3. Are valid tests available for Mexican American children?

The following will address itself to these concerns.

415

Related Research

First, the question of language handicap of Mexican Americans when measured on English *intelligence* tests will be reviewed.

Many investigators (Altus, 1953; Carlson and Henderson, 1950; Darcy, 1952; Garth, 1936; Havinghurst, 1944; Hill, 1936; Jamieson and Sandiford, 1920; Kittell, 1959; Kittell, 1963; Pintner, 1922; Pintner and Keller, 1922; Seidl, 1937) have attempted to determine the effects of bilingualism on the measure of intelligence of elementary school children. A method frequently used has been that of comparing the performance of bilingual children on verbal and nonverbal intelligence tests. *In general, the findings of the studies tend to support the conclusion that monolingual Spanish speakers and bilingual children suffer from a language handicap when intelligence is measured on verbal testing.* Kittell (1959) indicates that I.Q. scores may be misleading for bilingual children, and that I.Q. scores and socio-economics may be related in measuring I.Q.'s of bilingual children. Adler (1968) indicates that there seems to be a unanimity of opinion among psychologists that intelligence tests are not free from "cultural" bias. Many psychologists, as well as some anthropologists and sociologists, question the very fact that it is even possible to construct a test which is free from cultural loadings. As early as 1932, Sanchez (1932) showed that Spanish bilinguals increased their I.Q.'s on successive verbal intelligence tests when they received language experiences between test administrations. The predictive validity of I.Q. tests has been questioned (Carlson and Henderson, 1950) and the findings raise the question of the appropriateness of the common practice in schools of recording the predictive validity as an index of intellectual brightness for a child who is not a member of the cultural group upon which the test was standardized, and especially so when the predictive index is to be used at some time subsequent to the testing period.

Other research (Phillips and Bannon, 1968) has indicated that the Binet norms are not adequate for populations that are entirely *English* speaking. The validity and reliability of intelligence tests is further reduced by research (Masling, 1959) which indicates that examiners tend to be more lenient with more friendly subjects as opposed to a cold role-playing subject.

Mathis (1969) has clearly demonstrated that aptitude testing has profoundly bad effects on disadvantaged applicants. The tests tend to bar them from suitable employment and destroys their aspirations of success during the process. He further states that aptitude tests are based on faulty assumptions and that aptitude test scores should be followed by training to prepare disadvantaged applicants for jobs rather than exclude them from consideration because of a low score on an aptitude test.

The predictive validity of achievement tests was summarized by Personke (1969) in his research which indicated that existing readiness tests do predict the ability of Mexican-American children to read based on our *present* teaching methods. The tests were valid descriptions of children's ability, but the *programs* were *not*.

Conclusions

The above literature clearly indicates that:

1. Monolingual Spanish-speaking children and bilingual children are handicapped when taking English examinations of all types: intelligence, aptitude, and achievement.

2. The predictive validity of existing English tests; especially I.Q. and aptitude tests, is lost for Mexican-American children.

3. Existing readiness tests may predict achievement for Spanish-speaking children in our present programs, but the test scores *should* clearly indicate different programs for different populations.

Present Situation

Because of organized Mexican-American concern, the California Department of Education has allocated funds to develop a Spanish version of an existing intelligence test. The basic premise in developing an I.Q. test in a specific language is that those *children who will be tested are monolingual in the language of the test. Since most Spanish surnamed children are bilingual, they will be penalized by a totally Spanish I.Q. test as much as they were penalized by the English I.Q. test;* unless, the norms of the test are designed to reflect a normal curve equal to that of the English-speaking Americans. The normal curve for bilingual children will not be totally accepted until unique curriculums are developed that insure academic success for bilingual children. Before the curriculums are developed, tests must be developed to measure the degree of bilingualism and the effect of such on various curriculums.

There are achievement tests available in Spanish which measure achievement in the Spanish language, but give little information concerning instruction in English for bilingual children. As a result of the above research, I feel that the following is needed:

1. A bicultural ability test in English and/or Spanish that measures ability equally in either language.

2. Tests to measure degrees of bilingualism.

3. A list of *academic* priorities for bilingual children.

4. Development of curriculums best suited for various degrees of bilingualism, and based on academic priorities and behavioral objectives.

5. Longitudinal studies designed to measure long term effect of special curriculums.

6. Establishment of language development classes for those bilingual Mexican-American children who are supposedly "functional" in English, but that lack language development necessary to improve their socio-economic status.

7. Conduct reverse longitudinal studies on successful Mexican-Americans to determine the predictive validity of most commonly used "entrance" exams (ACT, GATB, GRE, etc.) and aptitude tests.

Until these steps are properly taken, the testing of Mexican-American children will remain a scientific morass and a lucrative playground for misguided research.

BIBLIOGRAPHY

Adler, Manfred, "Intelligence Testing of the Culturally Disadvantaged," *Journal of Negro Education*, 37:258-67, Summer 68.

Altus, G. T., "W.I.S.C. Patterns of a Selective Sample of Bilingual School Children," *Journal of Genetic Physchology*, 83:249-8; 1953.

Carlson, Hilding B., and Henderson, Norman, "The Intelligence of American Children of Mexican Parentage," *Journal of Abnormal and Social Psychology*, 45:544-51; 1950.

Darcy, Natalie T., The Performanc of Bilingual Puerto Rican Children on Verbal and on Non-Language Tests of Intelligence," *Journal of Educational Research*, 45:499-506; 1952.

Garth, T. R., "The Administration of Non-Language Intelligence Tests to Mexicans," *Journal of Abnormal and Social Psychology*, 31: 53-58; 1936.

Havinghurst, R. J., and Hilkevitch, R. H., "The Intelligence of Indian Children as Measured by a Performance Scale," *Journal of Abnormal and Social Psychology*, 39:419-32; 1964.

Hill, H. S., "The Effects of Bilingualism on the Measured Intelligence of Elementary School Children of Italian Parentage," *Journal of Experimental Education*, 5:75-9; 1936

Jamieson, E., and Sandiford, P., "The Mental Capacity of Southern Ontario Indians," *Journal of Educational Psychology*, 19:313-28; 1920.

Kittell, Jack E., "Bilingualism and Language-Non-Language Intelligence Scores of Third Grade Children," *Journal of Educational Research*, V 52, N 7, 263-68, Nov. 59.

Kittell, Jack E., "Intelligence Test Performance of Children from Bilingual Environments," *Elementary School Journal*, N 63, 76-88.

Masling, J., "The Effects of Warm and Cold Interaction on the Administration and Scoring of an Intelligence Test," *Journal of Consulting Psychology*, 1959, 23:336-341.

Mathis, Harold I., "The Disadvantaged and the Aptitude Barrier," *Personnel and Guidance Journal*, V 47, 467-472, 1969.

Personke, Cark, and O. O. Davis, "Predictive Validity of English and Spanish Versions of a Readiness Test," *The Elementary School Journal*, Nov. 69.

Pinter, R., "Comparison of American and Foreign Children on Intelligence Tests," *Journal of Educational Psychology*, 14:292-95; 1922.

Pinter, R. and Keller R., "Intelligence of Foreign Children," *Journal of Educational Psychology*, 13:214-22; 1922.

Phillips, L. J. and Bannon, W. J., "The Stanford-Binet, Form L-M, A Local English Study of Norms, Concurrent Validity and Social Differences," *British Journal of Educational Psychology*, 38:148-61, June 68.

Sanchez, I., "Scores of Spanish Speaking Children on Repeated Tests," *Journal of Genetic Psychology*, 40: 233-231; 1932.

Seidl, J. C., *The Effect of Bilingualism on the Measurement of Intelligence*. Unpublished Ph.D. Thesis. New York: Fordham University, 1937.

NUESTRA CIRCUNSTANCIA LINGUISTICA

Rosaura Sánchez

La mayoría de nuestros educadores piensan que las minorías desventajadas carecen de medios de expresión y que hablan dialectos primitivos y, por supuesto, inferiores. Las instituciones educativas han llegado a deificar los idiomas que han producido las grandes obras literarias del mundo, pensando que la literatura—generalmente occidental—es prueba del valor inherente de ciertas lenguas y por consiguiente de ciertos grupos raciales. El pueblo que a duras penas puede proveerse de una alimentación adecuada y que desempeña los trabajos más arduos de la sociedad generalmente no tiene ni el tiempo ni la energía para producir grandes obras artísticas cuando regresa exhausto a su casa.*

Los educadores parecen no darse cuenta que los idiomas establecidos no son más que dialectos que han sido favorecidos por algún grupo política y económicamente poderoso. Al proclamarlos dialectos oficiales los han difundido por todos los medios de comunicación y les han señalado funciones importantes en el gobierno, en la educación y en los centros culturales. El dialecto oficial o standard se convierte entonces en la herramienta necesaria para poder avanzar en la escala socioeconómica. De allí que los grupos minoritarios en EEUU procuren asimilarse a la cultura de la mayoría, olvidando, en la mayoría de los casos, el idioma de sus padres y de sus abuelos. Claro que para poder competir en este mundo anglo-sajón, hay que dominar el inglés, el inglés standard. Por esta razón más y más padres de familia méxico-americanos, queriendo evitar que sus hijos sufran las mismas humillaciones que ellos por hablar un *inglés mocho*, ahora les hablan inglés a sus niños. Y hay que concederles la razón, en parte por lo menos, porque ahora nos vemos rechazados de las universidades que exigen determinado puntaje

---

*Véase William Labov: "Academic Ignorance and Black Intelligence" *Atlantic*, June, 1972.

en los exámenes de ingreso, para los cuales las escuelas de barrio no nos han preparado.

Pero para sentir que lo nuestro tiene tanto valor como lo de cualquiera, tenemos que retener nuestro español. Tenemos que exigir programas de educación bilingüe en las escuelas, pero programas bien planificados con profesoras bien preparadas, que entiendan que el hablar un dialecto no-standard no es un obstáculo para al aprendizaje de un dialecto standard o de otras lenguas. El obstáculo es la profesora ignorante de todo aquello que no sea la norma, la profesora que considera al niño minoritario incapaz de expresarse más que con gestos o inflexiones e incapaz de enfrentarse a lo abstracto, en otras palabras, una profesora repleta de prejuicios burgueses.

En los últimos años debido a la iniciación de programas bilingües por el sudoeste de Estados Unidos se han planteado algunos problemas en torno a la selección de idiomas, puesto que al querer especificar la lengua materna del niño méxico-americano se ha encontrado que no existe una uniformidad lingüística entre el pueblo méxico-americano. Los niños que vienen de las zonas rurales o cuyos padres son immigrantes mexicanos en las zonas urbanas sólo hablan español. Otros niños, de segunda o tercera generación en EEUU, hablan una mezcla de inglés y español. En la tesis doctoral de Roger Mark Thompson (1971) sobre el uso del español y el inglés en la comunidad méxico-americana, encontramos que la mayoría de los padres de segunda generación han dejado de enseñarles el español a sus hijos. Estos lo aprenden de vecinos y demás personas que aún hablan español.

A veces la selección de las escuelas participantes en los proyectos bilingües se hace a base de los apellidos hispanos y resulta que muchas veces estos niños de apellido García o Pérez no saben ni jota de español. La educación bilingüe es para todos, alguien dirá. Sí, claro, pero cuando el número de escuelas favorecidas es limitado, es preferible que el proyecto se dirija a esos niños que no dominan el inglés y que sin la ayuda de estos programas tendrían que repetir el primer año escolar.

Antes de que este problema se resuelva y de que la educación bilingüe sea para todos en general, habrá que investigar lo que se entiende por educación bilingüe. Algunas escuelas que reciben subvenciones del gobierno federal por participar en un proyecto bilingüe realmente dedican sólo 30 minutos diariamente a la repetición de ejercicios audiolinguales de substitución. El niño que repite como perico "Es un triángulo. Es un círculo. Es un cuadrado." por 30 minutos, no recibe una educación bilingüe. Lo único que hace es memorizar una serie de términos dentro de una estructura de poca utilidad.

Algunas escuelas utilizan materiales preparados en Puerto Rico con vocabulario desconocido para el niño méxico-americano. Otras escuelas tienen materiales preparados por las profesoras mismas. En una escuela que visitamos la profesora pedía que los niños subrayaran los dibujos cuyos nombres comenzaran con [m]. La hoja incluía el dibujo de un molino que debía subrayarse. Los niños lo identificaron como *papalote.* La mariposa les pareció *paloma, palomita,* o *palomilla.* Todo material que se prepara sin debida atención al dialecto local trae resultados mediocres y contraproducentes. Lo trágico sería que si antes los niños méxico-americanos aparecían como retardados por faltarles el. vocabulario en inglés ahora también se les frustre por desconocer los términos que trae el diccionario de la Real Academia Española. Debemos considerar que si el niño desconoce un término, por ejemplo *balde,* es que en esa región se emplea otro, como *bote, tina, cedrón,* o *cubeta.* Claro que hay que ampliar el léxico del niño pero también hay que concretar lo que se está examinando, o la asociación de [m] con el sonido inicial de determinadas palabras o el conocimiento de determinadas variantes léxicas. Ciertamente se necesitan especialistas en la preparación de materiales para la enseñanza bilingüe, que conozcan el español regional.

El español del méxico-americano comparte varios rasgos con los dialectos hispanoamericanos como la debilitación de las fricativas, la aspiración de la sibilante, la tendencia a la monosilabización de los hiatos y el relajamiento de las vocales. Los rasgos distintivos proceden de nuestro contacto con el inglés, lo que ha producido en parte el uso de una cantidad de préstamos que se han adaptado al sistema fonológico y morfo-sintáctico del español y en parte una mezcolanza de los dos idiomas. Esta interferencia se da dondequiera que haya dos lenguas en contacto y dondequiera que dos idiomas lleguen a desempeñar una misma función dentro de la comunidad.

Puesto que un dialecto representa un subgrupo de un idioma utilizado dentro de ciertos límites geográficos, podría hablarse del dialecto méxico-americano del sudoeste de EEUU. Conviene considerar que no sólo es un habla regional sino también una variedad social que identifica a una minoría étnica vista por los anglos y los otros hispanos en nuestro ambiente como un pueblo sin líderes, sin ambiciones, de escasos recursos, de poca educación y de un bajo nivel socio-económico.

Un pueblo que participa en la economía de este país sin gozar de los bienes materiales que disfrutan los adinerados o los de la clase media necesita un esfuerzo colectivo para cambiar una situación que comparte con gran parte del mundo. Nuestra lengua, lo que podríamos denominar un dialecto popular del español, nos une a un gran número de personas por todo el sudoeste de EEUU y por toda la America Latina. No vamos a dejar perder este vínculo, convirtiéndonos en un pueblo monolingüe, agringado. Ahora que nuestro idioma se ve amenazado con la desaparición, es imprescindible llegar a un acuerdo en cuanto a fines lingüísticos. ¿Cuáles son las variedades del español en nuestra comunidad? ¿Se puede establecer una de ellas como norma? Veamos algunos ejemplos del habla méxico-americana en Texas:

Un Vato Loco:

—Orale, carnal. Póngase trucha, ése. Esta noche en mi chante, si quieres, la calmamos un escante. Mi jaina se descuenta pal cantón de su jefa, ése, y ahi pistiando te periqueo. Nomás pa que capeyes cómo vamos a esponjarnos al perro, al que fregó a mi broda. Chale, ése, no se escame, vato. Lo apañamos al chota cabrón solano. Y lo-lo lo filoriamos. Después, de volada le taloniamos pal norte. Ahí nos maderiamos, camiando nel fil o nalgún jale. Tengo una bironga de aquellas, ése, nel chante. ¡Chinga! Me voy hecho madre, a ponerle al jale. Ni que rayara friegos de jando. Ahi lo guacho esta noche, ése.

Unas Comadres:

—Fíjate que anoche llegó Juan echándole trancazos a la Filomena. Hizo una rejolina que ¡Válgame Dios! Y pa cabarla de amolar pos no se le antojó a Pedro irse a meter al borlote quesque pa pararle el alta al Juan. A ése ni quién lo pacigüe pero Pedro es mu cabezudo.
—¿Y a poco se le rajuelió todo?
—Ande, si ni chanza tuvo, porque lo-lo vino la chota y cargó con toos. Diay la Filomena se dejó venir.
—¿A poco quería que se lo juera a sacar?
—Pos sí. Y como le dije yo, comadre: "No me vengas con lloriqueos. Amárrate las naguas como las meras mujeres y déjalo que se pudra nel bote". No sé pa que le habló a la ley. Ya no más por no andar dejando.

Una Jovencita:

—Hey, Mary, ¿por qué no vienes pa mi casa? Tengo un magazine nuevo that I got this morning nel drugstore. Tiene todas las new songs, muy suaves, de los ... cómo se llaman ... You know ... los que cantan ésa que tocaron ... ahi nel jukebox when we were at the store. No, hombre, not that one, the other one, la que le gustó mucho a Joe. I like it too porque tiene muy suave rhythm y las words también, muy suaves ... Yeah ... what? realllly???? ... te llamó? OOOOhhhhh, Mary. Ese está de aquellotas.

Un Chicano militante:

—Gente orita ya stá despertando y stá dijiendo pos que la única modo de ganarle al gabacho en el juego, este ... es meternos haciendo cosas de nohotros como de la política y economía, metiéndonos, gente mexicana, que tiene el corazón mejicano, que quiere yudar la gente mexicana ... Como orita van a tener gente correr en las elecciones de 72 en el estado de Texas. Toavía no han agarrao la persona. Yo creo que es una movida mal porque no tenemos la feria y las conexiones y todo eso. Tenemos que empezar en los pueblos chiquitos. Yo ha hablado con gente que sabe más que yo que cree los mismo.

Todos estos ejemplos tienen algo en común, representan el habla popular, mezcolanza de lo standard con lo no-standard y a la vez fuertemente influído por el inglés en cuanto a vocabulario y fraseología. Claro que se puede romper con las normas fijadas por la Academia Española, pero para que el habla popular se convirtiera en dialecto standard—aunque se horroricen por allí con sólo pensarlo—habría que ser un pueblo de mucha influencia que pudiera difundir esa variedad por medio de la prensa, diccionarios, libros de texto, gramáticas, manuales de estilo y emplearlo en el sistema educativo, el gobierno y los medios de comunicación. Un dialecto standard necesita ser escrito y tener una función de suma importancia. Y esto es casi imposible ya que hasta ahora el número de altos funcionarios méxico-americanos en el gobierno o el sistema educativo es bien limitado y el número de éstos que emplean el español en sus funciones, casi inexistente. Lo más factible sería aceptar el español standard ya existente de esta región, o sea el español standard del norte de México. Veamos más detenidamente nuestra circunstancia lingüística.

Bilingüismo y Diglosia

El méxico-americano es bilingüe porque posee dos sistemas lingüísticos—el del inglés y el del español—que usa alternativamente y que a veces mezcla. El termino *diglosia*, según Fishman (1971) se refiere al uso de distintas variedades de un idioma o de distintos idiomas para funciones específicas. En algunos países, como los países árabes, hay un dialecto culto escrito, que se emplea en el gobierno, en la religión y en la literatura y otro dialecto popular. En nuestro caso no se puede hacer una división tajante para señalar dos o más variedades del español. Se puede señalar una variedad standard mexicana que emplean algunas emisoras de radio y televisión y algunas iglesias protestantes, pero la mayoría de nosotros giramos en torno a esta norma en distintas órbitas, algunos bastante distantes, otros más próximos. Los más distantes, los que sólo poseemos una variedad popular del español, tenemos un repertorio verbal limitado. Nuestra sintaxis es sencilla con poca subordinación gramatical en la que se repiten los mismos adverbios y adjetivos de siempre como *suave, bueno, luego, entonces, ahorita*. Los sustantivos también se reducen a términos generales: *árbol, mata, pájaro*. Y en cuanto a los verbos, tomemos para el caso el verbo *agarrar* que ha reemplazado toda una serie de otros verbos:

1. Tienes que agarrar una tarjeta para registrarte. (conseguir)
2. Yo voy a agarrar tres cursos. (seguir)
3. Agarra al niño. (Tómalo en los brazos.)
4. Agarra al niño. (Detenlo.)
5. Voy a agarrar trabajo. (conseguir, obtener)

6. Voy a agarrar el libro. (tomar)
7. Ya lo agarraron. (arrestaron)
8. Es muy agarrado. (adj. derivado de *agarrar*—tacaño)
9. Ahi no agarran chicanos. (emplean)
10. Me agarró bien fuerte. (abrazó)
11. No puedo agarrar la estación. (sintonizar la emisora)
12. Agarró la paseada. (se tiró al vicio)
13. Ya agarró juicio. (ya entró en razón)
14. Ya le voy agarrando. (entendiendo)
15. Quieres agarrar los derechos de un americano. (disfrutar)
16. Al rato lo agarra el Army. (recluta)
17. ¿No me quieres agarrar una orden? (comprar)
18. ¿No me quieres agarrar este taquito? (recibir, aceptar)
19. Voy a agarrar el bos. (tomar el bus)
20. Me agarró bien fuerte la calentura. (dio)

Hay que ver también que la juventud méxico-americana va perdiendo el uso de las formas de respeto. Se tutea tanto a todo el mundo que el *usted* es casi desconocido entre ellos. En cuanto a formas infantiles, lo mismo dice un niño "¿On tá tu libro?" que un adulto.

El poseer sólo la variedad popular de un idioma no nos impide comunicarnos pero sí nos limita. Hay que ver el idioma como un arma, como un instrumento que nos permite desenvolvernos en distintas situaciones de distintas maneras. Entre más variedades del español conozcamos y sepamos emplear, mejor podremos enfrentarnos a cualquier situación y discursar sobre cualquier tema sin sentirnos avergonzados ni menoscabados. Pero el aprendizaje de otras variedades del español debe iniciarse en las guarderías, en los jardines infantiles, en las escuelas primarias y no dejarse para la secundaria o la universidad. Recordemos que el alumno recibe doce años de inglés y generalmente un año más en la universidad.

Como ya dijimos, actualmente el español standard no desempeña ninguna función importante en nuestra sociedad de manera que no se pueden señalar variedades formales sino solo variedades populares. Tampoco se puede clasificar el español estrictamente como el dialecto familiar y el inglés como el dialecto del trabajo, de la escuela y de los medios de comunicación ya que el inglés cada vez más está invadiendo el plano de la intimidad, especialmente entre la juventud. Lo más común ahora es la mezcolanza de los dos idiomas. Si pasáramos totalmente al inglés, la conversación perdería ese rasgo de intimidad, señal de pertenecer a la familia, al barrio o al grupo.

Se discute bastante si el cambio del español al inglés o vice versa se hace al azar o si operan algunas limitaciones sintácticas o sociales. John J. Gumperz y Eduardo Hernández Chávez han llegado a la conclusion de que las restricciones son de tipo social ("Cognitive Aspects of Bilingual Communication"), definidas por la identidad étnica de los integrantes que participan en el diálogo, por el tema que se discute y por el grado de informalidad de la situación. En cuanto a las restricciones de tipo sintáctico, indican que hasta ahora sólo se puede decir que hace falta ampliar la investigación sobre el asunto. Ya trataremos este tema más detenidamente en la última parte de nuestro estudio.

Un dialecto, cualquiera que sea, tiene su estructura, sus reglas fonológicas, sintácticas y semánticas. En el habla también figuran todo tipo de restricciones sociales. Lo primero que tenemos que hacer es reconocer la validez del dialecto chicano. Después tenemos que optar por ampliar nuestros conocimientos, por aprender otras variedades del español, porque francamente nos conviene hacerlo.

Compartiremos aquí las características lingüísticas de 30 hablantes méxico-americanos en la Universidad de Texas (Austin) de San Antonio, Laredo, Brownsville, Austin, Mason, Odessa, Lyford, Seguin y San Angelo. El análisis se basa en las composiciones escritas por los alumnos, en nuestras observaciones personales dentro y fuera de la clase y en entrevistas grabadas con 17 alumnos.

El grado de desviación de la norma standard varía según la procedencia regional, el estudio anterior del español (de poca importancia, francamente), el uso del español o el inglés en casa y el interés del alumno en adquirir una variedad standard del español. El uso de *cómanos* por *comamos,* por ejemplo, es común a todos pero sólo dos alumnos (Austin y Odessa) dicen *iba ido* en vez de *había ido*. La mayoría dice *vía ido* (y así lo escribe). De manera que el habla del méxico-americano es una mezcla de formas standard y formas no-standard. En seguida analizaremos éstas.

FONETICA

Los cambios fonéticos que se producen en el español del méxico-americano se encuentran frecuentemente en el habla informal, descuidada o rural de todos los hablantes hispanos. La mayoría de los méxico-americanos no estamos conscientes de otra norma lingüística simplemente porque nunca hemos tenido instrucción en español sino en inglés. Apuntaremos aquí los fenómenos más comunes entre los alumnos.

VOCALES

En general las vocales iniciales átonas y las protónicas tienden a perderse. A veces las vocales altas átonas se abren un grado y las medias se cierran un grado. Los hiatos se convierten en diptongos a menos que se introduzca una -y- intervocálica, generalmente en las palabras de dos sílabas; si las vocales son homólogas, se reducen a una.

A. Aféresis: la pérdida de sílabas iniciales

enfermedad > fermedad   estar > tar (toy, tas, tamos, etc.)
haber > ber (bía, biera)   hacer > cer
Pérdida de a- inicial: yudar, cordar, rodillar, silenciar, paciguar, cabar, reglar, hogar, prender, horcar, hora, horita

B. Sinéresis: la diptongación de vocales en hiato

ea > ia   pelear > peliar   (golpiar, desiar, mariar, etc.)
aí > ai   caído > caido   (traido, ahi, maiz, raiz)
ae > ai   traer > trai   caer - cai (a veces reducción: trer, quer)
oe > ue   cohete > cuete
oa > ua   toalla > tualla
eo > io   preocupa > priocupa   (a veces reducción: procupa)
peor - pior

C. Reducción de diptongos en sílabas acentuadas

ie > e   ciencia - cencia (setembre, pacencia, alenta, quero, sente, penso)
ue > o   pues - pos   luego - lo'o - lo   mueblería - moblería
ua > a   graduar - gradar
au > a   aunque - anque
ie > i   dieciocho > diciocho, dicinueve, etc.
ei > e   treinta y cinco > trenta y cinco (venticinco, etc.)

D. Vocales átonas que se abren un grado:

i > e   injusticia > enjusticia (estoria, polecía, decesiva, existerá, derición, defícil, ofecina, dejieron, enmagino)
u > o   rumbo > rombo (complir, tovimos, joventud, imposieron, recoperó, sepoltura, secondaria, caloroso)
Vocal ante nasal > a
invitando - anvitando   en veces - anveces
entonces - antonces

E. Vocales átonas que se cierran un grado

e > i   entender > intender (disilucionó, manijar, siguridad, disconfiado, dishonesto, impidir, dicir, siguida)
o > u   morir > murir, murirá

F. Apócope: la pérdida de sílabas finales

para > pa   clase > clas

G. Prótesis: la adición de sílabas al principio de las palabras

    tocar > atocar   yendo > ayendo   gastar > agastar

H. Reducción de vocales homólogas: ee > e

    leer > ler   creer > crer

I. Síncopa: la pérdida de sílabas pretónicas

    desaparecido > desparecido   desapareció > espareció
    necesita > nesita   desapego > despego
    zanahoria > zanoria   alrededor > alredor

J. Epéntesis: adición del deslizamiento -y- entre vocales

    creo > creyo   veo > veyo   cree > creye   tío > tiyo
    mío > miyo   leer > leyer   creer > creyer
    maestra > mayestra   quería ir > quería yir
    destruir > destruyir   oído > oyido

K. Relajamiento de vocales átonas: schwa

    pero > [pərə] le > [lə] me > [mə]

L. Metátesis

    iu > ui   ciudad > [swiḍaḍ] [swiḍá]

CONSONANTES

En general las fricativas se debilitan y se pierden, la sibilante se aspira; los grupos consonánticos se reducen; los sonidos coronales se hacen laterales y hay además los comunes casos de refuerzos consonánticos.

A. Aspiración de la s en cualquier posición:

    nosotros > nojotros   puertas > puertah
    decir > dicir > dijir   este > ehte

B. Aspiración de la f

    fuimos > juimos   fue > jue

C. Aspiración de la h como en el Siglo 16

    Se fue de hilo. > Se fue de jilo.   Se huyó. > Se juyó.
    Se halló. > Se jalló.

D. Pérdida de fricativas sonoras en cualquier posición

    a) intervocálica: b d g

todavía > toavía, tuavía   todos > toos   agua > [awa]
estado > [estau]   abuelo > [awelo]   iba > [i:a]

b) -y- intervocálica

ella > ea   ellos > eos   botella > botea
billetera > bietera   orilla > oría

c) final

vecindad > vecindá   usted > usté   muy > mu

E. Confusión de fricativas

aguja > abuja   boato > guato   abuelo > agüelo

F. Simplificación de grupos consonánticos

ct > t doctor > dotor   mb > m también > tamién
        nd > d andábamos > [aɖa:mos]
rr > r barrio > bario   correr > corer   agarrar > garar
        cierra > ciera   arriba > ariba   arrancar > arancar
rl > l tenerla > tenela   pensarlo > pensalo
rn > n, 1   pararnos > paranos, paralos

G. Metátesis

pared > pader   problema > porblema, pobrema
impresiones > impersiones   prejuicio > perjuicio
magullado > mallugado   estómago > estóngamo

H. Consonantes epentéticas

lamer > lamber   estornudar > destornudar
querrá > quedrá   podemos > podermos
mucho > muncho   nadie > nadien   aire > aigre
adrede > aldrede   huelo > güelo

I. Lateralización

d > l de > le advierto > alvierto desde > desle
n > l nos > los nosotros > losotros nomás > lomas

J. Arcaísmos: semos, asina, ansina, truje, vide, naiden, haiga, ende-
nantes

K. Cambios de acentuación: mendigo > méndigo   seamos > séanos
(todos los verbos en el presente de subjuntivo, primera persona plural)

L. Interferencia del inglés

u > yu que usaba > que yusaba comunicar > comyunicar
d > r puedo > puero medio > merio
        me quedé > me queré

c > s   noche > noshe   muchacha > mushasha
         choque > shoque
r > r (retrofleja)   carne > ca\ne

TIEMPOS VERBALES

El méxico-americano ha conservado la misma orientación de los tiempos verbales que se encuentra en el español standard, según la descripción del sistema verbal del Prof. Bull (1965). El tiempo verbal señala el enfoque (simultáneo, anterior o posterior) desde determinado punto (expresado o sobreentendido) en el tiempo. Lo que ha variado es la morfología y la selección de tiempos verbales utilizados para expresar esas orientaciones. En el español standard los usos sistemáticos de los tiempos verbales son los siguientes:

Tiempos verbales orientados al PRESENTE:

Simultáneo al Presente	Tiempo Presente	como
Anterior al Presente	Perfecto	he comido
Posterior al Presente	Futuro	comeré
Posterior al Presente pero anterior a un punto futuro	Futuro Perfecto	habré comido

Tiempos verbales orientados al PASADO

Simultáneo al Pasado, Aspecto Perfecto	Pretérito	comí
Simultáneo al Pasado, Aspecto Imperfecto	Imperfecto	comía
Anterior al Pasado	Pluscuamperfecto	había comido
Posterior al Pasado	Potencial (Cond.)	comería
Posterior al Pasado pero anterior a un punto subsecuente al pasado	Condicional Perfecto	habría comido

ESPAÑOL DEL MEXICO-AMERICANO:

PRESENTE: La orientación es la misma en el habla del méxico-americano pero hay una tendencia a añadirle duración al tiempo o sea de hacerlo progresivo en todos los casos en que se utiliza en inglés: Sí, sí te oigo. — Sí, sí, te estoy oyendo. (I'm listening.)

PERFECTO: Para indicar una acción anterior pero pertinente al presente, se emplea el perfecto o el pretérito más adverbio: *Se ha ido.* o *Ya se fue.* Los cambios se producen en la morfología (he > ha, etc.).

FUTURO: El tiempo futuro es raro y se usa el presente o la forma perifrástica *ir* más infinitivo. En cambio se mantiene el futuro para casos no-sistemáticos, como para indicar probabilidad: *Será tu papá.* (o también *Ha de ser tu papá.*) *No sé qué quedrá (querrá).*

FUTURO PERFECTO: Este tiempo es casi desconocido. Se emplean adverbios para indicar algún punto en el futuro: *Pa diciembre ya va a estar aquí.*

Los tiempos presente, perfecto, futuro y futuro perfecto quedan reducidos a dos: presente y perfecto.

PRETÉRITO e IMPERFECTO: Los tiempos simultáneos al pasado se mantienen con excepción de los cambios morfológicos que indicaremos más adelante. También hay una tendencia de añadir duración al imperfecto: *Comía cuando entró.* > *Estaba comiendo cuando entró.*

PLUSCUAMPERFECTO: Este tiempo se mantiene pero hay cambios morfológicos. En vez de *había comido* se oye también en algunos sectores *iba comido.* ¿Vendrá de *ir* o será caso de metátesis: había > bía > iba? Tal vez sea confusión de dos formas reducidas: había > bía > ía; iba > ía. O también podría ser que el verbo *haber* se confunde con los verbos en -ar: *habiba* (así como *teniba, sentiba*) > iba.

CONDICIONAL: Este tiempo es raro menos en los usos no sistemáticos: ¿Quién sería? Se ha substituido en su lugar el imperfecto de indicativo y el imperfecto de subjuntivo. A la pregunta: *¿Que haría Ud. si tuviera mil dólares?* se contesta: *Yo iba a México.* o *Yo fuera a México.* A la pregunta: *¿Qué habría hecho Ud. si hubiera recibido mil dólares?* se contesta: 1) *Yo fuera comprado un carro.* 2) *Yo (hu)biera comprado un carro.* 3) *Yo (ha)bía comprado un carro.*

También aquí se han reducido los tiempos verbales al pretérito, imperfecto y pluscuamperfecto. El imperfecto, igual que el presente, se utiliza para los casos subsecuentes. Tal vez podría hablarse de una división bipartita: de lo que es anterior a un momento dado y de lo que no es anterior. Entonces los tiempos de aspecto imperfecto indicarían los casos subsecuentes.

	Anterior	Simultáneo	Posterior
Con relación al Presente:	Perfecto	Presente	Presente
Con relación al Pasado:	Pluscuamperfecto	Imperfecto	Imperfecto
		Preterito	

SUBJUNTIVO

El subjuntivo (presente, perfecto, imperfecto, pluscuamperfecto) se usa en frases subordinadas (sustantivas, adjetivas, adverbiales) en al español standard.

En las frases sustantivas se emplea después de verbos de influencia, expresiones de negación o duda, y expresiones de tipo emotivo. En el dialecto méxico-americano existe la tendencia de no usar el subjuntivo según la norma, especialmente en los casos de verbos de negación o duda, a pesar de que también existe la tendencia de ampliar el uso: *No sé si venga.*

Indicativo después de expresiones de negación o duda:

No creo que tiene muchas ganas.
No creo que es necesario.
No creo que hay sólo una manera de hablar el español.
No hay nada que puede hacer.
No hay nada que yo puedo hacer bien.
No hay seguridad que hallas trabajo.

Algunas expresiones como *Ójala* (*Ojalá*) o *Ójali* (Ojalá y) siempre introducen el subjuntivo:

Ójala y venga.
Ójala que ténganos tiempo.
El espera que nos pórtenos bien.
El sueño de mi hermana es que algún día júntenos un poco de dinero.

En frases introducidas por verbos de influencia no hay uniformidad de uso:

A nosotros los católicos nos dice que estéyamos preparados.
El podrá decir que ténganos un buen tiempo.
Le gusta que lo van a buscar.
Hizo que abandonaban el pueblo.
Querían que la mujer les hacía la cena.
Quiere que vamos a San Antonio.
Perdón que no lo ha entregado.
A mi mamá le gustaba que volvíamos temprano.
Pedro no quiso que su hijo se casaba porque pierdía.
Mandó que paraban de ir.
Es mejor que fumamos.
Quería que me paraba.

La tendencia aquí parece ser de retener el subjuntivo con las expresiones de esperanza y en algunos casos de mandatos indirectos.

En las frases adjetivas el subjuntivo distingue lo indeterminado: *Se necesita una mujer que tenga 28 años.* (cualquier mujer) *Vi una mujer que tiene 28 años.* (una mujer en particular). Desgraciadamente esta construcción casi no se utilizó en las cintas ni en las composiciones. El único ejemplo apareció en combinación con una frase adverbial y aquí no se empleó el subjuntivo: *Pero con una ocupación como maestra no la puede hacer menos que se casa con alguien que es rico.*

En las frases adverbiales el subjuntivo introduce una acción posterior a cierto momento: *El vendrá a las cinco. Entonces iremos.* > *Iremos cuando venga.* o *Me dijo que vendría a las cinco. Yo comí a las tres.* > *Comí antes de que viniera él.* Como se verá por los siguientes ejemplos, en las frases adverbiales el subjuntivo aparece mucho menos aún en el dialecto méxico-americano:

1. Lo mandó pa que juera decirle a Demetrio. 2. . . . antes que me fui. 3. El gobierno gasta miles de dólares cada año para que no plantan varias cosas. 4. Chicano Studies serán necesario hasta cuando la escuela pública enseña, no adoctrina. 5. Cuando la sistema se cambia más, los chicanos no van a tener que depender en los gringos. 6. Antes de que comenzaba a pagar . . . 7. Dice que la vida es una cosa que nos pasa antes que llegamos al fin descanso, la muerte. 8. Cuando acabamos ¿vamos a tener un examen?

Hay que examinar el subjuntivo también en las frases subordinadas introducidas por *si* que indican improbabilidad o irrealidad junto a una frase principal de potencialidad: *Si tuviera dinero, iría. Si hubiera tenido dinero, habría ido.* En la lengua dialectal méxico-americana hay una variedad de posibilidades. Se substituye muchas veces la forma *fuera* por *hubiera* y se usan frecuentemente dos formas subjuntivas, dos formas indicativas o una mezcla de las dos. Conviene que examinemos los distintos casos:

Si _____ , _____
     subjuntivo   subjuntivo

1. Si viera tenido un auto, yo te viera visitado. 2. Si tuviera mil dólares, yo fuera a Europa. 3. Te dijiera si supiera. 4. Si ellos llegaran a nuestros escalones, fuera fácil para comenzar una revolución. 5. Si yo fuera sido el papá, yo fuera visto que mi hijo . . . 6. Si yo fuera el papá, yo le fuera dicho al hijo que lo que vía pasado, vía pasado. 7. Si fuéranos tenido bastante más tiempo, se me hace a mí que pudiéranos hablar con esos jóvenes para dicirles que no tuvieran miedo de platicar la verdá.

Si _____ , _____
     subjuntivo   indicativo

1. Te decía si supiera. 2. Si no fuera por la idea, ahorita no tuvíamos Chicano Studies. 3. Si le viera pasado algo a mi mamá, la familia no puedía, mi papá no puedía mantener la familia.

Si _____ , _____
    indicativo   subjuntivo

1. Te dijiera si sabía. 2. Le ofreciera trabajo si podía. 3. Le diciera que es muy difícil. Si no le puedía enseñar el mal de sus deceos, entonces le ayudara comenzar algún negocio.

Si _____ , _____
    indicativo   indicativo

1. Te decía si sabía. 2. Si yo era el papá, yo le decía de la vida. 3. Si yo tenía dinero, iba a las vistas esta tarde.

Otros usos del subjuntivo:

En algunos casos *hubiera* más *participio pasivo* se substituye por *tendría que;* en otras palabras, a la forma impersonal *habría que* se le añade sujeto:

Un buen católico hubiera que rechazar las cosas del mundo.

Esta misma construcción aparece como equivalente de *debería haber* más *participio pasivo:*

1. Y los gringos van a tener que ser lo que hubieran hacido años pasado. 2. En vez de hacer el edificio fueran ayudado la gente pobre en Austin.

La misma frase se da con el cambio de *fuera* por *hubiera:*

Para mí eso no fuera ver pasado.

A veces al substituirse *fuera* por *hubiera,* se repite el *haber:*

Puedo vivir la vida como si no juera ver pasado. (como si no hubiera pasado).

MORFOLOGIA DEL VERBO

Los verbos del español standard se dividen en tres conjugaciones según la vocal temática: -ar, -er, -ir. La primera conjugación es la de mayor rendimiento, ya que la mayoría de los verbos pertenecen a esta categoría y todos los préstamos modernos también figuran dentro de la primera conjugación (que también comprende el grupo que termina en -ear). En el habla del méxico-americano las conjugaciones se han reducido a dos en algunos casos porque las formas en -ir y -er se han fundido para formar un solo grupo en -er. El mismo fenómeno lo observó Espinosa (1930) en Nuevo México:

salir: salgo   comer: como
     sales   comes
     sale   come

        salemos < salimos   comemos
        salen   comen

Por lo tanto abundan las formas como

vinemos (venimos)   siguemos (seguimos)
sintemos (sentimos)   pidemos (pedimos)
vistemos (vestimos)   durmemos (dormimos)
mintemos (mentimos)   muremos (morimos)

Debe observarse que la vocal radical se cierra un grado (e > i; o > u)
al abrirse la temática (i > e). En algunos casos se regulariza el tema al
cerrarse la vocal radical:

pid - o   vist - o
pid - es   vist - es
pid - e   vist - e
pid - emos (< pedimos)   vist - emos (< vestimos)
pid - en   vist - en

Se dan otros reajustes del sistema verbal. Verbos cuya vocal radical se
diptonga cuando es tónica conservan el diptongo cuando la sílaba es
átona, y como consecuencia, de las formas diptongadas se crean nuevos
temas para otros tiempos o derivados:

piens - o   puedo/puedemos   vienen/vieneron
piens - as   cuento/cuentando juego/juegó
piens - a   pierdo/pierdía   despierto/despiertando
piens - amos (< pensamos) acuesto/acuestó   duermen/duermieron
piens - an   quiero/quieriendo

Se presentan también casos de cambios temáticos basados en otra
forma verbal, como por ejemplo, la del pretérito:

tuve/tuvía   quiso/quisiendo   pido/pidí/pidiste/pidía
fui/juíanos   vino/vinía

Puesto que la tendencia principal es la de simplificar la morfología
verbal, el resultado general parece ser un mayor número de verbos que
siguen la conjugación ordinaria:

seguí/seguió   decir/deciste   decir-dicir/diciera/dicía
componer/componí   poner/poní   sentí/sentió
producir/producieron entretener/entretení caber/cabieron/cabo
eres/ero   costar/costa   ando/andé
tú has/ yo ha/ nosotros hamos   forzar/forzan

Lo mismo ocurre con los participios pasivos. No sólo se encuentran
formas regulares de los verbos con participios irregulares sino que

también pueden observarse participios derivados de conjugaciones irregulares:

abrir/abrido (abierto)   escribir/escribido (escrito)
decir/decido/dicido/dijido (dicho)   hacer/hacido (hecho)
morir/morido (muerto)   poner/ponido (puesto)
resolver/resolvido (resuelto)   puedo/puedido (podido)
volver/volvido (vuelto)   romper/rompido (roto)
supe/supido (sabido)   niego/niegado
tuvo/tuvido

Otras veces los verbos regulares se conjugan como irregulares: entregar/
entriego. O un verbo en -er se conjuga como uno en -ar:

traer/traiba (traía)   tener/teneba (tenía)   sentir/sentiba (sentía)

Incluso aparece la regularización de la forma impersonal del verbo *haber*
al cual se le añade el sufijo de número: Había muchos accidentes. >
Habían muchos accidentes.

En el sistema verbal del español el afijo de segunda persona singular
es -s y aparece en todas las conjugaciones de todos los tiempos menos el
pretérito. En el dialecto méxico-americano se agrega la -s al final de
pretérito también, como en el habla popular de otros países hispanos.
Un rasgo característico de la lengua dialectal es la pérdida de la -s- del
afijo de persona:

fuiste > fuites   viste > vites
tomaste > tomates   viniste > vinites

pero en algunos casos, menos comunes se mantiene:

fuistes, vistes, tomastes, vinistes

El afijo de primera persona plural es -mos pero en nuestro dialecto se
convierte en -nos si el verbo lleva el acento en la sílaba antepenúltima.
Las formas esdrújulas son las siguientes:

condicional: comeríamos   comeríanos
imperfecto: comíamos   comíanos
imperfecto
(subjuntivo):   comiéramos   comiéranos

Ahora bien, ocurre que las formas del presente de subjuntivo se han
regularizado o sea que el acento se ha mantenido sobre la vocal radical,
lo cual ha alternado la acentuación de la conjugación de primera
persona plural. Una vez esdrújula surge conjuntamente el afijo -nos:

cóm - a
cóm - as

cóm - a
cóm - amos > cómanos
cóm - an

También conviene señalar el uso excesivo del reflexivo para indicar la fuerza de voluntad con la que se dispone a hacer algo (ref. Bull):

Me voy a comer el taco.	Me salí de la clase.
Me fui.	Me vine temprano.
Me tomé el vino.	Me leí todo el libro.

Otras modificaciones y reajustes del sistema verbal se explican fácilmente como cambios fonéticos o como formas arcaicas.

PRONOMBRES

Pronombres Personales. Se ha observado entre los jóvenes la tendencia a descartar el *usted* aún con los mayores y con los extraños. La forma *nosotras* tampoco se usa y debido a la distribución n > l suele oírse también *losotros.* Las formas nominativas que se mantienen son las siguientes:

Yo	Nosotros
Tú	Ustedes
Ella, El	Ellas, Ellos

En cuanto a los dativos y acusativos, el fenómeno más característico entre nosotros es el uso de un acusativo proclítico plural cuando el complemento directo es singular pero el indirecto es plural. Por consiguiente se producen los siguientes cambios cuando al faltarle una marca evidente de pluralidad al dativo se añade a otra forma:

Les di el libro a ellos. > Se los di (a ellos).
Les di la mesa a ellas. > Se las di (a ellas).

Un problema análogo es la reducción de *nos* a *no* cuando le sigue otro pronombre enclítico o proclítico. Debe tenerse en cuenta que dentro de la norma el verbo pierde la -s cuando el *nos* es enclítico (Vamos + nos > Vámonos). De manera que esta reducción es sólo una extensión de la regla:

Nos dio el dinero. >	No los dio.
Véndanoslo. >	Véndanolos.
Véndanoslos. >	Véndanolos.

Por otra parte la forma *me* se asimila frecuentemente a una *o* anterior o posterior:

Me lo dio.   > Mo lo dio.

No me gusta. > No mo gusta.
Se me olvida. > Se m'olvida.

y a veces se convierte en *mi:*

Me dijo que no.   > Mi dijo que no.
Me encontré. . . . > M'incontré. . . .

Si reconsideramos el caso de los pronombres enclíticos encontramos
que tras imperativos se producen casos de metátesis y de epéntesis:

Dénmelo. > Démenlo.
Vénganse. > Véngansen.
Bájense. > Bájensen.

Como ya hemos observado, la lateralización de la nasal produce el
uso de *los* junto a *nos,* a veces en el mismo hablante:

1. Quiere que los salgamos.   2. Nos dice que los paremos.
3. Pasamos día tras día sin jamás pensar en lo que los pasará.
4. Los encontramos con unos jóvenes.

Pronombres interrogativos y relativos. En el habla dialectal méxico-
americana se ha generalizado el uso de *qué* por *cuál* en aquellos casos en
los que se emplea el correspondiente *what* en inglés:

¿Cuál es tu dirección? > ¿Qué es tu dirección?

Así mismo se encuentra la reducción de los pronombres interrogativos a
la forma singular:

¿Quiénes son? > ¿Quién son?

Tal vez se deba a que en inglés existe sólo una forma: *who.* Otro
resultado de la interferencia del inglés es el uso de *que* por *lo que:*

Esto es todo que puedo decir de mi comunidad.

También debemos notar la variante *acuál* por *cuál:*

Ahi estaba el Piporro no sabiendo acuál quería.

En cuanto a los pronombres indeterminados se encuentran com-
puestos y combinaciones como los siguientes: *algotro (algún otro),
algotra, algotros, algotras, un otro* (debido a la forma del inglés *another*)
y *cada quien.*

SUSTANTIVOS/ADJETIVOS/ADVERBIOS

Las reglas de concordancia de género y número del español formal se
simplifican en el habla popular de Texas. La norma, por ejemplo, exige

que los sustantivos femeninos singulares que se inician con a- tónica vayan precedidos por *el*. En nuestra lengua dialectal, en cambio, el artículo se elide a *l'* ante todos los sustantivos singulares—masculinos y femeninos—que se inician con vocal, tónica o átona:

el agua > l'agua	la amiga > l'amiga
la hermana > l'hermana	el oro > l'oro
el aguacate > l'aguacate	el humo > l'humo

Un caso análogo se plantea con respecto al género de los sustantivos. En español el género es inherente al sustantivo y no hay correspondencia entre terminaciones y género, puesto que todos los sustantivos que terminan en -*a* no son femeninos. Así palabras como día, problema, sistema y toda una serie de préstamos del griego terminan en -a pero son sustantivos masculinos. En el habla local, en cambio, toda palabra que termine en -*a* es femenina (menos *día*):

la sistema   la síntoma   la diploma   la mediodía

Se observa otra modificación del sistema standard en la inflexion de número. Generalmente se añade a las palabras que terminan en -*a* o -*e* tónicas el morfema de pluralidad -*s*. En el habla méxico-americana, sin embargo, se añade -*ses*.

pie/pieses   papá/papases   café/cafeses   mamá/mamases

Además en el español standard los sustantivos llanos (acento en la penúltima sílaba) que terminan en -s mantienen la misma forma cuando son plurales (afijo de pluralidad > Ø), como por ejemplo, *el lunes, los lunes*. En esta región, zona de seseo como todos los países hispanoamericanos, se dice también *el lápiz, los lápiz*, dado que lápiz es una palabra análoga a *lunes*.

Otro rasgo bastante difundido entre la juventud es la falta de concordancia entre sustantivos y adjetivos. Bien podría ser por interferencia del inglés ya que la mayoría de los alumnos méxico-americanos a pesar de hablar español en casa y con los amigos, casi siempre traducen del inglés al español cuando escriben composiciones o están conscientes del habla. Veamos algunos ejemplos:

los escuelas   muchos cosas   Una mujer hecho para pelear.
Una cadena que está conectado.   El televisor es vieja.
Las personas que son gordas son muy alegre.
Yo creo que el tercer persona es hombre.   No son igual.
Estas dos maneras son universal con nuestra gente.

A veces un mismo hablante varía en la selección de géneros para un sustantivo:

las ideales, el ideal	el pared, la pared
el función, la función	el parte, la parte

La concordancia de numerales sustantivos también se simplifica. Si el numeral termina en *un*, se hace singular el sustantivo: *Tiene veintiún año*. También existe la tendencia de usar la forma apocopada de ciento: *ciento cincuenta > cien cincuenta*. En los numerales de cantidades superiores a cien generalmente falta la concordancia a menos que el *cientos, cientas* esté inmediatamente antepuesto:

400 mujeres - cuatrocientas mujeres; 343 mujeres - trescientos cuarenta y tres mujeres

En cuanto a afijos derivativos, es característico de esta región el añadir diminutivos a un gran número de vocablos:

más tardecita, al ratito, un momentito, lo'o lueguito, orita, orititita, muchita (muchachita), muchito (muchachito), el negrito, la tiendita, toitito (toditito), toíta (todita), frijolitos o frifolitos, carrito, etc.

También abundan las formas con sufijos aumentativos, comunes a otros países hispanos. Algo más característico es el intensificar adjetivos, adverbios y verbos por medio de la repetición y los afijos *re-* o *rete-*:

Está azul azul.
Está fuerte fuerte.
Está retebonito.
Vino luego luego.   Vino lo'o luego.
Ponlo recio recio.   (más fuerte)
Iba recio recio.   (bien rápido)

Ese hombre no más trabaji trabaji y tú de hoquis. (trabaja y trabaja)
Anda canti canti.   (cantando)
Lo vi corri corri.   (corriendo)
Estaba chifli chifli.   (silbando)
El niño está brinqui brinqui.   (brincando)

INTERFERENCIA DEL INGLES (Según el esquema de Weinreich)

Conviene señalar que como resultado general del contacto entre el inglés y el español no sólo se encuentran innumerables préstamos en el habla local sino que también se puede observar algunas modificaciones de tipo estructural. Dada la constante alternancia entre los dos idiomas, el inglés también ha influído sobre la entonación del méxico-americano que en gran parte sigue la curva de entonación del inglés (231↓) para afirmaciones simples y no la del español standard mexicano (1221↓).

Entre los reajustes morfo-sintácticos puede observarse que en el habla del méxico-americano se añaden morfemas de número y posesión donde la norma los elimina:

Tengo las manos sucias.   Mis manos están sucias. (My hands are
                                                        dirty).
Se pusieron el sombrero.   Se pusieron sus sombreros. (They put on
                                                        their hats.)

Por otra parte ha habido identificación de segmentos gramaticales del
inglés con los del español. Así por ejemplo el *to* del inglés que introduce
el infinitivo se traduce literalmente como marca del infinitivo en español:

1. Querían a comenzar. 2. Déjeme atocar la colcha. 3. Lo quieren a
quechar. 4. Quedé de a ir para México. 5. Ofreció a prestárnolas. 6.
Porque es difícil a presentar todos los lados. 7. Es importante a yir.
8. ¿Pero es asesinato a quitarlas del cuerpo? 9. Es difícil a leer.

Como extensión de esto, después se añade una *a* epentética a todos los
verbos. Un alumno escribió: *No puedo hagastar tiempo a cambiar el
mundo.* Y otros dijeron: *Tuvimos a registrando. Tuvimos a buscando.
Andamos a vendiendo unos posters.*

Cuando hay formas correspondientes de los tiempos verbales en
inglés y español se suele seguir el sistema del inglés. Por lo tanto es más
frecuente la forma progresiva en el habla de los méxico-americanos, si el
caso así lo requiere en inglés. Lo mismo acontece con el gerundio, que
funciona en inglés como sustantivo pero no en español, donde se utiliza
en tales casos el infinitivo. El méxico-americano, como cualquier
alumno ánglohablante, utiliza el gerundio no sólo como adjetivo, lo cual
es algo conocido si no aceptado por toda la América hispana, sino como
sustantivo:

1. Para mis hermanitos viviendo en el proyecto era bueno.
2. El hijo quería poner al papá en una posición de sintiéndose
   culpable de los problemas del hijo.
3. Autorizando abortos es algo que exige mucho pensamiento.
4. Usándolas es una manera de afirmar su mexicanidad.
5. El ideal de la hombría consiste en nunca permitiendo que el
   mundo exterior penetre en su intimidad.
6. El dinero que gana lo gasta en tomando.

El inglés también ha causado la pérdida de algunas distinciones
obligatorias dentro del español standard. Como ya señalamos, se ha
dejado de usar en gran parte la forma *nosotras,* lo cual reduce las formas
de primera persona plural a una sola, *nosotros,* como el *we.* Así también
se pierde en muchos casos el pronombre de segunda persona *usted,*
quedando el sistema reducido a un *tú* singular y un *ustedes* plural, o sea
un *you* y un *you-all.*

Consideremos otro caso de interferencia: el español standard exige el
uso del artículo determinado ante un sustantivo genérico o colectivo: *El*

hombre es mortal. El arroz es bueno. Como en inglés el artículo se elimina en estos casos (*Man is mortal. Rice is good.*), el estudiante méxico-americano generalmente omite el artículo al escribir y al hablar:

1. Capitalismo es un sistema económico.
2. Religión es algo muy personal.
3. Gente ya orita está despertando.
4. Todos creen que cambios son necesarios.
5. Estadísticas revelan que . . .

A veces surgen construcciones sintácticas imposibles dentro del sistema español al traducir los verbos del inglés que llevan una preposición añadida, la cual en el habla informal puede aparecer al final de la frase. En español esto no sucede, de allí que los siguientes ejemplos resulten extraños:

1. La muerte es un tema que todos piensan en a veces.
2. Quieren quedar vivos porque su vida es la única vida que están seguros de.
3. . . . significa en realidad lo que nosotros tenemos fe en.

Las preposiciones ofrecen muchas posibilidades de variación ya que muchas veces se reproduce la cognada que no corresponde:

1. Lo hizo en una manera. . . . (de una manera)
2. No estamos pidiendo por más caridad. (pidiendo más caridad)

Préstamos

En cuanto a los préstamos, éstos se han integrado al sistema morfológico y fonológico del español. Si se trata de verbos se integran a la conjugación más productiva de -ar o más frecuentemente -ear, que casi siempre se reduce a -iar. Por ejemplo:

shine > chainear	tiss > tisear	dust > dostear
mop > mapear	quit > cuitear	watch > huachar
spell > espelear	catch > quechar	match > mechear
miss > mistear		

Los sustantivos derivados del inglés también tienen género y número aunque la terminación y el género pueden variar según la región. Así en algunas partes se dice *plogue* (m.) y en otras *ploga* (f.), aunque la forma masculina parece ser la corriente, y lo que es *magasín* para algunos es *magasina* para otros. Hay cierta medida de uniformidad en cuanto a las palabras de mayor frecuencia; por ejemplo casi en todas partes se dice *troca* (f.) (aunque a veces se oye un *troque* por allí). Podría decirse que en algunos casos se usa el género del sustantivo español reemplazado por el préstamo, sólo que como regla general se recurre al inglés porque no se conoce el equivalente en español. Así el que dice *la troca* no la está substituyendo por *el camión*, ni el que dice *la yarda* por *el patio*, ya que los patios de México son algo muy distinto. En cuanto a *birria* y *bironga*, ciertamente reemplazan el término *cerveza* pero estos dos ejemplos ya son casos de variantes de una jerga y no del español general del tejano.

Cuando el préstamo termina en -er en inglés, se adapta al español como sustantivo femenino terminado en -a:

la dipa (dipper)   la juila (wheeler)
la mira (meter)   la rula (ruler)

En otros casos, en cambio, hay concordancia de género y sexo:

el bosero (de *bus*)   la norsa (de *nurse*)
la huayfa (de *wife*)   el broda (de *brother*)
el troquero (de *truck*) el hueldeador (de *welder*)

Ocurre que algunas veces se emplean términos que ya existen dentro del español con otros significados como por ejemplo *yarda* y *mecha*. En estos casos se mantiene el género original. En cuanto a los préstamos que terminan en consonantes o que se integran con una -e final se encontrará que casi siempre con masculinos:

el fil; el yin (gin); el cloche; el bil; el bos; un daime; el cheque; el fone; el estare; un nicle; el suiche; el faite; el saine, etc.

En cuanto a consideraciones fonológicas, vale decir que en las transferencias sencillas los términos tomados del inglés se adaptan al sistema fonético del español. Las palabras que comienzan con sh- generalmente se pronuncian con la africada ch-: *sheriff* > *cherife; show* > *cho; shampoo* > *champú.* Si la palabra termina en consonante que no sea d, l, r, n, s generalmente se le añade una vocal, y la de más frecuencia parece ser -e: *puche, sete,* etc. Si comienzan con s- más consonante se le añade una e- inicial: spell - espelear; skip - esquipear.

Extensión de significado:

Puede observarse que cuando existen términos en español cuyas cognadas en inglés tienen otro significado, se pierde el significado original. Por ejemplo, *colegio* para la mayoría de los hispanos significa escuela o escuela secundaria y no los primeros cuatro años de universidad. El méxico-americano usa la palabra como equivalente de *college* ya que en EEUU se distingue entre *college* y *universidad.* Para escuela secundaria generalmente se dice *jaiscul* (high school) o *secundaria.* El fenómeno de las cognadas falsas es bien extenso y sólo señalaremos algunos ejemplos:

Se dice _____	en vez de _____	por influencia de _____
librería	biblioteca	library
carpeta	alfombra	carpet
conferencia	reunión	conference
lectura	conferencia	lecture
suceso	éxito	success
realizar	darse cuenta	realize
parientes	padres	parents

Mezcolanza fonética y morfológica:

En otros casos se altera la forma del español para que corresponda mejor a su equivalente en inglés sin cambiar el significado:

competición (competition) por competencia
populación (population) por población
telefón (telephone) por teléfono
perpetual (perpetual) por perpetuo
materialístico (materialistic) por materialista
asistante (assistant) por asistente
exploitación (exploitation) por explotación
practical (practical) por práctico
distincto (distinct) por distinto
farmacista (pharmacist) por farmacéutico
sadístico (sadistic) por sádico
incapable (incapable) por incapaz
correctar (correct) por corregir
directar (direct) por dirigir

Frases compuestas

Las frases del inglés se pueden reproducir textualmente con formas inexistentes dentro del español como por ejemplo *objetores concientes* (Weinreich, p. 50) que se ven en el español de Florida. Otras veces se hace una traducción literal de la frase, palabra por palabra. Se sobre-entiende que estas frases no tienen significado ni uso en el español de otros países hispanohablantes:

to have a good time	tener un buen tiempo	en vez de: divertirse
How do you like it?	¿Cómo te gusta?	¿Qué te parece?

to run for office	correr para oficina	ser candidato
to figure the problems out	figurar los problemas	resolver los problemas
to throw in the can (jail)	echar al bote	encarcelar
Your town is run by anglos.	Su pueblo está corrido por anglos.	está dirigido, gobernado
he grew more confused	"creció más confusido"	se puso más confuso

A veces las frases del inglés sólo sirven de modelo y se reproducen un tanto alteradas:

to get a college education > agarrar colegio
to call back > llamar pa' trás
to come back > venir pa' trás
to get a kick out of > agarrar patada

En algunos casos la frase del inglés causa la creación de un término nuevo en español para designar un concepto ajeno al español, como por ejemplo: *teenager*, que un locutor de radio en Austin traduce como *quinceañera*.

Compuestos híbridos

A veces se traduce una porción de la frase y la otra se reproduce en forma de préstamo en casos como:

flour > harina de flor   bedroom set > sete de recámara
light meter > la mira de la luz
light bill > el bil de electricidad, el bil de la luz
traffic sign > saine de tráfico

Al integrarse los préstamos al inglés se ha desarrollado una confusión entre el término nuevo y el viejo aunque en la mayoría de los casos, como ya indicamos, se tomó la palabra del inglés por desconocerse el término en español, especialmente en los pueblos ubicados lejos de la frontera mexicana. Algunas confusiones han resultado entre *huachar (guachar)* y *mirar*, eliminándose en muchos casos el *ver*. Otros ejemplos de varios términos para lo mismo son: *quechar, agarrar, pescar; tochar, tentar, tocar; sainear, firmar; el cho, el mono, las vistas, le película, el cine*, etc. Algunos términos como *deletrear* son casi desconocidos para la juventud y por lo tanto se usa *espelear* y así sucesivamente en muchos casos.

Cuando hay más de un término, a veces uno de ellos adquiere un significado especial. Según un alumno, por ejemplo, en su casa utilizan un *mapiador* para trapear con agua y un *trapeador* para encerar el piso.

Trueque de sistema

En el habla del méxico-americano aparecen frecuentemente cambios repentinos de un idioma a otro, con el mismo interlocutor. El hablante hace el cambio conscientemente y prueba de ello es que al preguntársele si habla español o inglés en casa generalmente contesta: "Pos hablamos revuelto. Inglés y español." Lo mismo se observa en los cuentos, los poemas y los ensayos enviados a las revistas chicanas. En la revista *Magazín* de San Antonio, apareció la siguiente oración: "Se encerró in the recamara and cried over her mala suerte."

En el habla los términos del inglés que se insertan en la conversación retienen la debida pronunciación dentro del sistema fonético del inglés. No puede decirse que la selección de términos sea al azar ya que existen algunas limitaciones. Dentro de los dos idiomas hay reglas gramaticales parecidas o elementos gramaticales semejantes que pueden desempeñar otras funciones, o sea las funciónes que tienen dentro del otro idioma. Sólo en estos casos se permiten los cambios.

Por ejemplo, no se hacen preguntas en español con las formas interrogativas del inglés:

Se dice: Lo hizo slowly.   pero no *How lo hizo?
         Vino early   *When vino?

Bien podría deberse al hecho de que estas frases requieren una partícula inexistente en español: *do*

1. How *did* he do it?
2. When *did* he come?

De igual forma, tampoco se dice:

1. Con quién Peter come?
2. Cuándo is Mary coming?

porque el español exige anteponer el verbo al sujeto:

1. ¿Cuándo viene María?
2. ¿Con quién viene Pedro?

Cuando hay elementos parecidos no hay problema. En inglés por ejemplo, la preposición aparece ante un gerundio y no ante un infinitivo como en español. En nuestro español mezclado si uno de los dos elementos va en inglés, opera la regla del inglés y el complemento es gerundio:

1. I'm talking about conociéndonos.
2. Está hablando de integration, de understanding other people's cultures.
3. Estoy por lowering the standard.

Lo único que podemos presentar aquí es lo que los alumnos dijeron en las grabaciones aunque nos guiaremos un tanto por lo que decimos también en casa.

A. Dentro de la frase nominal, que puede contener los siguientes elementos: articulo + sustantivo + oración adjetiva, el sustantivo en inglés va precedido por un artículo en español:

1. el wedding
2. el building
3. los officials
4. metieron un suit.
5. Tenemos un newspaper.

Si se trata de un sustantivo en español popularizado por la prensa, éste puede aparecer con un artículo en inglés:

Most of the barrio va por Gonzalo Barrientos.

En cambio no se dice: *The muchacho está aquí; ni *A mujer vino.

El sustantivo en inglés puede ir modificado por adjetivos en español:

1. Tiene todo el building agujerao.
2. en cualquier facet of school life.

El sustantivo y el adjetivo pueden ir en inglés y el artículo en español.

Hay un friendly atmosphere.

Si no se necesita el artículo, toda la frase nominal puede aparecer en inglés:

1. Te dan greater yields.
2. Puede dar better results.
3. Si hay run-offs.

El sustantivo en español puede ir modificado por una oración adjetiva en inglés:

Una cosa that turns me off . . .

Un sustantivo en inglés puede ir modificado por una oración adjetiva en español:

1. That's another bitch que tengo yo con los chicanos, que ponen música americana.
2. La most beautiful thing que nos ha pasado.

B. Los adjetivos y sustantivos del predicado (Predicate Adjectives and Predicate Nouns) pueden aparecer en inglés después de un verbo en español:

1. Me quedé surprised.
2. Te digo que está prejudiced.
3. Apá es el dominant.
4. La vida no nomás es un party.
5. Esa es una cosa que ya estamos brainwashed los mexicanos.
6. Es self-employed.
7. Parece que soy sensitive.
   pero no *He is carpintero.
   ni tampoco *She is sensible. i.e. (She is sensitive)

Los adjetivos en inglés pueden ir modificados por adverbios en español:

1. No quieren ser muy "radical." (radical - en inglés)
2. Es muy friendly.

En cambio nunca se usa un adverbio en inglés con un adjetivo en español. No se dice: *Es very amistoso. De igual manera tampoco se usa un adjetivo en inglés con un sustantivo en español: *un friendly hombre.

C. En una forma verbal progresiva, el elemento auxiliar puede aparecer en español y el gerundio en inglés:

1. No está hurting a la tierra.
2. Te están brain-washing.
3. Cuando van aging . . .
4. Estaban striking Kelly (AFB).
   pero no *He is trabajando.

D. En una cláusula, subordinada o independiente, si el verbo aparece en español, el sujeto en inglés funciona como elemento del español porque va marcado por el artículo:

1. Dice el announcer . . .
2. Una cosa . . . que es un fact.

E. Como en la forma progresiva, en las construcciones perifrásticas de *ir + infinitivo*, el segundo elemento puede ir en inglés:

1. Si va take una muchacha el dominant role . . .

2. En cambio no se diría nunca *If you're going to tomar . . .

F. Después de preposiciones en español, el sustantivo puede ir en inglés:

1. Yo estoy hablando de interaction, de power.
2. Siempre ando con hate.

Después de una preposición en inglés, rara vez se oye un sustantivo en inglés, a menos que la palabra esté de moda:

I'm talking about interaction with la gente.

Si el préstamo verbal del inglés tiene un elemento preposicional adicional, se incluye en el español:

What would it be like si un perrao estuviera afuera watchando over quien sale para perseguirlos.

G. Los complementos pueden parecer en inglés después de un verbo en español:

1. Si no tienen integrated parties . . .
2. Tiene todo el publicity.
3. Agarra el moisture.
4. Te dan greater yields.
5. Se caba cuando va al cemetery, halla el grave de su madre . . .

H. La introducción más grande es la de expresiones de moda, de modismos, como por ejemplo, "I mean," "right off," "in that sense," "Maybe," "in other words," "so like que."

* * * * * *

Además de términos—adjetivos, verbos, sustantivos, etc.—se introducen frases enteras. Si seguimos con esta tendencia, acabaremos hablando inglés sólamente, con un "Orale" o un ¡Jijo! introducidos por allí como únicos vestigios de nuestro español.

BIBLIOGRAFIA

Bernstein, Basil. "Some Sociological Determinants of Reception. An Inquiry into Sub-cultural Differences," *Readings in the Sociology of Language,* edit. by J. Fishman. Paris: Mouton, 1968.

Bull, William E. *Spanish for Teachers.* New York: Ronald Press, Co., 1965.

Espinosa, Aurelio. *Estudios sobre el Español de Nuevo Méjico.* Vol. II. Buenos Aires, 1930.

Fishman, Joshua A. *Sociolinguistics, a brief introduction.* Mass.: Newbury House Publishers, 1971.

Labov, William D., Paul Cohen and Clarence Robins. *A Preliminary Study of the Structure of English Used by Negro and Puerto Rican Speakers in New York City.* Final Report, Cooperative Research Project No. 3091. Washington, D.C.: Office of Education, 1965.

Weinreich, Uriel. *Languages in Contact.* Paris: Mouton, 1968.

Dissertation

Thompson, Roger Mark. "Language Loyalty in Austin, Texas. A Study of a bilingual neighborhood," The University of Texas at Austin, 1971.

PART V

CHICANOS EN EL ESTADO MODERNO

INTRODUCTION

There are those who have a predilection to structure human activities in hierarchies, with some above and some below, with some superior and some inferior, some advanced and some traditional, some modern and some old. This, however, is not the intent in the use of the term *modern* for this final section. Instead, *modern* is intended here only as descriptive in terms of time and place, with no hierarchical connotations whatsoever.

The section on the modern state opens with Fernando Vazquez' "El Acre: A Study of Space." This sociological work is a good example of empirical description, something that is always needed to form the foundation of good research. Vazquez' brief study is also important because it provides data that can be of use in the future. For example, how many individuals today have searched for data on the Pachucos of the 30's only to discover that virtually no one bothered to just describe their life styles?

A closely related work, Alvidrez' "Narcotics and Drug Use Trends in California," follows "El Acre." Alvidrez' work is important because it seriously questions one of the favorite causal explanations found in sociological and anthropological works, that is, the notion that poverty, or the "culture of poverty," is the principal cause of drug use trends. Mr. Alvidrez competently and forcefully demonstrates otherwise.

Jorge del Pinal then investigates the penal population in California. Here, he opens new areas for investigation, new areas such as differential jail sentences along ethnic lines, and the viewing of the rates according to the "risk" population, rather than basing such interpretations only on total populations when discussing rates of crime and sentencing.

Armand Sánchez then writes about "Affluence Amid Poverty" in which he strongly suggests that welfare assistance can easily be seen as a process by which certain business establishments are virtually subsidized, and then he suggests that curtailments in such aid could conceivably have a negative effect on the economy of certain business sectors. There is much more in the article by Mr. Sánchez, as the reader will see.

"Advertising and Racism: The Case of the Mexican-American," by Thomas M. Martínez, is an article that has gained wide circulation. It is concerned with a subject matter that is only all too familiar to Chicanos today. Whether or not such advertising will end, or merely change in form but not in substance, is something that one may well ponder.

This section concludes with "Notes on the Modern State." To the best of my knowledge, this is the only effort in contemporary scholarship to bring all these data together in order to view the entire spectrum of institutional influence upon the population in a contemporary state such as California. That the figures of people in one form or another under institutional care are so high has surprised some, and not others. Whatever the case may be, this situation suggests questions regarding either theory or practice with respect to social mobility in a modern state, ethnic distribution, economics, and a host of other questions which Chicanos, just as other people, not only ponder but intend to research as well. Transcending these questions is still another that bears directly upon the high degree of institutionalization that exists today, and that relates to the growing role of the professionals and their relationship to the society in general, and to the people who are under institutional care in particular.

EL ACRE

A Study of Space

Fernando D. Vázquez

A Description

Physical Location

El Acre is a small (.94 acre) park in a city of 28,000. It is located approximately seven blocks from the center of town in the direction of the barrio. El Acre is considered by some to be the line of demarcation between the barrio and the rest of the city. El Acre has been in existence since the 1800's, and it was part of the original subdivision of this early San Joaquin Valley settlement. It was then known as North Park. Later, during the turn of the century, its grounds served as a campus for the city's growing school system.

El Acre is an oval-shaped park covered with sparse grass and shaded by numerous Modesto Ash and pine trees. There are five cement tables and various benches placed around it for public use. A drinking fountain is in the center of the grounds. There are no restrooms. A cement walkway (that floods in the rain) stretches the length of the park, detouring only around a large, round, and perenially dry fountain in the center of El Acre.

Year round, there is activity at El Acre though it slows considerably during the coldest winter months and during the rainy season. It is in the warm and hot months from early spring to late fall that El Acre's population noticeably swells. Even when normal activities were disrupted once by the plowing under of the grass, people used to frequenting the park hung around watching the city workmen replant and waiting for their favorite place to become available.

On an average day, weather permitting, a person driving around El Acre can observe old men chatting, playing cards or just taking sun; young men standing around in groups or squatting, smoking; and perhaps some others engrossed in a game of dominoes. Occasionally too, a couple may be tossing a ball. Smaller groups may be gathered close to the edge of the park, or on the curbs by parked cars listening to the radio and talking. What may not always be visible to the passing motorist is that there are very distinct groups in the park interacting with each other and with anyone else who might happen to intrude, whether unknowingly or by design.

Physical Interrelationship with Environs

El Acre has a number of physically significant factors which take form in various ways. These factors, not necessarily in order of importance, are as follows:

1. It lies in the center of the East-West line of demarcation for the city. The street dividing the city is a northbound one-way thoroughfare that runs directly into El Acre, causing traffic to move counter-clockwise around it.

2. The park, being oval shaped, changes the pattern of north-south east-west street direction, and causes a fanning effect of its avenues of approach. Consequently, there are six possible directions from which it can be approached by car and seven different directions to which one may take his leave. The difference is due to one-way traffic patterns.

3. The one-way traffic connects with outbound traffic routes to nearby towns to the north and northeast. It is also necessary for all traffic to and from most of the northern residential areas to traverse the route around or immediately adjacent to El Acre.

4. It seems a happy financial consequence for the merchant doing business in the commercial zone surrounding this nucleus of activity. Not only is his establishment accessible to traffic, but also to the walk-in trade from the neighboring residential areas.

5. The Police Department also has a particular interest in the park, for different reasons. Though these reasons may concern high traffic count, population density, or the type of populace El Acre draws, the park is the pivotal point in police beat assignments.

There are two major beat systems used in this town, and both cue off of the park. The "6 Beat" system is characterized by a disproportionately small, concentrated, sixth beat being drawn around the Acre area. This beat is immediately adjacent to four other beats that may be called for assistance, each approximately three to four blocks from the park itself.

When the "5 Beat" system is employed, the smallest (Acre Beat) is eliminated and its area is divided three ways. While Beat Four actually is assigned the park, Beats Two and Five back it up from their particular assignments, three and two blocks away respectively.

Observations and Assigned Roles

Basic Distinctions

Though the people who generally occupy the park may seem fairly homogeneous to the passing motorist, there is much more than meets the eye at a fleeting glance. The first and most obvious distinction that might be made is race. The park population is approximately 70% of Mexican descent while practically all of the remaining are of Black ancestry.[1] An immediate comparison can be made with the opposite side of the street where shopkeepers and shoppers alike display a more varied racial spectrum. The next distinction to be made is chronological. Approximately 35% of the Mexicans and 50% of the Blacks are over the age of 30. Closer observation reveals a median age of 60 for the Mexican and 35 for the Black.[2] On the lower end of the scale, the ages fluctuate from about 15 to 28 with the majority falling in the 17 - 19 and 24 - 26 age groups.[3] This of course is an admitted interpolation as the younger groups are relatively unstable and most of the documented observation took place well after the school year began.

A third distinction to be made concerns the sexual composition of park inhabitants. Almost without exception, there are no Mexican females to be found at El Acre. The exceptions are: (a) Middle aged women who walk to or from town, usually accompanied by a daughter, comadre or a younger son; rarely alone; (b) Young girls walking to and from school, usually in groups. When alone, except for the more adventurous, or those having a brother or cousin present on the grounds, some walk around rather than through the park; (c) In addition, house-wives with their children sometimes stop for lunch in the shade of the numerous trees. They are always accompanied by another woman and her children. Other females in the vicinity of the park might be seen in cars parked around El Acre for the following reasons: (a) They shop in nearby stores. This presence is only coincidental, and usually not by choice since all the shops are on the opposite side of the street, and the

---

1. This fluctuates from day to day however and is one factor that is infinitely affected by weather. Though the Black population may rise as high as 50% on a given day it may drop to "0" on a particularly cold day.

2. The sampling for the Mexican man was taken from the late summer/early fall day-time attendance and did not take into consideration the late afternoon/ early evening card playing crowd that would bring the median down to the mid-forties.

3. This statement would hold true for the Mexican youth observed only, as the number of Black youth observed for this purpose was negligible.

women may be inviting unwanted attention just by their presence; (b) They may stop to talk to a boyfriend, though this occurrence would be rare. Usually, though not always correctly, unaccompanied girls are considered "free game" and are readily "hustled." For this reason males prefer that their women, particularly wives, do not approach them there. Such exceptions as exist are not relevant to this paper.

In the Black section of the park (territories to be discussed below), the average day will find more females per capita than elsewhere. The rough breakdown is approximately 60-65% male to 35-40% female. There is considerably more sexual cohesiveness observed in this group than elsewhere in the park. The females may be seen to sit and rap while knitting, reading or watching a game of dominoes.

If an exclusion of Anglos in park life has been noticed, it is only because of the relatively little interaction on a day to day basis that they have with the park "Insiders." The exceptions in this case are three: (a) A young blond lad that grew up in the neighborhood and is accepted as "O.K.," "a right guy," and "one of the dudes"; (b) One or two women considered "regulars" in the Black group; and (c) One of the city employees assigned to clean up the park (not much interaction here except that he or one of the other city employees is expected to clean up regularly). Other Anglo participation in the Acre may take the form of an occasional intrusion by blue collar workers (utility company, mail carriers, construction, etc.) during a lunch break. These are viewed as a definite invasion of privacy by the "regulars." The only other Anglos seen on the grounds are those buying or selling drugs, and an occasional "savior" trying to show the "poor heathens" that somebody "really cares." The latter are usually tolerated or ignored, in the knowledge that they'll soon tire and go away.

Sub-Groups and Territories

In making the distinction between types of territories and their uses, the terms "primary" and "secondary" can be applied. A "primary" area is the space within a geographically defined boundary most often occupied by a group and to which it holds a right acknowledged by peer groups. A "secondary" area is one which is not normally occupied by a given group but one into which it will "spill over" should its primary area become crowded or temporarily unsuitable. (See map #1)

Beginning with the Blacks in the extreme North end of the park, one can see this territory as being both the smallest and most ambiguously defined. Groups will "float" from primary to secondary areas if their size increases enough to extend their perimeters, but not enough to infringe upon other primary areas.

Though usually these sub-groups show at least a surface tolerance to one another, they have been known on occasion to purposely provoke their neighbors by intruding into their space. (See Werthman and Pili-avin, 1967: 58-59) These territorial domains are informally delineated and not as strictly adhered to as, apparently, the more rigid urban centers have experienced. (See Suttles, 1968: 114-115) For example, a Black may choose to "hang" nearer the Chicano area if it is not oc-cupied. A Chicano, upon seeing him there may mutter some unendear-ing epithet to himself at such lack of "courtesy," but here it stops, both knowing that had the area been occupied the intrusion would have been avoided.

The younger Chicanos normally "hang" around the center of the eastern half of El Acre. This domain is by far the largest of the primary areas and is exceeded only by the breadth of its own secondary area.

Of special interest is the interaction between the young and old sub-groups among Chicanos. Though the Youths' primary area overlaps the Oldies' there is no need for the Old Ones to have a secondary area as they may freely traverse the park and stop where they wish. For the most part, however, Oldies prefer the extreme South end and the soli-tary bench in the southeastern quarter.

Pursuing the deference given the older citizens by the younger dudes, disrespectful conduct by an individual will be negatively and more vigorously sanctioned by his peers than by another of the older crowd. Another form in which respect is shown is that rarely if ever would one "toque-up" or (toke) in the "presence" of an "elder." "Pres-ence" in this case would be near enough to be offended by the odor, or to observe the too obvious passing (or flaunting) of a joint. Approxi-mately 20 feet, if the back is turned, may be considered appropriate; closer if dark.

Though the oldsters there for reasons other than card playing gen-erally may be described as retired, disabled or unemployed, the younger dudes' presence can be described more precisely. The youngest, 15-16, though considered men by most standards, are definitely on the low end of the "pecking order" as perceived by others. The older sub-group is divided between the regular "vatos" and the "veteranos."

A cultural attribute manifested by park goers is the use of the whistle. Though whistling is widespread in the barrio, it is only readily observable to "outsiders" who may notice the distinct patterns of pitch and duration as one vato greets another in this residential fringe area, El Acre.

In the Chicano culture it is unheard of for one man to raise his voice
to another, unless he's looking for a fight. While it is not appropriate to
shout at another person, even across the width of the park, it is nevertheless acceptable to whistle. The whistle peculiar to this particular area
is a short, three character expulsion of breath in two tones that might
look something like this: eeo-ee, and repeated in rapid series of one,
two or three repetitions. Once the whistler has the attention of the
person he is addressing, he may make known by gestures of head and
hands whether they must converse or merely exchange greetings at this
distance.

There are expressive whistles in almost every geographic area where
Mexicans are found as well as some personal family whistles. Though
there are somewhat standard silbos for nearly every expressive exclama-
tion; query, disbelief, disapprobation, assent, warning, etc., others have
a more specific intent. For example, though an irritated mother may
call her children in a melodic shriek, some fathers have been known to
have a special whistle for each male child (the only ones allowed on the
street), or a collective call claimed by all the children as "theirs." There
are also accepted norms regulating when and who may or may not
whistle at whom. Example: A child is expected to run to his father if
the latter's attention is desired; he does not whistle.*

The Status Quo

Surrounding this earthy isle of existence are the venerable members
of the Acre Merchants Association. The list of eligible members will
begin at a low six o'clock on Map #1 and continue counter-clockwise to
twelve o'clock, north on the right side of the street for one block,

---

*This measure of respect is carried even further by some people. As the late
Andrea Vázquez (mi abuelita) used to say "Nomás se le silba a los animales, a la
gente se les habla como es debido."

Further research in the area of whistling as a form of communication is continuing. At the suggestion of Leonard Olguin, UC Irvine, the Canary Islands may be
considered as a source of possible origin for our own chifliditos.

Other systems of communication by whistling do exist. But Gomera's (one
of the Canarios) is unique, according to Professor Classe of Glasgow University, who has taken the trouble to spend several months in the island
learning it. For he describes it "as the only system based, not on prosodic
notes, but on purely articulatory notes." In other words, it is "whistled
Spanish" in which the variations in the pitch and tone of the whistle
replace the vibration of the vocal chords. (Myhill, 1968: 159).

return on the opposite side of the street, and continue in the original direction to approximately nine o'clock:

1. A bar.
2. OEO funded training center office building.
3. A church.
4. Mexican food drive-in.
5. Barber shop.
6. Fresh produce market.
7. Liquor store.
8. Rummage shack.
9. Bakery.
10. Food market.
11. Rummage shack.
12. Coin-op laundry.
13. Gas station.
14. "Soul Food" cafe.
15. Shoe repair shop.
16. College assistance office (OEO).
17. XYZ enterprise (Junk store).
18. Italian food restaurant.
19. Doctor's office (General Practitioner).
20. Barber shop.
21. Drugstore.
22. Community credit union (OEO initiated).
23. Combination carpet sales and TV repair shop.

The location of #2, 16, & 22 are not coincidental since such locations were actively sought by the local Poverty War Lords in the early days of the Economic Opportunity Act. "Where the people live, that's where the action is," it was said.

To the surprise of many downtown merchants, this northern bastion of commercialism has one of the highest retail sales areas in town according to a city economic survey conducted circa 1967. On the strength of this fact alone, one would assume that the Acre's merchants would be somewhat sensitive to the area residents' particular needs and have at least a materialistic interest in their well-being. This assumption is partially correct, judging from the direct, indirect, first and second-hand responses to queries. The typical concerns voiced at an Acre Merchants Association meeting have gone something like:

> We oughta get that park closed up if you ask me. Those damned kids are stealing me blind. Close the park and that will solve the (my) problem.

XYZ Enterprises is a relative latecomer to the Association. The owner-manager has complained bitterly about high rates of pilferage, personal abuses and general harassment. It is his contention that "these Mexicans are no good, they're lazy and disrespectful . . . . their parents should be called on the carpet." At a more recent Association meeting, one at which the city manager, a local judge and the Acting Chief of Police were present, he was heard to ask:

> What constitutes loitering? Am I liable if I shoot one of 'em? Do they have to be inside the store?

The bakery shop owner, an establishment of longer duration, asked:

> What is considered loitering? Can they be cited for standing around on public property? (sidewalk) What about when they lean up against my wall putting their feet up . . . . wears out the paint, I have to clean up . . . also my plate glass windows have been broken. (The window has since been replaced with wooden paneling after an incident.) Can the curb be painted red? (The answer was no . . . it is part of a state road system that prohibits it.) Well, can the opposite side of the street (our side) be painted for diagonal parking, causing the street to narrow and making it impractical for them to park over there?

The liquor store owner has somewhat curbed the theft problem by using empty bottles for display. He also makes it plain there has been no love lost between himself and the park "Insiders" for the several years he has been there.

Another latecomer to the scene does not even tolerate anyone who *looks* young on his parking lot. A seemingly pleasant sort of person at first, he fairly bristles at the mention of "those hoodlums" and confides he's keeping a 30.06 under the counter and various handguns in strategic locations throughout the establishment.

It seems however that this is not the general feeling of all the merchants. One of the others volunteered that "Oh, those people just don't like Mexicans or Negroes, if you know what I mean."

The owner of the Italian restaurant did not complain of such episodes. Her major problem consisted of an unusual number of burglaries committed by parties of unknown ethnicity. "How can I blame anybody, I don't know who's responsible but I wish they'd stop." During the time this study was conducted her frustration was heightened by a burglar alarm that went off at will, day or night, and which the police tired of answering.

The pharmacist at the neighborhood drug store and a drive-in proprietess, both Mexican American, have no major complaints. The latter relates that "sometimes they (the guys from the park) get in the way, but I usually manage to discourage them from hanging around too much." The pharmacist, on the other hand says, "I guess the place just doesn't attract them. Most of my clientele is pretty stable, inventory remains constant, and there's a minimum of pilferage. I've been at this location since early '68 and have never had any incidence of vandalism, burglary or harassment." Further questioning revealed that this fact was resented by the majority members of the Acre Merchants Association who hinted at his having what we shall call "ethnic immunity." The druggist went on to cite the short (30 day) business history of a record shop that last summer occupied the building now housing the second rummage shop (#11).

"They killed him (businesswise). That Chicano never really had a chance to get established. High pilferage, low turnover; the loitering I'm sure inhibited trade."

Other members of the status quo, formal institutions like churches, social welfare agencies, etc. as well as agencies of control (police and probation) possess views so varied in perspective that it would take volumes to relate.

Meanings of Space

What does El Acre really mean to those who go there? It depends on who you ask. To the beautifully wrinkled old brown men who go there, it may mean anything from a warm place in the sun to a refuge from old age. It is a place where you can be alone with the grass and trees, or to go for companionship and reminiscinces of another era. It is a place you go to for escape from noisy grandchildren and nagging wives, or one at which you reflect upon the loneliness of not having them.

El Acre serves as a placita where information and social amenities are exchanged with courtesy and respect. It is a favorite gathering place of senior citizens, and one where they can interact with peers, join in a card game or just talk.

There is a younger (middle age) crowd that goes there after work, perhaps for a can of beer, a little conversation, or a card game with the other men after dinner. When the days become shorter and cooler the meetings are more infrequent. Saturdays after the weekly shopping is done or Sunday afternoons are preferable; similarly the beer is now replaced by the bottle of brandy or blended whiskey that passes around.

Of course the occasional wino may wander on the park to share a bottle with a contemporary, but this occurs more in the warmer months of the year. Besides, the slats in the only two wooden benches have splinters. (The rest of the tables and benches are concrete.)

One middle aged winito spoke about sleeping at the park:

I don't hang around here much . . . last time . . . last coupla times, was
picked up—drunk they said, man was I sick.

The majority population at the Acre is the vatos. In this "home"
away from home, the atmosphere is relaxed, informal and pleasant.
Generally no one is going to hassle you unless you're looking to be
hassled. Yet there is always a chance that "la placa" will show up.
Although they rarely stop at the park they cruise around regularly.

". . . maybe not man, but when they do, you know one of 'em is going to
cagar el palo."

What do you mean?

Shit, you know what I mean ése. They talk with their hands . . . they can't
talk to you man to man, they gotta start pushing you or pulling you here or
there . . . . no way you can blame the dudes for getting pissed. . . . and
that's just to talk . . . if they think you really did something, they don't
come looking for you here man, they go to your house.

This feeling seemed to be the general consensus. Though admitting
that not all the cops were alike in this respect, it was easier to lump
them all together than to distinguish one from the other. However,
particular antagonism is felt toward selected individuals on the force,
individuals of whom the chief is equally aware of as liabilities but that
remain on duty in and around the Acre area. One of these "peace
officers" has been known to cruise around the park in his squad car
with one hand on the wheel and the other giving the vatos "the finger."
After a similar incident the vatos decided to pay their respects to
this lawman. A butcher paper and poster paint 4' X 25' sign greeted all
passers-by with a statement that questioned the patrolman's masculinity. Though some of the area's residents did not object to this form
of retaliation, they felt it a breach of respect to so blatantly declare
that: REDNECK ES PUTO.

The vatos may be seen to hang around in groups of twos, threes or
in groups as large as fifteen. While the older ones are content in just
"cooling it," some of the younger ones may horse around playing
"ball" with a towel taken from one of the others' bare shoulders and
knotted tightly.

Just sitting there observing the happenings around the park, one is
at a particular advantage over the merchants from the other side. Yet,
even this is preferable to the eyeballing received from some cars very
obviously not from the area and circling more than once.

What are you looking at? Que somos? animales en el zoo?

There is a definite pride in saying that "this is our park man, and we don't have to take that shit from anybody . . . do we go bother them in their houses."

This pride was challenged last year when the trees at El Acre, especially a tall pine on the southernmost exposure, were not decorated for the Christmas holidays. In past years, colored lights have been strung all around El Acre. Many of the Acre area residents were considerably put out at being so slighted.

> Over en la pinchi courthouse, they got a tree over there that they decorate for some pendejo that dies . . . flowers and the whole bit . . . but en El Acre, not even lights for us to see . . . pero ya verán . . . (and they did).

Another incident that caused ill feelings was the inopportune decision to completely plow up the park and install a new sprinkling system days before a community-wide celebration was to take place on the grounds. A 16 de septiembre fiesta (1970) had been planned for a number of weeks and the city declined to issue a permit for use of the public facility on the grounds that revolutionary activity would surely ensue. That the affair was being sponsored by a coalition of responsible civic-minded and professional organizations was of no consequence.

One of the lasting scars of that action, and a most lamentable one to the vatos, was that along with the old grass and water pipes, many of the trees from the park interior were also removed.

> Hijo que puntada, they took our shade trees. Leave it to the gavachos, they ruin everything, then they bullshit about ecology.

A city employee offhandedly remarked that it looked much better this way . . . easier to keep clean and all, "besides, now we can see what's going on in there . . ."

When asked about getting along with the older men one 19 year old replied:

> Oh, alright . . . see that dude getting out of the car? (about 40 years old) Here comes a card hustle. Man that dude is *good*,—he can really play cards—So's that other dude, and the one with the hat . . . c'mon, this is going to be a good game.

Some of these younger dudes are allowed to play with the older crowd if 1) they have money, 2) they can keep their mouth shut, and 3) observe for a reasonable length of time before joining.

One young lad, a college freshman, confided that he was "glad to get the hell away from there."

> Sure, I had a lot of good times there but, man if I'm going to stay clean I can't hang around there anymore. Tú sabes, man. I know I'll go back to it if I stay here . . . . just came home to see my mom, I'll go back to school tomorrow.

His biggest fear was that if he didn't come up clean on the urinalysis he would be dropped from the methadone program. Hanging around the Acre would insure contact with his old crowd, and a temptation that was hard to resist.

Another student away at school found it necessary to return almost weekly (some two hundred miles each way).

> I got to man. When the carnalillos look up to you, you just don't let 'em down . . . you know what I mean? . . . you got to be around to help 'em.

Are you getting a bad time about going to school?

> . . . . Yeah, . . . they want to know if I'm better'n'em . . . . shit . . . . got time to give me a ride home?

Two weeks later he dropped out of school entirely.

To these people and others interviewed, El Acre has many meanings. A place where you go to meet the guys. A place where you decide what else it is you want to do—whether tonight, tomorrow, or next year—a place where you can watch the broads drive by, score a lid, or just get away from home.

After you've been out of town for any length of time, the fastest way to find out what's been going on is to go to the park. Sooner or later everyone you know or want to see will drive by, or walk across the grass, it's only a matter of time. Guys just out of the joint, back from college, the army, or just having been gone for a while, will make El Acre one of their first stops when they return. "It's kinda like coming home—¿sabes?"

Bibliography

Myhill, Henry
    1968 The Canary Islands. London: Faber and Faber Limited

Suttles, Gerald D.
    1968 The Social Order of the Slum: Ethnicity and Territory in the Inner City. Chicago: University of Chicago Press.

Werthman, Carl, and Irving Piliavin
    1967 Gang Members and the Police. pp. 58-59 in David J. Bordua (ed.) The Police, New

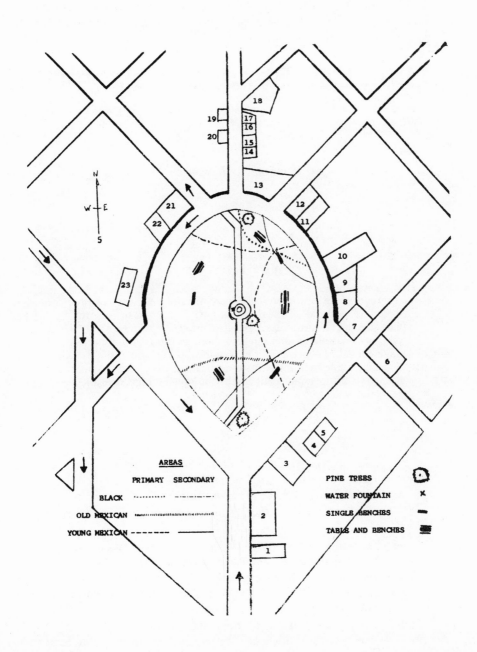

Drug Use Trends In California

Samuel R. Alvidrez

ABSTRACT

Years of intense attention to narcotic and drug use has produced a long series of theories that have been used to "explain" narcotic and drug use. As a result of what the social investigators have postulated, the public as well as the legal authorities have come to believe that it is people who live in sub-standard housing, suffer from inadequate medical care, and are the most numerous in unemployment roles, who are the biggest users of narcotics and drugs.

The following study demonstrates that these types of assumptions are incorrect and have been misapplied. The study shows, for example, that it is not the Mexican-American who is the biggest user of marijuana, but that the "White" youth are in fact the worst violators.

Another major contributor to the commonly held misconceptions is the belief that there are few crime census studies conducted that can be used for comparative purposes on a year-to-year basis. The California Youth Authority in 1964 started a uniform census of narcotic and drug users to run on a year-to-year basis. The following study is primarily based on the results of that census covering the last four years. Comparisons are made on a year-to-year basis with dramatic results. These comparisons show the Mexican-Ameri-

can dropping out of the drug scene and his "White" counterpart entering that scene in ever increasing numbers.

It is quite obvious from the graphs provided with this article that the generalizations which are widely held by lawmakers, police, judicial authorities, and the general public concerning the use of drugs and narcotics by Mexican-Americans are in need of qualification and revision.

———————

The reportedly widespread use of narcotics or drugs by present day youth has given rise to extensive research in many areas. To a significant extent, the interpretation of much sociological and clinical data is predicated on various assumptions which generally fall into one of three categories:

1. The etiology is genetic or physical.
2. The etiology is environmental or social.
3. The etiology is psychological.

The genetic or physical theories[1] have little empirical evidence to support them. They fail to explain why the majority of people who begin using narcotics or drugs, or experimenting with them, do not get more involved with them; unless, of course, we are to assume that those who do go on are the genetically determined ones. This category of theories also fails to explain why some narcotic or drug users stop using narcotics or drugs.

The social or environmental theories[2] are based upon a number of assumptions, including (1) narcotic or drug use is socially communicable, and (2) certain social environments are more conducive to narcotic or drug use than other environments.

The learning theories that are posited to explain narcotic or drug use are generally of the conditioning variety.[3] They suggest that the person becomes conditioned to internal and external stimuli. These theories likewise suggest that the stimuli may be similar for a variety of narcotics or drugs, as well as for initiation to narcotic or drug use. The lack of sufficient empirical evidence to understand the process of narcotic or drug use, the types of narcotic or drug users, and the factors involved in narcotic and drug addiction raises many questions about the feasibility of conditioning theory in explaining narcotic and drug use.

The changing patterns of narcotic or drug use pose questions and demand decisions based on realistic assessments of the role and extent of drug use, the impact and effect of narcotic or drug use on users, and the etiology and development of narcotic and drug use patterns. Although recent research emphases have tended to explore and develop a number of new and promising explanations, the literature in the field remains heavily weighted with poorly based conjecture, dubious generalizations and the perpetuation of subjective opinion as foundations for social action.

Methodology

The data upon which this paper is based was compiled in order to explore the validity of some of the basic assumptions and conjectures concerning narcotic and drug use, its etiology and trends *with respect to the ethnic characteristics of drug and narcotic users*.

The core of the data presented in this paper has been made possible by the on-going census of California Youth Authority Wards instituted on January 1, 1964, by the Youth Authority. The sources of information for the census are: (1) the Youth Authority Referral Document, which is completed by the county of referral and which contains an item on the past history of the use of any narcotic or drugs, as well as an item on the ethnic background of the individual concerned; (2) the Youth Authority Case Summary, which has similar items and is completed by the Youth Authority Clinic staff; (3) the Youth Authority Board Report, which provides information on the narcotic or drug use history of the wards on parole. Any history of the use of narcotic or drugs from any of the above sources is sufficient to place a ward in the user cateory.

Population Trends

During the time period (December 31, 1964/June 30, 1969) covered by this study, California's youth population in the 15 to 24 year age range increased from 2,575,000 to 3,328,900, an increase of slightly more than 29 per cent.[4]

According to the United States Bureau of the Census, California's Spanish surname population made up 7.2 per cent of the total state population in 1950. In 1960, the Spanish surname population had increased to 9.1 per cent of the total state population which indicates a growth rate of 88.1 per cent. By comparison, the State's total population grew by 48.5 per cent.[5] California's Spanish surname population in 1960 was concentrated in the younger age brackets — 70.4 per cent were under age 35. This compares with 64.7 per cent of nonwhites and 56.5 per cent of the total white population.[6]

Provisional estimates of the ethnic composition of California's population as issued by the State Department of Finance indicates that the Spanish surname population had by July 1, 1967, increased to 11.1 per cent of the state population, which was estimated at 19,478,000.[7]

Arrest Trends

On a year to year basis arrest data indicates an upward bound trend in all areas of crime which includes drug or narcotic use.[8]

The total number of juveniles arrested (as reported to the State Department of Justice), by law enforcement agencies throughout the state rose from approximately 269,584 in 1964, to 366,451 in 1969.[9] As a percentage of the total arrest (adult and juveniles combined) the figure shown for 1964 represents 27.6 per cent and nearly 31 per cent in 1968. This is, of course, accounted for to some extent by the much larger proportion of the population that falls into the general juvenile age group.

According to the State Department of Justice approximately 19.8 per cent of the total juvenile arrests for major law violations are disposed of within the arresting agency, and 3.6 per cent are referred to other agencies. The remaining 76.6 per cent are referred to probation. In the area of minor law violations, 52.4 per cent are disposed of within the arresting agency. Of the remaining balance 1.4 per cent are referred to other agencies and 46.1 per cent are referred to probation.[10]

About 43,000 more juvenile arrests were reported in 1968 than were reported in the previous year, resulting in a 12 per cent increase in the rate per 100,000 population. The biggest rate increase were for the series in the felony level (major), offense group. Drug law violations in 1968 show a 113 per cent increase over 1967.[11]

Examination of arrest data indicates that juveniles arrested on a felony charge tend to be treated more seriously than those arrested on a misdemeanor charge.[12]

Thus, the police tend to refer the felony arrestee to the probation department much more frequently than the other less serious category level of arrests. On a state wide basis, 77 per cent of the juveniles arrested for felony level offenses were referred to the probation department for further handling. In contrast, the misdemeanor and delinquency tendency levels had less than 50 per cent referred to the probation department.[13]

Youth Authority Wards

Since 1941, the California Youth Authority (Y.A.), has been the state agency responsible for the training and treatment of young persons found guilty of public offenses and placed under the jurisdiction of the Y.A. for correctional and rehabilitation purposes. Persons under 21 years of age at the time of commission of their offense may be referred to the Y.A. by juvenile and criminal courts. If accepted, the courts then commit the individual to the custody of the Youth Authority. Jurisdiction over juveniles first entering the Y.A. can be maintained until the age of 21; or those committed as misdemeanants until the age of 23 and, for those committed after conviction of a felony charge until after they reach age 25.

At the end of June, 1969, the total number of youths under Y.A. jurisdiction was 20,314, which represents a small percentage increase over the population figure of December, 1964, which was 19,808.

Exact figures for the Y.A. population during the study period are:

December 31, 1964	19,808
June 30, 1965	20,701
December 31, 1965	20,970
June 30, 1966	21,377
December 31, 1966	21,355
June 30, 1967	21,090
June 30, 1968	20,729
June 30, 1969	20,314

As the figures indicate a peak was reached on June 30, 1966, and from that date to June 30, 1969, there was a 5.1 per cent decrease. However, in the overall picture the Y.A. population has remained rather stable during the study period.[14] This situation can be attributed in part to the probation subsidy program administered by the Y.A.; wherein the Y.A. pays a county not to send youthful offenders to the Y.A. and instead place them under special supervision. As stated above, the subsidy program offers a possible (probable) reason for the lack of growth in the area of youths being placed under the jurisdiction of the Y.A. for any public offense.

By exploring the Y.A. population census for data relevant to sex and ethnic background, the data for Graphs 1A and 1B was ascertained and portrayed graphically.[15]

As Graph 1A indicates, those individuals classified as "White" males decreased in numbers from December 31, 1964 to June 30, 1969. Those classified as Negro males increased from 26.3 per cent to 28.9 per cent, an increase of 2.6 per cent. The Mexican-American males decreased from 19.9 per cent to 18.6 per cent, a decrease of 1.3 per cent. Those individuals classified as "Other" males increased by one tenth of a per cent.

In contrast, those females depicted in Graph 1B and classified as "White" did not change from December 31, 1964 to June 30, 1969. The Negro female increased by .6 per cent over the same time period. The Mexican-American female, like her male counterpart, decreased in numbers, but by .7 per cent only. As is indicated the decrease was not as significant. There was no increase nor decrease in the "Other" category.

This graph depicts the stability of the Y.A. population with respect to sex and ethnic background of the Y.A. wards.

Narcotic or Drug Law Violations

Graph 2A depicts the commitment rate for both males and females to the Y.A. for narcotic or drug law violations.

As the data indicates, those males committed during the six month period ending December 31, 1964, comprised 4.0 per cent of the total Y.A. male population. One year later, the commitment rate had increased to 4.7 per cent, which indicates a slight increase. By the end of the study period (June 30, 1969), the rate had jumped to 12.3 per cent, an increase of 8.3 per cent.

The overall increase for the females committed to the Y.A. for narcotic or drug law violations increased from 4.6 per cent to 8.8 per cent, which is an increase of 4.2 per cent.

Graph 2B graphically portrays the incidence use of drugs or narcotics by both males and females committed to the Youth Authority. As the graph indicates, females, on a percentage basis, are more inclined to use narcotics or drugs than their male counterparts.

It should be noted that the data shown on this graph pertains to all persons committed to the Y.A., inclusive of those individuals committed for narcotic or drug law violaitons.

All of the following graphs (Nos. 3A, 3B, 4A, 4B, 5A, 5B, 6A, and 6B) *are an expansion of the data presented in Graph 2B.* The data is displayed in categorical order as follows: specific narcotic or drug; sex and ethnic background.

In each of the eight graphs (3A through 6B), the dominant features are both the dramatic increase of narcotic or drug use by those individuals classified as "White," and the equally dramatic decline in the user population of the Mexican-American Y.A. wards.

As stated, the data plotted in Graphs 3A and 3B depict the incidence use of narcotic or drugs. Both of the distinctive curves for the "White" and Mexican-American youth population are present. The data for the Negro male and female populaiton indicates a slight increase for the male and a very slight decrease for the female. At first glance the curve for the Negro could be interpreted as a stabilized situation, however, when the population trends (State-wide) are taken into account, they are in reality decreasing. The same situation affects the Mexican-American, which in effect indicates a greater decrease than is shown by the graph.

The "White" male is by far the bigger offender of narcotic or drug laws. His female counterpart follows closely behind.

Dangerous Drugs

Graphs 4A and 4B continue to demonstrate the decrease of Mexican-Americans in the user population. The "White" male continues to dominate the field, with his female counterpart following closely behind. The Negro male shows a slight increase, while the Negro female is over-represented in this category. Those females classified as "Other" show an increase of 1.5 per cent.

Both of the graphs pertain to dangerous drugs only. The term "dangerous drugs" refers to amphetamines and barbituate type drugs. The data for the Mexican-American conforms to the data presented in Graphs 3A and 3B.

Marijuana

In the area of marijuana use, Graph 5A shows an almost equal amount of increase/decrease for the "White" and Mexican-American males. The Mexican-American females in Graph 5B continue their dramatic decline as is the case with the Mexican-American males. The "White" females in this area of narcotic use lead their male counterparts by 6.3 per cent. The Negro male shows a slight increase, while the Negro female shows a .4 percent decrease.

This set of Graphs (5A and 5B), are in keeping with the data shown in Graphs 3A and 3B with respect to the close proximity of the starting points for the "White" and Mexican-American males. The obvious difference is, of course, in the ending points of the respective curves which indicate a difference of 33.7 per cent.

Opiates

The incidence use of opiates as displayed on Graphs 6A and 6B indicates a dominance of users by those individuals classified as "White" regardless of sex. "White" females continue to lead their male counterparts as in the area of marijuana use.

Mexican-American males and females continue on their downward trend, as they have in all areas of narcotic or drug use. *A highly significant point in Graph 6A is the high starting point for the Mexican-American males and the 20.2 per cent decrease.* In contrast to this situation, the "White" male started at a relatively lower point than his Mexican-American counterpart, yet, the trend for the "White" male is on an upward-bound track.

The Negro female shows an increase of 2.2 per cent, however, as of the period ending June 30, 1967, a downward trend is indicated. The Negro male shows an increase of 2.0 per cent, which is consistent with the data shown for him in Graphs 4A and 5A.

Conclusion

There appears to be a glaring misconception prevailing in the field of narcotic or drug use. The misconception arises from a failure of the social science investigators to view this social problem from the perspective of history or in its relation to other problems. The causes and effects as described by various scholars change from discipline to discipline. Forty-two years ago, Terry and Pellens (1928), in their book "The Opium Problem," wrote as follows:

"Among the western nations, the United States seems to have acquired the reputation — whether deservedly or not, need not be considered here — of being more widely and harmfully affected than any other. Certainly, in this country there has been much more interest evinced in control measures both of an international and national character than elsewhere. Whether the problem is really greater in the United States than in other countries or whether, perhaps, the question simply has been more agitated here by virtue of a better appreciation of its extent are matters for speculation. Certainly, our news agencies have not minimized the importance of the problem or lessened the public's interest in it and today, on almost every hand, individuals, local organizations, scientific bodies, and legislative groups have become aroused to what is considered generally a health and social peril of magnitude.

C.Y.A. POPULATION BY ETHNIC BACKGROUND

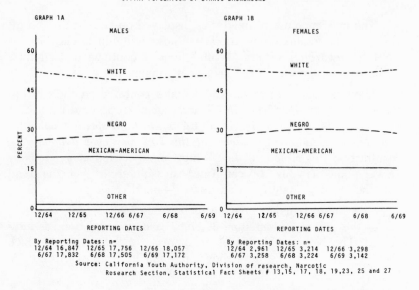

GRAPH 1A

MALES

GRAPH 1B

FEMALES

By Reporting Dates: n=
12/64 16,847   12/65 17,756   12/66 18,057
6/67 17,832   6/68 17,505   6/69 17,172

By Reporting Dates: n=
12/64 2,961   12/65 3,214   12/66 3,298
6/67 3,258   6/68 3,224   6/69 3,142

Source: California Youth Authority, Division of research, Narcotic
Research Section, Statistical Fact Sheets # 13,15, 17, 18, 19,23, 25 and 27

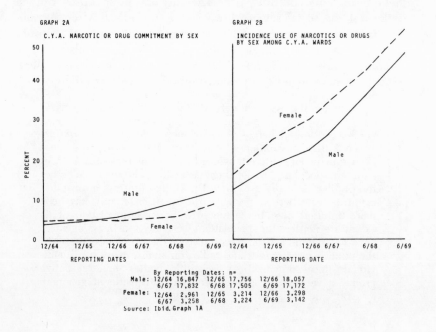

GRAPH 2A

C.Y.A. NARCOTIC OR DRUG COMMITMENT BY SEX

GRAPH 2B

INCIDENCE USE OF NARCOTICS OR DRUGS
BY SEX AMONG C.Y.A. WARDS

By Reporting Dates: n=
Male: 12/64 16,847   12/65 17,756   12/66 18,057
        6/67 17,832   6/68 17,505   6/69 17,172
Female: 12/64 2,961   12/65 3,214   12/66 3,298
        6/67 3,258   6/68 3,224   6/69 3,142
Source: Ibid. Graph 1A

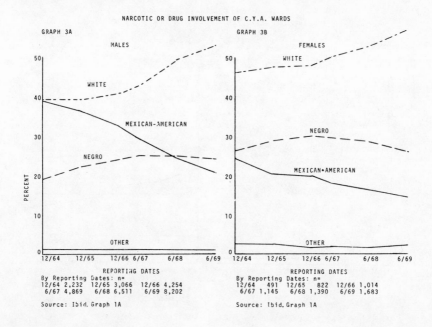

NARCOTIC OR DRUG INVOLVEMENT OF C.Y.A. WARDS

GRAPH 3A   GRAPH 3B

By Reporting Dates: n=
12/64 2,232   12/65 3,066   12/66 4,254
6/67 4,869   6/68 6,511   6/69 8,202

Source: Ibid. Graph 1A

By Reporting Dates: n=
12/64   491   12/65   822   12/66 1,014
6/67 1,145   6/68 1,390   6/69 1,683

Source: Ibid. Graph 1A

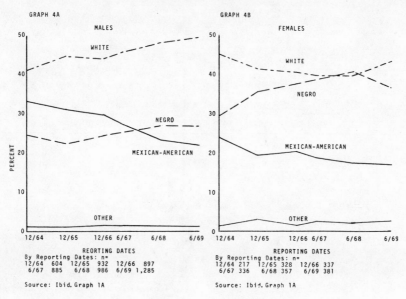

INCIDENCE USE OF DANGEROUS DRUGS BY C.Y.A. WARDS

GRAPH 4A   GRAPH 4B

By Reporting Dates: n=
12/64   604   12/65   932   12/66   897
6/67   885   6/68   986   6/69 1,285

Source: Ibid. Graph 1A

By Reporting Dates: n=
12/64 217   12/65 328   12/66 337
6/67 336   6/68 357   6/69 381

Source: Ibid. Graph 1A

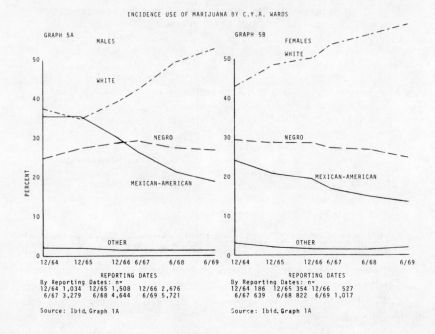

INCIDENCE USE OF MARIJUANA BY C.Y.A. WARDS

GRAPH 5A   GRAPH 5B

MALES   FEMALES

By Reporting Dates: n=   By Reporting Dates: n=
12/64 1,034   12/65 1,508   12/66 2,676   12/64 186   12/65 354 12/66   527
6/67 3,279   6/68 4,644   6/69 5,721   6/67 639   6/68 822 6/69 1,017

Source: Ibid. Graph 1A   Source: Ibid. Graph 1A

INCIDENCE USE OF OPIATES BY C.Y.A. WARDS

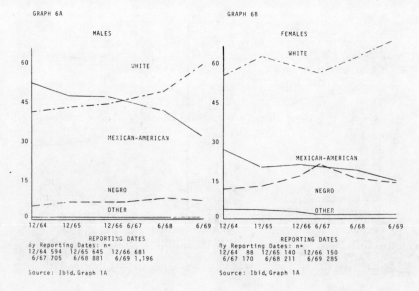

GRAPH 6A   GRAPH 6B

MALES   FEMALES

By Reporting Dates: n=   By Reporting Dates: n=
12/64 594   12/65 645   12/66 681   12/64 88 12/65 140 12/66 150
6/67 705   6/68 881   6/69 1,196   6/67 170   6/68 211 6/69 285

Source: Ibid. Graph 1A   Source: Ibid. Graph 1A

Unfortunately, among those who have become interested from a professional, legislative, administrative, sociological, commercial, or other point of view, there has been an almost continuous controversy as to practically every phase of the narcotic situation, with the result that all the way from the cause on through the development, course, and treatment of the condition, to say nothing of its underlying nature and methods of control, there has been a lack of unanimity of opinion. . . . In general, students and writers appear to have approached the subject from only a limited experience — with too meager a basis of fact — and to have emphasized unduly one or another feature to the total exclusion of related data. This tendency quite naturally may have led the more or less casual reader as well as legislators, administrators, and others officially or professionally connected with the individuals involved to prejudicial attitudes and unwarranted generalizations."[16]

This statement of 42 years ago implies that there is a great deal of concern over the problem of drug addiction; there is continuous controversy on the factors of causation or etiology; there has been a development of prejudicial and biased attitudes. This situation, as described by Terry and Pellens, is still valid and current in the United States today.

During the past several decades there have been numerous reports by legislative bodies, both on the federal and state levels, on this subject. As a general rule, they all start out with a historical review which notes with alarm the sharp rise in the number of addicts in the youth population of the post-World War II era, as compared with the previous two or three decades. These reports are either verbatim, or summary, and outline the effects of drug addiction on individuals. The reports either inadvertently or advertently also point out which minority groups are involved. This last statement is usually followed by a hypothesis on the factors of causation, which is governed by the peculiar bias of the majority members of the reporting group.

Almost the same thing can be said of the numerous papers and reports generated by investigators representative of their respective disciplines.

Apart from the polarities of limitless imputations to narcotic or drug use, there have been numerous attempts to attach the role of key causes to particular principles, activities, or conjunctures, as outlined in the introductory portion of this paper.

Keeping in mind the population trends for the "White," Mexican-American, Negro, and "Other" minority groups in the State of California, and also keeping in mind the arrest, narcotic and drug use trends in the state, can any one of the three general categories of theories explain the factors of causation and cessation of narcotic and drug use?

Of the three categories, the second category (of theories), the etiology of narcotic or drug use is environmental or social — fails to explain the factors of causation and cessation. There is meager evidence to indicate the narcotic or drug use is socially communicable, or that one environment is more conducive than another. According to one investigator (Clausen), the use of narcotics and drugs is to be found in slum districts, which are characterized by poverty, high population mobility, high crime and disease rates and, in general, a variety of social problems.[17] It is a well documented fact that in California the Mexican-American and Negro suffer from all of the conditions imputed by Clausen and the others cited, yet it is not the Mexican-American or Negro that are the most flagrant narcotic or drug users. It appears then, that most, if not all, of the theories in this general category were developed only because minorities were studied for involvement. It is also clear, in view of the trends, that *if* those theories are correct, the "White" juvenile is the one suffering from all of the social ills described by the social investigators cited, and not the Mexican-American or Negro.

The third and last category of theories — the psychological — offer even less plausible explanations than the preceding set of theories. Narcotic or drug use[18] has been described as a "retreatest" reaction of youngsters who are "double-failures" in relation to both legitimate and illegitimate opportunities.[19] It has been attributed to deep personality disturbances, including weak ego structure, inadequately functioning superego, and inadequate sex identity.[20] If we can believe these theories which were posited long before the data for this paper became available, we can conclude that those individuals classed as "White" and which come from the dominant faction of American society are suffering from each of those psychological ailments. On the other hand, we can conclude that while the Mexican-American and Negro may have suffered from those same ailments in the past, they are now well on the road to total recovery.

The President's Commission on Law Enforcement and Administration of Justice put forth three points which are still very applicable today:

(1) "If a serious effort to control crime is to be made, a serious effort must be made to obtain the facts about crime."[21]

(2) "Find out who commits crimes, by age, sex, family status, income, ethnic and residential background, and other social attributes, in order to find the proper focus of crime prevention programs."[21]

(3) "Project expected crime rates and their consequences into the future for more enlightened government planning."[23]

As was stated in the early stages of this paper, the main effort of this paper was not to offer an explanation of the etiology of narcotic or drug use, but rather to ascertain who, by ethnic background, uses drugs, and what the trends might be.

In conclusion, it must be remembered that when a particular social phenomenon such as narcotic or drug use is defined by law, social convention, or any institutional procedure, it must not be assumed that it can be referred to any one set of causes lying outside of the institutional system itself. Therefore, one must look to the discrepancies that exist within the system for an etiological explanation.

In the historical context, one possible explanation for the cessation of narcotic or drug use may be in the upsurgent human rights movement that encompasses the Mexican-American and Negro movements. Cultural Nationalism may, in the final analysis, be a main solution to narcotic and drug use as a major problem.

NOTES

1. D. R. Taft, *Criminology*, 3rd. ed., Macmillan, New York, 1956; G. B. Vold, *Theoretical Criminology*, Oxford University Press, New York, 1958.

2. Y. J. Kron and E. M. Brown, *Mainline to Nowhere*, Pantheon, New York, 1956; R. K. Merton, *Social Theory and Social Structure*, The Free Press, New York, 1957; R. A. Cloward and L. C. Ohlin, *Delinquency and Opportunity*, The Free Press, New York, 1960.

3. D. M. Wilner and G. G. Kassebaum (eds.), *Conditioning Factors in Opiate Addiction and Relapse*, in Narcotics, McGraw-Hill, 1965; I. Chein et al, *The Road to H*, Basic Books, Inc., New York, 1964.

4. Estimated and Projected Population of California 1960-2000, Table 10, California Civilian Population by Age and Sex, State of California, Department of Finance, Sacramento, California, 1968, pp. 30-33.

5. United States Bureau of the Census, U.S. Census of Population: 1960, Subject Reports, Persons of Spanish Surname, Final Report PC (2)-1B.

6. *Ibid.*

7. Financial and Population Research Section, California State Department of Finance, Sacramento, California, August 27, 1968.
8. Crime and Delinquency in California, 1968, State of California, Department of Justice, Bureau of Criminal Statistics, Table I-3, p. 22.
9. *Ibid.*, Table VIII-1, p. 124.
10. *Ibid.*, Table VIII-3, p. 125.
11. *Ibid.*, Table VIII-1, p. 124.
12. Crime and Delinquency in California, 1968, p. 128.
13. *Ibid.*
14. California Youth Authority, Div. of Research, Narcotic Research Section, Sacramento, California; Statistical Fact Sheets Numbered 13, 15, 17, 18, 19, 23, 25, and 27.
15. *Ibid.*
16. Charles E. Terry, M.D., and Mildred Pellens, *The Opium Problem*, Bureau of Social Hygiene, Inc., New York, 1928, pp. xiii-xiv.
17. J. A. Clausen, *Ddug Addiction in Contemporary Social Problems*, Harcourt, Brace and World, New York, 1961, pp. 181-221; J. Dumpson, *Gang and Narcotic Problems of Teenage Youth*, J. of Psychotherapy, April 1952, pp. 312-46; J. Fort, *Heroin Addiction Among Young Men*, Psychiatry, August 1954, 1964, pp. 251-59; J. Toolan, et al, *Adolescent Drug Addiction*, New York State J. of Medicine, January 1, 1952, pp. 72-74; P. Zimmering, et al, *Drug Addiction in Relation to Problems of Adolescents*, American J. of Psychiatry, October, 1952, pp. 272-278.
18. A. D. O'Donnell and J. C. Bell, *Narcotic Addiction*, Harper and Roe, New York, 1966.
19. Cloward and Ohlin, *Delinquency and Opportunity*, Free Press, New York, 1960.
20. Chein and Rosenfeld, *Juvenile Narcotic Use in Law and Contemporary Problems*, Vol. 22, 1957, pp. 52-68.
21. President's Commission on Law Enforcement and Administration of Justice, *Crime and Its Impact — An Assessment*, U.S. Printing Office, Washington, D.C., p. 123.
22. *Ibid.*
23. *Ibid.*

BIBLIOGRAPHY

Becker, H. S., *Narcotic Addicts*. Free Press of Glencoe, New York, 1963.
Clausen, J. A., *Drug Addition*. In Contemporary Social Problems, Merton, R. K. and R. A. Nisbet (eds.), Harcourt, Brace and World, New York, 1961.
Chein, I., D. L. Gerard, R. S. Lee and E. Rosenfeld, *The Road to H*, Basic Books, Inc., New York, 1964.
———, and E. Rosenfeld, *Juvenile Narcotic Use*. Law and Contemporary Problems, Vol. 22, 1957.

Clinard, M. B. (ed.), *Anomie and Deviant Behavior*. Free Press, New York, 1964.

Cloward, R. A. and L. C. Ohlin, *Delinquency and Opportunity*. The Free Press, New York, 1960.

Cohen, S., *The Drug Dilemma*. McGraw-Hill, New York, 1969.

Dumpson, J., *Gang and Narcotic Problems of Teenage Youth*. J. of Psychotherapy, April 1952.

Fort, J., *Heroin Addiction Among Young Men*. Psychiatry, August 1954, 1964

Freedman, A. and E. Wilson, *Childhood and Adolescent Addictive Disorders*. Pediatrics, August 1964.

Gitchoff, G. T., *Kids, Cops and Kilos*. Malter – Westerfield Pub., San Diego, California, 1969.

Gould, L. C., *Who Defines Delinquency*. Social Problems, Winter, 1969.

Hirschi, T. and H. C. Selvin, *Delinquency Research*. The Free Press, New York, 1967.

Horman, R. E. and A. M. Fox (eds.), *Drug Awareness*. Avon, New York, 1970.

Kron, Y. J. and E. M. Brown, *Mainline to Nowhere*. Pantheon, New York, 1956.

Lembert, E. M., *Human Deviance, Social Problems and Social Control*. Prentice Hall, Inc., New York, 1967.

Lingeman, R. R., *Drugs from A to Z: A Dictionary*. McGraw-Hill, New York, 1969.

Louria, D. B., *The Drug Scene*. McGraw-Hill, New York, 1968.

Merton, R. K., *Social Theory and Social Structure*. The Free Press, New York, 1957.

O'Donnell, A. D. and J. C. Bell, *Narcotic Addition*, Harper and Rowe, New York, 1966.
———, *A Follow-up of Narcotic Addicts – Mortality, Relapse and Abstinence*. Am. J. Orthopsychiat., Vol. 34, 1964.

Palmore, E. and P. E. Hammond, *Interacting Factors in Juvenile Delinquency*. Am. Social Rev., Vol. 29, 1964.

Russo, J. R. (ed.), *Amphetamine Abuse*. C. C. Thomas Pub., Springfield, Ill., 1968.

Schur, E. M., *Crimes Without Victims*. Prentice-Hall, New Jersey, 1965.
———, *Narcotic Addicts*. Prentice-Hall, New Jersey, 1965.

Taft, D. R., *Criminology*, 3rd ed. Macmillan, New York, 1956.

Toolan, J. et al, *Adolescent Drug Addition*. New York State J. of Medicine, January 1952.

Vold, G. B., *Theoretical Criminology*. Oxford Univ. Press, New York, 1958.

Williams, J. B. (ed.), *Narcotics and Hallucinogenics*. Glencoe, Beverly Hills, California, 1969.

Wilner, D. M. and Kassebaum, G. G. (eds.), *Conditioning Factors in Opiate Addiction and Relapse*. McGraw-Hill, New York, 1965.

Wootton, B., *Social Science and Social Pathology*. Macmillan, New York, 1959.

Zimmering, P. et al, *Drug Addiction in Relation to Problems of Adolescents*. Am. J. of Psychiatry, October, 1952.

State of California, Department of Finance, *Estimated and Projected Population of California 1960-2000*. Sacramento, California, 1968.

——, *Provisional Estimates of the Racial and Ethnic Composition of California, July 1, 1966 and July 1, 1967*. Sacramento, California, August 1968.

——, Department of Justice, *Crime and Delinquency in California, 1968*. Sacramento, California, 1968.

——, California Youth Authority, *Statistical Fact Sheets Numbered 13, 15, 17, 18, 19, 23, 25, and 27*. Sacramento, California.

United States Bureau of the Census, *U.S. Census of Population: 1960*. Washington, D.C.

President's Commission on Law Enforcement and Administration of Justice, *Crime and Its Impact — An Assessment*. Washington, D.C., 1967.

——, *Juvenile Delinquency and Youth Crime*. Washington, D.C., 1967.

THE PENAL POPULATION OF CALIFORNIA

Jorge H. del Pinal

The purpose of this study is to examine the penal institution population of the State of California and compare it, where possible, to the population of the State as a whole. More specifically, it is an effort to look at the California State Prison, Probation, and Youth Authority Wards populations, with special attention to the ethnic and age composition of these groups.

Table I presents the male felon population in California State Prisons for 1959, 1964, 1969, and 1972 broken down into ethnic groups. (Note: more figures for 1971 and 1972 appear in Table A of the appendix.) Several characteristics are immediately noticeable and striking about this table. First, we notice that the proportion of white felons has declined steadily since 1959, from 58.3% of the felon population to 50.3% in 1972. If one proportion in the population declines, at least one of the other proportions must increase. With this in mind, it can be noted that both the "Mexican descent" and the "Other" category have remained remarkably constant throughout the period. The Blacks, however, have seen a dramatic rise in their proportion of the felon population. In 1959 they constituted 22.6% of the population, and in 1972 they were 31.3%.

We also can discern that the felon population as a whole rose in absolute numbers, reaching 26,157 in 1970 (see Table A in appendix) but declined to 14,685 in 1972.

As can be seen, the ethnic composition has not remained unchanged. Since about 1964, we notice that the age of the felon population has become younger. This is clearly demonstrated by the median age (in Table I) which fell from 32.9 in 1964 to 30.2 in 1972. This may not seem like much of a drop, but it is quite significant as can readily be seen in the rise of the proportion under age 25, from 17.3 in 1964 to 22.9% in 1972.

The educational attainment of the male felon population is very low. The median grade attained has remained at 7.8 since 1970 (see Table C in appendix). Furthermore, there has been little progress in education within the prison environment itself. For example, the proportion of those in grade level 10 and over has only increased from 24% in 1970 to 24.8% in 1972. This slight rise seems to be due a shift from

Table I

ETHNIC GROUPS, Percentage Distribution of Male Felons in California Prisons, and Age Characteristics, Dec. 31, 1959, 1964, 1969 and June 30, 1972.

Ethnic Groups	1959	1964	1969	1972[*]
Total [1]	15,843	20,591	21,240	14,685[*]
Percent	100.0	100.0	100.0	100.0
White	58.3	54.9	53.6	50.3
Mexican Descent	16.8	16.8	16.4	16.9
Black	22.6	26.6	28.5	31.3
Other	2.3	1.7	1.5	1.5
Median Age in Years	31.9	32.9	31.8	30.2
Percent Under 21	2.8	1.7	2.0	2.8
Percent Under 25	18.5	17.3	19.2	22.9

SOURCE: California Prisoners 1969, State of California Human Relations Agency, Department of Corrections, Research Division, pp. 60,64.

[1] Excludes felons in the Reception-Guidance Centers and active parolees in the Narcotic Treatment-Control Units.

[*] From: Characteristics of Felon Population in California State Prisons by Institution, State of California Human Relations Agency, Department of Corrections, Administrative Information and Statistics Section, Research Division, Aug. 10, 1972.

grade level 10-11 to grade 12 and over, possibly from completion of high school and college courses while in prison. But as we have seen the educational level of the population as a whole has not risen, at least not since 1970. In 1972, 3.2% of the male felon population was classified as illiterate (see Table C in appendix).

Averaged over all offense groups, for male felons paroled for the first time in 1969, the median number of months served by whites was 35. The median time served by blacks was 36 months and 38.5 for those of Mexican descent. For some offenses, such as robbery in the first degree, whites served a higher median number of months than the other two ethnic categories. There are some offenses, however, for which the minorities served more time, such as rape, opiate derivatives, marijuana (see Table D in appendix).

Turning now to the female felon population, we notice a fall in the absolute number of the population since 1959, when there were 801 women in prison to 491 in 1972 (Note: more figures for 1970 and 1971 are in Table B in the appendix). Again, as in the case of the males, we notice a drop in the proportion of whites (62.5% in 1959 to 55.3 in 1972) but it has leveled off around 55% since 1970 (see Table II). Blacks rose in proportion since 1959 (29.5%) but had come back down to 31.4 by 1972. The "Mexican descent" category for women has seen a remarkable rise since 1959 (4.4%) to 9.4% in 1972, yet it is a much smaller proportion than the males of the same category.

The median age of the population has generally fallen from 32.3 in 1959 to 30.8 in 1972. However, the proportion under age 25 has not increased much. The women seem in general to have a higher educational attainment than men. The median grade level in 1972 was 8.4 (see Table C in appendix). The proportion in grade 10 or more has fluctuated around 30% since 1970.

Table III presents the Youth Authority population on December 31, 1971. White boys constitute 46.8%, while white girls 57.8%; Mexican-American boys 19.7%, girls 14.3%, and Black 31% and 24.7% respectively. The median age for boys was 18.9 years and 17.8 for girls.

Table IV presents the adult probation case load by ethnic categories. The Justice and Municipal Court case load probably under represents the amount of minorities that have actually gone through courts, because it excludes two counties which have heavy minority populations (Los Angeles and Alameda). Presumably ethnic statistics are not collected in these counties, but it may be assumed that the Municipal and Justice caseload closely approximates the Superior Court caseload in ethnic composition.

Table V gives the ethnic and age distribution for the Youth Authority wards on parole on December 31, 1971.

One way of seeing if minorities are over represented in the penal

Table II

ETHNIC GROUPS, Percentage Distribution of Women Felons in California Prisons
and Age Characteristics, December 31, 1959, 1964, and June 30,
1972.

Ethnic Groups	1959	1964	1969	1972 *
Total [1]	801	608	619	461*
Percent	100.0	100.0	100.0	100.0
White	62.5	52.5	57.5	55.3
Mexican Descent	4.4	5.9	7.4	9.4
Black	29.5	38.5	32.0	31.4
Other	3.6	3.1	3.1	3.9
Median Age in Years	32.3	33.3	32.5	30.8
Percent Under 21	3.2	1.8	2.7	3.0
Percent under Age 25	17.2	14.0	17.6	18.0

SOURCE: California Prisoners 1969, State of California Human Relations Agency,
Department of Corrections, Research Division, pp. 61,64.

[1] Excludes felons in the Reception-Guidance Centers and active parolees
in the Narcotic Treatment-Control Units.

* From: Characteristics of Felon Population in California State Prisons
By Institution, State of California Human Relations Agency, Department
of Corrections, Administrative Information and Statistics Section,
Research Division, Aug. 10, 1972.

Table III

Race and Age of Youth Authority Wards in California Institutions

December 31, 1971

Race and Age (last birthday)	BOYS		GIRLS	
	Number	Percent	Number	Percent
TOTAL	3,893	100.0	393	100.0
White	1,823	46.8	227	57.8
Mexican-American	766	19.7	56	14.3
Black	1,207	31.0	97	24.7
Other	97	2.5	13	3.3
TOTAL	3,893	100.0	393	100.0
13 years or less	17	.4	1	0.3
14 years	87	2.2	19	4.8
15 years	194	5.0	42	10.7
16 years	390	10.0	62	15.8
17 years	619	15.9	94	23.9
18 years	716	18.4	59	15.0
19 years	783	20.1	58	14.8
20 years	635	16.3	42	10.7
21 years	340	8.7	13	3.3
22 years	91	2.3	3	0.8
23 years or more	21	0.5	-	-
Median Age in Years	18.9		17.8	

SOURCE: Characteristics of California Youth Authority Wards, December 31, 1971, State of California Department of the Youth Authority, Division of Research and Development, Information Systems Section, p. 17.

Note: Percents may not add to totals because of independent rounding.

Table IV

ADULT PROBATION CASELOAD BY TYPE OF COURT AND ETHNIC GROUPS

December 31, 1971

	SUPERIOR COURT	MUNICIPAL AND JUSTICE COURT
TOTAL CASES	68,379	43,260
Male	59,092	36,080
Female	9,287	7,180
White	41,522	15,857*
Percent	60.7	72.8
Mexican-American	7,992	2,567*
Percent	11.7	11.8
Black	16,751	2,254*
Percent	24.5	10.4
Other	1,050	315*
Percent	1.5	1.4
Not recorded	1,064	774*

SOURCE: Adult Probation, Reference Tables 1971, California
Department of Justice, Division of Law Enforcement,
Bureau of Criminal Statistics, 1972, pp. 12,26.

* Excludes Los Angeles and Alameda Counties.

Table V

RACE AND AGE OF YOUTH AUTHORITY WARDS ON PAROLE IN CALIFORNIA

December 31, 1971

Race and Age (last birthday)	BOYS		GIRLS	
	Number	Percent	Number	Percent
TOTAL	11,219	100.0	1,898	100.0
White	5,742	51.2	1,032	54.4
Mexican-American	1,975	17.6	261	13.8
Black	3,290	29.3	544	28.7
Other	212	1.9	61	3.2
TOTAL	11,219	100.0	1,898	100.0
13 years or less	35	0.3	3	0.2
14 years	87	0.8	12	0.6
15 years	193	1.7	47	2.5
16 years	446	4.0	112	5.9
17 years	872	7.8	286	15.1
18 years	1,479	13.2	359	18.9
19 years	2,071	18.5	441	23.2
20 years	2,456	21.9	451	23.8
21 years	1,529	13.6	96	5.1
22 years	1,413	12.6	69	3.6
23 years or more	638	5.7	22	1.2
Median age in years ..	20.2		19.3	

SOURCE: Characteristics of California Youth Authority Wards, December 31, 1971, State of California Department of the Youth Authority, Division of Research and Development, Information Systems Section, p. 41

Note: Percents may not add to totals because of independent rounding.

population of the State is to compare the ethnic break down of the State to that of the penal population. According to the U.S. Census in 1970, California had:

		MEN	WOMEN
Total		9,817,543	10,140,172
	%	100.0	100.0
White		73.7	74.1
Black		7.0	7.1
Spanish		15.7	15.4
Other		3.6	3.4

For the purpose of this study, we have subtracted the "Spanish surname" population from the "white" population as enumerated by the U.S. Census. In actuality, the "spanish surname" population is identified as "persons of spanish language" and come from all of the ethnic categories. The great majority are enumerated as "white" and separately tabulated as "spanish surname." In order to simplify the procedure it was easiest to take them only from the "white" population. At the same time, because the "white" population is so large it will not be affected as greatly and little bias is introduced.

In any case, we notice the "white" population (even with the "spanish surname" subtracted) constituted 74% of the California population in 1970, but white male felons in prisons constituted only 53% of the prison population. On the other hand, Blacks were 7% of the State population but almost 29% of the felon population. Mexican Americans or persons of "Mexican descent" were over 16% of the felon population (see Table A in appendix) in 1970. The "spanish surname" population of the State was just under 16%. However, we must caution the reader that the "Mexican descent" category, as used by the Department of Corrections, may not include all persons of spanish language, and is therefore only a subset of the "spanish surname" population. If this is the case, there may be a bias introduced. However, for the purpose of this paper we will assume that these terms refer to the same population.

While these proportions give us an indication of the relative representation of the ethnic groups in the penal population, they are not good measures of the true distribution. One reason for this is that *the age structure of the separate populations differ from each other*. If we take the percent of people in each five year age group (0-4 to 75+) for each ethnic population and graph it by putting each older age group on top of a younger age group, we form a pyramid. An "age pyramid" gives a picture of the age distribution of a population. This has been done for the California ethnic populations of 1970 and presented in Figure 1. It allows us to compare populations of different sizes for

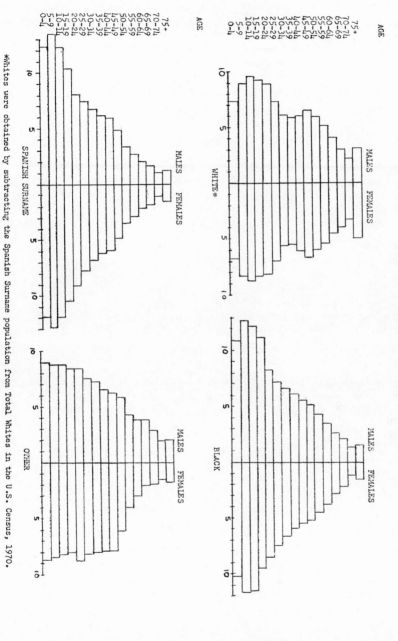

FIGURE I

CALIFORNIA ETHNIC POPULATION 1970 : Percent of each population in five year age groups (age 0-4 to age 70-74, and age 75+)

*Whites were obtained by subtracting the Spanish Surname population from Total Whites in the U.S. Census, 1970.

differences in age structure. Immediately we notice the age pyramids for both the "spanish surname" and the black populations have a much broader base than the white population. To a lesser extent so does the "other" population. These populations are said to have a much younger age structure, i.e., the young constitute a greater proportion of these populations than in the white population. This comes about mainly because of differences in birth rates (but may also be due to migration).

Live Births in California by Race of Mother

1969 *Mother:*	White	Spanish surname	Black	Other
	66.3%	20.2%	9.5%	4.0%

Source: California Department of Public Health, Health Intelligence Division.

We can clearly see that the minorities have a greater proportion of the births than their proportion of the total population. This leads to a broad base age pyramid or "overweighted" on the young side.

Since the felon population comes exclusively from people 18 years of age and older, to construct a proper measure we should use the population at "risk" of becoming felons in the denominator; i.e., the younger people should be excluded in constructing a measure for felons. If we took the felon population and divided it by the population *from which it comes,* and multiply this number by 100,000 (in order to simplify reading), we then have a felon rate per 100,000 of the total population 18 and older. We have in this manner eliminated the "overweightedness" caused by the young people. Below we have computed the rates for the California felon population in prisons on June 30, 1970, using the U.S. Census population in 1970 for the denominator. For example: the white male felons numbered 11,059 in 1970 (see Table A in appendix) and the white male population 18 and over in the State in 1970 was 4,946,183 (with Spanish surname subtracted out).

$$\frac{11,059}{4,946,183} \times 100,000 = 224$$

Felon Population per 100,000 people 18 and older, by Ethnic Category

1970	White	Black	Mexican descent	Other
Men	224	1536	402	183
Women	7	49	5	12

We can do the same thing for the Youth Authority Wards. However, we only have figures for December 31, 1971, but no general population figures for that time. This may mean our rates will be biased to the extent that the ethnic populations of California grew at different rates. Because of the higher birth rates of the minorities, they will become a greater proportion of the total population than they were in 1970. The rates we compute for the minorities are liable to be too high (because the denominator is smaller than it should be). The white rate, on the other hand, will be biased towards the low side (for the opposite reason). These biases will be present unless the populations grew at the same rate, which is not likely. In any case, we compute the rates bearing in mind that we are not using the appropriate denominator. The error due to the differing growth rates is probably not too great.

The Youth Authority wards come, for the most part, from the population 13 to 18 years of age, but since there are a few under 13, we will use the population age 10 to 18 as the denominator.

Youth Authority Wards per 100,000 population 10 to 18, by Ethnic Categories

1971	White	Black	Mexican descent	Other
Boys	166	949	263	177
Girls	22	76	20	25

Youth Authority Wards on Parole per 100,000 population 10 to 18, by Ethnic Categories

1971	White	Black	Mexican descent	Other
Boys	522	2588	679	387
Girls	98	429	92	118

For the Superior Court adult probation caseload on December 31, 1971, which includes both men (84%) and women (16%), we will have to use the total population 18 and over for the denominator. Here an additional bias will be introduced because men and women are lumped together, but we know that the sexes are subject to different risks of committing crimes. Our rate will be an average for the two sexes, yet it will be much lower than for men alone, but very much higher than for women alone.

Superior Court Adult Probation Caseload per 100,000 population 18 and over, by Ethnic Categories

1971	White	Black	Mexican	Other
	336	2034	458	969

Provided the proper denominators or reliable estimates of the proper population are used, comparisons over time may be properly made since the age structure and differential growth rates will be accounted for. The rates will show a more accurate picture of the change over time than using the proportions over time as we have done earlier in this paper. Proportions are affected not only by real changes but by changes in the other proportions. (At least one will have to be a residual category of doubtful meaning because it is affected by the other proportions.)

These rates are directly comparable, and we can see that in every case the Black rates were higher than the other categories. How much higher? If we take the white rate to be unity, we can compare how much higher or lower the other ethnic rates are than the white rate. This can be done simply by dividing each of the ethnic rates by the white rate. For example: the Black male felon rate was 1536 and the white rate was 224.

$$\frac{1536}{224} = 6.9 \text{ which is the ratio Black to white felon rates.}$$

We have computed the ratio of the various ethnic categories to the white rate:

Ratio of Each Ethnic Rate to the White Rate

	Black/White	Spanish/White	Other/White
Male felons	6.9	1.8	.8
Women felons	7.0	.7	1.7
Youth Authority:			
Boys	5.7	1.6	1.1
Girls	3.5	.9	1.1
On Parole			
Boys	5.0	1.3	.7
Girls	4.4	.9	1.2
Adult Probation	6.1	1.4	2.9

We now easily see that the Black male felon rate is almost seven times as great as the white rate. We can say that Spanish male rate is 80% greater than the white male rate. The Spanish women rate is 70% of the white female rate or 30% lower. The above table, in short, provides us with a quick picture of the ethnic distribution of the penal population in California.

REFERENCES

State of California Human Relations Agency, *Characteristics of Felon Population in California State Prisons By Institution*, Department of Corrections, Administrative Information and Statistics Section, Research Division, Aug. 12, 1970 to Aug. 10, 197

State of California Human Relations Agency, *California Prisoners 1969*, Department of Corrections, Research Division, 1970.

California Department of Justice, *Adult Probation, Reference Tables 1971*, Division of Law Enforcement, Bureau of Criminal Statistics, 1972.

State of California Department of Youth Authority, *Characteristics of California Youth Authority Wards, December 31, 1971*, Division of Research and Development, Information Systems Section, 1972.

Romano, Octavio Ignacio, "Notes On The Modern State," in *Voices, Readings From El Grito*, Romano, Octavio Ignacio, ed., Quinto Sol Publications, Inc., Berkeley, 1971

APPENDIX

Table A: Characteristics of the Male Felon Population in California State Prisons, June 30, 1970 to June 30, 1972.

Table B: Characteristics of the Female Felon Population in California State Prisons, June 30, 1970 to June 30, 1972.

Table C: Educational Attainment of Felon Population in California State Prisons, June 30, 1972

Table D: Selected Offenses, Ethnic Group and Time Served in Prison (California), Male felons paroled for the first time in 1969.

CHARACTERISTICS OF THE MALE FELON POPULATION IN CALIFORNIA STATE PRISONS
June 30, 1970 to June 30, 1972

	June 30 1970	Dec 31 1970	June 30 1971	Dec 31 1971	June 30 1972
Grand Total	26,157	24,105	21,789	19,449	18,479
Reception-Guidance Centers[1]	1,082	1,146	1,051	1,218	1,376
Narcotic Treatment-Control Units[2] ..	77	71	61	35	66
Other than adult felons[3]	4,126	3,574	3,097	2,462	2,352
TOTAL (Excluding above three)	20,872	19,314	17,580	15,734	14,685
ETHNIC GROUP	20,872	19,314	17,580	15,734	14,685
Percent	100.0	100.0	100.0	100.0	100.0
White	11,059	10,054	9,111	8,042	7,393
Percent	53.0	52.0	51.8	51.1	50.3
Mexican descent	3,446	3,198	2,925	2,601	2,474
Percent	16.5	16.6	16.6	16.5	16.9
Black	6,040	5,749	5,252	4,840	4,599
Percent	28.9	29.8	29.9	30.8	31.3
Other	327	313	292	261	219
Percent	1.6	1.6	1.7	1.6	1.5
Median Age	31.6	31.4	30.9	30.5	30.2
Percent Under 21	1.8	2.1	2.5	2.6	2.8

SOURCE: Characteristics of Felon Population in California State Prisons By Institution, State of California Human Relations Agency, Department of Corrections, Administrative Information and Statistics Section, Research Division, Aug. 12, 1970 to Aug. 10, 1972.

[1] Adult Felons only.   [2] Non-suspended adult felons.   [3] Includes mentally disordered sex offenders, county diagnostic cases, Mental Hygiene, Youth Authority wards, federal prisoners, safekeepers, and California Rehabilitation Center narcotic addicts received under W & I Code, Section 3000 et seq.

CHARACTERISTICS OF THE FEMALE FELON POPULATION IN CALIFORNIA STATE PRISONS
June 30, 1970 to June 30, 1972

	June 30 1970	Dec 31 1970	June 30 1971	Dec 31 1971	June 30 1972
Grand Total	1,125	928	891	845	764
Reception-Guidance Centers[1]	67	29	43	28	44
Narcotic Treatment-Control Units[2] ..	-	-	-	-	-
Other than adult felons[3]	419	340	331	323	259
TOTAL (Excluding above three)	639	559	517	494	461
ETHNIC GROUP	639	559	517	494	461
Percent	100.0	100.0	100.0	100.0	100.0
White	355	299	288	274	255
Percent	55.6	53.5	55.7	55.5	55.3
Mexican descent	44	44	40	38	43
Percent	6.9	7.8	7.7	7.7	9.4
Black	212	191	165	156	145
Percent	33.2	34.2	31.9	31.6	31.4
Other	28	25	24	26	18
Percent	4.3	4.5	1.7	5.2	3.9
Median Age	32.2	32.2	30.9	31.3	30.8
Percent Under 21	1.6	1.6	1.4	1.4	3.0

SOURCE: Characteristics of Felon Population in California State Prisons By Institution, State of California
Human Relations Agency, Department of Corrections, Administrative Information and Statistics Section,
Research Division, Aug. 12, 1970 to Aug. 10, 1972. [3] Includes mentally disordered sex offenders, county
diagnostic cases, Mental Hygiene, Youth Authority wards, federal prisoners, safekeepers, and California
Rehabilitation Center narcotic addicts received under W & I Code 3000 et seq.

[1] Adult felons only.   [2] Non-suspended adult felons.

APPENDIX: Table C

EDUCATIONAL ATTAINMENT OF FELON POPULATION IN CALIFORNIA STATE PRISONS
                June 30, 1972

	MALES	%	WOMEN	%
Grade Placement[1]	14,685		461	
Total less unknown	14,208	100.0	372	100.0
Illiterate	459	3.2	3	0.8
Grade 3	284	2.0	1	0.3
Grade 4	772	5.4	6	1.6
Grade 5	1,192	8.4	25	6.7
Grade 6	1,658	11.7	39	10.5
Grade 7	2,136	15.0	57	15.3
Grade 8	2,202	15.5	58	15.6
Grade 9	1,985	14.0	72	19.3
Grade 10-11	2,645	18.6	84	22.6
Grade 12 and over ...	875	6.2	27	7.3
Median Grade ..	7.8		8.4	

[1] Grade Placement as measured in reception-guidance center.

SOURCE: Characteristics of Felon Population in California State Prisons By Institution, State of California Human Relations Agency, Department of Corrections, Administrative Information and Statistics Section, Research Division, Aug. 10, 1972.

PERCENT IN GRADE 10 AND OVER OF THE FELON POPULATION IN PRISONS
               June 30, 1970 to June 30, 1972

	June 30 1970	Dec 31 1970	June 30 1971	Dec 31 1971	June 30 1972
MALES					
Grade 10-11	19.8	19.6	19.3	19.0	18.6
Grade 12 and over	4.2	4.5	5.0	5.6	6.2
Grade 10 and over	24.0	24.1	24.3	24.6	24.8
Median grade	7.8	7.8	7.8	7.8	7.8
WOMEN					
Grade 10-11	20.3	20.5	21.5	20.8	22.6
Grade 12 and over	10.4	8.7	8.2	8.6	7.3
Grade 10 and over	30.7	29.2	29.7	29.4	29.9
Median grade	8.5	8.3	8.3	8.3	8.4

SOURCE: Characteristics of Felon Population in California State Prisons By Institution, State of California Human Relations Agency, Department of Corrections, Administrative Information and Statistical Section, Research Division, Aug. 12, 1970 to Aug. 10, 1972.

SELECTED OFFENSES, ETHNIC GROUP AND TIME SERVED IN PRISON IN CALIFORNIA
Male Felons Paroled For The First Time
1969

	WHITE		MEXICAN DESCENT		BLACK	
			Time Served in Months			
	Median	Range middle 80%	Median	Range middle 80%	Median	Range middle 80%
All offenses[1]	35	18–69	38.5	21–72	36	23–72
(Number)		(2,603)		(580)		(1,189)
Murder 2nd	75	54–111	--	--	73	48–90
(Number)		(45)		(9)		(28)
Manslaughter	48	31–76	--	--	43	24–72
(Number)		(35)		(8)		(37)
Robbery 1st	50	35–87	48	32–74	48	36–80
(Number)		(359)		(51)		(224)
Robbery 2nd	39	25–68	40	22–49	42	30–60
(Number)		(128)		(19)		(93)
Attempted robbery	39	18–78	--	--	36	25–60
(Number)		(16)		(3)		(21)
Assault w/deadly weapon	40	22–72	42	24–79	40	24–70
(Number)		(95)		(33)		(77)
Burglary 1st	42	31–69	--	--	42	30–106
(Number)		(67)		(11)		(29)
Auto theft	24	18–42	24	18–48	25	18–42
(Number)		(150)		(22)		(38)
Rape	47	24–84	48	34–80	54.5	31–90
(Number)		(68)		(23)		(28)
Opiate Derivative	41	24–67	50	36–75	48	36–80
(Number)		(58)		(118)		(49)
Marijuana	30	23–48	39	24–60	37	23–61
(Number)		(186)		(83)		(119)

SOURCE: California Prisoners 1969, State of California Human Relations Agency,
Department of Corrections, Research Division, pp. 78–79.

[1] Includes offenses not shown.   Note: Median computed for 15 or more cases.

Affluence Amid Poverty

ARMAND J. SÁNCHEZ

"One individual represents the human race. He is one specific
example of the human species. He is 'he' and he is 'all'; he is
an individual with his peculiarities and in this sense unique,
and at the same time he is representative of all characteristics
of the human race. His individual personality is determined by
the peculiarities of human existence common to all men."[1]

"The State exists to serve the common man."

These two quotations contain the seed which is basically at the
very root of two fundamental questions: (1) What is the general
welfare of the individual? (2) What is the state's responsibility to
the individual?

True, these two questions have been debated philosophically
ad nauseam, for they are at the very core of the issue: the state's
responsibility in relation to poverty.

For purposes of logical and intelligent presentation, first we will
consider the concept of the welfare state: its historical background;
concept and philosophy; and the fundamental differences of opinions regarding the welfare state. Secondly, we will focus on poverty.
Various concepts of poverty and the frantic activity regarding poverty will be examined in view of proposed solutions to poverty.

I. THE WELFARE STATE

A. *Historical Background*

The welfare state has been attacked repeatedly with polemic rather than scholarship. Diverse characteristics of the welfare state have been in existence for some time. However, the term "welfare state" is of recent origin. In 1941 the term "welfare state" was originally used in contradistinction to the "power state" of the Communists and Nazis. The rationale for the use of the term was a defense of an enlarged role for the state based on religious values and moral principles.[2] William Temple's declaration that the state exists to serve the common man has provided a platform for welfare state protagonists upon which the welfare state programs rest. The term "welfare state" originated in Great Britain. The National Health Insurance Act of 1911 is regarded as landmark legislation. The old poor law, from which social services emerged both directly and by reaction, was not so much broken up as eroded away by depression, war, unemployment and the piecemeal introduction of remedial legislation. The social welfare legislation of the Labor government of 1945-50 has begun to be viewed historically, in view of its development over time.

In Germany, Bismarck's innovations resulted in the first comprehensive social insurance program of any modern country. Bismarck's reforms of the 1880's — laws of 1882, 1884 and 1889 introducing compulsory insurance against sickness, accidents, old age and invalidity, attracted immense interest in other European countries. Denmark copied all three German pension schemes between 1891 and 1898, and Belgium between 1894 and 1903.

In the United States, the struggle between the doctrine of laissez-faire and the concept of the general welfare state ensued. Ethical implications in the doctrine of non-interference motivated economists, social workers, polemicists, writers and others to attack the doctrine of laissez-faire.

> The protest against laissez-faire was not only ethical in character, it was also scientific . . . The emerging social sciences — economics, sociology, and political science — and the philosophy and psychology of William James and John Dewey all contributed to this development. The protagonists of these bodies of thought disputed the validity of the tenets of classical economics and social Darwinism and helped to undermine the theoretical foundations upon which the structure of laissez-faire had been reared.[3]

The traditional individualism of Protestant theology was aban-
doned in favor of the social gospel. The social gospel exerted a significant influence on the leaders and rank and file of Progressivism,
the religion of the Progressive movement. The social gospel movement became the institutional embodiment of the social gospel
point of view in American Protestantism. The social Darwinism of
Spencer and Sumner was strongly challenged by the arguments
of William James and John Dewey and the sociology of Ward,
Small and Ross. Political science was led away from laissez-faire
when Woodrow Wilson and W. W. Willoughby took issue with
John Burgess. The public at large appeared unimpressed by the
philosophy of the negative state; moreover, the public was less
inclined to entrust their fate to the laws of nature. "By the turn of
century," Commager accurately notes, "the philosophy had been
formulated, the instinct had crystallized into popular conviction,
and statesmen were preparing to translate that conviction into
legislation."[4]

The clear repudiation of laissez-faire came with the New Deal.
"It was largely owing to the Progressive movement, the New Deal,
and the Fair Deal of the twentieth century that theory was translated into practice and that the concept of the general welfare
state was embodied in legislation."[5]

The Employment Act of 1946 and the role it assigned to the
Council of Economic Advisers, the work-relief and public works
programs of the New Deal and the Fair Deal — all were transla-
tions of the concept of general welfare into programs. Sidney Fine
writes:

> As the mid-point of the twentieth century was reached, Ameri-
> cans would appear to have rejected the admonition that gov-
> ernment is best which governs least and to have endorsed the
> view that in the interests of the general welfare the State
> should restrain the strong and protect the weak, should provide
> such services to the people as private enterprise is unable or
> unwilling to supply, should seek to stabilize the economy and
> to counteract the cycle of boom and bust, and should provide
> the citizen with some degree of economic security. It had come
> to be recognized that the state had a responsibility with respect
> to the welfare of each of its citizens and each group of citizens
> and that this responsibility was to be discharged by such posi-
> tive action as was warranted in any particular case rather than
> by the invocation of the doctrines of laissez-faire and natural
> law. Thus had the ideological conflict of the late nineteenth

century between the advocates of laissez-faire and the advocates of the general welfare state been resolved in theory, in practice, and in public esteem in favor of the general-welfare state.[6]

B. *Concept and Philosophy*

It is to be noted that the welfare state is not the exclusive product of one political party. Both liberals and conservatives have contributed to its development. Hence political party lines are no sure guide to an understanding of the welfare state since both major parties support welfare state programs. Definitions of the welfare state are myriad. To most Americans the welfare state means a more limited group of services — social security, health and education, low-cost housing, unemployment insurance, and relief for the needy, the aged, the sick and the dependent. Asa Briggs defines the welfare state in comprehensive and more inclusive terms.

> A welfare state is a state in which organized power is deliberately used (through politics and administration) in an effort to modify the play of market forces in at least three directions — first, by guaranteeing individuals and families a minimum income irrespective of the market value of their work or their property; second, by narrowing the extent of insecurity by enabling individuals and families to meet certain 'social contingencies' (for example, sickness, old age and unemployment) which lead otherwise to individual and family crises; and third by ensuring that all citizens without distinction of status or class are offered the best standards available in relation to a certain agreed range of social services.[7]

Gunnar Myrdal, the eminent Swedish economist and political scientist, writes in his book, *Beyond the Welfare State:*

> In the last half-century, the state, in all the rich countries in the Western world, has become a democratic "welfare state," with fairly explicit commitments to the broad goals of economic development, full employment, equality of opportunity for the young, social security, and protected minimum standards as regards not only income, but nutrition, housing, health, and education for people of all regions and social groups.[8]

Myrdal's approach is an historical one in which the welfare state is distinguished by economic prosperity and universal political rights. However, these broad criteria fail to develop reliable guidelines for analysis of the welfare state. An analysis of established and operating programs presents a challenge to the welfare state to reinterpret the ethics of welfare and emerge with more equitable programs. Myrdal also makes it clear that in all countries the welfare state is still in the process of completion. Welfare state ideology lags behind welfare state programs because of a general unwillingness to change ideas and beliefs even though changing programs such as social security have rendered them obsolete. Proponents and supporters urge the fulfillment of the welfare state while its opponents feel that it has produced undesirable results such as irresponsibility and bureaucratic inefficiency. An added dimension to the welfare state proposed by its proponents is that the welfare state is more than a state dedicated to material well being. An ethical mission is associated with it.

In summary, fundamental concepts underlying the welfare state are expressed differently but generally involve the redistribution of income to assure minimum standard of living; equality of opportunity; minimum social services available to all; and a legal right to welfare state benefits.

C. Fundamental Differences of Opinion

The debates over the welfare state during the past twenty-five years have given rise to more heat than light. Both opponents and proponents have supported their arguments by assertions of belief rather than by analysis of the advantages and disadvantages of welfare programs. However, the dispute narrows down to just what is believed regarding the destiny, purpose, and place of man. *The welfare state emphasizes the place of man as a member of the group whereas the free enterprise economy emphasizes the fundamental dignity of man as an individual.* A more fundamental question is: Whose welfare state? *The point is that the welfare state benefits aid the middle class more adequately than the poor;* the middle classes receive good standards of welfare while the working classes receive a Spartan minimum. With rising standards of living, the goal of a subsistence minimum merely increases inequality. The true goal of a welfare state, therefore, must be to reduce inequality through a more equitable distribution of material resources.

II. POVERTY*

Resolve not to be poor . . . Poverty is a great enemy to human happiness; it certainly destroys liberty, and it makes some virtues impracticable and others extremely difficult.
— Samuel Johnson

*Michael Harrington's *The Other America* presented a dramatic documentation of poverty and deprivation among present day Americans. Other books, articles, institutes and seminars on poverty have also

The previous section addressed itself to the welfare state and its goals. However, the final part of the first section also raised the question: Whose welfare? An analysis of the distribution of wealth and income will reveal that a significant impact on poverty will be made only when economic structural changes are made. The war on poverty, the copious literature on poverty, and the frenzied activity regarding poverty will contribute but an iota to the solution of poverty; on the contrary, the synergistic effect will result in greater social unrest and upheaval, characterized by an increase in the poverty population and consequent intensified polarization between the poor and the power structure. The demand is for control of political and economic life rather than just more income. The theory of relative deprivation, if operative, indicates that more income changes the present social situation with little significance. Evidence suggests that the two groups that engage least in riot activity are the best educated and economically advantaged and the least educated and poorest.[9] Although the explicit goal of national policy is the elimination of poverty, this commitment is tempered by social and political realities. These realities have been tested out through the war on poverty, particularly the community action program, and the poor have found that getting more of the same does not solve their poverty problems.[10]

The reality of the economic structure does not correspond with the myths held and perpetrated by the dominant society, namely, potential affluence for all those who warrant affluence. The assumption is based on the equal opportunity theory. The issue is clearly an economic issue, not in terms of the absolute money income, which is a simplistic approach, but in terms of equal distribution of income and wealth.

Sociologically, we are entering the post-mortem phase of the war on poverty. The flurry of interest in the problem of poverty was politically occasioned and designed to aid political fortunes rather than the fortunes of the poor. Former President Johnson's

---

contributed to the exposure of the magnitude of poverty within our generally affluent society. John Kenneth Galbraith, in *The Affluent Society*, asserts that this country is an affluent society. Affluence amid poverty is a classic anachronism. More and more people assert that a nation that can, with seeming ease, spend thirty billion dollars a year on a war to alleviate oppression among a people unknown to most Americans, twenty-four billion to put a man on the moon, and an additional forty-five billion dollars for military defense should be able to devote a greater financial, legislative, and personal commitment to the problems of its own people.

definition of poverty was politically useful, altogether ignoring previous research as well as data produced by the Department of Labor. In 1964 the Council of Economic Advisers reported one-fifth of the nation to be poor. The political significance of the numbers game played with the size of the poor is obvious. The fact is that one-quarter of the nation's families and unattached individuals lived in a state of poverty and another one-seventh lived in marginal poverty, according to the United States Bureau of Labor Statistics. Equally important is the assumption on which measures to alleviate poverty have been based, namely, the universally accepted assumption that the poor and oppressed are responsible for their own plight; they are "by choice" uneducated and unskilled. To say that more education will automatically lead to more jobs erroneously assumes that the better educated are not unemployed. This very assumption is the issue of the poverty problem. Inequality is integral to a society wherein the richest tenth receives 30 per cent of the annual money income or 14 per cent of the nation owns 68 per cent of the net wealth. Some must profit if we are to maintain our economic structure in its present form; others must not. The poor will remain along with the inequality long after they have been studied, discussed, and forgotten by politicians and academics. The poor are likely to be with us more than ever before, not merely for a variety of economic and sociological reasons, but because the political paralysis that dominates American life today makes it extremely difficult to enact even the most minor genuine reforms. The American economic structure, with its deeply entrenched privileges and inequities, can hardly be changed, for no socially significant movement in American society today seeks to end poverty by attacking the basic, essential inequality upon which the economy rests, nor is there a broad vision of a new society. For this reason all the bills and measures advocated by political leaders, the unions, and the present day civil rights movement have little chance of altering the structure of poverty, wealth and economic power.

An analysis of the distribution of income indicates that while the income share of the richest tenth has remained large and virtually constant, the two lowest income tenths have experienced a sharp decline.

Table I further shows that the combined 6th through lowest tenth groups, which constitute the poorer half of the population, received 27 per cent of the national personal income in 1910, but only 23 per cent in 1959. Thus, for the only segments of the population in which a gain could indicate progress toward economic democracy, there has been no increase in the percentage share of the national income. *The deduction drawn from Table I is that no*

TABLE I

PERCENTAGE OF NATIONAL PERSONAL INCOME, BEFORE
TAXES, RECEIVED BY EACH INCOME-TENTH*

	Highest Tenth	2nd	3rd	4th	5th	6th	7th	8th	9th	Lowest Tenth
1910	33.9	12.3	10.2	8.8	8.0	7.0	6.0	5.5	4.9	3.4
1918	34.5	12.9	9.6	8.7	7.7	7.2	6.9	5.7	4.4	2.4
1921	38.2	12.8	10.5	8.9	7.4	6.5	5.9	4.6	3.2	2.0
1929	39.0	12.3	9.8	9.0	7.9	6.5	5.5	4.6	3.6	1.8
1934	33.6	13.1	11.0	9.4	8.2	7.3	6.2	5.3	3.8	2.1
1937	34.4	14.1	11.7	10.1	8.5	7.2	6.0	4.4	2.6	1.0
1941	34.0	16.0	12.0	10.0	9.0	7.0	5.0	4.0	2.0	1.0
1945	29.0	16.0	13.0	11.0	9.0	7.0	6.0	5.0	3.0	1.0
1946	32.0	15.0	12.0	10.0	9.0	7.0	6.0	5.0	3.0	1.0
1947	33.5	14.8	11.7	9.9	8.5	7.1	5.8	4.4	3.1	1.2
1948	30.9	14.7	11.9	10.1	8.8	7.5	6.3	5.0	3.3	1.4
1949	29.8	15.5	12.5	10.6	9.1	7.7	6.2	4.7	3.1	0.8
1950	28.7	15.4	12.7	10.8	9.3	7.8	6.3	4.9	3.2	0.9
1951	30.9	15.0	12.3	10.6	8.9	7.6	6.3	4.7	2.9	0.8
1952	29.5	15.3	12.4	10.6	9.1	7.7	6.4	4.9	3.1	1.0
1953	31.4	14.8	11.9	10.3	8.9	7.6	6.2	4.7	3.0	1.2
1954	29.3	15.3	12.4	10.7	9.1	7.7	6.4	4.8	3.1	1.2
1955	29.7	15.7	12.7	10.8	9.1	7.7	6.1	4.5	2.7	1.0
1956	30.6	15.3	12.3	10.5	9.0	7.6	6.1	4.5	2.8	1.3
1957	29.4	15.5	12.7	10.8	9.2	7.7	6.1	4.5	2.9	1.3
1958	27.1	16.3	13.2	11.0	9.4	7.8	6.2	4.6	3.1	1.3
1959	28.9	15.8	12.7	10.7	9.2	7.8	6.3	4.6	2.9	1.1

*Interms of "recipients" for 1910-37 and "spending units" for 1941-59.

Source: Data for 1910-37 are from National Industrial Conference Board, *Studies in Enterprise and Social Progress* (New York: National Industrial Conference Board, 1939), p. 125. Data for 1941-59 were calculated by the Survey Research Center.

significant trend toward income equality is identifiable. Income inequality is more evident when income-in-kind distribution is considered. Although existing statistics do not allow precise calculation of the percentage of total expense account outlays that represent personal income-in-kind, they suffice to indicate that income-in-kind is an item of major consequence to the share of the top income tenth, especially to the style of living enjoyed by many of the richest members of the economic elite.[11]

An additional factor to take into account in income-in-kind distribution is the underreporting on tax returns and non-reporting to interviewers. Low and middle income earners are dependent on wages or salary for their incomes from which automatic payroll deductions withhold the amount of money due for Federal income taxes. However, professionals, businessmen, and others receiving cash payments for their services are in an especially advantageous position to underreport their income on tax returns or to seek tax dodges.[12]

Taxation has not mitigated the fundamentally unequal distribution of income. It has perpetuated inequality by heavily taxing the low and middle income groups. The same factor that stimulated a higher tax rate on the rich also produced permanent and significant income taxation of low and middle income earners. Kolko writes:

> In this process of incorporating more and more of the American population into the Federal income tax system, a moderate degree of progressive taxation has been maintained. The income tax is practically the only major tax that is not basically regressive. Nevertheless, the income tax paid by the average family in the lowest income fifth — in 1957, amounting to 3.3 per cent of their income — constitutes a greater hardship for those living on an emergency budget than does the tax burden of 13.7 per cent paid in the same year by the average family in the richest income fifth.[13]

Taxes other than federal income tax must also be considered, for it is the local and state taxes that the low and middle income groups feel more heavily. Local and state taxes are regressive. More than half — 59 per cent in 1958 — of all state tax revenues come from sales taxes. About one-half of the expenditures of an average spending unit earning a cash income of less than $1,000 per year are subject to general sales or excise taxes, but only one-third of the expenditures of those earning $10,000 plus are so taxed.[14] This means that corporations present the public with additional hidden taxes, for taxes are another cost which corporations pass on to their customers. It has been variously estimated that one-third to one-half of this tax is shifted to the consumers. Furthermore, *at least two-thirds of American corporations add all payroll tax costs to their prices.*[15] Table II shows that state and local taxes are regressive, and that all Federal taxes combined fall much more substantially on the low-income classes.

It is to be noted that the figures in Table II include all local, state and Federal person-income taxes; inheritance, estates, and gift taxes; corporate-profit taxes (it is assumed that one-half of this is shifted to the public); excise and sales taxes; customs and property taxes. The highly regressive social insurance taxes, which take 7.3 per cent of the total income of those earning $2,000 or less, but

TABLE II

PERCENTAGE OF 1958 TOTAL INCOME PAID IN FEDERAL, STATE, AND LOCAL TAXES,* BY INCOME CLASS

Income Class (In Dollars)	Share of Taxes (In per cent)		
	Federal	State and Local	Total**
0-2,000	9.6	11.3	21.0
2,000-4,000	11.0	9.4	20.4
4,000-6,000	12.1	8.5	20.6
6,000-8,000	13.9	7.7	21.6
8,000-10,000	13.4	7.2	20.6
10,000-15,000	15.1	6.5	21.6
15,000-plus	28.6	5.9	34.4
Average	16.1	7.5	23.7

*Social insurance taxes are not included.

**Because of rounding, items do not always add up to totals.

Source: Tax Foundation, *Allocation of the Tax Burden by Income Class* (New York: Tax Foundation, 1960), p. 17.

only 1.5 per cent in the $15,000 plus class, are not included. The tax burden is substantially heavier for the lower-income classes in that income tax paid by the lower-income classes is money that would otherwise go for essential personal and family needs. Moreover, in view of the amount of Federal welfare expenditures, the lower-income groups paid for them. Taxation and welfare measures have not brought about a redistribution of income; rather, taxation and welfare measures impose an added hardship on the lower-income classes.

Table II does not take into account income undeclared in order to avoid paying taxes on it. It is estimated that about 10 per cent of the national personal income — $30 billion — never appeared in tax returns. Most of this $30 billion was received by the upper-income class. Capital gains, a deferred-compensation plan, stock-option, tax-exempt interest, gifts and trusts are means through which the higher income class avoids paying taxes, or pays at a low rate.

The concentration of economic power in a very small elite is an undisputable fact. This power is a function of both their direct ownership in the corporate structure and their ability to control it. Their possession of savings and wealth is possible because of the continuing basic inequality of income that is simply a part of a larger pattern of inequality in the United

States. The implications of this intense centralization of economic power are twofold. First, the concentration of income allocates a large share of the consumption of goods to a small proportion of the population. Second, a social theory assuming a democratized economic system — or even a trend in this direction — is quite obviously not in accord with social reality.[16]

Victims of Social Theory?

Some have defined poverty in psychological terms, while others have defined it in purely economic terms. Sociological factors such as age, occupation and race reflect only degrees of poverty. *Moreover, psychological aspects of poverty as well as sociological aspects of poverty are effects of poverty, not causes of poverty.* It is in this manner that social scientists are wont to engage in circular reasoning in trying to explain away poverty. Another example of circular reasoning is the internal causation argument. Talcott Parsons defined poverty as people who are not motivated to "get ahead" because of "qualities of personality."[17] Social theory reflects implicitly bipolar dichotomies which relegate segments of the population to lower class status and thereby creators and victims of their own poverty. Out of this nebulous thinking emerges the confusion between class and culture — they become one and the same. The anthropologist, Dr. Octavio I. Romano, has examined very critically the results of such thinking by sociologists and anthropologists with respect to the Mexican-American.[18]

Prior to the not-so-celebrated war on poverty, social scientists expounded the social theory that poverty had declined sharply as a result of radical changes in the economy — particularly the greater income equality.[19] Moreover, social scientists held that: "The poverty in America, in fact, is almost entirely outside the economic sphere proper."[20] Both pronouncements are totally erroneous. Recent studies by sociologists who have employed more honesty and rigorous methodology show that poverty has increased rather than decreased. Economists such as Robert Lampman have shown that poverty is not almost entirely outside the economic sphere proper.

Poverty is the economic inability to maintain minimum standards of nourishment, housing, clothing, and medical care. In addition to what has been said about taxation and inequality, distribution of income, and distribution of wealth, the hard fact is that unemployment, a guarantee of low income and poverty, always affects the lower income groups more frequently and for longer periods of time. Between 1960 and 1975, the population aged between eighteen to twenty-five is expected to grow more rapidly than the middle aged population.[21] With the more rapid expansion of the young and old population, both of which are low-income groups, an increase in the extent of poverty is probable.

It is estimated that in 1972 the poor population will be 28.9 million. In 1965 there were 27.4 million living in poverty, 14.3 million of whom were children under 18 years of age while 2.1 million were persons living alone. Of the 27.4 million poor in 1965, 25.3 million were children and adults living in families with children under 18 years of age.[22] It is important to point out that the poverty group is not homogeneous; the common factor is that their income falls below the Social Security Administration's poverty index. Recognition of the differential distribution of poverty is essential in the formulation of social policy.

Another very important aspect of the problem of poverty is the linear correlation between poverty and family size.

TABLE III

PER CENT OF FAMILIES IN POVERTY BY NUMBER
OF CHILDREN, 1965

Number of Related Children Under 18	Per Cent Poor
None	11.2
1	11.3
2	10.4
3	16.3
4	21.6
5	33.7
6 or more	43.5

Of the 14.3 million children in poverty, more than one-half — 8.2 mililon — live in families with four or more children. There seems to be two reasons for the poverty-family size relationship: (1) wages are insensitive to need; and (2) transfer payments (social security deductions, public assistance, etc.) benefit small families more than large ones.

In brief, poor population consists mainly of families with children. However, the national wage system favors single individuals or small families and a benefit system that favors small families among the poor. "Net transfers favor small families in low income classes, but favor large families in high income classes. The switch is at about $6,000 of pre-transfer income."[23] Poor families are predominantly *intact* families. Seven out of 10 poor families are headed by men. According to Social Security Administration statistics, in over 86 per cent of the male-headed families, the head worked at least part of 1965. The Eckstein-Harris report predicts that by 1972 relatively more of the poor will be persons in large families and female headed families, and aged persons.

TABLE IV

CHANGE IN NUMBER OF POOR PERSONS, 1959 TO 1964
AND PROJECTED 1968 TO 1972
(millions of persons)

Population Group	Number of Persons				Percentage Change	
	1959	1964	1968	1972	59-64	68-72
Total	38.9	34.1	31.1	27.7	−12%	−11%
Aged	5.9	5.4	5.1	5.0	−8	−2
Families with Children	27.4	24.0	22.1	19.5	−12	−12
Male Head	21.0	17.9	16.0	13.3	−15	−17
Female Head	6.4	6.1	6.1	6.2	−5	+2
Other*	5.7	4.6	3.9	3.2	−19	−18

*Non-aged unrelated individuals, and families with no children.

Source: Otto Eckstein and Robert Harris, *Income and Benefit Programs*. Office of the Assistant Secretary for Programs Coordination, U.S. Dept. of Health, Education and Welfare, October, 1966.

The Eckstein-Harris report has very serious implications. First of all, poverty will continue to be a national serious problem for many years, unless substantial measures are taken. Secondly, an alarmingly high number of poverty families will be *intact* families — families headed by men. A corollary to this implication is the implication that families, particularly large families, play a critical role in the perpetuation of poverty, for lack of adequate resources and the necessity to stretch very thinly meagre resources deter the families from providing the incentives, health and education which permit exit from poverty.

III. THE PUBLIC WELFARE SYSTEM

Widespread dissatisfaction with the welfare system is inevitably and inextricably tied to the concern for the elimination of poverty. However, two considerations in the elimination of poverty are a substantial reduction in the cost of welfare and the size of its bureaucracy. Existing welfare policies have become a huge political liability. Modern social welfare policy must be virtually unique among major policies in that it has no supporters one can discern. The welfare system itself — the direct provision of funds and services to carefully delineated groups in the population under a series of rules — has become an enormous political albatross. Rejection of existing welfare policy is understandable in the context that people want to control their own economic life. *The demand is for control of political and economic life rather than just more income.*

The charge of welfare colonialism addresses itself to the resistance of the poor to be manipulated. The poor want self-determination and control over their own lives as well as opportunity to select and develop their own life style and thus counter the sense of powerlessness and despair.[24]

It is clear that a dominant value in American society, industrial growth, is justified on the assumption of its universally beneficial results. However, this assumption turns into a blatant lie when we discover that those benefiting from industrial growth are but a handful. Moreover, it is becoming patently clear that the above assumption is but a guise for the maintenance of systems which perpetuate the social problems confronting our society today. It is particularly ironic that in this time of crisis these institutions seem frozen in the past, addressing themselves only to the casualties of a sick society.

A case in point is the welfare system. In the past, public welfare departments were charged by society with the responsibility for assisting those who are in need with the expectation that those receiving assistance are in need temporarily and will return to the mainstream in a relatively short time. While this expectation may have been valid during the depression of the 1930's, it is no longer valid in most instances.

A very pertinent question needs to be asked: in view of the fact that the welfare system was created for a time of economic crisis, the depression, why has it been kept in its original form when the rationale for its existence has changed radically? *Why continue with a structure created for depression years in an era of affluence?*

Thus the poverty group — the delineated group of the public welfare system — lives in a painful and constant ambiguity vis-a-vis the double message of the general public versus the explicit actions of those who control the system. Rules, regulations and policies are seen as deliberate "mystifications" that are promoted by an elite determined to keep clients at arms length and to shut them out from meaningful participation. It is becoming increasingly more clear that the Public Welfare System epitomizes a polarity between those who have economic and political power and those who are economically and politically poor. A corollary of this polarity is the discontinuity and confused thinking between authorization and practice. The system has the authorization and mandate "to rehabilitate" the poor. However, the practice of the system is nullified by the political and economic considerations in all communities. The incestuous nature of the funding base invalidates, contradicts and renders ineffective the authorization and practice. The socio-economic must be put ahead of "rehabilitative" issues. The welfare system can only respond to a program for the emancipation of the poor if the problem is conceptualized in economic and political terms. This is the heart of the dilemma. An institution cannot do battle against social problems at a causal level while its life depends on the largesse of political powers.

IV. A DEMOCRATIZED ECONOMY OR NOBLESSE OBLIGE?

The California *Welfare and Institutions Code,* Division 9, Part I, Chapter 1 (10,000) defines the purpose of Public Social Services as follows:

> The purpose of this division is to provide for protection, care and assistance to the people of the state in need thereof, and to promote the welfare and happiness of all of the people of the state by providing appropriate aid and services to all of its needy and distressed. It is the legislative intent that aid shall be administered and services provided promptly and humanely, with due regard for the preservation of family life, and without discrimination on account of race, national origin or ancestry, religion or political affiliation; and that aid shall be so administered and services so provided as to encourage self respect, self reliance and the desire to be a good citizen, useful to society.[25]

It is within this framework and philosophy that 700,000 children in California receive financial help through Aid to Families with Dependent Children (AFDC). It is within this same framework and philosophy that the legislature has not changed the payment base for the care of these children since 1957. During this time they did respond to the aged, blind and disabled by providing continuous raises and by providing cost of living increases.

The following chart which shows the increases over the last 12 years for the various categories will provide the initial understanding of the fiscal base. It is this fiscal base which is the root cause of the problem.

Table V graphically illustrates the problem. It is important to further understand how the State of California determines these different allowances for the public welfare programs.

TABLE V

MAXIMUM PARTICIPATING BASE

	Two Persons	One Person		
Year	One Adult and One Child	Blind	Aged	Disabled
1957	$145.00	$110.00	$ 89.00	$ 88.00
1966	148.00	183.50	179.00	150.00
1969 (Dec.)	148.00	202.00	195.00	166.00
Total Increase	$ 3.00	$ 92.00	$106.00	$ 78.00

The Maximum Participation Base (MPB) is the amount in which the federal, state and local agencies will share. The family or individual may have a larger amount to live on only when there is income from some other source, usually earnings, contributions, or OASDI benefits.

State laws provide for the public assistance recipients' budgets to be computed from state standards. These standards are set annually by the State Department of Social Welfare based on their determination of the amount of money needed to pay for minimal needs (W & I Code 11452). Changes in standards for families are reflected in the regulatory guidelines (cost schedules) county welfare departments must use in determining the amount needed by a family for its basic living. The amount of aid received by the family, however, is absolutely limited by the MPB, regardless of the State standard of need.

State laws provide for a cost of living increase when proven necessary in the adult programs. Section 44-205.1 of the Eligibility and Assistance Standards describes *"Cost of Living Adjustments — Adult Programs:* The Standard of assistance is adjusted on December 1 of each year to reflect changes in the cost of living as provided by statute." This adjustment assists aged, blind and disabled recipients in meeting increases in the cost of their minimum needs. No such provision is made for the AFDC family. The $3.00 increase in Table V is the result of a federal increase which the state was required to pass on to the families. While increased costs are reflected in the cost schedules issued annually, the legislators have not acted to permit increases in the MPB for families. If the standards for families were reflected in the MPB, the following would exist:

The amounts in Table VI are based on the standards provided for AFDC in Santa Clara County adjusted for cost of living increases for 1968-69. These figures take in only the basic need, as

TABLE VI

COMPARISON OF MPB STANDARDS

Number of Children	Average Amount Required to Meet Full Allowable Needs	Range	Present MPB	Average Difference
1	$192	180-203	$148	$44
2	228	207-250	172	56
3	279	247-311	221	58
4	322	279-366	263	59
5	372	319-426	300	72

determined by the AFDC standard, and do not reflect any special needs that may exist in the family's budget.

Rather than to rely solely on the standards which are determined by state staff in compliance with the law, and noting that the cost of living has risen by 30.6 per cent since the year 1957, it is important to take a look at the cost of living as it relates to the present MPB for AFDC. The Consumer Price Index (CPI) is used.

TABLE VII

COMPARISON OF MPB COST OF LIVING

Number of Children	Oct. 1957 MPB	Adj. to 9/30/69 CPI Increase (Rounded to nearest dollar)	Difference
1	$145.00	$189.00	$ 44.00
2	168.00	233.00	65.00
3	215.00	298.00	83.00
4	256.00	355.00	99.00
5	291.00	403.00	112.00

The October 1957 MPB used to compute the adjustment is basically the MPB adopted by the legislature in 1951 for various federal pass-on provisions occurring between 1951 and 1957. A comparison between the "Average Amount Required to Meet Full Allowable Needs" column in Table VI and the column headed "Adjusted to 9/30/69 CPI Increase" in Table VII clearly indicates the failure of the MPB to keep pace with the cost of living.

V. THE WELFARE DOLLAR IN THE ECONOMY OF A COMMUNITY

What role does the welfare system play in the economic health of a community. *How much does a community depend on the welfare system for its economic survival? Ultimately, who gets the*

TABLE VIII

COMPARISON OF MPB FOR 1950, 1957, 1968

1 child	$105	$145	$148	+$ 40	+$ 3	+$ 43
2 children	153	168	172	+ 15	+ 4	+ 19
3 children	201	215	221	+ 14	+ 6	+ 20
4 children	249	256	263	+ 7	+ 7	+ 14
5 children	297	291	300	− 6	+ 9	+ 3
6 children	345	320	330	− 25	+ 10	− 15
7 children	393	343	355	− 50	+ 12	− 38
8 children	441	360	373	− 81	+ 13	− 68
9 children	489	371	386	− 118	+ 15	− 103

welfare dollar? Who is profiting by keeping the system as it is? Is the welfare system a quasi-colony for the colonizer? However inadequate the welfare grant is, it contributes significantly to the economy of a community. *It is my hypothesis that the welfare dollar sustains and enlarges the economic and political power of a few in the community.* The corollary is that the welfare dollar does not contribute to the economic and social development of low-income communities. Since the possibility that there will be a radical change in the welfare system is very remote, are there ways in which the financial sources of the welfare system can be converted into resources for the economic development of a delineated community?

NOTES

[1]Eric Fromm, *Man for Himself* (New York: Rinehart, 1947), p. 3.

[2]Charles I. Schottland, *The Welfare State* (New York: Harper and Rowe, 1967), p. 16.

[3]Sidney Fine, "The General Welfare State in the Twentieth Century," *The Welfare State* (New York: Harper and Rowe, 1967), p. 47.

[4]Henry S. Commager, *The American Mind: An Interpretation of American Thought and Character Since the 1880's* (New Haven: 1950), p. 217.

[5]*Op. cit.*, Sidney Fine, pp. 51-52.

[6]*Ibid.*, pp. 68-69.

[7]Asa Briggs, "The Welfare State in Historical Perspective," *The Welfare State* (New York: Harper and Rowe, 1967), p. 29.

[8]Gunnar Myrdal, *Beyond the Welfare State* (London: Duckworth, 1958), p. 45.

[9]See Everett F. Cataldo, Richard M. Johnson, Lyman A. Kallstedt, "Social Strain and Urban Violence," in Louis H. Masotti and Don R. Bowen, eds., *Riots and Rebellion: Civil Violence in the Urban Community* (Beverly Hills: Sage Publications, 1968), pp. 285-298.

[10]See Daniel Moynihan, *Maximum Feasible Misunderstanding* (New York: The Free Press, 1969). James L. Sundquist, ed., *On Fighting Poverty* (New York: Basic Books, 1969).

[11]Cf. "Expense Accounts," *Harvard Business Review,* March-April, 1960, pp. 16, 172; *U. S. News and World Report,* August 16, 1957, p. 87 and p. 83.

[12]Cf. Gabriel Kolko, *Wealth and Power in America* (New York: Praeger, 1962), pp. 9-29.

[13]*Ibid.,* p. 35.

[14]Tax Foundation, *Federal Excise Taxes* (New York: 1956), p. 47.

[15]Lewis H. Kimmel, *Taxes & Economic Incentives* (Washington, D.C.: Brookings Institution, 1950), p. 182.

[16]*Op. cit.,* Kolko, p. 68.

[17]Talcott Parsons, "A Revised Analytical Approach to the Theory of Social Stratification," *Class, Status and Power* (Glencoe: The Free Press, 1953), p. 127.

[18]Octavio I. Romano, "The Anthropology and Sociology of the Mexican-American," *El Grito,* Vol. II, No. 1 (Berkeley: Quinto Sol Publications, Inc., 1968), Fall.

[19]Cf. Semour Martin Lipset and Natalie Rogoff, "Class and Opportunity in Europe and the United States," *Commentary,* Dec., 1954.

[20]Max Lerner, *America as a Civilization* (New York: Simon and Schuster, 1957), p. 338.

[21]Social Security Administration, *Illustrative United States Population Projections* (Washington, D.C.: Government Printing Office, 1957), Actuarial Study No. 46, pp. 23-24.

[22]For a profile of the poor see article by Mollie Orshansky in the *Social Security Bulletin,* January 1965, July 1965, April 1966, and May 1966.

[23]Robert J. Lampman, "How Much Does the American System of Transfers Benefit the Poor?" *Economic Progress and Social Welfare,* Leonard H. Goodman, ed. (New York: Columbia University Press, 1966), p. 147.

[24]Cf. *Report of the National Advisory Commission on Civil Disorders* (Kerner Report) (New York: Bantam Books, 1968), Chapter 17, Part III, p. 457.

[25]*Welfare and Institutions Code: and Laws Relating to Social Welfare.* State of California, Department of General Services, Sacramento, 1967.

BIBLIOGRAPHY

Books

Caplovitz, David. *The Poor Pay More.* New York: The Free Press, 1963.

Fromm, Eric. *Man For Himself.* New York: Rinehart, 1947.

Galbraith, John Kenneth. *The Affluent Society.* Boston: Houghton Mifflin, 1958.

Harrington, Michael. *The Other America.* Baltimore: Penguin Books, 1964.

Jacobs, Paul. *Prelude to Riot: A View of Urban America from the Bottom.* New York: Vintage Books, 1968.

Keyserling, Leon H. *Progress or Poverty.* Washington, D.C.: Conference on Economic Progress, 1964.

Kimmel, Lewis H. *Taxes and Economic Incentives.* Washington, D.C.: Brookings Institution, 1950.

Kolko, Gabriel. *Wealth and Power in America.* New York: Praeger, 1965.

Lerner, Max. *America as a Civilization.* New York: Simon and Schuster, 1957.

Memmi, Albert. *The Colonizer and the Colonized.* Boston: Beacon Press, 1965.

Mills, C. Wright. *The Power Elite.* New York: Oxford Press, 1956.

Morris, Robert and Binstock, Robert H. *Feasible Planning for Social Change.* New York: Columbia University Press, 1966.

Moynihan, Daniel P. *Maximum Feasible Misunderstanding.* New York: The Free Press, 1969.

Myrdal, Gunnar. *Beyond the Welfare State.* New York: Bantam Books, 1967.

Nisbet, Robert A. *Community and Power.* New York: Oxford University Press, 1953.

Schottland, Charles I., ed. *The Welfare State.* New York: Harper and Rowe, 1967.

Sundquist, James L., ed. *On Fighting Poverty.* New York: Basic Books, 1969.

Sorokin, Pitirim A. *Social and Cultural Mobility.* New York: The Free Press, 1957.

Theobald, Robert, ed. *The Guaranteed Income.* New York: Doubleday, 1967.

Will, Robert and Harold Vatter. *Poverty in Affluence.* New York: Harcourt, Brace, 1965.

Articles

Cataldo, Everett F., Johnson, Richard M., Kallstedt, Lyman A. "Social Strain and Urban Violence," in Louis H. Masotti and Don R. Bowmen (eds.) *Riots and Rebellion: Civil Violence in the Urban Community.* Beverly Hills: Sage Publications, 1968.

Cavala, Bill and Wildausky, Aaron. "The Political Feasability of Income by Right." Department of Political Science, University of California, Berkeley, 1969.

Harvard Business Review. "Expense Accounts." March-April, 1960.

Kain, John and Persky, Joseph. "The Nation's State in Southern Rural Poverty." Harvard University, 1967.

Lampman, Robert. "How Much Does the American System of Transfers Benefit the Poor?" *Economic Progress and Social Welfare.* Leonard H. Goodman (ed.) New York: Columbia University Press, 1966.

————. "The Low Income Population and Economic Growth." Study Papers Nos. 12 and 13. Joint Economic Committee Congress of the United States, 1959.

Parsons, Talcott. "A Revised Analytical Approach to the Theory of Social Stratification." *Class, Status, and Power.* Glencoe: The Free Press, 1953.

Rogoff, Natalie and Lipset, Seymour Martin. "Class and Opportunity in Europe and the United States." *Commentary,* Dec., 1954.

Romano, Octavio I. "The Anthropology and Sociology of the Mexican-Americans: The Distortion of Mexican-American History." *El Grito*. Quinto Sol Publications, Berkeley, Vol. II, No. 1, Fall, 1968.

Tax Foundation. *Federal Excise Taxes*. New York, 1956.

The Community Resources Project. *Dependency and the Poor*. The University of Arizona, 1969.

Government Publications

Social Security Administration. Social Security Bulletin, January, 1965; July 1965; April 1966; May 1966.

———. Illustrative United States Population Projections. Government Printing Office, 1957.

State of California. Poverty in California. State Office of Planning. Sacramento, 1964.

———. *Welfare and Institutions Code*. Department of General Services. Sacramento, 1967.

United States Commission. Report of the National Advisory Commission on Civil Disorders. New York: Dutton and Co., 1968.

Advertising and Racism: The Case of The Mexican-American

THOMAS M. MARTÍNEZ

Introduction

Emerging from a cloud of dust appears a band of horse-riding, ferocious-looking Mexican banditos. They are called to a halt by their sombrero-covered, thick-mustached, fat-bellied leader, who, upon stopping, reaches with the utmost care for a small object from his saddle bags. He picks up the object, lifts up his underarm, and smiles slyly — to spray Arrid deodorant. An American Midwestern voice is then heard over the television, "If it works for him, it will work for you." Message — Mexicans stink the most.

Flipping through the pages of a recent issue of LIFE Magazine, one will encounter a picture of a man painting a house, who appears to be of Mexican descent. He is covered with spilled paint except for his face, and the caption next to him reads, "You may get the shade you asked for." Underneath this is a description of Lark cigarettes ending with, "Tell someone about Lark's EASY TASTE and hard-working GAS TRAP FILTERS. Who knows? He may do something nice for you." Message — Mexicans are sloppy workers, and do not always do what is requested of them on the job.

The Functions of Advertising in American Society

Seldom a day goes by in the United States without at least one young Mexican-American being called, "Frito Bandito." Indeed, this cartoon caricature of a short, mustached two-gunned thief is a very effective prejudicial form of anti-locution[1] — effective in terms of making the out-group appear inferior, and the in-group superior. The Mexican-American children are paying the price in loss of self-esteem for the Frito-Lay Corporation's successful advertising attempt at product association. To understand how advertising can

521

create such racial stereotypes and inflame racism, we need to examine the functions of advertising in American society.

Advertising, like legal statutes and decisions, serves at least two functions: instrumental and symbolic. Instrumentally, an advertisement is meant to sell a product; its instrumental worth is measured in terms of how well the product sells due to the advertisement. Similarly, the instrumental function of law is to maintain order; how well these laws are obeyed, helped through enforcement, is a measure of their instrumental value.

The symbolic function of law, according to Joseph Gusfield, refers to, ". . . a dimension of meaning in symbolic behavior which is not given in its immediate and manifest significance but in what the action connotes for the audience that views it."[2] For example, the burning of a draft card is less noteworthy for its instrumental abuse than for its symbolic significance. Gusfield maintains, "A courtroom decision or legislative act is a gesture which often glorifies the values of one group and demeans those of another."[3] Thus, laws maintain the pecking order of society.

Likewise, TV commercials and magazine advertisements, of the type referred to above, symbolically reaffirm the inferior social status of Mexicans and Mexican-Americans in the eyes of the audience. Exaggerated Mexican racial and cultural characteristics, together with some outright misconceptions concerning their way of life, symbolically suggest to the audience that such people are comical, lazy, and thieving, who want what the Anglos can have by virtue of their superior taste and culture. The advertisements suggest to the audience that one ought to buy the product because it is the duty of a member of a superior culture and race.

Racist Messages and the Mass Media

The symbolic function of advertising is one level of understanding the racist implications of the mass media, especially regarding the Mexicans and Mexican-Americans. For another way of understanding, we turn to Marshall McLuhan. In his attempt to explain the influence of technological changes in communication, he told us, "The medium is the message." Later, of course, he termed it, "The medium is the massage,"[4] but the meaning is essentially similar; that is, *what* is said is less important than *how* it is said. As we move from the spoken to the written and to the televised, the media someway, somehow transforms our thoughts about ourselves, other persons, places, and things, as well as our relationship to them. The written world and the televised world (together with movies) have brought us closer to one another than the spoken world. Consequently, we are supposedly becoming involved in a "global village."

However, if McLuhan had been more sensitive to prejudicial racial and cultural stereotyping he might have felt less inclined to shift attention away from what is both said and pictured, especially in commercials and ads, regardless of media. Simply because different cultural and racial groups are brought into close proximity in our minds does not automatically lessen the influence of *cultural relativism* — we see different cultural and racial traits through eyes that are conditioned to see goodness and beauty as they are defined by our own cherished culture. We see beauty in things that we have come to accept as beautiful. That which is especially different from our own standards of beauty is often deemed distasteful. Television travelers and magazine mobiles take with them sacred values and beliefs that influence them to selectively perceive and interpret in a consistently self-fulfilling manner. A Peace Corps worker sometimes labels a foreigner as "primitive," an impression likely to be shared by television and popular reading audiences who judge from similar value standpoints.

Advertising media that utilize Mexicans and Mexican-Americans have selectively presented and exaggerated racial and cultural characteristics. The consequence is logical: an ethnic group is portrayed in a manner that renders esteem to the values and beliefs of the audience and, conversely, the ethnic group is perceived as "naturally inferior." To find nothing objectionable or distasteful about advertising's image of Mexicans and Mexican-Americans suggests tacit agreement with that image.

No matter what medium sends the message, the content and context of the message still have important ramifications, which in some cases supersede the importance of difference in media. Whether or not the "Frito Bandito" is pictured in a magazine or seen on TV (although the impact may be more widespread over the latter media), he still reaffirms the inferior social status of the people he is supposed to represent, which, to judge from advertising, encompasses everyone of Mexican descent. When Camel cigarettes presents a "typical Mexican village" in one of their commercials, it may, in McLuhan's sense, serve to involve the viewers in their village life. But what kind of village life is shown? All of the residents are either sleeping on the boardwalk, or walking around seemingly bored. The involvement, in this case, is one of the Anglo-American sensing superiority over the lazy Mexican villagers.

If we assume that the content and context of a message, as well as the medium, are extensions of man's thought system, then the conclusion is logically inescapable: almost all advertisers presently utilizing Mexicans or Mexican-Americans to sell their products are exhibiting racist thinking.

Not only are advertisers exhibiting racist thinking at the expense of everyone of Mexican descent, but they are also creating, in many cases, unfavorable racial and cultural stereotypes in minds that previously did not harbor them. When the image of an ethnic group is consistently similar over the mass media, there is the strong suggestion to the viewer that there is some validity to the image. Add to this power of suggestion the feeling of superiority that is aroused when another group is portrayed as inferior. Then, the result of such an insidious combination of forces might be the expectation, sprinkled with some desire, of perceiving the ethnic group as having many inferior traits, the worst one being that they are what they are — a mass of inferior traits. Individual members of such a group should not be expected to be exempt from these inferior traits (except perhaps in a very few cases), because this is how prejudiced minds think.

Whether or not this prejudice was learned through advertising or parents, the effect is similar. Even unprejudiced parents (of which there are few) are not equipped to counter the steady and subtle bombardment of prejudicial suggestions that advertisers conveniently communicate to their children. To many children, the "Frito Bandito" is highly representative of Mexicans. Besides, they can always have some fun calling the Mexican kid at school, "Frito Bandito."

Advertising is a significant part of what C. Wright Mills called the *cultural apparatus*, which involves all mass media.[5] The control of the cultural apparatus has important implications, as pointed out by Harold Cruse: "Only the blind cannot see that whoever controls the cultural apparatus — whatever class, power group, faction or political combine — also controls the destiny of the United States and everyone in it."[6] That is to say, advertising, at least in the treatment of Mexicans and Mexican-Americans, is an exercise in reaffirming the superior social status of one group (guess which one) and the inferior status of another. Advertising, then, functions as a tool of racist elites.

Where Lies the Blame?

Since advertisement is commonly conceived as a product of the advertising agency, there might be the tendency to attribute the bulk of the blame for creating and supporting racist notions to the agencies, rather than the advertiser. I say "blame" instead of "responsibility" because neither group could be considered socially responsible when they collaborate on racism.

It would be a simple explanation, not warranted by the complexity of the situation, to suggest that advertising agencies are amoral, image-exploiters, freely damning the image of anyone they damn please, or at least those who cannot damn them back. This is rejected out of hand, because advertising men and women are very much concerned with making a beautiful moral image of not only the product, but also themselves. Indeed, the advertising men and women see themselves as the most beautiful kind of people. It is not out of lack of insight, for instance, that Joseph Bensman (in his book, *Dollars and Sense*) conceptualizes the psychological state of advertising men in terms of narcissism, which is an intensified sense of self-love.[7] In his job, the advertising man must convince the public of the product's superiority. All the while, he must keep his cool. To "crack" is to admit weakness and invite failure, admitting that one is human. Under such working conditions, it is useful to develop the self-image of a "superman," in order to be really successful. The superman hangup, as we learned from Nazi Germany, is racist in nature, and scapegoating is taken for granted. The advertising supermen and women probably feel at ease in making an ad in which the advertiser, their client, finds no objectionable features, but which nevertheless casts someone of Mexican descent in an unflattering and stereotypical role.

An important point, however, is that ads are sold to clients, clients buy ads. The question then becomes why are so *many different kinds* of corporations [see chart] willing to be sold ads which support racial and cultural prejudice against people of Mexican descent? Searching for the most logical answer, the logic of illogical prejudice on the part of the corporations and advertising agencies is glaring.

Their prejudice was probed by students in my racial and cultural minorities course who wrote critical letters to firms who paid for commercials and ads that communicate racism. Not unexpectedly, the Frito-Lay Corporation was high in the racist standings. Their written reply took the following form:

> In response to your letter dated February 25, we did not and never have had any racist intentions in presenting the Frito Bandito cartoon character. It was meant to be a simple character which is intended to make you laugh, in turn we hope that this laughter will leave our trademark implanted in your memory.
>
> Again, our apologies if we have offended you.
>
> > Very truly yours (sic)
> > Director of Advertising
> > Frito-Lay Corporation

Tell this to the Mexican-American kids. They have the Frito-Lay Corporation to thank for adding another racial stereotype to our language.

Why would a business firm care so much about implanting their trademark "in your memory," when the implantation is fertilized with the seed of prejudice against Mexicans and Mexican-Americans? Again, is it really necessary to spell out the most logical answer?

Returning to the symbol of their racism, simply because the Frito Bandito is supposed to be a comical character, "to make you laugh," we might ask, is humor less harmful or more insidious than outright verbal statements expressing deeply held racial prejudice? Why are there so few, if any, jokes about rich Anglo-Saxons? And does it make any difference if some of the members of the victimized group itself freely laugh at the jokes about themselves?

A reasonably sound answer to these questions came in the form of B'nai B'rith's denunciation of all racial and cultural jokes, noting the rise in "Polish" and "Italian" jokes a few years ago, on the ground that jokes which ridicule exaggerated ethnic group characteristics promote ethnocentric thinking. Inasmuch as Polish and Italian jokes are usually similar, and often exactly the same except for the name, there is good reason to deem all ethnic jokes as ethnocentric.

Jokes in the form of comical characters seem to mislead the audience, as all ideal-types do when they are based upon biased data. The audience is deluded into thinking there is enough likeness between the comical character and his ethnic affiliations to render the character believable.

Freud believed that humor was a reflection of unconscious, repressed feeling.[8] Our true feelings are those which, due to social pressures to conform, are seldom made known or put forth as seriously-held beliefs. Many of the same people who claim not to be prejudiced easily laugh at ethnocentric jokes, and are amused by stereotyped characters. Consider, for example, the typical audience reaction to Jose Jimenez. Does such laughter reveal hidden prejuduce? It most likely does.

A commonplace contention is that it is healthy and harmless to laugh at oneself. However, it depends upon what aspect of self is being laughed at. For instance, if a person such as Jimmy Durante makes fun of his big nose because it is uniquely structured and "smiles" at people, then this is not psychically damaging to him. If, on the other hand, a person makes fun of his nose because he believes it to be an easily recognizable sign that he is a member of an ethnic group, of which he is somewhat ashamed, then this person is temporarily identifying with the superior group which looks down at such obvious traits. Self-ridicule in this latter sense is a form of self-hatred.

Shakespeare might differ with me: "What's in a name? That which we call a rose by any other name would smell as sweet." Yet, why do we call loved ones, "Honey?" Does not "Honey" suggest an image of something? Call her "vinegar," and watch her reaction. Apparently the Bard did not appreciate the influence of labels upon our perception and thinking. Ponder the thoughts of Erdman Palmore: "It may well be that if a rose were labeled 'stinkweed,' it would be perceived as smelling less sweet."[9] This idea tends to cast doubt on Shakespeare's insight into and sensitivity toward racial stereotyping, not to mention the forces that keep racial prejudice alive. But, then, he contributed his share through his creation of "Shylock."

The Brown Shadow

Today, no major advertiser would attempt to display a black man or woman over the mass media in a prejudiced, stereotyped fashion. Complaints would be forthcoming from black associations, and perhaps the FCC. Yet, these same advertisers who dare not show "step'n fetch it" characters, uninhibitedly depict a Mexican counterpart, with additional traits of stinking and stealing. Perhaps the white hatred for blacks, which cannot find adequate expression in today's ads, is being transferred to their brown brothers.

Much of the plight of Mexican-Americans is reflected in their collective powerlessness to combat the advertisers' image of them. Hanging onto the lowest economic rungs in American society, Mexican-Americans have been unable to cast a collective shadow in the minds of everyday Anglo-Americans, much less the power structure. We are invisible, and an invisible man has no shadow. The only racial shadow that advertisers have recognized and re-acted to, in addition to their own, is the black shadow, not unusual since all shadows are black; that is, any group which develops enough political power to influence their image-exploiters is visible. Mexican-Americans do not cast a shadow in this political sense.

Where, then, is the Mexican-American with his brown shadow? He has been, and still is, at the bottom of the white race ever since white Europeans invaded the New World. Until recently, the main races were distinguished by only four colors — black, red, yellow, and white. Brown people were considered to be members of the white race, on paper at least. There seemed to be little desire on the part of the whites to call Mexican-Americans any color other than white. It was too comfortable standing on top of the brown people, as opposed to recognizing them as officially a distinct group, although they were treated as disdainfully distinctive. Thus, it be-came easy to conceive of Mexican-Americans as embodying all that is worst in the white man. This analysis is supported by another re-sponse to a student letter complaining of racism in a specific advertisement:

> This acknowledges your letter of February 25 about an L&M TV commercial.

> We sincerely regret your reaction to this commercial be-cause we did not intend to be derogatory to any ethnic group.

> 'Paco' is a warm, sympathetic and lovable character with whom most of us can identify because he has a little of all of us in him; that is, our tendency to procrastinate at times. He seeks to escape the violence of war and to enjoy the

pleasure of the moment, in this case the good flavor of an L&M cigarette.

This commercial is the first in a new series for L&M, and it was tested carefully with many audiences, including Mexican-Americans, before it went on the air with no negative indications of any kind.

'Paco' is one of several commercials in the present L&M series, all with the same flavor, spirit and good humor, including the 'office secretary,' the Maine fisherman, 'the musical composer,' and the 'gypsies.'

We appreciate your taking the time to write and express your opinion. We are bringing your viewpoint to the attention of the advertising agency which produces our L&M commercials, and we will continue to examine all of our advertising carefully in our effort to avoid offending any individual or any minority group.

Sincerely,

Director of Public Relations
Liggett Meyers

According to this letter, "Paco" is an escapist who embodies the undesirable trait of procrastination. Yet, advertising men detest procrastination (they made the ad), and so do capitalists (L&M bought it). L&M, whether or not their public relations director realizes it, is actually revealing their prejudice against Mexican people by allowing such a commercial to be shown in their name.

It is noteworthy that L&M sent an almost exact replica of the above letter to another student of mine, who complained about the commercial that presented gypsies in a stereotyped fashion. To L&M, the only difference between the gypsies and "Paco" is the name: "The gypsies," replied L&M, "are warm, sympathetic and lovable characters with whom most of us can identify because he has a little of all of us in him; that is, our tendency to procrastinate at times." This easy exchange between ethnic groups strikingly resembles the phenomenon of ethnocentrism in Polish and/or Italian jokes.

L&M's justification for their ads, "a little of all of us in them," is a good example of *projection*, one of the dynamics of prejudice.

Gordon W. Allport's words on projection (from his famous book, *The Nature of Prejudice*) are still instructive:

> Suppose there are unwanted traits in oneself — perhaps greed, lust, laziness, and untidiness. What the sufferer needs is a caricature of these attributes — a simon-pure incarnation of these evils. He needs something so extreme that he need not even suspect himself of being guilty. The Jew is therefore seen as wholly concupiscent; the Negro as completely lazy; the Mexican as filthy. One who holds such extreme stereotypes need not suspect himself of having these hated tendencies.[10]

"Paco" represents L&M's caricature of undesirable traits within Anglo-Americans. And again, L&M, among others, takes it for granted that Mexicans are very amenable to caricaturization. We can also assume that the Mexican-Americans who supposedly were shown the commercial prior to its public release may not have had the insight into stereotyping and projection to offer more viable opinions on its offensiveness. Perhaps they have become accustomed or conditioned to accept "Paco," and others like him, as a reality rather than what he really is — an advertising fabrication.

NOTES

[1]Allport considers anti-locution the least energetic negative action: "Most people who have prejudices talk about them. With like-minded friends, occasionally with strangers, they may express their antagonism freely. But many people never go beyond this mild degree of antipathetic action." Gordon W. Allport, *The Nature of Prejudice* (Garden City, New York: Doubleday, 1954), p. 14.

[2]Joseph R. Gusfield, "Moral Passage: The Symbolic Process in Public Designation of Deviance," *Social Problems* 15:2 (Fall, 1967), p. 176.

[3]*Ibid.*

[4]Herbert Marshall McLuhan and Quentin Fiore, coordinated by Jerom Agel, *The Medium is the Massage*, (New York: Random House, 1967).

[5]C. Wright Mills, *Power Elite*, (New York: Oxford University Press, 1959).

[6]Harold Cruse, *The Crisis of the Negro Intellectual*, (New York: Wm. Morrow, 1967), p. 65.

[7]Joseph Bensman, *Dollars and Sense: The Meaning of Work in Profit and Non-Profit Organizations*, (New York: MacMillan, 1967).

[8]See S. Freud, *Wit and its Relation to the Unconscious*, (New York: Moffat Yard, 1916).

[9]Erdman B. Palmore, "Ethnophaulisms and Ethnocentrism," *The American Journal of Sociology* LXVII:4 (January, 1962), p. 445.

[10]Allport, *op. cit.*, p. 365.

CHART 1.
ADVERTISERS PROMOTING RACISM: A PARTIAL LISTING

Name of Advertiser	Context and/or Content of Ad	Racist Message
Granny Goose	*Fat Mexican toting guns, ammunition	Mexicans=overweight, carry deadly weapons
Frito-Lay	†*"Frito-Bandito"	Mexicans=sneaky, thieves
Liggett & Meyers	*"Paco" never "feenishes" anything, not even revolution	Mexicans=too lazy to improve selves
A. J. Reynolds	*Mexican bandito	Mexicans=bandits
Camel Cigarettes	*"Typical" Mexican village, all sleeping or bored	Mexicans=do-nothings, irresponsible
General Motors	†*White, rustic man holding three Mexicans at gunpoint	Mexicans=should be and can be arrested by superior white man
Lark (Liggett & Meyers)	†Mexican house painter covered with paint	Mexicans=sloppy workers, undependable
Philco-Ford	†*Mexican sleeping next to TV set	Mexicans=always sleeping
Frigidaire	*Mexican banditos interested in freezer	Mexicans=thieves, seeking Anglo artifacts
Arrid	*Mexican bandito sprays underarm, voice says, "If it works for him, it will work for you."	Mexicans=stink the most

†=newspaper or magazine ad
*=TV commercial

Notes on the Modern State

Octavio I. Romano-V.

Since the end of World War II there has unfolded before us a second major period of western expansion in the United States, again spearheaded by a great influx of people from throughout the midwest, the northeast, and the southeast. The results of this second westward expansion are well known in terms of western population growth, the development of highways, burgeoning cities and suburbs, and a host of other readily observable developments that have taken place and continue to take place in what seems to be an ever-accelerating tempo. In fact, such has been the nature of these changes, and the elements of routine everyday life that they impinge upon, that relatively few people have been able to stop and ponder the totality of what is developing in a state such as California. True, many individuals have focused upon a partial view of current developments limited to, say, mental health, or education, or social welfare, and the like. Most commonly, such partial views tend to be circumscribed because of a particular writer's frame of reference that is directly related to his particular field of professional specialization, be it social work, penology, medicine, or other similar activities. There is no professional field that one might call "totalology," that is, a discipline that specializes in the analysis and description of totalities such as institutions in an urban-industrial state such as California, unless, of course, one chooses to view some forms of systems analysis in this light. Even then, however, few indeed are knowledgeable about the totality of what current developments in California may augur for the future not only of this state, but for the future of urban-industrial society no matter when and where its manifestation and subsequent growth.

Nationally, some thirty years ago the State of California had the reputation of being a haven for retired people, navy bases, as a sunny locale for summer vacations, as an agricultural region abounding with broad expanses of colorful orange groves, and, of course, it was known for Hollywood and the products of Hollywood, both human and celluloid. Few people were aware of the Chicano population of the state, the history of labor movement in California and the role of the Mexican-American in this effort, the ultimate disposition of the lands that belonged to the relocated Japanese, or of the industrial potential of the state. In 1940 the population of the state was estimated at 6,907,387.[1]

Scarcely twenty-nine years later, in 1969 California was about to become the nation's most populous state, and its population was estimated at 19,834,000. In 1969 California ranked second in overall percentage of urbanization (86.4%), second only to the state of New Jersey (99.6%). There had developed also within the boundaries of the state the nation's second largest manufacturing complex,[2] second only to the State of New York.

The historical and interrelated processes of population growth, urbanization, and industrialization have wrought many changes for the population and the state, including those institutions that deal with education, social welfare, mental and physical health, and incarceration. Like other states, California has evolved sub-systems through which the state is involved in the training of youth for adulthood, in the field of unemployment, the care of dependents in families, care for the blind and the disabled, care for the ill, and in the care of the incarcerated. Involved in these efforts are manifest activities oriented to achieve certain ends that have been designated as either desirable or necessary as authorized through legislative and legal channels. These functions, generally, are claimed to be governed largely toward a philosophy, if not the practice, of rehabilitation in the broadest sense of the term. Thus they work toward the training and the re-training of individuals so that the process of entry and re-entry of citizens into the "productive sector" of society is hopefully propagated.

In an urbanized-industrialized state such as California, how extensive are the efforts toward and by the institutions of education, health, welfare, and penology? At any given time, what is the total number of the population that is under institutional care or control in one form of another? And, given such a picture, what are the implications for the future of society?

The Institutionalized

Whenever individuals come under the care of an institution, such as education, social welfare, health, or penology, a change in civil status takes place. For example, children who attend public schools do so under mandate of law, behave in a prescribed manner, and legal action can be brought to bear to enforce such behavior. Much in the same manner, recipients of social welfare undergo a change in civil status which results in the regulation and circumscription of permissable behavior. In hospitals, ingress and egress is controlled by formal regulations that affect the civil status of individuals and these regulations prescribe what a patient can and cannot do. Clearly the same applies to those individuals who are incarcerated, on probation, and on parole.

Once a citizen comes under the care of one of the aforementioned institutions, informal as well as legal sanctions come into play and a citizen then must exist under a set of taboos and restrictions which normally are not a part of his everyday "free" civil status. These restrictions go beyond simple behavioral rites of passage, since they are legitimized by legal means that define institutionalized status and they are brought into play the moment that the student, the indigent, the sick, and the criminal transgress the proscriptions that accrue to their status as institutional beings.

Toward an Assessment

For the institutions in question, the average daily census and the one-day census constitute the best sources of information. To extend the assessment beyond a one-day figure introduces many other factors such as recidivism and overlap for which there is virtually no reliable data available. The one-day figures, however, are available for public schools (K-12), private schools licensed by the state (K-12), adult and children's programs in social welfare, the mentally ill under institutional care, youth authority wards, camps, ranches, homes, correctional schools, as well as juvenile halls, county and city jails, hospitals and their related facilities. Information is similarly available regarding the number of employees engaged in institutional activities for any given day during the year of 1969.

Two broad categories divide the people who are involved in the institutions outlined above. First, there are those who are in charge of, administer, and service the various programs and departments. In the aggregate, these I call the *caretaker* population. Second, there are those who are under institutional care and control in one form or another, and to one degree or another. These I call the *subject* population.

Table I

THE SUBJECT POPULATION

An assessment based on a one day census by corresponding institutions

LAW ENFORCEMENT
Adult Felon Population[3] – December 31, 1969
Prisons 23,018
Parole.. 13,027
Adult Probation[4] – December 31, 1969 102,042
City and County Jail Population[5] – September 25, 1969 27,918
California Youth Authority Wards[6] – December 31, 1969
State Detention... 5,908
Parole.. 14,778
Juvenile Probation, Active[7] – December 31, 1969 94,724
Juvenile Hall Population[8] – January 1, 1969........................ 4,182

Sub-total   285,597

SOCIAL WELFARE
Cash Grant Persons[9] – September 1969 1,540,571
Certified, Medical Assistance Only[10] – September 1969 212,593
General Home Relief[11] – September 1969............................ 83,012

Sub-total   1,836,176

HOSPITALS
Mentally Ill[12] – June 30, 1969
Resident and on Visit....................................... 16,116
Extramural Care.. 5,406
Mentally Retarded[13] – June 30, 1969
Resident and on Visit....................................... 12,545
Extramural Care.. 11,591
Tuberculosis[14] – Average Daily Census............................ 232
General, Long Term & Other Special[15] –
Average Daily Census... 6,491
General, Short Term & Other Special[16] –
Average Daily Census... 51,087

Sub-total   103,468

SCHOOLS
Kindergarten through Twelve, Public[17] 4,645,000
Non-Public[18] 407,800

Sub-total   5,052,800

GRAND TOTAL   7,278,041

Bearing this dichotomy in mind, an assessment of the total number of people under some form of institutional care during a relatively average day in 1969 in California exceeded seven-million. (See Table I) This figure is based on one day census figures and the average daily census for the hospital population. Clearly there is some overlap, as when a child, for example, is simultaneously a charge of a school and also on welfare rolls. However, since this is a one day figure, and not the total for the year, this overlap is kept at a minimum.

Of course staff is required in order that institutional care can take place. Thus, for the categories listed in Table I, there is a corresponding group of caretakers. Table II is an assessment of the caretaker population required to fill this need. When totaled, the caretaker and the subject populations together approach the 8,000,000 mark (See Table III).

Table II

THE CARETAKER POPULATION
1969

Corrections[19]	22,242
Public Welfare[20]	29,842
Police Protection[21]	51,114
Local Schools[22]	315,165
Hospitals[23]	212,125
Private Schools[24]	17,500
Grand Total	647,988

Table III

THE INSTITUTIONAL POPULATION
Caretakers and Subjects 1969

The Subject Population	7,278,041
The Caretaker Population	647,988
Grand Total	7,926,029

The significance of the institutional population for any given day in 1969 is highlighted when it is viewed in comparison to the civilian labor force as itemized for the state for the month of June, 1969 (See Table IV).

Table IV

THE CIVILIAN LABOR FORCE AND EMPLOYMENT[25]
June 1969

Civilian Labor Force	8,440,000
Civilian Employment	8,052,000
Agriculture, Forestries, Fisheries	359,000
Mineral Extraction	33,000
Construction	380,000
Manufacturing	1,678,000
Transportation, Utilities	484,000
Trade	1,687,000
Finance, Insurance, Real Estate	406,000
Services	1,612,000
Government	1,413,000
Grand Total	8,052,000

For the present, some problem areas that seem most salient with respect to urban-industrial life, caretakers and subjects, are questions that concern social control and social institutions, social mobility, organizational behavior, minority peoples, and the extension of previously geographically limited institutions into the community.

Social Control and Institutions

Social control of the subject population is a function of the rules and legal regulations that govern the admission to, release from, and status as a subject. However, social control does not end at the boundaries of legal sanctions, for extra-legal standards and norms of behavior often come into play as means by which control may be exerted informally both among the caretakers and the subjects as well as between these two groups. Examples of extra-legal social control are many, some of which include standards of dress (it must reflect status to a high degree), personal grooming rules (control of dresswear in public schools), punishment or ridicule of children for speaking Spanish on a schoolground (or to speak English with a Spanish accent rather than a variant of an English accent), a taboo on sex practices while a patient in a hospital, a contrite demeanor before officers or judges, and a host of other similarly informal means by which behavior may be regulated.

Social Mobility and the Caretakers

Traditionally in the United States, the concept of social mobility has been closely associated with the belief that individual people will strive toward a higher rung in the economic and class structure. Upon achieving this goal, certain changes are said to follow, changes in personal, familial, and intergenerational life-styles. Thus, in general, the emergence of the American middle class is said to have taken place. However, such does not precisely apply to the ever-increasing number of people who have entered or presently are entering or moving toward entry into society as members of the caretaker population. Judging from the present enrollments in colleges and universities, the majority of students who are working toward entry into the caretaker population are already members of the middle class. Given the relatively low economic potential of caretaking status and employment, becoming a caretaker thus does not automatically constitute an elevation in class status in the traditional sense of social mobility. It is a possibility, therefore, that the personal and the societal forces that influence those who strive to become caretakers differ somewhat from the forces that guide others to become socially mobile.

Although, in this manner, caretakers may differ from other sectors of society, nevertheless they tend to share a general philosophy of training and rehabilitation regardless of their particular institutional affiliation. Overall, the common caretaking concern focuses upon the entry or the return of the subject population into the non-subject or the "productive sector" of society. From this perspective, caretakers can be seen as not only responsible for general institutional welfare, but also as gatekeepers of society at large. Thus, the control of deviation, however that deviation may be defined, becomes their prime programmatic, operational, and bureaucratic concern.

Caretaker and Subject Organizations

Over time there have developed many formal organizations whose membership is comprised of caretakers. There are, for example, educators' organizations, organizations for administrators, associations for counselors and psychologists in education, organizations for nurses, medical associations, police and law enforcement groups, organizations for technicians, etc. Usually such organizations are made up of people who band together because of mutual professional interests, or mutual agreement on general goals and purposes. On the other hand, the subject population has been most notable for its general lack of formal organization.

In recent years, however, changes in this traditional difference between caretakers and subjects are becoming more and more noticeable, and more and more efforts are being made toward organized behavior. Even secondary school students are grouping in order to address themselves to the status of student *per se,* and to voice interest in establishing input into areas previously reserved for caretakers. The largest such effort has been the Chicano school walkouts that took place in Los Angeles which spread far beyond the borders of California and which brought about considerable change in procedures that deal with school testing and bilingual education.

Still other groups of the subject population have made efforts directed to health, education, and welfare. Local groups the length and breadth of California have banded together on numerous occasions in order to address themselves to the administration of welfare programs. Local poverty groups, as well as others, are working toward community determined health centers and even toward a community based definition of mental health. The incarcerated and the recent incarcerated are participating in organized activity, such as in certain aspects of Synanon, the Seven Step Foundation, EMPLEO, and others.

Minorities in California

According to the figures of the 1960 census, there were 1,426,538 persons of Spanish surname in California, 883,861

Negro, 157,317 Japanese, 95,600 Chinese, 65,459 Filipino, and 39,014 American Indians. This comprised 16.9 of the total population. Although the latest census figures are not available at present, there is no question but that the ratio between "minority" and "majority" peoples has changed in the intervening years. For example, since 1960 the Spanish surname population in California has increased from 1,426,538 to 3,140,000. Some 2,980,000 of these are Mexican Americans. Thus one such ethnic group now constitutes 15.7% of the total population.[26] When considering the other minority peoples in the state, one can surmise that the overall percentage of the total now exceeds 20% and probably approaches 25% of the population.

As is well known, individuals from the minority groups make up but a fraction of the caretaker population, while their representation in the subject population is relatively high. This condition has been a source of friction in the past. To a high degree, the subject oriented organizations tend to cleave along ethnic lines.

Institutions in the Community

Current trends toward "outpatient" philosophy have tended to diminish the relative prominence of the traditional, *geographically based* institution. Thus it is becoming more and more common to find individuals within the community setting who are under institutional status and subject to institutional regulations. There are many examples of this condition, among which are adults and juveniles who are on parole or probation, hospital patients on leave but still under pre-release regulations, mental patients released to the community but not medically released, some forms of welfare, and students home on vacation from schools. In addition, overcrowded conditions in hospitals, jails, camps, juvenile halls, and the like often result in further release to the community.

Under the traditional and geographically localized institution there seemed to be a built-in limit to the construction of more and more buildings to house the institutionalized of the state. Such limitations were limited by both social and economic factors. However, under the "outpatient" approach no such limitation appears to exist. Thus, potentially, institutional care and status can become a more integral part of everyday community life, and institutional influences and controls no longer are limited by geographic boundaries and facilities.

Concluding Remarks

The nature and scope of institutional care in a modern state such as California promises to be among the most salient problems to be faced by the citizens whose lives will all be affected by these developments. To date, there is considerable shifting of individuals from one care status to another. However, the mere shifting of caseloads as reflected by the moving of individuals from nursing and convalescent homes to hospitals and then back again does not constitute a fundamental change either from the standpoint of the subjects or from the standpoint of altering the overall caseload. What most commonly is happening is that caseload shifts are merely jurisdictional. Much the same can be said of transfers from a police agency to welfare, or *vice versa*. In much the same manner, a change from inpatient status to outpatient does not significantly constitute a change. Briefly, such transfers may reflect a reduction in caseload for one agency, but simultaneously there is a corresponding increase in caseload for another. This being the case, there has been no significant change in the subject population as such.

Jurisdictional transfers are only caretaking actions that reflect bureaucratic decisions which, equally often, do not address themselves to the basic priorities that guide the functions of the institutions. Explicitly articulated priorities must supercede jurisdictional transfers if the concept of caretaking is to change toward better opportunities for human development, and if the subject population is to move toward a participating population.

The developments in recent years in the state of California clearly portend similar developments in other industrializing and urban areas and states throughout the world. Is it not proper at this juncture in history to ask what voice will the subject (consumer) population have in helping to guide the urban-industrialized state into the future? And given these developments, can a return to past history, and past solutions, be a feasible alternative? And what tax revenues shall be destined to better meet the problems of this future society which, it seems, is already upon us.

Insofar as the Chicano population is concerned, many answers to these questions are explicitly articulated or tentatively suggested within the pages of this book. Perhaps the title itself is indicative of the role Chicanos will play in this state of the future, for, after all, it is the prime purpose of this volume to let their VOICES be heard.

NOTES

1. *California Statistical Abstract – 1969.* California Department of Finance, Budget Division, State of California. Table B-1, page 9.
2. *Ibid.,* page VII.
3. *Crime and Delinquency in California, 1969.* Bureau of Criminal Statistics, Department of Justice, Division of Law Enforcement, State of California. Table I-11, page 37.
4. *Ibid.,* page 124.
5. *Ibid.,* Table I-13, page 41.
6. *Ibid.,* Table XI-1, page 182 and Table XI-2, page 183.
7. *Ibid.,* Table X-3, page 156.
8. *Ibid.,* Table X-13, page 174. This figure does not include certain categories in Los Angeles, San Diego, Santa Clara and Sutter Counties, thus the actual total may be higher than that provided here.
9. *1970 California County Factbook,* County Supervisors Association, Sacramento, California. "Public Assistance Caseloads and Expenditures," page 86.
10. *Ibid.*
11. *Ibid.*
12. Division of Biostatistics, State Department of Mental Hygiene, Sacramento, California. Personal Communication.
13. *Ibid.*
14. "Guide Issue: Hospitals," *Journal of the American Hospital Association.* Vol. 44, No. 15. August 1, 1970. Table 3, page 49.
15. *Ibid.*
16. *Ibid.*
17. Renetzky, Alvin and Greene, Jon S., *et al., Standard Education Almanac–1970.* Academic Media, Los Angeles, Table 37, page 64.
18. *Ibid.,* Table 46, page 71.
19. U.S. Bureau of the Census, *Public Employment in 1969,* Series GE 69-No. 1. U.S. Government Printing Office, Washington D.C., 1970. Table 8. Full-Time Equivalent Employment of State and Local Governments, by Function and by State: October 1969, page 22.
20. *Ibid.,* Table 8, page 21.
21. *Ibid.,* Table 8, page 21.
22. *Ibid.,* Table 8, page 19. (sic)
23. "Guide Issue: Hospitals," *Journal of the American Hospital Association.* Vol. 44, No. 15. August 1, 1970. Table 3, page 490.
24. Renetzky, Alvin and Greene, Jon S., *et al., Standard Education Almanac–1970.* Academic Media, Los Angeles. Table 54, page 77.
25. *California Statistical Abstract – 1969.* California Department of Finance, Budget Division, State of California. Table C-1, page 19.
26. "Mexican-American Population in California," *An Official Census Report By the Mexican-American Population Commission of California,* San Francisco, California. April, 1971. Page 7.